WITHOUT PRECEDENT

WITHout PRECEDENT

The Life of
Susie Marshall Sharp

ANNA R. HAYES

The University of
North Carolina Press
Chapel Hill

THIS BOOK WAS PUBLISHED WITH THE
ASSISTANCE OF THE THORNTON H. BROOKS FUND OF
THE UNIVERSITY OF NORTH CAROLINA PRESS.

Designed by Eric M. Brooks
Set in Arno and Sistina by Tseng Information Systems, Inc.
Manufactured in the United States of America

The paper in this book meets the guidelines for permanence
and durability of the Committee on Production Guidelines for
Book Longevity of the Council on Library Resources.

The University of North Carolina Press has been a member
of the Green Press Initiative since 2003.

Library of Congress Cataloging-in-Publication Data
Hayes, Anna R.
Without precedent : the life of Susie Marshall Sharp /
Anna R. Hayes.
p. cm.
Includes bibliographical references and index.
ISBN 978-0-8078-3214-1 (cloth : alk. paper)
1. Sharp, Susie. 2. Women judges — United States —
Biography. I. Title.
KF373.S46H39 2008
347.73'14092 — dc22 [B]
2008008442

Frontispiece: North Carolina Supreme Court chief justice
Susie Marshall Sharp
(Waller Studio, Raleigh, North Carolina)

12 11 10 09 08   5 4 3 2 1

University of North Carolina Press books may be purchased at
a discount for educational, business, or sales promotional use.
For information, please visit www.uncpress.unc.edu or write to
UNC Press, attention: Sales Department, 116 South Boundary
Street, Chapel Hill, NC 27514-3808.

For my parents

"Judges are but men,
encompassed by error,
seasoned with sin,
and fettered by fallibility."
What woman couldn't meet
those specifications!

SUSIE M. SHARP

CONTENTS

ILLUSTRATIONS

PREFACE

Why her? Why then? How did Susie Sharp become a legal icon at a time when women were all but nonexistent in the legal profession? These were the questions that gave birth to this book. Susie Marshall Sharp was not the first or only woman of formidable intelligence in North Carolina or elsewhere. Nor was she the first woman to aspire to a career in the law. And yet, indisputably, the number of women then at the pinnacle of public life, and particularly in the legal profession, was minuscule. She was the first in a number of significant ways, including first woman judge in North Carolina, first woman on the North Carolina Supreme Court, and first woman in the United States to be elected chief justice of a state supreme court. I wanted to find out how she had transcended the limits society placed on women in her time.

This is not, however, the book I expected to write.

My primary interest was in the historical facts — the events leading to her unprecedented status in the North Carolina judicial and political scene — as well as the use she made of her position to affect the lives of her fellow citizens. In this sense, the book is at least as much about North Carolina during this time as it is about Susie Sharp. Her activities as an attorney, judge, and politician must be understood in the context of the social mores, the legal profession, and the political battles of her era. Subjects such as women's education, legal education, and women's roles in public life bear directly on her life and career. To a great extent, of course, Susie Sharp's family background, private life, and personality closely relate to her career path and are inextricable from the story I wanted to tell. Here, I discovered a woman far different from the one I had imagined.

Susie Sharp was successful, spectacularly so, and gave every appearance of being an exceptionally well-integrated person. Her public image was that of a brilliant, personable, strict-minded woman who had sacrificed marriage and family to pursue her career. All this was true. But just as the era in which she rose to such a startling prominence was at once deceptively simple on the surface yet enormously complex underneath, she was a woman far more complicated than she appeared. How I came to discover the many paradoxes in her life is a story in itself.

When I began this book, Susie Sharp was still alive but her mind had abandoned her. With caregivers in constant attendance, she remained in her Raleigh apartment. Sadly, it was too late to interview her about her life. Her siblings, however, gave me access not only to their memories in the form of interviews and other recollections but also to all the letters, newspaper clippings, scrapbooks, and photograph albums at the family residence in Reidsville, in itself a mountain of material. It pained Susie Sharp to discard anything. There were old-fashioned letter boxes full of correspondence from her earliest years, down to and including schoolgirl notes passed in class. An early devotee of the typewriter, she also kept copies of most of her own letters. In addition to her private correspondence, I was able to examine what remained of the old Sharp & Sharp office files (also at the family home, stored in four metal file cabinets on the front porch), as well as the files that filled the Reidsville basement of Norwood E. Robinson, her father's former law partner. The latter were primarily the materials transferred from Chief Justice Sharp's office at the North Carolina Supreme Court when she retired.

I had been working steadily at reviewing, organizing, copying, and making notes from these papers for about two years when Susie Sharp died. At that time, her brother Kits Sharp asked if I wanted to come help clear out her apartment, thinking that I might find further useful material there. The apartment was packed solid with papers of all kinds, from newspapers to recipes to letters and mementos. I simply boxed up everything and brought it home. It was only after I had been digging my way through this second mountain for some time that I discovered and began to understand the significance of some of the things I was examining. One category consisted of old letters, or rather fragments of old letters, written by Susie Sharp, thrown in a box. She had dated each fragment by hand. Sometimes chunks of text had been lopped off the tops or bottoms of the letters. Delicate scissor work had excised words or phrases in the middle, leaving the rest. I called these the lace letters. They turned out to be Susie Sharp's letters to her lover John Kesler, routinely returned to her in accordance with their agreement, which called for each of them to destroy his or her own letters.

By far the best record of Susie Sharp's life after she went on the superior court, this correspondence continued in a substantive form from 1949 until the mid-1960s and contained lengthy and detailed reports of her experiences in court and of her family life, as well as political commentary. It was her hope to use this material when she sat down to write her memoirs, a goal she never achieved. She had therefore cut out most, but not all, of the parts about the personal relationship, while preserving the extensive record of her other activities and concerns.

Another important category of materials unearthed in Susie Sharp's apartment consisted of journals. She was an inveterate, if not a compulsive, journal keeper. Based on a letter from her cousin Earle Garrett dated October 7, 1944, twitting her about "the diaries you burned," it appears that she destroyed many years' worth, probably in 1943. But she could not bear to leave so much history unrecorded, and so she constructed a lengthy abstract of her journals ("Journal Abstract") dating from March 7, 1927, to November 12, 1943, which provides a detailed chronology of events for that time period. There is a gap between the end of this abstract in 1943 and January 1948, after which the journals continue until the mid-1980s.

Normally, a biographer would feel as if he had struck it rich to find such a gold mine. And indeed I did, except for the obstinate reality that the journals were mostly written in shorthand. Having never learned shorthand or aspired to do so, I despaired. A brief attempt to hire someone who could read shorthand was a failure for several reasons, not least of which was the would-be translator's lack of knowledge of the subject matter, which greatly hindered her ability to make sense of the material. Reluctantly, I embarked on a self-taught course in Gregg shorthand. The task of translating and transcribing the journals was a labor of another two years. Some passages remain impervious to my best efforts, but I am confident that I have deciphered most of the contents. Among other things, the journals document Susie Sharp's relationship with her first lover, her law professor Millard Breckenridge (universally known as "Breck"), and also reveal her affair with Judge Allen H. Gwyn, her political mentor who was one of the most important strategists behind her judicial career.

Then there were three small flip-top notebooks, about 3¾-by-5½ inches, advertising giveaways with "State Street" on the cover. At first glance, they appeared the least significant items I had yet come across. They were filled with entries in Susie Sharp's hand consisting primarily of line after line showing a date and, generally, a corresponding three-digit number. Occasional comments in shorthand were sprinkled here and there, along with some kind of running tally. Reading Susie Sharp's letters and journals in conjunction with these little notebooks, I realized they were a record of her rendezvous with Breck ("Breck Record") and with John Kesler ("JCK Record"), covering the time period from October 27, 1927, to March 15, 1968. The three-digit numbers next to the dates were, it turned out, hotel room numbers, as can be verified by contemporaneous references in the correspondence and her other, everyday journals. Additional shorthand notations included, for example, "at his house" or "in the car." The running tally I will leave to the reader's imagination.

Ironically, there is little correspondence between Susie Sharp and her constant companion for the last three decades of her life, Chief Justice William H. Bobbitt. Although they never married and maintained separate residences, they were virtually inseparable and thus had little reason to write one another.

Some who knew Susie Sharp may be surprised to learn that her private life was so different from her public persona. Some may wish that the information had never come to light. Her extramarital relationships, however, are a significant part of her story. All of the men in her life were trusted career advisers. Moreover, her perception that she could not do justice to both a career and a marriage was emblematic of attitudes common among both men and women of the period. Her determinedly single state provided her with the time and energy to indulge her overachiever's drive. Finally, it says a great deal about Susie Sharp that all of her lovers remained her devoted friends even after the romances had ended.

Inevitably, I suppose, revelations about Susie Sharp's private life will draw the attention of readers. It would be a shame, however, if this aspect of her life were to overshadow her enormous achievements in the legal and political world. Although at times it seemed as if her success occurred in spite of herself, she never wavered in her pursuit of excellence in her profession. This dedication, combined with her intellect and political skills, produced a jurist and public servant who had an immeasurable impact on the citizens of North Carolina.

Susie Sharp's extensive journals and her correspondence, not only with lovers and political confidants Kesler, Breckenridge, and Gwyn, but also with family members and friends, provided a far more complex portrait than that of the woman I had expected to describe when I began this book. It is possible that I know her better than any single other person ever did. Nonetheless, even now I do not presume to say that I know this woman, because some of the aspects of her personality and the choices she made remain mysterious. I have not attempted to psychoanalyze Susie Sharp, a task I am in any event not qualified to do. For the most part, I have set forth the facts to speak for themselves, allowing the reader to ponder the mysteries inherent in human beings without my interpretation, only occasionally acknowledging, here and there, the existence of the mystery.

INTRODUCTION

If, as F. Scott Fitzgerald said, "the test of a first-rate intelligence is the ability to hold two opposed ideas in the mind at the same time and still retain the ability to function," then Susie Marshall Sharp was a genius.[1]

Brains and a propensity for hard work were two of Susie Sharp's most obvious characteristics. On both sides of her family, these qualities had enabled her forebears to survive and even prevail over the difficulties of war, poverty, and the general benightedness of the backcountry in the South. In her parents were joined long lines of patrician plantation owners on one side and yeoman farmers on the other, both sides smelted in the furnace of the Civil War and the hard years that followed. Susie Sharp embodied the paradoxes of the South, with its twin strands of pride and humility, romance and pragmatism. The brutal years after the Civil War had imbued her family with a deep-seated fear of poverty, ignorance, and stagnation, but also with a dawning and determined optimism arising from unprecedented opportunities. In Susie Sharp, the determination and optimism were matched to an exceptional intelligence, which seemingly catapulted her far ahead of her times, even as she retained many attitudes typical of the nineteenth century.

The story of her career is a significant piece of North Carolina history, with implications not only for women but also for every citizen, because every citizen in the state was affected by her jurisprudence and her administrative initiatives. As a female pioneer in the state's legal profession, Susie Sharp saw North Carolina women gain the right to serve on a jury, achieved recognition as one of the earliest female political operatives on a statewide level, and influenced the national outcome of the vote on the proposed Equal Rights Amendment to the U.S. Constitution.

When she graduated at the top of her law school class in 1929, she was one of a bare handful of women in North Carolina, or in the country for that matter, with a law license. Moreover, she became one of a much smaller number of women attorneys who practiced courtroom law. Appointed to the superior court in 1949, the first woman judge in North Carolina, she earned a reputation during her thirteen years on the trial court bench as a judge of exceptional ability. When Governor Terry Sanford named her in 1962 to be the first woman to sit on the North Carolina Supreme Court, the appointment was greeted with widespread enthusiasm. In 1974 the voters of North Carolina made her the first woman in the United States to be elected chief justice of a state supreme court. The victory acknowledged the broad esteem in which she was held and offered her the opportunity to crown her career with both administrative and jurisprudential contributions to the state's legal system.

In her prime she was an attractive woman with a creamy complexion, which she protected from the sun with a parasol. She loved pretty clothes. A petite and proper southern lady, she carefully observed the rigid niceties of social conventions. (Few people knew that she packed a pistol in her handbag.) The question of why she never married was a favorite subject for discussion among her colleagues and the public at large. Although close friends were familiar with her sparkling wit, others tended to view her with a combination of respect and trepidation. Despite her size, she was a formidable figure of regal bearing who appeared to suffer none of the doubts or failings of average folks. Her achievements made her an icon of women's rights advocates.

She appeared complete, consistent, and infrangible.

The reality was quite different. Susie Sharp was a mass of contradictions. Ambitious, she often denied it even to herself. Loyal to a fault, she was no stranger to betrayal. Utterly pragmatic and realistic, she harbored the romanticism of a schoolgirl. She was an admitted racist, yet she delivered irreproachable judicial decisions dealing with race. A staunch believer in the value of precedent, she produced precedent-shattering opinions. Having scaled the barricades for women's rights, she worked to defeat the Equal Rights Amendment. She was obsessively image-conscious, yet she took risks in her personal life that would have destroyed her had they become known.

If she was a mass of contradictions, however, Susie Sharp was also a master of camouflage. Not for her the image of a woman bent on breaking the rules. She lived a life of freedom and professional achievement unimaginable for most women of her times, but the last thing she desired was to call attention to her disregard for boundaries. Under the guise of a straitlaced southern spinster, she enjoyed a remarkable romantic life. And as a jurist, a meticulous scholar, she carefully shored up her most far-reaching opinions with mountains of authority to show that, rather than overturning a long-held legal principle, she was merely shepherding North Carolina into the mainstream.

Hers was a life full of paradox, but even in this she mirrored her southern background, in which paradox could almost be considered the norm. Southerners often prized their local "characters," for example, even as they enforced the most rigid social conventions.[2] A prideful egalitarianism coexisted with strict social stratification. Deep-rooted conservatism shared the political landscape with a long tradition of liberal populism. The famous southern gentility and courtesy went hand in hand with a tendency to violence as well as the prevalence of dehumanizing racial discrimination. Truly, the hobgoblin of "a foolish consistency" did not overoccupy southern minds. Nor her own.

Although Susie Sharp's gender made her the focus of constant scrutiny, somehow she managed to achieve what she wanted, by and large, in both her public and her private life. In the end, her hard work and intellect made an enormous contribution to the state of North Carolina, its judicial system, and its citizens. Had she been less talented or less lucky, none of it would have come to pass.

PART I

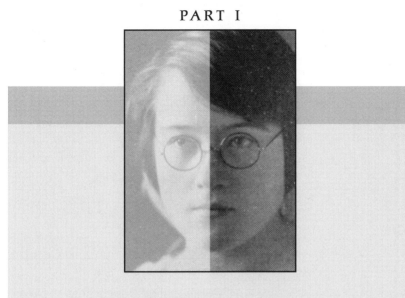

BEGINNINGS

CHAPTER 1

FAMILY

When Susie Sharp was born, her father was a thirty-year-old failure who had not yet reached bottom. James Merritt Sharp (b. 1877) was the son of a Civil War veteran from New Bethel Township, North Carolina, a yeoman farmer known for his well-tended fields and orchards. A 1930 retrospective newspaper article described the Sharps as "members of a well-known Rockingham County family . . . good citizens, debt-abhorring and honest . . . the sort who dignify toil."[1] Jim Sharp grew up in a family that, like many others, existed outside the cash economy, needing money for little beyond sugar and coffee.[2] The Sharps were not without broader horizons, however, for Jim Sharp's father was reputedly the only man in the community who subscribed to the *Atlanta Constitution*.[3]

Jim Sharp never lost his connection with the land and would be a farmer all his life, no matter what else he did. Nevertheless, despite his rural background—or perhaps because of it—he was motivated from a very young age to get an education. He got it "the hard way, by raising tobacco and 'sending himself' to school."[4] The poverty and turmoil of the post–Civil War years denied him the higher education he longed for, but he did manage to graduate from Whitsett Institute near Gibsonville, North Carolina, where he garnered "all the certificates they offered."[5]

At the age of eighteen Jim Sharp was teaching school in Madison Township, not far from the family farm. Having begun in the world of hand-to-mouth farming, he had worked his way onto the first rung of a brand-new ladder. Photographs from around this period show an attractive young man with regular features, a firm jaw, prominent ears, a fine profile, and a shock of hair combed to the side. Even as a young man he wore round-rimmed glasses. Showing him in a jacket and tie, regarding the camera with equanimity, his photograph reveals little of the determination within.

There was a story Jim Sharp liked to tell, the story of "Old Frog." He would later tell this story to his children, and Susie Sharp would repeat it many times to anyone in need of encouragement.[6] It was the tale of two frogs that fell into the milk crock as the lid was set in place. One of the frogs splashed around frantically until he got tired, and then he gave up and drowned. The other frog, however, just kept kicking. When morning came and the housewife lifted the lid on the crock, Old Frog sat high and dry on a sturdy mound of butter. The tale encapsulated Jim Sharp's approach to life and the philosophy he would do his best to pass on to his children.

Agriculture and education, both of which would be lifelong passions, had already claimed his attention. In 1900 he returned to New Bethel Township where he founded a nondenominational day and boarding school called Sharp Institute. When he petitioned for a local post office to serve the school, the U.S. Postal Service told him he would have to come up with a name different from any other in the state. Revealingly, he chose the name "Intelligence."

Sharp Institute was coeducational, with nearly equal numbers of boys and girls. The first term began with 50 students on October 22, 1900, three days after the school building was finished. The spring term of 1902 boasted 166 students "representing several counties," and the 1903 term exceeded even this. According to the school brochure,[7] nearly 2,000 people witnessed the closing exercises that year, and Governor Charles B. Aycock himself delivered the "Literary address."

Testimonials from nearby ministers and educators printed in the brochure bore witness to Professor Sharp's high standing in the eyes of the community, as well as to his awareness of public relations. Included in the brochure was a 1903 letter from U.S. congressman W. W. Kitchin declaring that he knew Professor Sharp and that he had "the reputation of an earnest, industrious, energetic, and progressive educator" who enjoyed "the confidence and esteem of a large and constantly increasing circle of friends." Professor Sharp was on the way up.

Then, on April 6, 1904, the main building of the school was destroyed by fire.[8] By the following year, however, the school had been rebuilt, and, at the close of the 1905 term, the enrollment had increased to "vastly over two hundred students."[9] The energetic Professor Sharp continued to be busy in his roles as headmaster, teacher, and coach of a well-regarded baseball team.

Among the faculty members at Sharp Institute was a young woman from nearby Vance County named Annie Britt Blackwell (b. 1884). Her family bore the weighty memory, perhaps embellished but never relinquished, of antebellum grandeur. She was the granddaughter of John Pomfret (or Pomphret) Blackwell Sr., known as "Marse Johnnie" to all, including his wife, a large landowner with more than 1,500 acres in what was then Granville County, just south of the Virginia line.[10] He was also a slave owner, although accounts differ as to the number of his slaves, ranging from seventeen to seventy-five.[11] Annie Blackwell's father had left home as a boy of eighteen to fight for the Confederacy, joining the cavalry because his father was able to supply him with a horse.[12] His enlistment in June 1864, coming at a time when the Confederacy had little cause for hope and no glamor left, bespeaks a youthful fervor reflecting the sort of obstinacy, pride, and gallantry for which the South was proud to be known.

Marse Johnnie was fifty-four years old and unable to fight when the Civil War began in 1861. In fact, he was so crippled by rheumatism that for thirty years he was unable to walk and instead "slided around" in an old split-bottomed chair. Most certainly by necessity, then, and perhaps by temperament, Annie's grandmother, Marse Johnnie's wife, Mary Ann Webb Blackwell, was "thoroughly business."[13] It was she who ran the farm during the Civil War and afterward until her death in 1885.[14] When the war closed down the schools, Mary Ann Blackwell took steps to continue the education not only of her own children but of other children in the area as well, hiring a schoolteacher to live on the place.[15] Annie Blackwell would remember her grandmother as ambitious for her children and hungry for education for them.[16] As a strong and capable woman, she set a high standard.

Five years after the end of the war, on February 1, 1870, the returned veteran John Pomfret Blackwell Jr. married Sallie Green Wortham, nicknamed "Mink" for her black hair. As a wedding gift, Mr. Blackwell Sr. gave his son 383 acres of land near Townsville, in the Nutbush District of what was then part of Granville County.[17] The young groom cleared the land and built a little two-bedroom log cabin between two hills. Sallie named it Valley Home.[18] A later photograph shows subsequent improvements resulting in a substantial two-story clapboard house with a small front porch and two chimneys.

The Nutbush area largely owed its antebellum prosperity to its rich soil, which was perfect for the type of tobacco then prevalent, as well as for diversified farming. After the war, however, the thin soil of the southern part of the county proved to be better for the new variety of flue-cured brightleaf tobacco that would transform much of North Carolina's agriculture and economy.[19] The farmers who were left out of the "Brightleaf Belt" boom in the latter part of the nineteenth century would not see much relief from the destitution they faced after Appomattox. The area in which the Blackwells lived declined steadily. A number of large estates were broken up, and the land gradually "passed into the hands of former overseers and some slaves."[20]

The Blackwells appear to have held on to much if not all of their land, but just a year before John P. Blackwell Jr. married, his parents had mortgaged a little more than 100 acres to pay a $400 loan. It would be sixteen years before the mortgage was paid.[21]

In the years after the Civil War, even as the state as a whole was "redeemed," violence and election fraud were not enough to secure victory for the Granville County Democrats,[22] so the legislature turned to gerrymandering. Vance County, as it is now known, was created in 1881, just three years before Annie Britt Blackwell was born. Reconfiguring county boundaries, Democrats in the General Assembly were able to consolidate Republicans in the newly established Vance County while preserving a Democratic majority in neighboring Granville, Franklin, and Warren counties.[23] The sacrificial county was named for thrice-elected Democratic governor and U.S. senator Zebulon B. Vance, who thereafter referred to it as "Zeb's Black Baby."[24] So it was that, although the Blackwells had not moved, Annie would be born in Vance County, not Granville. Cast to the wolves by the Democrats, Vance County suffered heavily from the postwar agricultural depression that continued into the late 1890s.

In Vance County and elsewhere, the struggle to retain their dignity and sense of superiority pervaded the lives of the North Carolina "aristocracy." Many years later, Susie Sharp recalled the atmosphere of determined gentility in which her mother, Annie Blackwell, was reared. As a child, she elaborated, she had been intrigued and puzzled by the word "aristocrat." According to her mother, "you either were or you weren't." Young Susie asked her mother, "But who decides and how can you tell?" Susie Sharp said she never got a satisfactory explanation. "My name was Sharp and not Blackwell and I got worried about the aristocracy of the Sharps. It certainly was not as noticeable as Mamma's. Daddy never mentioned it if his grandfather owned any slaves; so I jumped to the ominous conclusion that he must not have. I finally got up the courage to ask Mamma if Daddy was as aristocratic as she was. I didn't get a yes or no answer but, after the explanation was completed, I deduced that aristocracy was not as important in Rockingham County as it was in Vance and that honesty, integrity, and industry were almost as good as aristocracy. Furthermore, I was never to ask the question again; I might hurt my father's feelings. Since I idolized him, I never did!"[25]

In her careful explanation of the relative merits of birth and honest enterprise, Annie made her daughter Susie aware not only of her rightful status as a Blackwell but also of the value to be attached to plain hard work. There was never any question in the household that, although one's aristocratic origins should never be forgotten, it was hard work that brought success. It was also an article of faith that education was the scaffolding on which success, through hard work, must be built.

Annie's own mother had been determined that her daughters would get as much education and culture as they possibly could, even hiring, through an advertisement in the Richmond newspaper, a music teacher to give the children lessons in exchange for room and board.[26] In 1888 she defied her husband to find the money needed to send Annie's older sister Blanche to Greensboro Female College in Greensboro, North Carolina.[27] When Blanche married and followed her husband to Indiana, her little sister Annie, age thirteen, accompanied her to help take care of her growing family. Annie's reward was the opportunity to attend high school in Indiana, where the schools were vastly superior to those in North Carolina, which in the aftermath of the Civil War were considered among the worst in the country.

Back in North Carolina, Annie obtained her teaching certificate and went to teach (everything from "ABC's to Latin and Algebra") in a one-room schoolhouse with no running water in Granville County.[28] Soon she took a job at the private institute in Rockingham County founded by a young teacher named Jim Sharp. On July 3, 1906, Annie Britt Blackwell married Professor Sharp at Valley Home.

After a wedding trip that included a visit to Washington, D.C.,[29] Annie and Jim Sharp returned to Intelligence, where they took up their duties at Sharp Institute as before. Enrollment had grown to approximately 225 students and the institute appeared to be thriving. But on the night of January 22, 1907, just as the spring term got under way, fire broke out in the main school building again. By the time it was discovered, it was impossible to put out the blaze. The school was completely destroyed.[30] The *Reidsville Review* reported, somewhat opaquely, that the origin of the fire was "by incendiary" and that "[a]n attempt was made two nights before but the fire was extinguished."[31]

There were those who said Professor Sharp had burned the school, but if there was ever any evidence to support the charge, it has long since vanished. Certainly fire was a common hazard at the time; indeed, the county courthouse in Wentworth had burned in a spectacular fire the preceding October. Nevertheless, for some reason the fire apparently was considered suspicious. In any event, despite some encouragement by citizens of nearby Reidsville to relocate the school there, this time the professor was unable to get the financing to rebuild.[32] Subsequently, the residents of Intelligence raised the money for a new school to be called New Bethel Academy, but Professor Sharp was no longer involved. His career as an educator was over.

In March 1907 Jim and Annie Sharp moved to Rocky Mount, a town of about 7,500 people in eastern North Carolina, where Jim Sharp hoped to make a living selling insurance.[33] After the second devastating fire at Sharp Institute and the move to Rocky Mount, the couple had little if anything in the way of a nest egg.

On July 7, 1907, Annie gave birth to her first child, Susie Marshall Sharp, named for her own sister Susie and for Jim's father, James Marshall Sharp.[34] The new parents' joy, however, must have been undercut by their financial woes. Although the records have not been found to confirm it, family history says that Jim Sharp was forced to declare bankruptcy. Annie had to sell her heirloom furniture.[35]

Broke and with a new baby, the family retreated to the old Sharp homestead in Rockingham County. It must have been painful to return to the place in which Jim was no longer "Professor Sharp" of Sharp Institute, and to return in such dire circumstances. But if it bothered him, he did not let that prevent him from working toward his next goal. Like Old Frog, he just kept kicking. He had determined to become a lawyer.

Jim Sharp began studying law on his own without a mentor, reading his Blackstone while he walked behind the mule as he plowed the family fields.[36] He loved farming, but with the prospect of a young family to support, he was intent on finding ways to earn a better livelihood. To compensate for his lack of formal legal education, he attended a bar review course under the renowned Dean N. Y. Gulley at the Wake Forest College School of Law, then located in the small town of Wake Forest, North Carolina.[37] On January 27, 1908, he received his law license and promptly opened his office in Stoneville, North Carolina, not far from Intelligence.[38] He joined the Masons and began building his practice.[39]

That summer Annie's sister Susie Blackwell married Jim Sharp's first cousin A. Earle ("Early") Garrett, who was a teacher and principal of the Stoneville public schools. It was a measure both of family devotion and of hard times that Jim and Annie moved in with the newlyweds. Annie would long remember things like the time the two young wives were preparing fried potatoes for supper—it was *all* they had for supper—and Susie Garrett spilled them on the floor. Scooping them up, the sisters whispered, "Just don't tell."[40]

Jim Sharp practiced law in Stoneville for about two years. Then he and Annie moved a few miles away to Madison, North Carolina, a thriving tobacco manufacturing town on the railroad, which offered more opportunity for a young lawyer than the tiny town of Stoneville. In Madison two more children were born to Jim and Annie: a son and namesake, James Merritt Sharp Jr., in 1910 and a daughter, Sallie Blackwell Sharp, the following year.

Even as he attempted to get his law practice on firm footing, in 1910 Jim Sharp undertook a major agricultural investment just over the Virginia state line, borrowing $1,000 to buy 100 acres of land on Turkeycock Mountain, near the town of Ridgeway, Virginia. Known in the family as the Mountain Farm, the entire property eventually would amount to several hundred acres.

Sharp did have a scheme to make the land pay. The mountain was covered in timber. The plan was for his brother Bob Sharp, "Uncle Bob," to supervise the construction and operation of a sawmill on the mountain, transforming timber into lumber and thus into cash. Since the Civil War, demand had grown dramatically for lumber for new construction and for the furniture factories that were springing up along the route of the North Carolina Railroad.[41] It was not a bad scheme. Uncle Bob, however, was a hopeless reprobate with a weakness for moonshine whiskey. His supervision of the Mountain Farm left a good deal to be desired. Finally Jim Sharp determined that he was going to have to move his family to Virginia and look after the operation himself, leaving his budding law practice in Madison behind.

Susie, the eldest child, was about six years old when the family moved to the Mountain Farm. The house on the farm was a hastily constructed frame cottage, infested with bedbugs. There was no running water; indeed, there was not even a well. Annie Sharp had to carry all the family's water from a spring at the bottom of a steep hill, a constant chore that must have been especially arduous because she was pregnant again. Little Susie, who was forbidden to go to the spring because of the danger of snakes, lived in terror every time her mother went to the spring until she got back.

In winter the house was so cold that Annie tried to make the children stay in bed to keep warm. If that was too confining, they were made to sit, wrapped in quilts, in chairs. The farm was isolated and the Sharps had no feasible way to send the six-year-old Susie to school, so Annie, the former schoolteacher, began teaching her at home. It did not make matters any easier that Jim Sharp was often away overnight, trying to sell lumber or otherwise to raise some money for the payroll. Susie remembered that her mother was afraid of the black sawmill hands, although she did not explain why to the children. In the coldest part of the winter, in February 1914, Annie gave birth to a daughter, named Annie Hill.

The sawmill venture did not go well. In 1913 and 1914 the list of debts grew longer and longer. Sharp owed his laborers for work at the sawmill and his suppliers for fertilizer, feed, oil, and gasoline. He owed money for meat, for groceries, for shoes, for clothing, for dental work, for the doctor's "practice on family." He owed money for horses and mules, several of them dead. All told, it added up to more than $12,000 still owing. In 1914 it was a great deal of money, and on September 8 Jim Sharp filed a petition for bankruptcy in the United States District Court.[42] Years later, Susie Sharp recounted what happened:

> Well, to make a long story short, Daddy went broke absolutely, and he "went into bankruptcy." Appraisers came to the house and valued every sheet and pillow case; every sorry cot and bed; pots and pans; and every piece of clothing, etc. When they came Mamma had laid all our possessions out for inspection. . . . Of course, I did not then fully realize what was going on, but I felt the strangers were "mean men," up to no good. I was afraid and clung to Mamma. I must have asked her questions, but I do not recall what she said to me. I do remember, however, that she stood very tall; that she used her company manners and voice. She was gracious to the appraisers and they, in turn, treated her with deference.[43]

The family was all but penniless. A lifeline came from a lawyer in Reidsville, North Carolina, another Rockingham County native named Ira Humphreys, who suggested that Jim Sharp come to Reidsville to try his luck practicing law.[44] Like Jim Sharp, Humphreys was born in New Bethel Township. His father had served with Jim Sharp's father in the 45th North Carolina Regiment in the Civil War.[45] Ten days after Sharp filed his bankruptcy petition in Virginia, the Reidsville newspaper reported, "Attorney J. M. Sharp, formerly of Madison and Martinsville, has moved to Reidsville and will engage in the practice of his profession."[46] He was thirty-seven years old.

On arrival in Reidsville, the Sharps moved in once again with Uncle Early and Aunt Susie Garrett. Susie Sharp entered second grade.[47] The Garretts at that time also had four children, and the little house was crowded at best. Years later, Susie Sharp reflected on this time in their lives: "Mamma . . . was a proud woman. Remember, she was always a Vance County 'aristocrat!' She proved it the day the appraisers came and many times thereafter. I now realize how she must have hated to move her family in on Aunt Susie, and I can imagine that Daddy was embarrassed to 'impose' on Early, but both were grateful for the refuge which was lovingly offered."[48]

Susie Sharp was the only one of the children old enough to retain any memory of the Mountain Farm episode. It was a chapter in family history that was never talked about the way the old Vance County stories and other family touchstones were, told and retold, worn smooth with retelling. The children who were younger knew nothing about it until many decades later. Reidsville was a new start, and there was no point in dwelling on failure. Failure was not an option.

Once a stagecoach stop on the Indian trail between Virginia and South Carolina, Reidsville was barely a wide spot in the road at the end of the Civil War. By 1887 it was a town with a population of 2,500 to 3,000 with "ten tobacco factories, 14 barrooms, no water, lights or sewerage," in which "[t]hings was run wide open, with no sheriff to demur."[49] As one resident remarked, Reidsville "was inclined to be a little sporty," and boasted not one but two racetracks during the 1890s, which attracted some world-class racehorses.[50] Reidsville owed its healthy economy to a fifty-mile stretch of railroad built toward the end of the Civil War between Greensboro, North Carolina, and Danville, Virginia, which closed the only gap in a rail line connecting Virginia to the Deep South.[51] By the time the Sharps limped in from the Turkeycock Mountain disaster in 1914, Reidsville was a thriving little tobacco and textile town with a population of perhaps 5,000 people.

The railroad gave birth to a slew of tobacco manufacturing companies, which lined the tracks on the edge of town. One of these was swallowed up in 1911 by the American Tobacco Company, which then controlled 90 percent of the American market. Reidsville native Charles A. Penn became a vice president and director of the company in 1913 and recommended that a factory exclusively for the production of the company's popular Lucky Strike cigarette be located in Reidsville. Construction began in 1917. Lucky Strikes led all cigarette sales in 1918, and Reidsville became the largest per capita production center in the United States, known as the "Lucky City." For nearly three-quarters of a century, the American Tobacco Company would bring an unusual degree of prosperity and stability to the town, as well as a tinge of sophistication. The Penn family constituted local royalty and lived on a grand scale, constantly traveling to New York, Europe, or other far-flung places.

So Reidsville in 1914 was a busy and optimistic place, largely oblivious to World War I breaking out in Europe. Even as he suffered the humiliation of going broke for the second time in seven years, Jim Sharp plunged into his law practice. Although never a "clubby" man, he was a natural activist who participated in countless civic groups, including the Chamber of Commerce, the Rockingham County Farm Bureau, and the Reidsville Booster Club, that iconic organization of the New South.[52] He was also a passionate member of the Junior Order of United American Mechanics, a nativist fraternal order whose members were limited to American-born white males. Rooted in the antiimmigrant, anti-Catholic prejudice so deeply embedded in America at that time, the order feared that when the war in Europe was over, America would be "flooded with hordes of worthless immigrants."[53] Members lobbied in Washington for legislation restricting immigration. The organization enjoyed a certain success in North Carolina, where the 1900 census revealed that 99.8 percent of the population was native-born, the highest percentage in the country.[54] The Junior Order was an organization that would consume a great deal of Jim Sharp's energies over many years to come, and in which he would rise to a national position. His anti-Catholicism deeply marked his daughter Susie.

Jim Sharp also launched what would be a relentless participation in politics, running in the spring of 1915 for prosecuting attorney (now known as district attorney) for the Reidsville municipal court. Although Sharp lost, he garnered 194 votes to his opponent's 363, a respectable showing for a relative newcomer. Moreover, he had been unable to campaign, or even to be present on election day, because his son had to be rushed to Richmond, Virginia, to undergo brain surgery just at that time.

First stricken on his fourth birthday the year before, young Jim had been diagnosed with a brain tumor. He returned from Richmond with his head encased in bandages, but he bore his suffering so stoically that he acquired the nickname "Man-Boy," a sobriquet by which he would be known not only within the family but among all the neighbors and other residents of Reidsville who knew him. The dominant family memory would be of a little boy who wanted to become his lawyer father's "stenographer," as his secretary was called. All the family stories indicate that he was clearly marked to follow in his father's footsteps in the legal profession.

For the Sharps, the sorrow of Man-Boy's illness was offset somewhat by the birth in 1915 of a second son, Thomas Adolphus, to be called Tommy. This brought the total, for the moment, to five children. Such a large brood kept them busy but they seemed to thrive on it, despite the lack of financial security. One day when Annie was out with the entire contingent, she stopped to chat with an acquaintance who said, "My goodness, whose are all those children?" Annie regarded him sweetly and replied in her most genteel southern voice, "Mr. Sharp's."[55]

Man-Boy died in September 1916, about six weeks before his sixth birthday. Susie was nine years old. His father brought his body back to Reidsville from Richmond, where he had undergone another operation. Before they could put the coffin in the living room, bare of furniture, they had to clear out all the apples Jim Sharp had brought back from the Mountain Farm and spread on the floor for keeping.[56]

In 1917, a year after Man-Boy's death, two months after the birth of yet another daughter, named Louise Wortham, Jim Sharp paid $3,200 for a house at 629 Lindsey Street.[57] The neighborhood was one of the oldest in Reidsville, although not particularly distinguished. Middle-class, tree-shaded, it was a pleasant street, if not imposing. Situated on a pronounced S-curve just a few blocks from downtown, the wood-framed, tin-roofed house had been built about 1884, the original part consisting of three rooms and a porch, with old oak trees for shade. By the time the Sharps moved in, the house had been re-modeled several times with the addition of a second story, a bedroom down-stairs, and a bathroom. At some point, when the street was paved, a low wall had been built along the front from the discarded cobblestones. Over the years the Sharps would make other improvements and additions, including another porch and bathroom. The house was always full of family, friends, and relatives, prompting Annie Sharp to christen it "Chatterbox."

There was no central heat. The house had fireplaces in nearly every room and a pot-bellied stove on the enclosed back porch, which was where the family tended to gather. In the kitchen was a wood stove, which also heated the hot water. Daily chores included cutting kindling, bringing in coal, taking out ashes, all the necessary business of keeping the fires going in the fire-places. In summer the house was pleasant, except in the kitchen, where it was sweltering if the wood stove was in use for cooking and hot water. In winter, however, the house was impossible to keep warm or clean.[58]

The lot was narrow but like most in the neighborhood it was deep, run-ning 395 feet all the way to the next street in the back.[59] Jim Sharp soon had it under cultivation, operating the place as much like a farm as possible. He would come in from working in the garden, wet with sweat, and rush to get bathed and dressed in time to be in court at nine o'clock.[60] There was no end to work to be done. Many mornings the children woke to the sound of their father chopping firewood, and often they went to sleep at night to the sound of their mother's sewing machine.[61] The neighborhood was a lively one, full of children. It was the kind of neighborhood where people dropped in with-out knocking and helped one another whenever the need arose. The neigh-borhood children all walked to school and came home for lunch. It was a safe environment where, if there was little in the way of structured oversight, nevertheless little went unnoticed.

Meanwhile, in April 1917, the United States had entered World War I at last. As the forty-year-old head of a large household, Jim Sharp did his patriotic duty by serving as county chairman for the sale of Liberty Bonds in 1917 and 1918. The war changed little, however, in the family's daily life. About eighteen months after the birth of baby Louise, Annie and Jim were parents again, in April 1919, this time to another baby girl, named Florence Abigail. The summer of 1919 brought the Treaty of Versailles and Susie Sharp's twelfth birthday. As the big sister to five younger siblings ranging in age from an infant to a seven-year-old, she was often called upon to keep an eye on her brother and sisters, a duty she performed without protest and even with energy and humor. She nicknamed Louise and Florence, so close in age, "the Duplicates," addressing one as "'Cate" and the other as "Dupli-Cate." But she preferred getting off by herself with a book whenever possible, often climbing a tree to read in peace. On the many trips to visit Grandma Sharp in Intelligence, Susie would guard her solitude ferociously and was even known to bite if provoked.[62]

Grandma Sharp would come to visit in Reidsville, too. Annie would sew for her, black silk dresses to wear to the Primitive Baptist "Association" meetings that were Grandma's greatest joy in life. Religion, however, was an issue. As a strict Primitive Baptist, for example, Grandma did not believe in Sunday School, viewing it as "the Devil's workshop."[63] Once she told Susie that she would rather see her go to balls and card parties than to Sunday School, and she thought it a sin what Annie spent on Santa Claus.[64] Annie wrote in her diary, "Grannie is wonderful for her age, so clean and nice, but set in her ways in her religion. She thinks hers is the only one and has no respect for any other."[65] Members of the Primitive Baptist Church to which Grandma Sharp belonged believed that God had chosen those who would be saved before the creation of the earth and thus evangelism was useless, as was the hope of salvation among those who were not predestined to be saved. Annie could not accept Grandma Sharp's religious intolerance and could not imagine being a member of the Primitive Baptist Church. "I respect them, but can't think like them. One of them said God was only found in the Primitive Church. God made us all and why should some be the elect, predestined, and ordered before birth, or the foundation of the earth, while others were condemned. I can't believe it. God made us all, and . . . loves us all, although we are sometimes deeply punished, and 'tis hard to see through his ways."[66]

When Grannie was in residence, Annie would send the children to Sunday School at the Methodist Church despite Grannie's disapproval, although she discouraged their father from giving them their collection nickels in front of her. For his part, although Jim Sharp would often attend the Primitive Baptist Church when the preacher came to Reidsville once a month, he never officially joined it. He claimed allegiance to the Golden Rule rather than any particular church's teachings. He held to many of the fundamentalist church's ideas, but often he would attend the Methodist Church with his wife and family. Grandma's zealotry, however, had an impact. Because Primitive Baptists did not believe in infant baptism and Grandma was so strongly opposed, Annie and Jim did not have their children baptized in the Methodist Church or any other.[67]

Annie's tolerance did not extend to racial matters. Both she and Jim were strong segregationists, Annie perhaps more so than Jim. "November 7 was election day," she wrote in 1922, "and Daddy and I voted straight Democrat ticket, like our parents of old. The anti-lynch law the Republicans are trying to put over the South would disgust [any] decent white citizens."[68] Despite such chilling sentiments, a large part of Jim Sharp's law practice consisted of black clients. Attorney Sharp, while adhering wholeheartedly to the segregated customs of the day, could see the unfairness in the system and was known for fighting just as hard for a black client as a white one, even if he knew payment was only a remote possibility.

Susie Marshall Sharp, who would burst through countless barriers obstructing women to become an icon of modern womanhood, was deeply rooted in the previous century, retaining attitudes about race and class that she imbibed like drinking water from her parents. "As a child," she said, "I was an unreconstructed rebel,"[69] and she changed little. She also guarded old-fashioned ideas about women, never losing her southerner's appreciation for a man's courtliness toward the fairer sex, even as she proved herself the equal of any man in a tough profession. It was her father's refusal to acknowledge failure, however, that engendered in Susie a similar will of iron and was his most indelible legacy.

CHAPTER 2

FORMATIVE YEARS

By the time she finished high school, Susie Sharp had set her course in life. She had decided she wanted to be a lawyer and that she would never marry.

Reidsville High School achieved accreditation with the addition of a fourth year and implementation of a strong college preparatory curriculum in 1919. By the time Susie graduated in 1924, the school could boast a high-caliber faculty for its time and place. The principal and other male faculty members were educated at the University of North Carolina, except for one teacher in the commercial department, who had gone to Elon College. At the time, women were not allowed to attend the university as undergraduates, but many of the women faculty members had been educated at the North Carolina College for Women, which would later become the University of North Carolina at Greensboro.[1] All the female teachers except for one, who had attended Peace Institute and taught music, were college graduates.

Susie Sharp was a serious student, although the notes she and her best friend Janie Sands passed in class reveal a perfectly typical teenage sense of humor and silliness.[2] Jokes about fellow classmates and teachers, teasing remarks about boys, plans for after school, all the usual topics of teenage girls are there, spiked with the occasional pseudolegalism redolent of the Sharp household: "All allegations not denied are denied." In addition to Janie, Susie Sharp had other close friends, including Margaret Fillman and Margaret Reid Newnam, forever to be known as "the two Margarets." Somewhat surprisingly, Susie also got along with one of the prettiest girls in the class, a blonde with bobbed hair and a talent for frivolity named Constance Gwaltney. Still, Susie Sharp was known primarily as a conscientious and responsible person and was never part of the group that hung out downtown after school. "Susie was not a hanging out kind of girl," as one childhood friend put it.[3]

As for boys, her relationships were in the context of school and school activities, not after school or on weekends. A perennial member of the Honor

Roll despite a notorious inability to spell, she competed throughout high school for the top academic honors with a boy named Dillard Gardner. Susie Sharp would later declare that her main ambition in high school had been to make better grades than Dillard.[4] He was tall, nice-looking, a self-conscious intellectual, arrogant to a degree, already planning a career as a lawyer. In their banter there may have been a frisson of attraction, if only because their minds enjoyed the intellectual stimulation.[5] Janie passed Susie a note one day, saying, "When you said something cute, D. G. just raised his head and looked and grinned and smiled." Someone else passed Susie a note addressed to "Mrs. Dillard Gardner," but there was never any romance. Dillard Gardner would grow up to become the marshal-librarian of the North Carolina Supreme Court, where he would welcome Susie Sharp when she became an associate justice decades later.

Entering adolescence, Susie Sharp was not a beauty. She had a moon-shaped face and wore small round wire-framed glasses. She pulled her dark hair back, securing it with an enormous bow long after other girls had given up bows. All her life she would struggle with her weight, and at this point she was losing the battle if in fact she was even fighting it. Her clothes were bulky and shapeless. Nevertheless, her selection as president of the ninth-grade girls suggests that she was respected and well liked.

Throughout high school Susie was deeply involved in a wide range of extracurricular activities, including a social club called the Elite, whose motto, *Qui ne risque rien n'a rien*, she may well have adopted for her own: He who risks nothing has nothing. She began corresponding with a French pen pal, a fourteen-year-old girl named Eugenie Bouillat, nicknamed Nuion. Nuion wrote at length in fluent English, but also included long sections in French for the edification of Mademoiselle Sharp. The two teenagers would carry on their correspondence for several years, and although Susie Sharp's French never reached the level of fluency her pen pal displayed in English, they forged a long-distance friendship. Her senior year she was also vice president of her class, secretary of the French Club, and president of the Honor Council, the Debating Club, and the Old Maid's Club.

That same year she served as editor in chief of the school annual, the *Renocahi*. The *Renocahi* was an ambitious undertaking, consisting of a magazine that came out several times during the year, with a final issue that served as the school annual. As editor in chief, Susie Sharp not only created a good bit of the content but also oversaw the business side of the enterprise, including collecting payment from students, making payments to the printer, and soliciting advertising. She would work with Miss Donie Counts, the faculty adviser, well into the summer after graduation to tidy up the loose ends. Collecting students' purchase money required perseverance after the yearbooks had been distributed, and when the printer's bill finally had been paid, Susie Sharp wrote to Miss Counts that it might be smart to keep that bit of news under wraps for the moment. Miss Counts wrote back, "I don't know what I'd do without your letters. You *look* so *meek* but when you write you are bristling with something every time."[6]

But it was the Debate Club that absorbed most of her time and which would mark her life. Turned down for a spot on the glamorous girls' basketball team (due partly to her 5'2" stature but mostly to her lack of any athletic ability), she had set her sights on the next most prestigious group, the school debate team. Helped by her lawyer father, she made it. The team's main focus was the State Triangular Debate, an annual event in which regional schools qualified for statewide competition. Conducted under the auspices of the University of North Carolina Dialectic and Philanthropic Literary Societies and the university's extension division, the competition had been organized in 1912. In 1919, 250 schools had participated, with an estimated 80,000 people attending the events.[7] Winning schools in the regional debates advanced to the statewide finals held in Chapel Hill. A young lawyer who had hung out his shingle in Reidsville the preceding year, Allen H. Gwyn, volunteered to help coach the team, adding a degree of professional expertise to their preparations.

In an interview Susie Sharp gave at the end of her career, shortly before she retired as chief justice, she described how the experience led to her decision to go into law. "Well, I went out for the debating team, and our teams always won," she told a reporter from the *Philadelphia Inquirer*.[8] "Everybody commented then, 'Why, Susie, you ought to be a lawyer.'" Her memory that her team never lost, manifestly untrue according to the record, reflects the self-esteem debating gave her and the significance it had in her career decision. In fact, she considered the experience she gained to be the most valuable training she got in high school.[9] As she recalled in 1962, just after her appointment to the North Carolina Supreme Court, "The debates gave me an association and contact with my teachers and coaches from whom I acquired some special knowledge I would not otherwise have obtained; they introduced me to stage fright and got me over it; they taught me the beginnings of how to organize materials logically and to present an argument persuasively; I learned the value of a large vocabulary." Indeed, she wrote, "As a result of those debates I decided I wanted to be a lawyer and at the end of my senior year in high school I knew what I wanted to do."[10]

BEGINNINGS

Not the least important part of the experience was Susie's introduction to Allen Gwyn: "He praised me to the skies and I worked like a dog."[11] Their relationship, strong and complicated, would endure until he died nearly half a century later.

During her high school years, from 1920 to 1924, Susie Sharp had ample opportunity to observe not only the importance of debate in the public arena but also the role of women in public affairs. During the 1920 gubernatorial election in North Carolina, Cameron Morrison defeated O. Max Gardner, a result many attributed largely to the skillful manipulation of the women's suffrage issue, which had not yet been settled by ratification of the Nineteenth Amendment. Morrison opposed the amendment and used Gardner's support for it to imply that he also supported voting by blacks ("Did not the Amendment include Black women?").[12] That August, reflecting public opinion in the state, the *Reidsville Review* reported: "Women Suffrage Defeated by NC Senate 25 to 23."[13]

By fall, however, the Nineteenth Amendment to the U.S. Constitution had been ratified and the Democrats were stumping hard against a strong national trend toward the Republican presidential candidate, appealing to the new women's vote. The *Reidsville Review* exhorted the women to use their new voting privileges. Louise Alexander of Greensboro, a suffragist who passed the North Carolina bar in 1920 after attending the law school at UNC, spoke on behalf of the Democratic campaign in Reidsville, an event of which Susie Sharp was likely to have been aware.[14]

In addition to keeping up with debates on issues of the day, at home Susie Sharp also heard plenty about legal matters. As a child, she did not get to see her father in action as a lawyer because the courthouse was deemed no place for children—or for ladies either, for that matter. In high school, however, she began to accompany him to court occasionally when she was not in school, and enjoyed watching the trials.[15] In any event, the family was always aware that Jim Sharp was fighting regular battles in the courtroom. Court week bore an "awesome aspect." As Susie Sharp wrote decades later when she was a superior court judge, "We children did not understand what court-week was all about, but we knew that life—and Daddy—would not be normal until it was over. We knew that if he passed a wrong juror or Mr. G[lidewell] got the last speech or entertained some of the judges that great wrongs might result—i.e. Daddy might lose the case!"[16] P. W. Glidewell, a prominent and flamboyant attorney, was a colorful fixture of the Rockingham County bar for decades with whom Jim Sharp frequently locked horns in court.

At the dinner table, Susie's father would tell about the cases he had argued in court, and in the days before children bolted from the table to watch television, his vivid renditions of courtroom battles had great entertainment value.[17] Jim Sharp's mealtime reports of the legal world inevitably had a strong impact on the children, who saw so little of him. In addition to his law practice and civic activities, he was nearly always running for office.

The summer before Susie Sharp started the ninth grade, the large Sharp household had gotten even larger when Annie gave birth to twin boys, James Blackwell and John Pomfret. This event was cause for great rejoicing in the family, and Jim Sharp's elation was so apparent that the paper ran a humorous article, declaring that Attorney J. M. Sharp was "sitting on top of the world these days."[18] When the twins were about nine months old, Annie had to take little Jim to Richmond for a hernia operation at St. Luke's Hospital and was away for two weeks. She left Jim's twin brother John with a neighbor across the street while the rest of the children went to stay at Grandma Sharp's, where Susie was in charge of them. At the age of not-quite-fifteen, she was quite capable of taking care of five younger ones ranging from three to ten years old: Florence, Louise, Tommy, Annie Hill, and Sallie. Her sister Louise recalled, "She was used to managing us, and we looked up to her and did what she said."[19] If mutiny developed, Susie dealt with it by reasoning with the children, an approach that seemed to work back in those days when children minded their elders.[20]

This experience and others like it left Susie Sharp with no illusions about the joys of childcare. The following September, when her Sunday School teacher told her that she ought to be a kindergarten teacher, she replied, "If I ever go into a kindergarten, I hope someone will shoot me."[21] About this comment, however, Annie remarked in her journal, "All the 'chilluns' are cranky [crazy] about Susie and vice versa, but Susie does not want anyone to know it."[22]

In late spring of 1923 when Susie Sharp was in the tenth grade, disaster struck the family again. After a long spell in which nearly all the children had been desperately ill with measles, the twins, Jim and John, took sick with colitis and died within three weeks of each other.[23] Annie descended into a frightening depression. Although she acknowledged that her husband was just as heartbroken as she, and was aware that Susie had taken it the hardest of the children, she was lost in such overwhelming grief that she could not function. Her incapacitation left the rest of the family to manage their complicated lives on their own, and there was much to manage. Among other things, five-year-old Florence had been so terribly ill with the measles that she was having to learn how to walk again, four weeks after she was stricken. Then there were the more mundane matters—birthdays, a runaway puppy, the daily routine. Annie just went through the motions, trying to work herself "to a frazzle" so she could sleep. Meanwhile, Jim Sharp stepped up to the office of state councillor for the Junior Order, assuming leadership of the 50,000 North Carolina members, which meant he would be on the road even more than usual that year, making speeches all over the state.[24]

It fell to sixteen-year-old Susie Sharp to get the younger children clean and dressed, off to school. She was the one who refereed fights, organized chores, found lost belongings. On Sunday mornings, she got the entire brood all shined up and dressed in their Sunday best and marched them down to Sunday School. By every account she handled it all beautifully, but one day in September as she did the hated milking chores, the cow kicked her and she burst into tears.[25] No one seems to remember how long this went on. Eventually, Annie did get a grip on herself and reentered life.[26] Louise remembered that she knew it was going to be all right when her mother stopped wearing mourning clothes and bought herself a pretty pink hat. "It was a straw hat and it had a wide brim and it had flowers on it. We thought that was the prettiest hat in the world. It wasn't black."[27]

Whether or not being thrust into the role of mother to a large brood influenced Susie Sharp in her decision to remain single, it appears she made that decision early in her high school years. Perhaps she reacted defensively to the joking of her peers. "What Would Happen If?" queried one of several school magazine jokes about her. Among the answers was, "Susie Sharp had a date." If this sort of thing bothered her, there is no record of it. But years later Susie Sharp would recall that her mother used to tell her, "My ugly duckling will someday be a swan," a hope that applied to inner as well as outer beauty.[28] In any event, she projected a solitary life for herself.

Graduating from high school, she had the highest grade in the senior class, but Dillard Gardner's four-year average was higher by an eyelash, 96.64 to 96.37, winning him the title of valedictorian.[29] In the school yearbook, the class "Prophecy" peered a decade into the future and found that "Susie Sharpe [sic] is giving them strong competition in the law business," adding that "Susie is quite ambitious . . . making enough to support a husband in good style, though she does not seem inclined to do so."[30] In her "Commencement Memories" book, Susie Sharp's teachers wrote their advice for her. "Don't be frivolous," said Miss Janie Stacey. "Please don't be an old maid!" exhorted another. Her French teacher, Miss Pauline Whitley, wrote, "Soyez Gov. Sharp." No wonder Susie Sharp, in filling in the blank next to "My hopes and plans for the future," wrote, "To know my own mind."

In fact, however, she had made up her mind that she wanted to be a lawyer. That there was no more than a bare handful of women lawyers in North Carolina seems not to have deterred her in the least.[31] Years later she would jokingly claim that as the eldest child she had always been blamed for anything that went wrong and so she had to figure out how to defend herself.[32] "I was apparently quite argumentative," she explained, "and people started saying you ought to be a lawyer, like your daddy. I started taking them seriously."[33] Her debate team experience had strengthened her skill and her confidence, while her father's descriptions of his legal experiences had given her an understanding of what a lawyer's career was like.

Encouragement for Susie Sharp's legal career, however, did not come from her father, although he did not actively discourage her.[34] He must have felt there were easier paths. But both her parents were bent on sending their children out into the world equipped to make a living, an ambition that applied to the girls at least as much as it did to the boys.[35] Jim Sharp articulated this forward-thinking position quite succinctly: "You can't count on a man to take care of you."[36] This attitude was far from prevalent in a time when both husbands and wives were proud to say that the wife "did not work." Annie Sharp had worked as a schoolteacher, offering her children a role model as a working woman, and she joined her husband in the view that all women should be prepared to earn a living. Susie Sharp was fortunate in that she never imagined herself being supported by someone else. But to the extent that she received any encouragement to pursue a career in law, it came primarily from Miss Stacey and Miss Whitley. These two teachers "never minimized the difficulties but they encouraged me to try to overcome them," Susie Sharp wrote many years later, just after being elected chief justice of the North Carolina Supreme Court.[37]

The summer of 1924 was a transition time, not only for Susie Sharp but for the whole family. Her father was campaigning in what would be a successful race for the state senate as well as traveling on Junior Order business, and often she acted as his chauffeur. Annie, pregnant again at the age of forty-five, made ready for the new baby and complained to her journal about Jim Sharp's politicking. On July 17, 1924, James Vance Sharp was born, the last of Jim and Annie's children, known as "Kits." Coming just a year after the deaths of the twins, he was a beautiful consolation. No sooner had baby Kits arrived than his seventeen-year-old sister Susie left the family nest to go off to the North Carolina College for Women in Greensboro, known as NCCW. There had never been any question that she would continue her education. Over the years the entire family would sacrifice so that all seven children could go to college and graduate school. The house at 629 Lindsey Street would be mortgaged over and over again to help finance their educations.[38]

Twenty-four miles from Reidsville, NCCW was an exceptionally good launch pad for a young woman of Susie Sharp's ability and temperament. The first state-supported school in North Carolina for the higher education of women, it had opened in 1892 as the State Normal and Industrial School, changing its name in 1919 to North Carolina College for Women. (The school changed its name again in 1932 to the Woman's College of the University of North Carolina, reflecting its inclusion in the university system, and again in 1963, when it became coeducational, to the University of North Carolina at Greensboro.) A four-year college, it was an amazingly progressive institution, bent on producing "a 'New Woman' for the New South."[39] Charles Duncan McIver, the first president, was passionate on the subject of women's "right to be 'independent and self-supporting.'"[40] A strong faculty, primarily female, included women with degrees from the Massachusetts Institute of Technology, the Woman's Medical College of New York Infirmary, and Wellesley. Many faculty members had pursued graduate work at universities including Harvard, Columbia, Cornell, and Berkeley, as well as abroad. By World War I, the students had enthusiastically embraced the cause of women's suffrage.

Two professors in particular sparked the progressive attitude on campus: Harriet Wiseman Elliott and Walter Clinton Jackson. Elliott, who had a master's degree from Columbia University, taught history and government. She was "already a feminist and suffragist when she arrived on campus in 1913"[41] and would become a national figure, appointed by President Franklin D. Roosevelt to posts in his administration.[42] Affectionately known as "Aunt Hitt" by the students, she exhorted them to pursue the truth through original — not secondary — sources, to set high professional goals, and never to neglect their responsibilities as citizens. Susie Sharp's lifelong emphasis on keeping up with current affairs in the newspapers and on casting her vote may fairly be attributed to Miss Elliott's admonitions. Nor were Miss Elliott's girls to allow others to think for them — they were to think through problems for themselves.[43]

Walter C. Jackson, a *rara avis* in the Jim Crow South, was a charismatic liberal committed not only to women's rights but also to improved race relations.[44] Among his publications were *A Boy's Life of Booker T. Washington* and, with N. I. White, *Poetry by American Negroes*. A handsome man of forty-five when Susie Sharp was a freshman, he had a strong chin, a straight nose, and an eagle's gaze under a wavy widow's peak. He was an immensely talented teacher whose lectures were so packed that it was not uncommon to have to bring in extra chairs.[45]

In addition to challenging teachers, the students had the opportunity to hear an astonishing array of well-known speakers on a variety of subjects over the years, including, as a small sample, muckraking journalist Ida Tarbell and social worker Jane Addams, as well as Nellie Tayloe Ross of Wyoming, the first woman governor of a state, and Judge Florence E. Allen, the first woman elected to be a member of a state supreme court.[46] Clarence Darrow came, as did Bertrand Russell, Edna St. Vincent Millay, and Will Durant. Musicians and performers included Jascha Heifetz, Anna Pavlova, and Sarah Bernhardt.[47] The young women at the college, who came from farms and tiny towns across North Carolina, were exposed to a range of cultural and intellectual opportunities not even dreamed of in most households in the state.

By the time Susie Sharp arrived on the campus of NCCW, the school had grown from a teachers' college of 490 students and 23 faculty members in 1900 to a fully accredited liberal arts college with more than 1,600 students and 199 faculty members.[48] The sweeping changes on the NCCW campus reflected the dramatic progress women had made toward becoming true partners in the American enterprise. Ironically, however, the mid-1920s were a time of some backsliding, despite the prevalent image of the modern woman as convention-defying flapper. World War I was over; women had the vote. Women had largely won the battle for higher education, and by the 1920s it was no longer uncommon for daughters of middle-class families to go on to college. In the wake of victory, a degree of disillusion had seeped into the movement for women's rights. Women who had chosen to pursue a career generally found themselves in subordinate roles, with few real professional opportunities and precious few role models. Those who desired both a career and marriage faced enormous obstacles—logistically, socially, and emotionally.[49] The prevailing attitude among both men and women remained, as the motto of a Muncie, Indiana, women's club put it, "Men are God's trees; women are his flowers."[50] In 1920 only 12.2 percent of all professional women in the country were married.[51]

Although the tradition of progressive, proactive, and responsible women citizens remained strong at the college and among its faculty, feminism in general was on the wane, and it was apparent even at NCCW, where, for the first time, students were less concerned with social reform than with social invitations. In the South, in particular, college women stepped down off the barricades and onto the dance floor. At the same time, however, new freedoms and opportunities had fostered new attitudes, many of them shocking to the older generation. Technological advances had freed women from much of the drudgery associated with their homemaking duties and ratcheted up the speed of daily life. As one NCCW student put it in 1926, "A slow buggy ride is no longer attractive because it is now possible to go sixty miles an hour in an automobile."[52] She did not mention one of the most important social changes brought about by the automobile, which was its usefulness in the romance department. The shift from the front porch to the back seat matched up inclination with opportunity in a way not previously available. John Steinbeck, in his *Cannery Row*, remarked, "Most of the babies of the era were conceived in the Model T Ford, and not a few were born in them."

Ironically, independent thinking led more and more NCCW girls to the conclusion that marriage and a family ought not to be denied them merely because women now had other acceptable options. Marriage reemerged as a primary goal of young women who a decade before might have rejected such a fate as they fought for the right to a career. And although higher education was undoubtedly desired, whether as an adornment for women of the middle and upper classes or as equipment for making a living, there lurked a fear that too much education might derail a girl's journey to the altar, a fear the college recognized. For example, in the spring of Susie Sharp's sophomore year, a speaker giving a summary of "What North Carolina Women Are Doing" felt compelled to assure her audience, "Contrary to public opinion . . . college graduates do marry in large numbers."[53]

Susie Sharp, whose experience in life had not led her to think in terms of marriage, thus embarked on her college career at a time when by all rights she should have been validated for her already-avowed career goals, only to find that she was swimming against an outgoing feminist tide. But there she was: bright, energetic, strongly encouraged by her teachers and her parents to pursue a profession. No one had ever told her she could not be whatever she wanted. Moreover, she had been a close observer of the hardships and limits of her mother's life. Popular with her peers, self-confident in her abilities, but famously a wallflower with few romantic prospects, Susie Sharp had little reason to waver from her path.

Sophomore year sharpened Susie Sharp's focus on a variety of matters, academic and otherwise. In later years, she claimed that chemistry had almost diverted her from her intention to pursue the law, recollecting a sleepless night in which she walked the floor, deliberating.[54] Perhaps she was influenced in her decision by an article that appeared that fall in an issue of the *Alumnae News* entitled "Law as a Profession for Women," by a 1921 NCCW graduate who had received her law degree from the University of Michigan.[55] Without minimizing the handicaps, "some . . . imaginary, some real," confronting women lawyers in 1925, the author noted that the current number of women with a law degree in the United States exceeded 2,600, as compared to only 75 in 1880. Although a substantial number probably were not practicing, it was a dramatic increase, and the practicing women attorneys included Mabel Walker Willebrandt, who served as assistant U.S. attorney general from 1921 to 1929. In New York, there were four women assistant district attorneys, three assistant corporation counsels, an assistant U.S. district attorney, and a city magistrate. In the entire country, there were more than twenty-five female judges, including the best known, Judge Florence E. Allen of the Ohio Supreme Court. Susie Sharp often acknowledged that Judge Allen had been a role model for her. In North Carolina, meanwhile, a few pioneers had begun to clear a trail. From NCCW, five graduates had gone on to study law, of whom three were practicing; in addition perhaps half a dozen other women were actively practicing in North Carolina.[56]

Undoubtedly, Susie Sharp would have been aware of Kathrine Robinson, a 1913 graduate of NCCW who in 1920 was the fourth woman to graduate from the University of North Carolina School of Law and the eleventh woman to be licensed to practice law in the state.[57] When she applied to law school, the University of Virginia turned her down on the basis of her sex. At UNC Kathrine Robinson graduated first in her class, then made the top score on the bar exam. She was practicing with her father in Fayetteville when Susie Sharp was at NCCW, and her account in the *Alumnae News* of her trip as a delegate to the 1924 American Bar Association meeting in London made for intoxicating reading.[58] She reported on her visits to the courts in London, where she observed that women served on the juries, a privilege they did not have in North Carolina. She hobnobbed with women barristers in London and attended dinners in the Inns of Court, not to mention luncheons, teas, and garden parties, including one at Buckingham Palace. If, as is quite possible, Susie Sharp read this account, it must have thrilled her to the bone.

Clearly it was a time of rapidly expanding opportunity, and Susie Sharp — who had long envisioned herself as a lawyer — could derive encouragement from these reports of women who had begun to breach the barrier. The arguments of her Aunt Susie Garrett, who made a special trip from Danville, Virginia, to beg her not to go to law school because if she did she would surely never marry, were not persuasive.[59] "Besides," as Susie Sharp later admitted, "I didn't want to teach school."[60] With a chemistry major, school teaching would likely have been her only career option. If Susie Sharp struggled over the decision, however, once made she put it behind her and never thought to mention it again until she was well into her legal career, looking back at what she considered a fork in the road.

For the first time in her life, she was giving attention to her physical appearance. She was dieting and had begun wearing a bit of makeup at school, although she was careful to wipe off every trace before she returned to Reidsville for visits.[61] Very likely, this new interest in her appearance was partly due to the acknowledged crush she had on Mr. Jackson. A crush on Mr. Jackson was almost a curriculum requirement at NCCW. His charisma, intellect, anti-establishment views, and humor, as well as his looks, guaranteed classrooms of swooning girls. There is no indication that he encouraged Susie Sharp in any way other than academic, but for the first time she found herself powerfully attracted to a man, albeit an unattainable one. Not surprisingly, perhaps, he was an older man whose knowledge and intellectual accomplishments exceeded hers. In schoolgirl fashion, Susie Sharp freely shared the existence of her crush with her friends, but in her unique way she added a legalistic angle to her fantasy. Margaret Fillman wrote: "Susie, why do you wish to wreck homes by making divorce laws? . . . But, you are in love with an instructor and want him, so you would make a law to separate him from his spouse. I see it all now."[62]

Both girls may have been half jesting, but it is interesting that Susie Sharp's approach to her romantic dilemma was to look to the law. In fact, however, Mr. Jackson's unavailability may have been a substantial part of his appeal. The following summer while Susie was taking a summer school history course with her favorite teacher, one of her cousins wrote: "Don't worry so over Mr. Jackson. Probably you'll find a perfect married man in C[hapel] H[ill] that will suit you better. Live in hopes anyway."[63] Neither of them could have known how prophetic this remark would be.

With two years as an undergraduate under her belt, she was ready to move on to the School of Law at the University of North Carolina in Chapel Hill, the alma mater of the vast majority of the state's leaders, constitutionally required to provide an affordable educational opportunity to the state's citizens. Getting into law school was "no problem at all," according to Susie Sharp. "I just applied and they accepted me."[64]

More problematic was the requirement that students at NCCW had to know how to swim. Not only did Susie Sharp never learn to swim; it appears she may never have gotten wet. During her years as a superior court judge, she once regaled a dinner table with the story of how, as the line of girls would snake forward to jump into the school pool, she would deftly turn and rejoin the line at the rear as many times as necessary to avoid having to take the plunge. This story was mildly shocking to one of her listeners, Raymond Mason Taylor, who would later become marshal-librarian of the North Carolina Supreme Court during Susie Sharp's tenure. "I had always been taught, you know, you have to do everything exactly right, you've got to follow the rules all the time on all matters," he would recall. But he learned then that "Judge Sharp was very much of a pragmatist and was not impractical about things."[65]

PART II

PURSUIT OF THE LAW

CHAPTER 3

UNIVERSITY OF NORTH CAROLINA SCHOOL OF LAW

Susie Sharp sometimes said that her legal education began the day her father got his law license. As a student at the University of North Carolina School of Law, however, her formal legal training outstripped not only her father's but also that of the vast majority of practicing lawyers in the state. Indeed, her arrival in Chapel Hill coincided with fundamental changes taking place in legal education in general and at the UNC law school in particular.[1] These changes, which were related to the emergence of the New South as an increasingly integral part of the nation as a whole, were reflected in every aspect of the law school experience, from admission requirements to teaching methods and curriculum to graduation requirements. When Susie Sharp entered UNC as a first-year law student, she was right on the cusp of the school's transformation from a clubby bar review factory to a modern law school. In a very short period of time, between about 1923 and her graduation in 1929, the UNC law school underwent a major transformation. Susie Sharp was one of the very first to graduate with what today would be considered a proper legal education.

The university had expanded dramatically in the years following the First World War. Between 1917 and 1930, the university's enrollment grew from 855 to 3,017 students.[2] The modernization of the law school began under Lucius Polk McGehee, who served as dean from 1910 to 1923. It was under Dean McGehee that the law school added a third year of study, in 1919. Initially, however, very few students continued beyond the second year, which was then the minimum requirement to take the bar examination.[3] In 1923, for example, there were 12 third-year students out of a student body of 123, up from only 4 the previous year.

Dean McGehee also moved UNC away from the textbook-and-lecture system toward the casebook system, which was far better adapted to the increasing complexity of the law and to encouraging a vigorous intellectual facility in the aspiring lawyers. The case study method was developed by Professor Christopher C. Langdell at Harvard Law School, and it had triggered a transition in law schools nationwide. Under this method, students read the appellate court opinions on actual cases, then were drawn out in class by the professor's Socratic questioning, a technique that encouraged analysis and active thought rather than rote learning. Other changes included the reorganization of the moot court program in 1918 around a "law club" model developed at Harvard, in an effort to maximize the students' participation in the simulated progress of a case through the appellate process. And in 1923, after a long history of shifting from pillar to post on campus, the law school moved into the brand new law building, christened Manning Hall.

At McGehee's death in 1923, President Harry W. Chase sought to hire a dean who could catapult the law school into the first ranks, at least in the South. He visited the law schools at Chicago, Harvard, and Columbia and consulted men prominent in the field of legal education, as well as the Carnegie Foundation. "My conviction that the Law School stands at the cross-roads in its history has been strengthened," Chase said. At the time, the American Bar Association recognized thirty-nine institutions in the country as "standard law schools." The University of North Carolina was not among them. Chase proposed to the trustees a number of measures, including raising the admission requirement from one year to two years of college, which was the standard as defined by the American Bar Association in 1921.

In addition, President Chase urged a concentrated effort to persuade students to complete the full three-year course. He advocated the elimination of the existing summer school program, which was "frankly a coaching class for the bar examination," and the institution of a regular summer quarter with courses given for credit just like those during the rest of the year. He fully supported the case method of teaching, now universally used in reputable law schools, declaring, "Whatever may have been the case in the past, it is certainly true today that the body of existing law is so vast that the emphasis must be on method, and not on information."

President Chase had no doubt as to what was at stake. "The question . . . is whether it is the function of the University Law School to prepare an inferior brand of lawyers for law as a trade, or whether it shall prepare men for practice and leadership in law as a profession. . . . Times have changed. Not only has the existing body of law grown enormously, but the whole social and economic life of North Carolina is rapidly undergoing a transformation which affects legal problems as it affects problems in every other sphere of life." In his view, failing to develop a modernized law school meant the abandonment of "all thought of leadership."[4]

His view was not without opposition. Governor Cameron Morrison, himself a lawyer who had not attended college, argued that many fine attorneys had no college training and would not have been admitted to the law school under the proposed new requirements. But a number of alumni wrote to support President Chase, declaring, for example, that "the University Law Department has been hide-bound for 100 years by aristocratic and family and political ties" and that the law school dean "should be alive to world conditions, and should wish his men to have a knowledge and training in law as would immediately fit them for great commercial positions."[5] In June 1924 President Chase prevailed on all his issues before the trustees. It was a watershed. Chase's policies led to a series of law school deans with modern training in legal education, an increase in the number of faculty members, higher admission standards, the modernization of the curriculum, the institution of a full-credit summer school session, and a marked improvement in the law library.[6]

Among North Carolina attorneys, those who had gone to the university occupied a special position, for UNC was the holy ground on which most of the state's leaders were raised. Its mystique penetrated undergraduates and postgraduates alike to an extraordinary degree. Chartered in 1789, UNC was proud to be known as the first state university in the nation to open its doors. Around the perimeter of McCorkle Place, the original quad, the buildings included the two oldest state university buildings in the country, Old East and Person Hall.[7] The university was smugly situated in the beautiful town of Chapel Hill, shady and green, crisscrossed with low dry-stone walls, festooned with dogwood in the spring and exploding with brilliant hardwoods in the fall.

North Carolina was distinguished by its thickly interlaced network of men in positions of influence, not only in the handful of larger towns like the capital city of Raleigh but also in every county and in the numberless small towns that made up the texture of the state. Among these men the university was a potent common denominator. It was widely held that if a young man intended to make his life in North Carolina (and few saw any reason to go elsewhere), he would be better off to attend UNC than any of the ivy league schools because of the contacts he would make in Chapel Hill. He would know someone in an influential position in every nook and cranny of the state with whom he would have an immediate bond. In a state in which business of all sorts was conducted to a considerable extent on the basis of personal connections, a young man's future could depend on his UNC background.

In this powerful network, women were absent. Certainly there were a handful of accomplished women in the state who had achieved prominence in their fields, but as a rule they operated outside the old boys' club. Their outsider status was exacerbated by the fact that women attending the university were few indeed. As president of the university at the end of the nineteenth century, Edwin Alderman had interpreted the trustees' decision allowing women to attend the university as "postgraduates" to include graduates of two-year colleges, opening up the possibility for women to obtain an undergraduate degree at Chapel Hill, but only after transferring in their junior year. Acceptance of women on campus, however, was grudging at best. In 1898 Sallie Walker Stockard, the first woman to obtain an undergraduate degree, was not permitted to attend the graduation ceremony, but rather had to receive her diploma in private and, like other early UNC women students, was not included in the official class picture. Until 1912 women numbered only about 6 per year in classes of approximately 800 students. As of 1920, although junior and senior women were admitted into all departments, they were not allowed into all courses. It would not be until 1963 that women were free to apply to all university departments as freshmen and sophomores. Moreover, the legislature had refused to allocate funds for a women's dormitory, and because the majority of boardinghouses in Chapel Hill did not accept female boarders, women students had to scrabble simply for a roof over their heads.

In 1923 a proposal to fund a women's dormitory ignited a fierce battle in the legislature and on campus. The specter of coeducation on a large scale provoked a headline in the *Tar Heel*, the student paper, declaring, "Women Not Wanted Here." The *Tar Heel* editors labeled as "claptrap" and "sob stuff" the women's request to benefit from the best education the state had to offer. One editorial brutally rebutted the women's argument that they should be permitted a university education on the grounds that they were citizens of the state: "On the basis of that argument we could justify the admission of Negroes to the University. Perhaps we should permit them to do so, but where can we find a sane white man or woman in North Carolina who believes that we should?"[8] In the end, a coalition of enlightened professors, alumni, and politicians won the battle, and in 1925—the year before Susie Sharp arrived on campus as a law student—Spencer Hall opened as the campus's only women's dorm, albeit minus two wings originally included in the design.

Susie Sharp would never forget the "fear and trembling the first morning" as she mounted the limestone steps to the front door of Manning Hall. "Would anybody speak to me?" she wondered. "Would they laugh at me?"[9] But if she was fearful, she did her best to conceal it.

Theoretically, her presence should not have been disruptive, for she was not the first woman to attend the UNC School of Law. North Carolina, arguably, had an enlightened position on this issue, having become in 1878 the sixth state in the nation and the first in the South to allow women to obtain a license to practice law. Only six years before, in 1872, the U.S. Supreme Court had upheld the right of Illinois to deny a law license to a woman on the basis of her gender.[10] But when one Tabitha Anne Holton demanded the right to take the North Carolina bar exam in 1878, the state supreme court, after deliberating only ten minutes, held in her favor.[11] UNC admitted its first woman to law school in 1911 and had its first woman graduate, Margaret Berry, in 1915.[12] At both Trinity College (later Duke University) and Wake Forest College (later University), women were not formally admitted to the law school until 1927. Elsewhere in the country, many law schools continued to deny women admission well into the twentieth century, including Harvard, where women were not allowed until 1950.[13]

In comparison, then, the UNC law school had a liberal tradition.[14] But there had been only three female graduates since 1911. It had been six years since the redoubtable Kathrine Robinson (later Everett) graduated in 1920.[15] As the lone woman in her class of approximately sixty, Susie Sharp was more than conspicuous.[16] Her professors did not help matters by making an exception to the alphabetical seating chart for her alone, planting her in the first seat of the first row.[17] The heels of her shoes echoed distinctively on the uncarpeted floors.

Decades later, Susie Sharp would recall this period as a traumatic one. She was "so frightened by so much masculinity," she later declared, that it was days before she "saw anything of the law building except the floors."[18] She said, "I felt like I had the honor of womanhood on my shoulders. I was very conscious of my family obligations as well. I just couldn't flunk out."[19] But it was hard. Her childhood friend Janie Sands wrote, "I heard about you weeping over the telephone."[20] Perhaps it was a mixed blessing that her old hometown rival, Dillard Gardner, was also a first-year student and was only too glad to give her pointers. In class she found an anonymous note left in her seat advising her: "John Calvin said it was O.K. for a man to beat his wife, but he did not think he ought to rub salt in the wounds; *we* think Calvin was wrong about the salt."[21] Another note said, "One drop of kerosene ruins a whole barrel of flour."[22] Still another suggested she read the case of *State v. Black*, which she did, "the first time nobody was looking."[23] There she discovered that the North Carolina Supreme Court had upheld the exoneration of a husband who had dragged his wife around on the floor by her hair, on the grounds that, because he was responsible for her conduct, he was entitled to use such force as was necessary to achieve the correct result.

For about three weeks Susie Sharp continued to find these anonymous billets-doux on her seat when she arrived in the classroom each morning. She kept her eyes riveted on her books.[24] Eventually, however, the novelty of her presence began to wear off a bit, and at last she received one final anonymous note, advising her that rubber heels were on sale at Lacock's, the shoe store on Franklin Street downtown. She complied with the suggestion, and the epistolary harassment ceased. Perhaps it was significant that the boys no longer felt the need to hear her coming. Even so, she was still suffering from unwanted attention at least as late as January, into the second semester. Her father wrote that he was sorry to hear that she was being used "to amuse the class." He advised her to "stick to them and feed them out of the same spoon."[25] Susie evidently thought humor might help, but her father wrote, "I do not know of a good joke to hit the teacher with."[26]

From the safe perspective of half a century later, Susie Sharp would declare, "Being the only woman didn't hurt me at all. I was so conspicuous that I worked harder than I otherwise would have, and I wasn't lost in the shuffle."[27] In fact, as her male classmates realized that she had no intention of cramping their style, they began to appreciate her serious intellect and—equally important—her robust sense of fun. She was liked and respected well enough that she almost won the post of secretary-treasurer of the first-year class, losing the election by only two votes on the third ballot.[28] Many of her fellow students became lifelong friends.

She roomed in Spencer Hall, the new women's dormitory, which was home for female students from departments throughout the university. A large percentage were graduate students. Describing the group of women at UNC during her years there, Susie Sharp later said, "Lots of women were working on their doctorates and were very serious; it was a very attractive group of smart girls able to handle both academic and social problems easily."[29] Even the undergraduates, the juniors and seniors, were in general an exceptional group. By the time Susie Sharp arrived on campus, UNC coeds had established their credentials by consistently maintaining the highest grade point average of any group on campus.[30] In 1925 seven female students had made Phi Beta Kappa, which was extraordinary, considering their relatively small numbers within the student body.[31]

However great their accomplishments, UNC women nevertheless led a marginal existence at the university. As one historian has put it, "Women were present but peripheral, virtually a college within a college, *at* but not really *of* the University. Housing, admission standards, rules and regulations, governing bodies, and many extracurricular activities for women remained separate and distinct from those for men. Women shared classrooms with men but the University remained a man's institution."[32] Sarcastic remarks on coeds were a staple feature of the *Tar Heel*. Male condescension was simply a fact of life for women students.

In Professor Albert Coates's Personal Property class, Susie Sharp first began to grasp the nature of the challenge she had set for herself. Just three years out of Harvard Law School, where he had studied under Felix Frankfurter, Coates was irrepressible. He could quote by the yard from everything from the Bible to *Alice in Wonderland*, and did. He played tough mental games in class. Dean A. C. McIntosh caused elation among the first-year students when he was heard to say of the young professor, "You can always tell a Harvard man, but you can't tell him much."[33] Coates was largely responsible for the moot court program, supervising the students and obtaining prominent judges to sit on the bench during the final competition.

That September morning, as Professor Coates confronted the first class of the semester in his course on Personal Property, required of all first-year students, Susie Sharp felt her world drop out from under her. "I had come to Chapel Hill to learn the law, which—with naive faith—I then thought could be learned like the multiplication tables," she recalled more than fifty years later.[34] Professor Coates was exploring the acquisition of property rights in wild animals. The rule was simple: man "owned" the wild animal when he reduced it to possession. Yes, but—when was that? Professor Coates paced back and forth. Say, for example, you have set a mink trap, and it has captured its prey. You are a hundred yards away, but you hurry toward the trap. Just then another hunter gets to the trap and takes the mink. Was it your mink? To Susie Sharp's distress, Professor Coates did not answer. He just asked another question. "It was in that first class that Mr. Coates disabused my mind of the notion that the law and the multiplication tables had anything in common," she remembered. "My faith was shattered. There was no certainty in the law or anything else. When that class was over, I had despaired of ever 'mastering that lawless science of the law, that codeless myriad of precedent, that wilderness of single instances.'" By the end of that first week she was so upset by "the quicksands of the law" that she "suggested to Mr. Coates that the legislature ought to meet in special session and clear up some of those problems he kept raising by his repeated question, 'Where do you draw the line?'" Susie Sharp later averred, "It took me three years to dim the baleful impression I had made on my teacher by that suggestion."[35]

The modern "school larnin'" to which Susie Sharp was being subjected caused her father to snort, a common reaction among the older generation of attorneys who had learned the law largely on their feet. Commenting on a recent quiz, Jim Sharp said that he had been practicing law for twenty years and had never come across such "fool questions."[36] He was more concerned about her going and coming to the law school at night by herself, telling her that if she "couldn't get enough learning in the day, to leave it off."[37] But he was preoccupied with politics, speaking at or attending a political gathering nearly every night, running again for the North Carolina Senate. His law practice was busy too, and he had taken on a young lawyer named Harry L. Crutchfield to help him.

Jim Sharp was a scrapper, the kind of lawyer you wanted on your side, a frequent thorn in the flesh of his fellow attorneys. According to a widely held local observation, he had never had a guilty client. Nor had he ever ducked a confrontation. "Hurry up and get your law license," he wrote his daughter: "I may need you to defend me."[38]

On the way to getting that law license, Susie Sharp hit a bump. When Professor Coates released the grades for his Property class after first semester exams, she had made a D. She was not alone. In the class of fifty-two students, Professor Coates had dispensed fifteen Fs and a huge number of Ds.[39] The students responded furiously. There was talk of boycotting the class, of a petition calling for Professor Coates's dismissal. The school was in an uproar.

Susie Sharp reported the fracas in a letter home and received a reply from her father that focused forcefully on her priorities. "Mother said she had a letter from you saying that Albert's class wanted to go on a strike and that they wanted you to go with them," he wrote. "You do no such thing. You just go quietly along about your work and let them do as they please. I am working my head off to keep you there until you get through, and you have no time to lose." He did not care if she made the highest grades. "Just keep doing your best and it is alright. . . . Just so you pass and get through[,] it is all right. Whether you complete the degree course or not you can get to where you can pass the Supreme Court [exam], and then you will be able to take care of yourself."[40]

Susie Sharp's relationship with Albert Coates, marked by equal portions of deep affection and exasperation, would continue throughout her career.

By second semester of her first year, she was hitting her stride. She took a heavy course load while continuing with the moot court competitions, in which she was undefeated. Students were judged on both their briefs and oral arguments. By the end of the term, out of the fifty students who had begun in the fall, Susie Sharp was one of the four who remained standing, the winners who would compete for the final victory. She must have relished the moment that her rival, Dillard Gardner, fell by the wayside with a "favorable mention." In the end, the other side prevailed in the last round. Nevertheless, Susie Sharp could take much satisfaction in having been one of the finalists in the competition.

After the midyear Personal Property disaster, she approached exams with some trepidation, but she came through with flags flying: four As and two Bs. Her father, however, had not changed his opinion of the education she was getting. She sent him a copy of one of her exams, and his scorn was boundless. Swimming against the tide, he expressed his view that "[T]he sooner that bunch there who are trying to put over Harvard and Columbia methods find out that the State will not stand for it, the sooner we will get some common sense teaching and not til then."[41]

Despite his impatience with newfangled methods of legal education, Jim Sharp nevertheless approved his daughter's decision to attend the law school summer session.[42] For the first time, the school would offer a full session of courses for credit, and she could accelerate her graduation by forgoing the summer break. Although the school had feared that elimination of the old summer bar review course would cut enrollment, instead it nearly doubled.[43] Professors for the summer courses were an impressive group. They included North Carolina Supreme Court associate justices W. J. Brogden and George W. Connor and professors from Columbia University and Yale as well as regular UNC faculty members.

Undoubtedly Susie Sharp welcomed the chance to compress the time required to finish law school, but her decision to attend summer school may not have been entirely focused on her course work. Chapel Hill had many charms, and she was not as immune to them as she once might have thought. She had lots of friends, both male and female, and they could always find time to see a movie at the Pickwick Theater, known as the "Pick," attend a football game, or go for a hike in the nearby countryside. She was considered a good companion by her classmates, who included her in their outings, consulted her for advice, fenced with her quick mind, teased her, and generally enjoyed her company. Over the summer she got letters from at least one boy who had left town, full of news and gossip and general chitchat.[44] Susie Sharp did not lack for male companionship in the largely male environment. She had even enjoyed a flirtation or two. But more than that, the unthinkable had happened. She had fallen in love.

His name was John Columbus Kesler. Born May 23, 1899, he was the son of a Rowan County farmer and had gone to high school in the small railroad town of Spencer, just outside Salisbury, North Carolina. Neither of his parents attended college, but he had graduated from UNC in 1924 with a degree in history and was in his second year at the law school when Susie Sharp entered. He was outgoing enough to represent the law school on the student council and bright enough to be selected as an editor of the *North Carolina Law Review*, a prestigious honor based on scholarship. His 1928 class photograph reveals an exceptionally good-looking young man with abundant brown hair, large brown eyes, straight nose, and chiseled lips. As early as October of her first year at the law school, a friend's letter refers to Susie's "Secret Passion," a.k.a. "S.P."[45] Matters apparently had become so serious by February that Susie Sharp felt it necessary to call things off. Her old friend Janie Sands wrote to beg for details. "I can't learn all I want to know from your letter . . . I wanted to know more of the particulars (as usual) of that two-hour good-bye; and what were the agreements you came to. I don't believe you are worrying much over your ignorant family, or a law-partner for your father."[46] By the following May, however, the breakup appeared to have been temporary. Janie wrote to say, "It seems to me you are making headway with the S.P., and don't need any consolation."[47] But the path of true love did not run smooth. During summer school, the two apparently were not seeing each other, for Susie Sharp noted, "SP dates summer school girls every night."[48] Then, not long into September of her second year, the attraction reignited, and she was head over heels.

Students returning to Chapel Hill in September 1927 found a university in the throes of a building boom. At the law school, enrollment was up by 25 percent over the preceding year.[49] Three new law professors brought the number of faculty members to seven, "the largest full-time law faculty in the South, with one exception," according to the *Tar Heel*.[50] Miss Ruby Ross, who would become a good friend of Susie Sharp's, had been hired as secretary to the school, thus liberating Miss Lucille Elliott to devote her full attention to the law library, which had increased from 12,500 to 15,000 volumes the preceding year.[51] When Dean Charles T. McCormick formally opened the fall term, he defined the goal of the law school to be "not merely sectional eminence, but one of greatness measured by universal standards."[52]

As a second-year student, Susie Sharp began the year with a signal honor, selection to the editorial board of the *North Carolina Law Review*. Begun in June 1922, the *Law Review* was an important component of the law school's increasing stature. Under faculty supervision, the journal published notes, comments, and articles on legal issues written by students, faculty, judges, and leading attorneys. It served as a research and reference tool for the legal profession statewide, boasting a mailing list in 1927 of 1,464 lawyers. The responsibility of analyzing developments in the law in a comprehensive and authoritative manner was therefore quite significant and not limited to the law student universe. The faculty appointed the members of the student editorial board, headed by a student editor in chief, consisting of those second- and third-year students with the highest scholastic averages in their classes, along with the "willingness and ability to do the work required in investigating some legal problem involved in a new decision or a new statute and putting it in shape for publication."[53] During Susie Sharp's tenure on the *Law Review* the faculty editor in chief was Professor Robert H. Wettach, assisted by two to three other faculty members. One of these was a new professor, Millard Sheridan Breckenridge, who had just joined the faculty in the fall of 1927. He was to be one of the most important people in Susie Sharp's life.

Professor Breckenridge, or "Breck" as he was known to all, was thirty-six years old when he came to Chapel Hill, although he appeared much younger. Born in Chicago, he graduated from the University of Chicago and received his law degree from Yale, where he was on the editorial board of the *Yale Law Journal* and served as assistant to former U.S. president William Howard Taft, who was then on the faculty there prior to his appointment to the U.S. Supreme Court. Before joining the UNC law school faculty as a full professor, Professor Breckenridge, among other things, had taught at the University of Iowa and Western Reserve University.[54] Slender, of medium height, eagle-eyed, with a strong nose and a head full of dark hair swept straight back, he was an extremely handsome man. An outdoorsman, he was an enthusiastic bird watcher and preferred walking or riding his secondhand bicycle to driving. Ensconced in his automobile, however, he drove "like an aviator."[55] His wry sense of humor coupled with his powerful intelligence made him a favorite among students, especially the brightest, in whom he took special enjoyment. In class, he had "a matchless ability to keep long chains of connected ideas crackling with interest" and was "a master at provoking students into debates with him or with each other."[56]

During these years when the student body was small, students often developed close relationships with professors, and Breck was easy to like. His wife, Venitah, was happy to provide brownies or cookies whenever a group of students dropped by the house at 738 East Franklin Street to consult with the professor, as they often did. In particular, the student editors of the *Law Review* were frequent visitors.[57] The Breckenridges had two children, Jean, born in 1919, and Arnold, born in 1923.

As she began her second year, Susie Sharp was often thrown together with John Kesler as they participated in the Law Club moot court competition and worked on the *Law Review*. They were spending a good deal of time together outside of school as well. They had dinner dates, went to football games, made bets payable by treating each other to movies at the Pick. He had a car, and going to ride was a popular pastime. In October she went with him and another student to Salisbury, his hometown. At a football game in November, they ran into Judge Brogden, who had taught a class during the summer school session. "Still courting, I see," he teased them. "There is no law against it," John replied.[58]

Susie Sharp was not yet the attractive woman she would become, despite her blue eyes and creamy complexion. Her French pen pal, Nuion, upon receiving a photograph of her, remarked, "I see that now you are a bit dowdy, but where is the lady who is not dowdy."[59] Susie's long hair was yet unbobbed, pinned into a haphazard twist at the nape of her neck. Her face was round, her chin sharp. She wore the round tortoiseshell glasses common at the time. Still, John's interest was clearly more than that of a mere classmate or friend. As for Susie Sharp, she was experiencing the very feelings she had long feared and derided. Janie Sands wrote, "Just recall, for a moment, your opinion of the opposite sex and your views on matrimony, love, etc. at that (earlier) stage of our development; and then think of the letter you wrote me concerning *John*! I, then, never thought *it* would come to pass."[60] Susie Sharp's former teacher, Donie Counts, however, would have been less surprised. Miss Counts had once written her, "I know you a great deal better than lots of people do, and behind all your *pretended* aversion to the weaker (i.e., male) sex, you really are feminine to the core—and romantic."[61]

Frances Sharp, a cousin, wrote, "I'm still wondering what's happened to you. I fear you've eloped with Mr. Kesler. Is that true?"[62] Complaining of a former beau of her own, Frances declared that if he did not return the ring she had given him, "I am going to turn the matter over to Lawyers Sharp & Kesler. Does that suit you?"[63]

That undoubtedly would have suited her very well. Things were not so simple, however. Without question, Susie Sharp felt an obligation to return to Reidsville, where her father expected her to be his partner. She owed him an immeasurable debt for his support, financial and otherwise, which had enabled her to go to law school in the first place, and now he expected her to come home and take some of the load off his shoulders. As if to accentuate the point, in November he dissolved his partnership with Harry Crutchfield and was once again a solo practitioner. As for Susie Sharp, she did not have many options if she wanted to practice law. In the absence of a father—or a husband—to take her into his practice, the chances of a woman earning her living as a lawyer were remote. Given the choice, she might have seized the opportunity to begin her law practice as Mrs. John Kesler instead of Miss Susie Sharp. Love aside, life as Jim Sharp's partner held the possibility for disaster. Her friend Margaret Fillman questioned her thinking. "I am certainly sorry that you plan to come back here and begin the law business," she wrote. "Or are you so homesick and feel that your duty lies here? . . . I think it's a mistake for you and your father to be together. You are liable to get in each other's way and I'll bet there won't be a day that sparks are not flying. However, you know what you want to do, so be sure you're right then go ahead."[64]

In fact, she did not know what she wanted to do. Part of her considered the possibility of abandoning a career in law altogether. She did not know any women who managed to combine marriage, children, and a law career, and to the end of her life she did not believe it could be done. There is little doubt that she thought about marrying John Kesler and becoming an ordinary housewife.[65]

In any event, the choice appears to have been made for her. Right up until the Christmas vacation, she and John were still going out together. Her journal entry for December 19, 1927, reports that they had gone "to ride" after dinner. "He kisses me," she says. Then: "Christmas he does not write at all." After the holiday, something was askew with the relationship. John was apparently distancing himself from her, and she did not understand why. She was distraught and sought advice from her friends. One speculated, "Praps Brown Eyes thinks you are too brilliant. Men are funny that way. Or is this one an exception? You, being in so deep, will probably think so anyway."[66]

In February John left Chapel Hill to begin his law practice in Salisbury. Susie Sharp cut two classes to tell him goodbye. She would not be joining him as his wife or law partner or anything else. The existing record is unclear, but apparently John was the one to break off the relationship. Susie Sharp was devastated. They corresponded for a while, but he signed his letters "Yours truly."[67] Sometime that spring she wrote him two letters, the last of which went unanswered. These letters have vanished, but more than twenty-five years later, in trying to recall what she had said, she remembered "something about a pedestal, pride, and bureau drawers — in addition to the declaration."[68] Was it a declaration of love or independence?

With respect to John, the point was, as they said in the legal profession, moot. John was gone. Life had surprised the girl who had both scoffed at love and feared its tyranny. She had lost control over her feelings, only to be deprived of the mature expression of her love. More than ever, perhaps, she resolved never to be a man's captive, even as she acknowledged her capacity to love and be loved. She had come perilously close to detouring from her goals in life. Although she would be heartsore over losing John for close to another twenty years, Susie Sharp took a deep breath and moved on. She still had to finish law school and pass the bar. With five courses, law review, and moot court activities on her agenda for the spring semester, she had ample reasons to push John to the back of her mind.

She had begun spending time with a third-year student named George Shaw, with whom she had a jocular relationship. She liked to make him go on hikes with her. "Take GS on a hike which he thinks is 10 miles," she recorded. "He says I am a race horse."[69] George retaliated, chaffing her about his preference for "tall, stately girls." At this, she drew herself up to her full height, only to have him respond that she was just a "sawed-off runt."[70] He ragged her without mercy, telling her that if she was in love with John, she had better get over it.[71]

It was George Shaw who made an interesting observation about her interaction with her classmates, recorded in Susie Sharp's journal. Calling her a coward because she would not "talk up on class," he told her that although she would "laugh and joke with the boys," she would not "engage in a serious mental contest with them."[72] Susie Sharp did not record whether she deemed this a fair accusation. She had long used humor to cushion the impact of her superior intellect; it was one reason she rarely alienated her male colleagues. No stranger to sarcasm as a weapon, she was clever enough to use it sparingly. Rarely in doubt as to her view on an issue, she nonetheless would endeavor to make her point in a way that avoided humiliating her opponent. George Shaw's remark indicates a perception that — at least at this stage of her development — she refrained from direct confrontation. There could have been no question about her intellectual capacity, as she was regularly listed at the top of the class academically, but she was still learning how to navigate in the adversarial universe of the law while maintaining her femininity. Femininity had become surprisingly important to her since her relationship with John had revealed the unsuspected emotional capacities within her.

She had no qualms, however, about competing in the moot court exercises, where she was responsible for both the written brief and the oral arguments. By the end of the second year, she stood once again as a finalist. That summer she took two courses in summer school and began getting ready to take the bar exam in August, as she was entitled to do after two years of law school. Because the exams given by the supreme court tended to repeat the same questions year after year, students studied the old exams — which were widely available. Just how notorious was the similarity of exams from year to year was evident when Albert Coates allegedly overheard a conversation on the night before the exam in 1923. Walking down the street in Raleigh behind two law students, he heard one of the students pose a practice question and the other reply, "That is the twenty-first question in the nineteenth examination."[73] Well into the 1920s, forty-four out of sixty-six questions were repeated from previous years.[74] Jim Sharp advised Susie as early as February of her first year to begin reviewing the old exams. "At odd times, if I were you, I would study them and get up the correct answers to them. The next Supreme Court examination will contain some of the same questions. This is always the case."[75] As the exam date approached, he even did some research for her, going down to his law office to look up the answers to questions for her.[76] Never taking his eye off the goal, he chastised her for complaining about Justice Connor, who was teaching her summer school class in Constitutional Law. "Now if Connor does not know much law he has a real good vote when it comes to issueing [sic] licenses, and the thing to do is stay on the good side of that distinguished gentleman."[77]

The *Greensboro Record* ran a photograph of Susie Sharp, fetchingly posed with her legs crossed, spotlighting the "Pretty Reidsville Girl" among the candidates for the bar exam.

Unexpectedly, the fall 1928 bar examinations produced a shocking failure rate. Out of 181 candidates, seventy-seven did not pass, according to one newspaper. "Casualties Run High," headlined the *Greensboro Daily News*, reporting, "In the fallen are some of the best known and apparently best trained candidates." Chief Justice W. P. Stacy had put the questions, and in a break with tradition the applicants had undergone "a test not common in the interrogations of the Court."[78] So much for reviewing old tests. Fortunately, if

Susie Sharp was anxious about her fate, she had only to wait a few days until the results were in. And even before the list appeared in print, a Greensboro reporter, Tom Bost, was kind enough to wire her—"in code (not too hard to crack!)"—the news of her successful effort, thus endearing himself to her forever.[79]

She had passed the bar, but this apparently did not predetermine her future. The *Greensboro Daily News*, listing her as one of several notable names among the successful applicants, said, "Miss Susie M. Sharpe [*sic*], of Reidsville, will employ her brains to assist Dad John M. Sharpe [*sic*], unless she chooses to use her beauty for matrimony."[80] Matrimony did not appear to be in the cards, however. Although Susie Sharp had congratulatory letters from any number of friends and others, including her old debate team coach Allen Gwyn, her NCCW professor Walter C. Jackson, North Carolina Supreme Court justice Heriot Clarkson, and a Shelby lawyer named Clyde R. Hoey who would one day be governor, she did not hear a word from John Kesler.[81] Her friend Edith Averitt, a librarian at UNC who took some classes at the law school, consoled her. "You'll get over your affair but it will take time."[82] Several months later her cousin Frances Sharp, in what was at once the most prescient and the most out-of-date comment, wrote, "I am anxious to hear how John is being broken in by my esteemed cousin who is soon to be Judge of the Supreme Court and more than that—wife (we hope so, don't we?) of Mr. John Kesler."[83]

If Susie Sharp had any illusions about her new status as a licensed attorney, they were punctured on what should have been her proudest day. With the bar exam behind her, her next official step was to be sworn in as a member of the bar. The ceremony took place on November 30, 1928, in her home county of Rockingham before the Honorable John Henry Clement, judge presiding.[84] As she recounted in a speech delivered upon receiving yet another honor more than fifty years later, "On one never-to-be-forgotten day, my father, with great paternal pride, presented me to the Court and moved my admission to the Bar."[85] The draft of her speech contains the phrase, marked out, "[The judge] never swore in a more eager or prideful attorney, but, as always, pride preceded a fall." She told what happened: "Hizzoner dutifully administered the oath. Then, instead of making the usual congratulatory remarks and welcoming [the] neophyte into the profession, that Judge said to me, from the bench in a crowded and interested courtroom, 'Well, young lady, I congratulate you and all like that, but I'd be derelict in my duty if I didn't tell you that you will never make a lawyer. If you persist you will just be wasting your time, playing in the sand. I advise you to start right now trying to find something more appropriate to do.'"[86]

It does not take much imagination to conjure up how hot her flushed face must have felt. Susie Sharp did not relate her father's reaction. For herself, more than half a century later she wrote that "the memory of the deep hurt his unnecessary and inappropriate remarks inflicted upon me at the very moment I had achieved my great ambition to become a licensed lawyer never faded."[87]

With her license assured, instead of plunging into the practice of law, Susie Sharp returned to Chapel Hill in September 1928 to finish the optional third year of law school. Registration for the fall semester took place in the teeth of a hurricane that howled through the state from the south. In a year's time the economic holocaust would inflict far greater damage, but for the moment the community was concerned only with the broken branches and fallen trees covering the campus. President Harry Chase, in his opening address to the students, spoke again of his great theme, the knitting together of the New South and the wider world. "The most significant event of this generation is the extent to which this entire area is being linked up with the rest of the nation," he proclaimed. North Carolina was no longer an intellectual or economic backwater. At the law school there were two new professors, Frederick B. McCall and Maurice Van Hecke, establishing the UNC faculty of full-time law teachers as the largest in the Southeast.[88]

It was a time of intense national discussion of many issues, stimulated by the presidential election in November, which pitted Democrat Al Smith against Republican Herbert Hoover, with the added element of the Socialist Party nominee, Norman Thomas. As in most of the South, Al Smith encountered fierce opposition in North Carolina from Protestants, prohibitionists, and the newly resurgent Ku Klux Klan. Even the Democratic U.S. senator Furnifold Simmons, who had orchestrated North Carolina politics since the turn of the century, came out in support of Hoover, an act that would cost him his hold on power. At UNC, where the student body was the most cosmopolitan in its history with 20 percent from out of state, "a goodly portion of them from the North,"[89] a broader perspective existed if not prevailed. Speakers on campus included not only Norman Thomas but even "Mr. H. Hell Mencken, the Bad Boy of Baltimore."[90] The first-year law students passed a motion favoring Al Smith for president.

Meanwhile Susie Sharp was elected secretary-treasurer of the third-year class, now dramatically shrunk to fifteen in the aftermath of the post–bar exam exodus. It was her last semester. She had four more courses to take, and again she was heavily involved in the moot court exercises. Still, she had time to do some legal research for Allen Gwyn in Reidsville, who wrote to thank her for sending him some useful citations: "I really did not intend that you should take the time and go into the matter to the extent to which you did." He then spent two pages outlining another legal issue on which he would be interested to get her reaction. "But don't let me worry you with my troubles. Don't spend your time working on this question. Just write me what you think about it," he said. Having gone into considerable detail about the hypothetical case, which he did mention was "similar" to one he happened to have, he must have known she would send him a thorough analysis. "I hope that I may have the opportunity some time to reciprocate," he said.[91] He would.

The big event of that fall was the November election, in which Susie Sharp would be voting for the first time. She and Professor Breckenridge engaged in vigorous debate on the virtues and drawbacks of the presidential candidates. Never doctrinaire, Breck supported a candidate according to his merits, not his political party, and in this race he found all the merits on the Republican side. Back and forth they argued. He used all his superior experience and knowledge to persuade her to vote for Hoover, despite her "yellow-dog" Democratic family heritage. Certainly her anti-Catholic prejudice, as well as her upbringing in a "dry" household, gave her cause for concern about Al Smith. Smith's northern, urban, pro-immigration background was also offputting. At home in Reidsville her father initially did all he could to derail the selection of Al Smith delegates to the convention, fulminating in the newspaper against the candidate.[92] Once nominated, however, Smith became the diehard Democrat's avatar. In lengthy newspaper articles, Jim Sharp rationalized away all his previous objections and urged the voters to support the Democratic nominee.[93] He intended to vote for Al Smith, and he certainly expected Susie would too. Although he needed no reinforcement of his party affiliation, an encounter with President Coolidge on a Junior Order trip to Washington that fall had confirmed his deepest feelings about Republicans in general. After shaking hands with the president, Jim Sharp reported him to be "the coldest man he ever saw."[94] It was unimaginable that a Sharp might betray the Democratic Party. He sent Susie an absentee ballot along with detailed instructions about how to fill it out and send it in.[95] Breck was convinced he had converted her, however, and there is some indication that she did capitulate to his arguments, at least temporarily. There is no question that she left him with the belief that he had won the tug of war.

Closer to home, the elections had a measurable impact on the Sharp family. With the help of the "dry" vote, Republicans had won on the local as well as the national level. Jim Sharp wrote to Susie, "I will lose my job as county attorney on the first Monday. With it goes emoluments of about $1500."[96] The pressure on Susie Sharp to return to Reidsville and her father's law practice increased dramatically with this news. If she had nurtured any thought of bolting, she now had no acceptable alternative to becoming the junior partner in the law firm of Sharp & Sharp.

The semester ended in a ragged fashion. A virulent influenza outbreak swept through the campus in mid-December, and like a number of other schools from North Carolina to Missouri, UNC shut down prematurely. Exams were put off until the end of January. It was the first time since Reconstruction that the school had closed before the scheduled time. Even during the great flu epidemic of 1918, which claimed the life of university president Edward Kidder Graham, the doors had remained open.[97] Susie Sharp returned after the Christmas break to ace all her exams and prepare to leave Chapel Hill for good.

She was reluctant to depart for a number of reasons, but one in particular exerted a powerful undertow on her emotions. The semester that had begun with a hurricane and ended with the flu had disrupted Susie Sharp's life in other ways that were to have far more lasting effects. She and Breck were experiencing a powerful attraction to each other. That she was attracted to her youthful professor was not surprising, given his good looks, bright mind, and penchant for the kind of bright repartee she loved. Like her NCCW professor, Walter Jackson, he was prime material for a student crush. They had spent substantial time together since he arrived at the law school her second year, both in class and working on the *Law Review*. She was a frequent visitor in his home and a companion on the trips to Raleigh, Durham, and other destinations Breck made with other students and with his family. Spending so much time together, they developed a lively sparring style and a rich appreciation for one another's considerable intellect and wit. That Breck, who often voted Republican, could retain Susie Sharp's affection despite such a heretofore unacceptable sin was a measure of his charm and ability to engage her on the issues. Unquestionably he enjoyed baiting her, but she gave as good as she got. She knew full well that he was a self-professed happily married man. She herself was fond of his wife, Venitah, and the two children, Jean and Arnold. The family had enveloped her like an honorary daughter, which was no doubt a welcome source of warmth in the absence of her own family. None of this deterred her, however, from taking a romantic interest in her professor. Nor did she keep her feelings entirely to herself, as evidenced by a letter written in July 1929 by her friend Ina Young, denying that she could have been the source for another friend's comment that Susie was "interested in a married man."[98]

More surprising, the professor found himself drawn to his young coed student, who was becoming prettier, it seemed, all the time. Although Breck was far more conflicted over the attraction than Susie was, he did not put a stop to the developing situation. Their flirtation had begun as early as the fall of 1927, although she was then deeply involved with John Kesler. She had noted in her regular journal several incidents that testified to flirtatiousness on Breck's part, and her pleasure in it. Years later, when, at some point prior to the fall of 1944, Susie Sharp destroyed her journals, she took the trouble to make a lengthy and detailed abstract covering the period from March 7, 1927, to November 12, 1943.[99] She deemed these incidents with Breck of sufficient importance to include them in her distilled version of the destroyed journals. Also, on October 27, 1927, she began keeping a separate journal devoted solely to entries regarding Breck.[100]

By the time she took the bar exam in August 1928, more than six months after John had graduated, her journal records a distinct proprietary interest on Breck's part, as well as a dash of jealousy at her commitment to the legal profession. "I get a special dress for the bar exam. He was going to tell me it was pretty until he found it was for that purpose."[101] A week later they went for a ride in his car, and he told her that he wanted their relationship to be "open and honest,"[102] a clear indication that there was a possibility it might take another direction. But throughout the next year, they were thrown together frequently in the normal course of events, and, despite Breck's misgivings, the attraction continued. Susie's heart was heavy at the thought of leaving Chapel Hill.

A group of her girlfriends gave her a farewell party commencing with dinner and culminating in a trip to Durham to see *On Trial*, a recent movie enhanced by new "talkie" technology, the Vitaphone. Venitah Breckenridge had a party for her, too, at which Susie Sharp was presented with a clock. A few days later she was back in Reidsville, poised to take up the practice of law with her father. Her journal says: "The rest of my life on my hands."[103]

CHAPTER 4

FALSE START

Jim Sharp wasted no time in ordering new "Sharp & Sharp" letterhead and adding "Miss Susie Sharp" to his standard ad in the newspaper. Miss Sharp was ensconced in her own office in one of the law firm's three rooms on the second floor of the Whitsett Building in downtown Reidsville.[1]

Her father intended for her to become his equal in the law practice. Despite his determined equanimity, however, such an attitude toward women in the workplace was by any measure exceptional. For example, less than a month later the news that the vice president of the United States was going to have a "girl secretary" made the front page of the *Reidsville Review*, complete with a picture of the trailblazer, one Miss Lola Williams.[2] At the time, even the secretaries of important persons were male, as of course were nearly all important persons. In the United States, the percentage of lawyers who were women nearly doubled between 1910 and 1930, the year after Susie Sharp first entered practice, but this remarkable increase merely brought the figure from 1.1 to 2.1 percent.[3] The numbers were even lower in North Carolina, where women in the legal profession were virtually invisible.

Great fanfare therefore greeted the announcement that a young woman would be practicing law in Reidsville, North Carolina. Newspapers across the state carried reports, most accompanied by photographs. It was not the first such arrangement in North Carolina, following as it did the earlier partnership of UNC law school alumna Kathrine Everett and her father in 1921, but it was sufficiently novel that even the UNC campus newspaper initially reported that Sharp & Sharp was the first of its kind and then was compelled to issue a correction.[4] For the rest of her life Susie Sharp would be the subject (or victim, she might have said) of countless newspaper articles and photographs, and her experience with the press would be repeated over and over again: flattering attention, inaccurate information, and objectionable photos.

One newspaper even ran the story with the picture of another young woman, most emphatically not Susie, a long-necked beauty in pearls.[5]

Fanfare aside, her first attempt to practice law in Reidsville plunged her into a deep depression. In less than eighteen months, she would be back in Chapel Hill.

Years later, on learning that a niece was depressed and having a bad time, Susie Sharp wrote about "the depression which engulfed me in the spring of 1929."[6] She did not think she would make it as a lawyer. To begin with, everybody who came to the office "made it quite clear" that they did not even want to talk to her.[7] The Great Depression was cranking up and no one had any money, which only accentuated her inability to generate fees after all the sacrifices her family had made for her education. "To make matters worse," she wrote, "after five years in college — the last three in 'sophisticated Chapel Hill,' during both winter and summer, I was out of touch with life at home and in Reidsville. My parents seemed like such old-fashioned, mundane people as compared with the law professors and their wives." For the first time, she saw her parents as real people subject to human lapses in response to stress and strain.[8] One friend wrote to say, "[M]e heart aches when I think of me Susie trying so bravely to be the law partner her Dad requires, when the real Susie would love to be far away."[9]

She stayed in close contact with Chapel Hill. Although she had finished her classwork in February, the law school commencement exercises were not until the following June, and until she was an official graduate she remained a sort of quasi student with an interest in grades, honors, dances, and banquets. Soon after her departure, Breck wrote to tell her that, on the recent exams, she had bested her nearest rival, Jeff Fordham, by one point.[10] Her friend Ruby Ross, the law school secretary, reported on her own sleuthing about her grades with Dean McCormick, including "sounding him out on the Coif."[11] The Order of the Coif, a national legal honor society, had established a North Carolina chapter just the year before. The law school equivalent to Phi Beta Kappa, the order at this time had chapters in only twenty-nine prominent law schools in the United States. Members were confined to students in the top 10 percent of their class over three years, making inclusion a very high honor. Ruby relayed the word that the dean did not think there was any doubt that Susie Sharp would be selected.

All spring Susie Sharp returned to Chapel Hill at every opportunity, whether for school-related events or just for a visit, staying with various friends or the Breckenridges. In May there was an uproarious law school banquet at the Carolina Inn, complete with skits and parodies in a program that included a segment entitled "Cherchez La Femme."[12] It was on this evening that Susie Sharp and Jeff Fordham were named to the Order of the Coif, the only members of their class so honored.[13] Graduation took place a few weeks later, on June 10, and Susie Sharp received her LL.B. with honors.

She continued to visit Chapel Hill as often as possible, even in the face of pressure from her new law partner. "I know how hard it is going to be to impress on the 'Sweet Papa' the necessity of spending some of your days and nites on the Hill," Ruby Ross wrote to her, lamenting her absence.[14] One thing that kept her in close touch with the law school was the new project sponsored by the American Law Institute in which various areas of the law were to be reviewed and summarized in a standardized "black letter law" format, called a Restatement, in an effort to simplify and clarify the basic principles of American law. At UNC Breck was working on the Restatement for the law of agency. This was a research project well suited to her abilities, and which she could do when she was otherwise unoccupied. Albert Coates solicited her help, too, with his work on the annotation of the Criminal Code.[15]

Beginning a law practice is a humbling experience for anyone, but perhaps it is especially so for someone accustomed to receiving only the highest accolades. Susie Sharp's confidence and pride in her ability suffered considerably. It could not have been easy for her father either, faced with breaking in a neophyte lawyer who happened to be his daughter. Susie Sharp, full of book learning, was eager to apply it, while her father drew on a lifetime of experience largely unfettered by fine academic points. "If I found a law that did not suit his purposes," she once said, "he took it as an insult."[16] Nor did it seem that she would ever have clients of her own, because no one wanted to entrust his problems to a twenty-three-year-old single woman who by some fluke had acquired a law degree. "[T]hose who came to the office for my father," she would recall, "were careful to make it plain that they came in spite of me."[17] One story Susie Sharp often recounted (in language no longer deemed politically correct) illustrates the young lawyer's early days in practice. "[A]n old darky came to the office and actually inquired for me," she related. "My self esteem increased immeasurably. The old fellow was ushered in. 'Is you that lady lawyer,' he asked. I admitted the soft impeachment and inquired what I could do for him. He backed off in the greatest alarm and said, 'You can't do nothing for me. I just heard there was one in town and I kum up to see what she looked like.'"[18]

So in the beginning she did office work and legal research for her father, accompanied him to court, and despaired of pulling her weight as a full partner. Meanwhile, her father monitored her dealings with the firm's clients and did his best to give her experience without jeopardizing the clients' claims.

Even her friends expressed their doubts about her prospects for success. "I had to laugh at the idea of your giving advice on domestic problems," Chapel Hill friend Maude Brown wrote to her. "[O]n the face it appears absurd to come to a young miss, as yet unmarried, and ask for common sense advice on the subject of marriage relationships."[19] Howard Godwin, a former law school classmate and an admirer, delivered what was meant to be a supportive analysis: "I'm afraid you are not giving yourself the credit you deserve in reciting the dialogue between you and the irate client. I know you too well. It's a pity you are a woman. You will always be at a disadvantage for that very reason."[20]

Then, too, Susie Sharp had always held herself to high standards, and with the unmellowed zeal of youth she held others to the same. One surviving snippet of correspondence reveals a glimpse of an impatient and frustrated young woman sailing imperiously into waters with hidden currents and shoals. Writing to an attorney in Virginia about information he had repeatedly promised but failed to provide, she closed by snapping, "This time we trust [you] will cease to regard 'that as done which ought to be done' and do it."[21] Her father, on receiving the lawyer's reply (unfortunately lost to posterity), was obliged to try to mitigate the damage to a colleague's amour propre. "My Daughter," he wrote, "is just out of Law School at Chappel [sic] Hill, and has entered the practice with me. She was the Author, and after I received your letter, then she pulled the joke on me and showed me what she had written you. I trust you take this levity in the spirit in which it was written."[22]

Susie Sharp's disillusionment did not stop with fellow attorneys. Not long after she got out of law school, she faced a judge who rejected a basic point of law she was arguing on her client's behalf. As Susie Sharp recounted it, "I grabbed the first lawbook I could lay hands on and read Hizzoner some law directly to the contrary. He listened in gloomy disbelief and then said: 'Well, I don't care if that is the law; it's bad law and I'm not going to mess with it.'" She declared that the experience "shattered the naïve faith I had acquired in the L.S. that trial courts thirsted for knowledge and once informed as to the law, automatically applied it."[23]

She argued her first case before the North Carolina Supreme Court in April of 1929, just three months after leaving law school. Sharp & Sharp represented Rockingham County in a suit against the Norfolk & Western Railway, disputing the closure of a level crossing. Although she still lacked experience in the trial court, her father called on her fresh academic skills to fashion the brief and gave her the opportunity to present their argument before the high court in Raleigh. She must have been nervous, but her journal gives no hint of her mental state. "Argue my first case in S. Ct.," she recorded, without further comment.[24] If she was at all flustered, however, the newspapers were even more so. When the court's opinion came down, the *News and Observer* headlined the story on page one, "Woman Attorney Wins before Supreme Court."[25] In fact, however, she had lost, not won. That afternoon the *Raleigh Times* continued the confusion by running a correct version of the outcome even while lamenting her victory because of the (supposed) precedent it would set. Although their reporter got it right on the front page, the editorial writer complained that "[t]he appealing debut of Susie M. Sharp, Esq., flapper counsel," had resulted in a problematic ruling.[26] "Ready as we are to cheer first blood for Miss Sharp's legal lance, we would that she had won it in another cause," the *Times* editorial concluded. The next day the *Greensboro Daily News* gleefully blared, "Raleigh Editors Got Their Facts Mixed Up — Miss Susie Sharp Credited with Winning Case, When She Lost."[27] Laying it on, the article reported, "Both papers agreed that Miss Sharp is young. Both should have admitted that she is very, very pretty."[28]

The failure of Susie Sharp's first foray into the appellate arena was thus doubly humiliating. She was bound to have attracted attention in her first argument to the high court, but the mix-up in reporting the outcome amplified the news of her loss, especially in the Greensboro paper, which was widely read in her hometown of Reidsville. The coy references to the "flapper counsel's" youth and beauty heaped indignity on top of humiliation, although Susie Sharp left no record of her sentiments on that score. In truth, although she would have bridled at the "flapper" label, she was probably pleased to be described as an attractive young woman. It had not always been so, and she had worked hard on her looks.

Nonetheless, the defeat in her first major appearance was painful. Professor Breckenridge wrote immediately to bolster her morale. "If it will help any to have me re-iterate what you already know, that we down here, and especially yours truly, have just as much confidence in your capabilities as ever, then I hope you'll rest assured of that fact. If you are beaten in any case I know it's not because of a poor argument on your part."[29]

There were some victories. She successfully represented a defendant in a bad check case, which must have warmed the heart of Professor Breckenridge, who had taught her everything she knew about negotiable instruments.[30] Her old UNC friend Dorothy Fahs wrote in September 1929 to congratulate her on her "financial success as a lawyer,"[31] implying that Susie had managed to collect something in the way of fees. At that time a penniless graduate student, Dorothy said, "It makes little me look sick in comparison. But honest, I do think you have every reason to be happy, considering the odds against you."[32]

It was not until October 1929 that Susie Sharp made her first jury speech. Sharp & Sharp had been trying a land suit for a week, a long time in those days.[33] The firm of Glidewell, Dunn, & Gwyn represented the other side, the Gwyn being the same Allen Gwyn who had been her debate coach in high school. Like every jury she would face for the next seventeen years, her first was composed entirely of men: women in North Carolina would not be allowed to serve on a jury until 1946. She recalled, "How, I don't know, but I managed to pull myself by the table and, with my knees knocking and my throat getting dryer every step, I stumbled over to the jury box—and thus began the greatest ordeal of my life."[34]

Her handwritten notes for that jury speech, beginning, "Gentlemen of the jury," reveal an organized mind, a down-to-earth approach, and a skillful use of humor. Lucidity, logic, and common sense carried her to victory; the jury found for her client.

By early 1930, a year after joining her father in practice, she was beginning to make a place for herself, however small. Ruby Ross congratulated her on winning three cases.[35] The *Reidsville Review* noted, "Miss Susie Sharp, a member of the law firm of Sharp & Sharp [who] has the distinction of being the only female attorney in Rockingham County, is a regular attendant in the courtroom, her presence having a refining influence on the legal fraternity during the progress of cases at trial."[36] In at least one circumstance, however, her "refining influence" failed altogether. Over the years she told contradictory accounts, but the evidence shows that she participated in a breach of ethics that she never would have tolerated in later years, either in herself or in others.

As a result of some remodeling in the Rockingham County courthouse, the jury room had a hole in its ceiling. As Susie Sharp once described to an audience at a UNC law school banquet, "By climbing up into the attic, perching precariously on the rafter and clinging to the wall the lawyers could hear the deliberations in the room below."[37] For an attorney to eavesdrop on jury deliberations was, and is, of course, a grievous offense. Nevertheless, this was apparently a not-uncommon practice among some local members of the bar. Susie Sharp would tell several people over the years about this peculiarity of the courthouse and the advantage taken of it, usually denying that she herself ever did any such thing.[38] However, a letter written to her by Ruby Ross in the spring of 1930 remarked, "You surely stand in with the Judge to be listening in on the jury."[39] One Reidsville attorney who was a contemporary also remembers Susie Sharp telling the story on herself, naming P. W. Glidewell and longtime Sheriff Leon Worsham as her partners in crime.[40]

In the speech she delivered at the law school banquet, she made a true confession. Citing public policy and the threat of jail time for contempt of court, she did not recommend the practice of eavesdropping on the jury, but she used the story to illustrate her point. "It is like wire-tapping," she said, "illegal but you do hear some useful things. We early found that jurors are not as much influenced by the arguments of counsel as we had fondly believed."[41] The jurors quite sensibly felt that a lawyer argued the side of the client who paid him and therefore the jury should "go by the evidence and not what the lawyers say." Susie Sharp added, "And I want to tell you there is no more excruciating agony than having to remain silent in the attic while hearing a juror state his recollection of your side of the evidence in a case."

Extraordinary to contemplate, for those who came to know Susie Sharp either personally or by reputation, the idea that she would participate in such an ill-becoming, unethical, and indeed illegal activity. Perhaps she was reluctant to play the schoolmarm role, figuring that she got enough criticism along those lines as it was. Or perhaps, in those less regulated times, she was unable to resist the idea that the courthouse regulars accepted her enough to include her in this insider's game. Having been rejected so roundly when she first entered practice, she was undoubtedly hungry for any sign that she belonged. If this was her original motivation, however, she continued to participate in the improper activity for several years at least. In 1933 her friend Allen Langston, commenting on a case she had, wrote, "This is one time that something worthwhile was accomplished by a little judicious eavesdropping."[42]

Despite her lack of clients, Susie Sharp was in wide demand, if not always as an advocate. She was a popular public speaker, called on for speeches to church groups and schools, including a talk to the freshmen at her alma mater, NCCW.[43] Wearing a fetching green hat, she spoke at a "fair sex program" put on by the local Rotary Club. Her talk, entitled "The Business and Professional Women's Part in Life," was described by the paper as "chock full of humor and good sense."[44] One friend from law school wryly voiced his suspicion that she enjoyed the Rotary Club speech "much more than the talk before the Sunday School class," given what he characterized as the necessity for hypocrisy in the latter venue.[45]

Like any good advocate or politician, however, she did not require her belief or experience to be identical to that of her audience. When she was invited in July 1929 to speak to the PTA of a local school, for example, she acknowledged that she was "neither a parent nor a teacher." She reckoned, moreover, that she would never be an actual mother, because Judge Humphreys of the recorder's court had told her some time ago that "he never knew a man to marry a lawyer yet." (Susie Sharp told the judge she "didn't see what difference a license made as all women went in for law anyway: Some take it up while the others lay it down.")[46] Quoting Dr. Samuel Johnson's comparison of women preachers to mules walking on their hind legs, she begged the audience's indulgence, asking, "[P]lease, while you listen to me, don't think how badly I am talking but think how marvelous it is that I am talking to you at all."[47] This was a clever bit of psychology on her part, calculated to preempt and diminish any objection to taking advice from a woman speaking out of her "place." The members of the PTA must have thought she spoke well enough, for they invited her back the following May.

If she had any triumph during this time, it was her appearance in the North Carolina Supreme Court in April 1930, when she argued the appeal of *Ware v. Knight*, the case in which she had given her first jury speech the preceding fall. Despite the favorable outcome her performance had helped bring about at trial, the client had made a special trip to see her father, specifically asking him not to send "Miss Susie" to argue before the court in Raleigh.[48] But because she had done all the research on the case and because it never occurred to her or her father that the client would find out who argued the appeal, Susie Sharp got on the bus and went to Raleigh.[49] To her chagrin, however, she made the headlines.

According to the Greensboro newspaper, "Miss Susie M. Sharp, unbobbed barrister of the law firm of Sharp and Sharp, Reidsville, had the floor. . . . Allen H. Gwyn, chivalrous foe, had argued the plaintiff's side." When her turn came, she saw that the hands of the courtroom clock stood at ten minutes to two o'clock, when the court was due to recess. When the clock struck two, "[s]he was speaking like a house on fire."[50] But knowing that the court would adjourn not one second after two o'clock, she did not even wait to finish the word she was speaking when the clock struck and the justices rose to march off for lunch. The newspaper declared her a good sport and gave her credit for her argument. But the punch line was that the court had "ended the legend that nobody can head off a talking woman."[51] Luckily for her and for Sharp & Sharp, the court ruled in favor of their client.[52]

Despite this victory and other small gratifications, however, Susie Sharp remained unhappy. She was working very hard, but almost entirely behind the scenes where she would not frighten off clients. She complained that her father did not allow her to do enough in the courtroom and felt that she was not getting as much experience in the practice of law as she wanted and needed.[53] At home she was constantly battling to raise the level of civilization in a household with six siblings ranging from a college student to a preschooler. The less refined atmosphere of Reidsville grated on Susie, having spent so much time in sophisticated Chapel Hill. She did her best to impart some manners to the children, even making her mother, always anxious to do the right thing, self-conscious. Moreover, it was proving difficult to build a social life while living under her parents' roof. In an effort to leaven her daily grind a bit, she had joined an amateur theater group, which not only gave her a respite from work but also got her out of the house. For further diversion, she could attend movies at the Rockingham, the grand new movie theater built in the Spanish mission style in 1929, which was the first cinema in the region equipped for sound.[54] Still, she missed the freedom she had known in Chapel Hill. She had an occasional admirer, and she wanted to go out with whom she pleased. Her father's judgment as to acceptable companions for his daughter, however, was both uncompromising and insurmountable. More than likely, no one would have been good enough.

She took lightly the attentions of the occasional book agent or insurance adjuster, but there was a young attorney who began taking her out regularly.[55] It was apparently a rather staid relationship, and she never appeared smitten in the least, although she did wonder at his lack of ardor. ("I can't answer your question as to why he hasn't tried anything," Maude Brown wrote her.)[56] Susie Sharp did the best she could with such unpromising material as came her way in the daily course of events. Several months later, Maude teased her: "Your encounters read like the private life of a modern Cleopatra or some others of that tribe who were so fatally attractive to men. I'll not be at all shocked to hear of some gentleman dying a tragic death on your account. Honest, though, Susie, I'd like to know how you do it; I'd get a kick out of it, I'm sure, even if it was *only* book agents and insurance adjusters."[57] Her father was not the least amused, however, and took a dim view in particular of the young attorney, who, he informed her, was "the laughingstock of the bar."[58] Mr. Sharp put up with this situation as long as he could; finally, in the spring of 1930, he simply issued an ultimatum and forbade her to see him again.[59] Her heart was not broken, but the young man had offered her a social outlet. She was almost twenty-three, and she chafed under such heavy parental control. It did not help matters that her oldest childhood friend, Janie Sands, was getting married. Ruby Ross wrote to commiserate, saying, "I know just how you felt on receiving Janie's letter."[60]

Mr. Sharp had other things on his mind besides Susie's social life. His second-oldest child, Sallie, would go off to NCCW in the fall of 1929, and there would be extra expenses for her tuition, board, and upkeep. Sallie's ambition was to be a professional violinist. The family had always been supportive of her musical talent, which was evidently considerable. She had worked hard and received recognition. It was not unreasonable to hope that she might earn a living teaching music or otherwise using her gift, especially if her talent were enhanced by a college degree. But, of course, education cost money, and there were five more children lined up behind her. The family's finances were always precarious.

Financial troubles, exacerbated by the onslaught of the Great Depression, were a strong incentive to look for any sort of job with a regular paycheck, and in the spring of 1930 Jim Sharp made another run for office, that of solicitor for what was then the Eleventh Judicial District. His opponent in the June primary was Carlisle W. Higgins, a lawyer from the little mountain town of Sparta in Alleghany County, with whom Susie Sharp later would serve on the North Carolina Supreme Court. Higgins had served in the North Carolina House of Representatives in 1925 and was the only Democrat from the northwestern part of North Carolina to be elected to the state senate in 1929.[61] On the day of the primary, Susie Sharp worked all day at the polls. Once again, however, Jim Sharp's supporters were outnumbered by voters farther from home, in Alleghany, Ashe, and Surry counties.[62]

That summer was an eventful one for Susie Sharp. Among other things she underwent an operation for what the newspaper reported was appendicitis, but in fact was a procedure intended to alleviate her severe dysmenorrhea. Such was the misery caused by her monthly periods that her mother used to give her whiskey in ginger tea, a major exception to the family's teetotaling beliefs.[63] Migraine headaches and vomiting sometimes accompanied the cramps. Susie Sharp desperately hoped that the operation was the answer, and her doctor in Reidsville, William S. Hester, was optimistic. Unfortunately for him, he not only told her that the operation would cure her but made the mistake of guaranteeing it.[64] She soon found, however, that the operation had been in vain. And because Dr. Hester had guaranteed it would work, Susie Sharp refused to pay him. Her father backed her up: "As to paying Dr. Hester, I would not pay them a cent yet. Just let them wait awhile and see whether you are benefitted any at all. If not I would take my own good time, if I ever paid them anything at all."[65] Eventually she got an opinion from a doctor at Duke Hospital saying that the operation was not medically indicated and was poorly performed, after which she heard no more from Dr. Hester about the bill.[66]

But even more momentous, she made the decision to leave Sharp & Sharp. With the Great Depression deepening, the family financial situation was more precarious than ever. When an unexpected opportunity for her to earn a regular paycheck arose late in the summer of 1930, she zeroed in on it. In mid-August Ruby Ross wrote that Dean Charles T. McCormick's secretary at the law school had resigned. At Ruby's suggestion, Dean McCormick promptly wrote to Susie Sharp from New Haven, Connecticut, where he was spending the summer at Yale, to see if she would be interested. The salary, he said, was only $125 per month, although he felt "confident that a person of your training and capacity could develope [sic] the position into one of much greater scope than it now has, with corresponding salary advancement, but of course that would be a matter for the future" and would depend largely on "the future prosperity of the University."[67]

When Susie Sharp quizzed her about the prospects for a higher salary, Ruby advised that she needed to "put up a stiff fight with the Dean."[68] "*Don't let him think you want it as a secretarial job,*" Ruby urged.[69] The air thickened with correspondence between Reidsville, New Haven, and Chapel Hill. "I think you are entirely right in believing that your services are worth much more than $125, or $150, per month," Dean McCormick wrote, but he was doubtful that the school could increase the salary for the position. After consultation with the university comptroller, Charles T. Woolen, however, he proposed that her position might be designated "Secretary and Research Assistant," which would permit an addition of $250, bringing the annual salary to $1,750.[70]

There were other considerations, too, and Dean McCormick laid them out. "One problem facing a recent graduate such as yourself in such a position would be that of maintaining relations extremely cordial and at the same time extremely impersonal with both faculty and students," he pointed out, "but I know your tact and poise are easily equal to this." On a basic level, he wanted to know about her stenographic skills — could she take shorthand rapidly and was she a fast typist? She would be first and foremost a secretary, which led to his primary concern: Was the position an appropriate one for someone who wanted a career in law? There might be opportunities for her to assist with the work of the *Law Review*, to do legal research, and possibly to teach a course in Legal Bibliography, but the dean was clear that secretarial and administrative tasks would make up the bulk of her work. "The main interest would always need to be the management of the administrative and office side of the school, so vital to its progress. This I would turn over to you as fast as you find yourself able to handle it." She would be in charge of the admission of students, arrangement of curricula, keeping of records, control of expenses, and the like.[71] "To someone who is essentially interested in and enthusiastic about legal education as a life-interest, I think the job offers a fine outlet for ambition, and a pleasant dignified career." But if she took the position as "a temporary escape from a small-town practice, as a half-way house to something else," he said, "it would be a complete failure from the start."[72]

Reading the correspondence surrounding this move on Susie Sharp's part is painful. It was so clear to all involved that she was taking a step back, not forward. Yet she was drawn inexorably by the need for the salary and by the lure of Chapel Hill, at the same time that her unfulfilling "practice" in the shadow of her father propelled her away from Reidsville. She would be a glorified secretary and she knew it. She bolstered her decision with hopes of the expanded role she might create in the position, doing research, perhaps some teaching. In large part she was looking for a way out of practicing law with her father and hoped the law school job might be a stepping-stone to practice with another firm. But she was careful to be entirely candid with Dean McCormick, who had been so forthright with her:

> I want to say frankly that a purely secretarial job is not my ambition and could not interest me very long. I am intensely interested in law and everything I do is calculated, in the end, to make me more familiar with it.
>
> . . . I realize that what you want first and foremost is an efficient secretary and that the legal aspects must be subordinate now. So what I want to say is that if, at length, it should appear that in the Law School I am not doing the work which interests me most I would want to feel that I had not in any way deceived you. . . . If conditions are such that it is impossible for the job to develope [sic] as we hope, I shall not blame you, for you have been most frank and I would not want you to blame me if I found that my interest did not continue.[73]

With the reservations of both sides on record, Susie Sharp bit the bullet. She agreed to start on September 15, 1930.

How much of her desire to return to Chapel Hill was due to Breck's presence is impossible to say. Perhaps she herself could not have said. The negotiations for the job took only two weeks and—quite possibly by design—

Breck did not receive a letter from her in time to register his thoughts until the very end of her discussions with Dean McCormick. It does not appear, in fact, that she asked him his opinion, because his answer to her letter refers to the "news . . . of which I had an inkling before from Mrs. B." and "the plans that you were kind enough to let me know about."[74] In any event, she made up her mind without waiting to hear from him. By the time he sent his response, she had already communicated her willingness to take the job if she and the dean could come to terms.

When he did express his opinion, Breck did not mince words. "What I am about to say is merely a first reaction and may not be my considered judgment. Laying aside all personal gain to me from having your willing aid when I shall much appreciate it, and thinking only of the job as a stepping stone, etc., I can't see it."[75] Breck pointed out that the law school job would greatly curtail her contact with attorneys who might be looking for a lawyer to join them, nor would she enhance her chances to vault to another firm based on the recommendation by the law school dean, for she "could have had the dean's recommendation anywhere that a woman would be considered." There was the possibility, he supposed, that she might form an alliance with a new law school graduate, although he did not think that was what she had in mind. "My guess is that your best starting point on this would have been from an argument in court where opposing counsel had occasion to take your measure," he observed, irrepressibly noting, "Obvious additional remarks omitted."[76] He supposed her response would be "the complaint you have given me before — that you don't get to court when and as you'd like to. But you did and would some."[77]

Whatever his sincere beliefs about the job as a career move, Breck had reason to fear Susie Sharp's return to Chapel Hill. Their involvement had already progressed to a dangerous level, and neither of them could have had much doubt about where it would go if she were in such close proximity.

They had managed to see quite a bit of each other, both alone and with others, after she finished law school and went home to Reidsville. On the surface it appeared that Susie Sharp had adopted and been adopted by the entire Breckenridge family. Sometimes Breck would write to say that he and Venitah were coming for a concert or other occasion in Greensboro, where Susie would join them. His two children, Arnold and Jean, had already become honorary members of the Sharp family, riding back and forth to Reidsville with Susie to visit with Tommy, Florence, and Louise, who were nearest to their ages. In the summers Arnold came for Boy Scout Camp, located just outside town; his father, of course, had reason to visit him there, and Susie

Sharp would drive out.[78] When Breck was in Washington during the summer of 1930, she made a trip to see him there, although she apparently did not go alone; her journal indicates that she had a traveling companion, unnamed.[79] That same summer Venitah came to Reidsville to spend a weekend while Breck was in Washington, and Susie Sharp had a bridge party for her.[80]

She had, of course, spent a good deal of time in Chapel Hill all along, some of it working with Breck on the Restatement project, often staying at the Breckenridge home, where her status was ambiguous to say the least. There is no doubt that she was genuinely fond of "Mrs. B.," or that there was genuine affection in return. Mrs. B. was Susie Sharp's "other mother," as she was affectionately referred to by each of them. Nor is there any doubt of the genuine love between Breck and his wife. But matters were far more complicated than they appeared.

At the heart of things was Venitah, whose warmth embraced every living soul within her ambit. An orphan, she had been raised in a foster family.[81] After Arnold and Jean were born, a series of miscarriages had ended her hopes of more children, but she and Breck acted as foster parents to a series of abandoned "doorstep babies" who were too young to be taken by the facilities existing at that time.[82]

Venitah Ida Hunziker had met Breck one summer when he and his family were in Michigan, escaping the Chicago heat. Then a slim and pretty girl, Venitah was working in a dry goods store. She did not have a great deal of education, but she was smart, connected easily with people, and soon captured the heart of the bright, good-looking young man. Breck, born in 1891 in Chicago, was a year older than Venitah, and came from a more privileged background. He was the only child of Belle Sheridan and a lawyer named John H. Breckinridge — spelled with an "i" — who were divorced when he was about five years old. The stigma of divorce at that time was so great that until Breck's daughter Jean was well grown, she believed her paternal grandfather had died; he had in fact simply departed for California, to be heard of no more. The stigma may have been the reason that Breck changed the spelling of his name when he was of college age, something else Jean did not learn until many years later, after her father died.[83]

Breck's mother was also an only child, the daughter of Millard Sheridan, a well-to-do businessman with a seat on the Chicago Board of Trade. Mr. Sheridan took his grandson under his wing, taking the boy with him on his rounds to banks and businesses and acting as surrogate father. Reared in relative affluence, Belle was known as a fashion plate and an accomplished horsewoman, but she also graduated from Northwestern University, no small matter for a woman of her generation.

Susie Sharp was fearless, and she appears to have been the aggressor in the relationship with Breck, who may have felt that his initial, presumptively harmless, flirting had gotten out of control. He blew hot and cold, one minute encouraging her and the next retreating. Always, he made it clear that his first loyalty was to Venitah and his family. "He says he has not pulled the line of being misunderstood," Susie Sharp recorded on the weekend of her law school graduation, in the separate journal she had begun keeping, devoted solely to Breck.[84] The following December she reported, "He is getting squeamish. Says he is not being the right kind of father; that his colleagues have been teasing him about being a ladies man."[85] He did not work very hard at discouraging her, however. In May 1930, when he came to help with a children's camping trip just outside Reidsville, Susie Sharp took a carload of children out, and he and Susie went for a moonlight stroll. "He says that my telling him I did not mean to marry has made it harder for him and that he wants to appropriate me," she reported.[86] Several weeks later, he was back at the campground. "When he does not come into town as he promised I go out there," she wrote. "We walk to the pool and he takes me in his arms on the dam."[87] If she was the pursuer, he was willing to be caught.

So in mid-September 1930 Susie Sharp was back in her beloved Chapel Hill, beginning her job as secretary and research assistant to the dean of the law school. If she suffered any pangs of guilt at abandoning Sharp & Sharp, perhaps they were alleviated somewhat when her father wrote to her a week after she left Reidsville, "I am keeping very busy, but we are getting no money of any consequence. You will make twice as much this month as I will here."[88]

Susie Sharp would spend the next two years in Chapel Hill, staying on when Professor Maurice T. Van Hecke replaced Dean McCormick in the fall of 1931.[89] It was a time of confusion and often unhappiness for her, although there was much that gave her pleasure. Never again would she experience such a lengthy period in which she had no direction, no clear goal. Unsure about why she had fled Reidsville, uncertain where her life was taking her, she felt shredded by choices. With a few exceptions, however, most of her friends and colleagues were unaware that she struggled. In the dean's office, she soon exerted the power of her personality, and anyone with a connection to the school made it a point to check in with her whether or not he had business with the dean. She quickly mastered the administrative aspects of the job, although her notorious spelling remained a source of consternation and amusement. Nor did the new functionary hesitate to use her position in furtherance of goals not strictly within her job description. She was known, for example, to extract dime contributions for the Christmas Seal fund before relinquishing midterm grades to anxious students, no matter how desperately they pleaded poverty.[90]

Chapel Hill was a vibrant and stimulating place, particularly in contrast to Reidsville. Frank Porter Graham, already nationally known in liberal political circles and as a dedicated advocate for academic freedom, had just become the new president of the university. During his long tenure at UNC, Dr. Graham would serve in a variety of extracurricular capacities under both President Roosevelt and President Truman. In the emerging field of sociology, UNC professor Howard Odum had just published a new book to which the *New York Times* book section gave place of honor on its front page.[91] At the law school, Professor Van Hecke served as national president of the prestigious Order of the Coif. On the extracurricular front, the theologian Reinhold Niebuhr spoke at UNC in the fall of 1930; soon after, Susie Sharp went to hear the famous pianist Paderewski in nearby Durham.[92]

She delighted in inviting family and friends from Reidsville to come for the weekend to attend the football games and enjoy the attractions of the glamorous college town. Even her mother came and acquired a broader view of the world as well as a new understanding of Susie Sharp's efforts to raise the level of graciousness at home. After attending a football game and dining with members of the law school faculty, Annie Sharp wrote Susie, "[A]s I have not been out much, I found out that ladies do smoke in public and that Prohibition seems . . . a plum [sic] failure. The people were very refined, and now I see how you felt about the racket etc. at the table. We are all going to turn into white swans — in the future. I got along OK unless it was very bad about the jelly and olives in my plate. Albert [Coates] put his jelly on his plate too. Do you reckon he was that thoughtful — not to make me feel badly?"[93]

Susie Sharp still had friends in Chapel Hill from her law school days, even though most had scattered after they finished their studies at the university. While she worked in the dean's office, however, she got to know a group of law students who would remain some of her closest friends and advisers throughout her life. William T. ("Bill") Covington was one of them. A Davidson College graduate with a master's degree from Princeton, an editor of the *Law Review*, and a member of the Order of the Coif, he would become a prominent attorney in Charlotte, North Carolina. Another was Hugh L. Lobdell, known as "Cicero," a Mississippi native who also served as an editor of the *Law Review* and was tapped by the Order of the Coif. Covington and Lobdell would join forces in later years to form the nucleus of a highly regarded law firm based in Charlotte. Yet another friend who was on the *Law Review* editorial board and a member of the elite Order of the Coif was Hugh B. Campbell, a Phi Beta Kappa graduate of Amherst College in Massachusetts. Like both Covington and Lobdell, he went to Charlotte to practice law. He would go on to be a superior court judge and later was one of the original six judges Governor Dan K. Moore appointed to the North Carolina Court of Appeals when it was established in 1967. Interestingly, Susie Sharp does not appear to have been particularly close to Naomi Alexander, who as a woman was still quite a rarity in the law school, who was a student editor of the *Law Review* in 1931–32, and who was the lone female member inducted into the Order of the Coif in 1932 (and for many years thereafter).

Susie Sharp's relationship with the law students was based around her position in the dean's office and her work with the *Law Review*, but despite her status as quasi faculty she was also part of their social circle. She even went out occasionally with Cicero Lobdell, whom she also fixed up with her sister Sallie one weekend. Sallie later reported that he "wasn't as tame as he looked," having declared he was going to bite off her left ear and throw her off the high stone wall on which they sat if she didn't kiss him. (She escaped unkissed and with both her ears.)[94] Susie Sharp's Danville, Virginia, cousin Earle Garrett was attending law school, and his roommate John Gillespie was among her suitors, to Earle's great glee and terror. Her most constant admirer, however, was yet another *Law Review* board member named Allen Langston, who held a student job as an assistant librarian in the law library and teased "the Sekaterry" unmercifully about her spelling. He courted her devotedly despite his simultaneous romance with a blonde from another jurisdiction, a relationship Susie Sharp did her utmost to encourage even as she allowed him to take her out on a regular basis.

Despite the undeniable pleasures of Chapel Hill, however, Susie Sharp was if anything even more depressed than she had been in Reidsville. She felt acutely the disparity between her status as a practicing lawyer and as a secretary. "I felt that I had failed as a lawyer and compromised my future by taking a subordinate job when I had a law license," she later wrote.[95] Her Reidsville friend Margaret Fillman urged her, "Hold on and don't desert. . . . Please try to tough it out and forget about this selfish city—you don't want to be stuck here forever. All the good, sensible smart people really leave. Those who haven't enough brains to get away stay here."[96] But Susie Sharp was unaccountably homesick, and her mother made sure that she knew she could come back any time. "We certainly do miss you," she wrote, "and if you don't like [it], just come home as quickly as the bus will bring you."[97] Her mother also cautioned against taking on extra work: "Men will put it all on the women if they are cranks enough to do it."[98]

Her regular paycheck was a great consolation, and it was during this time that she began her lifelong practice of contributing to the family finances. Her father wrote, "If this Hoover prosperity continues much longer everybody, including me, will be bankrupt up here."[99] With Sallie at NCCW and Annie Hill due to graduate from high school the following spring, Jim Sharp knew there would be additional educational expenses on top of everything else. Over the next couple of years Susie Sharp would send amounts ranging from "four simoleans" to $100 and more, especially when school fees were due.[100] When Annie Hill enrolled at the Duke nursing school in the fall of 1932, Susie would take her shopping for shoes and underclothes or buy her dinner, recording the expenditures carefully: "Annie Hill came over for supper and cost me $1.90."[101] In May 1931 Susie Sharp bought the family its first radio, even though her mother worried that Susie needed to spend the money on having her eyes examined.[102] To the family, Susie's financial contributions made a critical difference in a variety of ways. "I know Daddy is glad he has a grown daughter, for more reasons than one," Sallie wrote to her mother after receiving a check from her older sister for $100 toward her tuition.[103] Bearing in mind that Susie Sharp's salary was only a fraction over $145 per month, it is clear that she was making a conscious effort to set something aside to send home.

As much as the money, however, the siblings appreciated Susie's love and attention. Annie Hill, for example, entered the nursing school at Duke after some of her Blackwell relatives in Richmond, where she had at first thought to go, made it clear they did not want any relative of theirs training to be a nurse in their hometown. According to them, nurses "all smoked, some drank, and part stayed out all night, and in general, they all had bad manners."[104] It was no occupation for a lady. Although Annie Sharp insisted that "nursing is a grand calling and you can behave or misbehave anywhere," Annie Hill must have felt slightly unloved and uncertain as she began her training in Durham. Her sister's regular visits meant the world. "Susie is so sweet," Annie Hill wrote. "I just wish I had half the good qualities that she does. Ever since she came I have felt 100% better. She gives me sympathy and most of all makes me feel a little bit important and that's what I need for a change."[105]

Susie Sharp herself needed no less, and she continued to flounder through the fall of 1930. By the following January, a scant four months after beginning her new job in the dean's office, she had made up her mind not to stay there.[106] Returning to Reidsville, however, was not necessarily her only option. For whatever reason, she had investigated at least one other secretarial job, in Durham. Her father's reaction to this idea, however, did not leave her much room to argue. "I will now tell you the truth of the whole matter," he wrote to her:

> I did not want you to go to Chapel Hill at all, but the money conditions were such that I felt it an injustice to say to you, stay on here.
>
> I did not expect you to stay more than this year unless you were perfectly satisfied. It would be the height of folly for you to spend your time on clerical jobs with the money invested in your legal education.
>
> I expect you to come back and help me if you want to. I had a lot of new envelopes printed yesterday with Sharp & Sharp on it.
>
> I would not think of considering the Duke Job or any other clerical job. You can make as much money as that in Normal times doing nothing but collecting and title work, and when times are good you can make twice that much.
>
> The thing to do is, if you can put up with it, finish out the year's work there and then come on back and let's practice law.[107]

He told her that he was managing to keep afloat financially, so worries about money should not prevent her from quitting the job. "The last two months, I have made about $1800 in cash fees. That is not bad. Of course this covered a much longer period but I never count it until I can put it on the books." He advised her to keep her decision secret until she was ready to give notice. It seemed that she would soon be back in Reidsville, but it took her another year and a half to extricate herself. There can be little doubt that the reason was Professor Breckenridge.

It was mid-October before he returned to Chapel Hill from Washington. Even as she anticipated his arrival, Susie Sharp recognized where things were headed and evidently attempted to tiptoe around the ramifications of such situations in a letter to Margaret Fillman, whose amused reply was, "I can't understand all you write on the delicate (?) [sic] subject of adultery—I suggest you learn to spell the word first."[108] In Chapel Hill, Susie Sharp and Breck immediately fell into a pattern of long walks and automobile rides, in addition to the time they spent working together on the *Law Review*, sometimes as late as midnight. At the law school her office was just across the hall from his, so they were together a great deal, day and night. Venitah presumed he was at the office if he was not at home. Sometimes he was, but so was Susie Sharp.

Sometimes they were ranging the countryside from Pittsboro to Hillsboro[109] in his car, stopping at their favorite spots. If Venitah suspected anything at this stage, the only evidence that she indulged her feelings is an entry in Susie Sharp's journal about the visit of Robert Hutchins to Chapel Hill.

Hutchins had been an undergraduate when Breck was at Yale Law School and graduated from the law school himself a few years after Breck. For a brief period after graduation, Breck had worked for the New York law firm of Baldwin & Hutchins, in which the "Hutchins" was Robert Hutchins's uncle. Something of a wunderkind, Robert Hutchins in 1927 became dean of the Yale Law School at the very young age of twenty-eight and then was named president of the University of Chicago two years later. It was Robert Hutchins who, among other things, introduced the Great Books method of study in higher education. Given Susie Sharp's interests and accomplishments, her position in the law school, and her close relationship to the Breckenridge family, there is only one likely interpretation of her notation dated October 30, 1930: "Mrs. Breck gives a tea for Robt. Hutchens [sic] but I am not invited."

In mid-December Susie Sharp once again took the initiative. "I tell him that I love him," she recorded, "and he says that if that is not his feeling for me he does not know what it is."[110] She did not relent. Over the next couple of months Breck made more than one attempt to back up, chiding her, for example, for not accepting an invitation from Cicero Lobdell ("Says I am not as sensible as he thought").[111] As if to emphasize that she was not going to disappear, she bought a secondhand Pontiac coupe, her first car, for the express purpose of traveling back and forth from Reidsville to Chapel Hill after her pending departure. To no avail, Breck told her that they must stop seeing so much of each other.[112] By early March they were lovers. When he asked her, several weeks later, how she felt psychologically, he was surprised when she answered, "No different."[113]

Then, as in later life, Susie Sharp's exterior concealed far more than it revealed. With utter sangfroid, she had entered into an affair with a married man, her former professor, into whose family she had been received as an honorary daughter. She plotted and connived and misled in a manner that would have killed her mother and made her father homicidal if they had known. Yet even with her reputation for high spirits, she still somehow came across as an old-fashioned girl, unschooled in the ways of the world. One of her male acquaintances in Chapel Hill, who prevailed on her to give him a ride to his bootlegger, called her straitlaced and accused her of not knowing the facts of life. He called her "the type a man ought to marry after he has had his fling."[114] Perhaps his characterizations followed a rejected pass, but another young man's remarks echo the same thought in a more wistful tone. This young man said he thought she was beautiful, adding that she was the only woman he had wanted to kiss who had not had some experience, as she reported dryly, with no further comment.[115] Susie Sharp was never tempted to discourage this perception, for it served her very well.

The situation with Breck, however, without question caused her stress and a good deal of unhappiness, even if no remorse. Like all lovers, illicit or otherwise, she and Breck experienced euphoria and depression in proportionate amounts, had spats, made up, despaired. Breck's internal conflict manifested itself regularly and was duly recorded by Susie Sharp. "Nice time but on the way back he says he loves his wife and does not want to do anything that she would not like and yet he likes to do this too."[116] Another entry reports, "Says he is old enough to be my father."[117] He forgot her birthday and then told her, "We are seeing too much of each other and must be careful."[118] What he really wanted was both his family and his Susie; he wished he could be honest with Venitah about it.[119] Susie Sharp's journal during these years when she was working in Chapel Hill is rife with notations of "terrible headache" and once even of a "crying jag."[120]

Stress may have contributed to the suffering she continued to experience with her monthly periods, which was so extreme that she even considered having a child, something popularly believed to alleviate such problems. In the spring of 1931 she wrote about this to her old UNC friend Dorothy Fahs, now Dorothy Beck, whose recent marriage was an early version of the flower child ceremonies adopted by so many in the 1960s, with vows written by the bride and groom.[121] Dorothy was the epitome of the intellectual Yankee with radical tendencies. She was well traveled, happily married, and—perhaps most important—living in Bronxville, New York, far from North Carolina. Dorothy replied, "As to this baby proposition I have had people tell me the same thing. There may be something to it. In any case if you seriously want to go through that physiological ordeal but do not want to marry or keep your child I believe the matter could be arranged." In Germany Dorothy had met a professor from Northwestern who, she informed Susie Sharp, was very anxious to have children, as was his wife, but unfortunately the wife was sterile. "He would like to have a child by another woman and she would consent, I am sure," Dorothy wrote. "I would never have thought of suggesting it if you had not written as you did asking for suggestions."[122]

Whether Susie Sharp contemplated a pregnancy by a stranger or someone closer to home, she did not pursue this option. Instead, she obtained from

Dorothy a scholarly bibliography on the subject of sex, marriage, and contraception, including volumes by Havelock Ellis and Margaret Sanger, as well as pamphlets on contraception that at the time could not be sent legally through the mail.[123] As for her dysmenorrhea, she consulted a specialist at Duke the following summer but apparently resigned herself to periodic misery after hearing the options he proposed, which included another operation or stopping her periods with x-ray therapy.[124] That she had contemplated such an extreme remedy as bearing an illegitimate child in an effort to obtain relief was a measure of the physical misery she endured; that she not only endured it but functioned on the level and on the schedule that she did over the years was a measure of her determination.

If Susie Sharp suffered from the stress of her affair with Breck, however, it had nothing to do with a desire on either side to disrupt the Breckenridge marriage.

"Where are we headed?" Breck asked her.[125] One thing was clear, the answer was not "to the altar." Breck had never led her to think that he would leave his family; on the contrary he had repeatedly told Susie how deeply he cared for his wife. His children adored him and he was active in their upbringing, very close to both of them. Moreover, he did not think he and Susie would get along together for, as he put it, she had ideas of her own.[126] For Susie's part, she did not desire marriage either, although there is no doubt that she genuinely loved Breck. She sometimes resented the power her feelings had over her, telling him she would as soon be a galley slave as in love with him (to which he replied, "Love is slavery").[127] The last thing she wanted was for him to leave Venitah, even though it meant, as she wrote upon finding herself in Reidsville "alone with a Xmas tree," that she could "never again enjoy a Xmas."[128] The arrangement, in fact, suited her well. Which leads to the question, What about Venitah?

There is considerable evidence throughout Susie Sharp's journal that Venitah knew, or at least strongly suspected, that Breck was involved with Susie. Although he claimed he had not told her, and indeed often said to Susie that he wished he could tell her so that matters would be on an honest footing, Venitah's intelligence, intuition, and knowledge of her husband would have given her reason to imagine the worst. In July 1931 the three of them attended a wedding in eastern North Carolina; at breakfast one morning it was not lost on Susie that Breck "would not sit with us and V. has tears in her eyes."[129] In October Breck told Susie of a talk with his wife "which left them both feeling terrible," and said that he must break off their affair, "as he had no right to make her suffer the way he does." He did not break it off, however; instead, the relationship intensified. In February 1932, Venitah confided to Susie that Breck had not always been faithful to her. There had been a woman, she said, when they were living in Cleveland.[130] Breck later acknowledged to Susie that "there had been a woman a long time ago, one that I loved and I have never gotten over it."[131] In a precise echo of what he had been saying to her, Venitah told Susie that Breck "never did want to give the other up after she found it out," that he wanted them both.[132] The following summer she told Susie that she "worries for fun if there is somebody else," that Breck did not get home until late and she noticed the mileage on the car.[133] Perhaps, without directly confronting her, Venitah was letting Susie Sharp know that she was not in the dark.

Susie Sharp never gave the least flicker of any intention to give Breck up. It seems clear that Venitah, as women have done for eons, made the choice to accept a distressful situation rather than disrupt her life and the lives of her children. Over many years, however, Susie and Venitah developed a warm relationship centered around their feelings for Breck but larger than that. The affection between Susie Sharp and the entire Breckenridge family was deep and abiding.

Any stress related to her affair with Breck thus did not result from a desire to wrest him away from Venitah or even from guilt, which apparently troubled Susie Sharp not in the least. Nonetheless, there was plenty of pain to go around, and the difficult situation certainly contributed to her unsettled and unhappy state. When she returned to Chapel Hill after Christmas in 1931, although she did not see less of Breck, she seems to have made an effort to go out more with the other beaux in her string: Allen Langston, Cicero Lobdell, and John Gillespie. Although he sometimes expressed his jealousy, Breck encouraged her in this.

On the professional front, too, matters were unwieldy and frustrating. She was helping her father on some of his cases, and he kept her generally up-to-date on his various trials, so she remained connected to Sharp & Sharp. In April 1932 she argued a case in the North Carolina Supreme Court, a will case involving allegations of insufficient capacity, fraud, and undue influence.[134] Susie Sharp represented the husband of a woman whose purported will left him out, in favor of her brother. Allen Gwyn represented the other side. Susie Sharp's successful argument must have helped to remind her of what she was supposed to be doing in life, and that she was not meant to be a secretary. As Breck said to her, the dean's office was no place for her to grow old.[135]

It had been more than a year since Susie Sharp had told her father she did not want to continue working as the law school secretary. She had dithered all spring about it, beset by events drawing her mind back home. In January, her mother had a cancer scare and underwent a hysterectomy at Duke. The outcome was successful, but the family was shaken. Susie's father beseeched Susie's aid in dealing with NCCW, which had sent a bill for $22.50 to cover the cost of Sallie's musical instruments, "an outrage." He asked Susie to go by the school on her way home and look into the matter, for "I think I would curse the whole Crowd out and do more harm than good if I should go."[136]

Through all this, Susie Sharp had slowly made her way to the decision to return to Reidsville before the fall term began. She must have felt a renewed sense of obligation when in midsummer she received an upsetting letter from her sister Sallie, who was very worried about their mother. "Today at the dinner table she broke down and cried," Sallie wrote. "Tommy and Louise were fussing, and even Kits was impudent to her. . . . I don't think Tommy could be much meaner if he tried. . . . I am losing all sympathy for Louise." Although it is likely there was nothing out of the ordinary in the children's behavior, it seemed to have had an unusual effect on Annie, who said that she wished she could take Kits and go stay with her sister Blanche in Indiana until school started. "Then she said she wished she could die, that she worked from morning 'til night, and heard nothing but fuss and noise." Sallie was terribly upset, for she was not accustomed to seeing her mother cry and had never heard her express a wish to go somewhere else. "Mamma is near the breaking point, if I am not mistaken," she wrote. "As long as she stays here she works all the time. I believe she wants to work herself to death. . . . I guess Tommy and Louise just can't realize that Mamma isn't as strong as she used to be."[137] Annie soon rallied after taking a few days away from the family, but Susie Sharp knew she could help her mother with the children's deportment if nothing else, and this knowledge must have reinforced her decision to go back home.

Margaret Fillman, astonished to learn that Susie Sharp was planning to return to Reidsville, tried to offer encouragement. "I do hope you will like it better at home, practicing there, than you did when you first tackled it, and I believe if you go at it with the determination to over-ride your father in some things that you will get along fine. You must make him let you argue some cases—I'll be horribly disappointed in you if you don't stand up for your rights," she wrote.[138] "[T]ake the bull by the horns and tell your well-meaning but often misguided father where to get off."[139]

Breck had told her in February that it was just beginning to dawn on him that he did not want her to go.[140] By May, however, when she informed him of her definite decision, he was resigned and said it was best for her.[141] But there was no decline in their relationship. On the contrary, they even finagled spending an entire night together, possibly for the first time, in a hotel in Durham. He made her leave at seven o'clock the next morning, but his parting words were, "I love you dear and when I have said that it is all there is to say."[142] He might not have booted her out so early if he had known she would spend the rest of the day with Allen Langston, winding up out at Gimghoul Castle at one o'clock the following morning. Deep in the woods, the turreted stone fantasy was the seat of one of the university's secret societies, the Order of Gimghoul. Susie Sharp recorded the dialogue: "Allen says that he wished he could take me home with him; oh, I like you, Susie. He's feeling my face and telling me about the skin you love to touch. I say, 'Want to feel my stubborn jaw.' He laughs and says, 'I like you more and more.'"[143]

It was common gossip around the law school that Susie Sharp was quitting her job and moving back to Reidsville because she and Allen were getting married, but, as Allen said to Susie when he reported hearing the rumor, although "[i]t may be true that 100 lawyers can't be wrong . . . this is one time that they are certainly sadly mistaken." Gallantly, he added, "I could very easily wish that the said rumors were not so utterly without any basis of fact."[144] For Susie's part, despite the considerable time they had spent together, the letters and the photographs exchanged, the flirtatious tone of their relationship, Allen had never given Susie "the slightest thrill."[145] The following summer he would marry the blonde from the foreign jurisdiction, and the three remained good friends. Indeed, Susie Sharp was the first person to receive an invitation to their small wedding to be held in the Chapel Hill home of Miss Lucile Elliott, the law school librarian.[146]

Breck went off to Washington again for the summer, where Susie Sharp visited him at least twice. Now that he knew he would no longer see her every day, his appreciation sharpened. "He tells me that there is so much more to his love than sex that he will love me when it is all over and that he wishes he could give me a child," she wrote, adding, "He says that sometimes he likes the adventure of all this."[147] Susie Sharp moved back to Reidsville at the end of July, but met Breck in Raleigh on August 12 when he came down to surprise Venitah the following day, which was both her birthday and their wedding anniversary. Drawing a very fine distinction indeed, he would not let Susie meet him on that day. Whatever sense it had made for her to rejoin Sharp & Sharp, when she saw him at this first reunion since she had departed from Chapel Hill, she grieved over the loss of their daily contact, saying that she had rather be across the hall from him and amount to nothing. "What shall it profit a woman to gain fame and fortune if she breaks her heart?" she asked. "You need not do that," he assured her.[148]

CHAPTER 5

SHARP & SHARP

If Susie Sharp had departed Reidsville feeling that she would never make it as a lawyer, especially in a practice with her father, her return two years later marked a sea change. Apparently having made up her mind that her place was in the Sharp & Sharp office, she caught hold swiftly, beginning a trajectory as a general practice lawyer that would carry her to a solid position in the Rockingham County bar.

At first, however, it seemed that nothing had changed, that clients still "wanted no part of that girl" when they sought legal counsel.[1] Clients continued to come to see Mr. Jim, not Miss Susie. But it was not always easy to find Mr. Jim, for he wanted to be out and about, politicking or farming on the land he had long since acquired not far from town. He often left Susie to take care of the office, and emphasized at every opportunity that clients should entrust their business to her. "Your letter was received in the office here this morning in the absence of my daughter who is handling this matter. . . . I am only doing what is necessary in her absence to protect the client's interest," he wrote to one lawyer.[2] And he chastised an insurance claim adjuster who had come to the office but left without accomplishing anything because Mr. Sharp was out: "My daughter who is my law partner was in the office at that time and would have been glad to discuss the above matter with you, but you did not mention it to her."[3]

She did not press, preferring to let the clients think she was a mere handmaiden. "Maybe they didn't know it," her sister Louise said, "but Susie was making the decisions."[4] In fact, before long it was Susie Sharp who held the office together. In Louise's opinion, "We wouldn't have had any law practice if she hadn't stayed there and tended to business. [Daddy] wouldn't stay in the office. . . . He wanted to be out in the fresh air."[5]

Susie Sharp too did not want to stay cooped up in the office. Like her colleagues, she spent much of her professional time searching real estate titles, drawing wills, and collecting debts, in addition to whatever office work she could do for her father. But she wanted to be in the courtroom, and because of her affiliation with a firm with an active trial practice, she had what was in those days—for a woman—a most unusual opportunity. Even in metropolitan areas where women lawyers were less rare, an office practice was the norm, trial practice the exception. The idea of a woman litigator was so unnatural that a marshal in federal court in Greensboro unhesitatingly tapped Susie Sharp on the shoulder and asked her to sit somewhere else, informing her that she was in the section reserved for lawyers.[6]

Susie Sharp's metamorphosis into a trial lawyer did not happen overnight, but she was less impatient than she had been before she bolted for Chapel Hill. For clients in the early days, as she put it, "the dignity of their lawsuit required Mr. Jim." Mr. Sharp "didn't care about pulling down the books and doing the research that I had learned to do in law school," she said. "So I would prepare the law in the cases that we tried." Soon she persuaded him that, to protect the legal arguments she had prepared and thus their client's position on appeal, she needed to be in the courtroom to make sure that the necessary objections got into the record. "So that's really how I got started into the trial business," she said. People got used to seeing her in court with her father. Clients began to say, "I've got Mr. Sharp and Miss Susie on my case."[7] Gradually she began taking more of a speaking role. Early on she gained praise from one judge, who told her that she "talk[ed] sense and discussed the evidence which was something few lawyers did."[8] In another case, the local newspaper reported "a pleasant surprise in the form of an able argument on points of law made by a very attractive young woman attorney."[9] The paper noted that she appeared with her father, who "allowed her to make the principal argument for the defense," and "so relevant and convincing was her argument that Judge Oscar O. Efird sustained a demurrer in the case."[10]

Still, acceptance in the courtroom came slowly. Courtroom arguments in those days tended toward the bombastic, a style most felt unbecoming to a woman. Jim Sharp was a practitioner of rafter-shaking rhetoric, considered necessary in many quarters for successfully persuading a jury. Susie Sharp's initial difficulty was "overcoming the presumption that no woman could be an effective trial lawyer," in the days when the common image of a working woman included "the school teacher, stenographer, seamstress or clerk in a store," but was not sufficiently elastic to embrace a female attorney in the courtroom.[11] "Clients believed that 'natural feminine timidity' would keep any woman from being the match for an aggressive, loud-talking male lawyer," Susie Sharp said.[12] But she was smart enough to realize that her worst mistake would be to try to act like a man, and that juries were likely to listen to her arguments *because* she was a woman, out of curiosity if nothing else.[13] She took care not to breach the public's expectations of a lady, even in the heat of a courtroom battle.[14] It was another example of her understanding that good camouflage could be as useful as more obvious battle apparatus.

As for her fellow members of the bar, she had to contend not only with the usual tactics and shenanigans of the courtroom but also with the extra flourishes and furbelows her gender elicited. In the early days of her career, lawyers developed a technique neatly designed to dispose of her and the case by flattering her "right out of court."[15] "Flattery from one's competitors is a danger signal," she warned.[16] Quoting a colorful old country lawyer, she compared it to "cologne water—nice to smell but not to be swallowed."[17] For the neophyte female lawyer, flattery signaled one of two things: either your opponent was attempting to blind you to a maneuver not in your interest, or you were not even in the race. Asked how she dealt with this tactic, she said, "I just endured it with fortitude."[18] It was not until her opponents stopped flattering her in the courtroom that she felt she had made progress.

Her father was not without qualms about some aspects of the trial practice, refusing at first to allow her to visit their clients who, doubtless through no fault of their own, found themselves behind bars. "That jail is no place for a woman," he told her. But it was not long before she overcame his objection.[19] Within eighteen months of her return to Reidsville, her friend Allen Langston, who was thrashing his way through his own apprenticeship in the law office of prominent Raleigh attorney Kenneth Royall, said, "You are getting some trial experience that I am afraid that I shall never have unless I get out for myself."[20] Clients who used to tiptoe up to the Sharp & Sharp office, hoping to catch Mr. Jim when Miss Susie was out, began to reverse their timing to find Miss Susie in when her father was out.

She was on her feet, in the courtroom and otherwise.

Small-town law practice in the 1930s and 1940s was no less intense than it is today, given the close proximity and long acquaintance of litigants as well as lawyers. Legal proceedings with one's neighbors or family members are fraught with a particular intensity not generally found between parties more distant. The familiarity of the members of the bar with one another in those simpler days, however, bred a far less stressful professional relationship in which civility and ethics were the essential implements of every attorney. If a lawyer made an agreement with another lawyer, his word was good; no one would have considered requiring the agreement to be in writing. In most counties, court was not held every week. In the normal course of events, there was time to indulge other vocations or avocations, time to linger at the post office and chat, time to walk home for lunch, perhaps to take a short siesta. This was true even in the absence of modern "time-saving" technology. Ballpoint pens did not exist, let alone word processors or email. Telephones had no dials or buttons because reaching another number entailed a conversation with the operator at "Central." Deed descriptions were copied out by hand. Duplicate copies of typewritten documents required accuracy, patience, or both because every mistake had to be laboriously corrected by hand on each carbon copy, or the entire document started over. Without air conditioning, the suffocating heat of the long summers exerted its own damp dissuasion to rapid movement. Papers had to be weighted against the hot breath of office fans.

Susie Sharp was schooled early on in the realities of trial practice. It was true then, as it had been before and would be thereafter in certain times and places, that there were two kinds of lawyers, those who knew the law and those who knew the judge.[21] Moreover, in the days before court reform, judges often owed their jobs to local power brokers like prominent local attorney J. Hampton ("Hamp") Price. When Price's portrait was presented at the courthouse many years later, Susie Sharp said in her remarks, "Hamp added a third dimension—he knew the law, the judge and all the jurors." In this he was not unique. Nor, in itself, did this necessarily imply chicanery; it was simply a fact that in those days a person who set about it could know just about every other person within his sphere of operations. Price, she said in her tribute, "had known the jurors as individuals long before their names were drawn for jury duty."

The art of picking a jury drew not only on detailed knowledge of personal backgrounds but also on a precise evaluation of loyalties. A lawyer would be aware, for instance, that it was not necessarily a good thing to have a personal friend on the jury because he might bend over backwards not to show favoritism, whereas a political friend could be counted on.[22] Flamboyant local attorney P. W. Glidewell was a known master at assembling a jury sympathetic to his cause. Susie Sharp once noted in her journal, "P. W. tries a liquor case with a man on the jury who helped defendant put up the still. Not guilty."[23]

One of Susie Sharp's own cases involved a miscarriage of justice, rooted in the county's complex sociopolitical environment, that would haunt her for years. It was a custody battle over the two sons, aged eleven and fifteen, of a prominent surgeon and his wife from nearby Leaksville, Dr. and Mrs. Carl V. Tyner. Sharp & Sharp, along with Leaksville attorney Harry Fagge, represented Mrs. Tyner. The doctor's four-man legal team included P. W. Glidewell and Allen Gwyn. Mrs. Tyner alleged, providing evidence in the form of affidavits and "mash notes," that her husband had engaged in at least three affairs, demonstrating his unsuitability to have custody of the children. The doctor countered that his wife had from time to time left the home and gone to stay with her family in New England without responding to his efforts to communicate with her. At one of several hearings on the matter, the newspaper reported, "They even dragged in a touch of the Battle of Gettysburg, arguing that Mrs. Tyner had despised the South," to which counsel for Mrs. Tyner responded that "if she was displeased with the South it was because she failed to find in her husband a Southern gentleman."[24] The paper declared that, out of the "routine of masculine voices," another voice stood out "brilliantly to those who heard" in "the quietly-couched[,] brief but stirring talk made by Miss Susie Sharp, a part of Mrs. Tyner's counsel and a lone feminine figure in this camp of men. The gentle forcefulness and directness of her speech brought applause from the audience and a demonstration of enthusiasm which made a call for order imperative."[25]

The doctor's case was supported primarily by testimonials to his good character made by prominent Leaksville citizens. When Judge Felix Alley awarded custody to the father, the mother's shock and grief could scarcely be borne. Worse was the way it happened. Thirty years later when she was on the North Carolina Supreme Court with Justice Carlisle Higgins, Susie Sharp described to Breck how "Judge Alley changed a record on me." The judge "announced from the bench that he had made a private investigation of his own into the facts of the case and, after doing so, he was awarding custody to the father," she said. "When I appealed and put that in the record, Allen Gwyn, who was representing Dr. Tyner, told Judge Alley that he was incapable of such unjudicial conduct and therefore could not possibly have made such a statement. Judge Alley, of course, agreed and almost put me in jail when I told him he said it and knew he said it."[26]

Mrs. Tyner, at least, was not one of those clients who wanted nothing to do with a woman lawyer. In a touching note to Mr. Sharp before the appeal was heard in the North Carolina Supreme Court, she wrote, "Please *take Miss Sharp with you to Raleigh. I feel her womanly manner will win the most hardhearted judge.*"[27] The high court, however, hewed to its solid tradition of refusing to find that a superior court judge had abused his discretion, and upheld the decision depriving the mother of custody.[28] Susie Sharp never doubted that the local power structure had rallied around one of its own to engineer an insider's victory against the unhappy Yankee wife.

Three decades later, what Judge Alley said in that courtroom, and later denied, was still on the mind of more than one of those present that day. Susie Sharp wrote in some wonder to Breck, "Judge Higgins, out of a clear sky, told me this week that he heard him say it. He volunteered the information a little late, I thought." The memory still rankled. "I doubt if it would have made any difference," she said. "The record is what the judge says it is in case of a dispute, and I was surrounded by crooks in that one. After 30 years that is my considered opinion—only one involved ever had pangs of conscience. AHG [Allen Gwyn] gave some evidence that he did."[29]

In the early 1930s, Allen Gwyn, Susie Sharp's former high school debate coach, was making a name for himself. Energetic and ambitious, he had an active law practice and was deeply involved in the political scene. In 1931 and 1933 he served in the state senate and was elected solicitor of what was then the Eleventh Judicial District in 1934. A contemporary described him as "a slim, youthful-looking, deeply earnest and friendly man, with a deliberate, gentle, yet firm manner of speech, who is intensely concerned with his fellow man, his state and his nation."[30] In 1933 he garnered extensive publicity when, after numerous appeals and reprieves, he marched all the way to the electric chair by the side of a client convicted of murder, a thirty-year-old white man named Clay Fogleman, and stayed to witness his execution, something that had never before happened on death row.[31] Some saw this as a tasteless publicity stunt. Allen Langston considered it "an unnecessary slap in the face of the Governor who had heard him so patiently and on so many different occasions."[32] Whatever the motivation, Gwyn's death row march foreshadowed his later interest in blighted lives caught up in the criminal justice system.

As it happened, the Fogleman case gave Susie Sharp what may have been her first experience with a death case. Fogleman had been accused of killing a service station operator named Carter in a holdup and a deputy sheriff a week later. The widow of the service station operator hired Sharp & Sharp to assist Solicitor Carlisle Higgins in the prosecution. Fogleman was tried for Carter's murder first and was convicted and sentenced to death on the basis of the widow's eyewitness testimony. It upset the entire Sharp family. Susie's sister Sallie wrote to her fiancé, asking if he had been following the case in the papers. "None of us believe in capital punishment," she said. "We were sorry that Daddy had anything to do with the case. He was one of Mrs. Carter's lawyers and collected most of the evidence. I don't know, but I don't think he will ever take another case like that. He and Susie and Mother have worried about it constantly."[33] If Susie Sharp opposed the death penalty at this point in her life, however, that view would change.

The practice of law, thankfully, was not without its lighter moments. Susie

Sharp enjoyed the inventiveness of a trial practice. She once won a case in which she represented the "poor defenseless wife of a G.I. overseas with two babes in arms . . . by the simple expedient of having the American Legion attend the trial in a body and sit on the front row."[34] She was fond of telling — with the aid of African American dialect — about the black couple who came to her office seeking, in no uncertain terms, a legal separation after five years and three children. Upon questioning, it developed that the couple had never actually married. Susie Sharp explained that no legal document was necessary and that "a simple walk-out" would suffice. The woman was adamant, how-ever, and insisted on an official document showing that she was through with that man for good. Moreover, she assured her lawyer, she had the money to pay for it. "At that interesting revelation," Susie Sharp said, "I capitulated." After some thought, she drafted two copies of a dissolution of partnership agreement replete with "whereases" and "party-of-the-first-parts," which the pair "signed, sealed and delivered to each other" before leaving with an "air of great finality and satisfaction."[35]

This story reflects two things of note in addition to Susie Sharp's ingenuity. The first is the reference to ability to pay. The partners in Sharp & Sharp held divergent views on pro bono work. Jim Sharp had always been willing to ac-cept the odd chicken or other bartered goods in lieu of his fee and, beyond that, had many times represented clients he knew could never pay.[36] Some-times it even went the other way. In the depths of the Depression, a client asked him to please send her some money from an estate Jim Sharp had handled for her, because her son had stuck a nail in his foot and she needed to pay the doctor. Mr. Sharp wrote her that the estate was in stocks, which could not be sold at that time without a great loss. "So," he wrote, "I am loaning you $5 out of my own funds, with the understanding that I am to take it out of your part when we ever get it. Now, please keep this to yourself. . . . I cannot loan out money as I do not have it, but am doing this for you because of your boy's accident."[37]

Susie Sharp was not averse to bartering. Her brother Tommy recalled the time she represented a young woman who came to Reidsville and opened a dance studio in the early 1930s. The dry cleaner ruined some of her clothes and refused to make good. When Susie Sharp won the case, instead of collect-ing a fee she negotiated dancing lessons for Tommy.[38] But she parted com-pany with her father when it came to providing services without payment, not to mention advancing loans to clients. Shortly after she joined the family firm, she confided to Tommy, "Daddy is willing to work for nothing, but I am not." Years later she also noted, "I sometimes felt that some clients thought

I shouldn't charge as much as a 'man lawyer,' but I disabused them of that notion."[39]

She even refused to waive her agreed-upon fee when the Pulitzer Prize–winning playwright and North Carolina native Paul Green enlisted her aid in the high-profile Burlington Dynamite case, a cause he had taken up. Recently returned to Chapel Hill, Green had intended to set aside most of 1935 to work on a new play.[40] But he was caught up in the seeming injustice of the labor dispute in Burlington and devoted much of his time and some of his personal funds to trying to help the defendants in the case.

The facts were simple. In 1934 at the height of labor unrest in the country, textile workers in Burlington, North Carolina, joined the general strike called by Francis J. Gorman, vice president of the United Textile Workers of America. When strikers tried to prevent other workers from entering the Holt Plaid Mill in Burlington, a melee broke out, and the National Guard dispersed the crowd with tear gas and bayonets. Five people, including a woman, were bayoneted. That night a bomb exploded outside the mill, causing what was later determined to be about $100 in damage. Arrests were swift and in some cases based on flimsy or dubious evidence. Seven defendants were convicted, and jail sentences of up to ten years imposed. At this, certain Chapel Hill liberals became outraged and launched a campaign to raise money for bail and appeals. Those active on behalf of the convicted bombers included not only Paul Green but also the young historian C. Vann Woodward and William T. Couch, the head of the university press, among others. As the case gained notoriety, the International Labor Defense, the legal arm of the Communist Party, stepped in, supposedly to assist with the appeals but in reality to further its own ideological goals. Friction between the International Labor Defense and the local union resulted in the withdrawal of the union's participation in the case in March 1935, as preparations for the appeals went forward.

On March 4, 1935, Paul Green called Susie Sharp to Chapel Hill to ask her to prepare the appeal.[41] She proposed a fee of $300 to do all the work in the case. Green got her to reduce her price to $250 because there were two other lawyers and a stenographer who could help, but the understanding was that Susie Sharp nonetheless would do most of the work. He wrote her a check for $100 out of his own pocket.[42] Subsequently, funds apparently dried up, and Susie Sharp "fell out along the way," according to Green, "for our lack of sustaining funds."[43] If she recorded her thoughts about the case or the participation of the Communist Party, any such record apparently has vanished. But she was adamant about being paid for her work. Her friend Ruby Ross sent her a *Daily Tar Heel* clipping about the case a couple of months later, saying, "I am glad you stuck them out for your fee for I don't feel that it is your responsibility or obligation to do all of that hard work for nothing."[44]

The second point of note in Susie Sharp's story about the dissolution of partnership agreement is that it concerned clients who were black. Like her father, she was a segregationist who nonetheless conscientiously represented black clients, who made up a large percentage of their practice.

Surviving Sharp & Sharp files include correspondence that vividly demonstrates her concern for one client, undiminished by her explicit racial prejudice, along with her modus operandi. The client was a black woman, a schoolteacher, injured in an automobile accident caused by another motorist subsequently convicted of reckless driving. Susie Sharp was negotiating for a settlement with the other driver's insurance company. The "colored doctor" in Reidsville had examined her client and declared that she had a spinal injury that might result in paralysis of the lower limbs, although at present she was still teaching school. Susie Sharp, concerned that they might settle for too little in the event the woman actually did have a permanent injury, arranged for a second opinion at Duke Hospital, which the client could not afford. By seeking a reliable medical opinion, of course, Susie Sharp knew that the resulting settlement might end up being less rather than more. The client, however, would know the truth of her condition, and Susie Sharp would see to it that she got a realistic amount. In the interest of an impartial and accurate diagnosis, therefore, Susie Sharp convinced the insurance company to provide thirty-five dollars for the examination. Susie Sharp herself would drive the client to Durham. Writing to confirm the arrangements at Duke with her sister Annie Hill, she asked, "Do you think that I should go with her any farther than the door? She is brighter than most Negro women but not as smart as a school teacher ought to be."[45] The files do not contain the outcome of the case, but the schoolteacher surely got everything to which she might be entitled.

By the mid-1930s Susie Sharp was a well-established figure in the local bar, accepted by clients and colleagues alike. In 1935, without advance notice or permission from her father, she bobbed her hair. Sometimes when she appeared in court in another county there were still incidents in which the bailiff might try to bar her from areas "reserved for attorneys," and the judge might feel free to comment from the bench that she was wearing "one helluva hat."[46] But on the whole she was recognized as a very good lawyer who happened to be female. With some pride she recorded in her journal a bit of dialogue at the end of a case handled by Sharp & Sharp: "Sheriff said, 'Well, I see that Mr. Sharp won this case.' Judge: 'Mr. Sharp did not win this case; the daughter did.'"[47]

One set of Susie Sharp's clients attracted national attention and engaged her services for roughly two decades. On May 23, 1946, quadruplets were born in the hospital at Reidsville to James Fultz, a fifty-nine-year-old black tenant farmer, and his thirty-seven-year-old wife, a deaf-mute named Annie Mae. Dr. Fred Klenner, who was married to Susie's sister Annie Hill, delivered the babies. Because they were identical, they were very rare indeed and were known as the first surviving identical African American quadruplets in the world. Within hours, photographs of the infants, weighing an average of three pounds, ten ounces at birth and given little chance of life, were flashed on the front pages of newspapers everywhere. When it appeared that the quads would survive, the family was deluged with offers of sponsorship from companies all across the country. Susie Sharp negotiated a contract with Pet Milk Company, which essentially provided for the children's upbringing, and she acted as trustee for the distribution of Pet Milk funds to the girls over the years.[48]

Pet Milk arranged publicity tours for the quads all over the country, beginning with a trip to Washington to meet President Harry Truman when they were about four years old. They made many other trips to New York, Chicago, Miami, Pittsburgh, and elsewhere and were twice on the cover of *Ebony Magazine*. They posed for pictures with black athletes such as Joe Louis, Floyd Patterson, Jesse Owen, and Althea Gibson. In 1962 they met President John F. Kennedy. It was Pet Milk that paid the medical bills and saw to it that the girls had whatever they needed, renewing their contract until they were juniors in high school, when they provided a $5,000 termination payment.

In January 1939 the city council named Susie Sharp to the post of city attorney. It was only a part-time job, which she held in addition to her regular practice, but, as she later recalled, "Oh! such a prestigious one."[49] It was the outgoing city attorney, Allen Gwyn, who recommended her.[50] Initially, she shared the position with P. W. Glidewell's son, P. W. Jr. (known as Pete), who had joined the bar a scant two years before. Susie Sharp's theory was that the council could not agree on a man. When she was appointed, it was the general understanding that she would do the heavy legal lifting, but a man would be available if needed to do something like walk a sewer line, which presumably was an assignment no woman could or would perform.[51] If the council was nervous about having a woman serving alone as city attorney, it was understandable for there had never been a female city attorney in North Carolina.

Eventually, in August 1946, the city council accepted the junior Glidewell's resignation and reelected Susie Sharp to hold the office on her own.

As a woman, fear of letting down her side was a powerful stimulant, never more so than in the only case she ever had referred to her by another woman attorney during the two decades that she practiced law in Reidsville. A female lawyer in Illinois needed to associate local counsel for a case in Rockingham County and consulted the standard attorney reference volume to see if there were any women practicing law in the county. She found, of course, only one. On arrival in Reidsville, she appeared in the offices of Sharp & Sharp with the job offer.[52] "An overwhelming wave of sex loyalty swept over me," Susie Sharp later said, "and I made that case the most important thing in my life. The man on the other side did not recognize the crusading gleam in my eye and was totally unprepared for the avalanche of authority which overwhelmed him."[53]

Life was not all work, thankfully. Susie Sharp particularly loved to travel. She routinely went to New York at least once a year, usually with Margaret Newnam or Margaret Fillman, seeing the sights and all the new Broadway shows. In 1939 she went to the New York World's Fair and got a tour of the offices of the white-shoe law firm, Sullivan & Cromwell. She also made extended trips to the Midwest, where she attended the 1933 Chicago World's Fair, visited her sister Sallie and her aunt Blanche, and toured many points of interest. She went fairly often to Washington, D.C., Baltimore, and Chicago to rendezvous with Breck. A trip to Canada took in Quebec, Montreal, New York, Yale University, Boston, Harvard University, and Gettysburg, among other places. She took her mother on a garden tour of Charleston, South Carolina. Nearly every weekend she jumped in the car and took off.

In August 1935 she took advantage of a cruise-convention organized by the North Carolina Bar Association to make a trip to Nova Scotia, along with her fellow attorneys Allen Gwyn and P. W. Glidewell. Also on board were Professor Albert Coates with his wife Gladys, and many prominent members of the legal profession in North Carolina, including Charles W. Tillett Jr., J. Melville Broughton, Henry M. London, and Kemp D. Battle, along with their families. Susie Sharp invited her friend Margaret Fillman to come along. They sailed from Norfolk, Virginia, on the SS *Reliance*, a ship of the Hamburg-Amerika Line, stopping in New York before arriving in Halifax, where Susie Sharp once again wound up in the headlines, this time through no fault of her own. "Six Tar Heels Almost Marooned When Barristers' Ship Sails," the headline read.[54]

Shortly before the ship was scheduled to depart from Halifax for the return journey, Susie Sharp, Allen Gwyn, P. W. Glidewell, Margaret Fillman, and two other passengers had decided to make a last-minute tour of Halifax. When they arrived back at the pier they saw the good ship *Reliance* well offshore, being nosed out of the harbor by tugboats. Solicitor Gwyn commenced what he described as an Indian war dance, and the others joined in, leaping and shouting. The German sailors who saw their plight merely gave "a Teutonic shrug," however, and the ship kept steaming steadily out to sea. At this point on board, Mr. Tillett and Mr. London realized their compatriots' dilemma and entreated the captain to turn back. "Turn back" was not in the captain's nautical vocabulary, but he did dispatch one of the tugs to rescue the party from the pier and ferry them out to the ship, where they had to clamber aboard, according to Susie Sharp, on something resembling a greasy pole.[55]

At home in Reidsville, she joined the Reid Players, a local drama group, took a short-story writing course, and tried her hand at turning some of her courtroom experiences into fiction. In her spare time, she read, listened to music, attended concerts in Greensboro, and kept up an astonishing array of photograph albums and scrapbooks. All her life she would be a tireless clipper of newspaper articles on subjects that interested her, accumulating drifts of newsprint that she worked constantly to contain and organize. One set of scrapbooks reflected what seems now like an odd obsession for a professional woman in her late twenties. Susie Sharp was completely gripped by the romantic drama of Wallis Simpson and King Edward VIII, later the Duke and Duchess of Windsor. Throughout the courtship and abdication crisis and for years thereafter, even until she clipped out the Duchess of Windsor's obituaries, Susie Sharp cut out every article and photograph pertaining to the couple that she could find and pasted them into her scrapbooks. Her high school friend Louise Tesh Wyrick, whose family operated a news stand in Reidsville, would save all the magazines and papers that contained anything about the beleaguered lovers, and Susie Sharp would come by daily on her way to the post office to collect them.[56] That the king had given up his throne for the glamorous Wallis was thrilling to her.

The great cynic, who belittled the institution of marriage and held few illusions about the rewards of male-female relationships, was at heart a thorough romantic. If her clear-eyed observation of the world had not led her to believe the odds were very good for success, she never relinquished the ideal, and, to her, the Duke and Duchess's love story was not tawdry but magnificent.

In the 1940s her own love life was becoming extremely complicated. Her affair with Breck had not abated, and she continued to see him at least every week or two on average in Chapel Hill or nearby towns, in addition to meeting him when he was in Washington on business or when he went home to Chicago, as he did with some regularity, without Venitah.[57] Breck was known as a walking compendium of train schedules, but Susie Sharp must not have been far behind. Despite bouts of jealousy, she maintained a close relationship with his wife and children, respecting his priorities and his deep feelings for them. On her part, Venitah evinced a genuine affection for Susie. That they both loved Breck sometimes seemed to strengthen rather than fracture their bond. Still, it could not have been easy for Venitah. Not long after Susie Sharp left Chapel Hill to return to Reidsville in 1932, she recorded in her journal a telling conversation with Breck. "[Venitah] tells him that she does not mind him being late if he is working and . . . it burns him like a hot iron for her to look at him with a hurt in her heart. I say I want her to be 1st. 'No, you don't; you think she ought to be and are honest enough to say so; that is the size of that.'"[58]

As for Breck, his ambivalence never overcame his ardor for Susie, but ambivalent he remained, and he did not refrain from expressing it. Although he was subject to jealous spells of his own, he often advised her to marry and told her that if she ever did get married, he would have some "black moments" but that he would give her up.[59] As the years progressed, however, they settled into a stable relationship in which he recognized that she loved him just as tenaciously as his wife did, and he grew deeply dependent on the pleasure she gave him in so many different ways. He was proud of her professional success, he enjoyed their intellectual sparring, and, as a man accustomed to being fussed over by the women in his life, he liked her aggressive care and concern for him.

At no time was her feeling for him more difficult for her to express than in May 1945, when his beloved son Arnold was killed. After graduating from UNC and, in 1942, receiving his medical degree from McGill University in Canada, Arnold joined the navy, becoming a flight surgeon. At the end of World War II he was serving in a combat air service unit in California and was assigned to accompany a commando unit preparing to go to Okinawa.[60] Tragically, he was killed along with seven others in a terrible accident, the explosion of a navy blimp near Santa Ana, California, on May 11, 1945, less than a week after Germany had surrendered.

Loyalty was one of Susie Sharp's strongest characteristics. She did not, however, believe that loyalty required exclusivity. Surely one could love and be loyal to more than one person. Obviously, in her liaison with a married man she had accepted this as truth. At least she knew of Breck's preexisting relationship with his wife; there is little if any evidence, however, that he knew she still saw John Kesler occasionally.

She had never stopped carrying a torch for John Kesler, as reflected in letters from friends well into the decade after law school. She did not see him often during the 1930s, once or twice or three times a year at most, but every time they were together the old flame flared up. Early in her career, in February 1933, she managed to spend an entire day with him when she had a case in his hometown of Salisbury, where he was building his law practice and dabbling in local politics. Her only comment on the visit was that when he heard her speech to the jury the next day, he criticized her for being too mild. It was more than two years before she recorded another meeting with him, again in Salisbury, where they spent a couple of hours together. Later that same year they had a conversation in which he claimed "the reason he never married was because he had never met a woman he thought capable of being completely honest in the marriage relationship."[61] Susie Sharp did not set down her interpretation of this statement, but she went on to report his theory that she was afraid of men, always expecting to be let down. Her response to him was, "Perhaps you are right."

Their paths continued to cross over the years, and their attraction escalated. Once they rode around until three o'clock in the morning. "He kisses me and I say that for the time being he is the first and last man I ever kissed. He wants to know about the others in between," she noted.[62] There was another encounter almost exactly a year later in August 1937 at a Young Democrats meeting in Winston-Salem, but not another until April 1939, when she stopped by his office on the way home from a trip to Chicago with Breck. John, she reported, "sits in the corner on the safe and kisses me time and again."[63]

The following July, John Kesler married a thirty-three-year-old schoolteacher named Sudie Grace West, originally from Dover, North Carolina, a small town in Craven County, near Kinston. If Susie Sharp made any contemporaneous record of her feelings about that event, it apparently has not survived.

But Susie Sharp had other lives to lead besides the one she had to keep hidden concerning her romantic involvements. One such was her increasingly important role within her family. When she moved back to Reidsville in 1932, there was no question about where she would live. Young women lived at home if they could and had few options if they could not. Even if there had been such a thing as apartments in small towns in those days, she would never have considered living anywhere except in the family home, occupying the same upstairs corner bedroom she had had since she was a child. In addition to the law practice, she was the family's "second mother and chauffeur."[64] Her brothers and sisters would always remember how Susie had either paid for or convinced their father to buy such additions to the household as an electric stove, electric refrigerator, radio, nicer furniture, reference books.[65] Louise later recalled, "She helped Mother teach us manners. She took us shopping, dyed the Easter eggs, decorated for Xmas, took us to Sunday School, let us use her car, bought us things Daddy didn't see the need for."[66]

Susie Sharp would play a major role in her siblings' lives not only while they shared the house on Lindsey Street but also after they had grown and left the nest, even as she remained.

The first to leave home was Sallie, next in age to Susie. She was often described as the prettiest of the girls, slender and with long black hair. She had majored in violin at Susie's alma mater, North Carolina College for Women in Greensboro. On weekends and holidays, she earned extra money by clerking in the Reidsville Montgomery Ward store, where she fell in love with the manager, a young man named Lawrence Arthur Taylor. Jim and Annie Sharp opposed their marriage on the grounds that Sallie was too young and inexperienced in the world, and also she was committed to teaching for two years in North Carolina public schools in exchange for reduced tuition at NCCW. Susie Sharp said that it would be a mistake to step straight from school into marriage[67] and warned her that marriage would take away her independence.[68] But the couple persevered. In the interim, the big sister acted as adviser and buffer. "Susie is such a help to me. She takes such a sane view of things," Sallie said.[69] From their romantic cocoon, the couple speculated on Susie Sharp's love life. "I have wondered too what Susie thinks about love," Sallie wrote. "She used to say she would marry only a very wealthy man. I wonder if she has ever been in love. . . . I remember her saying that she wouldn't marry a person she was in love with for she would be miserable."[70] Susie Sharp, the perfectionist, did not like to be out of control.

Eventually, after Sallie had taught for one year, Arthur offered to pay her remaining debt to the college, and he and Sallie were married in 1934. It was not a happy union. They would have two sons, who would later become among Susie Sharp's most challenging responsibilities.

No less distressing was Annie Hill's marriage to a young medical student named Frederick Robert Klenner, whom she had met when she was in nursing school at Duke. A native of Pennsylvania, he was handsome and charming. They married secretly on November 24, 1937. The secrecy is understandable in light of the attitude Annie Hill's family was certain to take to the idea that she might marry before she graduated. Even more certain to cause trouble in the family, however, was the groom's Catholic religion. It was not until a year later that the couple broke the news, claiming to have married in Saint Benedict's Church in Greensboro on October 12, 1938.

In 1939 the young Dr. Klenner opened his medical office in Reidsville. Described by one Sharp family member as a bigot and a racist and a Hitler admirer,[71] Fred ruled his household according to the authoritarian Teutonic model. He was the master and brooked no argument. In February 1942 he beat Annie Hill badly enough that she fled to the house on Lindsey Street. Jim Sharp, outraged, wrote a letter to Fred declaring, "Under the laws of North Carolina, a woman is not a chattel, but they have the same rights of life, liberty, property and the pursuit of happiness as a man, and no man has the right to order them around, and when they fail to move at his orders, to abuse and assault them."[72]

Annie Hill and the rest of the family prevailed upon him not to send the letter, hoping to prevent further trouble. Jim Sharp was prepared to take Annie Hill back under his roof, but to the horror of the entire family she chose to return to her husband. Jim Sharp's only comment was, "I just lost a daughter."[73] Indeed, he had. The following December Annie Hill gave birth to her first child, Mary Anne, who would be followed by Gertrude in 1944 and Fred's namesake, a son called Fritz, in 1952. The family lived a peculiar and secluded existence, the children forbidden by and large to play with other children. Annie Hill never sought refuge in her parents' home again. The Klenner union would disturb the entire family over the years and would ultimately lead to a terrible family tragedy.

Meanwhile, however, Dr. Klenner's medical practice, conducted for the entire duration of his career in offices with strictly segregated waiting rooms, grew. He pursued an interest in the effect of massive doses of vitamins, particularly vitamin C, on diseases of all sorts. At the height of the polio epidemic in the 1940s, his intravenous vitamin C treatment attracted considerable attention, not all of it favorable. In 1954, however, his theory achieved widespread credibility with the general public, if not with the scientific community, when the nutritionist Adele Davis included in her best-selling book, *Let's Eat Right to Keep Fit*, a purported polio cure Dr. Klenner had achieved with a single massive dose of vitamin C. Despite his eccentricities, Dr. Klenner acquired an almost cultlike following of patients for whom he could do no wrong. Many were the tales of Dr. Klenner's house calls in the dead of night and driving sleet, the brilliant diagnoses and the cures.

Susie Sharp's other brothers and sisters were growing up too, taking off like planes from an aircraft carrier, one after the other. Just a year after she came home from Chapel Hill, her brother Tommy left to enroll at UNC.[74] After graduating Phi Beta Kappa with a degree in chemical engineering in 1937, he went to work for DuPont in New Jersey. There he met a young woman from New Brunswick, New Jersey, Alice Robinson Carpender, called "Bobbie." She came from an old and wealthy family with ancestral roots in the South as well as old New York. Her upbringing, full of horses, travel, Broadway plays, and the like, had been at the other end of the spectrum from Tommy's, and she was not fascinated by life in a provincial North Carolina town. They married at Gray Gables, the Carpender family home in New Jersey. Tommy would go on to have a successful career at DuPont, Remington Rand, and, later, Sperry Rand, moving to Connecticut and then Pennsylvania. He and Bobbie had a daughter, Tyrrell, who would grow up to graduate from UNC like her father and to be a horsewoman like her mother. For all practical purposes, Tommy never came home again.

Next in line was Louise, nicknamed "Pokey" for her deliberate approach to life. A shy person who nonetheless held firm opinions, Louise's innate sweetness sometimes battled with a degree of rigidity in her personality. As a young woman, she once described her family as "hard to live with and hard to live without. They are public-spirited, big-hearted, kind and generous; they are stubborn, opinionated, quick-tempered and high-strung. They give me an inferiority complex; they also boost my ego."[75] Continuing the family tradition, she was salutatorian of her high school class although she claimed she had to work harder at it than her siblings did. In 1935 she followed her sisters' path to the North Carolina College for Women in Greensboro, where she graduated with a degree in elementary education. Teaching, however, was a trial for Louise, and after three years of it she entered the Duke Nursing School, obtaining her bachelor of science in nursing in 1946. The following year she joined the navy, where she found a home for the next twenty-one years. As she once wrote to Susie, "Smart people like you — independent thinkers — don't go in for military life. It's lame brains like mine who find more peace of mind in an organization where much of their thinking is done for them."[76]

Florence was the youngest sister, only eighteen months behind Louise. The least studious member of the family, she was perhaps the most popular, a lively and attractive girl with a level head. Susie Sharp once told Florence that she always thought she was their father's favorite "and deservedly so."[77] Speaking of how Mr. Sharp had always been so busy trying to make a living for the family that they did not see much of him, Susie told her sister, "But you were able to demonstrate to him the affection we all felt for him but could not articulate."[78] Florence went off to NCCW in 1937, graduating with a bachelor of science in secretarial administration. With firm good humor, she calmly diverted Susie Sharp's meddling in her social life. When Susie wrote at length to object to one of Florence's beaux, Florence teased, "I thought you were a better psychologist than your letter implied. After all, the psychologists say the more you say to a person about a certain subject the more determined they become."[79] She was not really interested in the young man, she said, but accused Susie: "You have made up your mind not to like him because he is a preacher."

Three years later, when she was teaching typing, shorthand, and bookkeeping at Walkertown High School in Winston-Salem, North Carolina, Florence met Robert W. ("Bob") Newsom Jr. and married him in 1945. After the war Bob went to work in the engineering department of R. J. Reynolds in Winston-Salem. By common agreement within the Sharp family, Bob was the only one of the sisters' husbands who lived up to its standards. He and Florence were a good match. On Christmas Eve 1946, their first child was born, a baby girl named for her aunt Susie Sharp but often called "Susie Q." Three years later they had a son, Robert W. Newsom III, known as Robbie or, when he was older, Rob.

Finally there was Susie Sharp's younger brother, James Vance, called Kits by all, except when his mother insisted on "Sugar Peaches." He was the baby, his mother's favorite who had been her salvation after the deaths of the twins. He did not leave home until 1942, ten years after Susie Sharp had returned to Reidsville. Like Sallie, Kits was talented in music, and it was Susie Sharp who contributed enough to pay for his clarinet when he was in high school. Kits was always grateful for that gift, which led to a lifetime of pleasure in music, as well as for financial assistance with big items like cars and college education.[80] He attended North Carolina State, UNC, and Duke before going on to get his M.D. from Bowman Gray School of Medicine in 1948, under an accelerated wartime curriculum.

Gradually Susie Sharp was stepping into her father's shoes not only at the office but also as head of the family. Grandma Sharp died August 22, 1938, at the age of ninety-three, freeing him from a major source of family responsibilities he primarily had shouldered. As her brothers and sisters left home, it was Susie Sharp they consulted whenever they needed advice and counsel. Her good sense combined with her knowledge of the wider world through the legal profession made her the oracle of first choice in matters ranging from financial to familial.

Another factor in the shifting of responsibilities was Mr. Jim's health, which was not good. One stifling hot afternoon in September 1935 he became overheated while arguing a case and asked the judge for permission to remove his coat. Permission was denied, after which his arm went numb and he collapsed in the Rockingham County courtroom. Susie Sharp, who was there, brought him home from Wentworth, his face still flushed, apparently having had a slight stroke. Of the judge who had shown so little compassion, she would say, "I may forgive him on my deathbed."[81]

Mr. Jim recovered, but his blood pressure remained high and his physical situation took a toll on him. Naturally, his impatience at having to curtail his activities only aggravated his condition. He continued to push himself to the limit. A friend wrote to commiserate with Susie about her father's predilection for running up his blood pressure, saying, "He is a wonderful man, and has done a grand job of his life, and I guess he just resents having to do a single thing that looks like slowing down."[82]

By the second half of the 1940s Susie Sharp was really bearing the burden of the practice. Her ability to handle it enabled her father to continue in the profession past the time when he might otherwise have been obliged to give it up. Just as he had carried some of her weight when she was not only a brand-new lawyer but a woman lawyer to boot, she now carried his. It was for this reason that, when the possibility began to emerge that she might be appointed as the first woman judge on the superior court, Susie Sharp's first thought was that it was out of the question.

CHAPTER 6

POLITICS AND PUBLIC LIFE

The very idea of a woman judge was almost incomprehensible in 1949, when the vast majority of United States citizens had never seen a female attorney, let alone a female judge. Certainly the citizens of North Carolina had never seen a woman presiding over a courtroom. Unlike a handful of other states, North Carolina did not even have any female justices of the peace or judges of such lesser courts as those with jurisdiction over municipal, county, probate, juvenile, or domestic relations matters. The court reporter or stenographer might be a woman, but a female clerk of court was rare indeed. It had been only three years since North Carolina women acquired the right to serve on a jury, something that in general they remained reluctant to do.

Judgeships were inextricably intertwined with politics, another area in which women were scarce. Then, as now, regular superior court judges were elected, although in practice most judges were initially appointed by the governor to fill a vacancy. Even more political, however, were the special superior court judgeships, appointed by the governor, who had the authority to appoint eight. Unlike regular judges, special judges were not tied strictly to one geographical section but served statewide. Created by the General Assembly in an effort to alleviate chronic courtroom backlogs without the difficulties inherent in redistricting, special judgeships inevitably had become coveted patronage plums.

Old-time politics, not so pure and not so simple, put Susie Sharp on the bench, a position she claimed never to have pursued. Even if the idea had crossed her mind — and it had — there were several reasons why it was not a good career move. Among other considerations, she had deep concerns about her father's health and his ability to carry Sharp & Sharp without her. Moreover, a quick glance around her could provide plenty of reasons not to view a judgeship as a realistic goal, the most persuasive being the resounding absence of women on the bench. But she was irrefutably up to her eyebrows in politics, mostly due to her father's active participation, which had earned him the moniker of "Mr. Democrat" in Rockingham County.

According to Susie Sharp, her father "had much in common with Woodrow Wilson's Vice-President Marshall, who once said: 'There are a great many things which I believe that I know are not so; for instance, I believe that the Democratic Party is always right.'"[1] In the 1928 presidential election, for example, after having worked furiously to prevent the nomination of the Catholic, anti-Prohibition candidate Al Smith, Jim Sharp had proved his loyalty by his willingness to stump the state at a time "when campaign orators for Al Smith were hard to find."[2] In 1933 he journeyed to Washington, D.C., where, he said, he "stood in the square in front of the nation's capital [sic] and saw the immortal Roosevelt take the oath of office and deliver his inaugural address."[3]

Although a perennial candidate, Jim Sharp had little success getting into office. He was elected to two terms in the state senate (1925 and 1927), but he lost at least four other races between 1915 and 1938 for solicitor of the old Eleventh Judicial District, the Reidsville municipal court, or recorder's court. In 1933 he mounted a campaign to be appointed U.S. district attorney for the Middle District, and Susie Sharp made a special trip to Raleigh, where she obtained endorsements of her father from four of the five members of the state supreme court.[4] Despite this support, as well as the endorsements of numerous other prominent members of the bar and the Democratic Party,[5] he was beaten out again by Carlisle Higgins, who had defeated him three years before in the race for solicitor of the judicial district. In 1937 Jim Sharp and Allen Gwyn both maneuvered unsuccessfully to be appointed to fill the unexpired term of Superior Court Judge A. D. Folger; that appointment went to one Samuel J. Ervin Jr. of Morganton.

Then in 1938 Sharp and Gwyn went head to head in a bitter contest for superior court judge in the Twenty-first Judicial District. There was strong support among the members of the local bar for Allen Gwyn, who was as energetic as "Mr. Jim" in his political activities, but better connected, smoother, and far more savvy. Indeed, there is some evidence that the local bar was dismayed by the prospect of Jim Sharp on the bench. One Reidsville lawyer wrote to Governor Clyde R. Hoey in support of Allen Gwyn: "I know of no lawyer in Rockingham County who would fail to support Mr. Gwyn, except Mr. Sharp and his daughter. . . . I prefer to speak kindly about [Mr. Sharp], but since this is a matter of public concern and since you want to know the truth about this situation I want to say that in my opinion the lawyers of this county who do the greater part of the practice and who are responsible for political affairs in this county would not support him if he were the only candidate in this county. Furthermore, his announced candidacy for Judge is not a surprise. In fact, it would have been a surprise if he had not announced. His rule seems to be to run for whatever office that may be available."[6] As P. W. Glidewell once remarked, "[L]ike Tennyson's Brook, he runs on forever."[7]

Against this background, Gwyn prevailed in the June primary. It was Jim Sharp's last race. Ironically, Gwyn's election in 1938 opened up his job as city attorney, to be filled by Susie Sharp and young P. W. Glidewell Jr. More important, it placed Gwyn in a position from which he could act very effectively as Susie Sharp's mentor and advocate—as well as sometime rival. Some members of the Sharp family would find it hard to forgive him for defeating Jim Sharp in his quest for the judgeship, but Sharp never spoke of it, and Susie Sharp would forge a strong relationship with Gwyn that would have an important bearing on her career in years to come.

If Jim Sharp was disappointed by the electoral process, his energy and loyalty to the Democratic Party were undiminished by his low success rate. From the time she returned to Reidsville from Chapel Hill in 1932, Susie Sharp found herself thrust into the local political scene on the basis of being Jim Sharp's daughter if nothing else.[8] It was not something she sought out. Only a week after she returned home that August, she turned down the opportunity to organize a chapter of the Young Democrats Club in Rockingham County. "After thinking the matter over from all angles I have decided that I ought not now to undertake anything extra," she wrote to Mrs. May Thompson Evans, president of the statewide organization, who had solicited her for the job.[9] She explained that she was already committed to help Albert Coates with the annotation of the Criminal Code, a task he had undertaken "years ago," and she had not yet begun despite an August deadline. She offered Mrs. Evans her help in less responsible capacities, however, and when the Young Democrats' organizational meeting was held a few weeks later in the Whitsett Building law offices of Sharp & Sharp, Susie Sharp was elected vice chairman.[10] As it happened, the Whitsett Building was a hotbed of political activity that fall, housing not only Mr. Jim's law offices but also the Rockingham County Democratic Headquarters.[11] Susie Sharp was promptly elected vice chairman of the county executive committee of the Democratic Party. Disclaiming any notion that she had done anything to merit the honor, she later claimed, "I owed my election to the rule which required the vice chairman to be a woman and the fact that I was Jim Sharp's daughter."[12]

Although women actively participating in politics in North Carolina were not unknown, they were relatively rare. Even many years later, after World

War II, when Susie Sharp was asked to give a speech on "Women in Politics," she began by saying, "If I merely arose, said 'There ain't no such Animal,' and sat down, I would have covered my subject fairly accurately and saved you a bad quarter of an hour."[13] When she returned to Reidsville from Chapel Hill, it had been only a dozen years since women got the right to vote in 1920, a right obtained without the assistance of the North Carolina legislature, which, on being presented with the first bill allowing women to vote in 1897, had promptly referred it to the committee on insane asylums. Even after the Nineteenth Amendment passed, many North Carolina women were reluctant to vote, prompting perennial hand wringing by those wishing for that half of the population to assume its civic responsibility.

Apart from the right to vote, a woman's right to hold office had been disputed. In 1915 the North Carolina Supreme Court struck down a statute authorizing the governor to appoint women to serve as notaries, on the grounds that a public office could be held only by a voter, that is, a man.[14] A year later, the court went out of its way to state that a woman could not serve as a deputy clerk of superior court.[15] Since gaining the right to vote in 1920, few women had come forward to run for office, and the prevailing view was that the local school board was the only acceptable venue for a female vote seeker.

There were exceptions. Lillian Exum Clement of Buncombe County became the first woman to serve in the North Carolina House of Representatives in 1921, and in fact was the first woman in the South to become a member of a state legislature.[16] In both the 1925 and 1927 terms, Mecklenburg County sent a woman to the state house, Julia Alexander and Carrie L. McLean, each of whom served one term. In 1931 Gertrude Dills McKee of Jackson County became the first woman in the North Carolina Senate; she subsequently would be reelected three times.[17] Susie Sharp's home county of Rockingham sent Lillie M. Mebane to the House of Representatives in 1931 and 1933. Outside the legislative arena, women like Gladys Avery Tillett were paving the way along other routes of political participation within the state and national political party organizations.

In addition to serving as vice chairman of the county executive committee, Susie Sharp did all kinds of menial chores for the Democratic Party, such as stuffing envelopes and getting voters to the polls. When U.S. Senator Josiah Bailey came to speak to the Rockingham County Young Democrats in 1933, she was one of the "special guests" formally recognized.[18] Three years later, she was the speaker selected to give the response to the welcoming address kicking off the Jackson Day program sponsored by the Young Democrats in

Rockingham County, reflecting her increasingly visible role in the local political scene.[19] She supplemented her political activities with occasional appearances before groups such as the Business and Professional Women's Club, as well as student and alumni groups at North Carolina College for Women and the UNC School of Law.

Susie Sharp was passionate on the subject of citizen participation in democracy—including the political process itself. The paucity of women in politics was a constant disappointment to her. In speech after speech to female audiences over the years, she preached the importance of active citizenship.

There had been some progress, however minimal. World War II undoubtedly increased the number of women actively participating in politics on every level, just as it swelled the ranks of women in the workplace. In Reidsville as elsewhere, men went away to fight, and their positions were often filled by women. As a town dominated by large cigarette and textile factories, Reidsville had been accustomed to women working outside the home even before the war, participating in some cases on a relatively equal level with the men. Within the tobacco labor union, for example, women held organizational positions. The local newspaper had been a longtime advocate of women's participation in public life. By some measures, Reidsville's view of women's roles was progressive, and wartime exigencies could only enhance public acceptance of women active in politics. Thus, although Susie Sharp by this time had been accepted on her own merits as a party loyalist, the prevailing winds were at her back.

When R. Gregg Cherry successfully ran for governor in 1944, Susie Sharp was a key part of his campaign in Rockingham County, serving as manager of "the women's division" of the campaign.[20] That there was such a thing as a women's division indicated the increasing weight of women in the political equation. Women activists in the party at the national level were hard at work to augment women's participation and influence, and North Carolina could claim a number of leaders in both the state and national organizations. Within North Carolina there was a consensus that the women's vote would swing the election, both because of the number of men lost or dislocated by the war and because of the increasing numbers of women exercising their right to vote.

Cherry carried the May primary election by approximately 50,000 votes statewide, out of approximately 320,000.[21] In Rockingham County his margin of victory was very slim, 2,204 to 1,915.[22] Regardless of the margin, however, Cherry's win in the primary assured that he would prevail over his Republican rival, Frank C. Patton, in November. Democratic women voters, it was noted, had turned out in numbers exceeding male party members by 10 percent.[23]

Cherry was the latest in a line of governors beginning with Shelby, North Carolina, native O. Max Gardner, who had challenged the old Simmons machine in the late 1920s and forged a ruling coalition that came to be known as the Shelby Dynasty. Reflecting the ongoing industrialization of the state, primarily in the Piedmont and centered around cities such as Charlotte, Greensboro, Winston-Salem, and Durham, the dominant forces in the state constituted what the eminent political historian V. O. Key Jr. labeled a relatively benign "economic oligarchy," noted for the aggressive pursuit of its interests. According to Key, the power structure recognized and supported the mutual benefits of improved education, better roads, and stronger health initiatives. It was nonetheless an urbanized group of leaders drawn primarily from the banking and manufacturing interests, supported by a strong network of elected and appointed state officials, most notably those connected with the highway and revenue departments.[24] Citizens in the more rural sections of the state did not always feel included in the state's progress.

Cherry's election boosted Susie Sharp into the ranks of what was sometimes referred to as "the state administration" or simply "the Administration," a euphemism for the network of Democratic Party regulars occupying state positions, forming the power base for the ruling political machinery.[25] In recognition of her efforts on his behalf, Governor Cherry appointed her to the board of corrections and training, which had oversight of the five correctional schools for boys and girls ("of both races") in the state.[26] She was well on her way to obtaining a substantial toehold in the political structure.

If Susie Sharp's active participation in the male-dominated world of politics was an indication of the changing role of women during the mid-1940s, nothing demonstrated the prevailing confusion on this issue more forcibly than the opinion issued by the North Carolina Supreme Court on November 8, 1944, one day after Cherry's election in which women voters had been such a prominent factor. In *State v. Emery* the court upheld the exclusion of women from jury service in the state.[27] According to the majority, Article I, Section 13, of the North Carolina Constitution providing that "no person may be convicted of any crime except by the unanimous verdict of a jury of good and lawful *men* in open court" (emphasis added) was to be interpreted in its most literal sense.

Susie Sharp, who had been arguing to all-male juries since 1929, would proudly claim that she had been one of the militants who fought for the passage of the constitutional amendment which ended that discrimination.

"That was my first battle for equal rights."[28] Even women who had no desire to serve on a jury said they would "fight for the right now that it has been denied them."[29] As one columnist declared, although freedom from whiskers and jury duty were two of the recognizable advantages in being born a woman, the wish to serve on a jury was a very different thing from the right to do so.[30] The *News and Observer* editorial labeled the court's decision "archaic" and declared that it "digs up more snakes than the court will ever be able to kill."[31] Referring to the standards for male jurors, the writer noted, "The women of North Carolina have not demanded service on juries. . . . But the women of North Carolina will not accept the status of legal inferiors to bootleggers, which has been conferred on them by the Supreme Court."[32]

In fact, many in the state had thought the question settled to the contrary, even though a woman juror was still almost unknown. Among other things, in 1921, following the passage of the Nineteenth Amendment granting women the vote, the North Carolina legislature had specifically enacted a provision declaring the word "juror" among others to be a word of common gender and applicable to man or woman alike.[33] Confronted with the *Emery* decision, the *News and Observer* stated the situation strongly, declaring, "Up until this week it had been almost universally assumed that the right to vote carried with it the right to hold office and all other rights and privileges springing from the franchise."[34]

The underlying mind-set of the *Emery* court may be fairly discerned in two other considerations laid out in the majority opinion. For one thing, the court pointed out, if women were constitutionally eligible for jury service, it "would require the commissioners of the several counties as well as the Federal authorities to place the names of all women, otherwise qualified, upon the jury list," causing an administrative imbroglio.[35] "Then too," the court continued, "*if some of the jurors may be women, all may be women.*"[36] That women routinely had their fates decided by all-male juries, and would continue to do so under the ruling in this opinion, bothered none of the justices in the majority.

In the country as a whole, eighteen states not including North Carolina expressly excluded women from eligibility for jury service in 1944 when *Emery* came down. In eighteen states, women had been expressly made eligible by statute, while the issue continued less settled in the remaining states.[37] Throughout the country, debate on the issue had yet to coalesce into sturdy strands of analysis. Was jury service a right, a duty, or a privilege? Were there differences between men and women that should keep women off of juries, such as their duties tending hearth and home, their (allegedly) emotional or irrational approach to problems, or their tender sensibilities? Conversely, women were sometimes viewed as having high moral character and a strong sense of responsibility in addition to a different perspective from that of men, which might be helpful in weighing evidence. If there were differences in the way men and women approached the sort of fact-finding mission required of a jury, some said, perhaps it was important to have diversity in the jury pool. Then again, perhaps men and women in 1944 should be viewed as equals, in which case it should not matter whether a jury was made up of all men or all women. But what about the rights of citizenship? Were women not citizens and therefore entitled to participate in the most basic functions of society?

There was scant guidance from the U.S. Supreme Court. In 1880 that Court held in *Strauder v. West Virginia* that the Fourteenth Amendment prohibited the exclusion of jurors based on race or color, while stating specifically that a state could exclude jurors based on other considerations, including sex.[38] Black men, on this issue, had thus benefited from the equal protection clause of the U.S. Constitution since the days of Reconstruction. But as of 1944, the highest court in the land did not recognize either a Fourteenth Amendment right of women as citizens to serve on a jury or a Sixth Amendment right of a defendant to a representative jury drawn from a pool made up of both men and women.[39]

During the battle for women's suffrage nearly a quarter of a century before, a poster circulated in North Carolina urging men to fight against giving women the vote because "Votes for Women Means Jury Duty for Women."[40] The densely printed attack, which focused entirely on the specter of jury duty, related horror stories of women forced to serve for weeks while they had sick children at home, of fathers rushing infants to court so mothers could breast-feed them during breaks snatched from court proceedings, of women subjected to "profanity, obscenity and the detailed narration of the immoral acts and doings of the lowest type of humanity." Few North Carolina women, in fact, had agitated specifically to be included on juries, and many viewed the idea with as much alarm as did the men. Nonetheless, 1944 was light years from 1920, and a substantial part of public opinion had leapt so far ahead that the reaction to the North Carolina Supreme Court's ruling in *State v. Emery* was one of shock.

The immediate reaction was swift and strong. A representative of the North Carolina Federation of Women's Clubs called the court's decision "a bombshell" producing a "unanimous group feeling . . . of astonishment and humiliation."[41] Another officer of the club declared, "That decision is not worthy to stand in a progressive state such as North Carolina, and we women must see to it that either that ruling is reversed or the necessary action

[is] taken so that such a decision can never be rendered again."[42] Requests for copies of the court's opinion poured into the clerk's office.[43] On the same day that the opinion came down, the Greensboro Business and Professional Women's Club voted unanimously to ask the General Assembly to draft a proposed amendment to the constitution.

Ten days after the supreme court had ruled, Attorney General Harry McMullan had drawn up, at the request of the North Carolina Federation of Business and Professional Women's Clubs, a proposed bill to give more protection to the rights of women. "It goes without saying," the *News and Observer* remarked, "that [the bill] would amend the Constitution of North Carolina to permit women to serve on juries."[44] As a part of a broader bill to render Article I of the state constitution (the Declaration of Rights) gender-neutral, the proposed amendment included language stating, "No person shall be excluded from jury service on account of sex." The legislature passed the bill on March 15, 1945, clearing the way for a statewide referendum in the November 1946 elections.

Despite the uproar caused by the North Carolina Supreme Court decision excluding women from jury service, the proposed constitutional amendment attracted relatively little attention leading up to the off-year election. Women's organizations such as the Business and Professional Women's Club took an active role in disseminating information about the issue, aided by the National League of Women Voters, which provided advice and practical suggestions about campaigning for the amendment. Other than the efforts of such organizations, however, there had been "no concentrated move to support the proposal," according to the *News and Observer* in an article two days before election day.[45] Another article stated, "Comparatively little interest has been manifested by North Carolina women in the State constitution amendment to be voted on November 5th to give women equal rights with men under the law."[46]

In fact, there was some opposition to the proposed amendment, grounded in the fear that placing women on an equal basis with men might result in a loss of certain statutory protections enjoyed by women, such as those relating to widows' shares in their deceased husbands' estates and those regulating hours and working conditions in industrial employment.[47] This perennial argument would resurface throughout the discussion about equal rights for women during the coming decades leading up to the failed Equal Rights Amendment to the U.S. Constitution.

On the eve of the election, leading clubwomen called for "a large and affirmative vote" for the amendment. This and other lobbying by the women's organizations apparently had an effect, and the day before the election the Democratic Party leadership issued a statement in favor of the amendment. William B. Umstead, chairman of the North Carolina Democratic Executive Committee, and Mrs. B. B. Everett, vice chairman of the committee, "agreed that the [amendment] appeared to provide a measure of justice to women of the State . . . [and] 'would serve the purpose of clarifying certain portions of the constitution which are not entirely clear with respect to the status of women.'"[48]

Nationally, the 1946 election produced a GOP landslide, but North Carolina remained solidly Democratic. The constitutional amendment making North Carolina women eligible for jury duty passed by a statewide vote of 186,540 to 133,396.[49] In Rockingham County the measure carried by a margin of 3,960 to 2,403.[50]

Eligibility for jury service, however, turned out to be just the beginning of the battle to get women onto juries. The week following the election, the *Charlotte Observer* reported, "The revolutionary nature of the amendment is just beginning to dawn on county officials."[51] All across the state, jury lists had to be updated to include women, and courthouses had to be remodeled to provide facilities for females (renovations that would be slow to be completed, or even undertaken). Moreover, as in many other states, North Carolina soon passed statutes allowing liberal exemptions for women, which resulted in a very low percentage of women who actually served. A woman could be excused if she had young children, for example, or was otherwise needed at home. Indeed, the judge had discretion to excuse women for any reason he deemed acceptable. Six years after passage of the constitutional amendment, the clerk of court in Guilford County estimated that at least 90 percent of women summoned for jury duty were excused.[52] One judge remarked bitterly, "The women of [North Carolina] clamored for equal rights; so we change the law. Now just try to get one of them to serve on juries."[53]

Women's organizations, in an effort to overcome women's reluctance, contacted Albert Coates to see if the Institute of Government in Chapel Hill could help educate their members about serving on a jury. Established in 1931, the Institute of Government was Coates's creation, conceived of as a "university for public officials" that would provide training for local and state government employees and elected officials.[54] With alacrity Mr. Coates arranged a seminar called "Ladies of the Jury" for groups from the women's organizations. As Susie Sharp would recall, "Since I had then been 'going to court' for about seventeen years without serious mishap, Mr. Coates subpoenaed me to help him with the seminar."[55] They did their best to explain the role of the jury in the judicial system and the court procedures involving the jury, all the while attempting to allay the women's fears of harassment or embarrassment, and to convince them that frequently women could make a substantial contribution to "a fair and impartial verdict."[56]

Many of Susie Sharp's speeches into the early 1950s would deal with the responsibility of women to shoulder their civic duty by not seeking exemption simply because it was so easily available. Of course, women on juries could still be dismissed by peremptory challenges, the overzealous use of which furnished yet another battleground not resolved until 1994, when the U.S. Supreme Court finally recognized a Fourteenth Amendment equal protection right prohibiting gender-based exclusion from juries.[57]

The 1946 election year was significant for Susie Sharp, and not just because it was the year that women were finally declared eligible for jury duty in North Carolina. Her long political seasoning had positioned her to make her mark as a political operative in the contest between John H. Folger and Thurmond Chatham for the U.S. House of Representatives. Incumbent Congressman Folger named her one of three co-managers for his campaign in Rockingham County.[58] Susie Sharp's extensive background in politics, however, could not have prepared her for the bitterness of that race, which was unprecedented (and which subsequently would be seen as a precursor of the vicious senatorial campaign in 1950 between Willis Smith and Frank Porter Graham). When she ran for chief justice twenty-eight years later, Susie Sharp characterized the Folger-Chatham election as her "most rugged political campaign experience."[59]

Folger had represented the Fifth Congressional District—made up of Rockingham, Forsyth, Stokes, Granville, Person, Surry, and Caswell counties—since succeeding his brother, W. A. (Lon) Folger, in June 1941. Tall, with a mane of dark hair and a trim mustache, known as a southern gentleman susceptible to a hard-luck story, John Folger had been a successful attorney in Mount Airy, the largest town in Surry County. Although well born and well educated, he was a New Deal Democrat and a vocal advocate for the less privileged. As a congressman, he was popular and respected. His opponent, Thurmond Chatham, also came from a prominent family, based in Winston-Salem and Elkin, North Carolina. A veteran of both world wars, he was a handsome, cultivated man of proven administrative ability who had reaped great wealth from his successful management of Chatham Manufacturing Co. It was said that his enormous energy was equaled only by his personal charm, which he extended to rich and poor alike. The Folger and Chatham families were well acquainted and had always maintained a cordial relationship, and no one would have expected the vituperation that resulted from the election.[60]

The campaign developed into a classic conservative-liberal split, in which Susie Sharp was on the side of the liberal New Dealer. Leading up to the May primary, Chatham took an aggressively conservative line, declaring that he was for "more business in government and less government in business."[61] Folger, as the champion of the farmer, the small businessman, and the working man, emphasized his bona fides as a Roosevelt Democrat. He attacked Chatham as a traitor to the Democratic Party who had voted for the Republican presidential nominees in 1936 and 1944 (Alf Landon and Thomas E. Dewey, respectively) and who had supported the Liberty League, a national organization heavily involved in opposition to New Deal programs. In turn, Chatham played on anti-union sentiment in the state with charges that Folger was backed by the "Communist dominated" labor group, the Congress of Industrial Organizations (CIO); he expressed astonishment that Folger "committed his vote in advance . . . on the side of those who would bring all the wheels of industry to a halt, array neighbor against neighbor, class against class . . . and even in our Southland, race against race."[62]

As this quotation indicates, underlying the linkage to the CIO and the threat of labor disruption was a none-too-subtle reference to the race situation. The reference was often explicit, as demonstrated, for example, in one surviving piece of campaign ephemera, an oversize Chatham campaign flyer. Printed on pink paper, it featured the banner headline "CIO SUPPORTS FOLGER!" above two large photographs labeled "Pictures Taken at CIO-Folger for Congress Rally."[63] The photographs, taken from the vantage point of a member of the audience looking toward the raised speakers' platform, showed large numbers of African Americans listening to what was described as an appeal to CIO members to support Folger. The caption under one picture carefully took note of the dignitaries on the platform, "Robert Black, colored, who acted as chairman of the rally . . . and Phillip Koritz, CIO official." Under the other picture, the caption identified a biracial duo, "Mrs. George Simpson, colored, left, and Miss Ann Matthews" singing "for the entertainment of the approximately 1,000 colored and 25 white persons who attended the CIO-Folger for Congress rally." The pair had also "led the crowd in the singing of union songs."

At a Lions Club gathering in Elkin, Chatham declared he was "informed reliably" that a CIO speaker at a pro-Folger meeting had spoken "disapprovingly of the customs of the south that enable each of the two races to live side by side comfortably, the natural social segregation that permits a minimum of friction."[64] Chatham queried the Lions Club audience, "Does this mean that a vote for Folger is a vote against segregation?" Dancing delicately on the head of a pin, he disavowed any "question of equality of opportunity," citing his record as a man concerned with "equal rights for all people, rich and poor, white or colored." But the audience surely had no difficulty deciphering his message.

If Red-baiting and race tactics were not enough, Chatham also accused Folger of using his office to obtain materials for a new warehouse in Reidsville, a sensitive issue in 1946 when wartime scarcities had not yet been overcome. Chatham claimed that the warehouse materials "would have built homes for 40 veterans."[65] The accusation brought heated denials from both Folger and the warehouse builders, further raising the levels of animosity between the two camps. As an example of the rhetorical extremes reached by some of the candidates' supporters, Marshall Kurfees, future mayor of Winston-Salem, delivered a blistering pro-Chatham radio address in which he compared the government of Folger's native Surry County to that of Hitler's Germany and, accusing the Folger family of nepotism, declared, "Never in history has a family so completely and selfishly ruled free men."[66]

For his part, Folger portrayed Chatham as a "'multimillionaire industrialist'" and "bigoted Tory, a tool of the NAM [National Association of Manufacturers] and an enemy of 'the little man.'"[67] He constantly reminded the voters that Chatham had deserted the Democratic Party on the national level, voting for two Republican presidential candidates and working against the sainted Roosevelt's New Deal initiatives that had meant the difference between eating and not eating for many of his constituents. Among the worst epithets he could find for Chatham was "'a Republican minded reactionary.'"[68]

In the days before television, a political campaign was waged like hand-to-hand combat, with personal visits to country stores, church meetings, and public rallies. A candidate would pay court to the local sheriff and clerk of court and register of deeds. A sheriff in one's corner could be very helpful because he had deputies in every community in the county, who were his political eyes and ears. Campaign materials consisted of letters to the editor, flyers, homemade ads pasted up for the newspaper, and the occasional radio speech. Nonetheless, it took money, including the sort known as "walking-around money." The Folger-Chatham race quickly became what Susie Sharp called "a battle between the 'Well-offs' and the 'Hard-ups.'" Her candidate, she believed, was a good congressman, but she soon realized he had no campaign chest, and the operation would have to be run on a hand-to-mouth basis. "I knew, of course, that properly informed voters could be counted on to vote in their own interests," she later reported. "But I soon learned that it took money to keep them PROPERLY informed."[69]

Setting the tone for ensuing events, on election eve some mishap resulted in the streets of Mount Airy being littered with ballots, a number of them already marked with Folger's name. Matters only deteriorated the following day when the voters — officially — went to the polls. In both Stokes and Surry counties, ballot boxes had to be impounded for multitudinous "voting irregularities." Accusations flew about Chatham's campaign expenditures, variously said to have been between $100,000 and $200,000, well in excess of the $6,000 legal limit for first primaries.[70] When a delegation of Chatham observers, including the aforementioned Marshall Kurfees, presumed to appear at the Stokes County vote canvass, the sheriff advised Kurfees that his safety was not assured, just moments before the register of deeds, a husky young man named Elmo Cromer, accelerated Kurfees's departure with a well-placed boot.[71] "This is the first time in Stokes County history that outsiders have felt it necessary to appear and question the activities of Stokes County registrars," declared one infuriated member of the Stokes County Board of Elections.[72] In both Stokes and Surry, Folger won by large margins. In fact, the margin in Stokes was 18 to 1, a result Chatham supporters could explain only by theories of serious hanky-panky. Folger also carried Rockingham and Caswell counties, losing only Forsyth, Person, and Granville counties to Chatham. In populous Forsyth with its county seat of Winston-Salem, however, Chatham's margin was nearly 2 to 1, ballooning his total. When all the ballots had been counted and recounted, Chatham led by fifty-nine votes out of a total of 42,505 votes cast.[73] Folger called for a runoff.

Leading up to the second primary, the bitterness only increased as the liberal-conservative contrast between the candidates grew even more pronounced. When national columnist Drew Pearson called for a congressional investigation of "the Chatham and Hanes money being spent to unseat 'liberal John Folger,'" Stokes County sheriff John Taylor "plastered his words in every newspaper in the district."[74] Charges and countercharges of intimidation and retaliatory firings prompted at least one lawsuit for defamation of character. Colonel William T. Joyner, secretary of the state board of elections, undertook an investigation in Stokes and Surry counties and issued a statement acknowledging evidence of "loose" election procedures but attempting to minimize any impact such laxities might have had. This report did nothing to calm Chatham's supporters.

On the morning of the runoff primary, June 22, it developed that Chatham's camp had devised a plan to place its poll watchers in every precinct in troublesome Stokes County, an intrusion that incensed the locals to a dangerous degree. The most interesting aspect of the plan was the roster of participants, which included prominent Winston-Salem citizens bearing names like Hanes, Gray, and Bahnson. One journalist joked that if it had been known at a number of national insurance companies that these gentlemen had set off that morning to oversee the ballot casting in Stokes County, it would have triggered unmitigated panic in those offices. "Here, wandering about peering into Stokes County voting boxes was, give or take a few hundred thousand, more than a million dollars worth of insurance policies on the hoof," he wrote, adding, "There probably are more dangerous hobbies for city slickers but right off hand I am unable to think of one."[75] And, in fact, at precinct after precinct, the pro-Chatham observers were either barred or ejected from the polling premises. Having been told they could either "get out or get carried out," the intruders withdrew out of range of the angry locals and, in most cases, out of range of observation as well. Several teams continued their surveillance with the aid of binoculars, whereas other teams found it expedient to withdraw to a point on the safe side of the Forsyth County line.

In Rockingham County, matters were somewhat less tense, but Susie Sharp did have to scramble to defuse a potentially disruptive problem. The names of registered voters were supposed to be entered not only in the general election registration book but also in the Democratic and Republican party registration books, which were used in the primary elections. A voter whose name appeared in the general election book but not in the appropriate party book was entitled under normal circumstances to show the registrar that his name had been omitted through registrar error and that he was qualified to vote in the primary. Because of the atmosphere surrounding this particular runoff primary, however, officials had ordered that registrars at the polls should have with them only the Democratic registration book, in an effort to eliminate any question of an unqualified voter participating in the primary election. This plan would have been a good one, except for the failure to transfer some properly registered Democrats' names into the Democratic registration book. Colonel Joyner of the state board of elections subsequently said in a letter to W. Benton Pipkin, a prominent Reidsville citizen who had contacted him about the problem, "[W]e had the very explosive situation on last Saturday morning that a number of voters who had voted in the first primary came to the polls and were told that they could not vote in the second primary because their names were not on the books."[76] On the morning of the runoff, Colonel Joyner, who was in Raleigh, received phone calls from several concerned citizens but was not in a position to evaluate the situation until, shortly thereafter, Susie Sharp called him to explain what had happened. Colonel Joyner then was able to advise the chairman of the county board of elections, P. W. Glidewell Jr., how to proceed so that qualified Democrats would be allowed to cast their votes.

There were some other dustups in Rockingham County, stemming from the public support given Folger's campaign by P. W. Glidewell Jr. and Judge Allen Gwyn. Both showed up on a list of Folger contributors. The *Reidsville Review* noted that Glidewell's name raised some eyebrows because of his position as head of the local board of elections, commenting that "in view of so many charges of election irregularity the chairman's partisanship proved interesting."[77] As for Judge Gwyn, he and his wife not only were listed as contributors but also had been active on the hustings, speaking at Folger gatherings across the county. Judge Gwyn received some editorial criticism at least as far afield as Charlotte and Raleigh for sullying his judicial robes with politics, even though, as one reporter said, it was "well known" that Judge Gwyn and others who were supposed to abstain from active politics "got the jobs in the first place because of proven political prowess."[78]

The voter turnout for the second primary exceeded that of the first by nearly 4,000 citizens, reversing the norm for first and second primaries. When the dust settled, Folger had won by a vote of 24,549 to 21,832, assuring that he would retain his congressional seat. Chatham conceded promptly and gracefully and announced that he would run again in 1948. This he did, without opposition from John Folger, thus achieving his goal of becoming a congressman. In the course of time, Thurmond Chatham's son married John Folger's granddaughter, and the river of North Carolina politics flowed on.

Were there voting "irregularities" in the 1946 Fifth District primary elections? Undoubtedly a number of allegations were based on little more than suspicion and ill will, but it is probable that some votes appeared or disappeared according to principles other than those legitimized by statute. There is no question whatever that the campaign tactics employed sank to new depths. As for Susie Sharp's involvement in the unsavory mess, Rockingham County did not suffer the indignity of uninvited out-of-county observers on election day. Nonetheless, the allegations that Reidsville businessmen had improperly obtained construction materials through Congressman Folger's good offices, as well as the issues involving P. W. Glidewell and Judge Gwyn's partisan participation, centered some of the candidates' animosities squarely within her jurisdiction as a campaign manager. Nor was the animosity alleviated by misunderstandings at the polls on the day of the second primary.

There is, however, no evidence or suggestion that Susie Sharp's actions were anything but aboveboard. Whatever she may have known about shenanigans at the polls elsewhere in the district, her instincts as well as her deeply held beliefs about the sanctity of "small d" democratic principles would have militated against any actual tampering with the voting process. She was no stranger to the use of dirty campaign tricks, having seen them used against her father in his many political races, but that was not her style. Before the election, the newspaper ads she wrote for Folger ran with her name alone signed below, as the representative of Folger's campaign committee, and contained nothing that could be characterized as negative campaigning. The harshest ad she devised was probably the one containing an exhortation to "Stop! Look! Marvel!" at a Chatham ad that ran two days before the second primary. Chatham's ad, she wrote, "looks as if it were copied word for word from the Roosevelt platform of 1936 and 1940." She accused Chatham of seeking "to ride into office on the platform he sought to defeat then," and urged the voters not to be fooled by "this zero hour repentance."[79]

More typical was a large ad proclaiming "Our Faith in Folger," which declared: "The purpose of our efforts has been to elect a liberal candidate to Congress who will help maintain a liberal government. By that we mean a government which recognizes human rights as well as property rights: A government which will be fair to capital, fair to labor, fair to all. A government which recognizes the value of private enterprise, private property, individual initiative, self responsibility and hard work. A government which secures to men not only freedom of thought, speech, and religion but freedom from fear of insecurity. A government which seeks to secure to the people the right to enjoy the fruits of their own toil."[80]

Over time, Susie Sharp's political views would shift toward the right, but during her lifetime the greatest part of her active political participation would be in support of old-fashioned liberals like John Folger, rooted in FDR's New Deal. When she chose to support the maverick gubernatorial candidate W. Kerr Scott two years later, in direct opposition to the Democratic machine choice, Charles M. Johnson, she based her position on Scott's sympathy for the farmer and the "little man," the citizens for whom she and her father had long fought battle after battle, both in the courtroom and at the polls. For a staunch party regular like Susie Sharp, forsaking party unity was a significant departure and a true indicator of her identification with the Democrats' liberal wing. It was not a gamble she made with any expectation of reward, because no one expected Scott to win.

Jim and Annie Sharp's wedding portrait, 1906
(Sharp family photograph)

"Chatterbox"
(Sharp family photograph)

A flock of Sharp children on a donkey: *left to right,*
Louise, Annie Hill, Sallie, "Man-Boy" (bandaged head), and Susie
(Sharp family photograph)

High school graduation picture
(Throckmorton Studio, Reidsville, North Carolina)

Professor Millard S.
Breckenridge
(Sharp family photograph)

Professor Breckenridge (*back row, second from left*)
with members of the University of North Carolina School
of Law faculty in 1937. *From left to right, front row*, Frank W. Hanft,
Maurice T. Van Hecke, A. C. McIntosh, John E. Mulder; *back row*,
Frederick B. McCall, Millard S. Breckenridge, Albert Coates,
Robert H. Wettach, Donald W. Markham
(*1937* Yackety Yack, *page 28, reprinted by
permission of Yackety Yack, Inc.*)

John Kesler, class
picture, University
of North Carolina
School of Law, 1928
(1928 Yackety Yack, *page 69,*
reprinted by permission of
Yackety Yack, Inc.)

Bar exam candidate
(Sharp family photograph)

Sharp & Sharp partners, 1929
(*Throckmorton Studio, Reidsville, North Carolina*)

First car, c. 1930
(Sharp family photograph)

PART III

SUPERIOR COURT
(1949–1962)

CHAPTER 7

APPOINTMENT TO SUPERIOR COURT

Susie Sharp's appointment as the first woman judge in North Carolina owed as much to a quirky gubernatorial election in which the courthouse crowd backed the losing candidate as it did to her exceptional qualifications. That the winner of that election, William Kerr Scott, was a showman and a populist who loved nothing better than shaking up the establishment certainly was a factor in her appointment to the bench. Perhaps equally as important was her alliance with her mentor and her father's old nemesis, Allen H. Gwyn. The explanation for her success that she herself most often cited — and perhaps believed — was that she simply was the right person in the right place at the right time. There was some truth to this theory, but as always the full truth was a bit more complicated.

Kerr Scott was not the first governor to think about putting her on the bench. According to her old friend, Tom Bost, the well-connected journalist who years ago had wired her advance notice that she had passed the bar, Susie Sharp had almost gotten appointed as a special superior court judge five years earlier, during the Cherry administration.[1] In his regular column, Bost divulged that, although it was "not generally, [or] even limitedly known," Governor Cherry had seriously considered naming Susie Sharp to the bench but had been dissuaded by several factors, including his recognition that women were not yet widely accepted in high public office and his now-quaint apprehension that such an appointment would be viewed, at a time when his popularity was low, as pandering to a particular segment of the voting population. Despite his political indebtedness to Susie Sharp as one of his campaign managers, and despite his experience as a state Democratic chairman working with some women with impressive political abilities, Cherry — unlike Kerr Scott — was no iconoclast.

In his article, Bost characterized Susie Sharp as "a good politician" and a "politico," rather than as a good attorney (although he surely believed her to be that), who would nonetheless make a good judge. He made this assessment, however, before she took the perverse position in 1948 of opposing Charles Johnson, the Democratic establishment's anointed choice for governor.

North Carolina politics in the late 1940s appeared on the surface to be relatively stable and predictable. Dominated by the Democratic Party, the state was still run by what political historian V. O. Key Jr. described as a "progressive plutocracy."[2] To the rest of the nation, North Carolina seemed more "presentable" than other states in the South and enjoyed "a reputation for progressive outlook and action in many phases of life, especially industrial development, education and race relations." For half a century, an enlightened oligarchy of business and financial interests centered in the increasingly industrialized Piedmont had governed according to the "capitalistic system liberally and fairly interpreted," as former governor O. Max Gardner put it.[3] V. O. Key's observation was that while many of the state's governors "may have been stodgy and conservative they have never been scoundrels or nincompoops."[4]

North Carolina's image as progressive, tolerant, and enlightened, however, obscured some hard facts. The state ranked at the bottom among the states in per capita income.[5] The textile, tobacco, and furniture industries, although thriving, paid notoriously low wages. Labor unions were ruthlessly suppressed, even as mechanization on the farms was driving more and more workers into industrial jobs. Illiteracy was a significant problem, and despite North Carolina's reputation for progressivism, opportunities for blacks were routinely limited.[6] In a state that was approximately 70 percent rural, most farmers were still isolated in areas without paved roads, electricity, or telephones.

Nonetheless, those in charge apparently had little sense of unusual political turmoil beneath the smooth surface. The old-fashioned Democratic political machine, built county by county and precinct by precinct, was "designed for use every day of every year and in every kind of political contest from sheriff and other county officers to Governor and United States Senator."[7] Future governors and other state officials were selected by the Democratic leadership, sometimes years in advance, with election in the one-party system virtually assured.

In fact, however, Democratic unity had begun to show some cracks, manifested most prominently in the gubernatorial candidacy in 1936 and 1944 of the liberal Ralph McDonald, against whom the "Administration" forces had closed ranks. After World War II ended, young voters who had just come of age, as well as returning veterans anxious to make their marks, were less bound by old traditions or political loyalties and constituted a new element of unpredictability. The deaths in 1946 and 1947 of two party stalwarts, U.S. senator Josiah W. Bailey and former governor O. Max Gardner, left large leadership gaps. Then, the appointment of William B. Umstead to Bailey's vacant Senate seat unexpectedly opened up the gubernatorial race.

Umstead, the state Democratic chairman, a former congressman, and Governor Cherry's campaign manager, had been the presumed next governor; his departure from the race left the way clear for state treasurer Charles M. Johnson to declare his interest in the position. When he did so, more than a year before the first primary, he was promptly anointed as the Administration candidate. Johnson was opposed by R. Mayne Albright, an energetic young Raleigh lawyer who cast himself as the antimachine candidate, touring the state with a trailer hitched to his car but brandishing the slogan, "Hitched to no machine."[8] The conventional wisdom, however, considered Johnson the certain winner. Planning for his inauguration was already under way.[9] So confident was Johnson himself that he allegedly had put in an order for his gubernatorial limousine well before the Democratic primary.[10] He wanted a Cadillac, and he thought perhaps the hubcaps should be embellished with the North Carolina state seal.[11]

So matters stood until mid-February 1948.[12] At that time Kerr Scott was commissioner of agriculture, a post he had held since 1937. As a champion of the farmer, he had traveled the state, lambasting the powerful electric power utilities, the feed and fertilizer companies, and a number of other special interests. He was popular with the farmers, and it was generally conceded that he could not be dislodged from his post as agriculture commissioner. There, however, it was felt that his future reached its limit.[13] Then, without warning, Scott resigned as agriculture commissioner, announced he was running for governor, and launched an all-out campaign—perhaps more accurately described as a crusade—focusing on rural electrification, better roads, telephone service, and other improvements for the farmer. "I was not invited to run by the so-called 'crown princes' in state politics," he declared in his first campaign speech. "They told me they had already picked your governor for you. I say to that you ought to be allowed to choose your own governor."[14]

Scott's understanding of the farmer's woes grew directly out of his own upbringing in a family of Alamance County dairy farmers. As he liked to point out, he was the only gubernatorial candidate who lived on a dirt road.[15] After graduating from North Carolina State College and serving in the First World War as an army private in the field artillery, he came home to the farm in Haw River to manage the family dairy business, an enterprise he continued throughout his career. From 1920 to 1930 he served as Alamance County farm agent, and then as master of the North Carolina State Grange from 1930 to 1933, during which time he witnessed the deepening of the Great Depression. In 1934 President Roosevelt appointed him regional director of the Farm Debt Adjustment Program, charged with providing debt-ridden farmers in seven states with some financial breathing room until their desperate situation improved. "Those were both heart-rending and happy days for me," Scott would recall. "Heart-rending because of the misery, want and hunger we saw on every side; happy because of the fear we were able to lift from the eyes of tens of thousands of men, women and children."[16] Two years later, in 1936, he ran for and was elected commissioner of agriculture, which seemed to be the perfect match of man and mission. Scott, however, believed he could accomplish more as governor.

Scott's candidacy threw the Democratic Party into turmoil. The self-styled country boy gleefully and with great effect fired salvo after salvo at the banking, utility, and business interests who supported Johnson, to the delight of the "branch-head boys," the farmers who lived way up where the creek began, who had no paved roads by which to get their crops to market, no electricity, no telephone. While Johnson "patted the Democratic Party fondly for its half-century of good government"[17] and boasted of the large surplus in the state treasury, Scott declared that "we do not have a real surplus, but actually a deficit in public services."[18] On at least one occasion, Scott publicly referred to L. V. Sutton, head of the Carolina Power & Light utility, as "Low Voltage Sutton."[19] There were those who believed that Scott sometimes "spoke Thursday and thought Friday,"[20] but the candidate relished his image as an unpredictable maverick. Terry Sanford, future governor of North Carolina, then a recently returned veteran and young lawyer, recalled watching Scott campaign. "He would ask everyone in the audience: 'Who wants a telephone? Raise your hand.' Nearly everyone in the audience would raise their hand. 'How many people don't have electric lights?' Half of them would raise their hands."[21]

If farmers prospered, so would the merchants in the numberless country towns dotting the state, who traded in everything from fertilizer to fabric. Thus, Scott gained a good deal of backing from small-town business. In addition to the large rural vote, he drew supporters from the returning World War II veterans, the blacks who managed to vote, and the small organized labor movement in the state.[22] He won no converts, however, among society hostesses, who cringed and cast about for cuspidors when Scott and his rough-hewn entourage breached the tranquillity of their parlors.[23] Big business and the professions, the "establishment," united almost unanimously in support of Johnson. This included virtually every lawyer and judge in the state. Judge Allen Gwyn of Reidsville was, according to his son Allen Gwyn Jr., the only superior court judge who supported Kerr Scott.[24] The "courthouse crowd" was solidly in Johnson's camp. As Terry Sanford would later put it, "And then the term 'courthouse crowd' had real meaning. The courthouse crowd *did* control the elections."[25]

For once, Judge Gwyn and Jim Sharp were in agreement: Scott was the clear choice for their constituencies, the farmers and small businessmen of Rockingham County. For Jim Sharp — "Mr. Democrat" — Scott's aggressive brand of populist agrarian activism outweighed considerations of intraparty politics. In both the Sharp and Blackwell families, the experience of rural privation was not a faded memory but rather a life-defining condition at a polar extreme from the board rooms and country clubs where the Piedmont's power brokers held sway. Sharp's understanding of democracy and of the Democratic Party was from the bottom up, not the top down. He had spent his life farming and working for farmers. He would work for Scott, not Johnson — the preordained winner, the bankers' drawing-room candidate — and damn the consequences. Susie Sharp joined her father and the judge in their apostasy, and the three formed a small but conspicuous outpost of Scott support in the legal community statewide.

Scott scratched the ground in a search for anyone of influence willing to manage his campaign in Rockingham County. In March he wrote various well-placed people, including Judge Gwyn, asking for recommendations. At least one prominent businessman allegedly turned down the post, and there were probably several others who did so.[26]

To the astonishment of many, what had been considered a sure thing instead turned out to be a very tight race. When the results of the first primary came in, Scott carried Rockingham County, although his margin of victory over Johnson was only 505 votes.[27] Statewide, Johnson led Scott by approximately 40.1 percent to 38.1 percent, with 17.1 percent going to Mayne Albright.[28] Scott called for a second primary.

Despite her heretical, bridge-burning support of Kerr Scott, Susie Sharp had never met the candidate. She was surprised, therefore, when she received a telephone call from his campaign headquarters in Raleigh. "The word was that Mr. Scott was disturbed by reports that his campaign in Rockingham County was not going well, and he wanted me to 'take over' as his manager," she later reported.[29] It was Judge Gwyn, his son Allen Gwyn Jr. believed, who was responsible for recommending her to the candidate.[30] Scott, of course, was well aware of the work both Jim Sharp and his daughter had done for him before the first primary.

Possibly Scott had his eye on the female vote. In announcing that he had named a woman, Mrs. Estelle T. Smith, as an associate campaign manager in his Raleigh headquarters, the News and Observer's "Under the Dome" column commented, "The women, if they want to, can roll up a whopping big vote, Kerr Scott decided after taking a glance at census figures."[31] Moreover, Mrs. Smith was not merely to head a woman's division of the campaign but was to be on equal footing with a male campaign manager.[32]

After considerable hesitation, Susie Sharp agreed to take the job. In her own words, it was a decision she never regretted.[33]

She and her father would always be given a great deal of credit for getting out the vote for Scott in Rockingham County. The effort was aided all across the state, however, by the disclosure shortly before the first primary that as state treasurer, prior to announcing his candidacy for governor, Johnson had deposited $170 million in state funds in banks around the state, at no interest. Although not illegal, this blatant political largesse boomeranged. Outrageous as a matter of fiscal policy, it was infuriating to the taxpayers. But even more pernicious was the support that such strategic, interest-free deposits of the people's money secured from bankers, their boards of directors, and stockholders.

Susie Sharp, working closely with Judge Gwyn, was merciless in her attacks on Johnson's maneuver. Two nights before the June 26 primary, she delivered a blistering radio speech devoted almost entirely to "the use of the state's money to advance the political fortunes of a particular candidate."[34]

Long before Mr. Johnson made the formal announcement of his candidacy for governor, she informed her listeners, "the word was being passed around in high financial circles that 'Johnson is the man.'" She said, "Johnson was indeed the man, ladies and gentlemen, who had strategically distributed 170 million dollars in various amounts in 243 banks throughout North Carolina. Of course, when Mr. Johnson deposited the money he did not say, 'Mr. Banker, I am planning to run for governor and I want to leave with you $500 thousand or a million dollars for such political advantages as it may give me with you, your board of directors, and your stockholders.'"[35] It was an attack worthy of a seasoned political operative. From Susie Sharp's point of view, it had the advantage of justifiable moral outrage.

In the second primary on June 26, 1948, Scott entered the record books. Not since North Carolina adopted the primary system in 1916 had a losing candidate in the first gubernatorial primary triumphed in the runoff.[36] Scott took the state by almost 35,000 votes (217,620 to 182,684).[37] Voter turnout, which the state Democratic chairman had optimistically projected at 270,000, topped 400,000.[38] The United Press correspondent in Raleigh wrote, "Even the most enthusiastic Scott backer must have been surprised at the runaway margin Scott posted."[39] Scott's statewide tally was a decisive 54 percent to Johnson's 46 percent. In comparison, in Rockingham County Scott received approximately 60 percent of the vote (2,976 to 1,772), carrying all but 3 of the 23 precincts.[40] Kerr Scott took note.

Susie Sharp's summary of her success as Scott's county campaign manager gave credit to "an enthusiastic committee" and focused on three main themes. "We were able to convince the farmers that they shouldn't lose an opportunity to elect one of their own. We also persuaded other voters that it was time for the banks to pay interest on state funds deposited with them. It was also time, we argued, to overthrow the 'political machine' which, for so many years, had chosen our governors."[41] As for herself, she had backed her candidate on principle, not party politics, and had unexpectedly been catapulted into the winner's circle. It changed her life.

Even before the November election, Susie Sharp's name was in play as a likely appointee to a position of importance under the new Scott administration. The *News and Observer* reported that Scott would support her for the post of vice chairman of the state's Democratic executive committee (although the post ultimately went to someone else). The *News and Observer* also reported that, at one point, she turned down a seat on the North Carolina Industrial Commission.[42] According to Susie Sharp, it was Rockingham County attorney and Democratic powerhouse Hamp Price who first suggested to the gubernatorial nominee that he appoint her to the superior court. Although Price had supported Johnson in the first primary, he had rallied to Scott in the runoff, and remained an important party leader. He himself had won the Democratic primary for the North Carolina Senate, to which he would be elected in the fall.

As Susie Sharp told it, in mid-July Price found himself seated next to Scott at the Democratic National Convention in Philadelphia as the delegates awaited Harry Truman's appearance to accept the presidential nomination.[43] "Hamp seized the opportunity to tell Governor Scott that the time had come to recognize women's participation in politics," pointing out that women had played an important part in his election and suggesting that Governor Scott might want to consider being the first governor to appoint a woman judge.[44] Playing to Scott's well-known propensity for doing the unexpected, Price allegedly mentioned that such an appointment would "attract a certain amount of attention."[45] Asked if he had anyone in mind, Price responded, "Yes, your Rockingham County campaign manager!"[46]

Many years later, Susie Sharp professed that "neither I nor the Governor had ever thought of such a thing" until Price made his suggestion. "When Hamp came home and told me about the incident, I was dumbfounded," she said. Price told her that Scott was "dumbfounded too at first but, when he had recovered from the initial shock, his comment was, 'You may have something, Hamp. I'll think about it.'"[47] Susie Sharp claimed not to take the report seriously, but less than two weeks later Scott himself mentioned the possibility to her. Her journal contains the brief entry for July 26, 1948: "Introduce Kerr Scott who says that he is thinking about appointing me a judge but he does not know." In a speech much later, she recalled the encounter this way: "I was astonished one afternoon when Governor Scott appeared unexpectedly at the law office of Sharp & Sharp and asked me how I would like to be a judge. I replied quite truthfully that I didn't know. He said, 'Well, you think about it, and I will too.'"[48]

One person had no doubts whatsoever. When Susie Sharp told her father about Scott's visit, he did not hesitate. "If the governor offers you a judgeship you will, of course, take it!"[49]

In November Scott handily defeated the Republican candidate, George M. Pritchard. Behind the scenes, the new governor wrestled with his patronage appointments, handicapped in the judicial sphere by the paucity of his support within the legal profession. He himself was the first North Carolina governor in the twentieth century who was not a lawyer,[50] and his legal contacts were therefore limited. Naturally he relied on Allen Gwyn, his prescient supporter on the superior court, for advice. With Scott's victory, Judge Gwyn's own long-held ambitions for the North Carolina Supreme Court saw the light of day, and his name was widely mentioned as the most likely appointee when Scott had his first opportunity to fill a supreme court vacancy. He also had reason to believe he was in a position to influence the new governor in his other appointments. He intended for Susie Sharp to get one of the special superior court judgeships.

Once her name had been mentioned among the cognoscenti, Susie Sharp found that she had friends who pressed quietly for her appointment. In early February 1949 her name surfaced in public. Newsman and friend Tom Bost reported, "Rockingham County friends of Miss Susie Sharpe [sic] had hoped earnestly to keep their ambitions for her quiet until they had made her a formidable candidate for appointment as a special superior court judge. . . .

Lawyer Susie's and Pop Jim's support of Governor Scott . . . justifies . . . this honor."[51] In Bost's opinion, "Judge Susie would be a natural for Governor Scott. He likes to do things never done by anybody else. There is a story in Raleigh that during the campaign last Fall Governor Scott intimated that he would like to appoint Miss Susie. Anybody who knows her would."

Bost's item prompted Scott to ask at least one Reidsville resident what he thought about the idea. In mid-February businessman A. P. Sands, father of Susie Sharp's childhood playmate Janie Sands, wrote the governor in response that he thought it would be one of the best appointments Scott could make. "I have . . . talked to a lot of people here about it," he said, "and I find that not only the women but the men likewise favor her appointment." Reminding Scott that Susie Sharp had "been like a member of my family since she was a child," he went on to say, "She has done a considerable amount of legal work for me and I have the utmost confidence in her and her ability."[52]

A less biased view was offered on the same date by W. H. Nelson, secretary-treasurer of Morehead Cotton Mills in nearby Spray, who did not know Susie Sharp "at all well" and disavowed any personal opinion. Scott had asked Nelson "to ascertain and advise" him as to the sentiment in the county regarding her possible appointment. Nelson reported that he spoke with about twenty people in his immediate area and also in Reidsville, looking for a representative cross section of citizens. His survey revealed reactions ranging from "hearty approval" to "equally hearty disapproval," with nearly all of her opposition coming from outside Reidsville. Although opinion was unanimous that Susie Sharp was smart and a good lawyer, a "considerable question" was raised "as to the ability of women in general and Miss Sharp in particular to act in an impartial and judicial manner." Actually, much opposition appeared based not on Susie Sharp's merits or lack thereof, but rather on antipathy to her father. As Nelson put it, "Mr. Sharp is not generally popular and seems to be deficient in tact." As to Susie Sharp's integrity and character, there was "not the slightest question raised."[53]

Scott himself was quoted as saying that "he wouldn't mind a bit appointing a woman as a judge, not even to the State Supreme Court. . . . If she was better qualified than the other candidates, fine. But if she was coming up merely because she was a woman, then it would be better to pick a man."[54]

Whatever reservations existed, however, a strong undercurrent was running in her favor. Various newspapers ran gossipy items like the one in the *Leaksville News*: "Don't say who told you, but there is a very good chance that Miss Susie Sharp, Reidsville attorney, will have the honor of being the first woman to grace the Superior Court bench in North Carolina."[55] From

Rockingham County, Senator Hamp Price forwarded a petition endorsing her appointment signed by the lawyers of the local bar association, along with a supporting cover letter in which he reminded the governor that he had spoken with him previously about naming her to the superior court bench.[56] Price also wrote to Judge Gwyn that "perhaps there might be a chance of Susie's being appointed in the near future. Several of the lawyers are trying to assist her and they are securing a few letters from Judges as to Susie's ability."[57] He added, "I hope in the very near future that I will have the pleasure of presenting your name to the Governor for appointment to the Supreme Court."

Gwyn's letter of recommendation dated March 5, 1949, expressed his profound admiration for Susie Sharp, her ability, and her character. "My interest in the matter arises from the desire to see better politics and better government in the State," he wrote. "Miss Sharp is one of the best politicians (among women) I have known." Gwyn praised her devotion to public service, declaring, "She is not like many politicians — hell-bent for personal, political preferment. She is not an office-seeker. She is one of the few constant workers who asks nothing for herself. She is a sort of crusader for Democracy."

Judge Gwyn reminded the governor of Susie Sharp's work during the campaign. "Illustrative of her political bent is a radio address made over WFRC in your behalf shortly before the last primary. A newspaper reporter in this community told me that that speech was the best political speech he ever heard on any occasion from any person. That reporter had previously voted for Mr. Johnson; he thereafter promptly voted for you." Gwyn extolled Susie Sharp's reputation as a skilled lawyer in both the trial and appellate courts, adding, "She has a mind of her own and the courage to use it and stand by her convictions. I have been impressed with the soundness of her legal philosophy."[58]

In a previous, unsent draft of a letter recommending her for a different position, much of which he copied directly into his letter to Scott, Gwyn had said, "She is not a 'me too' person. Important instances where she has differed with her close friends and even her father furnish the proof."[59] Governor Scott himself had reason to know that she did not necessarily follow the crowd. Perhaps the maverick governor would admire a kindred spirit.

Judge Gwyn called Susie Sharp the day after writing his letter to the governor and told her "she must accept."[60] Her chances appeared very good and had not been hurt by Jim Sharp's chairmanship of the Rockingham County campaign for passage of Scott's controversial $200 million bond issue for rural roads.[61] The bond issue, which would be one of the cornerstones of Scott's tenure as governor, passed in a special election on June 4, 1949.

The last week in May, Susie Sharp came under siege from the newspapers. She did her best to dampen the speculation by telling them "emphatically . . . that so far as she knew there was no foundation for the rumors."[62] Both the *News and Observer* and the *Winston-Salem Journal* called to ask if they could send a photographer and a feature writer to cover the story. She refused and "urged them with all the fervor of which I was capable" not to print the rumors. On June 3 the *Greensboro Daily News* man in Reidsville—most probably her old friend W. C. ("Mutt") Burton—told her that his paper would run a story the next morning on her possible appointment, and she begged him to stop it "at all costs." But the effort to stifle the story was in vain.

The morning of June 4, with the governor predicting passage of the bond issue by a 3–2 margin, the *Greensboro Daily News* ran a front-page article, with photograph, headlined, "Miss Sharp Is Rumored for Superior Court Seat." The first recognition of her possible appointment in a serious news article as opposed to various columns and behind-the-scenes reports, the article stated, "Efforts yesterday to verify the possibility of her appointment brought from one Reidsville source the comment, 'I imagine she will get one of the judge seats.'"

Susie Sharp was leaving for New York on her annual visit, to attend—in addition to the usual Broadway plays—two days of the Alger Hiss trial. She was horrified at the eruption of the behind-the-scenes speculation. She immediately wrote the governor to assure him she had "nothing whatever to do" with the story's appearance in the paper and to detail her efforts to suppress it.[63] "[T]his story to-day is such a flagrant violation of the proprieties that I feel I must apologize for being a victim of it," she wrote. "I cannot tell you how sorry I am to have been the cause—however innocently—of any embarrassment to you." Her anguish was no doubt genuine, regardless of her attitude toward the appointment. The public prognostication could work in her favor, or it could just as easily work against her, particularly given Scott's unpredictable tendencies. She was not naive about the media, however, and had a very clear understanding that the individual mattered far less than "the story."[64] As a general rule she understood the wisdom of making allies by helping the press do its job whenever she could, despite her natural inclination to privacy, but in this case she had done everything she knew how to do to prevent her name from appearing prematurely.

As for the putative "judge seat," she was still not 100 percent convinced that she should take it. The achiever, the perfectionist, the legal scholar, the father's daughter—all recognized the pull of the bench. How splendid to be the first woman. How splendid simply to be a judge. The position paid

$10,000 per year plus $2,500 in expenses. Why should she not leap at the opportunity if offered? She was nonetheless not inclined to take it.

There were several good reasons for her reluctance, beginning with the health of her father, who of course would have put a dagger through his heart before he would have impeded her from taking the seat he had so long coveted for himself. He had been operated on in March for appendicitis, his health in general was not particularly good, and he had a law practice to run. He would be running it single-handedly if she left, unless he could get someone to step in for her. He relied on her more than he even knew. "One word from him and I wouldn't have gone," she later said.[65] Susie Sharp also had strong doubts about whether she would be accepted on the bench by other members of the bar. Could she be effective as a judge, or would she be undermined at every turn? There were no role models for female superior court judges in North Carolina.

Moreover, all her hard work building up her share of the practice for the past twenty years might go for naught if she had to abandon her clients. A special judgeship, an appointive post, was for only a two-year term, as opposed to the eight-year term of a regular, elected superior court judge. Her clients would not necessarily remain with the elder partner of Sharp & Sharp, but rather were likely to be divided up among the other local attorneys. Susie Sharp later said that she fully expected to serve no more than her initial two-year term, partly because she "really didn't think the legal profession of North Carolina would accept a woman judge very long."[66] She had no illusions about the political nature of the appointment, and indeed once defined a judge — in a speech to the Georgia Association of Women Lawyers — as "a lawyer who knows a governor."[67] There was always the possibility that the next governor might not reappoint her, especially in light of her alliance with the political renegade, Kerr Scott. What if she were not reappointed, then had to return to a decimated law practice?

It was not an idle worry. The financial well-being of the entire family might depend on her decision. Jim Sharp, however, would not even listen to her objections.[68]

With the support of the Rockingham County Bar Association and that of resident Superior Court Judge Allen Gwyn on the record, the matter was more and more out of her hands. The new governor needed to proceed with his appointments and was not interested in the qualms of any potential appointee unless they were sufficient to derail the process. Scott departed for the National Governor's Conference in Colorado Springs, Colorado, leaving his office to make the announcements.

It was Susie Sharp's old law school friend Allen Langston, now practicing law in Raleigh, who called her about eleven o'clock on the morning of Tuesday, June 21, to tell her that he had seen the governor's list of special judges to be announced that afternoon, and she was on it. As fate would have it, Jim and Annie Sharp were in Baltimore at a convention, but Susie Sharp did not need to consult her father for his views. At quarter to three, the governor's office called, not to ask if she would accept, but to tell her they were announcing her appointment that afternoon. She asked when they were going to tell the press and was told, "In fifteen minutes." Immediately Susie Sharp displayed her savoir faire. As she wrote soon after, "I had promised the local paper if they would not print any rumors about me I'd tell them the minute I knew anything so that they could 'scoop' the Greensboro Daily. They resurrected a 10-year-old picture of me, stopped the press, and—I suppose—were the only afternoon paper with the story which made them feel most kindly about me."[69]

No sooner had the news hit the wires on Tuesday afternoon than her hairdresser called to see if she needed any "first aid." Susie Sharp was waiting for a long-distance call but dashed out the door, telling her secretary to transfer the call to the beauty parlor. As it happened, the secretary got her calls mixed up and put through *Greensboro Daily News* reporter "Mutt" Burton instead. His front page story headlined "Her Honor Gives Interview While Hair Is Shampooed" featured a vignette of the new judge wiping the soap out of her ears to take the call and his comment that he never thought he'd see the day he would have to "ferret out a judge of the Superior Court of North Carolina in a beauty parlor."[70] The story resulted in a long-distance tongue-lashing from Superior Court Judge H. Hoyle Sink, who called Susie Sharp that night to tell her that "he would never have thought that I would have been one to exploit my sex."[71] Recounting the incident, Susie Sharp said, "I think Hizzoner had had on a little too much because some of his conversation was startling." He told her he "was coming to see me in action and if I wasn't doing right he was not going to wait until later but he was going to interrupt on the spot and get me straightened out; that he had no doubt I was going to be chicken hearted and the first sign of weak-kneed shilly-shallying he saw in me he was going to start trouble; that I wouldn't like sentencing people to death but it would, on occasion, be my painful duty."

Then, she said, she made a big mistake, telling Judge Sink that she "never expected to be confronted with that emergency, that by the time I got through charging the jury on the recommendation of mercy, they'd all think it was their duty to do just that." At that, Judge Sink "really blew his top" and said "if

I was starting out with that line of conduct in mind I ought to be impeached now!" Susie Sharp allowed that the judge had upset her "a right smart," but she derived "a lot of pleasure out of thinking how much his phone bill would be." The next day, however, Judge Sink wrote her "a perfectly lovely letter" and later sent her some "judge's books," and she felt sure he did not remember all he had said to her on the telephone.[72] On Friday of that busy week, nonetheless, she dropped by to see him in Greensboro after taking her sister Florence home to Winston-Salem. She was too good a politician to leave a fence unmended if she could help it.

Susie Sharp gratefully accepted the assistance of friends and neighbors who answered the incessantly ringing telephone, greeted callers, and received telegrams (including one from her irrepressible cousin Earle Garrett with the wry comment, "MAY GOD HAVE MERCY ON THEIR SOULS"). Judge Gwyn came to the house along with floods of other well-wishers, newspaper reporters, and photographers. As it happened, she previously had invited company for dinner that Wednesday night and had set aside Tuesday night to boil, shell, and devein three pounds of shrimp. When the news upended that plan, her neighbor, Mrs. Balsley, rescued her. Susie Sharp got up at six o'clock the next morning to make a pie. Among her dinner guests was Hamp Price, for whom she may have held mixed feelings that evening.

But she managed, even if she was overwhelmed. "People have been so very kind and have expressed such confidence in me that I am literally scared to death," she wrote, adding that it would be better if they'd tell her what they really thought, because "maybe that would get me out of my present state of shock and make me mad enough to at least plan to show 'em." Throughout, she kept her sense of humor and a sure sense of self. For example, acknowledging to one reporter that she had never been married, she declared that she nonetheless had gotten more divorces than any other woman in North Carolina.[73]

In 1949 it was difficult even for women to picture themselves outside the kitchen. At the University of North Carolina, where women had struggled for decades to gain access, 96 percent of the women in the class of 1949 declared marriage to be their goal in life, and only 15 percent expected to work after marriage.[74] The press, besieging the new female judge, seemed equally unimaginative. When the News and Observer's feature writer called to ask a few questions, the first one was, "Can you cook?" The second one was, "To what clubs do you belong?" Susie Sharp lamented, "I have tried to cooperate with the press because I shall certainly need their indulgence, but I drew the line . . . when one reporter wanted me to don an apron, grab a pan, and be photographed by the kitchen stove."[75]

She could not suppress her femininity entirely, however. Unlike her fellow appointees, she was immediately confronted with the eternal female dilemma, "What should I wear?" This topic was of sufficient interest to appear in the *News and Observer*'s indispensable "Under the Dome" column, where most weighty political matters were aired. According to the paper, Susie Sharp made a trip to Raleigh to obtain the details on the swearing-in ceremony, during which she let it be known that she did not plan to adopt a more somber wardrobe when she took the bench. Superior court judges had not yet begun wearing the now-standard black robes, and her costume would be on full view for all onlookers. Susie Sharp, whose ensemble on this trip to Raleigh consisted of "a flower number which combined with a bright red straw hat that made her easily the prettiest superior court judge in the State," declared that she was opposed to wearing the judicial robe. In recent years she had trimmed up into a very attractive woman and a snappy dresser who had no wish to hide her carefully coordinated wardrobe under a robe. For the ceremony itself, and specifically the vexing issue of whether to wear a hat, she consulted fashion arbiter Colonel Frank P. Hobgood, prominent lawyer and former state senator from Reidsville, who decreed, "A lady wears gloves when she wears a hat; one never touches the Bible with a gloved hand." Therefore, "NO HAT."[76] He further admonished her against the wearing of flowered prints; only solid colors would do. She decided on a white suit for the big day.

The historic document commissioning Miss Susie Sharp as a special judge of the superior court of North Carolina, bearing the state seal and the signatures of the governor and the secretary of state, unintentionally reflected in its text the novelty of the appointment. Despite the "Miss" before the new judge's name, the boilerplate language plowed right on, expressing "special trust and confidence in his integrity and knowledge" and conferring "upon him" all the rights, privileges, and powers useful and necessary to the discharge of "his appointment." Susie Sharp took it in stride. She told "Mutt" Burton that "it was slightly startling," but she was not greatly disturbed by it since she herself was perfectly sure of her gender. She did allow, however, that when she went to Raleigh to be sworn in she planned to request a properly revised and feminized commission for the record, "if it's not too much trouble."[77]

The reaction across the state to the appointment of a woman superior court judge was largely favorable, at least in the press, perhaps due to the advance scuttlebutt, which had taken off some of the shock value. The *Reidsville Review* praised her selection in an editorial headed, "Our Miss Susie" and reported, "Close associates and fellow townspeople . . . are happy and thrilled over the honor that has been bestowed on 'Miss Susie' as she is popularly and affectionately called by her many friends here."[78] Despite innumerable feature stories with headlines like the one in Winston-Salem's *Twin City Sentinel* that read, "Charming Judge Sharp Wears Her New Honors Becomingly,"[79] her appointment was treated seriously and with respect. That same paper led its hard-news coverage with the sentence, "One of the State's outstanding female lawyers will become North Carolina's first woman Superior Court judge July 1."

Courthouse discussions were considerably more nervous, as Susie Sharp was well aware. "Since I was the first woman judge in North Carolina of any kind," she later said, "you can imagine the doubts and misgivings the men of the bar had: What about rape cases; can she keep flamboyant lawyers under control, that kind of thing. I had sense enough to know what was going on in their minds. They never talked to me about it."[80]

Her old friend Tom Bost gave her the opportunity to rebut the fear that a woman judge could not handle a rape case. In his newspaper column shortly after her appointment, he reported remarks overheard among "gallant gentlemen who wondered what Miss Judge Susie will do when she gets into one of these court cases full of filth and usually forbidden speech."[81] Susie Sharp promptly drew his attention to an address she had made to a meeting of the North Carolina Federation of Women's Clubs in August 1947 in which she attempted to ease women's discomfort at the thought of serving on a jury, where they might be exposed to unsavory facts.[82] Bost was happy to quote from her speech in a subsequent column. "[I]f the business of the court in which you serve as a juror is to try a sex crime there is no impropriety in your discussing the evidence of the case," she had said: "After all, you know the facts of life. You don't render yourself more alluring by pretending you don't. There couldn't have been a seduction or a rape in the first place if there hadn't been a woman present; so it's equally appropriate that there should be a woman at the payoff."[83]

Lest she be thought biased toward women at the expense of men, it is important to include what else she said: "[I]t's in this type of case that you may be able to make a peculiar contribution because you can furnish the woman's point of view — a woman can come nearer telling when another woman is lying than a man can, I believe. And women do sometimes accuse men falsely."[84]

Tom Bost was one of many who had no doubts about how Judge Sharp would do when she ascended the bench. As for Susie Sharp herself, she had qualms aplenty, despite her fundamental confidence in her abilities. In her letter thanking Governor Scott, she acknowledged the ground-breaking nature of her appointment: "I am fully conscious of the honor you have done me, but I am even more keenly aware of my responsibility to you and to the women of the State because I know that when you honored me you were honoring them. In making this appointment I know that you took a risk, and I promise that I shall do my utmost not to let you down or to disappoint the women of the State. I can only hope that my best will be enough."[85]

The morning of July 1, 1949, turned out to be sunny, and Susie Sharp wore her white suit, set off by a lavender orchid corsage sent to her by Colonel and Mrs. Hobgood. In addition to family, her entourage included friends like Janie Sands Smith, Margaret Fillman, and Margaret Newnam. Judge Gwyn was there, and Professor Breckenridge, the former bursting with pride and the latter proud but slightly disgruntled. "You don't like my part of this, do you?" she asked Breck. "I like you," he replied.[86]

Standing in the hall of the House of Representatives along with twelve other Scott appointees, both judicial and nonjudicial, forty-two-year-old Susie Marshall Sharp was sworn in by Chief Justice Walter P. Stacy.[87] Lieutenant Governor H. P. Taylor presided in the absence of Governor Scott, who spoke by telephone to the assembled crowd from the office of Governor Earl C. Clements in Frankfort, Kentucky, where he had stopped on the way home from Colorado. Those able to hear the poorly transmitted fifteen-minute address knew that Governor Scott specifically regretted being unable to be there in person "to see our first woman judge take the oath of office," but he expressed his confidence that she would "fill the office with credit." As to the court system in general, the governor relayed the complaints he had heard about the pace of justice in the state courts. Calling the judicial system "archaic," he criticized it for moving too slowly and urged the newly sworn judges to speed up the court processes.[88] This was a theme that Susie Sharp would repeat with far better transmission over the course of her career.

CHAPTER 8

JUDGE SHARP, PRESIDING

The new judge received a variety of advice as she awaited the assignment of her first term of court. Chief Justice Stacy counseled her to be careful of her sentencing power. "A new knife is very keen. It will cut deeply without you knowing," he warned. "You watch your sentencing power."[1] Judge Allen Gwyn passed along an admonition against arrogance, in the form of a quotation from Shakespeare's *Measure for Measure* that his mother had given him when he took the oath of office.[2] The old reprobate P. W. Glidewell Sr. cautioned her against "the blandishments of the Bar," saying, "You are going to have more eyes made at you than any other gal in North Carolina ever did. You be careful."[3] But it was her father's words to her that she would quote most often in the years to come, and which served as her touchstone. The sum total of his advice to her was, "Sue, plow a straight furrow and remember you are the boss."

Albemarle, North Carolina, the county seat of Stanly County, was to have the honor of the first court presided over by a woman judge, in the term beginning July 11, 1949. As a special judge assigned wherever the need might arise, Judge Sharp was to fill in for her close friend and colleague, Judge Gwyn, who had planned to be out of the state that week. Newspapers all across the state heralded the history-making assignment. The Saturday before court was to open on Monday, the new judge called the clerk of court to find out what was on the docket (a light schedule: two manslaughters, some divorces) and told him she would be in court on Monday. Sometime between that phone call and Monday morning, Judge Gwyn changed his plans and decided to go to Albemarle after all.[4] No one alerted the newspapers.

The result was a public relations disaster for Judge Sharp.

Farmers from all over the county had begun to arrive at the courthouse as early as seven thirty Monday morning, wearing their Sunday best, "their faces freshly shaven."[5] Nearly all the members of the Stanly County bar had turned out, whether or not they had a case on the docket, with their hair slicked back and dressed to kill in their best boiled shirts.[6] The Albemarle Woman's Club had sent a basket of flowers to the judge's hotel, and another floral arrangement graced the courtroom bench. The courtroom itself "appeared to have been given a thorough cleaning by the courthouse janitor."[7] By nine thirty the clerk's office was jammed with reporters, photographers, and lawyers waiting to welcome the new judge. The courtroom was filled to capacity with onlookers, including a large number of women.

As zero hour approached, Judge Sharp still had not been sighted. Meanwhile a rumor circulated that Judge Gwyn had checked into the local hotel, but the general consensus was that he must be in town to introduce Judge Sharp at her first term of court. The crowd was therefore quite shocked when at ten o'clock Judge Gwyn appeared and took the bench prepared for business as usual. He offered no explanation, merely commenting that he hated to disappoint those assembled, who he was certain had come to see a "jurist of another sex."[8] This observation proved accurate, for within moments the courtroom had virtually emptied, leaving only those unfortunates with actual business to transact. Photographers and reporters sent by newspapers from across the state had made the trip for nothing, and they joined the local crowd in expressing their disappointment.

With no information to the contrary, the disappointed populace leapt to the conclusion that the new judge had suffered a failure of nerve and backed out at the last minute. "Judge Susie Sharp Gets 'Cold Feet' and Fails to Appear in Court Here," headlined the local newspaper. Stood up, the locals shared the unhappiness expressed by the editorial writer who observed that it was "human nature to resent disappointment," and asked, "How easy it would have been for the new jurist to have picked up her telephone Sunday and called a newspaper office" to alert them to the change. "But not a peep from Miss Susie. And Judge Gwyn's explanation as to why he was present instead of the expected judge was powerfully unsatisfactory."[9]

Susie Sharp took it hard. The erroneous idea that the newly minted female judge had succumbed to cold feet and backed out of her maiden appearance scalded her pride. The uproar soon paled, however, against the events of her first term of court when she finally took the bench on July 25, 1949, in the Richmond County seat of Rockingham.

The system of special judges arose to standardize the practice of substituting for regular judges in an emergency when the 1925 legislature empowered the governor to appoint "any reputable lawyer" to hold court for a single term. Although for this limited time the special judges had the same powers as a regular judge, they lacked the same standing in the public eye. They were sometimes known as "Bevo judges," after a popular near-beer by that name, for reasons apparent in one fellow's description of the beverage: "I'll tell you, boss, it looks like beer, it tastes like beer, it smells like beer, but boss, it just ain't got the authority."[10] Special judges, whose terms had been increased to two years, had since gained respect. If any vestige of the Bevo judges lingered in the public mind, however, the new lady judge was about to obliterate it.

"No other experience in my life can compare with that first term of court at which I was the presiding judge," Susie Sharp once said.[11] Luckily for posterity we have a detailed idea of what it was like, thanks not only to numerous newspaper reports but also to the new judge's own description. When the week was over, she immediately sat down and wrote to Breck on her new letterhead printed with "Susie Sharp, Special Judge, Superior Court of North Carolina" at the top. It would have been an interesting account even if it had recorded no more than the first week of the first woman judge in the state, but as it happened the brand-new judge was faced with a case that dramatically revealed her substance. Moreover, because of the intense media attention focused on her that week, her handling of the case would result in changes in policy and law that otherwise probably would not have occurred.

Judge Gwyn had reserved a room for her at a tourist home called Cope's Inn, where he thought she would be more comfortable than at the hotel.[12] It was run by Mr. and Mrs. Corpening, an "attractive and unusual old couple" who treated her like royalty. "You don't look like any judge to me," said Mrs. Corpening. "You are young and pretty!" Judge Sharp appreciated the compliment all the more in light of the local newspaper's assessment that she looked like "a well-preserved school teacher." The most accurate description, however, was probably the radio report rendered at the end of her stay, declaring that she had arrived Monday "looking very fresh and youthful beyond her years — even girlish — but as the week passed the strain began to tell and she aged rapidly."

The July heat was brutal. She did not sleep. For her debut, she wore her white swearing-in suit with a sheer, lace-trimmed pink blouse, her only jewelry a cameo pin at her neck and pearl earrings. Conscientious newspaper reporting revealed that she wore light rouge and lipstick, as well as fingernail polish, in the same shade as her blouse. Her dark hair was "smartly coiffed back from her face." As the new lady judge departed for the courthouse, Mrs. Corpening sent her maid along to "tote" her books. "Ordinarily I would not have accepted a bearer," Judge Sharp said, but she was grateful for any help in the heat, which was rapidly ruining what one paper had described as her "Vogue-like" appearance.[13] When she entered the judge's chambers she noticed a thoughtful addition to the usual bare amenities of desk and chair — a new mirror.

If the light docket in Albemarle had offered a gentle introduction to the rigors of the judiciary, this was not the case in Richmond County. The court calendar, bearing the words, "Hon. Susie Sharp, judge presiding," laid out a criminal term of court with eighty or so cases on the docket, including two murders, five cases of assault with a deadly weapon with intent to kill, two manslaughters, one assault on a female, two first degree burglaries, four hit-and-runs, two cases of affray, and a number of morality offenses.

As the historic moment approached, she was "scared to death and hoping nobody knew it." The courtroom, packed with every member of the county bar plus an overflow crowd of 500 spectators, was already sweltering. Lieutenant Governor Pat Taylor was on hand to offer his formal congratulations. No one, including the lawyers, litigants, and new judge, knew what to expect. Judge Sharp believed that many feared the worst. She was well aware that the newspapers were present, prepared for any eventuality and hoping one would arise.[14] They would not be disappointed.

As Judge Sharp described it, "My wobbly knees got me up to the bench at 10 A.M. and my quavering voice said, 'Open Court, Mr. Sheriff.'" The first thing she did was declare the stifling heat cruel and unusual punishment and therefore unconstitutional, and inform the gentlemen in the courtroom that failure to remove their coats would constitute prima facie evidence of holes in their shirts. With that, she shucked off her own jacket and got down to business despite the trying circumstances. "The temperature in the courtroom was never less than 100 degrees, I know," she wrote to Breck. The noise from the fans situated all around the courtroom made it difficult for her to hear the witnesses. "The result," she told Breck, "was that I sat on the edge of my chair and strained to hear giving the impression that I was even more tense and nervous than I actually was — which was nervous enough! That big judge's chair simply swallowed me and the high back cut off what air there was; so I discarded that after the first five minutes and got one like I was used to and from which I could touch the floor." "Was she nervous?" she was asked during a lull in court. "Nervous? I have never been as nervous in my life. When I poured that first glass of water I wasn't at all sure I would get it to my lips," she replied.[15] Having survived thus far, she was not afraid to admit to her very human feelings.

She was already worrying about the case that would confront her Tuesday morning, *State v. Carpenter*, in which a prison superintendent was accused of assaulting an inmate in the name of prison discipline. Reviewing the North Carolina cases on punishment of convicts in prison, she found to her dismay that they were far from consistent and left her in a state of uncertainty on the law.

At the time the case arose, state prisons were run by the North Carolina Highway and Public Works Commission. Since the state had assumed responsibility for road maintenance in 1931, convicts sentenced "to the roads" had provided the labor; they were housed in specially built prison camps and worked in what were commonly called chain gangs. An inmate at one of these prison camps, a young white man, had violated a rule forbidding prisoners from talking to one another while working. On a hot August day when a beer truck passed the work gang, the prisoner had been heard to comment, "I would like to have me a case of beer." As punishment, prison camp superintendent N. L. Carpenter ordered the young man (who was serving an eighteen-month sentence for a misdemeanor) to be "hung up."[16] The prisoner was handcuffed to the bars of his cell in a spread-eagle position, his arms shackled at shoulder level and his feet just touching the floor. He was given water and allowed to use the bathroom for a fifteen-minute period every five hours, but otherwise was ignored. For somewhere between two and three days (fifty-two or sixty-three hours, depending on which evidence you believed), he remained suspended in this position without food or sleep. When he was "cut down" at seven o'clock Saturday morning, his feet and legs were painfully swollen, but he was required to work on the roads until noon, still without food.

Judge Sharp later said that her ignorance of the law applicable to the case was matched only by her surprise and indignation that such cruel and unusual punishment was inflicted on inmates of the state's prisons.[17] Lawyers for the highway commission — of whom there were four, including the prison division's chief counsel as well as a former judge — argued that their client had carried out his duties according to long-standing practices authorized by the commission's regulations governing prison discipline.[18] Judge Sharp was up all night working on her charge to the jury, a directed verdict of guilty leaving open only the question of whether the assault was simple or one involving the infliction of serious injury. If the latter, the judge would have the option of sentencing the superintendent to the very roads on which his former prisoner had toiled and expressed his longing for a beer. After returning to the judge for further instructions, the jury came in with the more serious verdict: guilty of assault resulting in serious bodily injury.

If history had intended to provide the maximum in testosterone-soaked parties for her first week on the bench, it could hardly have done better than the state highway commission and the prison system. Thanks in part to the $200 million road-building program of Judge Sharp's patron, Governor Scott, no state agency possessed a higher profile than the highway commission, which had always been a repository of enormous political clout. And the prisons that provided, as a form of punishment, the labor force for the expanding highway system were tough places into which the light of public inquiry rarely shone. At this time, midway through the twentieth century, for example, flogging was still a legally permitted means of prison discipline. Prison administrators were unaccustomed to interference from any outsider, not to mention a female judge whose tenure on the bench could still be measured in hours. Moreover, the commission had sent four of their best and most illustrious attorneys to argue the prison superintendent's case.

Judge Sharp might have been nervous about presiding over her first court, but she was not in the least intimidated by the powerful forces behind the defendant. It would have been far easier to defer to the argument that the superintendent was not responsible for actions taken under existing rules. But as her directed verdict made clear, she fully believed that any such rules constituted cruel and unusual punishment and could not be valid. When she pronounced her sentence, she took the opportunity to deliver a searing indictment of such practices, which she excoriated as "medieval." Nonetheless, her logic compelled a degree of mercy. Addressing the convicted superintendent, whom she had given a sentence of nine months "on the roads," she said, "I feel, Mr. Carpenter, that I ought to send you to the roads, so that you might see what it is like to be in the power of a prison superintendent; but because you did not make the rules, because you did have the approval of persons whose responsibility is greater than yours, because numerous other prison superintendents who are just as guilty as you will not be tried, and because of the fear that my outraged feelings about the rule and your conduct under it might lead me into an act of revenge, I am going to suspend sentence."

Her extensive remarks, reported in full by the newspapers, were based primarily on the theory that the purpose of imprisonment was deterrence, not revenge. In an oblique acknowledgment of rehabilitation as another goal of the penal system, she declared that any prisoner subjected to the type of "torture" in this case "would thereafter have such a contempt and hatred for constituted authority that all chance of reforming him is gone. You have opened the door and invited him to come in as an anarchist." She recognized that "prisoners are difficult to handle; that they cannot be treated like guests in one's home; they should not be coddled." Nonetheless, she reproached the superintendent: "For 52 hours you kept a man hung up . . . I cannot conceive how one man could do this to another."[19]

The case was appealed to the North Carolina Supreme Court as expected. That court felt obliged to order a new trial, not because of the merits or the outcome, but because of language in one of the judge's jury instructions.[20] The court made it clear, however, that the evidence admitted in the trial and the verdict should stand. Writing for the majority, Justice A. A. F. Seawell called the regulations "repugnant" and the interpretation of them "excessive." The court rejected the argument that the superintendent should be guiltless because he was acting under existing regulations: "We find [the regulations] so inconsistent with the rule of reason contemplated in the statute and so repugnant to natural justice that we cannot regard them as conferring any immunity on the defendant."[21] At the retrial before Judge Don Phillips the following January, the defendant entered a plea of nolo contendere to the charge of "cruel and unusual punishment" of a prisoner.[22] After hearing the evidence, Judge Phillips reimposed the sentence originally handed down by Judge Sharp, leaving the outcome for the defendant unchanged.

What did change was the prison system. Following some minor initial adjustments, Governor Scott ordered the highway commission chairman, Henry Jordan, to undertake a full review of prison system regulations in North Carolina as well as in other states. The three-month study culminated in several changes, the most significant of which was the elimination of hand-cuffing an inmate to cell bars as a punishment except as an emergency measure limited in duration to twenty-four hours. The study exhibited a serious and unprecedented effort to evaluate prison policy in the broadest terms.[23] It recommended such future improvements as hiring a full-time psychologist to work with the prison psychiatrist, hiring an education director to improve prison education and vocational training, and investigating the idea of incentive pay for work done by prisoners. Guard training was another area to receive attention. One editorialist, while disappointed that the immediate modifications had been less than sweeping, nonetheless acknowledged that prisons could be improved only by gradual, not revolutionary, changes and observed that "the commission's attitude seems to foreshadow a more modern prison system for North Carolina."[24]

This examination of the state's penal system was the direct result of Judge Susie Sharp's indignation when she heard the evidence against prison superintendent Carpenter. Brand-new at her job, confronted by a phalanx of male power figures, and performing under the close scrutiny of the statewide press, she had not hesitated to voice her disapproval of state-sanctioned regulations.

It was a gutsy stand for any judge, let alone one wet behind the ears and wearing pale pink fingernail polish to match her blouse. Arguably, she set North Carolina on a path toward reforms the state might not have considered for years, if at all. Prison reform was a subject in which she would remain deeply interested throughout her career.

Meanwhile, if the members of the bar across North Carolina had wondered what kind of judge she would be, *State v. Carpenter* had given them a powerful preview.

The Richmond County Bar Association presented her with a resolution of commendation "for the excellent manner in which she has presided over said term of court, always keeping a smooth temperament in the heat of the legal battles which have occurred at this term of court, together with her unerring desire to see that justice is done in every particular . . . and the calm, friendly and courteous manner exemplified by her excellent personality." Even more gratifying was the report from an Anson County paper, which, on inquiring as to "how the woman judge was getting along over in Richmond County," had been told that "the term of court was going on just like any other court."

The conversation that stayed with her the longest, the one she still quoted twenty-five years later, was with a deputy sheriff who told her, "Your Honor, I just want to say that you done better 'n I expected." She interpreted this—and later put the thought into the dialogue—to mean that in fact he "didn't expect nothing." She would always claim to have been the beneficiary of low expectations.

So began her career as an itinerant trial court judge. It was an arduous job, which until 1954 did not even reliably provide for a vacation. Year-round, the best a special judge could hope for was that no vacancy would arise requiring his presence, a rarity indeed. As Judge Sharp once commented, if by some fluke a special judge was unassigned for an upcoming week, "his or her great concern was to keep some regular judge from finding it out and suddenly becoming indisposed."[25] Moreover, unlike regular superior court judges, who circulated within a specified geographical area, special judges were called upon to preside over courts from one end of the state to the other. Depending on where in the state she was assigned to hold court, Judge Sharp would climb into her car either Sunday afternoon or Monday morning and set out in rain, snow, sleet, fog, or ice as well as sunshine—in the days before interstates smoothed the way—for some microscopic county seat that as likely as not had no decent hotel where a lady might lodge, or even a ladies' room in the courthouse. In Beaufort County, the only way to enter the judge's chambers was through the men's room.[26] As for a law library, there was no such thing in many of these little towns, and Judge Sharp relied on "a pretty good library in the trunk of her car."[27]

Often she would have to find a room in a local home, or she would stay in a nearby town and commute to the county seat. After a long day in court, she was often expected to deliver a dinner address to the local Business and Professional Women's Club or other civic group. On the road, she was subject to every sort of vehicular challenge from bad roads to breakdowns. In one letter she described a memorable occasion when a tire had a blowout in front of a house where a bunch of teenage boys were hanging about. Gallantly, they offered to help her change the tire, but immediately hit an impasse. They could change the tire, they said, but they didn't know how to get the fender skirt off. "I didn't either," Judge Sharp said, "so I got out the Instruction book which came with the car. No light there, however. The boys were just standing around with no progress being made. So I wrapped my raincoat around me and crawled under the car. In due course I found a protruding wire or rod, gave it a number of yanks and, after I'd given up hopes of its doing so, the skirt fell off. So did right much mud—right in my face." The boys were quite impressed, Judge Sharp wrote, adding, "So was I!"[28]

Back home in Reidsville for the weekend, she would spend half of Saturday either working in chambers or hearing domestic relations matters in recorders' court.[29] Less than three months after her appointment, she commented ("with emphasis") to a local newspaper, "I used to think a judge had a position. . . . I've found out this is a job."[30]

Whenever she held her initial court in a new county, there were invariably a few kinks to be worked out. "When I go to a courthouse for the first time, the lawyers are a little tense, and I am too," Judge Sharp told an interviewer early in her career on the bench.[31] "They don't know what to expect of a woman judge." But when they found out that she tried to perform her duties like any other judge and succeeded better than many, the tension dissolved. The most troublesome obstacle was always the issue of how to address her, and it gave rise to many humorous moments. "Your Honoress" was one of the least unconventional titles devised in the crucible of the courtroom, with "that She Judge" among the more memorable.

When Judge Sharp was holding court, the audience looked quite different from the way it looked on other days. Women spectators, previously scarce to nonexistent, braved the large crowds anxious to see the lady judge, sometimes bringing their children. One newspaper reported, "Among the spectators in the court room yesterday were a number of elderly and dignified women who looked as if they had never sat in a court session before. They left soon after the court session started, and it is our thought that they came by to catch a glimpse of Judge Susie and to pay tribute to this outstanding member of their sex."[32] In later years, it was common for strangers to stop Judge Sharp on the street to tell her that their mother or father had taken them down to the courthouse to see her when they were very young.

In contrast to the treatment given every other judge, newspaper accounts of Judge Sharp frequently described her clothes, jewelry, hairstyle, and overall appearance in detail. "The judge wore a suit of royal blue, buttoned to the neckline where she wore a silver pin of a dainty and feminine design and her earrings were of silver," went a typical write-up.[33] This reporter went on to say that, although Judge Sharp appeared attractive at a distance, "when we went to the front of the court room and saw her closer, we had no difficulty in deciding that she is definitely pretty. Newspaper pictures haven't really done her justice."[34] With this sentiment, Susie Sharp was generally in full agreement.

She ran a tight ship, but her discipline was tempered with common sense and compassion. Although she banned smoking from her courtrooms, she routinely allowed men to remove their coats and ties when the unair-conditioned courtrooms sweltered. She would never forget the heat stroke her father suffered that hot day in Wentworth when the judge refused his request to take off his jacket. Many observers remarked on her orderly court, not realizing that it resulted as much from a disability as from her innate lucidity and managerial skills. "People frequently comment on the order I keep in court. I haven't yet confessed to them that it is because the J[udge] is hard of hearing," she confided to one correspondent.[35] Although she could hear without difficulty so long as there was no competing noise, she was unable to distinguish between overlapping sounds, such as more than one person speaking at the same time. Her hearing problems would only get worse as the years went by.

What was the secret that enabled this first-ever woman judge to command a courtroom and earn the unqualified respect of her male colleagues without raising hackles? Part of it undoubtedly was her demeanor as a woman in charge but without a chip on her shoulder. Her training as a southern lady equipped her with useful antennae and techniques to avoid bruising male egos. But most important was her indisputable knowledge of the law. She knew what she was doing, and the lawyers in her courtroom appreciated that, despite any disappointment in not being able to outfox her. One colleague who knew her both as a fellow superior court judge and as a member of the supreme court explained, "[S]he had a reputation of just being one of those judges who was in control. And who knew the law. And who ruled accordingly. And who had no favorites. She was impartial. She was dispassionate.... She did the job the way they expected it to be done, and she was good at it. Very good at it."[36] It was also true that if she had high expectations for attorneys appearing before her, she made equally high demands on herself. If she gave no quarter, she asked none either.

Another secret of her success may have been that she took time to pay attention to the wives of the attorneys with whom she dealt, a duty she often found dull but which repaid her efforts in ways that, although unrecorded, were not unimportant.[37] She knew she could not survive if the lawyers' wives talked against her to their husbands at night.

It was one of the respected elders of the Wilson bar who bestowed on her the compliment she most cherished. Responding to an inquiry as to what it was like to practice before a lady judge, he replied, "I have not been aware of appearing before a lady judge."[38] Judge Sharp treasured this remark because she believed profoundly that "work has no sex, nor have brains."[39] In the first months of her judicial career, she expressed the hope that in the near future a woman on the judge's bench would not be a news item and that the publicity she received would not be because she was a woman, but because she was a respected and competent judge. This was a hope she would see only partially fulfilled during her half century in the legal profession.

If her professional life was demanding, her personal life was no less so. Although, as a single woman living with her parents in Reidsville, she was spared the normal responsibilities of running a household or keeping up with a husband and children, that did not mean her private life was simple. Indeed, the complicated nature of the personal relationships she was juggling almost defies comprehension. This is all the more true because her private life was in such contrast to the immaculate public image she maintained or, perhaps more accurately, that had been superimposed on her.

As a spinster lawyer and now judge, she had earned a reputation for honesty and probity. To observers and even to family and friends, she appeared to have no intimate entanglements. This puzzled many people, who often expressed the opinion that she was a very attractive woman and wondered why she had never married. Her family and oldest friends, of course, were aware of her long-held views, first expressed as a high school girl, that she never intended to marry but rather was determined to have a career, something she considered then and later to be incompatible with marriage and motherhood. Whatever change of heart she had experienced during her law school romance with John Kesler, the question of marriage had become moot when that relationship ended in 1928. Now, when asked, she would say that the law left her no time for a husband. In any event, she would point out, after she began spending every week holding court in a different town, a husband would soon "take up with a blonde" in frustration at her schedule. Moreover, she quipped, why should she get married and make one man miserable when she could remain on the bench and torment so many more?[40] To her nephew Jimmy Taylor, in response to his question as to whether she would ever get married, she once responded with a revealing comment. "Not unless I find a man smarter than I am and that's not likely," she reportedly said.[41] In any event, seeing no evidence of a man in her life, the public transmogrified her single status, her career, and her apparent lack of interest in romance into the image of a sort of strict but charming schoolmarm. Judge Sharp did not discourage this characterization, which protected her very well.

Judge Sharp's relationship with Professor Breckenridge had endured for nearly two decades. Meticulously recorded in a special journal, their affair had been a regular part of her life all those years, with frequent meetings in Chapel Hill or elsewhere. She and Venitah had long since bonded in a life-long compact based on their love for Breck and a genuine affection for one another. Susie Sharp was treated like a member of the Breckenridge family. "No one in the world, except my 'ain kin' . . . [is] closer and even then there is a very thin line," Venitah wrote to her in August 1949.[42] There is no evidence that Susie Sharp was ever troubled by the intertwined strands of carnal and quasi-familial love. She loved Breck in the wholeness of his existence, which included Venitah and his children. If after so many years their passion had subsided to a less demanding level, Susie Sharp and Breck had always been more than mere lovers. They were great friends and companions as well, bonded by their common interest in the law, their ongoing disputations on politics, their love of witty repartee. And, of course, it was a convenient arrangement for a woman who did not want the chains of matrimony applied to her own wrists and ankles.

What neither Breck nor anyone else knew at the time was that he was not her only lover.

In her separate journal dedicated solely to her meetings with Breck, she employed a simple notation system to record every romantic encounter, numbering each consecutively. It was a manifestation of the compulsive side of her personality and a habit she continued decade after decade, without a lapse. Meanwhile, in her regular everyday journal identical notations also appear beside references to her old mentor, friend, and colleague, Judge Allen Gwyn.

Although Susie Sharp destroyed her everyday journals for the period roughly between 1927 and 1943 (after first making a lengthy abstract of entries covering these years), and either did not keep journals for the following five years or destroyed them without making any record of their existence, in 1948 she took up her journal habit and did not abandon it again until her old age. In February 1948 an entry appears indicating that she and Allen Gwyn had had the forty-fifth romantic encounter of their relationship. Another entry about Allen Gwyn dated January 27, 1952, and annotated "18 years"—an apparent reference to an anniversary—suggests that the relationship had begun in 1934. (Her journals contain other references in this form to anniversaries.) In contrast to her obsessive record keeping regarding her affair with Breck, however, it does not appear that Susie Sharp kept a separate journal in which to record her encounters with Judge Gwyn, and the references in her ordinary journal are sporadic.

Allen Gwyn was a complicated man. Fourteen years Susie Sharp's senior, he was born in neighboring Caswell County in 1893 to a family of modest means but high principles. With a hiatus for World War I, during which he served as a lieutenant in the infantry, the young Gwyn worked his way through Trinity College (now Duke University), where he received both his undergraduate and law degrees. He began practicing law in Reidsville in 1921. As a young attorney in Reidsville, he volunteered to coach the high school debate team, where he first encountered Susie Sharp, the brilliant young debater. Gwyn was active and ambitious, heavily involved in civic and political life. Susie Sharp had known him well in his roles as, among other things, county court solicitor, city attorney, state senator, and Democratic Party stalwart, not to mention as her father's political rival.

In his long career on the bench, Judge Gwyn would become widely known for his thoughtful approach to criminal sentencing and innovative emphasis on rehabilitation. It was Judge Gwyn who virtually invented the concept of work-release in North Carolina, a program under which selected convicted defendants could avoid jail through holding a job. In a book entitled *Work, Earn and Save* published in 1963,[43] he described the methods he had developed for dealing with first offenders who, he believed, could be salvaged. Under a suspended sentence, the offender would work at a legitimate job, save his earnings above what he needed to live, and make regular payments to the court for the duration of the sentence. If all went well, at the end of the sentence he could claim the savings he had accumulated. Judge Gwyn believed that a young man could be diverted onto a righteous path by this system, and he was often proved correct. Many law enforcement officers and other officials, particularly clerks of court whose work load the scheme increased, were deeply opposed to Judge Gwyn's methods, but many others were converted, and over time his efforts had a profound impact on the North Carolina criminal justice system.[44]

For a politician, he was not afraid of controversy. Far ahead of his time on the racial issue, he publicly announced that no member of the Ku Klux Klan would sit on a jury in his courtroom.[45] When the North Carolina legislature passed the Speaker Ban Law in 1963, barring members of the Communist Party from speaking on the campuses of tax-supported institutions of higher learning, Judge Gwyn would be a vocal opponent to any such restraint on free speech and the spirit of inquiry so fundamental to academia.

He was a scholar and an intellectual with a deep understanding of the struggles of the underprivileged, having made his own way up from poverty. Never a glad-hander, he was nonetheless obsessed with and constantly immersed in politics. He was a tireless talker, indeed a pontificator, all of it pouring out of his bottomless interest in government and its effect on people. He had many admirers and not a few detractors.

Judge Gwyn was married to the former Janie Johnston, a Reidsville native. "Miss Janie" was his match, a formidable force, an energetic woman just as interested in politics as her husband was. They had two sons and a daughter. Their union appeared to be grounded in deep rock, unshakable. Judge Gwyn had, however, acquired a widespread reputation as a skirt-chaser, a "wolf" in the terminology of the day. It was said that in at least one county they refused to let him come and hold court, because of his harassment of court personnel.[46] Perhaps because of the judge's high moral stands on so many issues, and certainly because he was genuinely respected by a great number of his peers as well as ordinary citizens, many people refused to believe this sort of whispered allegation, but the whispers continued. Susie Sharp heard the rumors and for a long time sprang to the judge's defense, but eventually acceded to the evidence. Before the end of his life, she would include in her journal an exasperated report of his predations upon the nursing staff during a hospital stay.[47]

Perhaps Judge Gwyn pursued Susie Sharp because he was a compulsive womanizer, but there is no doubt that he also recognized her extraordinary talents and wanted her to reach for the stars. He encouraged her in every aspect of her legal career, plotted with her as to the politics of her advancement, and did everything in his power to boost her career. He would also, as will be seen, allow his own ambitions to thwart hers on at least one important occasion. They would maintain a relationship of one sort or another, despite innumerable opportunities for real bitterness, until Gwyn's death in 1969.

What, though, had led her in 1934 to embark on an affair with him? If she confided any information on the subject to her journal, this insight has disappeared with the relevant journals themselves. Susie Sharp had maintained a close professional relationship with Judge Gwyn throughout the years she had known him, despite the antipathy between him and her father. Interestingly, 1934 was the year that Gwyn defeated Jim Sharp in the race for solicitor of the Eleventh Judicial District. Their mutual antipathy would be further exacerbated when Gwyn beat Sharp in the 1938 election for superior court judge. For Susie Sharp, rabidly loyal to her father, to continue what was in fact a productive and fruitful connection with the judge in these circumstances reveals both a mature political mind and an ability to compartmentalize her emotions. She and the judge were involved in many of the same political and judicial activities, shared many of the same goals. It is not so strange that she could draw on her long acquaintance with him to overlook whatever ill feelings or lack of mutual respect existed between him and her father. But for her to embark on an affair with Judge Gwyn is not as easy to understand, because it is clear that she never believed herself to be "in love" with him, however warm her affection and respect.

If, as the evidence suggests, they had been lovers since 1934, the notation of their forty-fifth encounter in February 1948 would indicate that the sexual relationship had been intermittent over the years, at least until that point. It was in 1948 that the two worked closely on Kerr Scott's gubernatorial campaign and were thrown together even more than usual. Between July 1949 and May 1950 they had romantic encounters on an average of once a month, according to her journal entries. By the time Governor Scott appointed her to the bench, an appointment that Judge Gwyn had worked hard to see realized, they had an established relationship. Although there is no evidence whatever that Susie Sharp was in love with the judge, she occasionally burnished her notations with comments such as, "Very nice time indeed." She was certainly fond of him, even if he exasperated her at times. They enjoyed the kind of intellectual give-and-take that always invigorated her. And she had never had, other than her father, such a champion for her ambitions.

The two had many opportunities to meet in Susie Sharp's office downtown, which they often did at night. Once she was on the bench, it was not unusual for both of them to be assigned to hold court in Charlotte at the same time. As one of the largest cities in the state, Charlotte's courthouse accommodated multiple courtrooms and required multiple judges for every term of court, unlike the smaller county seats where one judge per term was the norm. Sometimes Judge Sharp and Judge Gwyn drove to and from Charlotte together, and they stayed at the same hotel. In a journal entry dated February 3, 1950, Susie Sharp related a conversation they had on the way back to Reidsville: "Nice drive home. . . . I cry because he talks about age, me etc. I tell him when I go out that door he no longer belongs to me and he says I belong to my public. That he plans for me like he does his boys."

Undoubtedly Susie Sharp saw that Gwyn was in a far better position to aid her career than was Jim Sharp. One is forced to consider the possibility that she sought to better her prospects by sleeping with her longtime mentor. Anything is possible, of course, but there is no conclusive evidence to suggest this was her motivation. If she had refused his advances, every indication is that Gwyn would have continued to be her ardent professional supporter. He had spotted her star quality early on, and he believed in it.

Indeed, in 1934 Susie Sharp had little reason to think that an affair with Gwyn would give her an assist onto the bench, even if such an unlikely ambition had entered her consciousness; she was barely accepted as a lady lawyer at that point in her career. Perhaps the possibilities of being Gwyn's protégée became apparent as both their careers matured over the years. There would in fact come a time when she continued to see him even though, for several reasons, she did not particularly want to, but this could easily have had more to do with the inertia of a long-standing relationship that is over yet not over than with ulterior motives on her part. Nothing in Susie Sharp's journals suggests that she had succumbed to any career-related pressure, either from the judge or from her own calculations.

More likely, he simply made his move at some propitious moment after she came home to Reidsville from her stint as secretary to the dean of the law school in Chapel Hill. She was no longer a schoolgirl and no doubt considered herself very sophisticated, having embarked on her love affair with her married law professor. She had returned to Reidsville with reluctance and feared being immured there. As one of the very few women in the state, indeed the nation, who had a career as a practicing lawyer, she may have felt herself not bound by the common mores. The country had recently emerged from the Roaring Twenties, and the rigid puritanism of the 1950s had not yet set in. She was not religious. And, although ostensibly a spinster still living at home in a small town, she secretly considered herself something of a femme fatale. Perhaps she was just bored enough to be intrigued.

Having an affair with a married man was not unknown even among Susie Sharp's closest friends, one of whom had been the paramour of a prominent local businessman for years. She had confided in Susie Sharp, who recorded in her journal, "[X] tells all, I advise caution."[48] When the lover became terminally ill and Susie Sharp's friend abandoned him to accept a marriage proposal from someone else, Susie Sharp was upset with her.[49] As for herself, she knew better than to return the confidences of her friend. She kept her own romantic arrangements to herself.

On the verge of turning forty, then, her private life was complicated if not necessarily fulfilling. Involved but not in love with the judge, she continued her relationship with Breck, although they were such old shoes together that the excitement was not what it once was. But her life was about to become infinitely more complicated. On May 26, 1947, she and her old flame John Kesler became lovers at last.

Susie Sharp began yet another special journal devoted solely to a chronology of her meetings with John beginning with that date in May, but it contains minimal commentary in general and none on the circumstances surrounding this event in particular.[50] Moreover, because her regular journals before 1948 have vanished, she left no record of how this long-deferred union with her oldest love came about.[51] We do know that over the years she and John had seen each other occasionally, usually when she happened to have a case in Salisbury, and on such occasions they would indulge themselves by rekindling the old embers a bit. Chances are they simply had an opportunity and took advantage of it. She did not see him again until September, when they arranged a weekend in Raleigh, staying in separate rooms at the famous old Hotel Sir Walter. It was not until a year later, on the following May 26, that they had another Sir Walter rendezvous, to mark the anniversary of their status as actual lovers. Susie Sharp's taciturn notes hint that the weekend was not entirely successful, and she did not see him again until February.[52]

John Kesler had been married since 1939 and had a little girl named Frances Sue. His schoolteacher wife, Sudie, was by her own description about thirty pounds overweight,[53] but she had a sweet face and an outgoing disposition. They lived on West Liberty Street in Salisbury, near downtown, in a neighborhood of modest houses set close to the curb, with long narrow back yards behind. Their corner lot was a popular playground for the children who lived nearby, who often gathered under a particular tree there. For a number of years in the late 1940s and early 1950s, Sudie Kesler organized a fondly remembered tradition, a Fourth of July parade for the neighborhood, with lots of flags, bicycles, crepe paper streamers, and little girls in organdy dresses. Grown-ups and children alike would march up and down West Liberty waving their flags, while John Kesler directed traffic. Sudie made lemonade and handed it out, along with chocolate chip cupcakes, from her post under the big tree.[54]

John had built a law practice in Salisbury, where he had also served as a judge and solicitor in Rowan County court. In 1945 and 1947 he represented Rowan and Cabarrus counties in the state senate. In 1949 he was appointed a trustee of the University of North Carolina, a position he would hold until 1957. He was active in the First Methodist Church, the Masonic Lodge, and many other civic groups. He still had a big wavy pompadour of black hair, parted on the left, and bushy black eyebrows over the liquid brown eyes that had always been one of his best features.

Susie Sharp and John Kesler each had ample reasons not to imperil the lives they had constructed. Most probably they told one another that the situation was impossible and hoped only for the occasional reunion, nothing more.

In 1949, the year Susie Sharp became a superior court judge, she and John managed to get together only four times, including their May 26 anniversary. Of course she was busy learning the ropes of her new job and was constantly on the road after her appointment in July. Moreover, she was still seeing Breck regularly, not to mention Allen Gwyn on occasion. And, in this particular instance, her instinctive defense system would have been working overtime to protect her from unrealistic expectations and—at least as important—from losing control over her emotions. Even as a high school girl, before she had ever fallen in love, she had been aware of love's disruptive effect and had feared the vulnerability inevitably involved. She had always said she would never marry for love, for she would be miserable in her powerlessness against her feelings. She had not forgotten how devastated she had been when she lost John before. One August day when she was in Salisbury to visit her friend Gladys Morgan Happer and stopped by John's office to say hello, she revealed her as-yet-uncommitted state of mind. "He wants me to go to his house and I run away," she wrote.[55] But she met him in Raleigh the next week, and again in November.

By the following year she was seeing Breck very little and Allen Gwyn quite a bit more, a situation that apparently created a strain in her relationship with Breck, who seemed to have had some awareness by this time that he was not the only man in her life. In February 1950 she reported a conversation with Breck "under great difficulty" and also his remark a couple of weeks later that "if I thought he was bitter the other night I ought to have been with him when he got my letter."[56] Meanwhile, at Christmastime Susie Sharp had made a scrapbook for John's little girl, for which she got a proper thank-you note from Sudie, and in March she went out to his house to "meet the wife and baby." She and John managed a dozen or so rendezvous into the fall, but then she did not see him for several months. When she got a letter from him in January 1951, she wrote, "It was a physical shock to see it."[57] A couple of weeks later he came to Winston-Salem where she was holding court. He had quit smoking and gained ten pounds, which were barely detectable on his lean frame.[58] When they were able to talk, he spoke among other things of his difficulty in writing her love letters. Sometimes he would write them, stamp them, and get all the way to the post office with them before losing his nerve—whether because of the emotions he had expressed or the risk of committing them to paper, she did not explain to her journal. On another occasion he confessed that he kept her most recent letter until he got another, prompting her to write, "That is not wise."[59]

They had a thrillingly audacious scheme in the works. They laid their plans during brief rendezvous, sometimes when she was holding court in nearby Greensboro and they would go out to a local park for a picnic lunch. "Here is a good place for me to kiss the Judge," John would say in the shelter of a secluded spot.[60] They were planning to spend a solid week together in New York.

The record does not reveal what pretext John had fabricated; Susie Sharp, of course, had a long history of leisure trips to New York and would have no trouble organizing her alibi. They could pose as a married couple. "He is going to make an honest woman out of me," she recorded.[61] She had a term of court beginning July 16 in Currituck County, the last far outpost of North Carolina in the remote northeastern corner of the state, wedged between Virginia and the Atlantic Ocean, and then she had a week's vacation, the only week off she would have for the entire year. She and John could scarcely wait until they could meet in Raleigh and start driving north—together. "If I am not in Raleigh," John said, "You can just start checking the hospitals."[62]

Judge Sharp left home in the middle of the afternoon on Sunday, July 15, to drive the 256 miles to Currituck County, a tortuous and sweltering trip in the July heat. She had no place to stay in the county seat because the clerk of court had advised her when she wrote to inquire that there was no motel in the vicinity, nor could he get her a room in a private home for the week. She would have to commute every day from Elizabeth City, more than twenty miles away. It was eleven o'clock that night when she rolled in.

When court opened Monday morning, Judge Sharp was appalled to see that the courthouse windows had no screens. Ever phobic as to insect and animal life of all kinds, she noted warily the black wasps circling the attorneys and members of the jury, not to mention the judge. "They say they don't bite," she fretted, "but if not I don't see why they are so attracted to humans."[63]

In any event, her attention was soon drawn to the first case, a land suit that had been pending, unbelievably, for eleven years. She dispatched that one without much difficulty and then confronted the next case, which — when she called the calendar Monday morning — the lawyers had told her would take two days at most. At least two judges had previously started the case but declared a mistrial. As Judge Sharp recalled it, "Well, we got into that case and I found out that that wasn't any two-day case." She discovered that the two other judges had extricated themselves by declaring mistrials because the case was a whopper. According to the court reporter, "Every time a judge would find out what the case was about, they'd make some excuse not to try it." The lawyers had lied to her about how long they expected the case to take. The court reporter told Judge Sharp, "They figured that if you got into it, you wouldn't do like the others had done, call a mistrial, you'd go on and finish it. But they expect it'll take all next week."[64]

Judge Sharp was livid. She called in the lawyers and laid it out. Without telling them the source of her information, she said, "I understand that this case can't be tried in the time you all estimated it would. Now, I've got plans to go to New York on Saturday afternoon. And I plan to go. But I don't plan to bust up this case either. We will have court, we'll have night sessions. We'll start court at 8:00 in the morning. We'll work until I get tired at night. And we'll have about an hour for supper."

The lawyers were horrified. "Judge, you can't do that," they said. "The mosquitoes are out here at night. The courtroom isn't screened. And the mosquitoes come in droves."

Judge Sharp said, "Where's the sheriff?" When he appeared, she told him, "Sheriff, you've got until tonight to get these windows screened. I've been mosquito-bit before, but these jurors, they might not vote right next election if you let them get mosquito-bit." By that nightfall he had nailed mosquito netting over the windows and requisitioned a flit gun for good measure. It was a good thing because on Wednesday night court was in session. Meanwhile she had fired off a letter to John to tell him to sit tight. And by God the case was finished by the close of court on Friday.

Before she left, the clerk of court who had been so unhelpful about her accommodations said, "Judge, the next time you come, we'll be able to get you a room."[65]

The trip to New York was a honeymoon in every way, except for the minor detail of not being married. They took turns driving. In the big city, they went to Broadway shows including *South Pacific* with Mary Martin, took in the Rockettes at Radio City, rode the subway to Yankee Stadium for a ball game, and toured Wall Street. They went for a boat ride and watched the USS *Queen Elizabeth* come into port. They ate at Susie Sharp's favorite restaurants. They shopped at Saks, Macy's, and B. Altman's. It was a week they would both always remember and would refer to as a sort of high-water mark in their relationship. They had proved to be utterly compatible, completely at ease with each other. Any hope Susie Sharp had of not succumbing to her feelings for John was lost forever.

Although she continued to visit "the Bs" as usual on her many trips to and through Chapel Hill, her romantic relationship with Breck was on hold for the entire year of 1951. Some evidence indicates that this may have been his choice, such as an entry in her journal during June in which she noted: "Go by the Bs and stay a while with him after [Venitah and Jean] leave.... On his bed for a while then he tells me to leave."[66] It seems clear that, although Susie Sharp still cared deeply for Breck, as she would continue to do all the days of her life, she had made him aware that he was not her primary love interest any longer. It was causing him a degree of distress that may have surprised him. Not long after this June visit, she met him in his office the morning of her birthday, July 7, a Saturday, and they went for a drive so they could talk. "We ride to Durham 3 times," she reported.

All that fall she saw John regularly. They spent the last weekend in December together in Raleigh, and her journal records his tender words to her. She admitted, "I nearly cry when I leave him."[67]

The following Saturday she was in Chapel Hill, where she spent a snowy weekend holed up at the Carolina Inn. Of her time with Breck, she wrote, "The old magic was gone." Not long after this he told her, "Susie, we are getting old. Our relationship is a much more honest one than that of a lot of married people."[68] Perhaps. Perhaps Susie Sharp was not as honest with him as he thought. But the deep affection between them remained. She told him of a certain superior court judge who had insinuated that she had no business in the big leagues, and Breck said, "When it is over you may have nobody to come back to but me." "Would you take me back under those circumstances?" she asked. "Will I!" he responded.

Less than a week later they met for the last time as lovers. But their friendship continued, and Susie Sharp's role as an honorary family member did not diminish.

It took her a little longer to extricate herself from her relationship with Judge Gwyn, and the process was greatly complicated by the ambition they each harbored, one more publicly than the other, to sit on the North Carolina Supreme Court.

CHAPTER 9

AMBITION

Susie Sharp was always disingenuous about her ambition, perhaps even to herself. There is no doubt that initially she had been conflicted about accepting Governor Scott's appointment to the superior court, primarily due to her concerns regarding both her father's health and the short-term nature of the special judge's tenure. But whether or not she had ever aimed for the trial court bench, there is evidence that she had long imagined a seat on the North Carolina Supreme Court, although she rarely admitted it.

It was a subject she and Breck had discussed for years, as revealed in a poignant letter to her shortly after her appointment to the superior court in 1949.

Breck's admiration for Susie Sharp never completely obscured his desire to be the dominant partner in their relationship. Part of him was jealous of her achievements. He had once had higher aspirations himself, but he "did not have the drive" to do what was required to achieve them, he wrote to her in September 1949.[1] "I shot my longest bow some time back and whatever I might have done, I am pretty well assured of not doing now." He had come to the realization that she was "on the up" and he was "on the down." He lamented that he was not even prepared for his class the next day. Reviewing his own failings, he contrasted his waning energies and abilities to her surging career. "Specifically, I think you are headed for the Supreme Court, as I have long said," he wrote. It is clear that he had envisioned and articulated this unprecedented goal, that she might claim a seat on the North Carolina Supreme Court, long before she was even visible on the general public's radar.

Meanwhile, as for Judge Allen Gwyn, he had not relinquished his higher aspirations. When Kerr Scott actually won the gubernatorial election, Gwyn believed that he would be Scott's first supreme court appointee. Not only had he worked hard and efficaciously for Scott during the campaign, but he was a lonely advocate among the superior court judges in his support for the dark horse candidate. Scott well knew that Gwyn wanted a seat on the court, and Gwyn was not alone in thinking there was no reason he should not have it. As a local newspaper put it not long after Scott's inauguration, commenting on possible Scott appointments to the court, "He doesn't have much choice if he wants to name somebody who was on his team, for the jurists flocked to [Charles] Johnson. However, Judge Allen Gwyn, of Reidsville, was a Scott man so look in that direction when the vacancy occurs."[2]

This expectation was widely shared. Speculating on Susie Sharp's prospects as a potential appointee to the superior court, Tom Bost of the *Greensboro Daily News* had discounted the fact that Reidsville already had a superior court judge in the person of Allen Gwyn, because his supporters were "counting on Judge Gwyn's early ascent to the Supreme Court."[3] In light of his experience and stature as a superior court judge, as well as his solitary support for Scott, Gwyn could be excused for thinking he had a sure shot at the next appointment.

The first vacancy occurred when Justice A. A. F. Seawell died on October 14, 1950. Among Governor Scott's papers are numerous letters of recommendation for more than twenty individuals to fill the post.[4] Most are in support of Jefferson D. Johnson Jr., who had previously served as a special superior court judge appointed by Governor J. Melville Broughton, and Itimous T. Valentine, a popular Nash County lawyer. Superior Court Judge William H. Bobbitt also received a large number of recommendations. If the file is complete, Judge Allen Gwyn received only four letters in support of his appointment, one of them written by Susie Sharp.[5]

Governor Scott, characteristically, appointed none of these candidates, but rather selected an old friend whom he had known at North Carolina State College (later University), a hitherto unknown small-town lawyer named Murray G. James. It was completely in keeping with Scott's pattern of doing the unexpected. Indeed, Scott's propensity for filling appointive positions with unlikely if not wholly unsuitable individuals had bolstered his reputation as a loose cannon. His appointment of Susie Sharp to the superior court and his selection of the nationally respected Frank Porter Graham, president of the University of North Carolina, as U.S. senator (a bombshell delivered without advance warning) were widely considered brilliant choices, but more often his appointments verged on the incomprehensible. James's only qualifications were a law degree and an early acquaintance with Kerr Scott.

One can imagine Judge Gwyn's reaction.

In any event, Justice James scarcely had time to warm the bench after he took the oath of office on October 20, 1950. The state executive committee nominated Jefferson D. Johnson Jr. as the Democratic Party candidate in the November election, which he won handily.[6]

The next opportunity came within the year. On September 13, 1951, Chief Justice Walter Parker Stacy died. He had been on the court for more than thirty years, serving more than twenty-six of those years as chief justice. Judge Sharp learned of his death when she turned on the radio just before eight o'clock that morning. As she wrote to John Kesler, "He's the only Chief Justice we ever knew and I feel as if the Supreme Court were dead. If the right appointment is not made it could indeed be the beginning of rigor mortis for our high tribunal. Let's burn a few candles!"[7]

She did not elaborate on who she thought might qualify as "the right appointment." Without question she knew that Judge Gwyn considered himself to be the man, but whether she shared that view is not evident. Regardless, in the wider world her own name instantly appeared on the lists of possible appointees, which understandably caused some strain between her and her erstwhile mentor and champion.

She was a credible candidate. Her first two-year term on the bench had been a great success. She had more than proved her ability to run a courtroom and to render justice in a disciplined, knowledgeable, and evenhanded manner. Her Democratic Party credentials were substantial, and she had been of service to Governor Scott. She was popular and respected among members of the bar as well as the public. Judge Gwyn himself had written her a congratulatory note on Christmas Eve 1950: "You are now completing your first full 'calendar' year as a Superior Court Judge. You have made good in a big way. We all are proud of you. . . . You have added much to the over-all worth of our judicial system. You have done more than any other woman in the State to gain for women their appropriate place in governmental matters."

She had been formally recognized for her accomplishments. In the spring of 1950, her alma mater, NCCW, renamed Woman's College, expressed the desire to award her an honorary doctor of laws degree at commencement. At the time she was only halfway through her first term as a special judge and had no assurance of being reappointed. It seemed unwise for a potential flash in the pan to accept such a high honor, she thought, particularly because the other two honorees were Dr. Helen Brooke Taussig of Baltimore, who with a colleague had originated the famous "blue baby" operation to correct a congenital cardiac malformation,[8] and North Carolina's beloved U.S. senator Frank Porter Graham. Judge Sharp begged the college to hold off at least until she finished her first term, at which time her performance might be evaluated, and she either would or would not have been reappointed. "I explained that nobody could then predict how that 'woman judge' would turn out; that if I were a flop I'd be a blot on the escutcheon of the College; and that would grieve me greatly."[9] Her entreaty was brushed aside, however, and, when she sought his advice, a proud Judge Gwyn advised her to accept the honor. "He kisses me and cries," she wrote in her journal.[10]

She did accept and subsequently got a laugh when told that the honor was arranged posthaste because no one thought she would last two weeks, let alone the two years of her initial appointment.[11] She later said of the occasion that she was "given a doctorate and overpraised for a performance, which, by a man, would have caused no comment at all."[12]

On May 30, 1951, Governor Scott announced her reappointment for another term. The news was greeted with enthusiasm across the state.

No doubt Judge Gwyn would have been the first to lobby for a seat for Susie Sharp on the highest appellate court in the state had his own ambition been achieved, but he certainly had not envisioned that his prospects might be undermined by his protégée or that she might ascend to the supreme court before he did.

Some observers said that she had as good a chance as Judge Gwyn. Once again, however, Governor Scott confounded the odds makers. After elevating Justice William A. Devin to chief justice, he appointed his old friend Itimous T. Valentine to take Devin's place as associate justice. A native of Nash County "down East," Valentine had a long history of service to the Democratic Party, and, although he had never been a judge, he was one of the few in the legal profession who had backed Scott in the gubernatorial election.[13] In explaining his choice to the press, Scott placed emphasis on the support received by the eight or ten candidates he had considered for the associate justice post. All had strong support from various groups, he said at a news conference, "but Itimous had the strongest."[14] Without mentioning Susie Sharp by name, Governor Scott confirmed the widespread speculation that he had considered appointing a woman. Even given the governor's penchant for unlikely appointments, few could think of any woman in the state other than Judge Sharp who might have been on his list, and newspaper accounts uniformly named her as the woman in question.[15] John told her that the next vacancy could be hers if she was willing to play the game.[16]

She may have believed it. Her journal indicates that her rivalry with Judge Gwyn had acquired a reality she probably had never anticipated. For two years she had basked in a warm and flattering spotlight as the first and only female superior court judge. The publicity she attracted simply because of her gender was almost entirely glowing and had made her well known to the general public across the state. Beyond mere novelty, however, she had earned nearly universal admiration among members of the bar. As a measure of her standing, at the annual meeting of the North Carolina State Bar on October 26, 1951, the two featured speakers were U.S. senator Willis Smith and Judge Susie Sharp. Judge Sharp's topic was "A New Judge Looks at the Bar," and it was a substantial address in which she delivered an unflinching report on the state of the court system and the courtroom arts to the practitioners themselves, a report so expertly cast in the (ostensibly) wide-eyed point of view of a newly minted judge and so warmly leavened with humor that the medicine slipped down their gullets without protest. "Maybe Judge Susie told some more than they cared to hear, but they asked for it," said one editorial. "Certainly the judge's words showed that her wide and increasing popularity devolves from her refreshing frankness, her determination to hew to the line, her sense of humor and her insight into the problems of her own profession."[17]

On November 11, 1951, less than two months after Governor Scott had passed over Judge Gwyn for the second time, Gwyn called and asked her to come to see him. He had decided to run for the North Carolina Supreme Court in the 1952 election, he said, but he wanted her blessing. He would run "if I tell him to," she wrote.[18] It had long been his ambition, he reminded her, and he did not know how long he would want to do it. He assured her, she recorded, that "he feels that every step I take gets me nearer to Raleigh, etc. etc." She knew she was being manipulated. Interestingly, nothing in her journal or her letters indicates that she was at all accepting about being asked to defer to his position of priority. If anything, she appeared resentful that he might obstruct her path, now that it had opened to her.

Three days later, the *News and Observer* carried the announcement that Judge Allen Gwyn intended to run for the seat occupied by Justice Valentine. Gwyn wrote to Governor Scott to explain his decision. "I wish to say that [I] have not been prompted by any vindictive motives or by the feeling that I have been denied anything I had a right to expect. I have not requested of you that you favor me with any appointment." Noting that he had just turned fifty-eight, Gwyn said, "If I am to reach the goal which I have set years ago, I must fight now or turn from the course I have cherished so long."[19]

In reply, he received a lukewarm letter from the governor, saying that he had "noticed the other day that you had decided to enter the race for a place on the Supreme Court." The governor continued, "I certainly will not do you any harm and it is questionable how much I could do for you. Naturally, I have been interested in you all along because you were one of the few in your profession who was for me."[20] If it had not been apparent before, Gwyn saw that he could not count on Scott to further his long-nurtured ambition.

As for Susie Sharp, when she told John Kesler of Gwyn's plans, "It made him mad as fire," she wrote, "as I knew it would."[21] She said to John, "Daddy despises Allen Gwyn," and John replied, "I knew I liked your daddy."[22] Susie Sharp herself was clearly unhappy about the turn of events, however predictable they might have been. The day after this conversation with John, she noted in her journal, "Fiasco Sat[urday] aft[ernoon] with Allen; I can't come across."[23] If she was angry or resentful, however, she did not go so far as to break off their relationship. The situation continued to smolder over the next month or so, with John declaring that Judge Gwyn was "increasingly vain and ambitious."[24] Meanwhile, Gwyn fretted and even summoned her to his office to tell her that she should go ahead, that he "would rather see me on the S[upreme] Ct. than to get there himself."[25]

In any event, Judge Gwyn proceeded with his candidacy, formally announcing in January 1952. Shortly thereafter, Judge Sharp received some national attention when she was featured in the February 1952 issue of the *Ladies' Home Journal*, along with twelve other prominent women in politics, including Connecticut's secretary of state, a state senator from Rhode Island, a mayor from Virginia, and state representatives from Ohio, Oregon, and Massachusetts. Judge Sharp was quoted as remarking that the public expected a woman judge to be "'fashion plate, legal encyclopedia and after-dinner speaker' all in one." Her renown had vaulted beyond that of Judge Gwyn, and although she surely took the magazine's notice with a grain of salt, she was well aware of her growing public visibility.

The 1952 supreme court race was exceptional. In the first place, it was rare for Democrats to oppose each other for a seat on the court. The normal pattern was for the governor to appoint someone to serve the unexpired term of a justice who retired or died in office. At the next election the incumbent then ran unopposed or with only token opposition from the Republicans. Justice Valentine, however, appointed by Governor Scott to fill the new vacancy, was considered vulnerable. So discredited were the majority of Scott appointees that Valentine took his post without the normal assurance of longevity in office. His seat attracted five prominent members of the legal profession seeking to oust him. The candidates included four superior court judges: Judge R. Hunt Parker of Roanoke Rapids, Judge F. Donald Phillips of Rockingham, Judge William H. Bobbitt of Charlotte, and Judge Allen H. Gwyn of Reidsville. A Winston-Salem lawyer, Oscar O. Efird, also entered the race.

Judge Parker, in the twenty years since his appointment in 1932 as the state's youngest superior court judge, had presided over some of the most widely publicized trials in the state. A graduate of the University of Virginia, a former member of the General Assembly, and a former district solicitor, he had focused his entire life on attaining a seat on the North Carolina Supreme Court. Judge Bobbitt, a University of North Carolina graduate, had practiced law in Charlotte for seventeen years before he was appointed to the trial court bench, where he had earned a solid reputation. He was widely thought to be just as determined as Judge Parker to become a justice of the supreme court. Judge Phillips's background was also distinguished and quite cosmopolitan. After graduating from the University of Georgia, he took his law degree from the University of North Carolina. He served as district solicitor and as judge of Richmond County court, a position he resigned to serve in World War I, seeing action in France as an infantry lieutenant. He was appointed to the superior court bench in 1934. After World War II he went to Germany to serve as a war tribunal judge. Oscar Efird, the only candidate who had not been a solicitor or superior court judge (although he had been a judge of the Forsyth County recorder's court for fourteen years), had studied at Princeton, UNC, and Harvard. This was the second time he had run for a seat on the supreme court.[26]

Allen Gwyn certainly had the stature and the desire to compete in this field of contenders. He threw himself into as much of a campaign as he could manage while doing his job as a sitting superior court judge. In addition to his own efforts, he promoted his candidacy "with the help of his wife and a map," as the *News and Observer* noted.[27] Taking up her husband's cause, Janie Gwyn toured the state distributing campaign literature and stirring up support. The map in question showed North Carolina divided into three regions, with three of the seven supreme court justices coming from the eastern part of the state and three from the western part. Without mentioning Justice Valentine, Gwyn argued that as a citizen of Reidsville he was the logical choice for the seventh seat, to represent the populous central or Piedmont section. He hoped to capitalize on the regionalism deeply rooted in state politics, a legacy dating from colonial days when the seats of power were in the eastern part of the state, later to come under pressure as the population increased in the west.

It was a race that no one seemed able to decipher or analyze. Contrary to common assumptions, Justice Valentine's status as a Kerr Scott appointee seemed to matter less in such a crowded field than local friendships and loyalties. There was little interference from the several factions of the statewide Democratic Party, with each candidate relying heavily on strong support from his own district. Judge Sharp was privy to countless speculative conversations and reported—selectively—on what she picked up in her peregrinations across the state not only to Judge Gwyn but also to Breck and John. In Charlotte, where there was a lot of support for Bobbitt, who had lived there most of his life, she was in close touch with her old classmate Cicero Lobdell. He was the current vice president of the local bar and was "leading the hoopla for Judge Bobbitt."[28] Susie Sharp wrote Breck that Gwyn had called her "long distance" and wanted her to "keep him posted on the Charlotte situation as well as to have me make strategic suggestions that Judge B. ought not to run for this and that good reason. Well, it was too late." In an aside that would be even more amusing some years in the future, she remarked about Judge Bobbitt, "I was amazed to learn in his announcement that he was born in 1900. He has looked middle-aged ever since I first saw him."[29]

John Kesler was adamant that Susie Sharp must not campaign for Judge Gwyn, but he acknowledged that his motives were mixed. "He says I talked about him so much and that all my experiences in the last 20 years have included him and that he may be jealous," she noted in her journal.[30]

She did not campaign for Gwyn, but a week or so after the conversation with John, she donated $100 to his campaign fund. She continued to provide the judge with snippets of political news, courtroom anecdotes, and collegial inquiries on issues of law. In a chatty and friendly letter dated April 22, 1952, for example, she reported that Judge Bobbitt's term of court had been canceled, "so it looks as if he has two weeks off in which to politick!" She enclosed two clippings from the Charlotte newspapers in which she thought Gwyn would be interested and reported that the previous week had been "full of political activity," with Mr. Efird and all four candidates for governor in town.[31] She would be glad when the campaign was over, she said, and "law becomes important once more." Soliciting his advice on courtroom matters, she said, "I have a list of questions to discuss with you. For instance, I want to know how long a man can be kept in jail for contempt for failing to pay alimony." She had had a case in Charlotte in which a man deliberately refused to pay, spending his money for other things. Incarcerated, he was unable to pay. "Nobody would pay for him and it looked as if he had a life sentence!"

she wrote. "That was entirely satisfactory with his wife and his wife's lawyer . . . What would you have done with it?"

Nothing in her tone indicated that she harbored any animosities toward Gwyn or suggested that he need worry about her friendship and support. "Mrs. Waddell, the court reporter here this week, tells me that you captured Brevard," she ended. "I hope all goes well with you."

In addition to the unusual and unusually large field, the supreme court race was complicated by other major elections that year on both the state and national levels. William B. Umstead was running against Hubert E. Olive for the Democratic nomination for governor, two old warhorses, each with solid backgrounds in public life. Meanwhile, Adlai Stevenson and Dwight D. Eisenhower would be the Democratic and Republican candidates for president, respectively. With so much action on so many political fronts, it was no wonder that neither the pundits nor the public had a particularly good grasp of the race for a seat on the North Carolina Supreme Court. When Hunt Parker was the victor in the second Democratic primary on May 31, 1952, unseating Justice Valentine, a prevalent theory held that the voters had confused his name with that of a better-known judicial figure, John J. Parker, who as chief judge of the U.S. Fourth Circuit Court of Appeals had been nominated and defeated for a seat on the U.S. Supreme Court more than twenty years before.[32]

Susie Sharp wrote Judge Gwyn a letter of consolation notable for its careful hypocrisy. Dated June 2, 1952, the letter begins with her apology for missing him when she tried to find him at home to express her "amazement and consternation" at his loss, but immediately goes on to point out, "The only good thing about it is that the 21st [judicial district] will not lose you," and to remind him that he once told her that "a Superior Court judgeship offered the greatest opportunity to serve, to do good, there is in the state. So perhaps the plan was to keep you in the greatest field." Try as she might, she could not sound too downhearted: "I know just how you are feeling about now—just exactly like there had been a death in the family, but remember this: We can only feel intensely bad for just so long. (That was certainly a merciful plan!) Therefore, since you know that in time you will feel better in spite of all you can do, why not skip the waiting period and feel better now?"[33]

But Judge Gwyn was not yet in the frame of mind to see the bright side, nor was Miss Janie. As Susie Sharp wrote to the Breckenridges, "They blame Judge Bobbitt for his defeat and are very, very bitter about it all. They resent the local bar's endorsement of Bobbitt in the 2nd primary," which, she added in a stunning revelation, "I suppose they will find out sooner or later if they don't already know, was stirred up by the undersigned."[34]

One scarcely knows what to make of this. Had her irritation with Gwyn simply seeped into an irresistible impulse to poison his effort? Did she genuinely feel that Bobbitt was the better candidate? Without documentary evidence, her motives are obscure. Although it was clearly a betrayal, it did not seem to offer her anything in return, particularly because she seemed to feel that Gwyn would eventually learn of it. It may have been an attempt, conscious or otherwise, to sever her ties with Gwyn altogether.

There is no evidence, however, that Judge Gwyn ever learned of this perfidy. Certainly there is no hint of rancor in the letter he wrote in September 1952 to William B. Umstead, congratulating him on his selection as the Democratic gubernatorial nominee and taking the occasion to urge Judge Sharp's reappointment when — as was certain — Umstead became governor. "[I]n my opinion Judge Sharp is doing a fine job," he wrote. "The better lawyers of the State who first had doubts are now commending her and her work. She has a fine legal mind. She is a hard worker. She looks after the business of the court with meticulous care. . . . I believe the people of the State would be greatly disappointed if she were not continued in office."[35]

Judge Gwyn continued to champion his protégée, writing again on May 4, 1953, to the governor recommending her reappointment. His lengthy and earnest letter praised her record and pointed out her broad support among women voters. "If Judge Sharp were not continued in office, I believe the women of the State would consider it a 'slap in the face' and their disappointment would be great indeed." He described her as "one of the best politicians I know . . . because her interest grows out of a sense of personal responsibility for good government." He lauded her for having convictions and the courage to follow them, pointing out that, when Umstead was running for senator, Susie Sharp had broken with her family, which supported Melville Broughton, and had declared her support for Umstead. "Her entire family later became your ardent supporters," Gwyn wrote.[36]

Gwyn's enthusiasm, although undoubtedly sincere, may have been stimulated by Susie Sharp's waning interest in their personal relationship. By spring of 1953, she could not sustain her physical involvement with Judge Gwyn any longer. Her journal is replete with references to phone calls from the judge asking her to meet him and her ever more frequent response: "I do not go." Finally, on May 23, 1953, she recorded, "A. G. calls and I go to the office to meet him. I tell him it is all over and he is sweet and says good bye. I tremble and almost break down." Her relief was palpable. But she was careful thereafter not to rupture their professional relationship, which continued as before.

Interestingly, Allen Gwyn was the only one of Susie Sharp's lovers who truly wished her to reach the heights of her profession, even though he was the only one whose ambitions directly clashed with hers. In this he was most like her father, to whom he stood a close second in his hopes for her. Both Breck and John were conflicted about her career, particularly after she went on the bench. Breck, who, like Allen Gwyn, was older and established in his profession when Susie Sharp met him, was a willing mentor but sometimes expressed jealousy of her professional commitment and accomplishment. John, who fashioned a very respectable but nonetheless ordinary career as a small-town lawyer and occasional legislator, was in every way Susie Sharp's professional inferior. Her evident ability and ambition were possibly the primary reason for his apparent rejection of her when he left law school and went to set up his practice in Salisbury, just before the Great Depression complicated plans of all sorts. If she never seemed to feel it mattered that he was not her equal, and she certainly never intimated such a thing to John, it is clear that he felt the gap in their standing. Susie Sharp eventually would eclipse virtually every lawyer and judge in the state, but her heart belonged to the least distinguished of her admirers.

In due course, on July 30, 1953, Governor Umstead reappointed Judge Sharp for another two-year term. Whatever flurry of excitement had been generated by all the talk about the supreme court, she began to settle in earnest into the role of a superior court judge. Indeed, she had reason to focus on whatever aspects of her career were the most reliable and predictable rather than to take risks in swirling political waters. Although by this time she had weathered a great deal both professionally and personally, she was still struggling to absorb one of the gravest blows of her life — the death of her father in August 1952.

Jim Sharp had not been well, of course, for several years. After Susie Sharp was appointed to the bench, he hired a young lawyer named Norwood E. Robinson to help him with the practice and broke him in fast. In fact, Mr. Sharp had the recent law school graduate arguing to the jury before he even had a law license. The way it happened revealed a great deal about Mr. Jim.

The summer of Susie Sharp's appointment young Robinson had come looking for a job in the Piedmont, which was economically less depressed than his native region of eastern North Carolina. Hamp Price, the prominent Rockingham County lawyer and politician, suggested he go to see Jim Sharp.

"He needs someone," Price told the young man. "His health is bad and he can't handle his business. If he doesn't get someone, he's going to have a problem."[37] After a satisfactory interview, Robinson returned to his home in Washington, North Carolina. Not hearing anything further from Mr. Sharp, however, he decided to open a practice in the northern part of Rockingham County. In the course of making his arrangements, he came to Reidsville to buy furniture and stopped by the offices of Sharp & Sharp to let Mr. Sharp know his plans. As he walked in the door, the secretary cried, "Where in the world have you been?" "Why, I've been in Washington," he replied. "Well, Mr. Sharp has been very disappointed," she told him. "He called the law school and he inquired about you and wrote a letter to you that very day for you to come up. He was very disappointed. He thought maybe you didn't want to practice law." "No, I didn't get a letter," said Robinson in surprise. "Wait a minute. I bet I know what I did," the secretary said. She pulled her letter from her files and saw that in fact she had sent it to Washington, D.C., rather than to "Little Washington" in North Carolina.

That was on a Wednesday. Mr. Sharp had a civil case to try the following day and told Robinson to come down to the office that night to listen to him talk to the witnesses. "You will sit in the courtroom with me tomorrow," Mr. Sharp told him, even though the recent graduate had yet to be sworn in as a member of the bar. As Robinson recalled it, he went and sat at the counsel table, "all eyes and ears." On the other side were Hamp Price and his equally well-known partner, Floyd Osborne. At the close of evidence, the judge ascertained that both Mr. Price and Mr. Osborne would have closing arguments and inquired of Mr. Sharp how many his side would have. "Two," said Mr. Sharp. And Robinson found himself on his feet in front of the jury.

It was quintessential Jim Sharp. He had the utmost confidence in himself, and if he had selected this young man to come into practice with him, then that young man was ipso facto capable of anything he might be asked to do. Undoubtedly, it was this attitude that had invested Susie Sharp with the confidence to take on challenges most young men, let alone most young women, would not have considered.

Judge Sharp herself swore Robinson in, in September 1949, just two months after her appointment. As her father reported to Mrs. Sharp, who was then visiting their daughter Sallie and her family in Missouri, the young man was now "armed to practice."[38] That first year was an intensive introduction, in which Robinson tried what were, at least to him, some very complicated cases. Mr. Sharp did everything he could to push him out in front, to expose him as much as possible. Robinson would later say that in the three years he practiced with Mr. Sharp he got the same amount of trial experience it would take many lawyers starting out on their own ten or fifteen years to acquire.

Judge Sharp was thankful that the young man was able to take up so much so quickly. She still did not know if she would remain on the bench, but it was important to keep the practice going whether or not she returned. After about a year, Mr. Sharp brought Robinson into a fifty-fifty partnership, with the understanding that she could always come back into the practice. Meanwhile, she could endure the grueling life of a traveling trial court judge more easily, knowing that her father had some much-needed help. For his part, her father followed her career closely, watching the papers for news of her court sessions and monitoring her record of reversals by the state supreme court. Needless to say, it upset him when, as is the lot of any judge, she got reversed. Judge Sharp said, "[H]e would fuss at me just as he used to when I was a child and had done something really stupid. But I understood, of course, that it was only his way of expressing his chagrin that I had made a poor showing."[39]

In May 1950 Mr. Sharp had a very bad spell. His blood pressure hit 300. He got numb, his face was drawn, and he lost motion in one side. "But it was only temporary, thank God," Susie Sharp wrote to Breck. He was not paralyzed. Fred Klenner, his doctor, told him to stay in bed until his blood pressure stabilized, but, she wrote, "as a result of the election excitement it's been 200 the past two days. Fred let him go vote yesterday on the theory he'd have a stroke if he didn't."[40]

The election of which she spoke was the first primary in the infamous race between Frank Porter Graham and Willis Smith for the U.S. Senate, and the Sharps were strong supporters of "Dr. Frank." That election raised blood pressure all over North Carolina. Graham missed winning an outright majority in the first primary by one percentage point, which entitled Smith to call for a runoff. A young news director at WRAL radio in Raleigh named Jesse Helms orchestrated a rally to encourage Smith not to give up. Judge Sharp said that the very thought of the runoff, in which she saw Graham's prospects as dismal, gave her "spastic indigestion." The campaign proved to be a watershed in the state's politics and is still considered perhaps the most vicious in North Carolina history. Dr. Graham's liberal sentiments left him vulnerable to race-baiting and to attacks for membership in "Communist front groups." His loss to Willis Smith shattered North Carolina's image as a state in which progressivism and tolerance were watchwords.

Although Mr. Sharp survived to cast his vote, Frank Graham's defeat could not have improved his condition. His health worsened steadily. At one point, perhaps feeling the breath of Time on his neck, he "suddenly could not wait one day longer to know how much income tax he had to pay." Knowing that it would compel her attention, he threatened to file his own return that week if Susie Sharp did not stop everything and do it for him. "In as much as he has never filed a return in his life and I do not want him to spend his declining years in Atlanta, that got me—as he well knew it would," she said. "So, for the past two days, I have done nothing but attempt to find a way thru the maze of his activities, especially farming. It was an opus magnus, I assure you."[41] (In truth, Mr. Jim's taxes were probably simple compared to others for which Susie Sharp took responsibility. One of his brothers, a farmer in Caswell County, came by to discuss his return. His reply to her inquiry as to how much he had spent on supplies was, "Whoo-ee! Just a WHOLE lot; I don't know HOW much!")[42]

In the summer of 1952, Mr. Sharp began to fail drastically. The July heat seemed to wilt him, and his prolonged high blood pressure was causing small hemorrhages in his retina. His eyesight was going. The specialist he consulted in Durham told him that there was nothing to be done and that total blindness might eventually result. Susie Sharp feared the worst. She wrote the Breckenridges, "He and Mamma will have been married 46 years tomorrow. Mon[day] he told me to get her an anniversary present for him to give her; that he had forgotten it *last* year and he wanted to be prepared this year. So far as I know he never remembered the date before in his life and I'm afraid it's a bad sign."[43]

Susie Sharp did as he had asked but "it upset mamma a lot more than if she hadn't got it. She *knows* it's a bad sign and says it's the first one he ever gave her."[44]

Meanwhile, matters were going from bad to worse out on the farmland Mr. Sharp had tended so lovingly. "His Negro farm tenants have just about stopped work since they learned that he can no longer check up on them," Susie Sharp wrote to John. "I suppose the crop will ruin. My brother went out there yesterday and found the truck had been left outside the shed. Its bed was full of water, the battery dead, the tires down. . . . I begin to realize that I should have taken greater interest in his farms all these years. I do not even know how to sell tobacco—in the unlikely event there is any to sell!"[45]

By the middle of July, Mr. Sharp was unable to walk and, worst of all, had "lost the optimism which has always been his stock in trade."[46] Dr. Klenner remained hopeful and said it was just a "spell," but Susie Sharp was not convinced. "He has heretofore avoided all mention of death and has taken the attitude that if he ignored his condition it would not trip him up. Today, however, he told me where his will was, what insurance he had, etc."[47] Despite being too weak to walk, he remained as alert as ever mentally. There were things she ought to know about his business, he told her. She took two pages of notes on the resulting conversation "which we both managed to keep matter-of-fact."[48] But she found it difficult to be upbeat. "In many respects I'm just a case of arrested development," she told John.[49]

James Merritt Sharp died on August 8, 1952, at the age of seventy-four.

For the family, and for Judge Sharp in particular, the notice that Mr. Sharp's passing received was gratifying. They were moved to hear him referred to as the dean of the local bar. The newspapers ran lengthy obituaries, and a generous editorial appeared in the *Reidsville Review* highlighting his work as a tireless advocate for the farmer among his other civic activities. As a final mark of respect, the route of the funeral cortège to Greenview Cemetery was lined by local police officers and members of the highway patrol who saluted as the hearse passed by.[50]

Norwood Robinson beseeched Judge Sharp to "quit the road" and rejoin the law practice, arguing that they would both make more money.[51] But the financial considerations were not sufficient to convince her to give up the bench. Her reappointment by Governor Umstead scarcely a month before meant that she had nearly two years remaining in her current term as special judge. And within a few weeks, her mother rented a room to the high school math teacher, which eased her mind about being away from home.

She was intent on grinding forward, although she was far from her best during the months following Jim Sharp's death. In addition to the emotional toll of losing the father to whom—she felt—she owed everything she had achieved, she had to consider the loss of income from his law practice, however diminished it had become, on which her mother depended. There were matters like tenant farmers and taxes to be dealt with, not to mention the needs of her brothers and sisters and their families, all of whom now looked to her even more than ever for guidance. The entire weight of responsibility for the family that her father had borne, although she had gradually assumed a great deal of it, now fell squarely on her.

It all took a toll. Constantly tired and often weepy, she herself described her state during the autumn following her father's death as "emotionally unstable."[52] A session with the artist who would paint the portrait of Mr. Sharp that would hang in the Rockingham County courthouse was particularly upsetting, even though she believed that "the portrait is the one thing which Daddy would appreciate more than anything else I can do for him now."[53]

Her run-down condition reached the point that when Breck ("who has never thought this job in my best interest, and who is always happy to blame everything on it") remarked that her looks were suffering, she was not up to her usual standard of banter with him.[54] "Part of the trouble was that he wanted to argue about politics. He is voting for Eisenhower," she reported.

Judge Sharp was an ardent supporter of Adlai Stevenson, whom she found "almost too good to be true."[55] Four months before, she had been "a disillusioned and despondent Democrat" but had become more enthusiastic about Stevenson with every speech he gave. "Today, while I'm still convinced we need a change and that there is a mess in Washington, I'm charmed enough by the Dem. standard bearer to believe he's the change we need," she declared.[56] But in her current state she did not have the energy to argue with Breck. "Arguing with B is ordinarily one of my great pleasures, but . . . I declined their invitation to supper and went straight to where I was staying. When I got there I went to bed without any supper and cried myself to sleep."[57]

Despite her grief and the complicated nature of her life, however, she coped through sheer force of will. "One foot up and one foot down, That's the way to London Town," was a mantra she often recited to herself and to others. Still, the family was not finished with grief. Little more than a year later, Judge Sharp had to abandon her courtroom on short notice yet again.

She was in the mountains on the Tennessee border presiding over a first-degree murder trial in Marshall, the county seat of Madison County, infamous for its Republican majority and political shenanigans. There she received a telephone call from the rector of her sister Sallie's church in Poplar Bluff, Missouri, where she had been living with her husband and two sons. The rector had tracked down Judge Sharp despite endless obstacles rather than call Mrs. Sharp. Sallie was dead, he said.[58] At the age of forty-one, she had suffered an attack diagnosed as gall bladder trouble. The doctor's treatment had apparently overburdened an already overburdened heart.[59] It was up to Judge Sharp to call home and break the news. Before returning home, she reconvened court at seven o'clock that evening to declare a mistrial. Despite many offers to drive her back to Reidsville, she insisted that she preferred to do it alone. She set out at eight o'clock to drive across the mountains and reached home at two in the morning.

She struggled to control her feelings, believing that "uncontrolled grief is very, very selfish." She wrote, "I did my best to get rid of mine on the ride from Marshall Wed. night when I was alone."[60] She had a strong role model in her mother. "So far as I know she broke down only when the casket came in Sat. noon. She said to me that we had to be schooled in sorrow just as we had to be in arithmetic and geography. She has learned lessons and has a strength of character which not many people have."[61]

The Monday following Sallie's burial in Reidsville, Judge Sharp was back on the bench, holding court in Greensboro. The initial novelty of her appointment had subsided, and her apprenticeship was over. She was beginning to hit her stride.

CHAPTER **10**

THEORY AND PRACTICE

Almost five years passed before Judge Sharp was assigned to hold court in her home county, a hiatus designed to put some distance between the new judge and her former colleagues in the local bar. Even so, old friends found it difficult to substitute "Your Honor" for "Susie."[1] Judge Sharp herself was acutely conscious of presiding over the Wentworth courtroom in which she had practiced law for twenty years. About the prospect of holding court at home, she had remarked shortly after going on the bench, "I hope that I will be spared this ordeal for some time to come, as life's worst moment will be when I have to try a case with my father on one side and his lifelong rival on the other."[2] Her father's death, of course, did spare her that experience, but there were plenty of former colleagues among whom she would have to allocate justice.

The judge wore a black dress with touches of red for the first day, opening the March 1954 criminal term of superior court for Rockingham County "without fanfare or ceremony."[3] She looked at the portrait of her father hanging just behind the judge's bench, swept the familiar courtroom with her glance, then picked up her gavel to commence the business of the day.[4] She did not get far, however, before she had to rectify an uncomfortable situation. The judge's bench had been designed for a "rangier jurist" and Judge Sharp, at barely 5′2″, found that her feet did not reach the floor. Ever practical, she asked Deputy Bernard Young, an old friend, to find her a box on which to rest her feet. In good time he would construct a small platform precisely calibrated to her height, a "foot box" that she used thenceforth whenever she was presiding in Rockingham County.[5]

She would return to Wentworth from time to time during her years on the superior court, almost always complaining to her journal about those—lawyers and litigants alike—who hoped to trade upon long familiarity or, in the case of certain defendants (some of whom she herself had represented), who hoped she had forgotten their colorful histories. Norwood Robinson remembered one of his clients who "tuned up and started crying" in court. Judge Sharp put one hand over her eyes and crooked her finger to beckon Robinson with the other. When he approached the bench, she asked, "Norwood, did you tell him to cry?" He denied any such thing. "Are you sure?" she insisted. "You know I can't stand to see a man cry."[6]

After one especially trying stint, the judge wrote to John Kesler, "The last week of the term at home ended this afternoon at 3 o'clock, and I repaired immediately to the beauty parlor to 'wash those men right out of my hair.'"[7] Adjudicating among her former colleagues always added a layer of interest if not stress to her sojourns in Rockingham County, but she took it in stride, as she did everything else.

Statewide, the public continued to pay special attention to her career. The idea of a woman wielding the ultimate authority in a workplace, let alone a courtroom, was still so novel in the mid-1950s that one reporter told her he had heard there was a Judge Susie Sharp, but he thought it was a man by that name and was very surprised to see a woman.[8] In 1955 a Greensboro reporter devoted an extensive article to the question, "When Judge Susie Sharp Presides, How Do Lawyers, Jurors React?"[9] He wanted to know how she was perceived by "the men who come under her authority at court—the lawyers, jurors, sheriffs, witnesses, defendants and even the gallery spectators." "[D]oes it boost the female ego of Judge Sharp to have power over [men]," he inquired, "knowing as she undoubtedly does that most men feel superior to women?"

At this point, she had held court in 46 of the state's 100 counties and had earned a solid reputation. As the reporter acknowledged, she had "handled a vast miscellanea of cases from murder to rape" and had sentenced one man to the electric chair. "Decisions like this and others were big ones to make for a member of a species which is supposed to jump up on a chair and scream when a small mouse is seen," he pointed out. She had many admirers outside the courtroom. But, he asked, "[H]ow about Tom Bowie, the fiery little lawyer from West Jefferson? When he gets wound up on one of his rip-snorting orations in which he often quotes poetry by Robert Burns to impress the jury, how does he feel to be called down by a lady judge and told to cut the dramatics and get down to facts? How did janitor Tommy Roark feel when the lady judge complained about the cold court room and he had to get up at 4 a.m. to start fires in the court room's two pot-bellied stoves so the room would be warm by 9 a.m.?"

It turned out that, for publication at least, attorney Bowie had nothing but praise for Judge Sharp, and janitor Roark just laughed and said, "I never minded getting up to make those fires. The judge is a nice lady." One juror remarked that women bosses did not bother him: "You get it from them at home; might as well get it away from home."

Judge Sharp herself would have been grateful if her gender had not provoked such articles, but she made the best of it. It was inevitable that when she arrived to hold court, the local newspaper reported not only on the proceedings in the courtroom but also on the lady judge herself, usually sending around a feature reporter to do an interview. Typical was the account given by one reporter for the *Charlotte Observer*, who said, "She presides with dignity and poise. . . . She is an interviewer's delight. At the end of a long day on the bench, she was charming and gracious in manner, and most cooperative and un-hedgy in replying to questions. . . . [O]ne is immediately impressed with the feeling that she is sincere with no affectedness about her." Also typical was the attention given to the judge's appearance: "She was completely and smartly feminine in a kelly green suit with a glimpse of a frilly, crisp white blouse and a bit of green velvet ribbon and silver pin at her neck. Her shoes were green, too. Jeweled earrings contrasted with her utilitarian 'spectacles'—which she half wears and half holds."[10] Another writer noted, "There is nothing ordinary about her complexion. Her skin glows with the soft, unblemished tones of youth—of girls twice as young as she."[11] Yet another declared, "Sharp is an attractive woman with a reserve that borders on shyness. She is a bright conversationalist who likes to talk about her job."[12]

If she liked to talk about her job, at least part of the reason was that it provided her with so many wonderful anecdotes. Some of them she shared only with trusted correspondents like John or Breck, but others she retailed in her unremitting role as dinner speaker wherever she went. Often these stories portrayed the lady judge as more lady than judge, a self-deprecating image that went over well with her audiences, whether made up entirely of her male colleagues or complicated by the presence of their wives. A variant of her use of camouflage, this pattern did not change from her earliest days on the bench right through speeches she would give after nearly half a century in the legal profession, when she often tailored her talk to the local audience by recalling her adventures as a superior court judge in that particular venue.

One tale involved an instance, not uncommon, when she stayed late to work alone in the judge's chambers, long after the courthouse had emptied out for the day. She had been holding court in Lumberton, heartland of the Lumbee Indian tribe, where poverty and racial unease greatly afflicted the populace. Judge Sharp told a meeting of the Sheriffs' Association:

I was deep in the toils of the law about 6:30 when I heard a scratching on the office door. I looked up and realized that it was dark outside and there wasn't another sound in the building. I waited apprehensively as somebody slowly pushed open the door, and suddenly there stood before me the biggest Indian in Robeson County. If he'd had on war paint and feathers, he couldn't have looked any more formidable to me, for I recognized him as the defendant whom I had sentenced for nonsupport that very afternoon. I'd put him under a suspended sentence, but I'd really given him a good lecture, generously sprinkled with threats of jail if he didn't support his family. When I saw who it was, I said in as stern a voice as I could manage, "I'm very busy; what do you want?" He stood first on one foot, then the other, and finally quavered, "Little Missie, can I have 'til Saturday to pay my nonsupport?"[13]

Her habit of working alone in a deserted courthouse worried many a sheriff and clerk of court. It is unclear whether she shared with them the fact that she rarely went anywhere without her "protection," a handgun in her purse. It was not something she advertised and, in fact, on several occasions she did her best to deny it. "I'd be more afraid of the gun than I would the person. I've always relied on the sheriff," she would claim years later, after decades of packing a concealed weapon.[14] She was genuinely grateful for the protective attitude she inspired in her male co-workers. When she discovered, however, that there was at least one, a deputy sheriff in Charlotte, who refused to leave the building before she did, she felt so guilty for causing him extra work that she had to give up working in chambers after hours.[15]

Perhaps the toughest challenge to her femininity on the bench came in 1958, when the North Carolina Conference of Superior Court Judges (which Judge Sharp referred to privately as "the union") voted to adopt the wearing of judicial robes when presiding in the courtroom. State court judges in North Carolina had historically been reluctant to put on robes, and, indeed, until 1940, when the state's supreme court moved into the new Justice Building and adopted the wearing of robes, North Carolina was the only state in which the justices of the highest appellate court still wore regular clothes on the bench.[16] Until 1958 superior court judges still wore civilian garb, and Judge Sharp had been able to indulge her pleasure in dressing well. She had worked hard on her looks and had come a long way from the lumpy young student she once was. For decades she had guarded her beautiful complexion against the sun by carrying a parasol, and she paid close attention to her wardrobe.[17] At this point in her life, it could be said — and often was — that she was a very attractive woman. Considering the effort she had put into her transformation, it was little wonder she was reluctant to cover herself in voluminous black robes.

The edict went into effect on January 6, 1958, and she wrote to Albert Coates, "That shroud hanging in my closet has ruined my Christmas. To think that the *vanity of men* has brought me to this pass!" The robe was too short despite the addition of a supplementary three inches and made her look, she said, "exactly like an apple dumpling."[18] In early May she was still complaining. "Life has been much more complicated since we started wearing those things," she told an interviewer. "The sleeves, the shoulders and the backs are padded and hot, and the billowing sleeves get in the way when I'm writing. I always step on the thing when I start up to the bench."[19]

One of the primary advocates of the judicial robes was Superior Court Judge Will Pless Jr. Perhaps in response to Judge Sharp's remarks about the heat, he had, in his capacity as president of the "union," engaged a seamstress in his hometown of Marion, North Carolina, to run up cotton summer robes for the judges. Though Judge Sharp conceded that this was an improvement over the original, "it was still hot and looks so cheap."[20] Seeking further improvement, she found some lightweight China silk, boxed it up with her cotton robe, and mailed the package to the seamstress with instructions to copy the cotton robe in silk. When the silk robe was delivered to her, however, there was something different. The cotton robe fastened with three invisible hooks. But, as she related to John, "You can imagine my horrified surprise . . . when I discovered that [the seamstress] had put a yard-long *zipper* down the front which not only bulged but completely changed the neck line." Aghast, she demanded to know "how come." The seamstress said that Judge Pless "had decided that I would look better in a zipped-up robe and he had gone downtown and bought the zipper himself and brought it to her with instructions to put it in!"[21]

Surely this degree of sartorial interference was the last peril she had imagined when she took her oath as a member of the judiciary.

Judge Sharp continued to be in constant demand as a speaker before every sort of audience, from graduating classes to bar associations to an endless array of civic organizations. In addition to grand occasions, it was rare that she did not have to sing for her supper as many nights as not after the day's business was done in the courtroom. Often exhausted at the end of the day, she found it difficult to refuse, even if it meant she had to prepare for the next day in court after she returned to her lodgings for the night. If she chafed under this burden, however, she also used many such occasions as a bully pulpit for her concerns and deepest beliefs. Her career gave her a unique perspective on the issues confronting America in the post–World War II era. Her speeches, like her life, both reflected and challenged deeply held beliefs of the general public, particularly with respect to African Americans and women.

Democracy was her touchstone, the starting point for her reasoning on every issue, and the rule of law was the unalterable principle on which democracy depended. She had an evangelical zeal on these subjects and lost no opportunity to exhort an audience to shoulder their duties as citizens.

She had no patience with the argument that politics was unsavory. "To let politics become a cesspool and then avoid it because it is a cesspool is a double crime," she declared.[22] Nor did she find the epithet "party politics" pejorative, joking that a "partisan" was always someone belonging to the other party. Despite her own efforts to maintain the one-sided status quo in North Carolina, she defended the two-party system as essential to democracy.

She did not share the common distaste for politicians. "The politician is vastly different from the way he is commonly pictured," she told a gathering of Young Democrats, quoting from William S. White's *A Defense of Politicians*: "'The politician's business is leading people by persuasion; his daily necessity is somehow to average out the bitterly competing views and wishes of constituents, parties, business, and labor interests. . . . It is actually the politician who makes democracy work, and when we consider the numerous varied pressure groups which are constantly pulling at him it is a wonder that he does as well as he does.'"[23]

Despite her ardent idealism, her worship of the democratic process was never less than clear-eyed. She had been reared, after all, in the realpolitik of Rockingham County. Certainly no one had ever qualified as a more ardent partisan, a capital-D Democrat. In the Sharp household, the party was paramount. When her teenage nephew announced to Annie Sharp, for example, that he was a Republican, Susie Sharp wrote to John, "Next to a Leper or a Catholic nothing could be as black a blot on the family escutcheon in Mamma's opinion."[24]

Judge Sharp admitted to her share of zealous party activities, such as over-enthusiastic get-out-the-vote efforts. "The job of getting out the vote is, of course, one very important part of the work of the professional politician because clearly there is no substitute for a majority of ballots marked for you," she once explained. "Getting out the vote is always a partisan operation, and, in my time, I have bent every effort of which I was capable toward doing just that and I'm afraid I didn't care too much whether the voter knew why he was doing it if he voted the way I wanted him to."[25]

She heartily agreed with Edmund Burke's declaration, "The only thing necessary for the triumph of evil is for good men to do nothing." This statement, however, she would have enlarged to include both "men and women." In speech after speech to female audiences, she chided women for what she called their "spectator attitude" to public affairs. She trotted out statistics showing that women owned 75 percent of the country's corporate wealth, managed 85 percent of the family budgets, and formed 33 percent of the labor force.[26] Yet women continued to abstain from active participation in politics, including the basic act of showing up at the polls. Citing a Gallup report that, although there were 2 million more women than men of voting age, fewer women than men would vote in the upcoming 1952 elections, she lamented what she perceived as "irresponsible indifference to government."[27] Theoretically, she liked to point out, "it would be possible for women to elect the President, pack the legislatures, and pass laws against stag parties and moustaches."[28] Men, however, exhibited no signs whatever of being worried about a female takeover. "They continue to enact the laws," Judge Sharp said, "and every time they enact one it affects more women than men."[29]

During the 1950s it was popular to question the existence of the jury system, criticism that never failed to provoke Judge Sharp to comment. In the first place, she viewed the jury as an indispensable adjunct to democracy. The right to a trial by jury, she would point out, was not something found behind the Iron Curtain.[30] "Courts are a very important part of our government because the chief function of the court is to protect individual rights," she said in a 1955 speech to the UNC-G Alumnae Association.[31] Jury duty, like the duty to be an informed voter, was one of the sacred responsibilities of a good citizen.

Judge Sharp objected to the elimination of the jury on both philosophical and practical grounds. As a small-"d" democrat, she would always favor the people's participation over delegation of power to an individual. "[A]s long as juries find the facts, the fate of a citizen is in the hands of his fellow citizens who have the power of the court. If you give to the judge the power to find the facts, to pass on a man's guilt or innocence, you have concentrated very great power in the hands of one person."[32] She took it as a given that "concentrated power is always abused."[33] Because the jury system provided for a new jury at every term of court, power was not vested in a single person or group of persons. She also argued that resentment would inevitably build against a judge, no matter how wise and good, as he made decisions over time, until "eventually his usefulness would be destroyed."[34] But because the composition of a jury was always changing, resentment could not accumulate against it.[35] Judge Sharp also felt that the jury offered some protection against the fallibility of a single arbiter. "I'm convinced that the jury system is better than one in which a judge or a panel of judges decides the verdict. Juries make mistakes sometimes, but I don't believe as many as would be made by judges."[36]

Responding to a *New York Times* article advocating the abolition of the jury in the interest of efficiency, she demonstrated her understanding that sometimes process was more important than result: sometimes merely having one's day in court sufficed even in the case of defeat. "If by increased efficiency in court one means only the disposition of a greater number of cases then certainly a judge can try more cases in less time without a jury," she granted. "However, I say that to be efficient the court must not only dispose of cases but the litigants whose cases have been disposed of must feel that they have received a fair trial."[37] Efficiency, viewed in the context of democracy, could not be measured by numbers alone.

Her most interesting argument in favor of the jury system, however, revealed her understanding that "a court of law is not necessarily a court of justice."[38] In an expression of support for jury nullification, she told one interviewer, "A judge owes a stronger responsibility to the law than a jury does. Sometimes a case may be set in such circumstances that a jury may reason that 'I just don't care what the law says, this is not right.'" The judge might feel the same way, said Judge Sharp, but whereas the jury had the power to decide as it wished, the judge had an obligation "to abide by the law," despite the temptation of a more "just" justice.[39]

In her courtroom she delivered talks to the members of the assembled jury pool calculated to inspire them to fulfill their jury duty, or at least to shame them into stifling their prepared excuses. At the same time, she was both sympathetic and realistic when considering a potential juror's situation. When one woman begged to be allowed to go home because she could not remember if she had turned off the oven, Judge Sharp let her go, knowing that her mind would not be on the jury's business.[40] Another time, an older gentleman begged to be excused because, even with his hearing aid, he had difficulty understanding what was being said. He bolstered his argument by telling the judge, "Why, I am so handicapped I can not even hear my wife talk at the breakfast table." Judge Sharp may have been persuaded on the basis of sympathy due to her own hearing problems, but her witty response was: "Since you consider not being able to hear your wife a handicap, I'll excuse you from jury duty."[41]

Following passage of the amendment to the North Carolina Constitution permitting women to serve on juries, Judge Sharp had been deeply disappointed by the numbers of women who took advantage of the lenient exemptions that allowed them to be excused. Sparse indeed were the women who actually sat on a jury, and in some counties women jurors remained almost unknown well into the 1950s. Tirelessly, Judge Sharp encouraged women to accept their responsibilities, to become "mature citizens."[42]

Although she did not believe that "women's intuition" played a role in making a female juror more valuable than her male counterparts, Judge Sharp did believe — quite apart from her feminist convictions that women should serve — that women added a much-needed balance to the makeup of any jury. "Generally speaking women make very conscientious jurors and I am convinced that their presence on a jury materially improves the administration of justice. The varied experiences and view points of men and women, when combined in the jury room and brought to bear on a case, are more apt to result in a just verdict than if the jury were either all men or all women."[43] She liked to tell the story of the women jurors who pointed out to the male members of the jury that the claim of a woman suing for a severe back injury was undercut by her high heels with ankle straps.[44]

It was a constant torment to her that women held less than 1 percent of all elective and appointive offices in the country. In 1950 no woman had won a statewide election in North Carolina.[45] Judge Sharp laid the blame largely on women themselves. The female "spectator attitude" may have kept dainty feet out of the mud, but it also kept women out of positions of influence. Besides, she noted, keeping your feet clean was not the way to improve matters. "[W]omen are fearful because they believe politics to be crooked, dirty, a double-crossing game. But dirt seems to follow people around and it will linger where they have been — unless perhaps we can get some good scrub women on the job and keep them there! Can you imagine a good housewife refusing to wash the dinner dishes because they are dirty?"[46]

The stubborn fact was that women had thus far proved they were unwilling to pay the price of active participation in politics and therefore they remained insignificant in their influence. "Chivalry is not dead," Judge Sharp noted, "but a politician who has fought, bled and died to get himself elected to office is not going to hand out appointments to any person, man or woman, who has not, in his opinion, earned his patronage."[47] If women refused to get into politics, they would continue to receive nothing more than "superficial amenities" from the politicians.[48]

Finally, however, the intractable problem of woman's primary role as wife and mother could not be made to vanish with rhetoric. Even with the emergence decades later of the modern husband willing to share some of the household and childcare tasks, the vast majority of working women did not escape their full-time jobs at home or the particular concerns of motherhood. The indomitable Judge Sharp herself believed that a woman's domestic responsibilities would always erode her ability to participate on a wider stage. On at least one highly public occasion, her 1949 address to the Georgia Association of Women Lawyers in Atlanta soon after her appointment to the bench, she declared that she was not one of those who thought a woman could do it all. "I used to think that it was just as possible for a woman to have a home and children and a career as for a man. Now, unless she is surrounded by unusually favorable circumstances, I do not think she should essay both in the absence of a compelling necessity."

Judge Sharp would be distressed when quoted in newspapers as having said in essence that a married woman belonged at home, that a woman could not be a wife, mother, and career woman without sacrificing too much in each role. But she did say it more than once, and it would remain a firmly held belief. As for the future of women in public life, she said, "I think it comes down to this. Women will always be a minority in public affairs but they should not continue to be the microscopic, less-than-1% minority they are today. That figure is unjustifiable and inexcusable."[49]

For those women who did find that there was a role for them in the professions or in public affairs, Judge Sharp was a tireless cheerleader. She was all too familiar with the burden on the shoulders of the trailblazers. As she told the women lawyers in Atlanta, "It seems to me that as of the date I took office I ceased to belong to myself, but—in some esoteric fashion which I do not understand—I now belong to 'The Women.' . . . [T]he obsession that I may slander my sex haunts my days and mars my nights."[50] It was not a new feeling for her. Ever since her first day in law school when she discovered that she was the lone woman in her class, she declared, "this fear has been with me."[51] She frequently reminded her listeners that "if a man makes a foolish mistake other men say, 'What a fool that man is.' If a woman makes one, they say, 'What fools women are.'"

Judge Sharp believed that a woman could and should do any job a man did, with obvious exceptions requiring physical strength beyond her capabilities. "Work has no sex," she repeatedly declared. "A trained legal mind has no sex." A successful woman lawyer would represent both men and women clients who hired her because she was a lawyer, not because she was a woman.[52] "The idea of any segregation or classification on account of sex in the professions, government, or business is fundamentally wrong."[53] In her 1949 address to the Georgia Association of Women Lawyers, she said, "It will be a happy day when there is no need for a woman's bar association as a professional organization."[54] For example, "You would not think of joining a woman's little theater group. If there is a play to be produced, the director has to have both men and women because a play attempts to portray a bit of life."[55] In her view, "The proper concept of feminism is not a sex war but mutual cooperation between men and women; no favors asked and no disqualification on account of sex."[56]

But if she insisted on women's right and responsibility to participate in virtually all aspects of life, she did not wish to be considered an unreasonable zealot. In all sincerity she hastened to assure her audience, "I am not, of course, suggesting that the Lions, Elks, Kiwanis or Rotarians become co-educational. These are not the sort of sororities and fraternities I am campaigning against. We girls will always want to get together so that we can let down our hair and be sure of a sympathetic audience when we say, 'just like a man.'"[57]

Indeed, although she wanted women to compete with men in the real world, she was careful to deny that this would entail women trying to act like men, whatever that might mean. In a speech at a woman's college, she advised the young women, "You should never try to be like anybody but yourself. . . . Be yourself with everybody—including your young man—and take the consequences. They will not be nearly as dire as those which flow from a misrepresentation. . . . So, develop all the feminine charm you can and use it."[58]

If her positions on women were at times far in advance of the general populace, she nonetheless exuded an air of common sense that, coupled with her demonstrated abilities and her ease with colleagues and public alike, softened her leading edge and made her views easier to accept than they might have been if accompanied by a more abrasive personality. Both men and women admired the starch in her backbone, without fear that her stance on the "woman thing" would cause undue problems in their less rarified lives.

Along with the postwar era of progress for women, Judge Sharp's years on the superior court overlapped with the nascent civil rights movement. She did not, however, draw useful parallels between the two. Despite her conviction that both the principles of justice and enlightened self-interest mandated fair treatment for black Americans, she never overcame her racism on a visceral level, remaining a prisoner of her upbringing.

Her views did not change much if at all from those in a speech she gave on race relations in 1948.[59] In this speech, she acknowledged that "[r]ace prejudice is bad because all prejudice is bad." At the kernel of her belief was the view that "it is one thing to have a feeling and it is quite a different thing to allow it to have full sway over one's conduct. We don't have to like a person to give him justice; it's harder to do but it can be done." Even as her aversion and outrage were amplified by what she perceived as indefensible tactics of the civil rights movement, she would not allow this kernel to be destroyed. Neither, however, did she allow it to grow and blossom. Her acceptance of black aspiration was an inescapable conclusion stemming entirely from her intellectual honesty.

She was willing to admit that the foundation of her prejudice had to do with the specter of racial intermarriage. "It is, of course, fear of the fusion of the races which has prompted our segregation laws." At the time of her 1948 speech, the North Carolina Constitution prohibited the marriage of whites and blacks "or persons of Negro descent to the third generation." Statutory law made such intermarriage a felony punishable by as much as ten years in the penitentiary. This policy met with Judge Sharp's complete approval. Paraphrasing Booker T. Washington, she advocated "the continuance of the white and colored races in the U.S. as 'separate as the fingers yet as united as the hand.'"[60] To those who criticized this goal as unrealistic, she cited "the success of the Jews and Gypsies in maintaining racial integrity in many lands" and asserted that "Democracy does not demand fusion of the races any more than it demands the fusion of religions."

Segregation, however, must not be confused with discrimination. Moreover, it was in the whites' self-interest to promote certain kinds of progress for the black population. Sanitary conditions in the black parts of town, for example, should be upgraded because "we have learned that a disease germ knows no color line." Similarly, it made sense to encourage Negro homeownership "because the property owner is usually a good citizen and not a candidate for the communist party."

But the fundamental concept was "separate" no matter how "equal." She identified herself as one of those middle-ground whites who recognized, "willingly or grudgingly, the validity of every Negro goal except the ending of general segregation." Moreover, as early as 1948 she warned that federal intervention to abolish segregation would not succeed in changing whites' deeply held feelings on the issue and that it would be "tragic" for the South, the Negro, and the nation if the federal government should attempt such intervention.[61]

North Carolina's reaction to the 1954 U.S. Supreme Court declaration in *Brown v. Board of Education* that segregated schools were unconstitutional, unlike that of some other southern states, was measured. It was in fact very carefully calibrated to achieve the same goal as that sought by the more radical states: little or no integration of the school system. It would be a decade after *Brown* before the state's schools exhibited anything more than the barest token integration. Susie Sharp's views on the race question were solidly within the mainstream of public opinion at the time.

Under governors William B. Umstead and Luther H. Hodges, state leaders walked a tightrope, endeavoring to mollify hard-line segregationists while avoiding a confrontation with the federal government. Federal intervention to compel rapid integration would create the worst of all possible worlds: desegregation, destruction of the public school system, and economic disaster.

Nonetheless, prevailing sentiment teetered on the knife edge. In March 1956, 92 of the 106 southern members of the U.S. Congress, including almost the entire North Carolina delegation, signed a "Southern Manifesto." Written in part by North Carolina senator Sam Ervin, the manifesto declared *Brown* illegitimate and put a seal of approval on defiance. Largely due to his fear of a challenge in the 1956 elections from Assistant Attorney General I. Beverly Lake, a diehard segregationist with strong support, and despite his concerns about its adverse effect on the schools and economy, Governor Hodges endorsed what was known as the Pearsall Plan, which proposed, among other things, a constitutional amendment allowing tuition grants for students to attend private schools and local referenda permitting a community to close schools rather than desegregate.[62] Undoubtedly, had Lake run, the election would have taken on a strident racist tone that could have torn the state apart.

The atmosphere, then, was heavily charged with racial feeling in the mid-1950s when Judge Sharp was faced with a lawsuit in Charlotte demanding desegregation of the city's only municipal golf course, known as Bonnie Brae. The golf course was part of a public park made up of several tracts of land used as a whole. One of the tracts had been deeded to the city with a reversionary clause, stating that if any part of the whole were ever used by Negroes the tract would revert to the grantor. Another tract reverted if any part of the park ceased to be used for park purposes (for example, if another tract reverted). Although the golf course itself was not subject to a reversionary clause, the existence of the encompassing public park hinged on the golf course remaining segregated.

In early 1952 sixteen blacks had attempted to play on the Bonnie Brae course and were—predictably—denied the privilege. The black players sought an injunction prohibiting the Charlotte Park and Recreation Commission from barring them from the course; the city, however, contended that the reversionary clauses provided legal justification for maintaining the whites-only policy. By the time the case came before Judge Sharp in Mecklenburg Superior Court in December 1956, the U.S. Supreme Court had refused to review the North Carolina Supreme Court opinion holding the reversionary clauses valid. The facts being undisputed, the case landed solidly before Judge Sharp presiding in a nonjury court. Spottswood W. Robinson III, an attorney from Richmond, Virginia, specializing in civil rights cases, represented the black plaintiffs, arguing that the only question was whether the plaintiffs were denied their rights under the Fourteenth Amendment to the U.S. Constitution. He cited three U.S. Supreme Court cases in which the Court had ruled in favor of desegregating state and municipal recreational facilities, including bathing beaches and bathhouses in Maryland, a golf course in Atlanta, and state parks in Virginia.[63] After hearing the arguments, Judge Sharp was constrained to state, "I think that the court has no alternative but to grant the injunction."[64] Her ruling was the first court order directly affecting segregation in Charlotte's public facilities, according to the *Charlotte Observer*. She loathed having to accede to her own legal reasoning. As she wrote to Professor Breckenridge,

> The NAACP sent its 2nd wheel horse, Spottswood Robinson of Richmond, Va. (salary reported to be $25,000 a year). I asked him from the bench if his clients would be satisfied with another, public, non-segregated golf course and leave Bonnie Brae with its reversionary hazards alone. I knew, of course, what his answer would be but I made him say that nothing but Bonnie Brae would satisfy them and that the City's loss of 60 acres of valuable park land meant nothing to him . . . and them. I could feel his hatred and I had the impression that he could feel mine because I had to grant him the injunction but despised having to do so. Perhaps I imagined it all, but I think the undercurrents in court

that day were really shock waves. . . . [W]asn't it the irony of fate that I, who would almost have preferred to close it down, had to *order* the course opened to them.[65]

The difficulty of her ruling was exacerbated by its political implications. Although the newspapers had sympathetic editorials, recognizing that she had been bound hand and foot by legal precedent, Judge Sharp told Breck "my stock with the majority is at an all time low and . . . I couldn't get elected dog catcher at the moment."[66]

North Carolina would inch slowly forward with piecemeal integration, largely as a result of litigation brought by the National Association for the Advancement of Colored People. With a few exceptions, enlightened self-interest in the dominant business community permitted just enough progress to forestall violence. Attitudes among whites in the 1950s, however, remained heavily prejudiced, and Judge Sharp's were no exception, even as she accepted the reality of the changing world. In the privacy of her letters, she commented freely. "I'm really getting soft in my old age," she wrote the Breckenridges in 1958. "In Greensboro last week I put a colored woman who was guilty of murder in the first degree on probation and a colored man who was guilty of rape got off with a suspended sentence after a week in jail. You simply cannot judge animals by human standards."[67] As late as 1961, she would remark to John about a black couple, a schoolteacher and a railway mail clerk, seeking a divorce in her courtroom: "They both take home about $4,800 a year and have a better than average education, but the social veneer is very thin. It took little provocation for them to act as persons of color usually do."[68]

Understanding how strong Judge Sharp's racism was allows one to admire her all the more for her unwavering adherence to the rule of law, even when it went against her grain. In a 1956 commencement address,[69] she laid out the dilemma caused by *Brown*: "Most of us consider that decision the greatest calamity to befall the South since reconstruction; that no nine men had the right to try to overturn the mores and customs of a region so radically and so suddenly and that we are morally bound to protect both white and colored from it to the limits of our ability—which simply stated means to resist the decision by every lawful means."

"Lawful means." Therein lay the rub.

"The decision presents a soul-searching problem to lawyers who have sworn to support the constitution and who have always understood the constitution to be what the Supreme Court said it was," she continued. "If people can defy one decision of the court they can—and will[—]defy another and the Pandora's box is wide open. So, the evil potential of the decision may be much more far reaching than even those who abhor it foresee. For the first time in their law-abiding lives many good citizens now regard a law as so wrong and offensive that they not only feel no obligation to obey it but every obligation to defy it."

There was no doubt in her mind as to the greater of evils, desegregation or subversion of the rule of law. In a speech delivered in 1950, prior to the decision in *Brown*, she said, "Enough of either ignorance or selfishness here at home, I keep repeating, could wreck democracy from within quite as effectively as Joe Stalin is trying to do. Take the KKK for instance. Hooded or summary punishment has no place under our constitution; yet it rears its ghostly head with monotonously discouraging regularity."[70]

Judge Sharp's profound understanding of the American system of government forced her to accept changes with which she powerfully disagreed. Over the decade following *Brown*, the civil rights movement's increasing reliance on civil disobedience would only deepen her commitment to the concept of a nation of laws, not of men, even as it intensified her racial antipathy.

Nonetheless, her animosity toward the demands and tactics of civil rights agitators was not so strong as to render her immune from revulsion at the sight of white racists taunting demonstrators. Emerging from a movie theater at about nine o'clock one night in 1961, she found eight or ten young black men and women marching back and forth in front of the theater, carrying placards protesting segregation. At the end of the marching line, as she described the scene in a letter to John Kesler, "[T]here was a white boy. . . . walking backward, prancing on his toes and facing the leading Negro. His body was slightly arched and he had his face in the Negro's face. Their noses were almost touching—no segregation there! On his back was a crudely printed placard which said, 'Negro, go home—you can't win.' The Negro was pretending the white face was not there; his face was as expressionless as a cigar store Indian's—but the expression on the white boy's face was not nice to see. He should not have been there. . . . The scene gave me a feeling of nausea; I felt terrible and left as quickly as I could."[71]

Such were the complications of the times.

As a general rule, a trial judge in the state court system was not compelled to wrestle with the race issue, because most civil rights litigation was handled in federal court. Judge Sharp did not confront the legal aspects of race or segregation in any more prominent case than the Bonnie Brae Golf Course matter, although of course she dealt in racism—her own as well as that of jurors, lawyers, court personnel, and the general public—every day that she sat on the bench. The death penalty, however, was an issue no superior court judge could avoid. She had to face it before she had been on the bench three months.

The case was particularly harrowing from beginning to end. The defendant was a thirty-three-year-old white man named Claude E. Shackleford, a sandy-haired 200-pound army veteran repeatedly described as "husky" in newspaper reports, accused of twice raping the ten-year-old daughter of his rural next-door neighbors, Mr. and Mrs. Nathan Hunt. The child's parents found their daughter Shirley Ann in Shackleford's blood-stained car on the morning of August 12, 1949, after looking for her all night. Newspaper and radio stories spreading the distressing details of the investigation were so prevalent that defense counsel in the Guilford County trial successfully petitioned for a special venire of jurors from adjoining Davidson County. It took three venires of 150 prospective jurors each and the better part of three days to seat a jury.

Eventually, the jury was chosen and the trial began. While the defendant sat beside his widowed mother, his face calm and expressionless, the courtroom bulged with spectators. As one reporter described the scene, "They stood on each other's toes, got on each other's nerves, craned their necks, and scrouged into every nook and crannie. One fellow offered a youngster two bits for his seat. The kid held out for half a dollar."[72] Many in the crowd were women, curious to see the lady judge, who in addition to dealing with the sensational nature of the case had to rule on some critical legal questions. According to the reporter, she handled herself beautifully: "She ruled on objections quickly, called attorneys when they edged toward the legal borderlines, lectured sharply to veniremen, and just plain entranced the spectators. Despite the crowded conditions in the court, she had to rap for order only once."[73]

The jury returned a verdict of guilty as charged with no recommendation for mercy, which meant that the death penalty was mandatory. Judge Susie Sharp thereupon became the first woman in North Carolina to pronounce the death sentence on a convicted defendant. It could not have helped her nerves that Shackleford, upon hearing the sentence, burst out loudly that he had been "kangarood through court" and hurled threats at the deputy sheriff who had testified against him. Judge Sharp banged her gavel and ordered, "That's enough." But the case was not over.

Shackleford appealed on the grounds that Judge Sharp had excluded certain testimony from a psychiatrist and that, given the statute allowing a recommendation for mercy, it was error to exclude evidence calculated to influence the jury to make such a recommendation. The North Carolina Supreme Court rejected these contentions and upheld the verdict on June 9, 1950.[74] Barring commutation of the death sentence by Governor Kerr Scott, the convicted rapist would die in the gas chamber on June 30. Defense counsel presented the governor with a petition for clemency signed by, among others, ten of the twelve original jurors, the victim's parents, and 539 neighbors of the Hunt and Shackleford families.[75] Some petitioners indicated that they felt Shackleford was mentally deficient and thus should not be executed.[76] Governor Scott, however, refused to intervene, stating that he had not found sufficient support for the petition in reports by the medical experts.

On June 30 the condemned man waited on death row, dressed in the customary white shorts with a stethoscope taped over his heart. A black hearse drove up to the prison gate. State's witnesses had crowded inside the small observation room adjacent to the gas chamber, while newsmen waited in the warden's office. But at nine minutes before the appointed hour of ten o'clock, the warden announced there had been a reprieve: the child victim and her mother had signed a statement saying that the child had not told the truth at trial. Faced with this development, Governor Scott granted a five-day stay of execution. Further investigation showed that little Shirley Ann and her mother had signed a document presented to them by two of Shackleford's cousins, who apparently told them that it would "save Claude's life." The problem with the statement, however, was that, although Mrs. Hunt could sign her name, she could not otherwise read or write, and the little girl, according to her father, was "slow to learn" and could not read "to amount to anything."[77]

Faced with the reality of the death penalty, the victim and her family appeared to share the feeling of many in the community: because Shackleford had not killed the little girl, he should spend the rest of his life in prison but should not be executed. However, when questioned about the alleged recantation, Shirley Ann and her mother declared they had told the truth at trial, had signed the cousins' statement without reading it, and in fact did not recant their testimony. Despite a last-minute plea by the Hunts, in which they said they did not want to be responsible for Shackleford's death and which included Shirley Ann's plea "that he be spared from the gas chamber because she did not want to be haunted by the memory of his death," the rescheduled execution went forward and Claude Shackleford died in the gas chamber on July 21, 1950.

It was certainly not an easy case for the new judge, even though she had not exercised any discretion in pronouncing the death sentence, mandated by law in view of the jury verdict. The nature of the crime, the age of the victim, the pathetic circumstances of both the defendant and the victim, the "recantation" and its subsequent withdrawal, the last-minute reprieve, the ultimate outcome—all created whipsaw emotions. Judge Sharp was not unaffected, although she did not feel that she had done or left undone anything essential. "Yes, I was bothered by that case," she admitted several months later. "But not any more than a man would have been. No one could take a case lightly which involved the taking of a man's life. There was no doubt about the defendant's guilt. And he attacked a 10-year-old child. Still I worried about it."[78] On another occasion she said, "Even though the jury made my sentence mandatory with its guilty verdict, I was numb."[79] She told another reporter that sentencing a man to death had been "the most sobering experience of my life, I assure you."[80] Revealingly, it was the media spotlight that had fortified her. "I felt terrible, but the newspaper reporters, who were there expecting and hoping that I would break down or do something unusual which would make a good story about 'that woman judge,' helped me through."[81]

She would sentence two more defendants to death during her tenure on the superior court. One was a "strapping" twenty-nine-year-old black garage worker named Richard Scales who entered the home of a young mother of four on the pretext of wanting to use the telephone. He confessed to attempting to rape her and to stabbing her and her seven-year-old daughter to death with the kitchen knife the mother had tried to use in self-defense. Under the statute, any murder occurring as a result of attempted rape was murder in the first degree for which no premeditation or evidence of willful malice was required. The jury, which included three blacks and whose foreman was a Quaker, deliberated less than an hour before finding the defendant guilty with no recommendation of mercy.[82] Once again, Judge Sharp was in the position of pronouncing a death sentence made mandatory by the jury's verdict. Speaking softly, she said, "Stand up, please, Mr. Scales," and then ordered that "the prisoner be taken 'to the place of execution to inhale lethal gas of sufficient quantity as to cause death.'"[83] According to the *Greensboro Daily News*, an "ominous clap of thunder from the dark clouds burst above the courtroom just as Judge Sharp spoke that part of the order." If the judge flinched, it was not noted in the newspaper. After an unsuccessful appeal to the North Carolina Supreme Court, Scales was executed on July 15, 1955.

Another death sentence Judge Sharp pronounced, her last, did not result in an execution. The defendant was a white, twenty-six-year-old truck driver named Roy Oakes, who was convicted of blowing off the head of his estranged wife with a shotgun in March 1958. Once again the jury's verdict of guilty was not accompanied by a recommendation of mercy; indeed, the jury's mercy went to the defendant's three motherless children, to whom they turned over their jury pay, more than \$200.[84] As was her duty, Judge Sharp sentenced the defendant to death, but this time the North Carolina Supreme Court reversed her and granted Oakes a new trial.[85]

Later, serving on the North Carolina Supreme Court, Judge Sharp would encounter considerable controversy surrounding the death penalty. Some of her opinions on the issue would be construed — or, rather, misconstrued — to paint her as an opponent of capital punishment. In fact, by the time she was required to pronounce the death sentence as a trial judge, she was not opposed to it, but that is not to say she found it simple or palatable. In 1956, after she had sentenced two defendants to death, she related in a letter to John an interesting exchange she had with John J. Parker, chief judge of the U.S. Court of Appeals for the Fourth Circuit. She wrote, "He took me quite by surprise at the beginning of the evening when I caught him looking at me across the room. Said he: 'Guess what I was thinking?' I opined that there was no telling. He said: 'I was wondering how an attractive, sweet girl like you could possibly bring herself to sentence a man to death.' Imagine him thinking of a thing like that. I told him I wondered too."[86]

As a member of the judiciary, Judge Sharp was not supposed to engage overtly in politics, but her job depended on her political skills as much as her judicial performance. Her speeches to the local worthies from the Kiwanis Club, the Rotary Club, the Business and Professional Women's Club, and the like constituted a form of politicking, serving to keep her in the public eye. Although she spoke often before groups of lawyers or judges, she also rarely declined an invitation to speak to ordinary citizens. She spoke to graduating classes (and the proud parents), church groups, sororities, and teachers' organizations.

As a special judge, she owed her appointment to the governor, but she was well aware that a high profile with the general voting populace was an important kind of job insurance, making it difficult for a governor not to reappoint her each time her two-year term expired. It was true that she had earned a solid reputation within the legal community. Retaining her seat on the bench, however, depended a great deal on her popularity with the public. Every time she worked into the early morning hours on a speech, every time she summoned the energy for an after-dinner oration following a long day in court, every time she gave up precious weekend time to make a commencement address, she was building a base of political support. Short of a professional or personal disaster, no governor could fail to reappoint her without confronting an uproar not only from her professional colleagues but also from a wide variety of ordinary citizens, male and female, whom she had cultivated as assiduously as any elected politician, all the while refraining from "politics."

In the mid-1950s, however, it appeared that all her efforts might go for naught when a judicial redistricting plan proposed to abolish all special judgeships. She narrowly escaped the fate she had half expected ever since Governor Scott appointed her to the bench in 1949—being sent home to practice law in Reidsville. It was a fate she contemplated with a degree of equanimity, given that she remained surprised by her success in achieving career goals for which she had had no supporting precedent. Nonetheless, she knew she was doing a good job and it was a job she loved. Despite periodic perusals of architectural plans for the house she fully expected to build on a lot she owned in Reidsville someday, she would not have relinquished her seat on the bench voluntarily.

There was widespread recognition that the judicial system needed an overhaul. Thoroughgoing court reform to centralize and unify the patchwork of unstandardized courts across the state would not come for another ten or fifteen years, but many inefficiencies in the system were the result of an outdated judicial district map and other structural infelicities that could be addressed separately.

The last large-scale reorganization of judicial districts had been in 1911, and expansion in the intervening decades had been haphazard at best. As needs arose, a judge might be added here or a solicitor added there on an ad hoc basis. When the second half of the twentieth century opened, North Carolina had twenty-one judicial districts, gerrymandered "to split up Republican strength,"[87] with a resident or regular judge based in each district. In addition to the regular judges and one active emergency judge, there were eight special judges, like Judge Sharp, appointed by the governor to travel the length and breadth of the state, holding court wherever there might be a temporary absence of the resident judge. The judicial districts were divided into two large divisions, east and west, within which the regular judges rotated. Even though the regular judges' territory was only half that of the special judges, they were still required to travel over great distances, a drain on the judges' time and energy. The chief justice of the state supreme court was in charge of assigning the superior court judges to the various terms of court within their divisions. Prior to the legislative designation of an assistant to the chief justice in 1951, little if any attention was given to balancing judicial resources with judicial needs. Many terms of court were wasted because counties requested terms "pretty much like requisitioning supplies in the army," asking for more than they needed, canceling later.[88]

Judges, lawyers, and citizens alike complained of lost time and taxpayers' money resulting from inefficient allocation of resources. In 1951, in her major address to the North Carolina State Bar entitled "A New Judge Looks at the Bar," Judge Sharp recognized among other things the distressing condition of the court system. "It has become obvious," she said, "that the courts cannot handle the increasing number of cases and continue with their present methods unless both the number of terms and court personnel is doubled." She did not, however, believe the taxpayers were likely to approve such an expansion.

Failing this sort of assistance to the overburdened system, she argued for reforms to increase the efficiency of the courts. Many of these had been resisted by lawyers comfortable in their familiar patterns and leery of changes that might deprive them of a tactical advantage over an opponent. For example, the expedient of a pretrial conference had been widely resisted as an "unsportsmanlike effort on the part of the judge to make [a lawyer] expose his hand to his opposition" or prevent him saving for trial "some little legal trap he has baited for what he hopes and fondly believes is an unwary adversary."[89] Judge Sharp warned that "the public sees in the contrast between the efficiency of modern business methods and what we are pleased to call due process of law only inefficiency and backwardness."[90]

Conscientious and efficient attorneys could not be created overnight by the legislature. But dissatisfaction with the court system had grown by 1951 to the point that the General Assembly began to take notice. The Judicial Council, a legislative advisory group made up of prominent lawyers and the recently appointed executive officer of the chief justice's office, John M. Strong, worked to formulate plans for major surgery on the mechanics of the judicial system. Reform bills presented to the 1953 General Assembly focused on judicial redistricting, a touchy topic, but did not arrive at an ultimate solution. Governor Umstead, however, was authorized to name up to twelve special judges. He appointed only seven, including five new judges. Only two of the incumbent special judges were reappointed, one of whom was Susie Sharp.

The 1955 legislative session finally produced a Judicial Redistricting Act, which added two new divisions to the two existing ones. In addition, the legislature increased the number of regular judges to thirty-two, which was the total of the former regular and special judges combined. No provision was made for any special judges. Many people were in favor of abolishing special judgeships entirely, at least partly on the grounds that the posts were political spoils determined by the results of a gubernatorial election rather than by merit, or at least by the will of the voters. Arguably, increasing the number of regular judges would take care of the needs of the courts, without requiring additional judges whose jobs were dispensed from the governor's patronage pouch. In a letter to the editor published in the *Asheville Citizen*, Chief Justice M. V. Barnhill acknowledged a widely held view when he wrote, "You and I know that the promises of judicial appointments have been, and will continue to be, made in exchange for political support."[91] There remained, however, the real problem of how to fill temporary vacancies on the bench, which was the original rationale for special judges. Filling in as a special judge was a full-time job. Emergency judges could not be expected to fill the gap, because by definition an emergency judge was retired, and likely to be subject to the vagaries of age and health as well as less interested in full-time employment. Even with the increased number of regular judges, therefore, it could be argued that there would still be occasions when a special judge would be needed. Clearly, however, the number of special judges, if they were authorized by the legislature, would be substantially decreased.

Under the new redistricting plan to become effective July 1, 1955, special judges who lived in newly created judicial districts could become the regular or resident judge in their home districts. Judge Sharp, however, lived in an existing judicial district that already had a resident judge: Judge Allen Gwyn. If the legislature did not authorize any special judgeships, she would have to go back to practicing law.

In recognition of the need for replacement judges, a "special judges bill" backed by the Judicial Council was introduced in the legislature on March 22, 1955, calling for the creation of four special judgeships to be appointed by the governor. Terms were to be for four years instead of two. On the floor of the legislature, however, the bill ran into trouble. Hot debate over the necessity of additional judges in light of the increase in the number of regular judges masked the underlying opposition to judgeships as political patronage.

In mid-April, Judge Sharp wrote to the Breckenridges, "I fear the special judge bill is in extremis." Her representative (who was doing what he could to save it) had informed her that the enemies of the bill were spreading the rumor that she was indifferent to its passage and did not care one way or the other. Surprised, she said, "It had not occurred to me that I was important enough to be misrepresented. I'm very much interested in seeing it pass whether I'm reappointed or not. Those judges are needed for more reasons than one."[92]

Allen Gwyn, ever alert to opportunities for both himself and Judge Sharp, summoned her to his office to discuss the possibility that he might get on the state supreme court, thus opening up his position as regular judge. No scenario would have pleased him more, undoubtedly. Judge Sharp's seat on the bench would be assured regardless of what happened to the special judges bill, and he would ascend to the post he had sought for so long. In fact, the possibility of an imminent vacancy on the court was not out of the question. Chief Justice Barnhill had gone into the hospital about the time the special judges bill was introduced in the General Assembly, as Judge Gwyn, who monitored the health of the sitting judges at least as assiduously as did their personal physicians, well knew. Gwyn told Judge Sharp that "he might have a better chance" than she did to get on the supreme court, and perhaps they should start working on it. With the special judges bill in jeopardy and a possible vacancy on the horizon at the supreme court, he must have hoped that the prospect of a regular judgeship would both mollify and galvanize Judge Sharp in support of his efforts to become an associate justice.

In the end, the special judges bill did pass. Judge Sharp got a report of the behind-the-scenes maneuvering from Breck, who had heard all about it when he visited Chief Justice Barnhill in the hospital. True to form, Breck took particular delight in the irony of how the matter had played out, with recently appointed North Carolina Supreme Court justice Carlisle W. Higgins as the critical lobbyist. "Dear entrenched judge," he wrote, informing her that "just possibly the man who, as I recall, took a federal post from your father was instrumental in bringing about this legislation to provide you with a sinecure."[93] Breck wrote, "It seems that, hearing that the [special judges] bill was about to languish and die, [Chief Justice Barnhill] from his bed of discomfort put in a call for one Higgins, J. and asked him to go around and see the boys and tell them that they might better have not passed the most excellent redistricting bill at all than to leave it without provision for four special JJ; that Higgins, J. enlisted the support of Assemblyman Doughton and others previously opposed and the job was done."[94]

Judge Sharp's term was due to expire the end of June. Even with passage of the special judges bill, she was not out of the woods yet, for there were seven former special judges without new districts in which they could become regular judges. With only four special judges authorized under the new legislation, three would not get new appointments. Moreover, opposition to the bill had been strong, and it was not clear that Governor Hodges would fill all four slots, at least not immediately. Her chances, however, were deemed good. As Breck reported to her after his conversation with Chief Justice Barnhill, the chief justice fully expected her to be one of the two "specials" from the western part of the state "because, as to you, 'Miss S. has made good' (a thing you may recall that I along with many others predicted from the first) *and* that 'unless he had another qualified woman to appoint, it would be a great political blunder not to appoint the woman incumbent who has made good' (the ladies wouldn't like it) which is also something that several of us have been thinking."[95]

When the governor called her on June 5, in fact, it was to tell her that she would "head the list" of his special judge appointments but that initially there would be only two, herself and Judge George M. Fountain of Tarboro.

Throughout, however perilous the politics, there had been widespread agreement among judicial sources that Judge Sharp would keep her seat. She had made a particular impression as a hard worker, in contrast to the not-uncommon public perception that judges were all too prone to disappearing from the courthouse around midweek. Knowledgeable observers gave her "a lot of credit for reducing a huge backlog of cases."[96] No matter how unpopular or difficult a case, Judge Sharp would try it. As one contemporary later said, "She'd try anything on the calendar."[97] Commentators were virtually unanimous that the only woman on the bench had "made an outstanding record."[98] But, without question, her high profile, bolstered by constant contact with the general public and her resulting popularity among the voters, played a large role in raising her stock among the cognoscenti. Known familiarly by all and sundry as "Judge Susie," she was a popular and respected figure.

She now had another four years, under the longer term limits of the new law, before she had to think about reappointment again. Meanwhile, she continued crisscrossing the state, holding court, giving interviews, and making speeches. Perhaps, as she shored up her base of support while an itinerant superior court judge, the thought occasionally crossed her mind that the justices of the North Carolina Supreme Court, although they were usually appointed by the governor to fill a vacancy, retained their posts by statewide election.

CHAPTER 11

THE ROAD TO THE SUPREME COURT

If Susie Sharp was nurturing ambitions to become a member of the state's highest appellate court, she was not willing to sacrifice John Kesler to them.

In vivid contrast to her feelings for Venitah Breckenridge, she found every mention of Sudie Kesler by John or others to be painful. She hated to hear him refer to "my wife" and would sink into silent despair until he reassured her of his feelings for her. Once, when someone told her about meeting Sudie with John before they were married, Susie Sharp recorded that it had made her sick to her stomach.[1] (Her revulsion, however, did not prevent her, on one occasion when she was holding court in the county where the Keslers were married, from examining courthouse records to look at the marriage license.)[2] In the time-worn lament of countless other "other women," she told him that "my idea of heaven is to be able to go openly thru the front door of places with [you] and where I can call all and sundry and say: 'I want you to meet John.'"[3] John said, "If we just loved each other less, it would be simple."[4]

After a visit in 1952 in Salisbury with John, his wife Sudie, and their little girl — a rare occurrence — Susie Sharp wrote that she had left "with a terrible pain and ache in my heart. I think that the best solution of the problem would be for me to have that wreck he worries so about."[5] For his part, John never gave any indication of plans to leave his wife and daughter. Early on, he told Susie that he did not see any future for the two of them.[6] Yet he too was willing to jeopardize all he had. Emblazoned across the top of a page in her 1952 journal: "He says, 'We know we are gambling. We must take what comes without getting too upset about it.'"[7] As for Susie Sharp, she sustained a deterministic composure, a belief that "[w]e are not punished for our sins, but by them."[8] Actions had consequences. It would be astonishing if they escaped the consequences of their affair, but it was a risk she was willing to take. Perhaps she did believe, as she once said, that having been born the eldest of seven children on the seventh day of the seventh month of the seventh year of the century, she was lucky.[9] Part of it, too, was a willful streak that she acknowledged. "Perhaps you have noticed that nothing I really want to do hurts me at all but that doing something I don't want to do might kill me!" she had once pointed out to John.[10]

John was haunted by what might happen if one of them were to die and leave evidence of their relationship.[11] The letters were a particular problem, for there were many of them and the evidence was there for anyone who read them to see. Susie Sharp's sentimental side and realistic side were hopelessly conflicted, for she could not bear the thought of destroying the letters. In the summer of 1954 John pursued the issue. "We talk about burning [letters] and I cry," she recorded.[12] They attended a bar association meeting on the coast the following week and had planned a bonfire. But Susie Sharp could not bring herself to do it. "We park off on the road to the right and get out the letters and I cry and cry so that he tells me to burn them at home," she wrote.[13] Ultimately, the two lawyers agreed to a system in which they would routinely return each other's letters as they were received, so that each of them could be assured of their disposition.

Susie Sharp did not burn all the letters John returned to her, but at some point in the coming years she undertook to censor them with her scissors, cutting out John's name and most—but not all—of the tender language.[14] Partly this was an effort to preserve the many anecdotes that she sent him about her daily experiences in the courtroom and elsewhere. Indeed her frequent letters to John were the most detailed record of every aspect of her life, both professional and personal, far more complete than her journals. Susie Sharp had an idea that someday she would want this record, perhaps for her memoirs, and was reluctant to lose it for reasons quite apart from sentiment, despite its incriminating nature. Her solution created what might be called "lace letters" in which she delicately cut around anything she deemed too personal, leaving the rest. She dated each fragment carefully by hand. Much of the record of their relationship was thus lost to posterity, but through haste perhaps and the burden of so much to censor, much was spared.

Her feelings for John overpowered her good sense in many ways. As one example, in early 1954 he showed her a building in Salisbury on which he owed $4,500. A year later she recorded a conversation about the building in which they "got nowhere at all."[15] John then owed $3,500 and the discussion involved a loan from Susie Sharp. She told him that "if every time he looked at me he thought: 'I owe her 3,500' he could go to the poor house before I'd let him have it." She had been schooled both as a lawyer and as a woman in the pitfalls of lending money to a man, especially the man one loved. Less than a week later, however, she went to the bank and got thirty-five hundred-dollar bills.[16] John, after further discussion, "finally declares he wants it." On his way to Reidsville where Susie Sharp had put the money in her safe, he thought, "Suppose something happened to me and that note was found in my effects."[17] When he told her this, she said, "I don't want a note."[18] Susie Sharp reported in her journal that he told her to write up the note, but that he did not insist. The subject never reappears in the surviving record, so apparently her fears proved groundless. But she was surely correct in recognizing the potential for trouble. That she allowed his request (which must have cost him dearly to make) to override her better judgment was a measure of her trust in him.

As the decade unrolled, they maintained their steady routine of letters and meetings in Charlotte, Winston-Salem, Salisbury, or elsewhere. He gave her a $155 watch and, far more useful, a portable typewriter that freed her from the need to borrow one from the clerk of court at every courthouse.[19] It was a tremendous help to her in her work and, not incidentally, made it easier for her to write to him. Often they spent the weekend in Raleigh where they could both claim some sort of business, especially John in his capacities as state senator and university trustee. Susie Sharp compulsively noted their separate hotel room numbers, but her journal makes clear that they did not occupy separate rooms. For years they had a tradition of staying at the Hotel Sir Walter during the Dixie Classic, the famous basketball tournament of the era that was always held in Raleigh the week after Christmas. Sometimes in the mornings they would go down to the coffee shop separately, but join each other for breakfast. The dining area would be full of people they knew, many of whom kept a permanent room at the Sir Walter, where all the politicians, lobbyists, and other movers and shakers carried on business in the state capital. There was a clubby feel to the place, where the insiders felt free to join one another for a bit of early morning business or simply for company, so that in itself sharing a breakfast table would not necessarily raise eyebrows. Other times they would eat separately, Judge Sharp working on the newspaper puzzle.

When they were in Raleigh, they like everyone else they knew ate many of their meals at the s&w Cafeteria (and later, its successors) near the hotel. At the s&w they had a regular waitress named Ethel who, year after year, fetched them coffee, cleared their table, and bantered with them. It was slightly thrilling to think that Ethel must know they were not "just friends." Once, Susie Sharp recorded, John left Ethel a dollar tip "and tells her she don't know nothing." Did he wink? Did Ethel smile? All we know is that she agreed, she "didn't know nothing."[20]

Susie Sharp's lifelong fear had come true. She was helplessly in love. Knowing her heart was tender, she had always hoped to escape the painful feelings she was sure were the inevitable price of loving. In this sector of her life, though, she had lost control, and that in itself was a source of distress. Her relentless rationalism was powerless against what she perceived as true love. Her fierce loyalty, engendered by the side of her that held a surprisingly romantic and sentimental view of the world, once engaged was not to be dismissed. This was a woman who grieved like a teenager when Princess Margaret was forced to give up the love of her life, Captain Peter Townsend, in 1955.[21] Susie Sharp no longer had any interest in any other man. She was revolted by Judge Gwyn's continued importunings. For Breck she had the deepest affection, but no longer any romantic feelings. She was John's, plain and simple.

Once, after she delivered her standard discourse on The Lady and the Law to a Chapel Hill audience, one woman in the back of the room raised her hand to inquire if the judge were married. Judge Sharp reported to John that she "answered legalistically."[22] "Legalistically" she was not married, but in her mind, body, and soul she was as married to John Kesler as it was possible to be.

She and John spoke sometimes of the years they had lost, the two decades between their law school days and their reconnection. He agreed with her that they had been victims of the Depression, but when he said he feared he would have stood in the way of her advancement, she replied that together they would have been more than the sum of their parts.[23] Fresh from a new hair cut, she asked him if their love would last until her hair grew out. "I would love you baldheaded," he replied. Her journal gives unceasing testimony to her feelings for him. "I lie down with him and we burst into flames," she wrote.[24]

John was not her only distraction from her judicial duties, however. Since her father's death, she had shouldered all the head-of-family responsibilities, from managing the farming operation to advising siblings and an ever-growing number of nieces and nephews on colleges, careers, and cars.

Along with her other duties, Judge Sharp routinely balanced her mother's checkbook and continued to do the tax returns for family members, friends, and the famous Fultz quadruplets, who remained in her legal care as trustee. In 1956 she facilitated the quads' adoption by the couple who had taken care of them since their birth and remained involved with their affairs until the mid-1960s.[25] She was the chief decision maker and more often than not the financial aid office for the entire family. It was due to Judge Sharp, for example, that her mother had a fine radio and her sister Louise had a car. Susie Sharp enjoyed the radio, too, of course, and especially loved spending a Saturday afternoon listening to the Texaco-sponsored weekly broadcast of the Metropolitan Opera.

She had not succumbed to the charms of agriculture. "Early this morning," went one typical description of her efforts, "I had to go out to the farm to check on the report that one of the tenants had been drunk ever since he sold his first load of tobacco. It was not intended that I should farm."[26] She was not, however, without a sense of humor about her various travails. She entertained Breck with one funny story that ensued after she decided that "in lieu of expensive hail insurance mamma should take out the cheaper and less remunerative gov't crop insurance." On the last day before the deadline, Judge Sharp made the requisite visit to the bureaucrat in charge, only to learn that he was not sure she could "sign up" for Mrs. Sharp. "Are you her agent?" the man asked. As Judge Sharp told it, she replied, "'Well, I attend to all of her business and run her errands but I haven't got any written power of attorney, if that's what you mean.' He still didn't know whether to let me sign; so I said, 'Oh, it's quite all right; I'm her general factotum.' 'Oh,' he said, 'Well, in that case sign right here.'"[27]

In 1958, however, family matters took a serious turn that would claim an exceptional amount of her time and energy in the next few years. On Christmas Eve of that year, her sister Sallie's husband, Arthur Taylor, suffered his third heart attack and died in Missouri. Although he had remarried after Sallie's death five years earlier, the marriage had lasted only a matter of months and the two Taylor boys, Larry and Jimmy, were left alone. Larry at twenty-one was already in college at the University of North Carolina in Chapel Hill,[28] but sixteen-year-old Jimmy was still in high school.

Judge Sharp found herself in charge of a household that included, for the first time in many years, two young men. Immediately, she had herself appointed the brothers' legal guardian.[29] Larry, attending UNC, was away at school most of the time except for vacations, although no less present for all that in Judge Sharp's sense of responsibility. She would often stop in Chapel Hill and get someone to fish him out of his dormitory so they could get a bite to eat in the dining hall on campus, or she could take him to dinner at the Carolina Inn.[30] Jimmy, on the other hand, was living at the Sharp homeplace at 629 Lindsey Street. During the week, his grandmother was the resident adult, with Judge Sharp arriving on the weekends to render decisions and try to bring order out of chaos. Judge Sharp described her mother as "a little more forgetful, but she is still waiting on and looking after all of us."[31]

The judge did her best to relate to a teenage boy with sports, cars, and who-knows-what-else on his mind, but it was not easy. She encouraged him in his sports and even joined the country club for his benefit, so that he might play golf on the course. As for herself, she had never been attracted by country club membership. Despite her interest in her family's links to the southern aristocracy, despite her ceaseless attention to appearances and the proper way to do things, despite many friendships with club members, she had no desire whatever to join or frequent the country club. Perhaps it was her father's influence, the memory of his plain-dealing ways that would have jarred the golfers and cocktail drinkers, the imprint of his "small d" democratic beliefs, which had kept her from joining. Whatever it was, Judge Sharp joined for Jimmy's sake but did not take advantage of her membership privileges until two and a half years later, when, to ease some of the pressure on her mother, she took the family to the buffet dinner for the first time.[32]

The shock of assuming an in loco parentis role flummoxed Judge Sharp as had nothing else in her experience. "Up to this change in my life and routine I have always felt that I could cope," she wrote to John, "but I'm faced with something now I am afraid I can't handle successfully."[33] Like any ordinary parent with a teenager, she suffered the usual tremors and trepidations, for which she had had far less time to prepare. "[Jimmy] got his driver's license this morning," she reported to John. "When he drove off alone—for the first time—in my car, I think I know how Daddy must have felt the first time he turned over his beloved new Nash to me."[34] She found herself sitting up into the wee hours of the morning, waiting for Jimmy to get home from a dance or, more maddening, being awakened at one o'clock in the morning by a dutiful phone call to tell her where he was and not to worry.[35] At least as disturbing as having a teenager in the house was the fact that the teenager had a dog. "Life was so simple before we acquired a boy with a dog," she lamented. "That dog has a skin ailment and how do I know that humans can't catch it?"[36]

Following one especially exhausting Thanksgiving with family, after which "the house looked like a professional wrecking crew had been thru," someone asked Judge Sharp what would be the name for an old-maid aunt with children. Her quick rejoinder was, "Anti-maternal."[37]

If a resident teenager posed a challenge, however, she also saw him as an opportunity to atone for what she felt was her failure to be of sufficient help to Sallie before she died. Jimmy graduated successfully from high school and went on to begin his grown-up life at UNC, but Judge Sharp continued to act as a parent, as best she could.

Whatever the strains in her personal life, when it came to her career she continued to build a solid reputation as a trial court judge and a savvy member of the political club. She genuinely enjoyed her work. Nevertheless, the shiny prize of a seat on the state supreme court continued to glint and glimmer.

Susie Sharp's public admissions of ambition were virtually nonexistent. Whether she believed an overt acknowledgment of her aspirations would be unbecoming and off-putting to men and women alike, or whether she was simply superstitious about voicing her unprecedented goals too loudly, she spoke of them to very few people. The question arises: would a man in her situation have been so reticent? Probably not. But even after Governor Scott had reappointed her to the superior court in 1951, Judge Sharp preferred to characterize her initial elevation to the bench as a lightning strike rather than as the culmination of her long service to the Democratic Party, magnified by the support that she, her father, and Judge Gwyn almost alone in the legal profession had given Kerr Scott, and capped by the calculation on Governor Scott's part that the appointment of a well-qualified woman to the bench would be popular. In public, she had even flatly denied any knowledge that she was being considered for appointment to the superior court, telling at least one reporter that it had come "as a complete surprise."[38] In a 1952 interview, she allegedly said, "I didn't seek it, didn't know I was being considered, and of course didn't anticipate the honor coming my way."[39]

As she continued to be mentioned as a candidate for the North Carolina Supreme Court, however, she grew bolder about acknowledging her goal, at least within the inner circles. She discussed it with Allen Gwyn regularly, with Breck occasionally, and also with John, as well as with a handful of key lawyers and politicians. Nonetheless, her behind-the-scenes positioning was so closely held that years later her own sister Louise, by nature the most literal and retentive of all her siblings, would say of her appointment to the supreme court, "She didn't know it was coming."[40] By and large, the support for her appointment was handled by others on her behalf so that her modesty was unbesmirched. There was no question, however, that she wanted it.

Judge Gwyn continued to be both a mentor and a rival. In mid-January 1954 he performed a maneuver that he must have felt would increase his chances in the long run even if it bumped him from the next appointment. Perhaps with his exquisite attention to the situation of each sitting justice, he had divined that there were at least two potential vacancies in the near future and he calculated that by throwing out a bone for the first go-round, he might win the game on the second. In an unsolicited and no doubt surprising letter to Governor Umstead, he wrote, "Permit me, please, to say a word with regard to the filling of any vacancy which may occur in the office of Associate Justice of the Supreme Court," and proceeded to recommend the appointment of Superior Court Judge William H. Bobbitt.[41] "If there is a person in the State who is better qualified to serve on the Supreme Court, I do not think I have met him."

Judge Bobbitt, of course, enjoyed wide support and would be a most appropriate choice for the next seat on the court. Gwyn probably believed he lost nothing by his gesture on behalf of a likely appointee, even as he gained both the further attention and the goodwill of the governor by his generous endorsement. However, when Chief Justice William A. Devin announced his retirement effective the end of January, Judge Gwyn felt compelled to fire off another letter to the governor. On January 28, he wrote: "Friends of mine have called throughout the day making inquiry as to my interest in an appointment to the Supreme Court. . . . I do not wish to be understood as having no interest in becoming a member of the Supreme Court. . . . I ran for the office but was defeated. . . . In the light of all the circumstances, I felt that it would be presumptuous of me to ask for the appointment. Furthermore, I prefer not to cause you any embarrassment which might arise in a contest between Judge Bobbitt and me."[42]

On February 1, 1954, Governor Umstead elevated Associate Justice M. V. Barnhill to chief justice and appointed Judge Bobbitt to fill the vacancy thereby created. Bobbitt would have to run in the November elections to keep his seat. Judge Sharp recorded in her journal that Kerr Scott told her "it has been suggested to him that I run against Bobbitt." She rejected this idea without a moment's hesitation. Undoubtedly she knew it would be an uphill race, but she also had a horror of having to run in a contested election. Speaking of the special judges' four-year term, she once said, "Of course, I think we ought to have the same eight-year tenure as the regulars, but I would prefer the hazards of changing administrations to a primary. I'd have an awful time 'running.'"[43]

In June, the second shoe dropped when Associate Justice Sam Ervin Jr. resigned from the supreme court to accept Governor Umstead's appointment to the U.S. Senate following the death of Senator Clyde Hoey. Rockingham County lawyer and backroom politico Hamp Price called Judge Sharp and told her that Judge Gwyn did not have a chance. He told her that he thought she would make it eventually. "I don't," Judge Sharp wrote in her journal.[44]

On June 8, 1954, Governor Umstead appointed Carlisle W. Higgins to fill Ervin's seat.[45] Judge Gwyn had been passed over again.

Following Umstead's death in November 1954, Rockingham County native Lieutenant Governor Luther H. Hodges became governor and was elected in 1956 to serve another term. For Judge Sharp and the Democratic Party, this was a bit of good news amid the unfortunate national election results, which returned the Republican ticket of Eisenhower and Nixon to the White House. Judge Sharp, in addition to being an ardent supporter of Democratic candidate Adlai Stevenson, had long nurtured an intense dislike of Richard Nixon. She even claimed to be willing to vote for a Republican presidential candidate if Stevenson failed to get the Democratic nomination, "unless Nixon is the V. Pres. in which event I shall inquire about conditions in Canada," she informed the Breckenridges.[46] After the Eisenhower-Nixon victory in November, she told another correspondent, "Nixon to me would be the fate worse than death."[47]

At least on the state level, the Democrats were still in charge. In August 1956 Chief Justice Barnhill retired. With little ado, Governor Hodges appointed Associate Justice John Wallace Winborne to the chief justice slot and named Attorney General William Blount Rodman to fill the vacancy created by Winborne's ascension. Although these appointments do not appear to have caused too many ripples, there was at least some behind-the-scenes maneuvering as would be expected when a justice has been rumored to be considering retirement. Evidence that Judge Sharp's was one of the names put forward appears in a letter she later wrote to Leonard S. Powers, a former law professor who had been Chief Justice Barnhill's administrative assistant. In her letter to Powers, written to thank him for his support after her eventual appointment to the supreme court, Judge Sharp remarked, "I was certain that you were promoting my interests back in 1956."[48]

Her name surfaced again in speculation in 1957, even though none of the sitting justices relinquished their posts. This time it was clear that she had the kind of support bespeaking both an articulated desire for the job and some coordination of efforts on her behalf, whether organized by herself or through proxies. In October 1957 the *Winston-Salem Journal* ran an article in its "Around the Northwest" column, headlined "Judge Sharp Is Backed for N.C. Supreme Court."[49] The article's lead paragraph stated, "The word circulating in court circles these days is that many attorneys hope to persuade Gov. Hodges to name Judge Susie Sharp of Reidsville to the State Supreme Court the next time a vacancy occurs." While acknowledging that no immediate vacancies were foreseen, the writer pointed out that, in light of the age and health of the current members of the court, it seemed likely there would be one before Governor Hodges's term ended in early 1961. Chief Justice Winborne at seventy-three was the oldest of the seven, Justice Carlisle W. Higgins was nearly seventy, Justice W. B. Rodman was sixty-eight, and Justices E. B. Denny and R. Hunt Parker were both sixty-five. Only Justice William H. Bobbitt, who turned fifty-seven that month, and Justice Jeff D. Johnson Jr., who was also fifty-seven, were relative youngsters.

After a social evening at the Governor's Mansion in February, as Judge Sharp told John Kesler, retired chief justice Barnhill, according to his wife, had said that due to health problems Justice Johnson "would have to get off the bench soon and that the Governor could not do better than with me."[50] Judge Sharp did not demur.

Court watchers continued to monitor the health of the supreme court members throughout the coming year. Justice Johnson in particular suffered several bouts of illness that kept him off the bench for extended periods. In September 1958 Justice Hunt Parker had a heart attack at the age of sixty-six. Meanwhile jockeying had already begun for the 1960 gubernatorial elections, and Judge Sharp had reason to hope that one of Kerr Scott's protégés, a young lawyer named Terry Sanford who had managed Scott's successful 1954 campaign for the U.S. Senate, might be the next governor. If so, Scott told her, he had advised Sanford that he ought to appoint her to the supreme court.[51]

If Judge Sharp was engaged in a quiet campaign for the high court during this time, she did not allow it to infringe on her regular judicial duties, or such extracurricular commitments as serving on the search committee appointed in June 1956 for the new chancellor of her alma mater, Woman's College of the University of North Carolina in Greensboro. In November 1957 Governor Hodges appointed her to a fifteen-member commission created to review the state constitution and present proposals for constitutional amendments. The constitutional commission would not only consume a good deal of her time but also immerse her in a wide variety of judicial politics. Eventually, her work on this commission would make a significant contribution to the sweeping court reforms that came to fruition in the early 1960s.

By 1959 the drumbeat had grown louder. Judge Sharp's name surfaced ever more prominently in each discussion of the supreme court's makeup. In January, Justice Jeff Johnson finally made the decision to step down, sparking speculation on his replacement. The *News and Observer* predicted that Governor Hodges would act swiftly to "avert a shoving match among supporters of a host of candidates bound to pop up."[52] Possibilities, according to the newspaper, included Superior Court Judges Frank Huskins of Burnsville, J. Will Pless of Marion, Clarence Hall of Durham, and Allen Gwyn of Reidsville. But there was no clear favorite among these names. "If there was any one candidate standing head and shoulders above the field, veteran observers of the political scene had failed to notice him," the paper said. "Their most intriguing bit of speculation was that it might not be a 'him' at all, but rather a 'her.' The name of Judge Susie Sharp of Reidsville, only woman on the State's Superior Court bench, was being dropped by men familiar with the Hodges penchant for surprise appointments."[53]

Governor Hodges, however, appointed Superior Court Judge Clifton Moore, a former "Klan bustin' solicitor" before his appointment to the bench by Governor Umstead in 1954. In 1952 he had won convictions against ninety-three Columbus County Klansmen, including the Grand Dragon.[54] The appointment gave the governor a triple play. In addition to the supreme court seat, the governor could then appoint a new superior court judge to replace Moore, and because Moore had served as chairman of the state probation commission, Hodges also gained an opening there. Another consideration was the geographic composition of the high-court bench, which by tradition was roughly balanced between the eastern and western regions of the state. North Carolina had a long history of power sharing between the two sections, alternating the terms of governors between representatives of the East and West, for example, and allocating one U.S. senator from each region at all times. Had Judge Sharp been appointed, the balance on the supreme court would have shifted further to the West, which already had four of the seven seats.[55] Governor Hodges, responding to a Rocky Mount attorney's telegram lauding her "native intellect, scholarship, industry, fairness, courtesy, firmness, and courage,"[56] said, "I couldn't agree with you more, but I felt like we ought to keep a balance of three Eastern Judges and four Western Judges."[57]

What is odd about the reported backroom speculation is that no one mentioned the obvious obstacle to the appointment of either Judge Sharp or Judge Gwyn to the supreme court. At this stage of Judge Sharp's career, making a choice between the two of them would have been difficult for any governor, but particularly so for Governor Hodges, who was from Rockingham County. Any governor in his right mind would sidestep that dilemma. Judge Sharp was philosophical. To Breck she wrote:

I note the comment that sumuvum thought this time might be "it." Many thanks for the thought in that connection! [Leonard Powers] once, when he was [administrative assistant], told me in "sacred confidence" . . . that I *was* the topic of discussion. However, the vagaries and vicissitudes of politics are such that current events can become ancient history very quickly. I have no illusions about that at all, and it is right much to expect lightning to strike twice in one life time. Of course . . . I would not turn *it* down if 'twer offered, but as long as I feel as well as I have for the last three weeks I'm satisfied with the status quo. There's fun, varied experience, opportunity, etc. in my present job which is provided by no other job in the whole wide world.[58]

It helped that she approved of the choice. "The Governor appointed a good man to the S. Ct. when he named Clifton Moore," she wrote to John. "He has had a variety of experience and is a scholar and a gentleman."[59] He had been an ally in the Battle of the Robes, a subject on which he and Judge Sharp had seen eye to eye. To John, she added, "I note that the score is still four Westerners and three Easterners."

Failing to win this appointment may have been the last straw for Judge Gwyn. In March 1959 he came to see Judge Sharp in her Reidsville office one Saturday and talked about getting her onto the court. "He says he still loves me," she noted without comment.[60] Her future was not, of course, a new topic between them, but his own ambition had always been intertwined with his hopes for her, and of late her potential for becoming a supreme court justice had become a threat rather than what he had always envisioned: an honor decorating his own record as well as hers. The protégée had shown alarming signs of leapfrogging her mentor. Meanwhile, Judge Sharp's advocates were not dormant. In October she sent her résumé to Charlotte lawyer Paul Ervin. "I don't know why you have requested the enclosed information," she wrote, "but I do know that it's in an effort 'to further the cause,' and to continue to encourage me."[61]

Then, what had become the greatest roadblock to her appointment — greater than her gender or the identity of the governor — was unexpectedly removed. Allen Gwyn gave up. Beyond that, he took on the role of backroom mastermind and enlisted his son Allen Jr. to be her "campaign manager." It was 1960, a watershed election year on both the state and national levels. Terry Sanford, ex-paratrooper, Kerr Scott protégé, former president of the state Young Democrats organization, and successful lawyer, was running for governor. One day in early January, Judge Gwyn told Judge Sharp "in strict confidence" that his sons would be key organizers for Sanford and that he was going to ask Sanford to put her on the court.[62] "He says that he has lost his desire for the place and that he loves me," she wrote.[63] Shortly thereafter,

Allen Jr. came to see her. In light of his health and age, he told her, his father was no longer interested in pursuing a seat on the supreme court. Now "they wanted to do what they could to actively promote and secure the appointment for me," Judge Sharp reported to John.[64]

Allen Gwyn Jr. recalled being surprised when his father told him he had given up his ambition and wanted to support Judge Sharp's appointment. But, according to the son, his father "said that he wasn't in the running and that Susie would make a terrific one, and she wanted it, and that would be the place for her, being the scholar she was. And he told me to go, he suggested I go talk to her." So young Gwyn dutifully sought her out and told her "that I wanted to do what I could to help her get on the supreme court, and if she would tell me what she wanted me to do, then I would certainly do it."[65]

Terry Sanford had begun running for governor well in advance of the usual campaign schedule, opening an office in Chapel Hill shortly after the death of Kerr Scott in 1958. His tightly run political organization was staffed by an extraordinary group of men—and women—whose names would be prominent in Tar Heel politics for the next two decades. Among his most effective organizers was Martha McKay, whom he had known at UNC, where she had made a place for herself in what was then the boys-only club of campus politics. Now she was in charge of organizing women all over the state for Sanford's election, a job she fulfilled far beyond any precedent. Another woman who played a key role was Guion Johnson, women's advocate, civic leader, and author of a seminal book, *Ante-Bellum North Carolina: A Social History*. In Charlotte, Doris Cromartie was prominent, as was the former suffragist Gladys Tillett. In Winston-Salem, Register of Deeds Eunice Ayers was a strong Sanford supporter and a close ally of Bert Bennett, the Winston-Salem businessman who would manage Sanford's campaign.

Sanford took education as his main theme, which resonated particularly well among women but had broad appeal across the state. Opponents charged that higher taxes would be required to support his programs, and he left himself open to the nickname "high-tax Terry" when he refused to rule out a tax on tobacco, the sacrosanct money crop that undergirded much of the state's economy. But it was the racial issue that roiled his campaign. The old Democratic power structure was on the verge of fracturing.

In early February 1960, four black college students occupied stools at a Greensboro dime-store lunch counter, sparking a wave of civil rights sit-ins that began to change the South and the nation.[66] Former Wake Forest law professor I. Beverly Lake took up the banner of segregation, swiftly consolidating support for his own bid for the governorship. In the first primary that spring, Lake's strong second-place finish sent shock waves through the state and led to an intense runoff campaign in which race took a central place in the debate, despite Sanford's efforts to dampen the issue. North Carolina, with its record for racial moderation, suddenly appeared on the brink of joining states like Mississippi and Alabama in the civil rights wars.

Sanford, who was at pains in his public statements to deny that he was in favor of integration, nonetheless urged voters not to imperil the schools by adopting the sort of massive resistance advocated by Lake. Like it or not, the U.S. Supreme Court had the last word. Lake's approach, Sanford charged, would lead North Carolina "directly down the road to complete integration, to federal troops, to closed schools."[67] He worked hard to keep the tone positive. He could not hope to win if he explicitly espoused integration, but he did his best not to confront the issue directly: "I take my stand for keeping the schools open and improving them." He suggested that the candidates ought to be discussing how to improve industrial development in the state, rather than "how we can scare it off by racial strife."[68]

Judge Sharp, despite her beliefs on race, was horrified by Lake's campaign. She feared that if he were elected, "we would have another Little Rock."[69] Although Lake, who was known as a scholar and a gentleman, based his opposition to integration on what were then considered respectable arguments for keeping the races "separate but equal" rather than on sheer race hatred, in the superheated atmosphere of the times the populace did not always appreciate the subtleties of his position. To Judge Sharp's distress, John Kesler announced to her that "Lake will be the next Gov. and that he is going to support him."[70] When Sanford won the second primary, she exulted, "The Bugle's headlines this morning were beautiful indeed. In black letters, an inch and a half high, it is proclaimed: 'SANFORD BEATS LAKE.'"[71]

For the moment, at least, Sanford had survived and, if nothing extraordinary happened, he would, as the Democratic candidate, be duly elected governor in November. But it was a year for the extraordinary, and when Sanford jumped onto the bandwagon for John Fitzgerald Kennedy, the young Catholic presidential candidate, he came close to wrecking his own election.

Sanford had made no statement as to which Democratic presidential candidate he would support, wanting to be sure of his own nomination first.[72] With his advisers, he weighed the choices. Senate Majority Leader Lyndon B. Johnson would be the favorite among the southern states, although realistic observers including Johnson were well aware that no southerner-*qua*-southerner had won the presidency in over a century. Adlai Stevenson had the highest name recognition among the possible candidates, but he had lost twice to Eisenhower, diminishing his appeal. Hubert Humphrey of Minnesota was interested but was not well known; what was known of his support for labor unions and civil rights would not win many votes in North Carolina. The young senator from Massachusetts, on the other hand, had made a creditable run at the vice-presidency in 1956. It was true that he was Catholic but, like Sanford, he represented the fresh new breeze of postwar leadership. With the exception of old-school "pols" like Ben Roney, Sanford's coterie of close advisers favored Kennedy. However, Sanford knew that Lyndon Johnson would be the popular choice for the North Carolina delegation. Sanford himself knew Johnson well and had if anything more confidence in Johnson than in the less experienced Kennedy as an occupant of the Oval Office.[73] It would have been the natural and easy thing for him to back the southern candidate.

But Sanford, who turned forty-three that summer, identified with Kennedy, back from the war and burning to seize the reins of leadership. And he was "tired of the old routine of Southern politicians backing a regional favorite to protect their reputations at home when they knew a Southerner would never lead the ticket."[74] A vote for Johnson's nomination would be wasted. Kennedy, on the other hand, had a chance of defeating Richard Nixon.

Bert Bennett, the shrewd Winston-Salem businessman who was Sanford's campaign manager, urged him to endorse Kennedy.[75] Giving public support to Kennedy at this juncture would shake up the process, and if Kennedy were successful in November, Sanford's early and unexpected support would give him exceptional entrée to the White House.[76] Bennett believed that if they wanted to be part of the nation they should work for a candidate with the possibility of winning.[77] "'History knocks seldom,' Bennett said, 'and when it does, you'd better open up. And history is knocking in this opportunity.'"[78] Kennedy's pollster, Lou Harris, who had been at the University of North Carolina with Sanford, flew to Raleigh with JFK's brother Robert Kennedy to try to persuade Sanford to make the endorsement.[79]

Change was in the air everywhere in the summer of 1960. The day before the Democratic Convention began in Los Angeles, Martin Luther King and other civil rights figures led more than 5,000 marchers through the streets to the Sports Arena for an NAACP-sponsored rally. A civil rights plank would be hotly debated at the convention and ultimately adopted as part of the Democratic platform.

Terry Sanford landed in Los Angeles and promptly announced his support for John F. Kennedy. Not only that, but Robert Kennedy persuaded him to give a seconding speech when his brother's name was placed in nomination, an act that enraged such party powers as U.S. senator Sam Ervin Jr. Most damaging, on the morning of the nomination national columnist Drew Pearson published a column in which he strongly insinuated that a substantial "contribution" of campaign funds offered by Robert Kennedy during a "quiet trip to North Carolina" had diverted Sanford from his previous support for Johnson.[80] Sanford issued a vigorous denial. In the end, he was able to deliver six votes for Kennedy out of the thirty-seven allotted to North Carolina. Kennedy won the nomination on the first ballot. Lyndon Johnson would be his running mate, with the responsibility of holding the South. What Sanford would call "A New Day" was dawning.

But Sanford had underestimated the reaction in his home state.[81] In one irate telegram after another he was accused of betraying the South, of grandstanding at the expense of North Carolina and his party. Many party stalwarts let it be known they would not be working for Kennedy in the fall, despite Johnson's presence on the ticket. The issue was primarily religion. Religion had helped to split North Carolina before, when the Catholic Al Smith was the Democratic presidential candidate against Herbert Hoover, resulting in a Republican victory in the state and in permanent power shifts within the state Democratic Party. According to one well-regarded commentator, North Carolina was "the least Catholic state in the nation."[82] Prejudice against Catholics was pervasive. Questions were raised, both serious and verging on the hysterical, about whether an American president would have to take orders from the pope. "We want 'In God We Trust' on our coins, not 'In the Pope We Hope,'" one Republican rally speaker said.[83]

Religion was not the only issue connected with Kennedy that troubled voters, although it was the most resonant. In addition, Sanford lost some significant support to the hard-core segregationists still smarting from Lake's defeat. In fact, North Carolina was in the early stages of becoming a two-party state, with the Republicans gaining adherents in the wake of *Brown v. Board of Education*. It was true that in parts of the state, especially down East, the Republican Party was still linked in many minds to Reconstruction; these voters would stick with the Democrats even if, as the saying went, they had to vote for a "yellow dog." But in the mountainous western counties, the Republicans had always maintained a strong presence. And in the Piedmont the postwar population shift from farms to factories had produced suburbs, country clubs, and a concomitant increase in Republican voters.[84]

Judge Sharp had hoped until the last hope was gone that Stevenson would get the nomination. Her initial reaction to Kennedy's nomination was that she could not support the national Democratic ticket. For the dyed-in-the-wool party loyalist, this apostasy reflected the depth of her anti-Catholic prejudice. With Kennedy's selection, she said, "In the face of this disaster I am attempting to remain calm."[85]

Like other thinking citizens, she and John debated the best direction in the new political landscape. Two days after Kennedy won the nomination, she set out her views on the candidates: "I regret very much that Sanford took the course he did at the convention but I do not regret having voted for him for Governor. On the issues in that campaign . . . the moderate, intellectually-honest voter, concerned about education and the general welfare of the state, had no choice but to vote for Sanford."[86] She appealed to John not to regret his support of Sanford over Lake. "It would have literally put a crack in my heart if you had done anything other than what you did. You are not 'a Lakeite' and you would have demeaned yourself if you had espoused his cause for some extraneous reason which seemed compelling at the moment."[87]

Kennedy, however, was another matter. Nor did the presence of LBJ on the ticket give her any reason to get on the bandwagon. "[W]hat of Johnston [sic] who 'makes a whale of a lot of difference?'" she asked. "If he didn't compromise and sell the South down the river, I misread the signs. I shall support the local ticket, but I cannot vote for Kennedy."[88] Recognizing that others would feel constrained to support the Democratic nominee, she said she would not "fault" those who did, "because he may be the lesser of the two evils and I have preached the duty to choose the lesser and now I find myself in a situation where I cannot vote for either Kennedy or Nixon."[89] Kennedy's Catholicism was the ultimate sticking point that threatened to drive her out of the Democratic fold. "If we elect the first Catholic President the ice is broken and the next one will come easier."[90]

Her objections to Catholicism, in addition to concerns about separation of church and state, were numerous. For example, she would rail that "the offer of prayers in return for money outrages me. It smacks of the 'sale of dispensations' we studied in our history books."[91] Perhaps priests involved in this practice might be able to "put a different light on the transaction" if she could discuss it with them directly, but "they are not presumed innocent in this forum."[92] Indeed, she admitted, "I'm so afraid of the Roman Catholic Church and its policies, for 'doctrines of infallibility are just as dangerous whether they come from Moscow or Rome.' If the Pope succeeds in catholicizing India, I wonder what effect that would have on that already over-populated country?"[93]

"Well," she remarked, if you reached her age without developing "some darn good prejudices, you haven't got any character."[94]

She would make her position clear in a case over which she presided a year later, in October 1961. A child claimed he was injured in an automobile accident, causing him to limp. Evidence suggested that his limp predated the accident, but according to Judge Sharp, the "little Catholic boy and his parents" lied about the preexisting condition. Defendant's counsel informed Judge Sharp that "when he told a Catholic sister that she would be needed as a witness to testify that the Plaintiff limped before he was in the wreck, she said she would have to have the permission of the Father before she could come to court." To Judge Sharp's amazement, "the Father" declared that the sister could not come. Judge Sharp's response to the lawyer was unequivocal: "I told him he would see if the Catholic church or the Superior Court ran the courts of North Carolina and to subpoena her *if* he wanted the witness and the jailor could prepare the cell."[95] She would have loved to slam the sister into jail for contempt of court.

Drew Pearson published a retraction of his allegations against Terry Sanford in August, and even included a ringing endorsement of the candidate: "I came to the conclusion that Sanford had been considerably more careful than the average politician in raising campaign funds and that North Carolina will be in the hands of an able and scrupulously honest man as governor if he is elected."[96] By this time, however, voters were so polarized that it made little difference.

Judge Sharp continued to support Sanford at every opportunity if for no other reason than that she could not abide the thought of Republicans gaining control of the state. Recounting a conversation she had with one of her cousins from Statesville, formerly a Lake campaign manager but now in the Sanford camp, she said, "He agreed the vast appointive powers of the governor and what a Republican would do to the commissions, boards, courts, etc. etc. of the state made any other course unthinkable. So, we had a satisfactory meeting of the minds. I assured him that turning this state over to the Republicans would be like turning the Congo over to the Congolese — they aren't ready and able — in spite of being willing!"[97]

But she continued to struggle with the national situation. In the end, she could not desert the Democrats. In September she wrote to John, "Ever since you told me that you thought I ought to vote for Kennedy I have been going thru an agonizing reappraisal of my position. I have come to the conclusion that you are right and that I can do nothing else. I shall vote for Kennedy. You and recent events have convinced me that I should do what I can to save the country from Nixon. That decision represents a struggle, but it is made."[98]

Interestingly, it was the second time her presidential vote had been swayed by the opinion of a man in her life. In 1928 she had debated with Professor Breckenridge, among others, about whether to bolt the Democratic ticket and vote for Hoover instead of the Catholic candidate, Al Smith. She had not forgotten that struggle either. In late August 1960 she dropped by to see Breck in Chapel Hill. "[I] tell him that I voted for Al Smith; that he almost had talked me out of it but Daddy saw me last," she wrote in her journal. "He wanted to know if that was the story of my life. He added that he used to be there last."[99]

In November Kennedy was elected president and Sanford became the next governor of North Carolina. The former owed more to the latter than the latter to the former. Terry Sanford had poured his energy into shoring up the Democratic Party in the state and using it for Kennedy's benefit. It was not too much to say that without the highly focused efforts of Sanford and his organization, Kennedy never would have carried North Carolina. JFK was grateful for Sanford's early and unwavering support.[100] Prominent guests at Sanford's inauguration included Robert and Ethel Kennedy.

For his part, if Sanford owed his election to anyone, arguably it was the women of North Carolina. His education theme had struck a deep chord in a state that suffered from inadequacy in every area from teacher pay to curriculum to physical facilities. It had appealed especially to the state's mothers. Thanks largely to Martha McKay's organizational skills and energy, countless new female voters had been motivated to go to the polls to vote for Sanford. Many observers acknowledged the key role women had played in the election.

Meanwhile, Judge Gwyn, always thinking ahead, surprised Judge Sharp shortly after Governor Sanford's inauguration in January by telling her that she should join the church.[101] It was not an addition to her résumé that she had ever considered. Although she frequently went to church with her mother in Reidsville, her attendance was more social than religious. Indeed, her antagonistic views of organized religion—which were not limited to the Catholic Church—were long-standing and well known to her friends and family.[102]

Nearly a decade earlier when her name appeared in the Winston-Salem newspaper in a column called "Churches Are My Beat," her sister Florence had sent her the clipping along with the comment, "That my dear friend was the last place I expected to see your picture."[103] Not long afterward, her brother Tommy and his wife Bobbie asked her if she would be willing to take their daughter Tyrrell in case they both were to die, and she agreed but expressed her astonishment at the request, especially because Bobbie's sister was "well endowed with worldly goods." Bobbie explained, according to

Judge Sharp, "that her sister had too much religion and I didn't!" To this she remarked, "If that omission qualifies one for guardianship, I suppose I meet the requirements without doubt."[104]

On another occasion she took pains to correct the record when, after she spoke to a Methodist women's organization, a dignitary chided her introducer "for leaving out 'the most important fact about me,'" that she was a member of the Methodist Church. "Since I'm not, I felt I could not let that go uncorrected," Judge Sharp said. "So I had to explain that I was merely a sympathizer."[105] Her failure to join an organized church did not mean, however, as she declared on another occasion, that she was an unbeliever. Quoting Abraham Lincoln in a letter to John, she once said, "I am frequently driven to my knees for I have nowhere else to go," adding, "I pray so much that sometimes I fear I 'nag' the Lord and you and yours are often included in those prayers."[106]

Becoming an official church member was nonetheless the farthest thing from her mind. Judge Gwyn, however, undoubtedly was thinking of every possible angle to her pursuit of a seat on the supreme court. It would not hurt to be able to add "member of the Methodist Church" to any write-up about her, and the lack of any church membership possibly could be used against her. This might be true as the governor weighed the choices he might have in filling future vacancies on the court; it could also be true if and when she would have to be elected in order to hold her seat. Odds were she would be unopposed as a sitting justice, but it was impossible to know. Why not just eliminate any potential problem? Judge Sharp listened, but took no immediate action.

Meanwhile, all the indications were that she was on Governor Sanford's short list. Guion Johnson, for example, told her in April 1961 that "T. S. says he would give me the next vacancy on the S. Ct."[107] On another occasion, in the fall of 1961 after Sanford had filled four new special superior court judge positions recently authorized by the General Assembly, Judge Sharp and her clerk of court went to lunch with one of the appointees, the well-connected Judge H. L. ("Chick") Riddle Jr. of Morganton.[108] He was a virtual font of judicial and political gossip and among other things informed Judge Sharp, as she reported to John, that "Sanford thought very well indeed of Yours Truly and that if, during his administration, he had the opportunity to fill three vacancies on the S. Ct. that, in all probability, I would get one."[109]

It would be over a year after Sanford took office before an opportunity arose. It would be the only vacancy occurring on the supreme court during his term in office.

January 1962 found Judge Sharp holding court in Charlotte, along with Judge Gwyn. On January 9 she noted in her journal that Gwyn had eaten breakfast in the hotel coffee shop with Bert Bennett, Sanford's former campaign manager and now state chairman of the Democratic Party. Nothing happened without Bennett's approval, as was well known throughout the state. Writing to Bennett several months later, Judge Sharp acknowledged that his "approval was a prerequisite."[110] That night after the breakfast meeting, Judge Sharp and Judge Gwyn ate supper together in the K&W Cafeteria. Judge Gwyn "says that something is happening to me that I do not realize and he wants me to come by his room to discuss it," she wrote. "I say no. We talk on the mezzanine but he will not talk unless. We do not talk."[111]

The next morning Gwyn was more forthcoming. At breakfast he told Judge Sharp that he had instructed "Bert Bennett and his boys to get ready."[112] The time had come. He did not think he could get the appointment to the supreme court for himself, he told her. In any event, as she knew, he had given up. He had told Sanford of his decision to stand aside, knowing that Sanford was aware of his long-standing ambition, to free the governor from any sense of obligation. Gwyn "wants to atone because Daddy wanted to be a judge and did not get to be," Judge Sharp recorded. "I told him he did not owe me anything but that I owed him much."[113]

The reason for the renewed activity was Chief Justice Wallace Winborne's health. At seventy-seven, he had served on the supreme court for twenty-four years. He had become less and less able to carry out his responsibilities, a fact not acknowledged publicly. In addition, his eyesight was failing him, and it had become almost impossible for him to read.[114] Those paying attention, as Allen Gwyn surely was, realized that the chief justice might have to step down before long. In January Winborne underwent a cataract operation, but it was not a success. By the third week in January, Judge Sharp was working on a list of prominent lawyers and political figures across the state for her "campaign manager," Allen Gwyn Jr., to ask to contact Governor Sanford on her behalf in the event of a vacancy on the court.[115] According to the younger Gwyn, she also provided such a list to political leaders and members of the bar in other parts of the state.[116] Women's groups and their leaders were also on active alert. Meanwhile Allen Gwyn Jr. wrote the governor to ask that he not make a decision on any vacancy that might arise on the court without giving people in the Piedmont an opportunity to make the case for Judge Sharp.[117]

Despite a report in the News and Observer's "Under the Dome" column on Sunday, February 4, 1962, declaring the chief justice to be "in fine fettle and ready to preside Monday when the Court opens its Spring term,"[118] he was unable even to attend the brief opening activities and did not appear the following day for the first oral arguments of the term.[119] In the absence of the chief justice, Associate Justice E. B. Denny, next in seniority, presided.

The following Sunday in Reidsville, Judge Gwyn and Judge Sharp went to her office to work on a letter from Judge Gwyn to Governor Sanford, typed by Judge Sharp.[120] "No one has intimated to me that any one of our Supreme Court Judges intends to retire soon," the letter began. "However, in the event of such a vacancy, I would like to join with Allen, Jr. in his request to be heard before the vacancy is filled." Judge Gwyn went on to recount his long acquaintance with Judge Sharp, her brilliant record, and the universal esteem in which she was held. Then he touched on a factor that had never before played into the selection of a North Carolina Supreme Court justice: "For the first time in our history the women of our state have come to regard themselves as having a definite, tangible part in the judicial branch of our government. They look to Judge Sharp as their champion. They are proud of her. They say so in no uncertain terms. If the women in North Carolina could have their say as to who should occupy the next vacancy on our highest court, there would be no doubt as to whom they would choose."

Her record and her high profile were not the only factors to recommend her. "When it comes to the selection of a member for our Supreme Court, however," Gwyn continued, "popularity is not so important as one's philosophy." He wrote, "She is a firm believer in capitalism and a free, competitive system. Her democracy squares with that of Thomas Jefferson. I have been impressed with her regard for the affairs of defenseless people and her desire to do equal justice between the high and the low."[121]

When Judge Sharp had typed the letter, Gwyn "signed it and we laughed about this and that," she reported to her journal.[122]

It was almost a month before the logjam broke.

The first full week of March Judge Sharp was in Reidsville, unassigned to hold court. "I'm having my winter week off," she wrote a friend. "I don't know how I rated it. The Boss just wrote that he was giving it to me. It was like money from home, and will probably save my sanity."[123] The week was set to be a full one, although Judge Sharp had no idea just how full. Her sister Louise was home on leave from the navy. Her mother had celebrated her seventy-eighth birthday on Sunday, and sister Florence had brought all her family from Winston-Salem to dinner. Shortly after the birthday guests had left, Judge Sharp had "a caller," an apparently deranged man who "had been brooding over a case" she had tried three years before in Pittsboro, involving his sister. Judge Sharp could not for the life of her remember the case, but the gist of her visitor's grievance was that every time his sister had tried to tell her side of the dispute, Judge Sharp had "objected." He did not want any advice or help, he said. "He just wanted to talk about how wrong I had done," she wrote. "I had a terrible time getting him out of the house."

As if that were not enough, over the weekend she had managed to get a permanent, have some major repairs done on her car, and mail off her tax returns. She had finished her mother's, but still had to prepare the returns for her nephew Jimmy Taylor and the Fultz quadruplets. In addition, there was "also the little matter of three speeches to write this week."[124] Writing a speech was the worst sort of drudgery for her.[125] "Woe, woe, woe," she wrote to her friend. "I'm so afraid that I will not make the most of this week off that I have practically got the shakes."

Thursday night, with only one of the three speeches drafted, she "greased up [her] hair good with olive oil"—in the service of Beauty—and went to bed.[126] When Governor Sanford called her at nine o'clock the next morning, she must have been grateful that he could not see her through the telephone.

The evening before, having been notified by Chief Justice Winborne that he would like to "wait upon" the governor, Sanford had received him at the Mansion after dinner.[127] Knowing that the visit most probably related to Winborne's retirement, Sanford had reviewed in his mind and with a few key aides the names of various possible appointments. But, in fact, although he did not know Susie Sharp personally, he had long nurtured the idea of putting her on the court and thought this might be the moment. As a lawyer himself, he had a grasp of her solid reputation on the bench. Over time he had discussed her as a potential justice among a handful of his close associates and advisers, including his mentor, Kerr Scott, years before.[128] "I had no doubt tried it out on several people," he would later say. "You know, I wasn't just shooting in the dark."[129]

Beyond Susie Sharp and her particular qualifications, Sanford wanted to give women in general a higher profile in state government. He believed sincerely that it was time to move forward on women's issues; he also recognized the critical role women's support had played in his margin of victory in the election. In the first year of his administration, he would name to important positions the largest group of women any North Carolina governor had ever appointed.[130] He even wanted to put a woman on the highway commission, but that proved to be so unthinkable to most people that he "let himself get talked out of" making the appointment.[131] He believed, however, that he could put a woman on the North Carolina Supreme Court. "And it became pretty obvious that if you were going to put a woman on the supreme court, it almost had to be Susie Sharp," Sanford would say in recalling the appointment years later.[132]

Sanford and his administrative assistant Tom Lambeth received Chief Justice Winborne in the formal parlor of the Governor's Mansion. The chief justice handed his resignation letter to the governor, and Sanford expressed his regret that he should have to resign. Then he broached the subject of the vacancies thereby created. As Sanford recalled it, he told Winborne that unless he had some objection to it, he would like to elevate Justice Denny to the post of chief justice. As the next senior member of the court, Denny would by tradition and precedent be the expected choice. "Oh, that would please me very much," said Winborne. Sanford then mentioned three or four people as possible appointees to the associate justice position vacated by Justice Denny. "I threw Susie Sharp's name in there," Sanford recalled. But he was unable to get a great deal of reaction from Winborne on most of the names. "He quite properly said, 'That's not any of my business.'" Nonetheless, as the chief justice rose to depart, Sanford pressed him a bit. "I'm not sure I've caught your opinion on one of my suggestions," he said. "What would you think if I put Susie Sharp on the supreme court?" Sanford never forgot Winborne's response: "Governor, the supreme court is a man's court."[133] According to Tom Lambeth, Winborne was extremely upset and distressed by the very idea.[134]

When the chief justice had left, Sanford said to Lambeth, "I think I'm going to appoint Susie Sharp."[135] Lambeth then called the legal assistant to the governor, Joel Fleishman. The two of them were delighted at the prospect and resolved to get to the office early the next morning to make sure that Sanford did not get talked out of it.[136]

Prior to Chief Justice Winborne's resignation, apparently only Judge Gwyn, his son Allen Jr., and Charlotte attorney Joe Grier had actually sent letters to the governor advocating Judge Sharp for the court.[137] There had been telephone calls and other conversations, however, with her supporters. For example, Forsyth County Register of Deeds Eunice Ayers, who was close to Bert Bennett and well connected within the power structure of the Sanford organization, was active in Judge Sharp's behalf early on, conferring with both Bennett and the governor.[138] Ironically, Sanford did not consult his liaison for women's interests, the formidable Martha McKay.[139] If for some reason he backed out of appointing Susie Sharp after mentioning her as a front-runner, Martha McKay could be counted on to make the governor's life a misery.[140]

Once Judge Gwyn had relinquished his hopes for the appointment, Sanford's options were simplified. Moreover, he was spared the usual scenario in which his campaign manager, attorney general, or other close political ally coveted a seat on the supreme court. His close allies during the campaign for one reason or another were not interested in the job.[141] There was only one applicant who both desired the post and had enough political influence to be troublesome: Superior Court Judge J. Will Pless. If anything, his supporters had done a far more pervasive job of putting his name into play than had Judge Sharp's advocates, beginning long before Chief Justice Winborne finally conceded that he could not continue on the bench. Although Sanford later said that "ten or twelve" supreme court candidates had been proposed to him at one time or another,[142] Pless was Judge Sharp's only substantial competition. Years later, Guion Johnson would tell Judge Sharp that when she went to see Sanford about appointing Sharp to the court, he told her he would but that he would need help because there were strong pressures from Superior Court Judge Will Pless.[143]

Sanford, who for his own reasons was not inclined to appoint Judge Pless, nonetheless had a political situation on his hands. Chief Justice Winborne was from Marion, in the western part of the state, and his resignation left the court with only one true western representative, Justice Higgins of Alleghany County. Pless, who was also from Marion and therefore did not expect to be named to the court while Winborne was still a member, had made no secret over the years that he felt he should be appointed to fill the slot once Winborne retired. Many members of the bar, particularly in that part of the state, agreed with him and had made their support known. Traditionally, justices like Bobbitt (Charlotte) and Denny (Gastonia) had been counted as "Westerners," but more accurately speaking they were from the Piedmont, and were "western" only in the sense that they were not "eastern." The Piedmont, however, with its denser population and economic power, was a far different place from the western mountains. Comparatively isolated both culturally and economically, the western part of the state was closer in many ways to Tennessee than to North Carolina, and many of its residents did not consider Justice Bobbitt or Justice Denny to be one of theirs. Western North Carolina had a long history of feeling like a stepchild in state politics, and the paucity of justices from the western counties was a glaring defect in the court's lineup. Even though Sanford was prohibited by the state constitution from succeeding himself, no governor could afford to ignore the sentiments of a substantial portion of the population, particularly when the sentiments emanated largely from the legal profession.

When the news broke on March 9, 1962, that Chief Justice Winborne had resigned, a deluge of telegrams and letters poured in to the governor's office. Judge Sharp's advocates outnumbered those of the nearest contender by almost two to one. In an unprecedented show of support, six professors from the UNC law faculty[144] sent a telegram urging her appointment, largely composed by Mr. Breckenridge (who sent "Your Honorissima" a copy of the working draft with his revisions, pointing out how "the original as it was knocked out was greatly improved in the hand of one of your ardent supporters").[145] Professor Hanft's wife wrote separately and said that three other Chapel Hill women including Venitah Breckenridge had asked their names to be added to her endorsement of Judge Sharp. Guion Johnson weighed in, as did the heads of women's organizations across the state. Kerr Scott's widow, "Miss Mary," later described by Governor Sanford as "on the ball," picked up the telephone and called him.[146] With a few exceptions, however, most of the telegrams and letters urging the governor to appoint Judge Sharp came from ordinary people, not lawyers. They were from cousins, clerks of court, members of women's groups. They came from all across the state.

In contrast, Judge Pless had an enormous outpouring from members of the bar.[147] Interestingly, the majority of these communications came from attorneys in Charlotte, where Judge Sharp had held court more than anywhere else in the state. It was a natural power base for Pless as a representative of the western interests, but Judge Sharp's extremely small showing is startling considering how much time she had spent in Charlotte and how many good friends she had in the legal community there. Perhaps the memory of the Bonnie Brae Golf Course integration case still lingered, but the real answer seems to be that her name simply did not cross the minds of most Charlotte lawyers, who had been more thoroughly cultivated by the Pless forces. Even Judge Sharp's old and dear friend from law school, Hugh Lobdell, was among the first to send in his support for Judge Pless.[148]

What no one knew when they fired off their earnest appeals to the governor was that he had already offered the appointment to "Judge Susie."

As she was applying olive oil to her coiffure that Thursday night, March 8, Governor Sanford in the wake of Chief Justice Winborne's visit was already planning the next day's events. Thinking about Winborne's reaction, Sanford said, "I got to laughing about that again about six o'clock in the morning. And I couldn't wait until a decent hour to call Susie Sharp and ask her if she would accept."[149]

He waited until nine o'clock Friday morning, just as she was about to run out the door to the beauty parlor to get her hair washed. As she recorded in her journal, he asked her how she would like to be named to the supreme court.[150] Governor Sanford remembered that she did not hesitate.[151] Her recollection was slightly more detailed. "That is the ambition of every superior court judge, you know," she replied to his inquiry. "Do you think you would like to work with all those men?" he asked her. Judge Sharp said, "The question would be, 'Would they mind working with me?'" "I hope you will accept." "Are you offering me an appointment?" she asked. "Oh, you did not know that Judge Winborne had retired last night?" he asked.[152]

When she finally declared that she would be honored to accept, Sanford warned her that she would have to run to keep her seat. He hoped she would not have any opposition, but said that if she did he would get behind her.[153] The announcement would be made at midday.

She dashed downstairs to tell her mother and Louise. "The Governor called and you are looking at an Associate Justice of the Supreme Court," she exulted.[154] Her mother was making bread, her hands covered in flour. Louise said to her mother, "Aren't you going to kiss the new Justice?" "I'll get flour all over her," Mrs. Sharp protested. Judge Sharp called the beauty parlor to say she would be a few minutes late and that she could not tell them the reason but they had to make her beautiful.[155]

As soon as she could manage it, she slipped upstairs to call John and give him the news. She had not seen him since the previous November. She spoke in code, trying to relay what had happened without mentioning any names or job positions. Finally it dawned on him. "You mean you are in!" Yes. "Well, congratulations," he said. "I could not be happier."[156] The next day he made his official congratulatory call. "Here are *two* women who want to talk to you," he said, putting first his daughter Frances Sue on the line, then "Mrs. K." When he took back the receiver, Susie Sharp told him she wanted to see him as soon as she could.[157]

Her life went into overdrive. It would be a long time before the pace relented.

The phone started ringing. She gave the governor's press secretary her life history over the phone in the beauty parlor. By ten o'clock the governor had notified all the members of the court and other interested parties of the new appointments. The media storm, reminiscent of when she was first appointed to the superior court bench in 1949, swept over her even as she struggled to handle the mundane details of taking on the new job. Among other things, it meant that she would have to leave 629 Lindsey Street and move to Raleigh. She drove down on Tuesday, the day before her swearing-in, and arranged for a room at the Hotel Sir Walter.[158] Her intention was to look for an apartment in Raleigh as soon as she got "her feet on the ground,"[159] but it would be nearly fourteen years before that happened. That night, even before she was sworn in, she began studying briefs for the cases to be heard the following week.[160]

The next morning before the swearing-in ceremony, she dashed to Belk's department store for some white lace to put in the neck of her judicial robe. Nearly all of her family was going to be there, everyone except her brother Tommy. Cousin Earle Garrett from Danville, whose father had told her not to accept Governor Kerr Scott's appointment to the trial court bench in 1949 for fear she would soon be out of a job, was coming. Her old high school chums Margaret Newnam, Janie Sands Smith, and Margaret Fillman (now Chaney) would be there, along with several neighbors. Former professors from the law school and other friends from Chapel Hill including Dean Henry Brandis, Mr. and Mrs. Maurice Van Hecke, Albert and Gladys Coates, and, of course, the Breckenridges would attend, in addition to such professional colleagues as Irving Carlyle and Hamp Price. Judge Allen Gwyn, his wife Janie, and Allen Jr. would certainly be there. Governor Sanford, of course, would attend. Among the missing was John Kesler, but he sent her a letter she received that morning, a letter that made her weep all the way to the ceremony.[161] "I shall be there beside you more closely than I could be in person," he wrote, in part. "Congratulations to one I love very much indeed. You are set."[162]

The North Carolina Supreme Court occupied the Justice Building, on Morgan Street opposite the State Capitol in downtown Raleigh. The high-ceilinged courtroom on the third floor, although wood-paneled and thickly hung with imposing portraits of deceased chief justices, was saved from gloom by a row of towering windows along one side. The invited guests who entered through the ten-foot-tall double doors opposite the windows looked to their left to the elevated bench running the width of the courtroom. Fifty-six green leather armchairs were neatly arranged in rows facing the bench. Seated on the bench, the justices would look down at tables for counsel, the clerk of the supreme court, and the marshal-librarian, as well as the lectern in the center from which counsel addressed the bench during oral arguments.

There was an overflow audience, among the largest turnouts any of the regulars had ever seen.[163] The history-making ceremony took only ten minutes. Judge Sharp wore a black suit "of some duration" and a double strand of pearls. Her old high school rival, Dillard Gardner, in his capacity as marshal-librarian of the supreme court, called the court to order promptly at eleven thirty. Justice R. Hunt Parker administered the oath to the new chief justice, Emery B. Denny, who then swore in the first woman to sit on the state's highest court. After she took the oath, Dillard Gardner escorted her into the justices' conference room directly behind the bench, where with flashbulbs popping she donned her robe before being escorted to her seat, the farthest to the left of the chief justice.[164]

Following the ceremony, she and the new chief justice greeted a long line of friends, relatives, and top state officials who filed by to shake their hands. Chief Justice Denny remarked to the newest associate justice, "You are not nearly as important as you were yesterday." Judge Sharp, much astonished, said, "What do you mean? I thought I'd been promoted." "Oh, no. You can no longer sentence anybody to jail," the chief justice replied. "Why, you can't even let a man off the jury and you've got no sheriff to look after you anymore."[165] At least, unlike Judge Clement on the day she was sworn in as a member of the bar, he did not tell her she was wasting her time.

Years later Judge Sharp would claim, "I never dreamed that I would one day be a member of the Supreme Court,"[166] a statement that can most charitably be interpreted to mean that she had not imagined her dream could be realized. In fact, more than two decades later she would tell Terry Sanford that he had "made the dream, which I had thought to be unobtainable, come true."[167]

It would be more accurate to say that, although she had long contemplated the position, the timing of her appointment was unexpected. In a thank-you letter to one of her supporters, she said that no one had known the chief justice planned to retire when he did. "Some of my friends, using Sherlock Holmes' methods, had deduced that he might, and they had taken steps in my behalf," she related. "My friend, neighbor, and colleague, Judge Allen H. Gwyn, masterminded the campaign and his son, Allen, Jr. was my 'Manager.'" Nonetheless, she declared, "When the appointment came I was quite unprepared for it. I hadn't expected a vacancy so soon and I had never really thought that it could happen to me anyway."[168]

Having come this far, however, she appears to have resolved to do everything necessary to keep her seat. Three weeks after her swearing-in, on April 7, 1962, she joined the Methodist Church.[169]

The new judge, 1949
(*photograph by W. C. Burton, reprinted by permission
of the* Greensboro Daily News)

The new judge in evening dress, 1949
(*photograph by Bernadette Hoyle*, Raleigh Times,
reprinted by permission of the News and Observer)

Flowers for the judge
(*Sharp family photograph*)

Judge Sharp and Judge Allen H. Gwyn at the
Reidsville Jaycee Harvest Jubilee, 1954. *Seated, left to right,*
former governor and U.S. senatorial candidate Kerr Scott,
North Carolina representative Radford Powell, Judge Gwyn,
and Judge Sharp; *standing,* Mayor George Hunt
(Sharp family photograph)

Judicial robes, 1958
*(photograph by Bill Futrelle, reprinted by permission
of the* Goldsboro News-Argus*)*

Judge Sharp, presiding in Harnett Superior Court, 1958.
Left to right: D. K. Stewart, Archie Taylor, District Solicitor
Jack Hooks, Robert Bryan, Duncan C. Wilson
(T. M. Studio, Lillington, North Carolina, Dunn Dispatch)

North Carolina Supreme Court associate justice Susie M. Sharp being
sworn in by Chief Justice Emery B. Denny, March 14, 1962

(photograph by Ken Cooke, reprinted by permission of the News and Observer*)*

opposite:
North Carolina Supreme Court chief justice Susie M. Sharp and her court,
1975. *Seated, left to right,* Justice I. Beverly Lake, Chief Justice Susie M. Sharp,
and Justice Joseph Branch; *standing, left to right,* Justices J. William Copeland,
J. Frank Huskins, Dan K. Moore, and James G. Exum Jr.

*(photograph by Robert Schulenberg, "The Supreme Court of North Carolina,"
reprinted by permission of the Administrative Office of the Courts)*

245

Retired chief justices Susie M. Sharp and William H. Bobbitt
(photograph by Hugh Morton, reprinted by permission of Catherine Morton)

PART IV

NORTH CAROLINA
SUPREME COURT
(1962–1979)

CHAPTER 12

TAKING THE VEIL

The morning after she was sworn in, she reported for her first day at work as an associate justice. Her attention was diverted, however, by a furor in the press over issues related to her appointment.

Most distressing for Justice Sharp was an article on the front page of the *News and Observer* in which the lead paragraph read, "Judge Susie Sharp, the first woman ever to become a justice of the State Supreme Court, believes that the average woman's place is in the home."[1] The story was picked up by newspapers all over the country and as far away as Puerto Rico and Germany. Many people sent her copies of a version that appeared as a "Special" to the *New York Times*.[2] Written by reporter Roy Parker Jr., the *News and Observer* article gave the impression that the quote was from an interview he conducted with the newly appointed justice. In fact, alone among the newspapers of statewide circulation, the *News and Observer* had not contacted her.[3] Judge Sharp had never met Parker, who took his quotes from a 1952 story by a reporter in New Bern, North Carolina, which had run in the Raleigh paper.[4] In *that* purported interview, which Judge Sharp did not recall, she was quoted regarding her opinion on women in political office. "Judge Sharp seriously doubts that women will seek political office to any considerable extent, but she thinks many of them are capable of filling high office," the article read. "'I wouldn't hesitate to vote for a woman for governor or for president,' she says, 'if the right woman ran for the job. However, I'm of the opinion that the average woman's field is in the home, as a wife and mother.'"

The words may have been particularly ill-chosen or even inaccurately quoted, but they manifested her genuine belief that women, unlike men, could not manage both a job and a family. It was a view that, despite her denials, she expressed similarly in other times and places. Indeed, in an interview with another *News and Observer* reporter later in the week, when asked about "the age-old conflict of career versus marriage," she declared, "You can't serve two masters and serve them well."[5] The article went on: "She believes a woman's children are her first obligation. 'Had I married and become a mother, I wouldn't be sitting here being interviewed,' she reasoned. 'I could never work and raise a family and be a success at both. It's hard to reach the top with a husband and family to care for.'"[6] To women involved in expanding women's horizons, her repeated assertions that most women — including herself — could not successfully manage both a family and a career were unwelcome.

The newspaper articles upset the state vice chairman of the Democratic Party, Doris Cromartie, longtime women's advocate from Charlotte, who immediately called Governor Sanford and Bert Bennett to express her outrage. Sanford suggested that she call Judge Sharp, which she did. As Judge Sharp reported to John Kesler, she gathered from the conversation that Mrs. Cromartie "thought I thought I was above average and would like to sentence the others of my sex to a life of drudgery in the kitchen and over a wash tub!"[7]

Martha McKay, Governor Sanford's formidable organizer, now a member of the North Carolina Democratic Executive Committee and a Democratic national committeewoman, fired off a letter to Judge Sharp in which her efforts to bite her tongue are almost palpable. After expressing her congratulations on her appointment, Mrs. McKay continued, "With your permission, I would like to be very frank. It is generally thought that the women of the state had a great deal to do with electing Terry Sanford governor, and thus indirectly with your appointment. . . . I wonder if there is any chance you were misquoted in your statement saying that woman's place is in the home. At any rate, may I humbly suggest that it would be a great help if in the future you could instead point to the contributions women have made and are capable of making to their communities, state, and nation."[8]

Judge Sharp, horrified at the uproar, emphatically claimed to Doris Cromartie, Martha McKay, Governor Sanford, Bert Bennett, and anyone else within range that she had never said anything resembling the quoted remark in either public or private. She spent time she did not have composing letters and telegrams to everyone who had written or called her, or even simply sent her a clipping containing the offending quote along with their best wishes, declaring herself both innocent and appalled. She was well aware that she had no choice but to take whatever time was required to undo as much damage as she could. As she said to John, "You never know when a tempest in a teapot like that can become a hurricane."[9] She seemed incapable of recognizing that she had without doubt made remarks from time to time that were, at a minimum, susceptible to the interpretation the newspapers had given them.

Her first impulse had been to contact Roy Parker, the transgressing reporter, but she accepted the advice of Bill Snider, then associate editor of the *Greensboro Daily News*, not to fan the flames by responding. "Newspapers can make it very hard for a thin-skinned person," she commented.[10] It was something of a relief when she encountered Parker a couple of months later and had "the opportunity to discuss the matter with him."[11] He explained that ordinarily he would not have written such a story "without checking it with 'the subject,'" but that he had tried repeatedly without success to reach her by telephone the day of her appointment.[12] Judge Sharp, though sure this was the truth, lambasted him for using alleged quotes from an old story while giving the impression that he interviewed her on the day of her appointment.[13] He apologized, but privately Judge Sharp said, "He will never know how much joy he took out of a momentous occasion for me."[14]

The governor's failure to appoint Judge Pless also created some editorial sniping in the western part of the state. In Asheville, an editorial remarked, "Women's organizations over the state pressured the governor in the Sharp appointment."[15] One particularly biting commentator stated that although the mountains had produced all sorts of talented people, including scholars, writers, business and professional men, a Miss America, and a member of the Football Hall of Fame, "somehow the word never gets to Raleigh."[16] The editorial acknowledged Justice Sharp's qualifications and expressed pride in having a woman on the high court, but nonetheless regretted that Judge Pless had not been appointed, adding, "We don't know exactly how [Governor Sanford] appraises these things, but we do know that if Raleigh continues to ignore the West there may be even more Republicans than we have now."[17]

If Governor Sanford was worried by the westerners' disappointment, he did not let it disturb him. In his office the deluge of congratulatory letters was so overwhelming that it took two secretaries to process it all.[18] Many who had written him to propose that he appoint Pless wrote again after Judge Sharp was named to say that, although they had endorsed Judge Pless, they were extremely pleased about his choice. Several Charlotte attorneys, including Judge Sharp's law school friend Hugh Lobdell, admitted that it had simply not occurred to them that Judge Sharp might be considered.[19] "You and Governor Scott were one jump ahead of most of us in thinking of this fine lawyer as judicial material," Lobdell wrote. Attorney Joe Grier, who had contacted the governor on Judge Sharp's behalf early on, reported that her appointment seemed to have "met with universal approval, even from those members of the Bar who might initially have favored some other candidate."[20]

Sanford had essentially made up his mind that he would appoint her, even before the vacancy occurred. He had acted swiftly to prevent other candidates from organizing. As he explained to one Pless supporter who criticized him for not allowing time for people to weigh in with their thoughts on the appointment, "I did not wait very long because having reached a decision I could see only disappointment and confusion for many if I allowed a number of campaigns to build up."[21]

Sanford's instincts had been right on target. All over the state the reaction was primarily one of delight and enthusiasm. Putting Judge Sharp on the supreme court would turn out to be one of his most popular and well-regarded acts as governor. The new justice was particularly touched by the celebratory dinner given her by the members of the Rockingham County bar, at which she was presented with a gift-wrapped and be-ribboned parcel that contained the Rockingham County "foot box" made years ago for her by Deputy Bernard Young, which he had "covered handsomely with rich velvet befitting her new rank."[22]

Nor was it lost on interested observers that, as the youngest of the justices, she had an excellent chance of remaining on the court long enough to become chief justice. Albert and Gladys Coates were among those to suggest this possibility shortly after her swearing-in. The Coateses took Judge Sharp the gift of a plant, which, as Albert informed her, they had "christened 'Justice' with the hope and belief it will grow into the 'Chief Justice.'"[23]

As for Justice Sharp, having reached her goal, she was in danger of being overwhelmed. "It has been my ambition," she wrote to John, "but now that it is here I am beset by doubts, fears and such a feeling of inadequacy that I almost wish I could turn back the clock."[24] Driving back to Raleigh after a weekend in Reidsville two weeks after her appointment, she was so exhausted that she fell asleep at the wheel and ran off the road—something that had never happened to her before, even during all those thirteen years on the road as a peripatetic judge.[25] Perhaps the old adage, "Be careful what you wish for," crossed her mind. Her new license plate read "J-7," but her monthly check was actually $1.57 less than before.[26]

In a matter of days her entire life had changed drastically. From living in Reidsville in her childhood home, she had moved to the state capital and taken rooms in the Hotel Sir Walter. Instead of leaving home on Sunday or Monday to drive to some far-flung courthouse, she would now have her center of gravity in Raleigh, driving back to Reidsville on the weekends to check on her mother. As a member of the supreme court, she would spend her days looking for error rather than for truth, as she had done as a trial judge. Instead of ruling orally from the bench, she would have to render her opinions in writing, which for such a perfectionist was a wrenching adjustment. If people had had low expectations of her when she was appointed to the superior court, now she feared that they expected too much.

She was not the first woman to sit on a state supreme court, a fact that would have done little to diminish her standing in North Carolina even if it had been widely known. That honor went to Florence E. Allen, who served on the Ohio Supreme Court from 1922 to 1934, before becoming the first woman to be appointed to the U.S. Court of Appeals when President Franklin D. Roosevelt named her to the Sixth Circuit. Justice Sharp herself had no idea if she had any current company in her rarified category, and one of the first things Supreme Court Marshal-Librarian Dillard Gardner, her childhood friend, did was to research the question. He found that in two states, Arizona and Hawaii, the highest appellate court boasted a woman justice, both of whom had previously served in the state attorney general's office. Justice Lorna E. Lockwood had joined the Arizona court the year before, in 1961; Justice Rhoda V. Lewis had been on the Hawaii court since 1959. Another woman, Anne X. Alpern, had been appointed to the Pennsylvania Supreme Court in August 1961, but was defeated in the ensuing election.[27]

Given the amount of publicity Judge Sharp's trailblazing had always brought her, it was probably just as well that she was not burdened with the designation of first woman supreme court justice in the entire country. Any more media demands than she already received would have been difficult to handle. She found her work load overwhelming. "I am left with the feeling that I have taken the veil and the doors of the cloisters have closed and locked behind me—and I'm terrified," she wrote.[28]

It did not help that she was under immediate and intense pressure from the political side to accept a variety of speaking engagements, requests for which poured in. The most troublesome of these came from key bases of her support, such as, for example, the Democratic Women of Forsyth County, home of political kingmaker Bert Bennett, without whose support she would not be on the North Carolina Supreme Court. No neophytes, the president and program chairman sent Bennett a copy of their letter requesting a dinner speech from the new justice, and he personally wrote Judge Sharp urging her to accept.[29] Judge Sharp, although committed to fulfilling her speaking engagements already scheduled, balked at any further such obligations and in particular to any such overtly political speeches. She brought the matter up with the other justices, who bolstered her position; the chief justice himself went down to the Hotel Sir Walter "to explain to Mr. Tom Davis, the executive secretary of the State Democratic Executive Committee, that [she] could not with propriety accept the invitations" for speeches to political groups or participation in political programs.[30]

In addition to a long, careful letter to the Democratic Women explaining her position, Justice Sharp also wrote Bert Bennett, begging his understanding and cooperation. She noted that the canons of the American Bar Association and the policies of the supreme court did not permit a justice to take any active part in politics. This created "an anomalous situation because a judge is no less a Democrat the day after he (or she!) was appointed and he must be elected if he stays a judge." The supreme court, however, stood in judgment over both Democrats and Republicans. "It is not only necessary that in its judicial acts a court be non-partisan, it is almost equally important that the people have confidence and faith that it is so," she wrote. "It would simply be impossible to keep this faith and confidence if the justices of the Supreme Court participated in any political activities such as speech making. It would be particularly unfortunate if I should do it because of the amount of publicity I would get."[31]

She felt compelled to add that there was "another reason which has nothing to do with politics" that prevented her from accepting speaking engagements. "There is no time; the work of the court is too demanding." During her first week as a supreme court justice, there were fifteen cases for which she had to read the entire (often voluminous) record and briefs, hear arguments, and write opinions; the second week there were twenty-one. "I have barely been able to keep up," she confessed to Bennett.[32]

In addition to her new regular duties, court tradition decreed that the newest justice serve as secretary to the court. Susie Sharp, to her vocal distress, was inevitably chosen to be the secretary of every organization she ever belonged to, from the local Democratic Party organization to the Conference of Superior Court Judges of North Carolina. "I was born to be a secretary!" she often lamented.[33] She told her old friends Bill and Winona Covington that her latest position as secretary to the supreme court was "a condition comparable only to college hazing."[34] Among other things such as keeping the minutes of the justices' conferences, she was responsible for all the writs of habeas corpus, petitions for certiorari, motions, and the like that came to the court. Attending to these alone required one full day a week.[35]

Fortunately for her health, her sanity, and the business of the court, she was able to hold firm on the issue of speaking invitations. Her diplomatic and persuasive letters to those requesting her presence, backed up by support from Chief Justice Denny and Governor Sanford, had their intended effect. The governor wrote her what she told John Kesler she would almost call a "sweet" letter in which he assured her "that he understood perfectly the situation in which I found myself and that I should 'not worry at all' about pressures from The Chairman BB et al to make political speeches; that he knew I could not and would explain it to him and others."[36]

One speech request, however, was difficult to refuse. Judge Sharp's sister Louise, serving as a navy nurse at the Cherry Point, North Carolina, military base, had asked her to be the guest speaker at a May 1, 1962, banquet, sponsored by the Camp Lejeune–Cherry Point Bar Association, in its observation of Law Day, U.S.A. It was not Louise's idea. After Judge Sharp was appointed to the supreme court, a delegation of marine officers paid Louise a visit and asked if she could get her sister to be their speaker. Louise, knowing full well how her sister felt about the burden of speechmaking, especially since her recent appointment, said, "Well, she can't do that. She doesn't have time!" At this, the delegation said they would send a special plane for the justice. Under pressure, Louise said she'd ask. Characteristically, knowing that it would be helpful to Louise, Judge Sharp agreed to do it despite her lack of time, not to mention her fear of flying.[37] As it turned out, however, she enjoyed the trip very much. Not only did the officers send a special plane for her, but they also presented her with an orchid to wear at the banquet held at the Marine Corps Air Station Officer's Club and in general behaved with a gallantry guaranteed to perk up any girl's spirits.[38]

As the junior justice, she moved into Room 317, formerly occupied by Justice William B. Rodman, who took advantage of the opportunity provided by a new member on the court to move into nicer chambers.[39] Justice Sharp's office, high-ceilinged albeit not overly large, was on the back side of the building, and although it had a window, utilitarian venetian blinds were kept closed to hide the dismal alley view. Her chambers, like those of all the justices, had a private powder room adjoining. Justice Sharp told an interviewer, "The floor's a lovely teakwood. I won't need a rug, but I do plan to rearrange the furniture a bit. The walls need some pictures and I'll need a filing cabinet for personal notes and mail. I'll probably keep some cut flowers about."[40] One of her first official actions was to exercise her privilege of borrowing paintings from the North Carolina Museum of Art. After consultation with Dr. Justus Bier, director of the museum, she selected two landscapes, inoffensive if not particularly distinguished.[41]

In truth, the state's highest judges carried out their duties in quarters that were shockingly spartan. Since the supreme court had moved into the newly constructed five-story Justice Building in July of 1940, there had been essentially no changes, redecoration, or modernization.[42] Although the courtroom itself was soberly impressive, the justices' chambers on the third floor were devoid of any trace of grandeur, elegance, or, arguably, comfort.

Only the courtroom itself had air-conditioning when the Justice Building was built. Some window units had been installed in the judges' chambers over the years, making for an unaesthetic hodgepodge. When, however, funding later became available for central air-conditioning to be installed, the justices rejected the idea. Judge Sharp feared the dust and disruption involved in tearing out walls and installing new ductwork. In addition, all of the justices had spent nights in hotels and motels where you could not open the window to get some fresh air or turn off the air-conditioner. They all had memories of trying to blunt the icy blast of the air-conditioner with a blanket or pillow to avoid freezing to death and, as individuals accustomed to control, did not wish to surrender sovereignty over the temperature of their chambers.[43] For Justice Higgins, it was important to be able to open the window because, in winter, he kept his five o'clock beer cold on the windowsill.[44]

Except in the justices' inner chambers, the floors were of a hard terrazzo thinly covered by a coarse, reedy matting or — in the hallways — by rubber runners. As each of the three cushions on the couch in the chief justice's reception room grew tatty, it would be sent out singly to be recovered, the result being three not-quite-matching cushions. Fluorescent lights dangled from the ceilings. Compared, for example, to the palatial highway commission's offices with their elegant paneled walls and fine accoutrements, the supreme court chambers were almost primitive.[45]

This state of affairs was at least partly due to the attitude of the justices themselves, who considered austerity a badge of honor. In addition to what was a peculiarly North Carolinian distaste for trappings of power deemed inconsistent with "little-d" democracy, the notion that the court might owe anything whatsoever to the legislature was anathema. Justice R. Hunt Parker was known to have claimed, "I have never asked the State for anything! The only time I have ever asked for anything is when my chair fell from beneath me, and I asked that it be repaired."[46]

Judge Sharp did dare to make one innovation. When the members of the previously all-male court assembled in the conference room prior to filing out to take their seats on the bench, they had never felt the need to check their appearances before emerging, so there had never been a mirror in that room. Judge Sharp took it upon herself to remedy the situation. She was well aware that the court would never submit a funding request for such an item. Her initial solution was to bundle up her Green Stamp booklets and redeem them for a mirror, which she installed in the conference room.[47] Not only did no one object but, to her surprise, no one said anything at all about it.[48] The Green Stamp mirror was not elegant, however, and several years later Judge Sharp undertook to replace it with something much grander. This time it created a great deal more uproar.

Around 1970 when the justices' chambers were finally undergoing some decorative renovations, Judge Sharp found an attractive antique mirror and persuaded a majority of the court to recommend its purchase. Justice Higgins, however, took the trouble to write the state purchase officer to record his objection. "In my antiquated and humble view," he wrote, "the expenditure of Seven Hundred Dollars for the purchase of a mirror for the Supreme Court conference room is unjustified. This sort of thing encourages more waste and will cut another hole (although small) in the state's money bag."[49] Undeterred, in September 1971 a determined Judge Sharp offered to buy an "antique pier mirror with gold leaf frame and accompanying miniature marbletop table" and donate it to the court.[50] Her offer was accepted unanimously, and although several justices offered to share the expense with her, she declined.[51]

When Judge Sharp went on the supreme court in 1962, the deprivations went beyond the cosmetic. For example, all the records and briefs were printed by mimeograph machine. The justices' secretaries typed the court's opinions on onionskin, seven sheets separated by carbon paper. Every typo meant erasing the error on the original and each of the carbon copies, then retyping. The opinions were circulated to the justices with legibility of the copies correlating to seniority, thus ensuring eyestrain if not complete mystification for the newest member of the court. Although the photocopier had begun to be indispensable in the modern office, it would be sometime in the late 1960s before the court acquired a copy machine, and it was in spite of rather than because of the justices. After strenuous efforts by Marshal-Librarian Raymond Mason Taylor, the justices finally allowed Senator Robert Morgan to insert the request as a line item in the budget bill, while expressly refusing to request such an action.[52]

Judge Sharp was pleased, however, with her new quarters in the Hotel Sir Walter. The ten-story hotel, built in 1923, was home for a number of legislators and government personages, including at least one of her new colleagues, Justice R. Hunt Parker, and his wife. Indeed, at one time most of the supreme court justices lived at the Sir Walter. In an era before apartment houses were common, the hotel claimed a number of full-time residents, including Mrs. Wilbur Royster, mother of Vermont Royster, who became the editor of the *Wall Street Journal*; Mrs. Mabel Claire Maddrey, a legendary grande dame; and Mrs. Blanche Manor, known as "Miss Blanche," who held a nonstop salon that served as politicians' news central, where she not only provided the latest gossip but also offered welcome and guidance to new legislators. The hotel dining room was filled with movers and shakers of all kinds. Local clubs met at the hotel, and debutantes with their families and escorts took it over once a year during the annual ball weekend. So much legislative business was transacted at the Sir Walter that it was known as "the third house of the North Carolina General Assembly." As one former member of the legislature recalled, "Nightly the spacious lobby and plush sofas were filled with solons, lobbyists, state officials and plain folks bending ears or eavesdropping. Agreements were made and committee votes assured. Anyone you wanted to see might pass through the lobby."[53] Upstairs were lobbyists' hospitality rooms, well-stocked with food and liquor, and generally a poker game somewhere.

Judge Sharp had taken the apartment occupied by Chief Justice Winborne until his resignation. The newly decorated living room, bedroom, and bath cost only twenty-five dollars a month more than the single room in which she had been staying when she first arrived in Raleigh. It was furnished with hotel furniture, nice enough although nothing special. She had a double bed, a sofa bed in the living room, and plenty of lamps. From Reidsville she brought pictures and a few pieces of special furniture, along with three sofa pillows her mother had made for her.[54] She bought a small refrigerator, a toaster, and a hot plate so she could do some light cooking.[55] In addition to the house phone that came with the apartment, she installed a separate private line, partly because outside calls would be cheaper without the hotel's additional charges, but primarily for reasons of privacy. "My calls will not go thru the switchboard and long distance callers can dial my number knowing that if the phone is answered it will be I," she explained to John Kesler.[56] The pièce de résistance was a brand-new Fisher stereo hi-fi, a combination radio and record player on which she listened to her beloved operas.[57]

At the court itself, her acceptance appeared to be both immediate and sincere, whatever private misgivings some justices may have harbored. "Congratulations on your appointment as a member of this Court. A warm welcome awaits you," read a telegram signed by Chief Justice Emery B. Denny and all five of the other associate justices. Knowledgeable court watchers speculated that the profoundly traditional Justice Parker must be horrified. As one observer would later describe Parker's views on women's place, "Judge Parker thought that [all women were] like Mrs. Parker. You were just supposed to stay upstairs and to be there for meals."[58] Perhaps Parker's public reaction was muted by the sentiment Justice Higgins expressed when he told Judge Sharp that "they were so afraid of what they were going to get that they were perfectly delighted" with her appointment.[59]

They were from the old school, her new colleagues, all of whom had served on the court for a number of years. Born in 1892, Chief Justice Emery B. Denny had been appointed as an associate justice twenty years before, in 1942. A bald-headed gentleman, he was once described as "kind-looking" by a reporter,[60] an accurate characterization. Next in seniority was Justice R. Hunt Parker, also born in 1892. According to the same reporter, his visage was "severe, hollow-eyed and thin-lipped." By the time of his death in 1969, he would have served almost seventeen years on the court, nearly four years of that time as chief justice. It is doubtful that any justice before or since has had more stories told about him than Hunt Parker, whose Anglophilia and exceptional self-regard were legendary. He was so conservative that he claimed never to have appeared in his shirtsleeves outside of his bedchamber. A stickler for precedent, he prided himself on never having written an original word in his supreme court opinions.[61]

Next most senior was William H. Bobbitt, appointed to the court in 1954. A warm personality did not obscure his keen intellect, and he was held in high esteem by everyone from the lowliest employee to his fellow justices. Carlisle W. Higgins, Jim Sharp's old adversary, was the member of the court whose eccentricities came closest to equaling those of Hunt Parker. Born in 1887, Higgins's experiences were the stuff of legend. He was a big game hunter with a mountain named after him in Alaska, a marksman who—despite the loss of his left eye in 1929—would be able to fire two bullets through the same hole at a distance of 100 yards the day after his ninetieth birthday. After World War II he had served as a prosecutor at the Tokyo War Crimes trials. Prone to dozing during a particularly dull argument before the court, Higgins disconcerted more than one attorney when he dropped off, his good eye closed while the glass eye remained open.[62] Justice William B. Rodman Jr., the grandson of a former justice who had served from 1869 to 1878, had been on the court since 1956. The youngest in seniority, although he had a head full of snow-white hair, was Clifton L. Moore, appointed by Governor Luther Hodges in 1959. Bobbitt and Moore at sixty-two were the youngest members of the court until Judge Sharp joined them approximately four months before her fifty-fifth birthday.

The members of the "man's court" were rarely less than cordial and normally were even courtly toward the newest associate justice, whatever qualms they had about her gender. Her only special request was that she not be addressed as "Miss Justice." Soon enough they came to respect her as at least their equal. For her part, Judge Sharp's newness coupled with her perfectionism caused her to take pains undreamed of by her fellow justices. After the first few weeks on the court, she wrote to John Kesler, "I am producing very slowly. Apparently I have been reading the records and studying them more closely than my colleagues prior to argument."[63] Several months later, she was still lamenting her inability to get ahead of the work load. "If the load is not to crush me," she wrote to John, "I must learn to put it down quicker — but I do not seem to be able to learn to do anything except my way, the hard way."[64] She would improve her speed over the years, but she would remain the slowest worker on the court.

Hunt Parker was indeed perhaps the least amenable to the notion of a female justice. During Judge Sharp's first year or so on the court, he could not seem to let one of her opinions go by without a dissenting vote. She found, however, that if she made a point of including an opinion written by Justice Parker among the supporting authorities in her draft opinion, his objections dwindled markedly. After several months of success along these lines, Judge Sharp remarked to her law clerk, "It's just unbelievable how we now have no trouble with Justice Parker."[65] Before long, Justice Parker to his credit decided that she was a brilliant judge even if she was a female, and they formed an excellent working relationship.

Not all of her adjustments were reflected in the judicial record. "Here where the secretaries in the Justice Bldg. put on hats and white gloves to go to lunch at the s&w I have suffered sadly by comparison — especially on the hem line," she wrote to John.[66] First Lady Jackie Kennedy's fashion influence was being felt all over the country, and Judge Sharp lamented that skirts seemed to be getting "shorter and shorter."[67] She simply had not had time to get her wardrobe up to date, but the last straw came when one of the secretaries "tactfully suggested" that she would "look more youthful in a shorter dress."[68] Judge Sharp persuaded her alterations lady to skip church on a Sunday so they could have a hemming session.[69] Nor did she waste a particle of time otherwise available to her. "As the Court walks to the s&w to lunch each day the gentlemen keep their eyes straight ahead, but I turn mine to window shop," she confided to her friend Evelyn Ripple.[70] "That is the only time I have to do it and, believe it or not, I collected my costume for [a] luncheon that way. I saw a white linen with red and blue trim in the window at Teachy-Womble's; at Mother and Daughter I saw an aluminum mesh bag; in Adler's I saw some white shoes with red and blue trim, and in the Em-Dee Hat Shop, I saw a red Bretton [sic] hat."

Even with such diversions, however, she found that the freewheeling atmosphere she had enjoyed in the trial court was absent. "We don't have the fun here which occasionally brightened the day in the Superior Court, and my efforts to get a little are always squelched by somebody," she wrote to her Charlotte friend Lelia Alexander, one of the few female lawyers in the state.[71] Moreover, she was uncomfortable with the fawning attention that accompanied her position. "I can't get used to a lot of bowing and scraping," she complained to John.[72] She had been horrified when she called the clerk of court and asked him to come up sometime during the morning at his convenience to transact some business and he was in her office almost before she hung up the telephone.[73] She was grateful for a more realistic attitude from the two black messengers who were longtime employees of the court. "They know I'm new and scared. I have not pretended to be otherwise and they do seem to want to help."[74]

After interviewing several applicants, she hired a secretary named Virginia Lyon. It was a gut decision, one that she would never regret. She wrote candidly to one unsuccessful applicant, after apologizing for subjecting her to unnecessary pressure by failing to alert her to the time involved in the interview, "I have selected Miss Virginia Lyon, not because I think she would do better work—I do not believe she will. It was a matter of temperament. I may be one hundred percent wrong; I have not had much experience in selecting secretaries. However, I too am inclined to be nervous under pressure and it was this which formed the basis of my decision."[75] She needed someone with a steady disposition as her closest aide, not someone else for her to worry about.

Virginia Lyon, a fading redhead who had never married, lived with her mother in Raleigh and had worked in the attorney general's office, background that Judge Sharp felt would be helpful to her at the supreme court. From the beginning they were a team and would become friends, almost like family. Partly because Judge Sharp did not have the time to cultivate many close friendships, she enjoyed the opportunity to talk about "girly" things with someone she saw daily. The two of them shared a love of beautiful clothes, and Virginia was always telling Judge Sharp she ought to go have a look at a blouse or a dress or a hat she had seen on her lunch hour. Virginia liked to wear yellows, reds, and oranges—colors considered taboo for redheads— and she could carry it off.[76] She was loyal and protective without being overbearing, and, like Judge Sharp, she was interested in getting the work done properly rather than getting caught up in office politics. Dick Jones, who was Judge Sharp's first law clerk, recalled that Miss Lyon had a "wonderful personality."[77] She would be the only secretary Judge Sharp would have during all her years at the supreme court. So valued was she that when Judge Sharp took out flight insurance before leaving on various trips, she listed Virginia as a beneficiary along with her siblings.

Routine at the court was carefully defined and followed. The court held two terms each year, a spring term beginning in February and a fall term beginning in late August. During hearing weeks the court sat from Tuesday through successive days, hearing oral arguments from ten o'clock to two o'clock, until the cases on the calendar had been heard. In the afternoon the justices met in conference to discuss that day's cases. Every third week of a term was devoted exclusively to drafting opinions, and the court did not hear oral arguments.

A typical day when the court was sitting began with a quiet, respectful buzz building up in the solemn paneled courtroom, in the attorneys' room off the hall at the back of the courtroom, and in the adjacent corridors. Lawyers and interested parties filtered through the tall double doors into the courtroom to take seats in the green leather armchairs. Behind the bench two Ionic columns reached to the high ceiling, one on each side of the full-length portrait of Chief Justice Thomas Ruffin (1787–1870). If the weather was warm, the soaring windows might be open to admit the sound of traffic three floors below, along with soft southern breezes. From down the hallway might come the faint sound of a typewriter. The ticktock of the grandfather clock against one wall exerted a hypnotic power.[78]

The courtroom session was scheduled to begin promptly at ten o'clock, and so it would. Often, however, punctuality depended on a manual adjustment to the grandfather clock just beforehand. "Supreme Court time," it was called. As the hour approached, an attendant placed water pitchers on the marshal's desk and beside the attorneys' lectern. Justices had their own water goblets, and each had a buzzer under the bench to summon refills or anything else required. The marshal emerged and addressed the audience: "Upon the opening of court, please remain standing until the clerk and the marshal sit. Please do not sit when the court sits. Thank you."

At the first stroke of the grandfather clock announcing the hour, the marshal buzzed the adjacent conference room where the justices waited. As the last bong sounded, he cracked his gavel and intoned, "The Honorable, the Chief Justice, and the Associate Justices of the Supreme Court of North Carolina." The conference room door opened and the black-robed justices entered the courtroom in single file, in order of seniority, led by the chief justice. The presence of a woman among the justices was still so novel that at least one southern gentleman, Supreme Court Marshal Raymond Mason Taylor, felt distinctly uneasy when Judge Sharp had to let all the male members of the court precede her through the door, and wait to be the last to file out of the courtroom at adjournment.[79] The justices' seats along the bench were also assigned according to seniority, with the chief justice in the center, and the associate justices in alternating order to either side, the most junior justices on either end and the most senior justices next to the chief justice. As the newest member of the court, Judge Sharp had the seat on the end next to the windows, from which she could watch the squirrels on the Capitol grounds, a diversion she would miss when she graduated to the other end of the bench.[80] Once the justices, in unison, had taken their seats, the marshal banged his gavel again, proclaiming, "Oyez! Oyez! Oyez! The Supreme Court of North Carolina is sitting for the dispatch of business. God save the State and this honorable Court."[81]

Each attorney had thirty minutes to present his side of a case, interrupted by questions from the bench. As an appellate court, the justices were concerned only with questions of law, not of fact. The justices were each responsible for reviewing the record and briefs of every case to be heard, and had before them black notebooks containing their synopses of the facts and points of law. North Carolina was one of the few states in the country in which the justices of the supreme court observed this discipline. In New York, for example, cases were assigned to justices in the order they were filed, and only the justice who would write the opinion read and briefed the cases assigned to him.[82] In some states the cases were divided among committees, which briefed the other members on the cases it had prepared.

When Judge Sharp joined the court, the tradition that "every Judge does his homework" was very strong, and she declared to an audience of lawyers, "I, for one, would not incur the disdain of my brethren by coming to Court without having my notebook up to date."[83] She was not without help, as each justice had, at that time, one law clerk to assist with research. The degree to which a justice might depend on a clerk for drafting an opinion varied with the justices, but every opinion bore the name of the justice writing for the majority (or that of the author of a dissenting or concurring opinion), so most justices were reluctant to abdicate to the wisdom of a brand-new law school graduate, no matter how brilliant.[84]

E. Richard ("Dick") Jones, Judge Sharp's first law clerk, had been clerking for Chief Justice Winborne before Winborne resigned. Due to the chief justice's health, Jones—who had recently graduated from the University of North Carolina School of Law—carried a heavier than usual amount of responsibility for the opinions issuing from the chief justice's office. Although Judge Sharp joked about his abrupt descent from No. 1 to No. 7, the young man was frankly relieved to be working for someone who was less reliant on him.[85] Nevertheless, when Judge Sharp handed him a draft of her first opinion, he was appalled. Spelling and punctuation had never been her strength, as her clerk now learned. But, in addition, he felt that the opinion was disjointed and overly long. (He had, it was true, majored in English.) "I didn't know quite what to do about it," he would recall. He wanted, if possible, to spare her unnecessary criticism from the other justices, but he did not know her well enough yet to gauge whether he could level with her. His solution was to make two copies of her draft. On one he jotted a few token remarks and corrections, and on the other he made all the changes he felt were necessary. "I red-lined the hell out of it. I just tore it all to pieces."[86]

When they met to discuss the opinion, he found that Judge Sharp pressed him repeatedly for his honest opinion, so he complied. "As it turns out," he said, "I have another copy here that I've made a few corrections on." Judge Sharp looked at the hacked-up draft and said, "Oh, my. Is it that bad?" "Yes, ma'am, I'm afraid so," Jones replied. Her response was to ask him to sit down and tell her why.

She was a fast learner. According to Jones, she rewrote the opinion, and it was fine. "[I]t wasn't my opinion, and she didn't incorporate all my suggestions by any means, but nonetheless she saw what I was talking about and went ahead. She was a very intelligent woman and she was just out of practice at that sort of writing."[87] He never had to edit her again, although she continued to rely on him for careful proofreading.

Judge Sharp appreciated constructive suggestions, whether she took them or not. Another of her clerks recalled that she told him, "Remember that whenever two people agree about anything all the time, one of them is unnecessary."[88] This did not mean, however, that she was not susceptible to a certain wicked glee when the tables were turned. "I put the Jones boy in his place this morning," she chortled to John. The clerk had spent two full days on a will case. "He wrote me a voluminous report in which he said no error could be found and he wished me good luck (in writing) in trying to rationalize the Conference vote," she said. "It didn't seem to me that he hit the point; so, while I was waiting for the Secretary to finish the first final draft in the adoption case so that I could leave, I began trying to search myself. In less than ten minutes I had found a one-page opinion which disposed of the matter summarily and flatly in accordance with the vote. . . . I suppose that was just one of those things and that I had a happy accident, but 'I wouldn't have taken a pretty for it.'"[89]

The justices' conferences, held to discuss the cases heard in that day's oral arguments, were almost as formal as the court proceedings, subject to written rules, the most important of which was the rule of strict confidentiality. Everything the justices said in conference was to remain within the walls of the conference room.[90]

The justices sat in high-backed chairs in order of seniority around the conference table, the chief justice at the head, facing the junior justice at the foot. Three of the chairs were reputed to be those of the first state supreme court, which had only three members.[91] The first case discussed was the last case argued, and so on, in reverse order. The junior justice had the unenviable honor of being the first to give his views on a case and how it should be decided. (Justice Higgins, when he was the newest member of the court and faced with making the first comments on a particularly terrible case, reportedly met this burden by stating, "Well, just to tell you the truth, I'm mighty sorry it all happened.")[92] After all the justices had spoken, in order, back up the chain to the chief justice, the junior justice cast the first vote. A majority of four votes decided a case, but justices could still change their votes right up to the last minute before the opinion was released to the clerk for publication.

At the last conference of the week, the justices chose which opinions each of them would write. The shucks containing the records of each case heard that week were placed on the conference table. Then, following an unbroken rotation initially established according to seniority, each justice chose in order from among the cases, limited only by the requirement that the justice writing the opinion had voted in the majority. Thus if Justice Bobbitt (J-3), third in seniority, had been left with the last case at the preceding week of arguments, then Justice Higgins (J-4) would have the first choice, Justice Rodman (J-5) the second, and so on. Because every justice was familiar with all the cases, each was in a position to decide which to tackle. The last case left on the table was known as "Hobson's Choice," because it was no choice at all and invariably was the most difficult or undesirable case in the lot.[93]

In a speech to the North Carolina State Bar, Justice Sharp once elaborated on the court's system of assigning opinions: "This method of assigning opinions, which combines choice and chance, is designed to keep down specialization on the Court, to keep every member abreast of the law, and to make certain that each participates in every decision as an informed Justice. In this way, from time to time, every Justice must write an opinion in every branch of the law."[94] The method had the additional advantage of sparing the chief justice the thorny job of assigning the cases.

Drafts of the majority opinion as well as any dissents or concurrences were circulated among the justices. Informal discussion might be held between or among justices, and the shape of an opinion was still subject to metamorphosis. It was possible, although unusual, for members in the minority to prevail at this stage, converting votes, and the opinion would be reassigned to a member of the new majority. More likely, a member who had voted against the opinion would find that enough changes had been made, perhaps at his suggestion, so that he could either join or concur in the majority opinion. If he wished, he could state his differences in a concurring opinion, or the opinion might simply note, for example, "Sharp, J., concurring in the result."

The justices worked hard, always, to minimize splits and dissents in an effort to make the court speak as much as possible with one voice. Dissenting opinions were invariably a sign of significant and irreconcilable differences among the justices, not only because of the court's preference for unity, but also because writing a dissenting opinion often took just as much time as a majority opinion, sometimes more, and time was a scarce commodity. A dissent entailed substantial extra work for a justice who, having voted in the minority, had no responsibility for writing an opinion. Moreover, the burden of persuasion was heavier than in a majority opinion, often involving extensive legal research as well as special attention to the legal argument. Dissenting (and concurring) opinions were therefore important indications of serious disagreements. Sometimes they pointed the way to the future. Although the North Carolina Supreme Court was extremely conservative in adhering to precedent, it could and occasionally did overrule prior decisions, particularly if a persuasive dissent was already on record.

The final showdown came on opinion day, which occurred once a month during the fall and spring terms. In the original conference ballot, the court had voted on whether to affirm or reverse the lower court's ruling (or to make some other dispensation of the case). Now the court would vote on whether to approve the written opinion. The justice who had written for the majority "tendered" the opinion to the other justices in conference. If it passed with at least four votes, it "went down," becoming law and precedent for subsequent cases. If not, it remained in the drafting stage until a majority approved it.

Once ready for release, the opinions were put in a two-handled basket, which a messenger carried downstairs to the clerk's office, where the new opinions were made available to the concerned parties and the press. Savvy reporters knew who had written each opinion the moment they were spread onto the press table because their jackets were color-coded. Justice Higgins's opinions, for example, were covered in a lemon yellow jacket, Justice Bobbitt's in pale green. Justice Sharp chose lavender for her opinion jackets and sometimes remarked to close friends and associates that they would find "a touch of lavender" in the basket on opinion day.[95]

The most public of all the supreme court traditions was the justices' daily luncheon procession from the Justice Building, down Fayetteville Street. Over the years the lunchtime venue changed from time to time, from the s&w Cafeteria to the cafeteria in the Hudson-Belk Department Store, for example. But one could set one's watch by the sight of the supreme court justices en route to take their midday meal together. An out-of-town observer, astonished to see the North Carolina Supreme Court stand in a cafeteria line like everyone else, once remarked that in Virginia "you would likely find the Justices of the Virginia Court dining at one of the swank clubs and dining privately."[96]

Lunching "en banc" was not compulsory, but most of the justices valued it as an opportunity to be together in an informal setting, to joke a bit, to get to know each other outside the third floor of the Justice Building. Occasionally, a knotty problem that had seemed insoluble might come unraveled over lunch. "If we have any pre-argument conferences on the cases to be heard they come about as spontaneous discussions at lunch," Judge Sharp would later write, as chief justice, to a law professor who had requested a description of the North Carolina Supreme Court's operating procedures. "[M]any things are decided at lunch in the Capital Room at Belk's Department Store."[97] Over the years Judge Sharp endured an unimaginable amount of sports talk, a subject on which she maintained a nearly impervious ignorance. A colleague once claimed that, until he explained otherwise, "Justice Sharp thought the Harlem Globetrotters were a traveling orchestra."[98] Justice Parker, ever aloof, was one of the few who generally chose not to join the other members of the court at lunch. "I'm in the middle of a sentence," he commonly explained, until "he must be in the middle of a sentence" became the tongue-in-cheek insider's explanation for someone's absence.[99]

The justices' camaraderie was reflected in a creative security measure devised by Justice Higgins for the lady justice, who generally drove herself around alone. Higgins, Judge Sharp wrote to John, "had a very fine western hat which cost $25. He thought very highly of it until somebody gave him a $50 hat. This week he had the old one cleaned and blocked and presented it to me to put on my back seat. No doubt it will do the work, for anyone seeing it will think I am carrying either LBJ or a 2-gun boyfriend."[100]

After all the hoopla accompanying her March appointment, it was hard to believe but Justice Sharp would have to run in the November general election in order to keep her seat for the remaining four years of the term to which she had been appointed. On June 1, 1962, the Democratic Party's state executive committee nominated her in the hall of the House of Representatives as the Democratic candidate.[101] She was opposed by the Republican candidate, Irvin B. Tucker Jr. from Raleigh. It was an off year, without a presidential race to bring voters to the polls. But there was a constitutional amendment on the ballot that split the legal profession, and indeed the North Carolina Supreme Court, down the middle. The issue was court reform.

By the late 1950s the North Carolina court system was an outdated hodgepodge, badly in need of reorganization. Below the superior court at the trial level, there were more than 180 lower courts variously denominated recorder's courts (county, municipal, and township), general county courts, county criminal courts, special county courts, and mayor's courts in addition to juvenile and domestic relations courts. Judges were usually part-time and could be either elected or appointed locally. No one was sure exactly how many such courts existed, because they were established by the local governing bodies without notice to any central agency.[102] In addition, there were as many as 925 justices of the peace, who were a serious blot upon the escutcheon of justice. The justices of the peace, with jurisdiction over minor civil and criminal cases, were compensated by the fees they exacted from those they themselves found guilty.[103] Judge Sharp had inveighed against the abuses inherent in this system for years. Although there were other issues to be addressed (such as the need for an intermediate court of appeals between the trial court and the supreme court), the lack of centralization and standardization, as well as the conflict of interest inherent in the justice of the peace system, had first priority.

Governor Luther Hodges, in coordination with Chief Justice M. V. Barnhill, initiated the lengthy process of court reform in the mid-1950s by encouraging the North Carolina Bar Association to study the court system and make recommendations.[104] The bar association established a study committee chaired by Charlotte attorney J. Spencer Bell, which called for reorganization of the court system in its 1958 report. Simultaneously, the North Carolina General Assembly created a constitutional commission to make its own report. As a superior court judge, Susie Sharp had been a member of the commission, which completed its report in early 1959. At least one commentator gave her credit for having "the key role in developing the judicial section of the proposed revised constitution."[105]

The two groups agreed on the identification of many of the problems in the court system but differed on how to solve them. Most of the disagreements related to the question of whether the North Carolina Supreme Court or the General Assembly should have authority over such questions as jurisdiction, rules of procedure, and general supervision of the court system.[106] There was broad common ground, however, on the desirability of a new all-inclusive, uniform court system with authority centralized in the state. The maze of local courts was to be abolished and replaced by a new district court system to handle the wide range of relatively minor civil and criminal matters. The justice of the peace was to be replaced by the newly created magistrate, who would function within the district court as a judicial officer inferior to the district court judge. Fees and court costs would be standardized.

Legislation to amend the constitution passed the House of Representatives in 1961, preparing the way for a statewide referendum in the November 1962 general elections. The final version, which adopted proposals from both the Bell committee and the constitutional commission, gave the legislature the authority to fashion the new uniform system of justice, while creating an Administrative Office of the Courts to oversee the operation of the courts. The legal community was deeply divided, the newspapers full of both endorsements and statements of opposition from judges and lawyers across the state. The bar association appointed Superior Court Judge J. Will Pless to chair a committee of thirty lawyers from each of the state's judicial districts to promote approval of the proposed amendment.

Some opposition focused on the provision stating that the General Assembly would not have the power to "establish or authorize any courts other than as permitted by this article." Opponents to the amendment believed that such a provision would hamstring the legislature, which might find it desirable to create courts in the future. Other opponents, fearing an excessive concentration of power in the supreme court, disapproved of the creation of an Administrative Office of the Courts, whose director and assistant director would be appointed by the chief justice.

Additional considerations were less philosophical and not part of the public debate. For example, all personnel in the judicial system would cease to be county officials and would become state employees. Salaries that had been determined by county commissioners would be standardized by the state. The clerk of superior court in a given county, whose attitude might be that, as an official elected by the voters, he did not have to answer to some bureaucrat in Raleigh, would find that, if he wanted a pay raise or additional office help, he needed to be in good odor in the state capital. Moreover, equipment in county offices ranging from telephones to record books to filing cabinets would become state property subject to state purchase and contract procedures, thus stripping the clerk of court of what had been a significant amount of patronage involved in the power to select one office supplier over another.[107] This sort of thing could pay off if a clerk had opposition at election time, when, for example, it would not be unusual for a printer who had a county's court printing business to donate campaign brochures, signs, and handbills to the incumbent clerk.[108]

A more profound difficulty with the new Administrative Office of the Courts was its potential for political manipulation. The power of the chief justice and his appointee, the director of the new administrative organization, would reach like no other state authority into the heart of every courthouse.[109] Opponents could conjure up nightmare scenarios. For instance, although tradition and other considerations might inhibit a governor from appointing one of his political cronies to be chief justice, ignoring the long-standing tradition that the senior associate justice would normally be the appointee, the governor had the power to do so. The new chief justice could then appoint a political operative as director of the Administrative Office of the Courts. And in every courthouse across the state, clerks of court might find that they were under pressure to see that their counties and precincts were in the correct column on election day.[110]

Shortly before the November election, Governor Sanford sent a handwritten note to Justice Sharp while the court was in conference, asking, "Have you given any thought to making a statement of endorsement for the Court Amendment? I don't know of anything that would be more influential."[111] Initially reluctant to be the only justice taking a stand on the issue, Judge Sharp conferred with Chief Justice Denny, the governor, and Allen Gwyn, as well as John Kesler.[112] The matter came to a head when a United Press International reporter came up to poll the justices as to where each stood, causing "much consternation and running around."[113] The subsequent article reported that Justices Higgins, Bobbitt, and Rodman would vote against the court reform amendment, while Chief Justice Denny and Justices Parker and Sharp would vote in favor.[114] Justice Moore declined to comment.[115] "High Court Justices Split on Court Plan" was the headline in the News and Observer, with similar ones running in papers across the state.[116] Superior Court Judge Pless, after declaring publicly that he thought Judge Sharp "might pull the Amendment through," called on Chief Justice Denny to encourage her to make a statement.[117]

Justice Sharp responded with a six-page statement she released to the press three days before the election.[118] It was given wide play in the papers, both as news and in editorials, and perhaps it did make a difference. In it she voiced her wholehearted support of the measure, even though it was not perfect. She labeled as "scandalous" the system under which a justice of the peace decided the guilt or innocence of a party, knowing that the J.P. would "get no pay unless he convicts the defendant." She criticized the jumble of lower courts with their "different rules, regulations, jurisdictions, procedures and court costs," noting that costs of $7.50 in one county and $27.00 for the same offense in another county might mean that "if John Smith were tried in X County he could pay out, but if he were tried in Y County he would have to go to jail for thirty days." She added, "It is the purpose of a court to dispense justice — not collect revenue to help run a town. The pyramiding of costs in some courts which follow the policy of revenue collecting agencies rather than dispensers of justice gnaws at the vitals of the system."

She addressed the notion that the amendment was unnecessary because the legislature already had the power to reorganize the courts if it chose to do so by pointing out that "[p]ractical politics had demonstrated the utter political impossibility of remodeling 400 separate courts in various counties and towns in North Carolina." If, however, under the new amendment all previously existing inferior courts were abolished, the legislature would have a clean slate on which to establish the proposed district court system. Ever mindful of the courts' effect on the average citizen, she pointed out that it was at the level below the superior court that most cases were tried, and that the lower courts' decisions "may be of earth-shattering importance to the man being tried." It was at this level that most people got their idea of justice in North Carolina, because comparatively few came in contact with the superior court and it was "a rare litigant who ever sees a supreme court justice."

To those who distrusted the idea of an Administrative Office of the Courts, she described "the fear that the amendment will create a judicial dictator in Raleigh" as "totally unfounded." Recalling her days as an itinerant superior court judge, she noted that "the administrative assistant to the Chief Justice told me each week where I should go to hold court. Without this instruction and the commission from the Chief Justice I would have stayed at home. . . . Without some administrative office it would be impossible to run the courts of North Carolina. They are a big operation. We would not call the traffic director in the control tower at the airport a dictator or a czar. We know that he is indispensable to the operation of the airport, and so it is with the administrative office of the courts."

Without going into some of the murkier scenarios floating about, she accused opponents of basing objections "on fears which could never materialize unless the legislature and the people become so callous and indifferent to their obligations as free men that representative government will be impossible in any event. When you analyze these fears and objections they stem from a lack of faith in representative government."

Finally, as a pragmatist she argued that despite imperfections, despite the fact that it did not contain "many of the ideas which I myself advanced as a member of the Constitutional Commission," she did not think "the next legislature could propose a better constitutional amendment."[119] The alternative, doing nothing about the inconsistent and unappetizing hodgepodge of lower courts, was inconceivable. There would be time to fight again for other reforms.

When elections finally rolled around on November 6, 1962, Judge Sharp listened to the returns "all by myself alone."[120] If lonely, she had to have been cheered by the results. The court reform amendment passed, making North Carolina one of the first states in the nation to adopt a unified court system.[121] And she was elected to finish the remainder of her appointive term on the supreme court.

It was even better than that. When all the votes were in, she turned out to be the top individual vote getter in the elections. The only woman on the statewide ballot, she had "led the ticket" with 494,169 votes against her Republican opponent, who garnered 311,577. (Judge Sharp's sister Florence reported that her children were "absolutely appalled" that anyone would vote against her, causing Judge Sharp to muse, "How does one explain Republicans to little children?")[122]

Some commentators were so elated that they threw her name out as a possible gubernatorial candidate. The News and Observer's "Under the Dome" reported that her name had come up at a meeting of newspaper editors, one of whom described her as the ideal candidate for the Democratic Party in 1964, pointing to "the fact that she led the ticket in votes on November 6, that she has a Statewide reputation as a Superior Court judge, and the respect of just about all elements of the party."[123] Judge Sharp wrote to John that she was "touched, flustered—and embarrassed," adding, "I don't suppose, however, that I'm the first person to be put in that condition by the press and especially by 'Under the Dome.'"[124]

Now that she was duly elected in her own right, she went out and bought a "stand up desk" at which she could work without aggravating an increasingly bothersome back problem.[125] Many of her clerks, when they recalled their clerkship days with Justice Sharp, remembered going over their work with her, standing at that desk. They also remembered that she liked to work in her stocking feet, an image not shared with "Under the Dome."

CHAPTER 13

OPINIONS

The lady justice, a term recently deemed an oxymoron, had garnered more votes than any other candidate on the ballot statewide. It was just one indicator of a rapidly changing world.

The civil rights movement had been gathering steam in North Carolina since 1960 when four black students in Greensboro staged the nation's first lunch counter sit-in. Vietnam, a country few North Carolinians could have located on the globe not long before, was becoming a topic of discussion. Betty Friedan published her watershed book, *The Feminine Mystique*. Then, on November 22, 1963, President John Fitzgerald Kennedy was shot to death as he rode in an open parade car in Dallas, Texas.[1] The photograph of Lyndon Baines Johnson being sworn in as president on Air Force One, with the shell-shocked Jackie Kennedy looking on in her blood-stained suit, was noteworthy for many reasons, not the least of which was the fact that it was a female judge, U.S. District Court Judge Sarah T. Hughes, who administered the oath of office.[2]

Ironically, although the revolutionary social changes and political tides that swept over Justice Sharp like all other Americans during the 1960s and 1970s affected every aspect of her day-to-day life, there was perhaps no sturdier shelter from the storm than within the walls of the North Carolina Supreme Court. The constitutional issues of the day were mostly questions for the federal, not state, courts. With a few exceptions in which the state supreme court had to grapple with ripple effects emanating from the Great Society and the Vietnam War, Judge Sharp was largely spared the agony of wrestling with the more inflammatory aspects of national public policy from the bench. This did not mean that she did not agonize.

She was more and more alienated from the national leadership of her beloved Democratic Party. The Kennedy family's Catholicism, rumored shady dealings, and strong-arm tactics disturbed her. She shared the fear and loath-

ing of Robert Kennedy that was a common sentiment among white southerners and had never been an unequivocal admirer of President Kennedy himself. His assassination nonetheless stunned her. To John Kesler, upon hearing
the news, she wrote, "Goodness knows, I have many times regretted my vote
for him, but I never would have wanted his administration to end in this bar-
barous fashion. . . . This afternoon brings back the memory of the shock I felt
when I heard the news of Pearl Harbor and the death of Roosevelt."[3] With the
rest of the nation she watched the television obsessively as events unfolded
with the murder of Lee Harvey Oswald and the long goodbye to JFK: the
riderless horse; Jackie Kennedy holding the hands of her children, little Caroline and John-John, by the graveside; John-John's soldierly salute. "Terrible,"
said Judge Sharp.[4] Her prejudice nonetheless overcoming her genuine horror
at the tragedy, she could not help remarking to her journal, "Catholic mass
was quite unimpressive to me."[5] As president, Lyndon Johnson would offend
her on every level, from political to personal, prompting journal entries such
as one on March 15, 1965: "Listen to Johnson's speech on Negro voting in
Democracy. I wish I could take back my vote."

Frustration and alienation did not, however, mean that she ceased to be
engaged as a citizen, both intellectually and as politically as she dared within
the constraints of her judicial position. This would be especially true in her
opposition to efforts to pass the Equal Rights Amendment, as will be seen,
but it extended even to such small gestures as a letter to President Johnson
in which she lobbied for a long-standing cause. "The objective of your War
on Poverty must be realized if, in the long run, our capitalistic system of free
enterprise is to survive. It seems to me, however, that this War will never
be won unless immediate and effective steps are taken to insure birth control."[6]

More striking, she did not hesitate to jawbone North Carolina legislators
in the aftermath of the legislation known as the Speaker Ban Law, which prohibited known Communists from speaking at state-supported institutions of
higher education. Passed, without a single public hearing, in nineteen minutes under a suspension of the rules at the very end of the 1963 session, the
speaker ban caused an uproar.[7] Such an assault on freedom of speech and
academic freedom not only embarrassed the state but threatened the funding
and accreditation of its tax-supported colleges and universities. Comparisons
were made to the infamous 1925 Scopes "monkey trial" in Tennessee. Despite—or rather because of—the furor, Governor Dan Moore called for a
study commission instead of attempting to get the law repealed at the next
legislative session in 1965.

In an example of the hard feelings caused by the gag law, Judge Sharp's former law school classmate Jefferson B. Fordham, then the dean of the University of Pennsylvania Law School, cited the speaker ban as his reason for declining an invitation to a class reunion organized by Judge Sharp and Governor Dan Moore. He particularly blamed Governor Moore for preventing repeal during the 1965 session by his recommendation for a study commission.[8] Judge Sharp spent part of her birthday writing her own letter to Fordham, defending Governor Moore and describing her efforts to get the ban off the books. "I assure you that I too deplore the speaker ban law and, equally, the manner in which it was passed. In my opinion, however, it was not the Governor's recommendation of a study commission which prevented its repeal this year. On the contrary, Dan's recommendation offers the only hope of repeal in the foreseeable future." She was frank about her own lobbying on the issue, telling Fordham, "Because of my deep concern about the law and the situation which produced it, I took every opportunity this spring afforded to talk to the legislators, a large number of whom lived at the Sir Walter and ate in the s&w—as do I. As a result, I became convinced that the ban could not have been repealed this session."[9]

Ultimately, after an inadequate revision of the statute by the legislature, a lawsuit was instituted and in 1968 a three-judge panel in the U.S. District Court in Greensboro ruled the law unconstitutional.[10]

When the social and political issues of the day did find their way into cases before the North Carolina Supreme Court, Justice Sharp generally did not allow her personal views to influence her. During her seventeen years on the appellate bench, there were several occasions when her judicial opinions dealt with some aspect of the era's upheaval, such as school integration or capital punishment. For the most part, her handling of these cases reflected her overriding respect and reverence for the rule of law, even when it ran counter to her personal feelings or jeopardized her politically.

During Justice Sharp's tenure, civil rights was the overriding issue in the country and in North Carolina. The aftershocks of the 1954 U.S. Supreme Court decision in *Brown v. Board of Education* still reverberated. From 1953 to 1969, the much-reviled Warren Court persisted as the South's bogeyman, and once LBJ succeeded in arm-twisting the Civil Rights Acts of 1964 and 1965 into existence, their interpretation in the Court was a battleground for years.

In 1964, ten years after *Brown*, less than 1 percent of black elementary and high school students in North Carolina attended school with white students.[11] In 1971 the U.S. Supreme Court decided an important case originating in Charlotte, North Carolina, *Swann v. Charlotte-Mecklenburg Board of Education*,[12] which held that busing could be used as a tool of school desegregation. Inexorably, black activists pried open hotels and motels, swimming pools, and even cemeteries. Landmark civil rights statutes and court decisions seemed to rain down on a white populace still unreconciled to the reality of integration.

Segregation, integration, and civil rights were subjects Judge Sharp had pondered for many years without altering her fundamental feelings. She would be the first to admit she was prejudiced. When Mississippi governor Ross Barnett gave a speech on "states' rights" to an audience of law students in North Carolina in 1963, Judge Sharp's reaction reflected both her political sentiments and her standards: "I agreed with his words but I wished for a more intelligent champion. He looks like a sly countryman come to town in the hope of 'doing' some city slicker."[13]

On a personal level she occasionally made an effort to rise above her prejudice, but too often she failed. At a 1963 Phi Beta Kappa dinner, for example, she found herself seated at a table "with the President of Meredith [College], a lawyer's wife and a colored girl," she reported to John. "I did my best to do the right thing and tried to talk to her, but I finally gave up. It wasn't worth the effort."[14]

On the level of public policy, however, Judge Sharp had long been a pragmatist, albeit an angry one. She gave Governor Sanford high marks for his handling of the racial issue in North Carolina. "The nature of the problem is that a really satisfactory solution would not be palatable to either side; so, poor Sanford, in the middle, garners little affection from those whose interests he has served in spite of themselves," she wrote to a friend in Winston-Salem.[15] She did not know what the effect of the federal civil rights legislation would be on race relations, but, like many other whites, she was convinced that "interference by outsiders" would "simply stir up violence and harden resistance."[16] She recognized that it "would be futile to say that the Negro has not been oppressed in both the South and the North," but was unprepared to support remedial measures. "Those who would sell the Negro on the idea that because he has not had a fair chance in the past he is now entitled to special privileges and that the law no longer applies to him are simply creating a worse situation and one with which we cannot cope," she wrote to one of her former college teachers, Miss Jessie Mebane.[17]

Nonetheless, two basic factors forced her to accept racial integration: the fear of an underclass with nothing to lose and her unshakable faith in the rule of law. "All responsible people recognize that the threat of an uneducated, irresponsible, have-not racial group is so serious that self-preservation requires corrective measures," she wrote Miss Mebane. "We could become a Viet Nam fighting a guerilla war!"[18] As for the law, she said, "Our system (a government of laws, not men) cannot tolerate the philosophy that obedience to law rests upon the personal likes and dislikes of any individual. This means, of course, that the South must obey the civil rights law."[19] But she pointed out that it would have been much easier to enforce the law had its advocates not pursued their goals by way of civil disobedience.[20]

Judge Sharp wrote this letter to Miss Mebane in September 1964. The subject was fresh in her mind, thanks to a recent contretemps with the U.S. Supreme Court. That June, Justice Sharp had written an opinion for the North Carolina court, *State v. Cobb*, upholding the use of a state antitrespass law to enforce segregated seating in a movie theater.[21] The antitrespass law had been a widely used tool across the South for combating civil rights sit-in demonstrations on private property. In *Cobb*, Judge Sharp was pleased to hew closely to the doctrine of separation of powers, declaring, "A man's conduct must be judged by the law as it exists at the time his conduct is called into question and not by the law as he and others think it should be rewritten in the interest of social justice."[22] In language deemed to be thinly veiled criticism of the U.S. Supreme Court, she stated, "If the law is to be changed, it is the firm conviction of this Court that our system requires it to be changed by the legislative branch of the government and not by the judiciary. When a court, in effect, constitutes itself a superlegislative body, and attempts to rewrite the law according to its predilections and notions of enlightened legislation, it destroys the separation of powers and thereby upsets the delicate system of checks and balances which has heretofore formed the keystone of our constitutional government."[23]

Ten days later, the U.S. Supreme Court effectively overruled *Cobb* when it decided *Robinson v. Florida*, a case in which blacks had conducted a sit-in at a Florida restaurant. Without ruling on the question of whether the Fourteenth Amendment prohibited the arrest and prosecution of persons who had refused management's request to leave the premises, the Court looked to Florida Board of Health regulations requiring restaurants to provide segregated restrooms. "While these Florida regulations do not directly and expressly forbid restaurants to serve both white and colored people together," the Court stated, "they certainly embody a state policy putting burdens upon any restaurant which serves both races, burdens bound to discourage the serving of the two races together."[24] The Court concluded that such regulations were sufficient to constitute state action for purposes of invoking equal protection under the Fourteenth Amendment. Because the state law compelled discrimination on the basis of race, the proprietor's personal decision to eject the demonstrators under the antitrespass law was not relevant.

On the same day, the U.S. Supreme Court sent back two North Carolina cases similar to *Cobb* in which sit-in demonstrators had been convicted under the state antitrespass statute. In per curiam decisions the Court vacated the judgments and remanded the cases "for consideration in light of *Robinson v. Florida*."[25] North Carolina, with racial discrimination laws similar to those in Florida on the books, could not hide behind its antitrespass law to enforce segregation. *Cobb* was no longer valid.

Two years later, Judge Sharp demonstrated her recognition of reality. In 1966 she wrote the majority opinion in a case arising in the wake of the 1964 Civil Rights Act, *Dilday v. Beaufort County Board of Education*.[26] Prior to passage of the civil rights legislation, the citizens of Beaufort County, North Carolina, had approved a bond issue to finance construction of a new school consolidating three white high schools, as well as to make improvements at two black high schools. The schools would also benefit from federal funds. In light of the intervening Civil Rights Act, which forbade segregation where federal funds were received, the school board requested the county commissioners to reallocate the funds to build a single integrated high school, accommodating students from all five existing high schools. A citizens' suit sought to enjoin the expenditure of the bond proceeds for construction of a single integrated school on the grounds that voters had not approved the bonds for such a purpose. Justice Sharp's opinion did not mince words. With or without federal funds, she said, Beaufort County schools could not be segregated.

[I]t is not within the power of the Board of Education or the Board of Commissioners of Beaufort County to provide their constituents with racially segregated schools. The provision of . . . the Constitution of North Carolina which provided that "the children of the white race and the children of the colored race shall be taught in separate public schools" was invalidated on May 17, 1954, when the Supreme Court of the United States handed down its decision in Brown v. Board of Education of Topeka. . . . The Constitution of the United States takes precedence over the Constitution of North Carolina, and, for all practical purposes, the Federal Constitution means what the Supreme Court of the United States says it means. . . . The Brown case is binding upon us.

. . . Under the decisions of the Supreme Court of the United States and the Acts of the Congress, the Board of Education of Beaufort County can no longer legally impose segregation of the races in any school.[27]

Because certain formalities had not been completed, the North Carolina Supreme Court ruled that the bond proceeds must remain enjoined. However, the opinion held that the Beaufort County citizens' only remaining choice was whether to have a single integrated high school or several integrated high schools, subject to formal reallocation of the funds by the county commissioners. "The question whether the schools of Beaufort County will be integrated in the future is no longer open," wrote Justice Sharp.[28]

Indicating the degree to which these matters remained unsettled, Associate Justice I. Beverly Lake, appointed to the court by Governor Dan K. Moore in August 1965, filed a separate opinion, concurring in the majority's ruling that the funds should remain enjoined but disagreeing that the voters must now accept the expenditure of the funds for integrated schools, a purpose that had not been within their contemplation at the time they approved the bond issue. Justice Lake declared, inter alia, "I cannot agree with the statement in the majority opinion that the Constitution of the United States means whatever five out of nine members of the Supreme Court of the United States may see fit, from time to time, to say that it means."[29] Although he agreed that the North Carolina Supreme Court and all other courts, both state and federal, must decide the cases before them "as if the decision of the U.S. Supreme Court in Brown v. Board of Education . . . were a correct interpretation of the Fourteenth Amendment to the U.S. Constitution," he deemed Brown to constitute unconstitutional interference of the federal government.[30]

However much Justice Sharp regretted the outcome, she was not one to tilt at windmills or to undermine the authority, as she saw it, of the U.S. Supreme Court. The children of Beaufort County, black and white, needed schools. She recognized explicitly that, despite Brown, at the time the bond issue passed, the county commissioners and members of the school board "apparently did not believe that the situation which now confronts them could possibly materialize."[31] Nevertheless, they were now required by their oaths of office "to face realities" and "to take the steps which, in their best judgment, will serve the highest good of all the children, for whom they are trustees," for — as she deeply believed — "[t]he preservation of our form of government . . . depends upon an adequate system of public education."[32]

Justice Sharp's opinion in the Beaufort County school case came down on June 16, 1966. In November, having completed Judge Denny's unexpired term to which she had been elected in 1962, she had to stand for reelection. Considerations as to political repercussions did not enter into her handling of the sensitive issues in the case, however. She called it as she saw it, even if she herself did not like it and even if it might cost her votes at the polls. It helped that she ran unopposed that fall, but if she had lost any support with the general public it was not reflected in the totals. Justice Sharp again was the leading vote getter in the November election with a total of 524,659 votes, more than any other candidate for any office on the ticket.[33] She had won a full eight-year term on the high court.

But it was not in the arena of civil rights or other areas of federal constitutional law that Justice Sharp would leave her mark on the North Carolina Supreme Court and thus on her fellow citizens. As just one of seven members of a deeply traditional court, all of whom had an equal vote on any given case, she was limited in what she could accomplish. Nor was she by nature or training predisposed to making waves. Nonetheless, she was the author of a goodly handful of opinions that, notwithstanding her avowed judicial conservatism, demonstrated an ability to make the law breathe rather than remain corseted in moribund precedents outstripped by new realities and practicalities.

Without question, she was acutely attuned to the separation of powers and the dangers of "legislating from the bench." As both a former lawyer and trial judge, she had a full understanding of the need to adhere to precedent in order to provide stability within the judicial system and predictability in the affairs of men.[34] Within the steely architecture of stare decisis, however, she was a meticulous yet agile scholar who was capable of finding a way to accommodate necessary change.

Perhaps the best example of her willingness and ability to "push the envelope" came relatively early in her career on the supreme court, in a case entitled *Rabon v. Rowan Memorial Hospital*.[35] It began in 1959, before Judge Sharp joined the appellate bench, when the plaintiff, a textile worker named Homer D. Rabon, went as a paying patient to Rowan Memorial Hospital for treatment of an infection. There, he alleged, a hospital nurse negligently injected a drug "into or adjacent to the radial nerve" in his left arm, resulting in the permanent paralysis and loss of use of the hand and arm. The issue as to whether the hospital had been negligent in its hiring or management of the nursing staff was not raised. The hospital in its defense relied on the doctrine of charitable immunity, based on its characterization as a nonprofit charitable organization offering free hospital services to patients unable to pay.

The doctrine of charitable immunity was well established in North Carolina and provided that "a charitable institution may not be held liable to a beneficiary of the charity for the negligence of its servants or employees if it has exercised due care in their selection and retention."[36] Under a line of North Carolina Supreme Court cases, a paying or nonpaying patient injured by the negligence of an employee of a charitable hospital could recover damages only if the hospital was negligent in its employee selection or retention, or perhaps if it provided defective equipment or supplies.[37] Thus, for example, a laboratory technician at a public hospital in North Carolina "could kill a patient with mismatched blood and the institution goes free."[38] Likewise, as in Homer Rabon's case, there would be no recourse for a patient partially paralyzed by a nurse's negligence.

Various rationales supported the doctrine of charitable immunity. An 1876 Massachusetts case was the earliest in America to enunciate the rule, relying on already discredited English law barring the payment of damages from donations to a charitable hospital, which constituted a "trust fund" for the operation of the hospital only.[39] Another theory held that anyone who entered a charitable hospital for treatment impliedly consented to assume the risk of negligent injuries and therefore waived any claim for damages.[40] Yet another line of cases, adopted by North Carolina, declared that the doctrine of respondeat superior, whereby the institution could be held liable for the negligence of its employees, did not apply to charitable hospitals. Finally, the public policy argument was that, because charitable institutions provided a vital public service, it was desirable to protect donations from liability claims.[41]

Judge Sharp, conferring with her law clerk, Henry Manning, initially thought *Rabon* to be an open-and-shut case in favor of the hospital, based on existing North Carolina law. As he recalled it, she said, "Henry, I think North Carolina is pretty clear on this. Draft up a little opinion. You might even do it per curiam."[42] A per curiam or "PC" opinion is issued "by the court," on behalf of the majority, with or without concurring or dissenting opinions, and without identifying any specific justice as the author; it is used in cases where there is little to discuss. Often a per curiam opinion is no longer than a paragraph or two.

Manning, however, was struck by arguments he found in his research that supported overturning the doctrine of charitable immunity in circumstances similar to those in *Rabon*. In accordance with his instructions, he drafted a short per curiam opinion affirming the lower court's denial of relief to Homer Rabon. But he also made a brief abstract of authority for the opposite view and asked Judge Sharp to look at it before committing to the PC. A day or so later, she told him that she was intrigued by his abstract and asked him to tackle an opinion from that perspective. Recognizing that overturning such an entrenched legal doctrine would be, to say the least, an extraordinary thing for the conservative North Carolina court to do, she drew on Shakespeare, telling her clerk that if they were going to shoot at the king, they had to have all the bullets because they could not afford to miss. "I'm going to give you this for a project," she said, allotting him the next couple of weeks to focus on it. Henry Manning made the most of it, producing a mountain of research in support of overruling prior North Carolina Supreme Court decisions on charitable immunity.[43]

The *Rabon* case was ideally situated to capture Judge Sharp's interest and determination. It was not simply that the result in the trial court, denial of relief to Homer Rabon, a textile worker whose life had been irrevocably damaged by the negligence of a hospital nurse, seemed unfair. An appellate judge deals daily in "unfair" outcomes that must stand because of the weight of precedent and/or overriding public policy considerations. Rather, when she examined the foundations of precedent for the charitable immunity doctrine as applied to public hospitals, she saw that changing times had undermined or outmoded them. The old rule had made sense at one time, when charity was a small-scale operation and the local charity-supported hospital could not afford to have its donations diverted to pay damage claims. But by the mid-1960s charity was big business, and public hospitals received revenue not only from donations but also from paying patients and government funding. Under these circumstances, many believed they could no longer be considered a "charitable institution" entitled to immunity.[44] Moreover, the availability of liability insurance shifted the balance between the hospital and the patient, as to which should bear the full burden of an employee's negligence.

Additionally, the charitable immunity exception to liability for negligence was "judge-made law," and as such offered more latitude for judicial examination than statutory law. There was an abundance of legal authority from other jurisdictions, which appealed to Judge Sharp's scholarly disposition, and much of it supported reversing North Carolina law. A cross-country survey revealed that thirty states no longer allowed charitable hospitals immunity from the actionable negligence of their employees, and fully eighteen of these had abandoned the doctrine by judicial decisions overruling prior opinions.[45] Only one state, Nevada, had repudiated the doctrine by statute. In proposing to overturn the North Carolina law, Justice Sharp might even be described as being in the mainstream rather than the avant-garde. And as someone who found the spotlight more of a hindrance than a help, she was not anxious to be perceived as leading a quixotic charge.

She had an opportunity, if she could persuade a majority of the court, to effect a needed change in North Carolina law. But such a complete reversal of policy, with such wide repercussions, was just the sort that in the belief of many well-respected authorities should be left to the legislature. Indeed, the North Carolina Supreme Court had addressed this very issue in the case most closely controlling the *Rabon* case. As her majority opinion would acknowledge, the North Carolina Supreme Court had previously concluded that, "no matter what the merits and demerits of charitable immunity as applied to hospitals, the doctrine was so deeply embedded in our common law that the court's withdrawal of it would constitute an act of judicial legislation in the field of public policy; that whether to change the rule was 'a question of broad public policy to be pondered and resolved by the lawmaking body.'"[46]

Some insight into Justice Sharp's view of useless precedent may be gained from a rather startling note she wrote to Justice Parker during her second year on the supreme court, regarding a troublesome case in which it was difficult to reconcile the law with justice. Judge Sharp recommended simply laying down the decision without worrying overmuch about the niceties of the applicable case law. "If we are to save Mr. Gaskins from his duly licensed attorney, I favor just bodaciously doing it," she wrote. "As a precedent, I apprehend that this case will not bother us." It would be another 150 years, she reckoned, before a similar situation might arise.[47] Once again it was her pragmatist streak that rose to the fore.

A more lyrical expression of her judicial philosophy appeared in the letter she wrote to Governor Kerr Scott in 1950, little more than a year after he appointed her to the trial bench, in which Judge Sharp recommended her friend Judge Allen Gwyn for the supreme court vacancy created by the death of Justice A. A. F. Seawell. Lamenting the loss of Justice Seawell, Judge Sharp told the governor, "I regarded him as the most liberal of them all."[48] Judge Gwyn, she said, believed that "the law is not a morgue." She continued, "We depend upon the Supreme Court, as well as the Legislature, to see that law changes with the times and grows to fit the body politic."

Justice Sharp finished her first draft of the *Rabon* opinion in early August 1966.[49] Immediately it drew criticism from Justice Bobbitt, who encouraged her to rework it. Despite her efforts, at the final conference of the spring term on August 26 she could not muster a majority. The court had a vacancy due to the death in July of Justice Clifton L. Moore, and the vote was tied three to three, with justices Bobbitt and Higgins on her side. Chief Justice Parker and

Justice Lake were opposed, as was Justice J. William Pless Jr., who had joined the court in February of that year.[50]

In August the court regained its full complement of seven members when Joseph Branch was sworn in to take Justice Moore's seat. All that next fall Judge Sharp battled to get the votes, but could not get firm commitments. In an effort to shore up support and persuade fence-sitters, she drafted a provision making the decision prospective, applicable only to Homer Rabon's case and future cases, thus allowing charitable hospitals the opportunity to procure liability insurance.[51] For Branch, it was difficult to be the deciding vote because he was personally and politically close to Chief Justice Parker. They were both from the town of Enfield, and Parker had been a mentor, almost a father figure to Branch. It was no small thing to oppose Chief Justice Parker even without such a long and close relationship. To vote against Parker, as the court's marshal-librarian Raymond Mason Taylor put it, risked Parker's "eternal condemnation."[52] It took Branch the entire fall term to make up his mind, but in the end he broke the tie and the decision went down 4–3 in favor of overturning the old rule.[53] Chief Justice Parker and Justices Lake and Pless dissented, with Parker and Lake both writing strong dissenting opinions. "It is a traumatic experience for this Court to overrule 'a uniform line of decisions,'" Judge Sharp wrote to Dean Jefferson Fordham at the University of Pennsylvania Law School. She noted that "[t]he prospective overruling feature was one of the means by which overruling was accomplished."[54]

If a 4–3 split was unusual on the North Carolina court, so was the activist tenor of the majority opinion. As one editorialist pointed out, members of the "relatively conservative" state appellate court were more likely to criticize the U.S. Supreme Court led by Chief Justice Earl Warren for what they deemed legislating from the bench than to emulate it.[55] Justice Sharp herself had certainly expressed this view about the federal court. At the same time, she recognized that when the legislative branch dodged its responsibility, "there's a vacuum and somebody's going to fill it."[56]

Ironically, some commentators have pointed out that the U.S. Supreme Court decision in *Brown v. Board of Education* was a powerful example of this principle, overruling the "separate but equal" doctrine set forth in *Plessy v. Ferguson*,[57] in what some saw as "the model of how judges should operate to impose progressive solutions that legislatures were afraid of, or hadn't gotten around to."[58] Although the passage of time was necessary before *Brown* could be viewed with perspective, even hidebound strict constructionists would eventually concede that on balance the Court was right, even if not correct.

In her *Rabon* opinion Justice Sharp noted, "This Court has never overruled its decisions lightly. No court has been more faithful to *stare decisis*."[59] Yet she had chosen to annul the old rule, quoting former North Carolina Supreme Court justice Sam Ervin, who said, "[T]he doctrine of *stare decisis* will not be applied in any event to preserve and perpetuate error and grievous wrong."[60] Her opinion was a scholar's tour de force, employing "all the bullets" of legal research to demonstrate that North Carolina had substantial grounds for abrogating the old charitable immunity rule. Ultimately, she made the opinion overruling the North Carolina precedent sound almost conservative in its application of authority and public policy. In an approving editorial, the *News and Observer* declared, "The majority did not brush aside precedent; it looked behind precedent to see whether the substance of it had not already been brushed aside. . . . The notion that the court should not 'make law,' but leave that to the legislature would seem to be a too simple assertion. The court often 'makes law' when it interprets it."[61]

Scholars and members of the legal profession consider the *Rabon* immunity case to be a towering landmark in North Carolina jurisprudence. One commentator described it and a later case in which Judge Sharp revisited the immunity issue as "among the most brilliant the Supreme Court has written in a quarter century."[62] It was an example of Justice Sharp's willingness and ability to move the law forward from the bench. Her exhaustive opinion, however, made it clear that, in overturning established doctrine, the North Carolina court was far from blazing trails and, in fact, was merely joining a significant if not overwhelming trend. In this, the case reflected Judge Sharp's lifelong ability to be in the vanguard without appearing to violate accepted norms.

Long after Justice Sharp's career on the bench had ended, those who remembered her would be split as to whether they viewed her as judicially "conservative" or "liberal." Like the rest of the court, in most cases she was far more likely to adopt a straightforward application of existing precedent than to strain against it, even in certain cases where there might have been good arguments to do so. Asked on a 1973 questionnaire to rate her position on a quote from U.S. Supreme Court justice Benjamin Cardozo that stated, "I think adherence to precedence should be the rule and not the exception" (in which he went on to acknowledge that some percentage of cases offered an opportunity for "the creative element in the judicial process"), Justice Sharp marked her agreement at 80 percent.[63] Her general preference was not to appear too far out of the mainstream, due in part to her deep respect for mechanisms promoting consistency and stability in the judicial system, in part to the additional demands on her time that any exceptional position required, and also in part to her awareness of the extra attention to which any deviation from the well-worn path invariably subjected her. Moreover, she was after all an elected official and had to consider just how far she could stretch her base of support.

Nevertheless, she was fond of quoting the old saying that, like the turtle, you could not get anywhere without sticking your neck out (and sometimes wore a turtle brooch in silent reference to the adage). Some of her opinions, combined with her provenance as a Kerr Scott–Terry Sanford appointee, earned her a reputation in some quarters, deservedly or not, as one of the most "liberal" justices on the court.

Justice Sharp's intellectual honesty was without stain, but as a legal scholar she knew that precedent did not necessarily equal stagnation in the law. In the same 1973 questionnaire, she agreed 100 percent with a quote from Karl Llewellyn's *Jurisprudence*: "You must know where you want to go in the case in hand before you can utilize the precedents effectively. They can limit you, before you decide, but they cannot deprive you of choice. . . . The precedents are multiform, ambiguous, never fixed, and . . . the tradition-hallowed techniques for dealing with them permit you to squeeze out of the same set of precedents any one of a dozen different conclusions or rules."[64]

Rabon was one of a number of cases in which she did press against the boundaries. Beyond the rarified arguments of judicial philosophy, she was both intellectually engaged and also willing to shoulder the extra work that writing ground-breaking opinions entailed. With her meticulous, even obsessive, nature and her determination "to have all the bullets," launching an assault on established law meant even longer hours than she normally worked. She lamented that the burdens of her job were so great that she could not "follow the gleam" as often as she might like,[65] but when she got her teeth into this kind of opinion, she spared nothing in the effort. In defense of her colleagues, it was true that as an unmarried woman living alone, she had more latitude to indulge in a workaholic's hours. It was simply routine for her to return to the office at night after dinner.

Another opinion in which she "followed the gleam" also advocated the abandonment of legal principles that seemed no longer useful. It would lead to a major change in North Carolina law. The case involved a consumer who alleged that she became ill after discovering a green fly in a bottle of Sun-Drop Cola which she purchased in a lunchroom. The plaintiff relied on the legal theory of implied warranty of fitness, claiming that the ultimate purchaser was entitled to hold the manufacturer responsible. The trial court dismissed the case and the plaintiff appealed. Justice Higgins, writing for the majority, disposed of the case in four paragraphs, applying the long-held doctrine known as privity of contract under which the consumer could not sue the manufacturer.[66] Unlike a claim brought by the consumer against the manufacturer for negligence, claims under a theory of warranty, whether actual or implied, depended on contract. Any implied warranty of fitness was deemed to apply only to the parties to a contract, and the consumer who bought a product from a retailer had no contractual link to the manufacturer.

Justice Sharp concurred in the result denying the plaintiff the right to be heard because the evidence permitted the conclusion that the bottle had been open for an indeterminate period of time before the fly was discovered; therefore, it was possible that the fly got into the bottle after it left the bottling plant. Nevertheless, she wrote a lengthy concurrence (or a "dissenting concurrence," as she called it) arguing for elimination of the privity requirement where a consumer purchased a food product in its original container. Once again, the doctrine had made sense "'in the good old days' when marketing was simple, products were uncomplicated and open to inspection, and the buyer was able to evaluate their quality."[67] But in modern times products were mass-produced and marketed through intermediaries, with demand created by advertising.[68] Again, as in *Rabon*, North Carolina was in the minority on the issue, and there was substantial authority from elsewhere to buttress the trend toward eliminating the privity requirement. "In this opinion I shall advance not a single idea new to legal writers, but I shall try to marshal the most salient of the ideas to support the position I take," she wrote.[69]

It was revealing that Justice Sharp took on the labor of writing this long, scholarly concurrence despite the plaintiff's slender case.[70] "All sympathy accorded for plaintiff's unhappy experience," she wrote, "she suffered minimal damage, and I should have preferred to assault the citadel in behalf of one who, victimized by lack of privity with the manufacturer or supplier, had been more ruinously afflicted."[71] But, she continued, "I have felt compelled to champion her cause, lest this and previous pronouncements of the instant rule by this Court be strengthened by silence, with, in consequence, 'futility the fate of every endeavor to dislodge them.'"[72]

Justice Sharp's "dissenting concurrence" would be a major factor in the state's adoption of strict liability for food manufacturers. Less than three years later, Justice Higgins, writing for a unanimous court in another case involving unsavory contents in a cola bottle, carved out an exception to the privity requirement. Citing Sharp's *Terry* concurrence, Higgins stopped short of eliminating the privity requirement but noted that it had been under "vigorous assault" across the country.[73] Finally, in 1979 the General Assembly passed a new Products Liability Act effectively eliminating the privity requirement in implied warranty cases found in prior law.[74] Thus, the purchaser of a bottle of contaminated cola, for example, could seek damages directly from the manufacturer. Elimination of the privity requirement, of course, had a far broader effect, applying to numberless consumer transactions for all sorts of products. With a substantial push from Sharp's "dissenting concurrence," North Carolina came into line with the national trend on privity.

On another front, one of Justice Sharp's dissents was influential in bringing about a fundamental change in North Carolina divorce law, leading to the enactment of statutes mandating equitable distribution of marital property. The result in the 1979 case, *Leatherman v. Leatherman*,[75] was so manifestly unfair under the law as determined by the court's majority, and Justice Sharp's dissent so forceful, that the General Assembly made North Carolina an equitable distribution state in the next session.[76]

Bessie, a mill worker, married Floyd Leatherman in 1947. At that time he was "hauling lumber" for a living. In 1951 Floyd bought a bulldozer from his father and started a one-man, one-machine grading business, aided by his wife, who did the office work as well as taking care of the couple's three children. Over the years the business grew, and Bessie continued to handle all the office duties. She "handled the money and did the book work. She made deposits, paid the bills, answered the telephone, kept up with [her husband's] whereabouts on the various jobs, and kept in touch with callers."[77] By 1963 the business had twenty-eight employees and had added operations out of state. Bessie Leatherman was working more than forty hours a week, taking care of "increased payroll and other expenses, quarterly reports, 'federal forms,' individual work sheets, tax record keeping," and the like. It was Bessie Leatherman to whom the job foreman reported every afternoon, and in the absence of her husband she would deal with problems that arose, including those related to broken machinery. Her signature was on every loan application and performance bond. The couple filed a joint federal tax return, which included the business; they never filed a separate business return. Bessie was not paid a salary until 1971. For most of the time that she worked with her husband, income from the business was deposited into a joint bank account from which both business and personal expenses were paid.

In 1965 the business grossed $500,000. At this point Floyd Leatherman sought advice about changing the organization, and the business was incorporated in 1966. All the stock was put in Floyd's name. When Bessie protested, her husband said it was for "tax purposes" and that he would make a will leaving her the business. In 1975 the parties divorced, and Floyd refused to give Bessie any part of the business they had built and operated together.

Under the law in North Carolina at the time, ownership in a corporation was determined solely by the name on the shares of stock, absent proof that, for example, a husband had made a gift of stock to his wife or otherwise agreed to an ownership interest for her. The presumption in the law was that Bessie Leatherman had rendered her services to the business without expectation of compensation of any sort. Moreover, money earned by the business and deposited in the joint bank accounts of the husband and wife belonged to the depositor, here deemed to be the husband; thus Bessie was deprived of any claim on the business's earnings.[78]

The majority of the North Carolina Supreme Court held that Bessie Leatherman had no claim on "her husband's business." Rejecting theories that might impose a "resulting" or a "constructive" trust to benefit her, the court found that under North Carolina law Bessie had no claim on the business whatsoever.[79] No one in the legal community was surprised. The majority opinion was on solid ground.

Justice Sharp's dissent argued that the majority had misconstrued Bessie Leatherman's theory for her case. Rather than analyzing Bessie's claim under a theory of quantum meruit, where the law implies a contract to compensate a party for services rendered, Justice Sharp argued that the relationship between husband and wife with respect to the business was that of a partnership, which can be created by an implied agreement, and her recital of the facts underlined just how full a partner Bessie Leatherman had been in the business. With this analysis, it was possible to find that Bessie had a claim under a resulting trust theory. In addition, Justice Sharp found that a constructive trust arose because Floyd Leatherman's assertion that putting all the stock in his name was better for tax reasons was a patent "snow job," and his reassurance that she would be named in his will as the owner of the business at his death was calculated to lull her into a false sense of security.[80] It was a respectable argument with sympathetic facts, argued under an alternate legal theory rather than public policy. But in the end Justice Sharp was able to persuade only one other member of the court, Justice Huskins, to join her.

For Bessie Leatherman the cause was lost. But the case led directly to action in the General Assembly, which in 1981 joined approximately forty other states in adopting equitable distribution legislation. The Equitable Distribution Act drastically changed the law relating to ownership of property after divorce, placing the emphasis on a fair division of property between the divorced husband and wife, without regard to title. Complicated, expensive, and not without its own problems, equitable distribution did not prove to be a panacea, but it would be safe to say that if it had been in existence when Bessie Leatherman got divorced, she would not have come away with nothing after working side by side with her husband to build their family business for more than three decades.

Yet another area in which Justice Sharp moved the law forward was workers' compensation. *Booker v. Medical Center*,[81] which involved a laboratory technician at Duke University Medical Center, would have a particularly significant impact on a spate of brown lung cases soon to make their way to the supreme court.

Robert Booker's job required him to handle blood samples on which he performed various chemical tests. In July 1971 he was diagnosed with serum hepatitis, a viral disease of the liver transmitted when infected blood is introduced into the blood of an uninfected person. Only one exposure to contaminated blood is necessary to cause transmission of the disease. Although he was a careful and experienced technician, inevitably blood would spill on his fingers as he handled the vials of blood to be tested. As an avid gardener, Booker often had cuts and abrasions on his hands. The evidence revealed no possibilities for the source of his infection other than contact with contaminated blood as part of his work.

Booker died in January 1974. His widow and four minor children filed a claim for death benefits under North Carolina's Workers' Compensation Act. Duke appealed the decision of the North Carolina Industrial Commission favorable to Booker, and the North Carolina Court of Appeals reversed, on the grounds that serum hepatitis was not listed specifically in the schedule of occupational diseases compensable under the statute nor did it fit under judicially determined definitions requiring a gradual onset of the disease through prolonged exposure to harmful conditions, as found in a 1951 case.

First enacted in 1929, the North Carolina workers' compensation statute, like others nationwide, was designed to provide some relief for employees who suffered an unexpected, employment-related accident during working hours. The earliest laws did not cover diseases of the workplace, even including such well-known examples as lead and arsenic poisoning. Many early cases dealt with the distinction between "injury by accident" and "occupational disease," because the former was compensable while the latter was not. The emphasis on defining "occupational disease" therefore tended to focus on the suddenness of an accident as opposed to the gradual onset of a disease.

In line with the national trend recognizing that some diseases were clearly caused by working conditions, North Carolina amended its statute in 1935 to provide coverage for certain specified occupational diseases. As the inadequacies of limiting coverage to quickly outdated lists of diseases became apparent, many states expanded coverage to encompass any disease that met the criteria linking the cause to the workplace, and in 1971 North Carolina further amended its statute to allow coverage for "[a]ny disease . . . which is proven to be due to causes and conditions which are characteristic of and peculiar to a particular trade, occupation or employment, but excluding all ordinary diseases of life to which the general public is equally exposed outside of the employment."[82] Because serum hepatitis was not a listed "occupational disease," Booker's claim had to be found valid under this catchall provision.

The question in those states with comprehensive coverage for occupational diseases was no longer whether the injury resulted from an accident or the onset of disease, because both were compensable, but rather whether the cause of the disease could be "distinctively associated" with the workplace.[83] In applying criteria from cases decided long before the 1971 amendment to the workers' compensation statute, the North Carolina Court of Appeals had relied in *Booker* on language whose original purpose was to distinguish claims arising from an "accident" from those arising from "occupational disease," characterized by its gradual development. Because serum hepatitis did not have a gradual onset, but rather resulted from a single (although unidentifiable) incident, the court of appeals held that it was not a compensable occupational disease under the statute.[84]

Justice Sharp's opinion, a masterly summation of the development of workers' compensation law combined with a humane and commonsense approach, demonstrated that Booker's claim clearly fell within the intent of the legislature in amending the statute to "bring North Carolina in line with the vast majority of states by providing comprehensive coverage for occupational diseases."[85]

As a preliminary but significant matter, Justice Sharp first determined that Booker's claim accrued at the time of his death in 1974, not at the time he contracted the disease (which was prior to the effective date of the amended statute), thus bringing him under the 1971 catchall provision.[86] Next, she declared that the catchall provision must be interpreted "independently of any prior definition of 'occupational disease'" and that a disease contracted in the workplace, even though by a single unidentifiable exposure, was compensable.[87] In addition, she held that serum hepatitis, although found in the general populace, was not excluded as an "ordinary disease of life" under the statute, because Booker's job exposed him to a far greater risk than that faced by the general public.[88]

Booker gathered up loose ends resulting from the evolving law affecting workers' compensation and cleared the ground for further development into the 1980s, when the court continued expanding coverage to include brown lung disease, a significant change in a state where the textile industry was an enormous economic engine. Chief Justice Sharp herself wrote the first opinion opening the way for recognition of occupational lung disease in North Carolina in *Wood v. J. P. Stevens & Co.*[89] slightly more than two weeks after *Booker*. Expanding on *Booker*'s holding that a claim accrued at the time of death, *Wood* determined that an employee's claim for disability from an occupational disease similarly accrued at the time he actually became disabled rather than at the time he contracted the disease, resulting in broader coverage. Later the court would consider such "occupational diseases" as repetitive motion injuries and job stress.[90] It was *Booker* and *Wood* that opened the door to the liberalization of workers' compensation law in North Carolina.

In perhaps one of her most far-reaching cases, *Sutton v. Duke*,[91] Justice Sharp was largely responsible for setting on a firm footing the new Rules of Civil Procedure, which replaced the old North Carolina Code in 1970. This body of procedural rules, governing every aspect of a civil trial from the filing of the complaint to the conduct of the appeal, is the scaffolding supporting the facts and law of a case, without which chaos would ensue. The rules are among the so-called technicalities upon which a case might be won or lost despite its substantive aspects. The new rules had been greeted with considerable consternation and confusion among members of the bar and judiciary. Here, it was not a question of her propensity or lack thereof for breaking new legal ground. Rather, the court was obliged to interpret statutes, newly enacted by the General Assembly, that radically changed the nature of trial practice.

In her opinion interpreting the new rules for drafting a civil complaint, she set out to draw up as clear a road map as possible for the lawyers and judges who would have to adapt to the new way. Her goal was ever to marry the theoretical with the practical; having laid the theoretical base, she always tried to leave as little room for confusion as possible for the practitioners in the real-world courtroom. Arguably no other case in her career had a broader impact, because her lucid explanation of the new world in which the legal profession found itself affected every civil case filed thereafter. Few if any of her cases brought forth so many expressions of gratitude from the practicing bar.

Then there were the cases that, though of less significance, contributed to her notoriety. Perhaps the most notorious was the one in which she declared the widespread practice of "brown-bagging"—bringing one's own liquor to public establishments—illegal.[92] In theory North Carolina was one of the driest states in the country, having voted to go dry in 1908 before Prohibition and having voted against repeal of Prohibition in 1933. Although in "wet" counties consumers could purchase bottles of alcohol at state-controlled stores for home consumption, it was not legal to sell liquor by the drink. Under the statutes, a person could possess liquor only in his home or while transporting a limited quantity, less than one gallon, to his home. Nevertheless, it had long been common practice in restaurants and clubs for customers to supply their own liquor (in the proverbial brown paper bag) and pay the establishment for "set-ups"—ice and mixers. In fact, social drinking was a prevalent and deeply cherished part of life for a substantial part of the population, including not a few members of the legislature.

Judge Sharp's decision came out on November 30, 1966 (with a supplemental ruling on December 20), just in time to put a damper on the Christmas spirit. Despite the fact that she wrote for a unanimous court, her well-known status as a teetotaler further enraged those inconvenienced by the ruling. For the business community, it had been bad enough that one could not buy liquor by the drink, a policy that resulted in lost conventions and tourism, but at least customers could have a drink by bringing their own. A shrill chorus of protest from numerous businesses, and especially from restaurateurs claiming they would have to close their doors, lamented the impact of the decisions. In Charlotte, where a new 2,000-seat convention hall had just opened, it was said that fifteen conventions had canceled due to the ruling.[93] Public feeling ran so high that Supreme Court Marshal Raymond Mason Taylor demanded a highway patrolman to drive him to serve the mandate on the Mecklenburg County clerk of court. "So far as I know this is the first time a Marshal of the Supreme Court has ever been on a mission of this sort," he told the newspapers.[94] (His request for a pistol in addition to the highway patrolman was, however, denied.)[95]

Justice Sharp became known as "The Lady Who Dried Up the State," and Mayne Albright composed a song entitled "Little Brown Bag How I Miss Thee." The Wall Street Journal took note in an article headed, "The Brown-Bag Blues: North Carolina Has Wets Crying in Beer."[96] An anonymous correspondent sent Judge Sharp a brown bag decorated with her picture and two Old Crow labels.[97] Another correspondent declared that he hoped she would pilot the first no-return rocket to the moon, with Martin Luther King as copilot.[98]

Despite the bitterness of some citizens, the situation was sure to be (and was) quickly remedied by the legislature, and therefore could be viewed with a degree of humor. At a Wake County Bar Association dinner at the Hotel Sir Walter, the supreme court justices' places were marked with brown bags containing bottles labeled appropriately as "Old Jack," "Old Crabapple," and the like. Judge Sharp informed those assembled that her bottle was legal because she lived at the hotel.[99]

The opinion that undoubtedly gave Justice Sharp the most enjoyment was one involving baseball. Famously uninterested in athletics and often teased for her long-suffering silence during the lengthy sport-related discussions among her colleagues on the bench, she had not chosen the case on purpose. It was a "Hobson's Choice," the last case left on the table.[100]

The lawsuit arose from a Carolina League game between the Raleigh Caps and Greensboro Yankees played one June night at the old Devereux Meadow, now long-vanished, in Raleigh.[101] The plaintiff was the umpire who had the effrontery to make a number of close calls in favor of the Greensboro team. This so incensed the manager of the Raleigh team that his invective reached a level sufficient to inspire if not incite a riot, in the course of which the umpire sustained physical injury at the hands of an irate fan. The umpire alleged, inter alia, that the Raleigh manager was liable for damages, having goaded the crowd to attack him. To the glee of the press, including *Time* magazine,[102] Judge Sharp ruled that the umpire had no case. "For present day fans," she wrote, "a goodly part of the sport in a baseball game is goading and denouncing the umpire when they do not concur in his decisions, and most feel that, without one or more rhubarbs, they have not received their money's worth. Ordinarily, however, an umpire garners only vituperation — not fisticuffs."[103] She found no proximate cause between the manager's behavior and the injury inflicted by an unruly fan; therefore, the manager was not liable.

One commentator later described the opinion as "a priceless mix of good sense, good law and good fun."[104] Breck wrote to say that if she proceeded with her education, she might be "qualified as a sports writer" once she retired from the bench.[105] Judge Sharp herself proudly reported, "My baseball case made The Law page in Time Magazine of 10/2/64."[106]

Judge Sharp had consulted heavily with two law clerks, Harold Tharrington and Wade Smith, who undertook to educate her on baseball. Once the opinion was finished, she even attended a game in their custody.[107] She could not admit that she had seen a professional baseball game once before — with John Kesler on their secret trip to New York in 1951 — so the legend grew that it was the only one she had ever attended.[108] With delight, she recorded in her journal, "We see a rhubarb."[109] Eventually the legislature would strive to provide the umpire with a little more protection, but as one journalist remarked, "They can never legislate sympathy for the ref."[110]

It was a good thing that she could summon the energy for levity, because the court's work load was becoming impossible, even for a workaholic like Susie Sharp. When she went on the court in 1962, every case that was appealed from the trial court came to the North Carolina Supreme Court, for there was no intermediate court of appeals. Moreover, the right of appeal was virtually unlimited. As a matter of right, an appeal could be taken from any criminal conviction in superior court, and from any final order or determination made by a superior court judge in civil cases. Unlike the U.S. Supreme Court and many other appellate courts, the North Carolina Supreme Court could not decline to hear any properly presented appeal, no matter how many times the court had previously ruled on the issue involved or how well settled the law. As a result, the volume of cases was extremely heavy. The first year Justice Sharp was on the court, it issued 379 written opinions, or better than one a day on average.[111] Two years later, the number had soared to 473 written opinions (in addition to rulings on some 200 petitions).[112] In fact, the volume of appeals handled by the North Carolina Supreme Court was thought to be the heaviest in the country.[113] New Jersey, for example, with more than 6 million citizens to North Carolina's 4.5 million, had only 124 written supreme court opinions in the same year, while California, with a population approaching 16 million, had only 127.[114]

By the mid-1960s the situation had become dire. Rulings from the U.S. Supreme Court, such as those guaranteeing an indigent's right to court-appointed counsel and barring self-incriminating statements made by a defendant unless he had been advised of his right to remain silent and to have an attorney, had resulted in a vastly increased number of criminal cases in the appellate system.[115] The 1962 court reform amendment had not addressed the issue of an intermediate North Carolina court of appeals to buffer the supreme court and reduce its caseload. Some relief arrived for the supreme court's most junior justice at least when in 1964 the court began dividing up the work of processing prisoners' petitions, which, swollen by new constitutional issues, had surpassed the ability of one justice to handle.[116] But the court as a whole was inundated with cases on appeal from the trial courts.

Finally, an amendment to the North Carolina Constitution to establish an intermediate appellate court was proposed and passed in the fall of 1965. The court of appeals became operational on October 1, 1967, with an initial complement of six judges sitting in rotating panels of three.[117] The court began hearing appeals in January 1968. During that first year, the court of appeals heard 582 cases, many of which ended their journey through the courts there. As a result, the North Carolina Supreme Court issued only 162 written opinions, in contrast to 428 in the preceding year.[118] At last the justices could devote their time and energy to doing a more thorough job on the more significant cases.

CHAPTER 14

FEDERAL JOB PROPOSALS

Whatever the frustrations of her job, Justice Sharp found that she had to fight a constant battle to keep from getting "promoted" to the federal bench, either the Fourth Circuit Court of Appeals or the U.S. Supreme Court. Although she was ambivalent at best about the idea, she was a serious candidate for the highest court in the land for almost two decades prior to Sandra Day O'Connor's appointment in 1981. Her consideration at every vacancy reflected her national standing.

She had scarcely gotten settled in her new position on North Carolina's highest court when Governor Terry Sanford, in effect, offered her the opportunity to be the first woman on the U.S. Supreme Court. Had the timing been slightly different, it is likely that, as Sanford believed, he "could have probably put her on the Supreme Court of the United States" while John Kennedy was president.[1]

As a result of his critical role in Kennedy's election, Sanford was in a position to harvest a good deal of political gratitude from the new administration. He would later say that when Kennedy became president, he had "complete access" to the White House.[2] Sanford could claim credit for Kennedy's appointment of former North Carolina governor Luther Hodges as secretary of commerce, and he even secured the president as UNC's University Day speaker on October 12, 1961.[3] Among other benefits to North Carolina, Sanford's influence with Kennedy resulted in the location of the National Institute of Environmental Health Sciences and the Environmental Protection Agency facilities in Research Triangle Park, North Carolina.[4]

The first U.S. Supreme Court vacancy under Kennedy opened up scarcely two weeks after Susie Sharp took her seat on North Carolina's highest court, and the president filled it swiftly. Justice Charles E. Whittaker retired on March 31, 1962. His replacement, Justice Byron R. White, took his oath of office on April 16, 1962. In August 1962 Justice Felix Frankfurter, who had been appointed to the Court by President Franklin D. Roosevelt in 1939, also stepped down. This might have been an opportune moment for Sanford to put forward his suggestion for a nominee, but Frankfurter occupied what was generally known as the "Jewish seat" on the Court. In keeping with this twentieth-century tradition, Kennedy appointed Arthur J. Goldberg, who was sworn in on October 1, 1962.

It is unclear if he discussed it with Justice Sharp beforehand, but on October 29, 1962, Sanford wrote to Kennedy formally suggesting that the president consider appointing her in the event of another vacancy on the Court.[5] Briefly reviewing her distinguished career after being appointed as "a relatively young woman" to the superior court in 1949 and later on the North Carolina Supreme Court, Governor Sanford wrote, "Her record has been characterized by uncommon learning and education, remarkable wisdom, legal knowledge, and a genuine understanding of the human elements involved in all cases which come before her." The governor added, "Placing her on the Supreme Court was the most popular appointment of my Administration."[6]

Sanford had every reason to think that there would be broad popular support for getting Justice Sharp nominated to the U.S. Supreme Court. Indeed, the North Carolina Federation of Women's Clubs had sent him, several months before, a resolution commending him for appointing her to the North Carolina appellate court and urging him to pursue her appointment "as the first woman member of the U.S. Supreme Court."[7] Close political allies such as Superior Court Judge J. William Copeland also encouraged him. Judge Copeland, in an extensive political report to Sanford on Justice Sharp's native Rockingham County, included the remark: "Push Judge Susie Sharp hard for Sup. Ct. It would be the smartest thing for the Pres. He would help himself with a lot of people and she is qualified."[8] Many ordinary citizens as well as members of the legal profession wrote both Judge Sharp and the governor, expressing the hope that she might be appointed. Leaving aside the feelings of those who did not hold that court in high esteem, the elevation of North Carolina's own "First Lady of the Law" to the highest federal bench would have been a significant point of pride for the state.

Sanford assumed, not unnaturally, that Judge Sharp would be pleased to become the first woman on the U.S. Supreme Court. To his surprise, however, it was a possibility she rejected.

Sometime after an interrupted conversation in the governor's office in November 1962, Justice Sharp wrote to express her appreciation for his proposal and to explain her reasons for turning it down. Primarily, she claimed, she did not feel qualified to sit on the federal bench: "I never tried a case in any Federal court in my life. My experience has been entirely within the State system. I know that some have gone to high judicial positions in Washington who never tried a case anywhere, but that is not the way it should be."[9] She did not believe she "could be even reasonably happy under such circumstances." Beyond that, she told the governor, she did not feel that she had "yet come to grips with the position with which you so bravely entrusted me."

Next to the journal entry in which she noted, "Write to the Gov. re S. Ct.," Judge Sharp marked a big "X" in the margin. When she saw the governor a few days later, she told him that she had written him as she did because "feeling as I did about the job I did not want him to go out on a limb for me."[10]

Her lack of qualifications, as she termed it, could be described more accurately as a lack of desire. Of course, she could have mastered federal law if she had wanted to, however daunting the task. But for a perfectionist like Judge Sharp, still in the intense early days of her new job on the North Carolina Supreme Court when she felt so overwhelmed, it must have been difficult to imagine tackling an even steeper learning curve at this stage of her life, under an even brighter spotlight than any to which she had yet been subjected. Beyond that, events in recent years had done little to bring federal courts into better favor in North Carolina or the rest of the South, where they had never enjoyed universal admiration. Many considered the Supreme Court under Chief Justice Earl Warren to be the nadir rather than the apex of the federal judicial system. "Being a federal judge about now would never lure me from a state court," Judge Sharp wrote a friend.[11] To Governor Sanford, she left no doubt as to her wishes. "I feel that I should tell you that I have no ambition to go to Washington. My ambition is to continue to try to pay my debt to North Carolina in the position I now have."[12]

Left unexpressed were other, more personal reasons why she did not wish to leave North Carolina. She was irredeemably the head of her family and had only recently abandoned her mother, leaving her to rattle around alone in the old house in Reidsville. Her mother, despite the inroads of age, was not the type to slow down, which was a worry in itself. For her seventy-eighth birthday the week before Judge Sharp was tapped for the high court, for example, Mrs. Sharp had requested 100 pounds of fertilizer for her beloved garden. Judge Sharp occasionally received reports on her mother like the one from her neighbor who said, "Susie, I hate to tell you this, but I passed by today and saw your mother sitting on a pillow hoeing."[13] Judge Sharp's response was that she was helpless to do anything about it, declaring, "My jurisdiction doesn't extend that far."[14] It was Judge Sharp who had to tend to all matters like taxes, termite treatments, or roof repairs. She found it difficult enough to manage such details from Raleigh, and, as a constant worrier, Judge Sharp needed to go home to check on her mother virtually every weekend. This she would do as long as her mother lived. Moving to Washington did not appear practical.

She had not changed her mind by August 1963, when she wrote to John Kesler, "I told His Ex. that I was not interested in going Nawth in the unlikely event I got the opportunity. He called off his 'man' up there and that gent didn't believe she meant it. His X told him he thought I did. I did."[15]

In 1962 when Judge Sharp went on the North Carolina Supreme Court, she and John had been lovers for fifteen years. Her feelings were as strong as ever, but some evidence suggests that John was pulling away even before she was appointed. During 1961 the two of them had managed to spend three dozen or so nights together. Nonetheless, an increasing number of Judge Sharp's journal entries reflect unease and unhappiness. Several incidents had created some degree of paranoia about his attentions waning or straying. On one occasion when she went to Salisbury to meet him, there had been a misunderstanding, and when she finally caught up with him on the street, she felt that "[s]omething in the way he looks makes me know that he was not coming to meet me." In fact, he said, he'd been on his way to the sheriff's office. She said, "Well, if you were not looking for me I will not delay you." She went home, "hurt to the quick."[16] In addition, there was apparently some tension with his wife, who may have suspected something was going on, with Judge Sharp or perhaps someone else. John reported that "he was being watched."[17] He tried to reassure her and said that no finger was pointing to her, but she did not find him very convincing.[18] In early 1962, before she was appointed to the supreme court, she recorded in her journal, "Something has happened but I don't know what."[19] A month later John wrote that he had had a "[r]ow with wife who is on 24 hour alert."[20]

The year 1962, then, began with the relationship in an unsettled state. John's response to her appointment to the supreme court in March was a letter of loving renunciation she received two days after her swearing-in.[21] She did not, however, accept his renunciation, and the relationship continued, although they saw each other very rarely from then on. Ironically, it was at this time that the secrecy surrounding their affair was breached, just as it was at its lowest ebb. In April 1962 Judge Sharp received a letter from John that had been opened and resealed with Scotch tape, leading her to conclude, "Somebody in Raleigh knows I have a lover and I don't know how many others will be told."[22] If whoever had opened the envelope had read the contents, however, he or she must have been the soul of discretion. After telling John what had happened, Judge Sharp never mentioned the matter again in her journal.

Meanwhile, John was inattentive, forgetting their anniversary in May.[23] Repeatedly, he canceled planned trips to see her in Raleigh. Judge Sharp, of course, was swamped with her new job and had to go home most weekends to see her mother. Still, they did find the occasional opportunity to meet, and he continued to express his affection to her. "He says that I spoil him and he loves every minute of it," she recorded.[24] They had a weekend together at the end of October, very comfortable and tender. "[W]e sit on the sofa for a while and look at the paper. He leaves about noon — with some candy, 2 little donuts and an apple. He says, 'I love you, my sweet.' I say, 'I do too.'"[25]

This was the situation that fall of 1962 when Governor Sanford asked Judge Sharp if she wanted the nomination to the U.S. Supreme Court. In addition to her demanding new job and her worries about her mother, Judge Sharp had her longtime affair as another incentive to stay in North Carolina. Even if she was occasionally worried or depressed about the situation, she fully expected the relationship to continue and would not have wanted to do anything to cause further problems or put more distance between her and John. It was not difficult for her to reject Sanford's overture. Being on the U.S. Supreme Court had never been her ambition or even within her contemplation. Not even the immense honor of being the first female U.S. Supreme Court justice could overcome the pull of her established life in her beloved North Carolina, doing work that she deeply enjoyed on the state's highest court, and being within visiting distance of the man she had loved since her law school days. It was a decision her childhood friend Margaret Newnam reinforced when Judge Sharp told her that she had told Sanford she "was not interested in going to Washington." Margaret said that "she thought it was the wisest thing I ever did; that she is appalled at what I have given up for this [career]."[26]

At a certain point, her attitude about the U.S. Supreme Court would change, but not until after President Kennedy's term in office was cut short by assassination. In the interim, President Lyndon Johnson in his inimitable fashion worked behind the scenes to create vacancies on the Court, and Judge Sharp's irrepressible supporters worked to put her on the federal bench, one way or another.

Judge Sharp herself was focused on her reelection to the North Carolina Supreme Court. In 1966 her intention to run for another eight-year term was, however, complicated by a well-meaning but unsolicited and badly timed effort by her U.S. senators to get her appointed to the Fourth Circuit Court of Appeals. On February 9, 1966, along with four other members of the court up for reelection, she marched down to the state board of elections office to pay her filing fee of $230 for the Democratic primary in May.[27] The *News and Observer* obligingly published a photograph of the justices with an accompanying article, and the campaign was officially under way.

The next day, as Judge Sharp was having lunch at the s&w Cafeteria, someone told her that the radio had just announced that North Carolina's U.S. senators Sam Ervin Jr. and B. Everett Jordan had "recommended her for something."[28] Unbeknownst to Judge Sharp, they had nominated her for an upcoming vacancy on the Fourth Circuit Court of Appeals. Judge Sharp was horrified. Not only did she have no desire to serve on the federal court, but the nomination endangered her reelection to the North Carolina Supreme Court. She lost no time in calling off the senators and issuing a public statement saying she had asked that her name be withdrawn. Annie Sharp reported to her cousin in Danville, Virginia, that Senator Ervin "seemed quite surprised" that Judge Sharp did not want the position.[29] The senators had been unaware that she had filed for reelection to the North Carolina Supreme Court, but for Judge Sharp the timing was irrelevant to her choice. "Whatever the timing, my decision would have been the same."[30]

"My Senators put me in a most impossible situation," she wrote to her cousin William Blackwell.[31] "Having announced for reelection and paid my filing fee on Wednesday, the last thing on earth I would have ordered on Thursday was a recommendation for a Federal appointment!" Until the filing period closed on March 18, all the declared supreme court candidates were vulnerable to opposition that might arise. At least one attorney had announced his intention of running for the court but had not yet selected which of the justices he would challenge. "I would undoubtedly have been his target if I had not promptly repudiated the recommendation," said Judge Sharp.[32] Just as important was the perception in the minds of voters. "I do not see how any candidate could ask the electorate to return him and/or her to office in order to use that office as a springboard to a Federal job," she wrote William Blackwell. She worried that voters might think she was "both presumptuous and ungrateful" for the honor given her by the state's senators.[33] Some people, she knew, were under the impression she had actually declined a tendered appointment, as opposed to a nomination.[34] She was also apprehensive that her friends and supporters might think she had let them down or lost her ambition—"alternative calamities!"[35]

Writing to William Snider at the *Greensboro Daily News*, she reviewed some of her considerations. She considered the supreme court of North Carolina to be "quite as important a tribunal as the Circuit Court of Appeals."[36] Although the circuit court embraced five states, it was still only an intermediate court. It was true that the federal court offered life tenure and a larger salary, but North Carolina voters were not in the habit of replacing incumbent justices so long as they were doing their job, and "as a *feme sole*, with no dependents," the salary increase was not as strong a lure as it might be to others.[37] And there were other satisfactions. "On March 15th I will have been on this Court 4 years," she told Snider. "In that time I have moved up from J-7 to J-5, three notches. The work here is hard and totally possessive, but it is a never-ending challenge affording infinite variety. Actually I know of nothing else I'd rather be doing. I work with congenial and sympathetic people in familiar surroundings, and I feel that I can make a more certain contribution here than on the Circuit Court."[38]

To her cousin William Blackwell, she was frank about another consideration. "If I last long enough here and my seniors don't last too long, I could conceivably become Chief Justice of North Carolina — an honor I covet more than a Federal judgeship, even though it carries life tenure. After all one lives only so long. If I survive the coming primary and general election, I will be eligible for retirement at the end of that term."[39] A friend, Charlotte attorney Lelia Alexander, told Judge Sharp that another attorney had remarked, "Do you know that in turning down that job on the 4th Circuit she may have been turning down a position on the U.S." But Lelia had responded as she knew Judge Sharp would have — that even if it were true, she did not grieve over it.[40]

Her mother, for one, was relieved. "It would mean more money, but much traveling and the laws are different." she wrote. "She likes where she is. I told her not to consider me, if she wanted it, that I could make out. My! I was glad she didn't take it."[41]

But every time there was a vacancy on the U.S. Supreme Court, her name came up.

President Johnson, in what many observers felt was a two-birds-with-one-stone coup, persuaded Justice Arthur Goldberg to resign and take over for Adlai Stevenson, who had died suddenly on July 14, 1965, as ambassador to the United Nations. Stevenson had been useful to LBJ because his liberal credentials gave the president some cover even as he attempted to pursue the hawkish Vietnam policies begun under the Kennedy administration. "You are the only man who can bring peace to Vietnam," LBJ said to Goldberg, and implied that such a feat would make him the next president of the United States.[42] Goldberg, who was said to be restless as a member of the Supreme Court, took the bait. By appointing Goldberg, a brilliant negotiator, as ambassador to the United Nations, Johnson could appease the increasingly skeptical liberal wing while gaining a vacancy on the Court for his close adviser, Abe Fortas.

Ever alert, Judge Allen Gwyn sent off a letter to President Johnson dated July 24, 1965, one day before Goldberg's resignation, urging the president to consider Justice Sharp for the slot, but this was a seat earmarked for Fortas, who was sworn in on October 4, 1965. In writing to thank a supporter for his encouragement, Judge Sharp remarked that she did not think it likely that Johnson would appoint "a middle-of-the-roader like me, even though I am a woman."[43] In fact, she was skeptical about reports that LBJ had actually considered nominating a woman, referring to this White House disclosure, made after Fortas was named, as "painless chivalry."[44] "My life has been in the State courts," Judge Sharp wrote, "and I am happy here in Raleigh—even if we do work all the time!"[45] She did not, however, reject the idea as she had done as recently as two years before. In February 1966, in her letter to Bill Snider explaining why she did not want to be appointed to the Fourth Circuit Court of Appeals, she gave a hint that her attitude might be shifting. Compared to her job as an associate justice on the North Carolina Supreme Court, she wrote, "there could be only two other ambitions which would be promotions, and it would be both self-defeating and a breach of taste to mention either."[46] For the first time, she included in her thinking a seat on the U.S. Supreme Court, along with her long-sought goal of becoming North Carolina's chief justice.

The next time a vacancy arose on the nation's highest court, she was willing to consider it.

President Johnson had another opportunity to name a Supreme Court justice when Justice Tom C. Clark resigned in 1967. This vacancy was also engineered by LBJ. When Attorney General Nicholas Katzenbach resigned, Justice Clark's son Ramsey Clark was named as acting attorney general. In January 1967 Johnson told Ramsey Clark that he wanted to appoint him as permanent attorney general, but that if he did, Justice Clark could not stay on the Court because of potential conflicts of interest.[47] Ramsey protested that it would hurt the president if his father, the Court's toughest proponent of law enforcement, stepped down, but LBJ argued that "every taxi driver in the country" would see that there was a conflict of interest if a son argued cases before a court on which his father sat.[48] To Justice Clark, Johnson reportedly said he intended to make Ramsey attorney general, adding something along the lines of, "I'm sorry that's going to raise a problem for you, Tom, and I'm not going to do it if you don't want to resign."[49] Whether with or without an agreement as to the result, Johnson appointed Ramsey Clark to be attorney general the following month, and the same day Justice Clark resigned effective at the end of the Court's term in June.

As soon as they learned of the impending vacancy, North Carolina's U.S. senators Ervin and Jordan fired off a two-page letter to the president urging him to nominate Susie Sharp.[50] Whether Justice Sharp had advance notice is unclear, but she learned the recommendation had been made when a local television reporter called to get her reaction.[51] This time, instead of notifying her senators that she wished her name withdrawn, she wrote each of them, gracefully noting that it had been her hope that Senator Sam Ervin would be the next nominee, but acknowledging, "Although I am happy in my work here and it seems presumptuous of me even to consider the possibility that I might be appointed, I thought perhaps I should tell you that if the President should decide to name the lady from North Carolina, I could not decline the honor."[52]

She had a lot of support over the next few weeks. Her former law school classmate Governor Dan Moore wrote President Johnson a warm endorsement and solicited the support of the neighboring governors in South Carolina, Virginia, West Virginia, and Tennessee as well.[53] "Nothing would please me more than to see you appointed to the U.S. Supreme Court, and I am going to do everything in my power to help make it come about," Governor Moore wrote to Justice Sharp.[54] Members of the North Carolina congressional delegation introduced a joint resolution recommending that President Johnson appoint her "to fill any vacancy that now or hereafter in the reasonable future might exist upon the Supreme Court of the United States."[55] At home, the North Carolina General Assembly passed a similar resolution.[56] Allen Gwyn Jr. notified Judge Sharp that the Rockingham County Democratic Executive Committee had sent out telegrams to the entire congressional delegation in support of her appointment. His father, Judge Gwyn, wrote supporting letters to Senators Ervin and Jordan.[57] Professor James A. Webster Jr. of the Wake Forest College School of Law wrote the president to add "the voice of a legal academician."[58] The board of governors of the North Carolina Bar Association, "representing 2500 practicing attorneys," unanimously approved a resolution supporting her appointment.[59] In addition, numerous friends and colleagues wrote to Judge Sharp expressing their hope that she would get the nomination, and the press reported favorably on the efforts of her supporters.

Judge Sharp did nothing to discourage the movement on her behalf. She viewed it all with a large degree of skepticism, but for the first time she was willing to consider the possibility. She even had her law clerk, Tom Bolch, look up the salary and retirement benefits to which a justice of the U.S. Supreme Court was entitled.[60] He had no doubt in his own mind that she would have accepted the nomination.[61] Her law clerk from the previous year, Henry Manning, also believed she would have gone if chosen, primarily because she did not like the direction the Court had been taking and would have welcomed an opportunity to exert her influence on it.[62] Partly out of superstition perhaps, she nonetheless maintained a firm ambivalence, writing to one of her stalwart supporters, "It is my opinion . . . that the President has long since made up his mind whom he will appoint to succeed Justice Clark. It strikes me as beyond the realm of possibility that he would consider me. . . . One could not, of course — without a compelling reason for doing so — turn down an appointment to the Supreme Court of the United States, but I have no desire to go to Washington."[63]

What had changed in her life that caused her even to consider the move to Washington, D.C., at this time? To be sure, after five years she had settled into her job on the state's highest court, and if she was working hard she was feeling less overwhelmed. But she had no more experience in federal law than she had in 1962. And at home in Reidsville matters were certainly no less difficult. With her mother's advancing age, Judge Sharp had even more reason to remain close by. Writing to a cousin during the 1967 speculation about her appointment to the U.S. Supreme Court, she said, "I go home almost every weekend. Occasionally, something comes up which keeps me here, but it is not often. Mama was 83 on March 4th, and her strength, eyesight, and hearing are all failing."[64] The most significant change in her life was that she and John Kesler now rarely saw one another.

As early as January 1963, John speculated to her, for the first time, about what might happen if he were not married, expressing doubts, telling her that "he had so little to offer" her.[65] Almost exactly a month later, his wife Sudie had a heart attack, complicating his life and no doubt his emotions. On one occasion that summer, Judge Sharp went to Salisbury to see him, but after getting her room at the Holiday Inn she waited in vain for him. She was unable to reach him by phone and made several fruitless "patrols" in her car past his office and home. "My disappointment is so keen that there is a physical reaction," she wrote.[66] By early 1964 Judge Sharp was writing entries in her journal such as this: "No letter from John. I know that I have no right at all in his life and that his family, his partner and all his clients have prior claims — but I can't make myself like it."[67] In August she wrote, "Get a short note from John. I can not believe that he wants to see me anymore."[68] In 1964 they saw each other only twice.

The moment of truth came in September 1965 when once again John told her on the phone that he could not come to Raleigh to see her. It seemed like the last straw. When she hung up, Judge Sharp confronted reality. Her secretary Virginia Lyon came into her office and, perceiving that she was stricken in some way, asked, "Don't you feel well?" Later in the morning, Virginia persisted, saying, "I know something is wrong. Is something worrying you?" Judge Sharp wrote in her journal, "I could not tell her that I had just realized that an era had ended."[69]

So she was willing to ponder the possibility of becoming the first woman on the U.S. Supreme Court, even if she was not exactly on fire about it. The enormity of such a historical appointment could not fail to draw her. She did think that perhaps she could do her part to curb some of the more egregious excesses, as she perceived them, of the Court. Up until a certain point, as the selection process moved forward, she remained, if not hopeful, then at least watchful.

That point was the moment that the name of Thurgood Marshall surfaced in the preappointment speculation. Marshall, the prominent NAACP attorney who had successfully argued the case of *Brown v. Board of Education* before the Supreme Court, had been appointed to the U.S. Court of Appeals several years before. When he became a candidate, Judge Sharp knew that she would not get the nomination. The African American had trumped the Woman. To Henry Manning she remarked, "I am the wrong sex and the wrong color to qualify for this job. For this appointment."[70] In truth, she was also too conservative and too opposed to the civil rights goals that LBJ sought as his legacy. President Johnson announced Marshall's nomination in June. Any disappointment Judge Sharp endured was mixed with relief.

She continued to be mentioned seriously as a potential appointee over the next decade, although she never again felt that she had a realistic chance and ultimately began to feel the speculation was more of a nuisance than anything. Nevertheless, her name invariably surfaced as a candidate, inspiring her supporters to leap into the fray over and over again despite her efforts to squelch them.

Ironically, both of the Republican presidents who spanned most of the remainder of her career, Nixon and Ford, gave more serious consideration to naming a woman to the court than had Johnson, and her name was invariably on the White House lists. President Richard M. Nixon appointed four Supreme Court justices, but he had to nominate six candidates to get his appointments confirmed.[71] During his tenure Judge Sharp was under what seemed like incessant assault, because the nomination process was constantly in the news.

In 1969 President Nixon had two vacancies to fill on the Court. The first arose when Chief Justice Earl Warren retired; Nixon's nomination of Warren Burger as chief justice was quickly confirmed. That same year Justice Abe Fortas resigned. In 1968 President Johnson had tried to have him confirmed as chief justice when Warren had initially tendered his resignation, effective upon confirmation of his successor, but the nomination had succumbed to opposition from Republicans, including a filibuster by Strom Thurmond, the first ever mounted in opposition to a Supreme Court nominee.[72] Subsequently, Fortas came under fire for accepting funds from a private foundation. Although he returned the money, he gave up his seat on the bench, becoming the first U.S. Supreme Court justice to resign under pressure.

The vacancy incited Judge Sharp's champions into the fray. "Once again our Senators have submitted my name without my knowledge," she wrote to U.S. representative Richardson Preyer.[73] Over and over, she sent thanks-but-no-thanks letters to those who had written the president on her behalf. "Any woman judge, of course, would cherish the distinction of being the first one to sit on the U.S. Supreme Court, but this honor is not in the cards for me. . . . It is not realistic to believe that the President will appoint a lifelong Democrat who has never deviated," she wrote one supporter.[74] To her old friend Judge Francis O. Clarkson, she said, "The highest court can struggle along without a woman for a while, and the President can find a younger, more qualified Republican who will do for the present. Therefore, I refuse to worry about an invitation to go to Washington. . . . I would not swap my present associates for any others."[75]

Nixon's first nominee to fill this vacancy was a southerner, Clement Haynsworth of Greenville, South Carolina, whose appointment was torpedoed by suspicions over his commitment to civil rights and by no small degree of political payback from Democrats still seething over the Fortas defeat. The president's second nomination was G. Harrold Carswell of Florida, who inspired Nebraska senator Roman Hruska's infamous comment in defense of mediocrity. (Senator Hruska had declared, "Well, even if [Carswell] were mediocre, there are a lot of mediocre judges and people and lawyers. They are entitled to a little representation, aren't they, and a little chance? We can't have all Brandeises and Frankfurters and Cardozos and stuff like that there.")[76] Carswell also drew fire for his public endorsement of segregation in 1948 and was rejected by the Senate in April 1970.

By this time, Judge Sharp's supporters were increasingly insistent. To one, a self-described "pre-law student, career woman, and mother to three children" who wanted to circulate a petition in her behalf, Judge Sharp wrote a heartfelt plea to desist in which she laid out many of her reasons for discouraging further lobbying. "[I]t is ten years too late for me to aspire to that position," she said, noting that in two years and four months she would be eligible for retirement under the North Carolina Judicial Retirement Law, which status she would forfeit if she went to Washington.[77] In addition, she had "a family problem" she could not conscientiously ignore, by which she meant her mother's health. "It is not realistic to think that President Nixon would appoint a lifelong Democrat to the Supreme Court when there are so many 'deserving and qualified Republicans.' I am sure he does not want a woman on the Court enough to name a Democrat," she said. Moreover, she frankly stated, "While I have not made any speeches such as the one which brought down the avalanche upon Carswell, I believe I would be no more acceptable to the groups which are opposing him."

President Nixon finally nominated Harry A. Blackmun, who was confirmed in May 1970.

Two more vacancies occurred on the Court during Nixon's administration. In September 1971 both Justice John M. Harlan and Justice Hugo L. Black retired. At this time it became known that President Nixon was in fact giving very serious consideration to appointing a woman. Contrary to cynics' suspicion that he was dangling this possibility without any intention of following through, tapes of conversations in the Nixon White House released on October 16, 2000, by the National Archives and Records Administration reveal that Nixon pursued the idea doggedly, despite what he insisted was his own antipathy to the idea. On one occasion, for example, Nixon told White House aide John D. Erlichman, "There's a hell of a lot of stuff that has to do with women. I'm not for it. I don't think women should ever be allowed to vote even."[78] But if Nixon could go to China, perhaps he could also appoint the first woman to the Court.

The Nixon tapes contain extraordinary insights into the social and political environment surrounding the possible appointment of a female justice. By 1971 women had clearly made their political influence felt, but the old boys' clubhouse for the most part remained closed to them. It is fascinating to learn that the flamboyant southern belle, Martha Mitchell, wife of Attorney General John Mitchell, was lobbying her husband to push for a woman on the Court. Even the normally quiescent Pat Nixon, as well as the Nixon daughters, Julie and Tricia, were pressuring the president on the issue.[79] More to the point, the president and his advisers agreed that nominating a woman would have some political benefits.[80] For this reason, the president pressed the issue with some force, asking for recommendations of possible female appointees from all over the country. Of course, as one cartoon put it, the ideal candidate would be "a strict constructionist, Southern, Woman, Negro, who is a Catholic married to a Eurasian midget."[81]

Brainstorming in the White House, Nixon, Mitchell, and other advisers stepped all over each other to deny that they thought a woman on the Court was a good idea, apart from the political allure. "I'm not for women, frankly, in any job," said Nixon. "I don't want any of them around. Thank God we don't have any in the Cabinet. But I must say the Cabinet's so lousy we [might] just as well have a woman [there] too."[82] Chief Justice Warren Burger was adamantly opposed to a woman on the Court, an obstacle that Nixon and his inner circle spent considerable time discussing. At one point, Burger threatened to resign if a woman was appointed.[83]

Speaking to John Mitchell, Nixon said, "I don't think a woman should be in any government job whatever. I mean, I really don't. The reason . . . is mainly because they are erratic. And emotional. Men are erratic and emotional too, but the point is a woman is more likely to be. The second problem they've got is that in terms of the Court, I know that that's like living with somebody inside of a spaceship."[84] Nixon continued, "What about poor Burger? What he'd have to go through? So from the standpoint of that, I just think we shouldn't have a woman. There should never be a woman there." But then he switched sides, arguing, "Whatever you and I think about the woman thing, and whatever Burger thinks, and we all think alike, believe me, women's lib is here, [and] it is a growing thing. And the demand is there. And the woman's viewpoint probably ought to be on the Court. It isn't a man's world anymore, unfortunately. So I lean to a woman only because, frankly, I think at this time, John, we got to pick up every half a percentage point we can."[85]

Senators Ervin and Jordan could not refrain from sending the president yet another earnest recommendation of their perennial lady candidate for the Court.[86] The University of North Carolina law faculty signed a petition to the president in support of Judge Sharp's nomination.[87] The American Association of University Women telegraphed an appeal to Nixon to appoint a woman and called attention to North Carolina's Associate Justice Sharp along with five other women recommended by the National Women's Political Caucus.[88]

According to White House counsel John W. Dean, Justice Sharp was among the dozen female possibilities on the list submitted by a staff member for Nixon's review.[89] The list included liberals, conservatives, Republicans, and Democrats. Contrary to Judge Sharp's assumption that a lifelong Democrat would not be considered, Nixon did not reject the idea of a Democratic woman candidate, although, of course, a Republican would have been given preference. He was much more concerned about whether she was conservative enough. "Now if she's liberal, the hell with it," he said to John Mitchell. "I won't appoint any liberal [to the Court]."[90] In fact, the woman Nixon eventually settled on as his top female prospect, Mildred L. Lillie, a fifty-six-year-old judge on the Court of Appeals, Second Appellate District of California, was a Democrat.[91]

As the selection process went on, many friends, judges, lawyers, and women's advocates rallied to Judge Sharp's cause, only to receive gracious but firm letters from Judge Sharp disavowing any thought of going to Washington. "Mr. Nixon is 'Mr. Republican,' and I have been a lifelong Democrat," she wrote to one supporter.[92] Moreover, at the age of sixty-four she believed she was too old, from the president's point of view as well as her own. A constitutional amendment was pending in North Carolina that would, if passed, give her eight more years before compulsory retirement. "In that eight years," she wrote, "I hope to give my 'maximum utmost' to North Carolina. Were I to go to Washington, by the time I finished my apprenticeship, there might not be time enough left to do honor to the position of my sex."[93] Writing to University of North Carolina president William Friday, she was definite: "I hope there will be no more talk of my going to Washington. The time for that has passed. It is my desire to finish out my career on the Supreme Court of North Carolina."[94]

Nixon's choice for the woman nominee, Judge Mildred Lillie, had impressed those who met her or reviewed her background for the White House. Chief Justice Burger had been brought to heel under pressure and had acquiesced to Nixon's determination to nominate a woman. In the end, it was the American Bar Association (ABA) Standing Committee on Federal Judiciary that apparently torpedoed Judge Lillie, rating her as "unqualified" by a vote of eleven to one.[95] John Dean believed the committee had rejected her solely because she was a woman, although, as John Mitchell reported to Nixon, "They said . . . she was probably as good as any woman that could be considered for the Court."[96] Nixon made sure that the press got wind of that remark.[97] Regardless of the committee's reasoning, Nixon was happy to put the blame on the ABA for his failure to find a "qualified" woman candidate for the Court.[98] Safely off the hook with credit for having tried, he gave up any further attempt. He finally filled the two seats with William H. Rehnquist and Lewis F. Powell.

There would be one final effort in 1975, under President Gerald Ford, when Justice William O. Douglas retired. Once again, without consulting Judge Sharp, the entire North Carolina congressional delegation met and agreed to sign a joint letter of support urging her appointment.[99] The unanimous group, it might be noted, ranged from the more liberal members such as Representative Richardson Preyer from Greensboro all the way to the opposite end of the spectrum occupied by Senator Jesse Helms. Although Ford was under considerable pressure to name a woman to the Court, and Justice Sharp's name was included in the speculation, this time around no one really believed that she would be nominated. She was too southern, too old, too Democratic. When asked to comment, Judge Sharp discounted the idea, adding that "she didn't think being a Southerner would affect the President's choice so much as the fact that, 'let us say, I have been a Democrat for a good many years.'"[100] Another factor this time was her opposition to the Equal Rights Amendment, as mentioned in White House aide Pat Lindh's memo to the president explaining why there were no women on the final list of potential nominees. "Two or three of the candidates on the Attorney General's list are opposed to the Equal Rights Amendment, which really puts us in double jeopardy," she said, and of these Judge Sharp was clearly one.[101]

Once again the president of the United States failed to find a woman to put on the Court and nominated John Paul Stevens, who was quickly confirmed in December 1975. Writing to her sister-in-law Bobbie Sharp, Judge Sharp said, "I am . . . getting mighty tired of being 'mentioned' for the job every time a vacancy occurs. It begins to smack of the old Listerine ad, 'Oft a bridesmaid—never a bride.'" She had first thought Betty Ford would get a woman nominee, she said, but as time went on, she figured the president could not find the woman he was looking for. She told Bobbie Sharp, "I was definitely out, having been a Democrat for *too* many years. That is what I told all the reporters who called. The time for me to go to Washington—if there ever was one—has definitely passed."[102]

How close did Susie Sharp come to being the first woman on the U.S. Supreme Court? The two basic questions to be answered are whether Judge Sharp could have gotten the president's nomination and, if so, whether she could have been confirmed by the Senate.

Governor Sanford was quite sure in his mind that he had the political clout to get President Kennedy to nominate Justice Sharp to the Supreme

Court.[103] Kennedy was indebted to Sanford, and the idea of putting the first woman on the court might have appealed to him. Judge Sharp's bona fides as a loyal Democrat were beyond reproach. Certainly she had exceptional stature within the profession and, as a member of the North Carolina Supreme Court, had achieved a prominence equaled by very few, male or female. Very early in her tenure on the state's high court she had begun making a reputation as a legal scholar. She had exceptional political backing. As for her gender, it could work either for or against her.

In light of the fate of Nixon's top female choice, California Court of Appeals judge Mildred Lillie, the role of the ABA's Standing Committee on Federal Judiciary in the nomination process requires consideration. This committee was still relatively new when Kennedy came into office. It was President Dwight D. Eisenhower who in the 1950s first invited the ABA to rate potential nominees to the federal bench. Recognizing the pressures that all too frequently made judgeships a political reward, Eisenhower saw that the ABA could be an effective buffer that could improve the selection process and thus the quality of the federal judiciary. Without any requirement in the law, the practice was quickly established by which the ABA played an important role in nominations for federal judges at all levels.

Under its first chairman, Bernard G. Segal, the Standing Committee on Federal Judiciary instituted a set of criteria focused solely on the potential nominee's professional qualifications. Segal was a fierce advocate of nonpartisanship in judicial selection and strove mightily to encourage, as an intermediate goal, an evenhanded bipartisanship in appointments. Members of the committee were chosen without regard to political party. Despite both sincere efforts and wishful mythology, however, the ABA and its screening committee were more closely identified with the Republicans than the Democrats.

Presidents have paid varying degrees of attention to the ABA Committee on Federal Judiciary, particularly with respect to Supreme Court appointments, long considered an unfettered presidential prerogative.[104] The nomination of William Brennan in 1956 was the first time the president consulted with the ABA in advance of naming his choice for a seat on the Supreme Court.[105] When John F. Kennedy was elected in 1960, his subsequent actions revealed a clear disinclination to follow the ABA recommendations or lack thereof. During his first two years in office Kennedy appointed eight (out of a total of ninety-nine) lifetime federal judges deemed "not qualified" by the ABA.[106] As for the Supreme Court, the standing committee reports are vague as to whether Kennedy consulted it prior to announcing his choices of

Justices Byron White and Arthur Goldberg, but in both cases the ABA gave the nominees its highest rating. In fact, it is difficult to imagine that President Kennedy, along with his brother, Attorney General Robert Kennedy, would have allowed the ABA to evaluate in advance his choices for the Supreme Court, still less to exert a de facto veto.

Moreover, although he was not the first or the last president to follow the partisan trail, Kennedy's appointments to the federal judiciary in his first two years were overwhelmingly Democrats, contrary to forcefully expressed pleas from Chairman Segal for evenhandedness in judicial appointments. When Kennedy came into office, federal judges were for the first time in over a generation almost evenly divided between the political parties, with 160 Democrats and 161 Republicans. A year and a half later the tally was 223 Democrats to 158 Republicans on the federal bench.[107]

After Kennedy's assassination, President Johnson made it clear he was taking no advice from the ABA on his Supreme Court appointments. Despite his failure to consult the standing committee in advance, the ABA subsequently, in response to the request of the Senate Judiciary Committee, approved all three of LBJ's nominees: Thurgood Marshall in 1967 and, in 1968, Homer Thornberry and Abe Fortas as chief justice.[108] Only Marshall was confirmed, however, and the Fortas nomination launched the modern era of contentious Senate confirmation hearings for Supreme Court appointments. President Nixon initially made it clear that he did not intend to submit his nominees for the Supreme Court to the ABA in advance, and he picked Warren Burger as his choice to succeed Earl Warren as chief justice without prior consultation.[109] Nixon's controversial nominations to fill the vacancy arising when Abe Fortas was pressured to resign in 1969, Clement Haynsworth and G. Harrold Carswell, were also made without consulting the ABA, as was his ultimate, successful nomination of Harry Blackmun, who was confirmed in June 1970.

Following the ugly public discussion of Haynsworth's and Carswell's qualifications after their nominations were announced, Attorney General John W. Mitchell made an about-face and notified the ABA on July 23, 1970, that he had decided "to furnish the ABA's Standing Committee on Federal Judiciary the names of persons I may consider recommending to the President for nomination to the Supreme Court."[110] The ABA had long argued that this procedure would allow it to evaluate potential candidates before their names were made public, in the hope of avoiding exactly such embarrassing confirmation hearings as had just occurred. Fearing partisan revenge for the Republican filibuster against Fortas for chief justice, Nixon felt the Democrats would be hard-pressed to oppose a nominee given a high rating by the ABA. Thus, ironically, although he had been vociferously opposed to allowing the ABA to vet his prospective Supreme Court nominees, Nixon actually emphasized the evaluation committee as a factor in the selection process.

It was under this "experimental advisory relationship" that the ABA committee reviewed the prospective nominations to fill the vacancies created by the retirements of Justices Hugo Black and John M. Harlan in September 1971.[111] Attorney General Mitchell submitted a list of six names, including two women, California Court of Appeals judge Mildred Lillie and District of Columbia Superior Court judge Sylvia Bacon, and a bond lawyer from Little Rock, Arkansas, named Herschel Friday.[112] Mitchell directed the committee to focus on two of the names, Mildred Lillie and Herschel Friday.

Mildred Lillie, a 1938 graduate of Boalt Hall School of Law at the University of California, Berkeley, had served for eleven years as a municipal court and superior court judge in Los Angeles before going on the state's court of appeals in 1958. She was credited with reorganizing the domestic relations court in Los Angeles and was generally considered a good, fair-minded judge. She was a Democrat but also a former prosecutor. Her tough-on-crime opinions on the court of appeals, however, had a high rate of reversal, nearly two-thirds, by the California Supreme Court. Even if one considered the California Supreme Court's alleged list to the left, this was a disturbing number of reversals to legal observers. She had been married twice, and her second husband had had business difficulties, resulting in some twenty-two lawsuits against him for nonpayment of debts. Judge Lillie was, however, extremely personable and intelligent, and White House aide John Dean was very impressed with her when he met her for an evaluative visit.

Nixon's tentative inclusion of the ABA in the prenomination process blew up when the press got wind of the names submitted to the Standing Committee on Federal Judiciary for evaluation. The *New York Times* and the *Washington Post* both ran stories on Judge Lillie and Herschel Friday, including reports of substantial opinion within the legal community that neither candidate was of sufficient stature for the U.S. Supreme Court. The National Women's Political Council registered its disapproval of the two women candidates. Even Nixon's former law partner, Leonard Garment, arguing for Howard Baker and Caspar Weinberger as candidates, said, "A persuasive case has not been made for the appointment of Judge Lillie . . . and there is a growing feeling that she's not qualified."[113] Ultimately the ABA Standing Committee, made up of seven Republicans and five Democrats, rated as "unqualified" both the nominees the White House had submitted as the two most serious candidates, Mildred Lillie and Herschel H. Friday. For whatever reason, Judge Sharp apparently shared the view of the ABA evaluation committee. She commented in a letter to her brother Tommy Sharp, "I'm very sorry that Mrs. Lillie got such unfavorable publicity, but I am more thankful she didn't get the appointment."[114]

Following this disaster, Nixon once again terminated the ABA's role in pre-nomination evaluation of Supreme Court candidates. Not until Gerald Ford resumed the practice with the nomination to fill Justice William O. Douglas's seat did the ABA regain its advisory capacity before the announcement of the proposed appointee.

With respect to the putative nomination of Justice Sharp, then, the ABA committee would have had little if any influence, especially during the times when her nomination stood a realistic chance under Presidents Kennedy and Johnson, neither of whom was disposed to asking prior approval from the ABA for their Supreme Court nominees. Even if she had been vetted by the committee, however, Justice Sharp's credentials and professional standing significantly exceeded those of Judge Lillie, who, no matter how highly regarded, was nonetheless only on an intermediate state appellate court, whereas Justice Sharp sat on her state's highest court.

All else being equal, then, there is reason to believe Governor Sanford's claim that he was in a position to secure Judge Sharp's nomination to the U.S. Supreme Court. The next question is whether she could have been confirmed by the Senate. The answer to this is probably yes. Between 1959 and Judge Sharp's retirement, Democrats firmly controlled the U.S. Senate. With respect to presidential appointments to the Supreme Court, the Senate had been almost uniformly acquiescent. No Supreme Court nominee had been rejected by the Senate since 1930, when North Carolina's John J. Parker, then serving on the Fourth Circuit U.S. Court of Appeals, was defeated by two votes when opposition developed from labor unions and the NAACP. It would not be until President Johnson's heavy-handed manipulation of Supreme Court vacancies, culminating in his ill-fated effort to appoint Abe Fortas chief justice, that the twentieth-century trend toward contentious Senate confirmation hearings took hold. Thus, during the years in which Judge Sharp had a realistic chance of being appointed, the Senate was unlikely to present an obstacle.

Given that there is substantial reason to believe that Judge Sharp could have had both President Kennedy's nomination and the Senate's confirmation, the critical factor becomes timing. Between the fall of 1962, when Judge Sharp rejected Governor Sanford's proposal, and 1967, when she permitted her backers to pursue the vacancy created by Justice Clark's resignation, President Kennedy had died and been replaced by President Johnson. Although President Johnson thought highly of Sanford, and indeed had asked him to manage his 1968 reelection campaign,[115] LBJ did not have the same debt to Sanford that Kennedy had had. In any case, LBJ had his own agenda.

If Kennedy had lived into a second term, by which time Judge Sharp had changed her mind about going to Washington, the moment might have seemed right for Kennedy to honor his debt to Sanford. It must be said, however, that if Kennedy had remained in office, there might not have been any further vacancies, because it was LBJ's machinations that led to the resignation of Justice Clark and indirectly to that of Justice Fortas. Conceivably, Justice Goldberg, whose restlessness aided LBJ in enticing him into retirement in 1965, might have stepped down of his own accord while Kennedy was president, but that seat was so clearly designated for a Jewish member of the Court that to substitute a woman would have been more trouble than it was worth. Nonetheless, if President Kennedy had lived into a second term and circumstances had brought about another vacancy, Judge Sharp very well could have had the honor that did not come to a woman until 1981, when President Ronald Reagan appointed Sandra Day O'Connor to the U.S. Supreme Court.

But by the time President Ford, after failing to find a woman appointee, named John Paul Stevens to fill Justice William O. Douglas's seat in 1975, Judge Sharp's regrets about not attaining a seat on the U.S. Supreme Court, if any, were long since behind her.

CHAPTER 15

OUT OF COURT

When Judge Sharp moved to Raleigh in 1962, hastily arranging for rooms in the Hotel Sir Walter, she did not imagine that she would never again live in Reidsville. She had refused numerous opportunities to sell her empty lot in the Pennrose neighborhood of Reidsville, earmarked for her retirement, and she entertained herself from time to time with house plans. At first, of course, she had no idea whether she would remain on the supreme court, although after having been the top vote getter in the 1962 and 1966 elections, she knew that she could stay as long as her health permitted. Moving to Raleigh, however, had major repercussions on every aspect of her life.

The most immediate impact was on her relationship with John Kesler. To be sure, other factors such as the actual and psychological stresses of her elevation to the supreme court as well as complications in John's life contributed to the decline of their affair. But Judge Sharp's new base made it far more difficult for them to arrange meetings. Before, when she was holding court in Charlotte or Greensboro, for example, or even just passing near Salisbury en route to her assignment, it was much simpler for John to slip away for a rendezvous. In 1962, when Judge Sharp went on the supreme court, he was no longer a trustee of the university and had served his last term as a state senator in 1961, which meant he had fewer excuses to come to Chapel Hill or Raleigh. His only regularly recurring business in the area was as a member of the State Judicial Council, which met in Raleigh.[1] "Absence takes a toll," she lamented to her journal in 1966.[2]

She felt isolated in general. No longer did she travel about the state, renewing friendships and refreshing her outlook. She had been on the supreme court a little more than three years when she wrote John a sad letter shortly before her birthday. "Each year now, as I take inventory of the past one, I find less hope in it for the future," she wrote. "And sometimes when I'm very tired I feel very blue."[3] The narrowing of her daily horizons seemed to have turned her view inward, to unhappy effect. "I'm chained here these days and the friends I used to see so often because I traveled where they were, I see so rarely now. One can grow old without maturing and I suffer from so many of the pains and penalties of immaturity. Impatience, compulsiveness, wanting one's own way, and many other faults with which I am familiar, are the indicia of youth and not the philosophic mind which age is supposed to bring."[4]

Although in years past she had kept a similar pattern, spending the week out of town and returning home to Reidsville on the weekends, things were different now. As a superior court judge, her weeks had been full of people and activities. In court she saw a constant stream of lawyers, litigants, and ordinary citizens, while at night she was scarcely ever without a dinner invitation. By the time she went home on the weekends, she had had a week full of stimulation and social activity. On the supreme court, however, she saw the same six other members of the court and the same members of the staff day in and day out. Appearances by counsel before the court were strictly limited in time and scope by the rules; the cases dealt with questions of law instead of the colorful and sometimes outrageously entertaining facts overseen by the trial court judge. Most days she had lunch with the other justices. At night, more often than not she returned to the office to keep up with the heavy work load. And then, on almost every Saturday she went back to Reidsville, missing out on whatever weekend invitations might have come her way. Thus she formed few new friendships in Raleigh, even as she felt many old ones slipping away for lack of contact. The s&w Cafeteria and the coffee shop at the Sir Walter provided most of her opportunities for company, but she was not a table hopper or back slapper by nature, so she often dined alone. Perhaps it is no coincidence that during her early years on the supreme court, her journal mentions repeated migraine episodes when it was all she could do to keep from screaming and could not keep her food down.[5]

She was lonely, and the poor condition of her relationship with John depressed her. Six weeks after her realization that "an era had ended" and that things were no longer the same between them, she wrote him a poignant description of a wedding she had attended: "In his 'charge' to the bride and groom [the preacher] told them that their joys would be magnified because shared and their sorrows minimized. For the first time I realized why tears are the order of the day at weddings. I found myself crying. I didn't expect to; the tears just came."[6]

Her family responsibilities, too, contributed to her sense of isolation in Raleigh. She never considered abandoning the weekend trek to check on her mother, of course. Unfortunately, although her brother Kits and his anesthesiologist wife Gwen had moved back to Reidsville in 1958 to practice medicine, in 1964 Kits decided to rejoin the navy. When her mother was ill that year, Judge Sharp lamented that decision. "His home was just two blocks from ours and Mamma ate the evening meal with him and his family every day. It was such a reassuring arrangement."[7] In her eighties, Annie Sharp was still tough to slow down, however, although she took on tasks that sometimes seemed too much even for her. "A colored man, Mr. Porterfield, a mule and I planted my garden this a.m.," she wrote her sister Susie Garrett. "Oh! How I miss Daddy. There is so much to do."[8]

Mr. Sharp was much on her mind, too, on the day in 1965 she went to Raleigh with Norwood Robinson to see him argue a case before the supreme court. When the marshal banged his gavel three times and intoned, "The Supreme Court of North Carolina," Annie Sharp was deeply moved. As she described it, "All the audience stood as the seven marched in. Susie was at the end by the window. I had a tight feeling in my chest, and how I wished for Daddy. I could hardly choke the tears back. He worked so hard to educate the seven [children] and he would have been so proud."[9] For his part, Robinson forever after chuckled at the ribbing he got for bringing the mother of one of the justices to court for his oral argument. His rejoinder was, "Well, it's well known in Reidsville that Justice Sharp doesn't pay much attention to what I say, but when her mother speaks, she listens!"[10]

Matters reached a crisis in 1967, however, when Mrs. Sharp was critically ill. "We came very near to losing her," Judge Sharp wrote on that occasion.[11] Her mother spent two weeks in Baptist Hospital in Winston-Salem, suffering from a bad case of pneumonia and pleurisy. Judge Sharp believed the illness had "left her with a serious heart condition."[12] In addition, her mother's back was giving her trouble, and Judge Sharp felt it would be "a long time before she will be able to return to her home in Reidsville."[13] The situation became even more alarming a couple of weeks later when the family realized that Mrs. Sharp's mind had somehow been affected. Judge Sharp's letters to family members described her mother's condition. "I saw Mama Saturday, and I was shocked by the change which had occurred in her in two weeks. Physically she is much stronger and is getting better, but she cannot remember anything very long at the time," she wrote her Aunt Bertha.[14] "Mama appears to be much better physically; the change in her mental condition, however, will startle you," she warned her sister-in-law Bobbie Sharp.[15] It was clear that Mrs. Sharp could not return to live alone in Reidsville.

Judge Sharp's sister Florence Newsom and her family bore the initial brunt of Mrs. Sharp's illness, taking her into their home in Winston-Salem. It was not a long-term solution, but it was the only one until they could find someone to stay with their mother twenty-four hours a day. Meanwhile, Mrs. Sharp longed ceaselessly to go home to the house on Lindsey Street. "She begs so pitifully to be taken home that it breaks our heart," Judge Sharp wrote to her nephew Jimmy Taylor.[16] But it was out of the question without full-time help. For example, although her life depended on getting her medication regularly, her memory could not be trusted for this purpose or any other. "Each time Florence gives her her medicine it is a complete surprise to her; she does not remember that she ever had a dose before," Judge Sharp reported.[17] Her mother recognized everyone and seemed perfectly rational, but a few minutes later would have no recollection of the conversation.[18]

Judge Sharp telephoned her mother every night, using the office WATS line, which allowed free long-distance calls (a major perk of her job, of which she took full advantage). She took her turn staying with her mother at Florence's on weekends to give her sister a break; Florence could not leave the house without getting a "sitter." Judge Sharp took over all her mother's affairs entirely. There was the tobacco to be sold from the old Sharp homestead, of course, and small amounts of rent to be collected from family farms.[19] Astonishingly, it turned out, Mrs. Sharp held a small percentage ownership in a Reidsville establishment called the Blue Front Pool Hall, a legacy from her husband, and Judge Sharp took the necessary steps to cash out her mother's share in an effort to stave off invading principal.[20] She carried on a relentless correspondence with everyone from the newspaper delivery manager to the Orkin exterminator service, trying to stay on top of the daily details her mother could no longer manage, even if she had been in residence at 629 Lindsey Street.

Something had to give. The best solution appeared to be convincing Louise Sharp to retire early from her career as a navy nurse and come home to Reidsville to take care of her mother. For Louise, it was an enormous sacrifice. Among other considerations, she would have to give up a good salary along with free medical and dental care, her maximum pension, and other benefits. She knew that if she stopped working as a nurse anesthetist, it would be difficult if not impossible to return to it later. In addition, the old homeplace was in very poor physical condition, needing all sorts of improvements, like rewiring and kitchen modernization. Louise did not have many friends in Reidsville anymore and could look forward only to being incarcerated with her mother, who would require constant supervision. Moreover, she would not actually be in charge, because, as she said, it was Judge Sharp who "controls Mother's affairs."[21]

Push came to shove when R. J. Reynolds Foods named Florence's husband, Bob Newsom, director of industrial engineering at the New York headquarters and the family reluctantly made the move from Winston-Salem to Connecticut.[22] Louise did not want to truncate her career to take care of her mother, but in the end she did, and in December 1968 Mrs. Sharp was able to go back to Reidsville. Louise's siblings did what they could to compensate her for her sacrifice, which enabled their mother to remain in the old home she so loved, in the care of her medically trained daughter. It was no small sacrifice, as they all well knew. Sometimes Louise's natural resentment and exhaustion spilled over, something else for Judge Sharp to try to manage. She still went home virtually every weekend and any other time she could spare to give Louise a respite.

Nor did the other family members escape her devoted attention. When Bob Newsom was honored by being made a Fellow of the American Institute of Industrial Engineers, Judge Sharp made sure the Winston-Salem newspaper heard about it.[23] When Tommy and Bobbie Sharp's daughter Tyrrell enrolled as a freshman at UNC, Judge Sharp, who hated horses, joined the Triangle Hunt so that Tyrrell could keep up her considerable expertise as a horsewoman.[24] When her niece Susie Newsom got engaged to a young dental student named Tom Lynch, Judge Sharp hosted a luncheon for her at the Forsyth Country Club in Winston-Salem and sent the details, including guest list, to the society news editor at the Winston-Salem newspaper.[25] In response to a request from her niece, she composed a two-page, single-spaced typed dissertation on her skin care program.[26] She wrote countless letters of recommendation for children of friends and family members, including one for the sixteen-year-old son of her sister Annie Hill and Fred Klenner for a week-long turn as a Senate page in the North Carolina General Assembly — despite the fact that Fred had long since alienated the entire family.[27] "Fritz is an attractive, smart boy who has been over-protected by his parents," Judge Sharp wrote. "A week in Raleigh would be revelation I want him to have."[28] No family problem was too large or too small for Judge Sharp to notice and take action on, no matter how crowded her agenda.

She had been in Raleigh for about five years when something happened that alleviated her isolation. She began "walking out" with one of her colleagues, Justice Bobbitt.

William Haywood Bobbitt was best summed up by a *News and Observer* editorial headline: "A Great Mind, A Merry Twinkle."[29] He had been on the North Carolina Supreme Court since he was appointed by Governor Umstead in 1954. Asked to describe him, Judge Sharp's sister Louise would recall,

"Well, he was cute. He was friendly and he was a good conversationalist, and he knew how to put people at ease. He just had a wealth of information. He was easy to talk to."[30] Not much taller than Judge Sharp, he had a large square forehead and a sharp chin set over a large paunch. Seven years older than she was, he was born in Raleigh in 1900, the grandson of two Methodist ministers. His father was a pharmacist who moved the family to Baltimore for a period during the young Bill Bobbitt's childhood, while he marketed a patent medicine he had developed. There, the boy fell ill at the age of five or six and was not expected to recover. He did, although he had to learn to walk again. When he was seven, his mother died of complications of childbirth. About five years later, his father sold the patent medicine rights, and the family returned to North Carolina, ultimately settling in Charlotte.[31]

Bill Bobbitt went to the University of North Carolina on a scholarship. An outstanding student, he received many honors including Phi Beta Kappa, Order of the Golden Fleece, the Bingham Debating Medal, and the Wiley P. Mangum Medal in Oratory. He served as president of the Dialectic Society and was elected permanent president of his class. At Chapel Hill he was well acquainted with such figures as Jonathan Daniels, Luther Hodges, and Thomas Wolfe.

Although he had been drawn to the ministry as a career, he decided on the law. After three years in the general college at UNC, he completed one year of law school there. Because he had not yet reached his twenty-first birthday, however, he was not eligible to take the bar exam, even though he had satisfied the educational requirements in effect at that time. Returning to Charlotte, he clerked in the law offices then known as Stewart and McRae until he could take the bar. As a young attorney, he was fortunate in his association with this firm, whose members had distinguished careers. Plummer Stewart was an exceptionally talented trial lawyer, deemed the "absolute czar" of the trial calendar in Mecklenburg County. John A. McRae, prominent in both law and politics, ran for governor in 1936. John J. Parker, who had run for governor in 1920, joined the firm not long after Bobbitt, before becoming a U.S. circuit court judge in 1925. Parker, who came within a hair of being confirmed for the U.S. Supreme Court in 1930, served as a judge at the Nuremberg trials after World War II. At his death he was the senior circuit judge in the United States. Bill Bobbitt would say that the training he received from these superb lawyers made up for his abbreviated legal education.

Since his appointment to the North Carolina Supreme Court in 1954, Justice Bobbitt had become known for his capacity for hard work, his wit, and his carefully drafted opinions. His former clerk, Willis P. ("Bill") Whichard, who himself later served as a justice of the North Carolina Supreme Court, would say that Bobbitt "authored many opinions which, at the time were of great importance to the public and to the jurisprudence of the state, and . . . some of them will influence the jurisprudence of the state and the country for many years to come. . . . They reflect the author's extensive knowledge of the law, his capacity for clarity, and his soundness of judgment."[32] Judge Bobbitt was famous for his ability to remember names, a skill he cultivated. Revered for his scholarship and "steel-trap mind," he was self-deprecating and egalitarian. A gentleman and a gentle man, he was too nice to deflect unwanted visitors who sometimes found their way to his office, where they would find a willing listener.[33] He had a great store of anecdotes and tales and enjoyed the company of all sorts of people, from distinguished colleagues to cafeteria workers.

Judge Bobbitt had a long and happy marriage to the former Sarah Buford Dunlap whom he wed in 1924. They had four children—Sarah, William Haywood Jr., Buford, and Harriett. He was a deeply devoted family man, and when his wife died of cancer in 1965 he was shattered. His clerk that year was Bill Whichard, who would recall, "He was a very broken man."[34] Judge Sharp, who had known Bobbitt for many years as a superior court judge and for the last several years on the supreme court, wrote to John Kesler about his loss, remarking, "Her death was a release for her and the family but so sad nevertheless. They were devoted and so dependent upon each other."[35]

It was about two years after his wife's death that Judge Bobbitt began to take notice of Judge Sharp in a way that transcended their professional relationship. One day in March 1967 she dashed in to her office and saw a brown paper bag on her desk. She was too busy to look inside until lunch time, when she discovered a two-pound jar of country peanut butter that had been deposited there by "B-2," as she called Judge Bobbitt in the shorthand referring to his seniority on the court.

She had not been looking for a new romance in her life even though matters remained less than satisfactory with John. Nearly two years after she grieved "the end of an era," she still saw him from time to time, but in the main he evinced little enthusiasm for trips to see her in Raleigh, leaving her angry and sad over the state of things. Several times in the next few months after Judge Bobbitt's peanut butter gift, Judge Sharp remarked occasions when John's wife and daughter were visiting family out of town or he had some excuse to come to Raleigh, but did not. Once in mid-April, for example, she called him and he said, "My wife is down East." She noted in her journal, "I almost said, 'Once upon a time I would have known about this long before now.'"[36] In

May he did manage to come to Raleigh for their twentieth "anniversary," but it was bittersweet. "He was very tired," she recorded. "I told him that I had never wanted to take anything from the family—only give him a lot of extra but I suppose it could not be done. He said, that insofar as it could be done, I had done it."[37]

Meanwhile, Judge Bobbitt began accompanying her on the regular walks she took for exercise and inviting her to have dinner with him. Judge Sharp heard from several friends that she was rumored to be seeing her fellow justice. Although flattered, she remained somewhat wary. She told her friends there was nothing to it. Over the summer they continued to see each other outside of court, however, and Judge Bobbitt pressed his extremely Victorian suit. It was not until July that he told her she "could consider herself kissed."[38] In August he suggested that when they were socializing she should call him Bill. "That would mean that you would have to call me Susie," she replied.[39] (They eventually settled, however, on addressing one another as "Judge.")

A few days after this conversation, Judge Bobbitt fretted that she "acted bored" and wondered if his courtship was merely amusing her.[40] "Oh, Judge, I was thinking that the nicest compliment I ever had was that at age 60 I could interest you," she responded. He then confessed that he had not expected to fall in love with her, that he had considered asking her to marry him but decided against it because, in the first place, he did not want to be a rejected suitor and, in the second, he did not want to interfere with her career.[41] A few days after that he declared, "I want to say this to you: I love you and I do not use the word indiscriminately."[42] Judge Sharp told her journal, "I'm speechless."[43] The following week he apologized for "pestering" her on the telephone, to which she replied that she felt "so cherished" but she also told him that he did not have to get married again.[44] It was not until toward the end of August that he kissed her for the first time.[45] He suggested that they consider taking one of their colleagues into their confidence. "I do not buy that one," said Judge Sharp.[46] Over the next weeks as Judge Bobbitt elaborated on the idea that most of their life was over and that he would like to walk the rest of it with her, she waffled, giving him "quasi *feme sole* talk."[47]

Judge Allen Gwyn, with his ultrasensitive antennae, picked up some vibrations somewhere and invited Judge Sharp to breakfast for the specific purpose of telling her that Judge Bobbitt would undoubtedly fall in love with her now that he was a widower. Gwyn did not want that to happen, he told her. First of all, he would be jealous, but also he believed it would mean she could never be chief justice.[48] Indeed, he felt, it would be "highly improper" for a husband and wife to serve on the court at the same time. No matter what the reality, the perception would be that there were only six votes among the justices, not seven. As Judge Sharp reported to her journal, Judge Gwyn said "that he would always love me—in a way he never loved anybody else." He declared that, at one time, if she had said she loved him, "that would have been it." She replied, "I told him he wanted me but that he did not love me; that I was then just one of many."[49]

Judge Sharp did not need Allen Gwyn to tell her that a relationship between two justices on the court at the same time posed substantial problems. In October she and Judge Bobbitt had a serious discussion in which he told her he was willing to wait until she told him it was no use, but not to keep him waiting until he was "decrepit." Judge Sharp replied that she would not be a party to "deposing" him or endangering his future as chief justice, a position for which he, as the next most senior member of the court, was next in line. She told him that the "$64 question" was whether they could change their status and stay on the court. Judge Bobbitt said that he did not know, that this question "kept him awake at first but no longer." Finally they agreed that they were both happy with the present arrangement. "He says we will play it by ear from time to time; that there is no hurry."[50] Nonetheless, he assured her, he was "ready, willing, and able" to marry her "on very short notice"; all she had to do was say the word.[51]

Judge Bobbitt's courtship came at an opportune time, when Judge Sharp was vulnerable and glad for companionship. All spring and summer and into the fall of that year, she became accustomed to having Judge Bobbitt available, someone with whom she could take her meals, go for walks, attend events. It was the first time in her life she had had anyone who filled that role. As a single woman, she was at a disadvantage without an escort, and it was an enormous relief to have one. Once recognized as a couple, of course, they received even more invitations. As Judge Sharp once said, "No hostess wants a single woman on her hands."[52] She and Judge Bobbitt began to meet for breakfast as well as dinner, and as a matter of course they took their midday meal together in the company of the other justices, more days than not. The first time Judge Sharp and Judge Bobbitt ate all three meals together, she noted the occasion in her journal.[53] Regular patrons used to watch for what was known as "the shuffle" as the justices went down the lunchtime cafeteria line. Entering in order of seniority as they always did, the members of the court would maintain that order until they reached the trays, with Justice Higgins in his place between Justice Bobbitt and Justice Sharp. Then Higgins would drop back to allow Judge Sharp to precede him down the line, whether out of chivalry or as acknowledgment of her relationship to Justice Bobbitt was a matter for endless speculation and amusement.[54]

At the end of October when Judge Sharp made plans to attend the UNC–Wake Forest football game in Chapel Hill, she received her usual invitation to a pregame luncheon held in the Morehead Planetarium building. "For the first time I do not invite John," she wrote.[55] Judge Bobbitt took her to the game, where, she recorded, "I decide as I sit by him at the game that I could love him."[56] Not exactly a thunderbolt, but for the first time in many years she was open to a new possibility. The way forward was far from clear, however, and although she had confided in her secretary, Virginia Lyon, as the courtship had proceeded, she turned to another source for serious guidance—her former professor and first lover, Breck: "I tell him I need to talk to somebody and he is the only one. . . . I tell him to brace himself. He does and I tell him that B-2 thinks he is in love with me. He says that does not surprise him at all; that is the natural thing and he had suspected something of that kind. I say that I was taken by surprise and he wants to know how naïve I could get to be. He does not know whether we could get by with both of us staying on the bench or not. The more I talk to him the more I decide that I love Bill. . . . He wants to know if I am so involved with B-2 that I can not put my head on his shoulder. He says that once after he and Venitah stopped by our house . . . she said to him, 'If I should die you would marry Susie within one year after my death.'"[57]

Venitah Breckenridge had in fact died the year before, on January 21, 1966. As Judge Sharp walked Breck to the bus station after their visit, he admitted that he recognized the irony in the current situation. "You mean a very great deal to me," he told her. But he also said that he had not wanted to be "the husband of Judge Sharp."[58] She may have felt that he was not the only one. Still, she could appreciate the humor in her situation. Several months later when she was trying to solve the morning newspaper "Jumble" puzzle, she enlisted Virginia Lyon's help, saying that if she could not get it, "B-2 will have a very smug look on his face." Virginia's response, as Judge Sharp relayed it to Breck, was, "Judge Sharp, don't you know that if you are going to keep a beau you have got to let him be smarter than you are? You are too competitive." Judge Sharp's comment to her journal was, "Breck says that story is rich as cream."[59]

The very night after her heart-to-heart talk with Breck, Judge Sharp told Judge Bobbitt for the first time that she loved him.[60] "He takes it very calmly," she reported. At least they were equals; if anything she deferred to Judge

Bobbitt as her senior on the court. Of course, being equals was the problem insofar as their future plans were involved. In the meantime, they kept up an ever-increasing schedule of meals and walks and social events in each other's company. On at least one occasion, Judge Sharp made an effort to retain some semblance of independence by trying to pay for her own dinner. When she offered him money for her share, he said that "he can't clothe me but he would like to feed me." Judge Sharp replied that she did not want to embarrass him ever, but that unless it would embarrass him she would like to pay her way. Her journal does not say whether he accepted her offer.[61]

This was not a woman madly in love. Perhaps the most poignant entry in her journal was one she made in early 1968 after she and Judge Bobbitt had spent a Sunday together, having lunch at the old Colonial Inn in Hillsborough and then going on to Chapel Hill to see the "Star of Bethlehem" show at the planetarium. "He likes it very much," she wrote. "I think of John and when my heart was aflame."[62]

By this time, tongues were wagging all across the state. Friends and acquaintances were thrilled by the news that the popular Judge Bobbitt and the lady justice who was believed to have theretofore devoted her life solely to her profession were an "item." Sightings of the diminutive couple began to be reported with delight and affection. Marriage was rumored to be in the works. Jeannelle Moore, Governor Moore's wife, got Judge Sharp in a corner and told her that she could get married in the Governor's Mansion, that she would love to give the reception.[63] Judge Sharp, however, continued to tell those who inquired that there was nothing to the rumor of an impending wedding.

In mid-March 1968 Judge Bobbitt went away for the weekend. Judge Sharp made plans to see John. Underlining how long it had been since they had seen each other, he was "astounded" by her appearance. "Haven't you lost a lot of weight?" he asked. Judge Sharp broke the news to him about Judge Bobbitt. "I tell him all and weep. He says that he is very glad he heard it from me and not somebody else. I let him know that I felt neglected and he says that he is sorry he neglected me if that had anything to do with it." In the end she felt rather coldhearted about it all, and when he said that if she wanted to talk to him at any time, he would come, she remarked to her journal, "belated interest."[64]

In a way her news took some pressure off what had become an unhappy situation between the two of them, while allowing them to remain affectionate and caring. There were still phone calls and "I love you's" but no pressure for John to come to see her. Still, when a radio station called to ask Judge

Sharp if there was any truth to the rumor that she was planning to retire in the near future, her answer was, "Not at all." She and Judge Bobbitt continued to see each other at every opportunity, and continued to discuss marriage, but neither could find a way to reconcile it with their professional situation. Judge Sharp said that if they could both stay on the court, she would marry him tomorrow. But, as she told him, "I could not see him going to the office and leaving me at home and I said that I could not see him sending me off and staying there."[65] Judge Bobbitt thought the difficulty would come in an election year, when voters might think there were too many family members on the state payroll. He told her that he had considered the idea of getting married secretly, but decided it would not do. "When I marry Susie I'll shout it from the housetops," he told her.[66]

In the meantime, they were two grown-up people in their sixties. Judge Bobbitt was so old-fashioned that it was left to her to bring up the question of whether they might become lovers. "I tell him that since we can't get married, that I wonder if the same rules which my mother gave me applied at age 60."[67] "Are you asking if it would be morally wrong. . . ?" he asked. When she said she was, he replied, "No, but I do not think it would be advisable because if we started we would not stop and we would get into trouble."[68] Because they were long past child-bearing age, this remark was not entirely logical but perhaps reflected concerns he was not ready or willing to discuss at this point. "He said that his happiness did not depend on it," Judge Sharp wrote. "I tell him that he can decide; that I did not want to be Eve and tempt him. He poo-poos that idea and says that he is more experienced in such matters than I am."[69] Considering that he had told her he had never kissed anybody but her and his wife Sarah, "not counting pecks,"[70] one can imagine her thoughts as she recorded this conversation. Later that summer, they did embark on a physical relationship, but it was never to be entirely successful. This was upsetting for Judge Sharp, and doubtless for Judge Bobbitt as well. A year or so later, Judge Sharp wrote, "We decide we are not trying again for a long time."[71] She was very depressed about the prospects for the future.[72] Nonetheless, they continued to make the effort from time to time, with varying degrees of success, but it was a sad business.

As colleagues on the court, they were in constant consultation and almost always in agreement. Married or not, they were certainly perceived as a unit when the votes were counted, so much so that "Justice Shabitt" was the in-joke reference for their joint persona. Because their analysis of a case was truly a collaborative process, however, with neither justice dominating the other, their virtual unanimity was not viewed as a blot on the court. Rather, it was understood that they shared certain views, and if they came out in the same place on any given case, it was not because one or the other had dictated the result. Both Judge Sharp and Judge Bobbitt were deeply respected as judicial scholars, and everyone knew that each of them had brought the full force of his or her formidable intellect to bear on the case. Indeed, their constant back-and-forth undoubtedly strengthened their analysis and ultimately the opinions each of them wrote. Politically, they were balanced on the other end of the spectrum by former law school professor Justice I. Beverly Lake, himself a respected scholar,[73] and "Justice Shabbitt" was not always in the majority. But their near-perfect agreement on the cases that came before them was not generally considered a detriment to the court.

There is no question that Judge Sharp was deeply fond of her companion and the two of them enjoyed themselves enormously. Mornings they would meet for breakfast at the International House of Pancakes or some other venue. Judge Sharp often brought grapefruit for them to share before their orders came, being a firm believer in its health benefits. They became great friends with the waitresses wherever they became regulars, one of whom they even assisted in becoming an American citizen.[74] They were in attendance at every sort of public function in Raleigh and elsewhere, especially at UNC in Chapel Hill. Their public adored them and took great delight in their "special friendship," as Judge Bobbitt called it. For her part, Judge Sharp told Allen Gwyn, "[H]e looks after me and . . . I am happier in Raleigh than I ever was before."[75] It was the first time she had ever had a romance in which she could bask publicly.

This did not mean that she did not still yearn for John, with whom she stayed in regular contact. In October 1968 she talked to him on a Thursday before a meeting of the Judicial Council on Friday. "He did not want to come to the Judicial Council meeting unless he could see me," she wrote. But she had to go to Durham the next day. Friday night, having dinner with Judge Bobbitt, who was also a member of the council, she tried in a roundabout way to find out if John had attended the meeting, but finally had "to ask outright."[76] She and John made a few tentative plans to get together, but John kept his distance. "I would not interfere, Little One," he said in one phone call, signing off with "I love you."[77]

In November 1969 Bobbitt became chief justice following the death of Chief Justice Hunt Parker. Justice Sharp was now second in the line of succession, after Justice Carlisle Higgins. Chief Justice Bobbitt was sworn in on a well-worn Bible held together with a neatly tied black shoestring. It was a Bible he had acquired soon after his marriage, he explained, and he had always used it when he was sworn in. When asked about the shoestring he laughed. "It used to have a rubber band on it," he said, "But Justice Sharp said it just didn't look right and gave me a shoestring."[78]

The Friday before Easter in 1971, Judge Sharp's mother died of congestive heart failure in the hospital in Reidsville, at the age of eighty-seven. Judge Sharp had been to see her early that morning and knew it would not be long. The funeral was held the afternoon of Easter Sunday, and Judge Sharp had to be back on the bench on Monday. She was, naturally, the executrix of her mother's will, a duty that consumed vast amounts of time over the next two years,[79] not least because she had six siblings to inform and consult about every detail. It would be mid-May before she caught her breath and let the loss sink in. Writing to friends from her childhood, she said, "It was not until last week that I began to get a glimmer of what life was going to be like without Mamma. To my great surprise a gentleman from Edwards [&] Broughton Printing Co. (which was celebrating its one hundredth birthday) called and presented me with a book entitled 100 Years, 100 Men." It was a thick volume containing the pictures and biographies of 100 North Carolinians who the editors thought had made a "significant contribution" to the state during the past century. As the first female judge and supreme court justice, Justice Sharp was one of the "100 Men." (She did not comment on the book's title.) Her first thought was, "Won't Mamma be proud!" Then came the realization that she could not give her mother the book—or anything else ever again.[80]

After her mother died, freeing her from the relentless need to shuttle back and forth to Reidsville, Judge Sharp settled into life in the capital city. Louise, who had nurtured hopes that Judge Sharp might return home after she retired, began to think she never would leave Raleigh or build her house in Reidsville. Judge Sharp and Judge Bobbitt became, for all practical purposes, inseparable, although they continued to maintain their separate apartments. Now there was no reason for Judge Sharp to move back to Reidsville, where she would not have anything like the companionship or the social life she enjoyed with Judge Bobbitt. Even so, she often felt blue. Judge Bobbitt, generally considered the soul of joviality, was also in fact subject to "moods," the reason for which she could never divine.[81] Judge Sharp's sister Florence urged her to move out of the Sir Walter, which was not aging gracefully, and find a proper apartment. "You must get out of that hotel. No wonder you stay depressed. If I had to go back to those cramped, out-of-date, unkempt quarters after a hard day's work I would be in [the insane asylum]!" Florence wrote.[82] But it would be some time before Judge Sharp made the move.

In August 1972 John Kesler's wife Sudie died. For some while before that,

John had been trying to reconnect with Judge Sharp, but now she was the more reluctant one. "Call John and am sorry I did it. He wants to come back," she wrote during the summer of 1970.[83] "Call John and wish him Happy New Year. He says, 'I want to see you,'" reports a year-end entry that December.[84] "Get to the office before 8:30 to call John who said that he had hoped I could come by Salisbury on the way to Reidsville. That I could not do," she said in March 1971. In May of that year she forgot their "anniversary" on the 26th, something that had never happened before.[85]

Judge Sharp was unable to go to Sudie Kesler's funeral due to a judges' conference in Seattle. She sent flowers, of course, and later that day she spoke to John and his daughter Frances Sue on the telephone. "I know John will be simply lost," she wrote to an old friend from Salisbury.[86] In September she ran into him at a UNC football game she was attending with Chief Justice Bobbitt. John took her hand, and she told him she did not know any more about football than she had in 1928. "If that is true, you have a lot of explaining to do!" John said to Bobbitt.[87] "I try to catch his eye as we leave but have no luck," Judge Sharp wrote.[88] Although she was a regular at the football games during the season, she did not see him there again. It was not until nearly Christmas that they arranged a rendezvous.

Judge Bobbitt was headed to Charlotte for the holidays. Judge Sharp, who had long sent boxes of California dates to people on her Christmas list, called John to see if his had arrived. "He said that was not the kind of date he wanted with me," she reported.[89] Two days later she saw the chief justice off to Charlotte, then got in the car and drove to Lexington, near Salisbury, where she met John. They had lunch and drove back to Salisbury so she could see the improvements he had made to his law office. He asked her about her plans. "Do you mean Judge B.?" she asked. He did. "I try to tell him," she wrote, without elaborating. "When we leave he takes me in his arms and kisses me and says, 'You know I love you.'"[90]

In November 1972 North Carolina experienced a political earthquake when the Republican candidate for governor won for the first time since 1896. James E. Holshouser Jr. was a moderate, business-oriented governor whose very moderation belied the significance of his election. It was a major crack in what had long been a Democratic monolith. As in other parts of the South, North Carolina was still feeling the reverberations set off by the 1954 U.S. Supreme Court opinion in *Brown v. Board of Education*. Voters had deserted the Democratic Party in increasing numbers throughout the Great Society years under President Lyndon Johnson, as the party embraced civil rights and other so-called liberal goals. In 1972 President Richard M. Nixon was reelected in one of the most lopsided victories in American history, defeating George McGovern, who, after being chosen on the first ballot at the Democratic Convention, was never able to overcome the perception that he was a leftist radical. He carried only one state, Massachusetts. In North Carolina, Nixon received approximately 69.5 percent of the vote. For the first time since Reconstruction the Republican Party was a significant presence in the state.

The Republican earthquake had serious implications for Judge Sharp's political future, threatening her goal of becoming chief justice. In addition to electing a Republican governor, North Carolina voters had approved an amendment to the state constitution that would require members of the supreme court to retire at age seventy-two, complicating the succession question considerably. For Judge Sharp, the path to the chief justiceship was suddenly littered with obstacles and bereft of signposts. She did not know whether she would even remain on the court, a decision with ramifications for her personal relationships as well as for the final shape of her career.

In many ways, she was tempted to call it quits. Based on her length of service, she was eligible for retirement. She wanted to travel, and she wanted to build herself a house.[91] She was plagued with arthritis, cataracts, glaucoma, and a hearing problem, all of which made her long days sitting, reading, and listening to arguments particularly arduous. To one old friend, she wrote, "I am still doing my work here, but I can [see] the day looming when I will not be able to cope with the quantity of it. I now live from one day to the next and count it well spent if I have met its deadlines. But if I do that, there is no time left over for anything else, and I am beginning to feel inadequate — and that is a deadly feeling." She confessed, "For the first time I begin to think that perhaps I ought to retire. The changed political situation has created so much uncertainty about the future of several members of this court that we cannot now see even the outlines of future events."[92]

The entry in her journal for New Year's Eve 1972 records her phone call to John, in which they talked "$10 worth." The last words in her journal for that year were, "He said, 'I love you.'"[93] She began the New Year in a quandary. John, no longer restrained by his marriage, tentatively explored whether they might have a different future or indeed any future at all. So much depended on whether she would stay on the court and whether she would continue the relationship with Judge Bobbitt. In a heartfelt letter probably written in January 1973, John said: "You are herewith reminded that I have been careful in efforts not to upset the 'Status Quo.' . . . I want what is best for you.

"I walked away one time for that reason and have been sad many, many times. I realize that things as they now exist are very convenient.

"I know what I can say with assurance. I love you."[94]

Judge Sharp replied, "I have read your letter over and over again since I received it last Wednesday. This time I understand and know that every word in it came from the heart." She was grateful for many things, she said, not least that in the last quarter of life she had gained some understanding of the first quarter. "In understanding there is solace."[95] But she was not in a position to discuss the way forward. On the heels of the Republican governor's inauguration, she wrote, "The past two weeks have been hectic — tense and uncomfortable ones for me. They have brought into focus the physical and political problems which make my last quarter a most uncertain ballgame and any plans for the future futile. For the immediate present the goal is to meet the next deadline. Beyond that I cannot see."[96]

When it came down to it, Judge Sharp was not ready to relinquish whatever might remain of her career. Nor could she now imagine giving up her new life as the companion of Chief Justice Bobbitt.

At the end of January she called John and they "talked and talked."[97] John said he knew he had no claim on her, that he had no white horse or shining armor. All he knew was what he had written her. He was feeling very depressed, not wanting to get out of bed in the morning. Perhaps he would go live with his daughter, he said, but then again he did not want to be a burden.[98] A few weeks later he came to Raleigh, "in sad condition," as Judge Sharp described him. "First time it was not adultery," she recorded.[99] The next morning he told her that she had better marry Judge Bobbitt, that it was later than she thought. To walk away was the measure of his love for her, he said. "[T]his time I believed him," Judge Sharp wrote.[100] It would not be the last time she saw him. But in the meantime she had political battles to fight.

CHAPTER 16

CHIEF JUSTICE ELECTION

Not since 1902 had a North Carolina Supreme Court chief justice initially taken office by way of election. For seventy-two years prior to the 1974 elections, whenever a chief justice died or retired, one in an unbroken string of Democratic governors had appointed the next most senior justice to succeed him. The appointment amounted to a lifetime position, for under what was essentially a one-party system, an incumbent was unlikely to lose his seat or even be opposed when elections were held.[1] This procedure reliably ensured a Democrat as chief justice, given the scarcity of Republican justices. There had not been a Republican on the court in decades.[2]

Chief Justice Bobbitt turned seventy-two on October 18, 1972. Had he foreseen that North Carolina voters would deliver a double whammy in the 1972 elections—not only electing a Republican governor but also approving a constitutional amendment mandating retirement of supreme court justices at age seventy-two—he might have resigned beforehand, enabling the Democratic governor to appoint the new chief justice. Under the new law, both Bobbitt and Higgins could finish their terms expiring on December 31, 1974, but they were not eligible to run again. Prior to the 1972 election, however, resigning does not seem to have been on Judge Bobbitt's mind, nor would such a drastic step have been the obvious choice, given the track record of Republican gubernatorial candidates. "Republican governor" was practically an oxymoron. Thus it probably would not have occurred to many observers that even if the mandatory retirement amendment should pass, Bobbitt's forced retirement would coincide with the election of the first Republican governor in the twentieth century. And, of course, if the mandatory retirement provision failed to pass, Justice Higgins as well as the chief justice would be spared, leaving Higgins, second in seniority, as the traditional chief-justice-in-waiting. Not Justice Sharp.

The composition of the court in 1972, while for the most part congenial and inclined to unity wherever possible, nonetheless fostered undercurrents not apparent to the naked eye. After Chief Justice Bobbitt, Justice Higgins, and Justice Sharp, the remaining justices in order of seniority were I. Beverly Lake, Joseph Branch, J. Frank Huskins, and former governor Dan K. Moore. If for some reason Justice Sharp did not ascend to chief justice, Lake as the next in seniority upon Higgins's retirement would have the strongest claim to the top position on the court. Behind closed doors, the prospect of Lake as chief justice caused uniform dismay because of his political views and the extremely close relationship he had with Attorney General Robert Morgan, who had managed his 1960 campaign for governor.[3] Between them, they would be in a position to exert enormous influence within the judicial system, and the other justices wanted to forestall at all costs the possibility of Lake becoming chief justice.

The court, moreover, was not in a position to encourage, no matter how discreetly, the selection of anyone but the senior associate justice as chief, foreclosing the possibility of supporting a member of the court other than Lake, should Justice Sharp not take the position. Although the law did not require the governor to name the senior associate justice, the tradition had been unbroken since 1889, and the wisdom of the practice reinforced and encouraged its continuation. Any intimation by a governor that he might appoint as chief justice someone other than the senior associate justice — perhaps even someone not currently on the court — invariably threw the members of the court into a frenzy of opposition. As recently as 1969, Governor Robert W. Scott had caused a furor when he let it be known he intended to appoint former governor Dan K. Moore to replace Chief Justice Hunt Parker upon his death, rather than elevating Justice Bobbitt, then the senior associate justice. Serious pressure from the members of the court had blocked Governor Scott's attempted breach of tradition, however, and Moore had seen the wisdom of not jumping the line. Governor Scott subsequently appointed Moore to fill the vacancy created by Bobbitt's elevation to the top position. The court's insistence on the tradition under which the senior associate justice became the chief was fresh in recent memory in 1974, therefore, and any court-sponsored deviation from it would have required substantial explanation.

After the bombshell 1972 election, there was a good deal of behind-the-scenes speculation that Chief Justice Bobbitt and/or Justice Higgins might resign during the period before Republican Governor James E. Holshouser Jr. was sworn in, giving Governor Scott the opportunity to fill one or both of the slots.[4] According to Judge Sharp's journal, Justice Higgins initially said he would resign if Governor Scott would appoint Court of Appeals Judge Frank Parker to his seat.[5] This would have the effect of moving Judge Sharp into the senior associate justice position, from which she could smoothly ascend to chief justice upon Bobbitt's resignation. Following a back-channel inquiry, Justice Branch reported to Justice Sharp that Governor Scott had said he would appoint Parker if there was a vacancy.[6] Justice Sharp thereupon asked Justice Dan Moore to relay this news to Higgins, but Higgins promptly denied he had ever made such an offer, leaving matters at a most unsatisfactory point.[7]

Whatever motivated Higgins to reject the proposal, it does not seem to have been an effort to thwart Judge Sharp. Indeed, he came to talk to her just before Governor Holshouser was inaugurated and urged her to do nothing that would keep her from running for chief justice in 1974. "You are all that stands between the state and [Lake]," he said. "He and Bob Morgan will take charge of the state."[8]

Matters were not resolved in time to do anything before Holshouser became governor. Whether because of inertia, befuddlement, failure of imagination, crossed-up politics, or simply lack of time, neither Chief Justice Bobbitt nor Justice Higgins had stepped down before Governor Scott left office, and to do so thereafter would allow the new Republican governor to make the appointments.

The stakes were high with respect to the chief justice's position. Although not generally recognized by the average citizen, the chief justice occupied one of the most politically powerful posts in the state. Among other things, the chief justice appointed the director of the Administrative Office of the Courts, whose power and influence was felt in the day-to-day operations of the trial courts and the offices of the clerks of court in all 100 counties. The director of the Administrative Office of the Courts made decisions as to the salaries and number of employees in the clerks' offices, a potent political tool. Of special interest to the judiciary was the director's authority to make recommendations about judges' salaries and to decide which judges were assigned to which courts. (A judge in the director's good graces, for example, might be assigned to hold court in the mountains or at the coast during the best times of the year; conversely, a judge on the wrong side of the director might find himself holding court in the most benighted corners of the state, battling icy sidewalks far from the ski resorts or swatting mosquitoes many miles from any ocean view.) The director was not a perennial bureaucrat; rather he served at the pleasure of the chief justice. Thus he acted in every corner of the state as an extension of the chief justice, who also had many other more direct powers at his disposal in managing the judicial system.

In addition to the chief justice's seat, two others on the court would be up for grabs in November 1974.[9] The terms of both Justice Higgins and Justice Sharp also expired on December 31, 1974. Justice Higgins at eighty-five would be in the same situation as Chief Justice Bobbitt and would have to step down at the end of his term.[10] Justice Sharp would have to run no matter what, either for her existing associate justice seat or for chief justice.

"Risk" was not a word typically associated with judicial incumbents. But now, following nearly three-quarters of a century during which it was all but impossible for a Republican to be elected, Republican voters had demonstrated their newfound strength across the board. Not only had they elected a governor; they had also carried the state for Richard Nixon and sent Republican Jesse A. Helms to the U.S. Senate, and nobody knew where it might end. As governor, Holshouser would fill all vacancies arising in the judiciary from the supreme court down through the court of appeals to the superior court and district court. On top of this, he was entitled to name eight special superior court judges. All told, Governor Holshouser might have the opportunity to name dozens of Republicans at every level of the judicial system. Moreover, in addition to the three contested seats on the supreme court, seven of the nine court of appeals seats were vulnerable due to a combination of resignations and the ends of terms.[11] The old Democratic establishment was considerably unsettled, and throughout the judiciary the sense of uncertainty about the future was palpable.

For Justice Sharp, once she decided not to retire, the next question was whether she would seek to become chief justice. She could have chosen not to confront the issue. She could have chosen simply to stand for reelection to her existing seat without much worry of serious opposition. But if she wanted the top job, this was her last chance to pursue it because, under the new law, she would be forced into retirement at age seventy-two, before the end of her new term. It was the first time she had had to weigh such matters without the advice of her old mentor Judge Gwyn, who had died in 1969.[12]

In 1974 Justice Sharp was sixty-seven years old and had served twelve years on the supreme court. With the forced retirement of Justice Higgins, she would be the senior associate justice, who by tradition would be tapped to become the chief justice. In the normal course of events, it would be "her turn." Now, however, with a Republican governor in office, to reach the pinnacle toward which she had toiled for so many years she would have to get out on the hustings. As one who abhorred the idea of "running," she quailed at the thought of having to campaign, something she had never had to do. If she decided to run for chief justice, it was possible that she might face opposition in the Democratic primary, as well as Republican opposition in the general election. Most worrisome to Justice Sharp was the knowledge that in addition to a variety of hopefuls statewide, any or all of her fellow associate justices could choose to run for chief justice. Specifically, she feared that Lake might challenge her.[13]

From the point of view of her colleagues on the court as well as others interested in joining the court, her decision whether to run for the top position was of some consequence, for reasons including but going beyond their genuine respect for her and the fear of Lake becoming chief justice. Whoever won the chief justice post most likely would be in place for many years and could through sheer longevity rob ambitious current members of the court of the hope of rising to serve as chief. If, on the other hand, Justice Sharp ran and as expected was elected chief justice, her mandated retirement in 1979 would come just far enough in the future. Most observers believed that the Democrats would recapture the Governor's Mansion in the 1976 election, returning the court appointment system to Democratic control before she would have to step down. Under this scenario, current members of the court who might aspire to becoming chief justice would likely still be on the court and in a good position to move up, simultaneously opening a new associate justice seat.

Justice Sharp did not make up her mind for months. As late as the end of May 1973, she told her secretary, Virginia Lyon, arguably closer to her than anyone except Judge Bobbitt, that she did not know whether she would run for the top spot.[14] If she was not going to run for chief justice, however, there were others who would like to know so they might put in their own bid. Not long afterward, she had a "visitation" from Justice Joe Branch, who asked her directly what she planned to do.[15] He would support her if she decided to run but told her "not to mess around" because he would run if she did not.[16] (Upon hearing this, Chief Justice Bobbitt said, "Good for Joe.")[17]

The conversation precipitated discussions at lunch the next day between Judge Sharp and several of her colleagues. Higgins was there, along with Joe Branch and Frank Huskins.[18] Higgins brought up the subject, declaring that he had "led the delegation" for previous chief justices Winborne, Parker, and Bobbitt and that he would do the same for her if she chose to run.[19] "Frank and Joe both in and it was arranged," Judge Sharp recorded without further comment.[20] Confronting her worst fear, she went the next day to talk to Lake. To her relief, he said he would support her.[21] Dan Moore readily gave his blessing when she caught up with him the day after that.[22] She went home to Reidsville that weekend, and when she saw Judge Gwyn's son, Allen Jr., at church, she told him she was going to run for chief justice. That must have made it seem official.

There was still substantial talk among the justices, however, about whether Bobbitt should offer to retire if Holshouser would agree to appoint her chief justice, giving the governor a Republican appointment for her vacated seat. Lake was particularly persistent in pressing this idea, but it was shared by all the other members of the court except for Higgins.[23] Judge Sharp would have none of it, however, believing the Democrats would resent the conspiracy that allowed such a breach. And who could say how long the Republican might stay on the court, a blotch that would always remind her that she had cut a deal with the help of her close friend, Judge Bobbitt.[24]

If Justice Sharp ran and won the race for chief justice at the polls, however, neither she nor her colleagues could be accused of allowing a Republican on the court. Like her, the aspirants for the other two seats would have to prevail at the ballot box. Once past this troublesome four years with a Republican governor, surely the Democrats would regain control and judicial appointments would no longer pose partisan problems—at least not for the Democrats. Judge Sharp argued her position until she convinced everyone except Lake, who never concurred.[25]

At her first opportunity, Judge Sharp confided her plans to Bill Snider, editor of the *Greensboro Daily News*, who obligingly ran an in-depth article the following week, headlined, "Susie Sharp to Seek Top Chair."[26] The subhead spelled out what was perhaps the key to her decision: "Justices Encourage Female Associate." Without the support of the other members of the court, she would not have run. She declared, "I would have found no satisfaction in being elevated to a position for which those with whom I had worked over the years did not want me or for which they thought I was unqualified. It is very important for the Court and the State that the CJ not be at loggerheads with the other members of the Court."[27] The other members of the court had been appointed and/or elected in their own right and did not work *for* the chief justice, she pointed out. But it was critical that they would work *with* the chief justice.

Judge Sharp's old court reporter friend from Salisbury, Caroline Earnhardt, was among the first to hear the news and to contact her. "Yes, it is my present plan to run for Chief Justice," Judge Sharp replied, closing with her fervent wish: "I suppose it is entirely too much to hope that I could run without opposition, but that would be a happy way to run."[28]

Judge Sharp was very clear about her reasons for seeking the top job. When she came to set them down on paper, the first listed was, "My time had come."[29] She had paid her dues. After almost thirteen years on the court, with the mandatory retirement of Justice Higgins, she had risen to the senior position just below the chief. She had no doubt that she could do the job, and her colleagues had expressed their confidence in her. She had earned the prize. Moreover, she felt a responsibility to other women to reach for the top: "I felt that it might be some time before another woman would be as strategically situated to become chief justice and that I owed it to 'the situation' to run."[30] She recalled that when her name was proposed for the U.S. Supreme Court she had told "all the ladies who were trying to send me to 'Washington City' that I would rather be the C.J. of North Carolina if the opportunity arose."[31] Finally, she felt that her parents would have been disappointed in her if she did not reach for the highest goal. It was to her father that she owed the opportunity she had had to forge a career in the law, and she recalled his response when she expressed doubts, so long ago, about accepting Governor Kerr Scott's appointment to the superior court. "Certainly you will take it," he had said. She knew she would always be nagged by a sense of failure if she did not make the effort now to win the chief justice seat.

In preparation for her announcement, she sought a variety of advice. She must create an image of "a femme fatale who is a wise and learned jurist, a . . . competent court administrator and a stalwart character," recommended one counselor.[32] Bette Elliott, a local television personality, gave her hints about how to make up her face for television appearances.[33] (Enlisting a friend to help her try out Ms. Elliott's instructions, Judge Sharp warned that if she made her look like a showgirl, "the brethren" would withdraw their support. Not to worry, the friend replied, "You couldn't look like a showgirl if you tried.")[34]

On Thursday morning, January 3, 1974, all seven members of the court walked down to the state board of elections, where Judge Sharp paid the $390 fee[35] and filed as a candidate for chief justice with her colleagues standing behind her, both literally and figuratively. She read a prepared statement in which she touched on the long tradition by which the senior justice moved up to chief justice, a practice that "promotes internal harmony and assures a chief justice who is familiar with the operation of the Supreme Court and the state's entire system of courts."[36] She pointed out that in some states "you have the spectacle of judges running against each other for the chief justiceship. And that is not conducive to cooperation on the court."[37] But she wanted to campaign on her merits, downplaying as much as possible both political party and gender.

Downplaying her bona fides as a Democrat was something new for her. Perhaps like so many other Democrats, she had begun to see the advantages of nonpartisan judicial elections following the Republicans' first breach of the solid Democratic tradition in 1972.[38] The rapidly growing strength of the Republican Party in the state had led to an increase in the number of contested races. Nonpartisan judicial elections, as a side benefit to removing judges' positions from party politics, would also dilute to some extent the impact of Republicans in the judicial branch.

On the morning she went down to pay her filing fee, she took the opportunity to say that, although she was filing as a Democrat, she believed nonpartisan election of judges would make for a better judiciary.[39] As for her gender, it was her hope that voters could make their choice on her merits alone, and she discouraged reference to her status as "the woman" who had been first in so many things.

Judge Sharp had spent the previous afternoon contacting the media. She was pleased with the photo that ran in the next day's newspapers, showing her seated at a table before a bouquet of radio and television microphones, with all six of the other justices arrayed behind her. It was a photo that raised some eyebrows, because the court had only the year before promulgated a new code of judicial conduct, in which judges were forbidden to endorse candidates for public office.[40] Justice Sharp, however, expressed her gratitude to her colleagues, saying, "They wanted to be with me on this momentous occasion, and I am greatly honored by their presence this morning."[41] She would continue to refer frequently to the court's unanimous support, with both public pride and private relief.

She knew that becoming chief justice would represent a significant increase in her responsibilities. "Now that the die is cast I'm scared again," she wrote to former supreme court justice W. B. Rodman Jr. "[I]n following Judge Bobbitt I can only be an anticlimax. Few there are who have his wisdom, learning, temperament, and character; and I am not in his class. Today the chief justice has many duties in addition to writing the same number of opinions as the other justices. And you know what a slow writer I am! Should I be elected I will give the position all I have. Please help me pray that it will be enough."[42]

Her immediate concerns, however, were with the upcoming campaign.

Her candidacy had been greeted with near-uniform approval across the state, and few observers felt she would have any trouble whatsoever. Even the *Wall Street Journal*, in taking note of the election, ventured the opinion that "she may not have any opposition either in the primary or in the election."[43] Closer to home, the *Durham Herald* said, "Jurist Appears Shoo-In for Top Court Post."[44] Never one to take anything for granted, however, Judge Sharp was less sanguine. "All I want for Christmas is *no* opposition!" she had written a cousin just a couple of weeks before.[45] Months before her formal announcement, Superior Court Judge Frank Armstrong had admonished her, "It is my judgment that if you seek the office you are most likely to be nominated and elected, but I hope you will not assume that attitude. The political situation in North Carolina is not now stable enough to assume that position in connection with any office"[46]

She soon began to hear rumors about the thing she dreaded most—a Democratic opponent. A superior court judge from Statesville, Robert A. Collier Jr., was said to be "anxious to run and teetering on the brink."[47] At forty-three, a prominent lawyer and businessman, he had served in the state House of Representatives from 1965 to 1967 before being appointed to the trial bench by Governor Dan K. Moore. On January 28, 1974, the *News and Observer*'s "Under the Dome" column ran a lengthy report on Collier's potential candidacy for the chief justice slot. (Justice Higgins "nearly had a stroke," said Judge Sharp in her journal.)[48] Collier's two main rationalizations appeared to be that Judge Sharp had been away from the trial courts for too long and that, under the new mandatory retirement law, she would be unable to complete her eight-year term if she were elected.

One of the first people Judge Sharp called was John Kesler, who did not want her running with opposition, although he reassured her that she would defeat Collier. Distressingly, however, he reported that "they" were saying the chief justice did not want to step down as the new law mandated, that Bobbitt would continue to act as chief justice through her.[49] It was nothing she had not heard before, most likely, but no less unwelcome for that.

Judge Sharp's supporters went into action, writing Judge Collier and sending special delegations to dissuade him.[50] Nonetheless, she soon received from one of her countless allies a copy of a five-page letter Collier had sent to judges, lawyers, district attorneys, sheriffs, and clerks of court all over the state declaring that "at the urging of several trial judges and a number of lawyers" he was "seriously considering becoming a candidate for Chief Justice of our Supreme Court."[51] Collier argued that the policy of designating the senior associate justice as chief justice "is a policy that has outlived its usefulness and desirability in our state." The practice ensured that "the person furtherest [*sic*] in point of time from any trial court experience" and therefore least familiar with current problems the practicing attorney encountered every day was the head of the entire court system. Most unchivalrously, he pointed out that this same person, being the member of the court nearest retirement, was usually the "least able physically to effectively perform the job of running the court system with the vigor, interest and enthusiasm it deserves." Collier had a number of ideas, he said, about improving the court system, which would require "push and drive" to see to fruition through whatever steps might be necessary involving the judiciary, the legislature, and possibly even the voters if constitutional amendments were necessary.

Although Judge Collier's brashness in proposing his possible candidacy against "Judge Susie" earned him little but concerted and vocal discouragement from members of the legal profession, a number of his ideas about needed improvements to the court system were far from outlandish. For example, the use of trial court administrators to tame the multitudinous non-judicial demands that otherwise required so much time from the judge would be adopted in many jurisdictions in coming years. Nor was he wrong in saying there was room for improvement in the magistrate system, where better salaries and training could make a difference in the administration of justice at that level of the court system. Justice Sharp herself agreed with him that the Code of Judicial Conduct needed further study and some revamping.[52] Collier's strength was as an administrator, and he saw an opportunity in the post of chief justice to take hold of the judicial system at the top, like a real chief executive officer, and to make the operation more efficient, lobby the legislature, and ensure the kind of financial and human resources the courts needed to get things done.[53]

Collier's main offense was simply in daring to challenge Judge Sharp, whom few considered weak or feeble in any way, who commanded the respect and affection of lawyers, judges, and just plain folks all across the state, who had worked harder and to better effect than virtually anyone else in the history of the state judicial system, and who was widely felt to deserve this crowning conclusion to her career.

Judge Sharp did not deign to respond to the suggestion that she was too remote from the trial court to understand how best to administer the court system. No one seriously disputed her energy, stamina, or ability to get things done. As for the notion that a chief justice invariably served a complete term, Judge Sharp countered (having done some research) that in the past twenty-three years during which six chief justices had presided over the court, "their stays in office have ranged from less than three years to approximately five years."[54] Still, throughout the month of February Collier continued to act like a candidate. Franklin Freeman, who at that time was assistant director of the Administrative Office of the Courts, came to tell her that Judge Copeland had relayed word from a "reliable source in Winston-Salem" that she had better be making plans or she was going to be three weeks behind Collier, that she needed to raise between $75,000 and $100,000 and get a headquarters.[55] "I have a very bad night," Judge Sharp wrote after that news. To one old friend she wrote that if Collier decided to run, "we will just have to get the old steam roller out of mothballs, but Oh! How much trouble that will be."[56]

Meanwhile behind-the-scenes meetings and machinations continued apace, while rumors swirled. The filing deadline was noon on Monday, February 25. As the time approached, Collier seemed to be wavering. In fact, he sent out a letter to supporters dated February 22 saying that he had decided not to run, giving as his reason the inability to raise sufficient campaign funds without resigning his job as superior court judge.[57] On the morning of filing day, the *News and Observer*'s "Under the Dome" column declared, "Collier tests waters and finds them cool."[58] The previous day he had told the newspaper, "I have just about definitely decided not to do it, but I want to talk to a few more people." Collier said he had a tight court schedule with only one week free before the May primary, making it virtually impossible for him to campaign. "Reportedly," the newspaper said, "Collier also ran into what amounted to a brick wall of support for Justice Sharp among the state's judges and, to a lesser degree, the lawyers." The newspaper had done an informal survey of judges who had received Collier's five-page letter seeking support and found that a number had responded, advising Collier that "his entry into the race would be ill-considered at best" and conveying "a tone of 'you don't stand a chance.'"[59]

But just as Judge Sharp was breathing a sigh of relief over her morning paper, events were taking another turn.

In Salisbury, Judge Collier convened the Monday session of criminal court over which he was presiding about ten o'clock, but after making a few introductory remarks to jurors and conducting the calendar call, he abruptly announced a recess and withdrew to his chambers to go over certain "pressing matters." Five minutes later he emerged, accompanied by attorney Robert M. Davis and state senator Robert V. Somers, to announce that the recess would be extended until two o'clock. What followed was described by one reporter as a "Keystone Cop comedy. And no more believable."[60]

The "pressing matters" turned out to be the time of the filing deadline and the location of the state board of elections. The former was twelve noon and the latter was 120 miles away in Raleigh. The incredulous reporter, following the proceedings "in open-mouthed disbelief," described how the trio "lost whatever judicial calm they had and raced down the courthouse steps to a car." From there they sped to the Rowan County Airport, where "Somers' plane was panting in its hangar awaiting their arrival."[61] Somers, a Republican, in a burst of bipartisanship, had agreed to fly Collier and Davis to Raleigh. Davis, it seemed, had also been seized by the desire to run for the supreme court. According to the Salisbury paper, he had actually considered running against Justice Sharp for chief justice but, after meeting with Collier that morning, had agreed to seek an associate justice seat.[62]

Alas, once aloft the would-be candidates encountered severe winds that increased their flying time. After speeding from the airport in Raleigh to the state board of elections office downtown, they arrived "huffing and puffing" just a minute or two after the noon deadline. The door was closed. Judge Collier even pleaded the fact that he and board of elections chairman Jerry Alvis had both been members of the same fraternity, but the Greek connection was insufficient to persuade Alvis to open the door.[63] "The filings are closed," Alvis said, and he would not be moved.

"It's an ill wind that blows nobody good," Will Pless shot off in a note to Justice Sharp penned at one o'clock, upon hearing the news.[64]

So she was spared having any Democratic opposition, but the race only became more interesting. Two Republicans, each nearly unimaginable as a candidate, had filed to run in the primary for her seat. One was a black woman district court judge from Greensboro and the other a fire protection system salesman with no law license. The Republican establishment had not anticipated fielding a candidate against Justice Sharp and was just as surprised as anyone.[65] No one could recall another time when there had been a Republican primary for chief justice.

District Court Judge Elreta Melton Alexander was quite a personage in her own right. An attractive African American woman of fifty-five, given to flamboyance and informality in her courtroom, she was considered "good copy" by local reporters.[66] She had been born in Smithfield, North Carolina, where her father was a preacher and her mother a schoolteacher. Early on she had exhibited both intelligence and ambition. After getting a college degree from all-black North Carolina A&T State University, she married Dr. Giradeau Alexander, a young Greensboro physician, taught school, and then applied to Columbia University School of Law. As a black woman, she had a narrow choice of law school options. In fact, she was the first black woman to be admitted to the prestigious program at Columbia. After earning her law degree and passing the New York bar, she practiced briefly in Harlem, but decided to return to North Carolina, where in 1947 she became the first black woman admitted to the North Carolina bar.[67]

In Greensboro she had a thriving law practice. She liked the opportunity to "'flex her mental muscles' and show the world that 'brains are not sex or color coded.'"[68] It was at about the same time that the first woman judge in the state, Susie Sharp, was the news of the day wherever she went to hold court, and attorney Elreta Alexander similarly attracted curious crowds when she appeared in court in many a small town. She would later say that what she remembered as the "lonely, scary, tiresome days" of her early career made her especially pleased to see an increasing number of women attorneys in the courtroom.[69] She took special pains not to be overlooked and was known for her mink coats, dramatic makeup, outrageous hats, and Cadillac automobiles. Once in 1960 Judge Sharp surreptitiously composed a thank-you note to a Fayetteville cousin while she listened to "a colored lady lawyer," who was almost certainly Ms. Alexander, argue a drunk driving case to the jury. Judge Sharp described her as "the best Negro lawyer in the state" and noted that she had "made a pile of money." She wrote, "She wears a different and more striking outfit every day—shoes, hat, bag, complete outfit entirely different. The only things that do not change are the diamond rings and watch." With some glee, Judge Sharp appended a P.S. to say, "The jury convicted the lady lawyer's client. He was *very* guilty!"[70]

In 1968 Alexander changed her party affiliation from Democrat to Republican and won a seat on the district court, becoming the first black woman in the country to be elected to a district court judgeship.[71] In the courtroom she was innovative and loquacious, creating both admirers and critics. When the *Greensboro Daily News* conducted a survey in 1976 among Guilford County lawyers, Judge Alexander received by far "the most 'outstanding' ratings for her knowledge of the law, absence of bias, fairness of sentencing and courtroom demeanor."[72] As one of seven district court judges in the rankings, Judge Alexander was rated "outstanding" by twenty-eight lawyers, while the next highest-rated judge garnered only seven "outstanding" votes. Judge Alexander also, however, tied one other judge for the most "unqualified" ratings, the lowest category, illustrating her tendency to polarize opinion. One lawyer commented, "She lectures too much, loves to hear herself talk, and is given to theatrical histrionics. Yet I rate her the best damn judge we have on the District Court. She follows and knows the law and applies it with a gavel of concern and equity. She is noted for going out of her way to protect the female in domestic cases but again this does not distort her application of the law."[73]

One of the things Judge Alexander was best known for was her "Judgment Day," a controversial approach to misdemeanor first offenders who came before her in court. After hearing the evidence from the state and the defendant, Judge Alexander, instead of sentencing a guilty miscreant, often would simply withhold punishment. She would say, "Here is what you need to do," and lay out whatever she felt would get the offender back on track. He might be required to make restitution, go back to school, get a job, start supporting his family, or anything she saw as pertinent to his difficulties. "Now if you do thus-and-so," she would say, "at some point in the future it's going to come a Judgment Day and at that point I am going to render judgment against you." Then periodically she would set aside an entire session of court for Judgment Day, and all those whose sentencing had been suspended would appear to show her that they had fulfilled her conditions. If they satisfied her, she would deal with them leniently, finding them not guilty, or finding them guilty but suspending the sentence, or giving them prayer for judgment continued. If they had not lived up to her conditions, she would lower the boom.[74]

Justice Sharp was one of a number who found this sort of free-form justice disturbing. It was not entirely clear that Judge Alexander had the kind of legal authority she had assumed for herself in fashioning her second-chance sentences. Justice Sharp, from her viewpoint as an appellate judge and as one with a more traditional disposition, needed more uniformity, predictability, and certainty when it came to the dispensation of justice.

Judge Alexander was very popular with the public, however, and when she ran for reelection in 1972 she led the ticket.[75] Interviewed before the May 1974 primary, she like Justice Sharp dismissed attributes like race and gender as qualifications for the job. "I don't feel it is appropriate to campaign as a black woman," she said. "I am an American citizen. As my life has evolved, I have had to be labeled the first Negro or black or whatever you want to call it but as one lawyer who practices in my court has said, I am absolutely color-blind."[76] In the opinion of James G. Exum, then resident superior court judge of Guilford County, later a member and chief justice of the North Carolina Supreme Court, she would have made a formidable candidate in the general election.[77]

In many ways, Elreta Alexander and Susie Sharp had much in common, although probably neither of them would have found the other congenial.

Judge Alexander's opponent in the Republican primary was James M. Newcomb, sixty-five, a self-described "Christian family man" from the small town of Williamston in eastern North Carolina. He had dropped out of school in the seventh grade, then returned when he was seventeen to finish high school at the age of twenty-two. His career included stints as a farmer, fisherman, lighthouse keeper, and insurance salesman before he settled into the fire extinguisher and lightning rod business, which he operated under the name Fyr-Fyter out of his four-room home.[78] Father of ten children, he wore brass eyeglasses and an unruly brush of brown hair. His sole political experience consisted, he admitted, of "one time in 1954 [when] I hauled off out of a clear sky and ran for county commissioner in Wilson County."[79] He lost. An ardent Shriner, he had been a strong supporter of I. Beverly Lake in the racially charged 1960 gubernatorial election.[80]

As for Newcomb's qualifications for chief justice of the supreme court, the lack of any judicial background, not to mention the absence of a law degree, did not faze him. The state of North Carolina in its infinite wisdom did not require that a judge be first a lawyer, and Newcomb trusted to divine guidance to help him in his duties.[81] Justice Sharp would later remark that it was "probable that he is a religious fanatic and . . . his purpose in filing was to prevent a woman (me) from becoming chief justice."[82] As for Newcomb, he claimed his motivation was a belief that "the America he grew up in has somehow gone morally astray and must be righted," although he admitted he was not entirely certain how he might combat the situation from the supreme court. "I don't have a cut-and-dried plan for doing it. That would be like asking a man when he'll plant his garden. There's some things you just play by ear," he explained. "But I'll say this. Being a 'final tribunal' don't even constitute a half of what the Supreme Court ought to do. If I was on there I would see that everything in the state was kept under surveillance, and I wouldn't wait for a case to come up before I'd do something about it. If the Supreme Court don't do it, who's going to?"[83] In another stunning statement, he declared, "I don't feel the Supreme Court should just sit there and preside as an appellate court. . . . I would be concerned with violations not committed as well as those committed. You ought not to wait until the horse is out of the stable."[84]

Newcomb's campaign literature consisted primarily of a one-page "Pledge to the Voters of North Carolina," in which he suggested that his lack of legal credentials would prove to be an asset, and a flyer featuring a photograph of himself and his wife Betty surrounded by head shots of their ten children. Mrs. Newcomb, it was said, was "bitterly opposed" to his candidacy, fearing that her husband would be "destroyed by ridicule."[85] Newcomb acknowledged that his wife had "cried off and on for a week" when he decided to run.[86] His campaign involved little more than dropping in on his usual business customers and leaving a copy of his flyer. "I'm kinda like a man carrying a sack of flour with a hole in it; you know where I've been," he said, describing his campaign efforts.[87]

Newcomb's candidacy was indeed greeted with shock and ridicule, although it seemed obvious he would not survive the primary against Judge Alexander. Judge Sharp naturally assumed that Judge Alexander would be her opposition in the fall. "[I]t is inconceivable to me that a non-lawyer could be the nominee for chief justice — even allowing for the general public's lack of information about our appellate courts," she wrote to supporters.[88] In another among many such missives she said, "I am told [Judge Alexander] will not be a serious threat, but her filing statement suggests that there will be charges of racial discrimination in the courts and that race will be made an issue. This is a regrettable development."[89] It was true that Judge Alexander's statement contained veiled allusions to race, but they were far from polemical. Her statement said, "If 'we the people' are to achieve an orderly society, insuring domestic peace and tranquility, the courts must take appropriate steps to assure equal justice under law. The prevalent climate of fear of the courts and judicial processes must be eliminated if public confidence is to be attained." Her only mention of her race was oblique. "We have come a long way in this state," she said. "My election in 1968 as a District Court judge is a first for the United States. For this, I am grateful and we are justifiably proud." Those who were aware that she was black might have picked up on the reference, but the statement could hardly be called a racial call to arms.

Because Judge Alexander had filed without any advance notice to the GOP leadership, no one had any idea of her motives. Judge Sharp reported to her nephew Larry Taylor and his wife Barbara the reaction of her supporters to the announcement. "Half the folks think her candidacy is merely an effort to advertise herself for some other job; the other half are so appalled at the prospect that she might become CJ . . . that they insist we must organize every county, advertise by radio, TV and newspaper just before the election, and that I must do all the things any other candidate would do under the circumstances." It was unimaginable. "Of course, I can't," she said, "but I must make a commencement speech, introduce Sam Ervin at a to-do in Winston-Salem, go to Charlotte week after next for a clam bake, attend three rallies in the vicinity, get ready for court on the 14th, attend two commencements and write two opinions — all between now and May 20th."[90]

Her description of the sheriff's annual fish fry in Rockingham County in April gives an idea of her stamina: "It lasts from noon until 8 p.m. and no candidate in her right mind would fail to appear. At least 10,000 people came during the day. I stayed from noon until 3 p.m. when I had to leave to visit [the family cook] during visiting hours in the hospital . . . I went back to the fish fry and politicked until 7 o'clock. . . . I got back to Raleigh at 10 p.m."[91]

In fact, the Reidsville newspaper estimated that 15,000 had attended the dollar-a-plate shindig, describing the day as "long, crowded, hot and sunny."[92] Sheriff Carl H. Axsom, running for reelection, had ordered two tons of fish and two hundred gallons of coleslaw, "and had to send out for more twice." Country music had filled the air early on, but a combination of the heat and the high volume necessary to overcome the noise of the crowd blew out the amplifiers by midafternoon. U.S. senatorial candidates Robert Morgan and Nick Galifinakis were there, along with Congressman Richardson Preyer, all the Democratic candidates for the state House of Representatives, and the Rockingham County clerk of court. People stood under shade trees to visit, keep an eye on the children playing, eat their fish, and watch the candidates shaking hands in a line so long that "the end disappeared for several hours."

In an era when sheriffs were Sheriffs and county politics was not a spectator sport, this was not an unusual gathering, and Judge Sharp had to turn up in person to press the flesh at any number of similar occasions. To one fellow who went down the line and told her she had a handshake like a man, she replied "limply" that that was because she was a strong judge. (Telling about it in a letter to her nephew and his wife, she added an aside: "If there is one thing I can't abide it is a slithery, limp handshake.")[93] Physical stamina was a prerequisite for any candidate.

Judge Sharp primarily worried that voters had little interest in or knowledge of the judicial races. "I feel that if the voters are fully informed about the candidates and vote I will be elected. However, the danger of block voting, straight Republican tickets and voter apathy cannot be ignored." She also saw "danger in the frequently expressed view that I have 'nothing to worry about.' I hope that is a correct appraisal, but the situation will keep me running scared."[94] She wrote dozens of letters to friends and supporters outside the legal community explaining that she was in a contested race for chief justice, losing no opportunity to educate the public. She even wrote a cousin who was in the hospital and "very ill," reminding him that she was running and asking his help from his sickbed. "I'd be mighty proud if you would tell the nurses and doctors you see to vote for your cousin in November," she suggested.[95] In another approach to the medical community, when she sent a check to pay a doctor's bill, she added, "I take this occasion to send you several of my campaign brochures and to remind you of your promise to get me *at least* 100 votes from the Duke Hospital area!"[96]

With the help of the legal community, she had a network of campaign managers in place in every county as well as in many towns and cities. She had been quick to capitalize on her connections with women's groups both in and out of the Democratic Party. She was a prolific correspondent in the service of her campaign, and, although she begrudged the inroads on her time and energy, she understood the need to make appearances as a candidate. As the subject of gratuitous and often burdensome publicity all her adult life, she had a natural aversion to media attention. Adjusting to the reality of a contested race, however, she dutifully drew up lists of newspaper, radio, and television contacts and tried to make sure her candidacy was well publicized. But when CBS News called her, asking for an interview to be aired before the primary, she recoiled. "No!" she said, declaring that if she got elected chief justice that would be time enough to get on CBS national news. "Call back in November," she told the caller. Her colleagues could not believe it. "The brethren were horrified when they learned I'd turned down any free publicity and told me I should have my head examined," she wrote her nephew Larry Taylor and his wife. When CBS called to try again in a couple of weeks, she was therefore more receptive. "I allowed myself to be persuaded," she reported.[97] A four-person team from Atlanta came, "stayed two days and took miles of film," which translated into four minutes on the screen. Even in those more leisurely times, four minutes on the national news was quite a lot of attention. Justice Sharp hoped it would do her some good in North Carolina, although the exposure produced more mail from California than from her native state.[98] "No doubt I will carry the west coast!" she said.[99]

There were times she wondered why on earth she was putting herself through all this. "I keep thinking what a fool I was to run for chief justice instead of going back to Reidsville and building a house on my vacant lot that everybody wants to buy so much."[100] She continued to turn down offers for the property, the most recent having been in January. "I really have not yet given up the hope of building on it myself," she said. "Each year I get closer to the mandatory retirement age!"[101]

The November election may have worried Judge Sharp, but she sailed on toward the May 7 primary, like most knowledgeable observers, without any more thought than she had already devoted to it. The Republican primary was certainly a novelty, but it seemed unlikely to bring fresh surprises. As the *News and Observer* editorialized, after noting that in the Democratic primary Judge Sharp was deservedly unopposed: "District Judge Elreta M. Alexander of Greensboro is obviously a better choice for Republican voters than her opponent, who has no legal training. . . . She is evidently qualified for a place on this state's highest court. The record shows her to be intellectually competent, fair-minded and admirably committed to the rule of law."[102] The prospect of two women — one white, one black, both qualified — facing off in the race for chief justice had already begun to capture the imagination of those who paid attention to that sort of thing.

But when the votes were counted on May 7, the white man with no legal training had won the Republican primary.

What happened? Justice Sharp was stunned. "[I]t never entered my head that enough people would vote for a man with no legal training whatever for chief justice," she said. "The only politico of my acquaintance who prophesied that result was Allen Gwyn Jr., and I thought he had lost his mind."[103] Judge Sharp's foreboding about voters' knowledge of judicial candidates appeared validated. The Republican leadership, although surprised by Judge Alexander's decision to run, had deemed her a credible if controversial candidate. Believing her likely to defeat a candidate with no legal background even if he was white and male, the party had not devoted any resources to publicizing her candidacy. Judge Sharp said, "'People hadn't heard of either one (Alexander or Newcombe [sic]) but they knew one was a man and the other a woman so they voted for the man.'"[104]

Monday morning quarterbacks tended to agree that race probably was not much of a factor because most voters simply did not know enough about the candidates to be aware that Judge Alexander was black and Newcomb was white. What they could determine from the names on the ballot, however, was that one candidate was female. "If I had to guess," said state Republican Party chairman Thomas Bennett, "I'd say most voters probably looked at two names and didn't know either one, said 'Well, this is for chief justice, so I'll take the man.' I don't think race had a thing to do with it."[105]

Ironically, across the nation in 1974 women in public life had become numerous enough to be the focus of much media attention. There were about 1,200 women running for state legislative offices, an increase of one-third over 1972.[106] At the national level, nearly four dozen women were running for Congress.[107] Among the well-known female candidates was Ella Grasso, running for governor of Connecticut. Two years before, Texas had elected a formidable black woman, Barbara Jordan, to Congress. And in North Carolina, Susie Sharp was not the only woman running for high judicial office; she was joined by Judge Naomi Morris, who had been appointed to the court of appeals by Governor Moore in 1967 and was running for another term.

In short, women in positions of power and influence were reaching a critical mass, no longer anomalies although not yet unremarkable. Had the public (and the local media) been paying attention, voters would have learned about Judge Alexander's admirable legal career. But when it came time to mark the ballot, Republicans who knew little or nothing about either candidate chose the man over the woman.

Judge Sharp had another theory. Because Judge Alexander would certainly have presented a more credible opponent in the general election, Judge Sharp suggested, "everybody who voted for Mr. Newcomb was really voting for me."[108]

Whatever the cause, everyone was shocked at the result except Jim Newcomb. The Republican leadership, including Governor Holshouser and U.S. senator Jesse Helms, publicly repudiated him as the party's candidate. The *News and Observer* quoted Republican Party chairman Bennett: "There comes a time when party considerations must come second. As a party leader and attorney, I feel obligated to speak out on this.

"My personal feeling is that we have nominated a man of good reputation, a Christian gentleman, a good citizen, but a man whose background is not sufficient for him to perform the duties of chief justice."[109] Even in his hometown, the news of the local candidate's victory in the primary was greeted with, at best, bemusement. One longtime friend remarked with a grin, "'I've got a college degree and I know I don't have any business running for the Supreme Court. So I don't know why Jim should think he can.'"[110] Another friend said, "'Look, Jim's a fine Christian gentleman, but I don't think he'd get 300 votes in Martin County this Fall. Heck, I'm surprised he even got any votes in the primary.'"[111] In fact, Newcomb carried his home county by fifty-six votes out of a pool of 530 registered Republicans. Statewide he polled 59 percent of the primary voters.[112]

Newcomb's victory presented the Republican Party with a problem that transcended the contest for chief justice. A Republican was also running for the seat to be vacated by Judge Sharp, who, if she lost the chief justice election, would be out of a job. Court of Appeals Judge James M. Baley Jr., who had no opposition in the Republican primary, was considered a deserving candidate for the high court, and the GOP leadership wanted to get him elected. On the heels of their triumph in 1972 over a divided Democratic Party, the Republicans were profoundly conscious of the need for unity. But they could not ask party members to vote the straight ticket in the judicial races because of Newcomb's place on the ticket. Suggesting that voters mark their ballots for one but not the other Republican, however, conjured the risk of confusion and/or abstention resulting in almost certain victory for the Democratic candidate.[113]

The issue of straight-ticket voting was an even greater concern for Judge Sharp. As one commentator pointed out, "Newcomb's chances of winning are, at best, slim. But defeat for Justice Sharp is possible. Think what could have happened in 1972, for example, if Jim Newcomb had been on the ballot with Richard Nixon and Jesse Helms and Susie Sharp had been on the ballot with George McGovern in this state."[114]

A suggestion blossomed shortly after the primary that perhaps Mr. Newcomb might be persuaded to withdraw from the race, but Judge Sharp discouraged the idea. "I have concluded . . . that it will probably be better for me if he remains in the race. Were he to withdraw, the Republican State Executive Committee might name a more dangerous opponent. . . . I feel sure that the Republican hierarchy would welcome his resignation, but publicly I am not mentioning the possibility."[115]

In the middle of the summer, yet another candidate appeared. The socialist United States Labor Party, after an intensive drive, submitted the requisite petition bearing 10,000 signatures to the state board of elections for certification before the August 1 deadline.[116] Alex Brock, director of the board of elections, announced the party had thereby won a place on the November ballot. The Labor Party platform advocated such things as a moratorium on municipalities' debt service payments so that workers could receive higher wages. The accompanying rhetoric featured jabs at the Rockefellers and the Central Intelligence Agency. The party planned to field candidates for Congress, North Carolina attorney general, and chief justice of the North Carolina Supreme Court.

The Labor Party candidate for chief justice was a twenty-three-year-old Charlotte resident named Stanley Ezrol, who, like James Newcomb, had no legal training. Characterized in the press as a "full-time Marxist organizer," he said his candidacy was part of the party's attempt to organize as broadly as possible. Judge Sharp could not refrain from huffing "with decorously muted outrage" to one interviewer that she knew nothing about Ezrol except that he belonged to the U.S. Labor Party, "which, as I understand it, is pure Communist."[117] The very day the Labor Party became legal, supporters posted signs on Fayetteville Street in downtown Raleigh featuring a clenched fist, urging the "expropriation of Rockefeller holdings." Judge Sharp pointed out, "Of course if the government can expropriate Rockefeller's property it can also take John Smith's property—and you can be sure it will."[118] Other than focusing even more attention on the state's lack of any legal background as a requirement for its judges, Ezrol's candidacy merely provided a little extra color to the race, especially as Ezrol had a propensity for getting arrested. In Charlotte he was charged with obstructing a police officer during a Labor Party rally, and he was convicted on an assault charge by a Durham court in connection with an incident at a tobacco factory where he was campaigning.[119]

Judge Sharp left nothing to chance, despite the apparent unsuitability of her opposition for the job of chief justice. As she saw it, her real enemies were voter ignorance, voter apathy, and gender bias, all of which would be exacerbated by straight-ticket voting of the Republican ballot.

Of the problems facing her, none was greater than voter ignorance, which encompassed virtually every aspect of the chief justice race, including the fact that there was one. Her trips outside Raleigh had convinced her that "[a]n amazing number of people do not know that the chief justice is elected." In fairness, it had been seventy-two years since a new chief justice came into office by election. But even among those who knew that she was running, "[a] high percentage . . . do not know that the Republican candidate is a nonlawyer and totally unqualified," she wrote. "When told, their first reaction is one of utter disbelief, for they do not believe the law would permit such a thing to happen."[120]

Such ignorance was not limited to the politically apathetic. Particularly unnerving was a telephone conversation she had with the chairman of the Democratic executive committee in Cumberland County when she called to accept his invitation to a candidates' breakfast in Fayetteville the following week. After saying he was pleased she was coming, the chairman inquired, "Miss Sharp, what office are you running for?"[121] Even more unsettling was the discovery she made late in the campaign when she attended a First Congressional District rally (encompassing twenty-one counties) held in Jim Newcomb's hometown of Williamston. "There was a large crowd there, and I made a short talk," she related. "It was good that I went, for I learned that some people in the area were under the misapprehension that I was a black woman!"[122] Actually, she had heard that this same rumor was rampant in the far western part of the state as well. "I suppose I will never know whether it was started by some person who had me confused with Elreta or whether it was deliberately started," she mused.[123]

Many if not most North Carolinians did not know what the chief justice's job entailed. "I don't want the public to get the idea that the chief justice just sits in the middle of the six associate justices and is just a titular head of the court system," Judge Sharp told a helpful interviewer.[124] She took any opportunity to point out that the chief justice, in addition to presiding over the court and writing one-seventh of the court's opinions, also was responsible for overseeing the administration of the state's courts from the supreme court down to the lowliest magistrate's office. The work force of the state's judicial system, she would note, comprised approximately 2,500 judges, district attorneys, clerks of court, magistrates, juvenile counselors, court reporters, and supporting personnel. The 1974–75 budget was just shy of $40 million. Without mentioning her opponent or his lack of qualifications, she constantly emphasized the magnitude of the job and her ability to handle it.

The most substantive issue on which Judge Sharp feared public misunderstanding was her stance on capital punishment. At a time when many felt the U.S. Supreme Court was doing all it could to turn criminals loose on every sort of so-called technicality, elected officials in the state were careful not to appear "soft on crime," and of course that was of particular concern for members of the judiciary. In the 1970s, North Carolina death penalty statutes underwent considerable turmoil, and Judge Sharp found that she was unable to join the majority in upholding death penalties in a number of cases during this time, a circumstance that had nothing to do with her personal feelings about capital punishment.

In fact, her personal feelings about the death penalty had evolved over the years, placing her closer to the conservative viewpoint on the issue. "At one time in my life, when I was much younger," she wrote in 1973, "I was violently opposed to capital punishment. After I went on the bench and my experience broadened I began to change my mind. Under the conditions prevailing today, I think we should carefully weigh the consequences before we abolish capital punishment for first-degree murder and rape."[125]

Prior to 1941 in North Carolina, the death penalty was mandatory upon conviction for first-degree murder, first-degree burglary, rape, or arson.[126] That year the statutes were amended to give the jury the option to recommend life in prison instead of the death penalty for the capital crimes of arson and first-degree burglary. In 1949 the so-called mercy proviso was added to the statutes relating to rape and first-degree murder. During the 1960s a campaign to abolish capital punishment burgeoned across the country along with the civil rights movement, fueled in large part by a growing awareness of the correlation between race and the death penalty. In North Carolina a number of attempts to modify or abolish capital punishment had failed over the years to pass the legislature, the most recent in 1971.

In 1972 a 5–4 majority of the U.S. Supreme Court in *Furman v. Georgia*[127] invalidated death penalty statutes as administered across the country, including in North Carolina, where the judge or jury had discretion to decide whether a defendant convicted of a capital crime would receive the death penalty or life imprisonment.[128] When the case of *State v. Waddell*[129] came before the North Carolina Supreme Court on the heels of *Furman*, the issue was what part, if any, of the death penalty statute remained valid. Was the effect of *Furman* to *require* the death penalty or to *prohibit* it until the legislature revised the statutes? In a prospective ruling to apply to cases after *Waddell*, four members of the North Carolina Supreme Court held that the death penalty statutes were unconstitutional under *Furman*, but that the offending proviso permitting the jury to recommend life imprisonment in its unbridled discretion was severable, leaving only the words "shall be punished with death." The bare majority therefore held that the death penalty was once again mandatory for defendants convicted of capital crimes.

Chief Justice Bobbitt, Justice Higgins, and Justice Sharp dissented, believing that the effect of *Furman* was to invalidate the death penalty provision and that unless and until the legislature amended the statutes, punishment for these crimes was life imprisonment.[130] As Chief Justice Bobbitt further explained the position of the dissenting minority in a subsequent case, "In our view, the provisions of these statutes embody an indivisible and unified plan for punishment of the felonies referred to therein. *Furman* did not purport to delete, isolate or invalidate any particular portion of the statute."[131] Therefore, in the minority's view, the entire death penalty statute was invalid.

The North Carolina legislature enacted a new statute on April 8, 1974, making death the penalty for first-degree murder, and later added the same provision for first-degree rape.[132] A new offense of second-degree rape was defined and was not punishable by death; arson and burglary were also taken out of the category of capital offenses. Between the *Waddell* opinion and the effective date of the new statutes, the North Carolina Supreme Court upheld the death penalty for five defendants convicted of first-degree murder. Justice Sharp along with Chief Justice Bobbitt and Justice Higgins dissented in all of them, on the grounds that after the U.S. Supreme Court invalidated the North Carolina statutes governing capital punishment in 1972, there was no death penalty in North Carolina until the effective date of the new statutes on April 8, 1974. In another case the defendant was sentenced to die for what would be second-degree rape under the new statute and therefore not a capital crime, on the grounds that the new statute applied only to acts committed after its ratification.[133] Justice Sharp dissented, saying it seemed "inconceivable that, under these circumstances, the General Assembly could have intended that any person would thereafter be executed for a crime for which Chapter 1201 abolished the death penalty."[134]

Well aware that the public perception might be that she was against the death penalty per se, Justice Sharp was at pains to state her beliefs. In *State v. Jarrette,* for example, she said, "In my view the death sentence is not constitutionally impermissible as cruel and unusual punishment for first-degree murder and rape. The question of capital punishment, however, is one of momentous public policy to be determined by the legislature. It is not for this Court to declare either by unanimous decision or four-three division."[135]

Despite her best efforts, the *News and Observer,* among other newspapers, continued to describe her and her dissenting colleagues as being against the death penalty. Judge Sharp not only was frustrated to be misinterpreted but also feared the political repercussions. It is noteworthy that her dissents in the death penalty cases did not achieve any immediate purpose because hers was not a swing vote. The four-member majority would prevail whether she joined it or not. She could have joined the majority without altering the situation one iota, meanwhile avoiding the accusation that she was against capital punishment.

Among the three dissenters, Judge Sharp was the only one who had to face the voters in November because both Chief Justice Bobbitt and Justice Higgins were retiring. But she felt strongly enough about the separation-of-powers principle involved to stick her neck out on the chopping block. In this she demonstrated the difference between pragmatism, which she had so often embraced, and opportunism. It might have been expedient for her to remain silent on the death penalty issue, because she had nothing to gain from dissenting. But this silence would have been misleading, if not dishonest, and thus she spoke out. It was an echo of her early support for Kerr Scott despite his disfavor among the Democratic Party regulars, support that she never imagined would benefit her politically. As a useful comparison, her reluctant acceptance of racial integration, which reflected her profound belief in the rule of law as well as her recognition of reality, offers an example of true pragmatism. She did not, as a rule, pursue pragmatism at the expense of her beliefs.[136]

As a candidate she was restricted by the Code of Judicial Conduct, promulgated by the North Carolina Supreme Court the previous year at the request of the legislature, in what she could say other than what she wrote in her opinions for the court. Under the code, a judge—even one running for office—in addition to being prohibited from making a political speech was also prohibited from announcing his views on disputed legal and political issues. Capital punishment clearly fell under that heading. Justice Sharp tried to stay within the code, answering the frequent questions on the subject by saying that the legislature had enacted a new statute on April 8, 1974, making the death penalty mandatory for first-degree murder and first-degree rape, but that no one could be executed until the U.S. Supreme Court had ruled on the constitutionality of the new law.[137] She also drafted a form letter for the Administrative Office of the Courts to send in response to letters she received from members of the public, making an exception to the rule that "the Supreme Court speaks only through its opinions," which explained that her dissent in the death penalty cases was "no indication that she is opposed to the death penalty."[138] Her friend and adviser, the well-respected Superior Court Judge Hamilton H. Hobgood, drafted a letter for her to send to sheriffs across the state, declaring, "To clear up any possible misunderstanding I wish to state without reservation that I am personally in favor of capital punishment for the crimes of First Degree Murder and Rape."[139]

Although there would be further twists and turns in North Carolina's capital punishment law, until the election in November 1974 the would-be new chief justice could not do much more than state the basis for her dissenting opinions and try to be sure that the public understood it. Her law clerk that year would later recall, however, that she did take an extra hard look at noncapital criminal cases that could have gone the other way, raking them with a fine-toothed comb to see if there were grounds on which she could conscientiously affirm the trial court and thus bolster her tough-on-crime credentials.[140]

Voters' ignorance of the chief justice race could be blamed for Judge Sharp's second great concern, voter apathy, among the broader population. But what gave her sleepless nights was the apathy of those who were quite aware of her race but who could not believe she had anything to worry about.[141] Nothing made her more nervous than to be told that she was as good as elected. "Dangerous talk," she called it, "for many a candidate has been defeated by that attitude on the part of his friends."[142] She knew of at least one district court judge who had been elected on the slogan, "only layman running."[143] As one of her most valued advisers put it, "I am sure you will get the educated vote, but you must remember that the 'Jackass' vote counts just as much."[144]

Even the educated vote, however, was not a sure thing. Lest anyone think that public opinion unanimously supported the idea that judges should have a law license, at least one newspaper columnist inveighed against the "elitism" of such a requirement, calling it "intellectual and economic segregation."[145] Superior Court Judge James G. Exum, who was running for Justice Higgins's seat, recounted to Judge Sharp a conversation he had while politicking down East that illustrated just how widely such sentiment might extend. He had been going around shaking hands with anybody he could find and began talking to the pharmacist in a drugstore about his campaign.

Then, as he did whenever he had the opportunity, he tried to give a little plug for Justice Sharp. He gave his usual spiel to the pharmacist, saying what a capable woman she was and how much she deserved to be elected. "And by the way, you know, her opponent is not even a lawyer. He's a fire extinguisher salesman," he told the pharmacist. The pharmacist, an educated man, replied, "Well, I'm sure not going to vote for Miz Sharp." Exum, in amazement, said, "You're not going to vote for Miss Sharp? I just told you her opponent is a fire extinguisher salesman. He's not even a lawyer." The pharmacist said, "Well, that's why I'm going to vote for him. There're too damn many lawyers on the Supreme Court."[146]

Finally, if it were true that Jim Newcomb had beaten Judge Alexander based on his gender, then Justice Sharp was still in danger in November.[147] Her fear was that "uninformed voters, confronted with a choice between a candidate named James M. Newcomb and one with a little girl's nickname, might make the wrong choice."[148] Over and again she stated, "I'm not asking anybody to vote for me because I'm a woman. By the same token I trust that nobody will vote against me because I'm a woman."[149]

Overriding all the issues was the specter of Republicans voting the straight ticket. In the aftershock of the GOP victories two years before, no one knew how the system would work in what was suddenly a two-party state. Judge Sharp's informants indicated that in the counties west of Asheville, voters would vote a straight ticket, but whether it would be Democratic or Republican depended on who was running for sheriff and county commissioner.[150] The recent Watergate scandals added another dimension that could have cut either way. Voters might be so horrified at the Republican misdeeds that they would be reluctant to support the party of Richard Nixon. On the other hand, Nixon had resigned and Gerald Ford had become president on August 9, 1974. Judge Sharp feared that might increase the number of Republican straight-ticket voters, who would no longer have to overcome any squeamishness connected to the disgraced president.

She was even more worried after a late August visit to Reidsville, where she discovered that in certain quarters Nixon was actually revered. "I was utterly astounded at the pro-Nixon sentiment which I encountered in Rockingham County. His defenders were loudly proclaiming that Nixon's offenses would pale into insignificance if they could be compared with those of LBJ's. One man said that Watergate made no difference; that Nixon got us out of Vietnam and that was all that mattered. Others were saying that because of the way Sam Ervin had hounded Nixon out of office they were sorry he did not run again so that he could have been ignominiously defeated!" She recognized that "these people did not belong to the intelligentsia," but she pointed out that "some of the latter told me that the county was full of people who shared those sentiments." She told supporters, "I am running more scared every day!"[151]

She would never have forgiven herself if she had lost the election for lack of effort on her part. She threw herself into campaigning, leaving opinions unwritten as she traveled the state. Members of the legal community were both quick and generous with their offers of advice and assistance, for which she was grateful. Although steeped in politics all her life, it had been twenty-five years since she was actively involved, prior to her appointment to the superior court. As one of her staunch supporters, Superior Court Judge Hamilton H. Hobgood, said to her, "You are a smarter judge than I am—I'll stipulate that for the record—but you are not as smart a politician as I am."[152] She listened to her advisers and lost no opportunity to say how much she needed their help.

She felt particularly uncomfortable about her support in Charlotte, home to a number of powerful women's advocates, due to her opposition the year before to the passage of the Equal Rights Amendment in North Carolina. Her position, which had been made public during the fray, was that the rights to be protected under the ERA were already covered by the Fourteenth Amendment to the U.S. Constitution, and that further constitutional tinkering could well result in harming rather than helping women. ERA supporters were furious and blamed the amendment's defeat in the General Assembly to no small degree on her opposition. She counted heavily on Charlotte attorneys like Joe Grier and Lelia Alexander, among others, who did yeoman's work for her in Mecklenburg County.

She opened her campaign headquarters in Room 317 in the Hotel Sir Walter on September 25, declaring that she was running on her record as an "experienced lawyer, trial judge and supreme court justice."[153] Having used her position on the supreme court as an excuse to decline speaking invitations since the day she was sworn in, she now accepted any offer she possibly could. She spoke to bar associations, women's groups, political rallies, sheriffs' associations, church groups. Former governor Terry Sanford, in his capacity as president of Duke University, issued her an invitation to receive an honorary degree the week after the May primary, along with Canadian prime minister Pierre Trudeau, gaining her some widespread coverage.

Even among members of the legal profession, not all of whom knew her personally, she worked hard to make an impression. As one Greensboro attorney reported to Chief Justice Bobbitt about her appearance at a bar meeting, "Justice Sharp gave a tremendous speech. It was full of humorous sayings, little stories of great interest, and of course, she recited a number of little instances on the campaign trail principally with respect to mountain Republicans. All this was a side of her with which I was totally unfamiliar. . . . I do not remember when the Bar enjoyed a meeting as it did last night."[154]

As Judge Sharp put it, "Campaigning is strenuous business for the only state-wide candidate with no chauffeur, no speech writer and no patronage!"[155] Her sister Florence worried about her. "You are so exhausted it is scary," she said, urging her not to fret about unwritten opinions and to realize that she could not do everything.[156] "It would be terrible if you had a heart attack or a stroke and Mr. Newcomb was left with no opposition."[157]

Florence's words carried extra weight because on July 16 Chief Justice Bobbitt suffered a heart attack and did not leave the hospital for more than six weeks.[158] Once back home, his activities were severely restricted, and despite everyone's hopes, he was unable to return to the court for the opening of the fall term.[159] By the end of October he was still unable to work or preside at sessions of court.[160] Judge Sharp was thus burdened with worry about the chief even as her days were filled with the rigors of campaigning. It made her quest to succeed him all the more poignant.

But as election day approached, Judge Sharp went all out. Her October calendar shows her attending at least one campaign event every day that the court was not hearing arguments, crisscrossing the state: Greenville, Charlotte, Salisbury, Greensboro, Asheville, New Bern, Smithfield, Goldsboro, Chapel Hill, Durham, Selma, Rocky Mount. The news media in the final weeks finally woke up to the possibility of "swapping the witch for the devil" in the chief justice race and got busy. Radio stations gave her free time and conducted interviews designed to educate the voters, while the major newspapers ran feature articles followed by editorial endorsements of her candidacy.[161]

One week before the election, she wrote, "The last six weeks have been as grueling as any I ever spent. How much of the campaigning I have done was necessary I do not now know—perhaps the election results will provide some clue—but were an unqualified person to become chief justice the consequences would be so disastrous to our Court that I felt I had to do all I could."[162]

On election night, November 5, 1974, Justice Sharp presided over the "hospitality suite" at her campaign headquarters, watching the returns come in. Delegations of her family including sisters Louise, Annie Hill, and Florence had come to Raleigh to be with her. When the votes were counted, it had been a good night for Democrats, women, and Susie Sharp. She was the first woman in the country to be elected chief justice of the supreme court of her state.[163]

Nationally, Republicans under President Ford's three-month-old presidency were stunned by a Democratic landslide. Democrats had won 43 extra seats in the House, giving them a clear two-thirds majority of 291 seats, and had picked up three new Senate seats for a total of sixty-one. Democrats had a net gain of four governorships, including New York and California, giving them thirty-six states. In North Carolina, Democrat Robert Morgan had an easy victory in the U.S. Senate race, as did Democrat Rufus Edmisten, running for state attorney general. In the contested race for Justice Sharp's associate justice seat, Democrat J. William Copeland defeated his Republican opposition, while Democrat James G. Exum Jr., unopposed, would take Justice Higgins's seat.

Across the country women had won office in unprecedented numbers. Ella T. Grasso captured the Connecticut governor's race, and New York elected its first female lieutenant governor. In Congress, although the Senate remained an all-male bastion, five new women members would take their seats in the House. Another example among many was the new female mayor of San Jose, California, the first woman to take charge of a city with a population of more than 500,000. In the national news media, North Carolina's new chief justice, Susie Marshall Sharp, was prominently featured along with these and other headliners, with her picture in *Newsweek* and *Time*. (Judge Sharp said she was "satisfied the photographer who took that picture on election night is a Republican!")[164]

She had polled an overwhelming 74 percent statewide, or 745,376 votes, which was extremely gratifying. One cartoonist pictured her standing over a jungle animal trap, a hidden pit into which Governor Holshouser mounted on the North Carolina GOP elephant had fallen. The chief justice, dressed in her robes, laughingly crowed, "ME Tarzan—you Jane!"[165] Later, Justice Sharp would comment, "[I]t was fortunate for me that, as a Superior Court judge, I had held court in 64 of the state's 100 counties and that the local newspapers had given 'the lady judge' generous publicity. The 'name recognition' I had acquired was very helpful, for the voters know very little about judges and Supreme Court justices."[166] She was fortunate, too, that it was a banner year for Democrats in general.

The truly astonishing fact, however, was that the fire extinguisher salesman with no law degree had received 264,661 votes.[167] Undoubtedly some of these votes were the result of the straight-ticket voting that had worried her so much before the election. As retired Justice William B. Rodman Jr. remarked, "I attribute the fact that there were 1,100 idiots in Beaufort County who voted for your principal opponent against the 4,400 or 4,500 that you received to the simple fact that we had taught everybody never to vote anything except a straight ticket and stick by your party no matter what the nominee may be." Equally as certain, many voters had picked the candidate named Jim over the one named Susie.

The ultimate result, however, was that North Carolina had become the first state in the nation to elect a woman chief justice of its supreme court, and that woman was Susie Marshall Sharp. It was also the first time a woman had won any contested statewide election in North Carolina. At the end of her first year as chief, *Time* magazine put her on the cover along with eleven other women who collectively were recognized, in an exception to the usual Man of the Year, as "A Dozen Who Made a Difference."[168] The other "Women of the Year" included First Lady Betty Ford, Cabinet secretary Carla Hills (Department of Housing and Urban Development), Connecticut governor Ella T. Grasso, U.S. Representative Barbara Jordan of Texas, tennis star Billie Jean King, and Smith College president Jill Ker Conway.[169]

With deep satisfaction, Susie Sharp could finally put to rest the words of Judge J. H. Clement when he swore her in as a member of the bar in 1929: "You will never amount to anything as a lawyer."[170]

CHAPTER 17

CHIEF JUSTICE

At her swearing-in ceremony, Chief Justice Susie Marshall Sharp devoted her first official remarks largely to a tribute to retiring chief justice Bobbitt and associate justice Higgins, lamenting the mandatory retirement law that was forcing them off the court. The state would be the poorer for their absence, she said, but — referring to her own age-limited term — she quipped that "the law that impoverished the state in 1974 may very well save it in 1979."

The ceremony took only fifteen minutes, but it came nearly half a century after the pudgy young Susie Sharp had launched her unprecedented career when she entered law school at UNC. Twenty years as a practicing lawyer, thirteen as a superior court judge, and another thirteen on the state supreme court had earned her this day, January 2, 1975, when she was sworn in as chief justice. She was sixty-seven years old. The grand and familiar courtroom of the supreme court was standing-room-only, with the crowd spilling out the tall doors into the hallway. Although Republican governor Holshouser did not attend, dignitaries included (Democratic) Lieutenant Governor James B. Hunt, Attorney General Rufus Edmisten, and members of the court of appeals and the council of state. Chief Justice Sharp could look out into the audience and see all but one of her brothers and sisters along with their families, including lots of nieces and nephews. She could recognize childhood friends from Reidsville like Janie Sands Smith and Margaret Fillman Chaney; Norwood Robinson, who had come to Reidsville to practice law with Jim Sharp so many years ago; and Judge Allen Gwyn's widow, Janie. Judge Sharp's law school chums Bill Covington, Hugh "Cicero" Lobdell, and Hugh Campbell, now a judge, were there. Breck, who had been living in Virginia Beach, Virginia, for a number of years, had come with his daughter Jean. John Kesler attended with his daughter Frances Sue.

Judge Sharp's parents, Jim and Annie Blackwell Sharp, were certainly present in spirit if not in body. In fact, the room was full of ghosts and memories that swirled around the living, breathing, speaking forms of those listed in attendance.

The new chief justice, however, had no time for ghosts.[1] Her agenda, always full, now included the complete range of responsibilities carried by the head of the judiciary system. In contrast to her overwhelming initiation as a new member of the court in 1962, however, she stepped smoothly into her new role, familiar not only with the substantive aspects of the job but also with the court's quirks and customs. Describing her duty to "buzz the brethren" when it was time to make their lunchtime procession down Fayetteville Street, she once wrote Breck, "You'd think they were all farm hands who had eaten breakfast before sun-up. If I don't buzz promptly at twelve, they start buzzing me to know if I'm not going to eat today."[2]

Although most of the work of court reform instigated in the 1960s had been carried through, Chief Justice Sharp would take the lead in shaping new guidelines under the recently formed Judicial Standards Commission.[3] Within the confines of the Code of Judicial Conduct—and sometimes dramatically outside them—she would use her position as a bully pulpit on such issues as prison reform, judicial qualifications and selection, and the Equal Rights Amendment. During her tenure, the state and nation would continue to struggle with the issue of capital punishment. A battle to increase judicial salaries would give her a jolt of political reality, as would her experience as a member of President Carter's search committee to find a new director of the FBI. Meanwhile, despite these and countless other demands on her time and energy, she would continue to write her share of the court's opinions, some of which would be among her finest.

It was an interesting footnote to history that the year in which Judge Sharp became the first woman elected to be a state chief justice was also the year in which the first female law clerk breached the solid boys' club at the North Carolina Supreme Court. Fittingly, it was Judge Sharp who hired her. Elizabeth ("Betsy") Cochrane, a 1974 graduate of the law school at UNC, was a tall young lady given to short skirts and green eye shadow, both of which were on Judge Sharp's lengthy list of dislikes. But Betsy was recommended by Dickson Phillips, UNC law school dean and Judge Sharp's chief clerk-procurer, and moreover she had grown up next door to Judge Sharp's dear friend and fellow attorney in Charlotte, Lelia Alexander. After interviewing Betsy, the somewhat bemused justice consulted, among others, Judge Bobbitt and—equally important—her secretary, Virginia Lyon, about the prospect of hiring a female clerk. Miss Lyon did not want a girl, but conceded that if she was qualified she should not be deprived of the job on the basis of gender. Judge

Sharp noted Judge Bobbitt's reminder, "It was not held against me because I was a girl."[4] On the other hand, Judge Naomi Morris, the only woman on the court of appeals, was known to insist on a male clerk "to chaperone her at night."[5] Perhaps Judge Sharp counted on Judge Bobbitt to be her chaperone, for in the end she offered Betsy the job on condition that she would "leave off green eyeshadow, put her skirt to the knees and put up her hair."[6]

In retrospect, Betsy would conjecture that among the five or six women law students in her class, she was certainly the only one that Judge Sharp would have countenanced.[7] Her female classmates in that era were in the "aggressive, hard, pushy" mold, the type known as bra-burners. In comparison, Betsy, a southern debutante, was someone Judge Sharp could understand even if she did not care for all of her fashion choices. Betsy was "suitable." She had been brought up to be respectful of her elders, to say "Yes, ma'am" and "No, ma'am." Like Judge Sharp, she did not need to deny her femininity just because she had a brain. Her selection reflected Judge Sharp's belief that a little camouflage was sometimes a good thing. Judge Sharp was repelled by the militant unattractiveness of some of the more radical feminists and, moreover, considered it counterproductive. In the prevailing environment a woman was unlikely to get much accomplished by trying to appear like a man. Nor was it necessary. She had proved that. Betsy was both attractive and competent, qualities that Judge Sharp did not hold to be mutually exclusive.

It turned out to be a very congenial relationship. For Betsy, it was amusing that the other justices were protective of her, troubled about a young woman on her own in downtown Raleigh at night. Less appealing was their warning that she should not stay late to work in the Justice Building at night, because "people" would be concerned about her being there after hours with male colleagues. But Betsy was not the sort to let such things bother her. And she later recalled a bit of sisterly commentary from Judge Sharp, who told her, "You know, sometimes we run into male egos and male attitudes. We just have to find another way around. There's always another way around."[8]

This philosophy may or may not have been in Chief Justice Sharp's mind when she conferred with the president of the North Carolina Bar Association about her first major address, the speech traditionally delivered by the chief justice to the annual meeting of the bar association in July. The president suggested that "instead of talking about the 'work of the court and other related matters,' as chief justices have been wont to do when left to roam in an unfenced field," she might choose "'a subject of general interest to the members and their wives.'"[9] His thought was that she might entertain the dinner audience with some reminiscences about her experience as North Carolina's first woman trial and appellate court judge, a speech Judge Sharp might be pardoned for believing she had delivered on countless previous occasions. If she felt that the suggested departure from substantive, if less entertaining, subjects was condescending, she did not say so. But her speech was a brilliant riposte, commencing with a reference to the president's helpful topic suggestion followed by an entertaining rendition of some of the more amusing incidents in her career as a lady judge, then finishing with a blistering indictment of the state's prison system. Something for everyone.

Speaking under the rubric of her trial court experiences, she made a seamless transition. "I want to take you back for just a moment to 1949," she said to the unsuspecting audience, "and tell you about the first case which I tried as a superior court judge." She then recounted the story of the prisoner who had been suspended from the bars of his cell by his handcuffs for somewhere between two and three days without food, for the offense of making a wisecrack to a fellow inmate in violation of the "no talking" rule. Her outrage, which had resulted in the first serious examination of prisoner treatment in North Carolina, was undiminished, and she went on to charge that conditions in 1975 remained "inconsistent with the professed standards of a Christian people." Indeed, just the month before there had been a five-day riot at the Corrections Center for Women in Raleigh when inmates protested, among other things, poor medical treatment and hazardous working conditions in the prison laundry. The General Assembly, responding to public demand in the face of soaring crime rates, had legislated harsher sentences and fewer paroles but had failed to make adequate provision for housing the criminals, with predictable results. "Today 13,000 prisoners are being housed in facilities built to house 10,000," the chief justice said. "Surely we have no right to confine men and women under conditions which deprive them of all privacy, dehumanize and strip them of all self-respect and dignity, and subject them to homosexual attacks from which they are powerless to defend themselves."

To those who might suggest that prisons were "not supposed to be country clubs," Chief Justice Sharp responded that "if the moral aspects of this situation are not sufficient to arouse us, then an enlightened self-interest ought to do it." Rehabilitation, presumably a worthy goal of the penal system, was an unlikely result of a sojourn in the state's prisons. Nor, she pointed out, should the white, middle-class members of her audience think they were immune from personal acquaintance with a cellblock. "I am certain that all of you know at least one highly respected person, perhaps a revered friend, whose son, daughter, or grandchild has broken the law in this permissive era and been sent to prison. A criminally negligent homicide resulting from an auto-mobile accident can make a felon out of any motorist any day. One never knows when he may suddenly have a very personal interest in North Caro-lina's prisons."

If this were insufficient to get the attention of her audience, she insisted that prison reform needed to be the top priority of the General Assembly, with "first claim on the tax revenues of the state." More specifically, she said, "[U]ntil this explosive, unconscionable situation is corrected, schools, col-leges, hospitals, teachers' salaries and judges' salaries must all wait."

Franklin Freeman, then the assistant director of the Administrative Office of the Courts, later recalled that this last "didn't sit well with the judges."[10] It was "fairly remarkable," Freeman reflected, that her first speech to the bar "would not be about how overworked the courts are, how they ought to pay judges more, or a host of other issues related to court matters."[11] She had in-stead raised a broader public policy issue. Even if some members of her audi-ence had expected more from her address than amusing anecdotes, few had expected to be confronted with the shameful, hidden, and neglected problems of the prison system over their dinners. But the speech made headlines and the editorial pages of papers all over the state. The press was both vocal and virtually unanimous in cheering her appeal for action on prison reform. And she was prescient in her concerns, for ten years later would come a variety of lawsuits over prison conditions, which resulted in a federal consent decree compelling dramatic changes in the North Carolina prison system.[12] "She was on target. Precisely. Ten years ahead of the federal courts, basically," Freeman said.[13] In his address on the presentation of Chief Justice Sharp's portrait to the supreme court in 1996, Freeman stated, "Her speech before the 1975 North Carolina Bar Association's annual meeting advocating widespread, far-ranging improvements in the state's prison system even before judges re-ceived a pay increase, was a major impetus for the dramatic changes that have occurred in North Carolina's penal system in this last generation."[14]

As chief justice, Susie Sharp had nothing more than her moral authority and high profile to bring to bear on prison conditions, but she did have con-siderable power at her disposal to apply to the conduct of the state's judges. Both as the administrative head of the court system and as the author of several significant supreme court opinions, she played an important role in interpreting new judicial standards promulgated just two years before. She had no deeper concern than the conduct of judges on the bench.

Franklin Freeman, as assistant director of the Administrative Office of the Courts, had a close-up view of her decisive management style when it came to reported failings of a judge under her jurisdiction. There were occasions when she summoned a judge about whom she had heard complaints for a little "pep talk," and Freeman would escort him to her chambers. "[I]t was interesting to watch these grown, big men, you know," he later recalled. "The concern with which they would go downstairs to that meeting."[15] By this stage in her life, Chief Justice Sharp had acquired a regal bearing, which occasionally caused her to be compared to England's Queen Mother and which prompted her father's old law partner, Norwood Robinson, to address her jokingly as "Your Majesty."[16] She had the kind of formidable presence that could indeed reduce grown men to the quivers. Judge Sharp herself claimed that she preferred not to "haul them up here." Often she would have Freeman write or call judges who were in need of a suggestion or two on her behalf.[17] Dealing with judges "takes a great deal of diplomacy," she acknowledged.[18] But she wanted them to know she was paying attention. Her influence was particularly brought to bear on the district courts, which were still a work in progress, having been in existence less than a decade.

Although in superior court the chief judge in each judicial district was determined by seniority, Chief Justice Sharp was responsible for naming the chief district court judges, who served at her pleasure. She expected all judges not only to be competent, hardworking, and professional on the bench, but also to be above reproach in their communities and to lead by their example. A chief judge especially needed to be without blemish. In this she was implacable, despite her vulnerability with respect to her own private life. Her journals and letters reveal no instance in which she dwelled on this inconsistency or even seemed to notice it. She had long ago accepted the risk that her public life could come unraveled. Her justification for her hypocrisy, if that is what it was, would likely have been that she was doing a superior job in her position, a performance unaffected by anything in her private life, past or present. Of course, this would likely have been the same justification offered by those whom she called to task.

Chief Justice Sharp made her appointments quickly and decisively, and on the several occasions when she found it necessary to remove someone and appoint a different chief judge, she did so swiftly and never looked back. "She never second-guessed herself," Freeman said. Bert M. Montague, who served as director of the Administrative Office of the Courts during Judge Sharp's tenure as chief justice, would later say that she had taken "an affirmative action position" in her effort to raise and uphold the standards of the judiciary, especially in the district courts: "Judge Sharp has gotten the handling of cases off of street corners, out of hallways and into open court."[19]

The fact that a judge was not required to have a law degree was naturally fresh in her mind after her recent contest with the fire extinguisher salesman. In those same elections, three new nonlawyer district court judges had been elected, bringing the total to 10 out of 118 judgeships at the district court level. The three new judges had previously been employed as an auctioneer, a town policeman, and a personnel manager for a steel foundry, respectively.[20]

As chief justice she did what she could to demonstrate the folly of such a lack of qualifications on the bench. Before she became chief justice, the policy of the Administrative Office of the Courts had been to advise chief district court judges to assign lay judges only to criminal court and traffic court, where the procedures were comparatively straightforward.[21] Lay judges were kept out of civil court, where they would have to deal with issues above their level of competence. As Freeman recalled her policy reversal, "[S]he told the chief district court judges to assign lay judges to every court, that the people had elected them and the people needed to see what they were getting." If the lay judge was incapable of handling civil district court, the people needed to see that, needed to understand exactly what they were electing.[22]

In one instance, there was a judicial district in which only two out of five district court judges were lawyers, one of whom was the chief judge. The other judge with legal training was young and inexperienced, so Chief Justice Sharp had retained the senior man as chief judge even though she had doubts about his suitability on other grounds. But during the 1976 election year, when a lawyer was running against one of the incumbent lay judges, the chief judge let it be known that he supported the incumbent. When Judge Sharp heard about it, she summoned Franklin Freeman immediately. "She had me call him that day. She removed him as chief district court judge within twenty-four hours of finding that out," he remembered. "Just like that," he said, snapping his fingers.[23]

Prior to 1973 there were only two ways to remove a judge from the bench: either by "address," which was removal for mental or physical incapacity, requiring a joint resolution of two-thirds of all the members of each house of the General Assembly, or by impeachment through accusation by the House of Representatives and trial by the Senate.[24] Neither means of removal had proved effective. The last time a judge had been impeached was during Reconstruction in 1868, and no one could document an instance in which removal by address had been used.[25] Moreover, short of removing him, there was no provision for disciplining a judge.

In November 1972 North Carolina voters had approved a constitutional amendment creating the North Carolina Judicial Standards Commission, which was to be an independent, impartial body that could recommend to the state supreme court that a judge be disciplined or removed.[26] Under the new legislation, a judge could be censored or removed on any of several grounds, including willful misconduct in office, mental or physical incapacity, and "conduct prejudicial to the administration of justice that brings the judicial office into disrepute."[27] The Judicial Standards Commission statute further stated, "A judge removed for other than mental or physical incapacity receives no retirement compensation, and is disqualified from holding further judicial office."[28]

To give more precise notice of the conduct expected of a judge, the North Carolina Supreme Court promulgated the North Carolina Code of Judicial Conduct, containing principles and guidelines that could be used by the Judicial Standards Commission in determining whether a judge had engaged in conduct for which censure or removal was appropriate.

In short, North Carolina now had in place for the first time a framework for the evaluation of judicial conduct and for the discipline or removal of malefactors on the bench. What was lacking was a history of interpretation of the newly promulgated standards. There was no difficulty with the concept of discipline for such egregious conduct as embezzlement or moral turpitude. But what, for example, constituted "conduct prejudicial to the administration of justice that brings the judicial office into disrepute?" Was the supreme court bound by the commission's recommendations, or could it act according to its own interpretation of the findings? What if the commission recommended censure, for instance, but the court felt the judge should be removed — or vice versa? It remained for the commission to break new ground in making its recommendations and for the state's supreme court to forge a new body of precedent and further enlightenment in its subsequent actions against judges accused of misconduct.

During Judge Sharp's tenure as chief justice, the court published seven opinions relating to judicial misconduct. She was deeply involved in shaping these opinions and, as the author of two of the most significant ones, was responsible for much of the language and rationale governing the commission's oversight of the judiciary. "[B]asically all the questions about how the Judicial Standards Commission should conduct their business and what they should do are answered in those earlier opinions by her," Franklin Freeman has said.[29]

In the first three judicial standards cases, written by other justices, the conduct of which the judge was accused had been either admitted or established by uncontradicted evidence, and the supreme court had followed the Judicial

Standards Commission's recommendations for censure without discussing evidentiary standards.[30] In the fourth case to arise, however, District Court Judge W. Milton Nowell, accused of disposing of two speeding tickets outside of court without notice to the prosecutor, contended that the evidence did not support the commission's findings of fact. Chief Justice Sharp wrote the opinion and took the opportunity to discuss, among other things, the standard of review to be used by the court and the standard of proof required in an inquiry before the commission.

A survey of other states with judicial standards commissions similar to North Carolina's revealed unanimous agreement on the issue of the standard of review, concluding that the supreme court was not bound by the commission's findings and had as its scope an independent evaluation of the evidence.[31] Chief Justice Sharp saw no reason to go against the grain and declared that the North Carolina court had reached the same conclusion.[32] In a subsequent case, the North Carolina court would explicitly hold that the commission's recommendations were not binding on the court.[33]

What about the standard of proof? Should it be "beyond a reasonable doubt," applicable to criminal cases? Should it be the "preponderance of the evidence" standard used in civil cases? Or something else? In her opinion, Chief Justice Sharp explored the decisions made in other jurisdictions, ultimately holding that the proper standard should be proof by "clear and convincing evidence," a burden less than "beyond a reasonable doubt" but greater than "the preponderance of the evidence."[34]

In this she followed the lead of the Supreme Court of Alaska. Interestingly, as a relatively new state, having joined the Lower Forty-eight only eighteen years before, Alaska was creating new case law. With respect to the judicial standards legislation enacted in 1973, North Carolina had just as blank a page before it. That Judge Sharp was drawn to or persuaded by the fresh reasoning of a supreme court given the opportunity to forge new law ab initio was an indication of her willingness to look forward, not back. It was the polar opposite of former chief justice Hunt Parker's approach, in which he claimed never to have written an original word. Clearly it was within the purview of the supreme court to interpret the law as promulgated by the North Carolina General Assembly, but with such virgin territory before her, dealing with a subject on which she held strong beliefs, Judge Sharp's opinions came close to the line where interpretation crosses into legislation. Backed up by her characteristic legal scholarship, she answered questions that had not been specifically asked but for which answers were necessary, laying down in the process a road map for the Judicial Standards Commission to follow. It is probable that, as Franklin Freeman would later speculate, she saw it as part of her role as chief executive of the judiciary to shape and mold the way the judicial standards legislation should be implemented.[35] However justified, Judge Sharp's judicial standards cases reveal an activist at work.

One particular opinion involving judicial misconduct would be among her most controversial.

Linwood T. Peoples was a popular district court judge in the Ninth Judicial District. In 1977, as part of a routine audit, it came to light that he had formed a pattern of making special dispositions of traffic tickets and other violations for friends and acquaintances (known in the vernacular as "ticket fixing"), outside the normal court procedures. This he did without concealment and with no real monetary benefits.

On January 30, 1978, the Judicial Standards Commission instigated formal proceedings. Judge Peoples tendered his resignation, effective two days later, February 1, 1978. On the same day that Peoples resigned his district court judgeship, he filed notice of his candidacy for a seat on the superior court in the election to be held that year.

In April the Judicial Standards Commission recommended to the supreme court that Judge Peoples be removed from judicial office, that he receive no retirement compensation, and that he be disqualified from holding any further judicial office. In May Peoples won the Democratic primary in the superior court race; there was no Republican opposition.

Meanwhile, pursuant to a North Carolina State Bureau of Investigation inquiry, over the next few months Judge Peoples was indicted in three separate actions in Vance and Granville counties on five felony embezzlement charges and twenty-eight misdemeanor counts of failing to discharge duties as prescribed by law. The embezzlement charges stemmed from his handling of traffic court costs that totaled slightly more than $100. In all three cases Peoples was acquitted of the charges. The jury in one case required only fourteen minutes to render its verdict.

In November, being unopposed, Peoples won the election to the superior court judgeship. Ironically, the vacant seat was that of retiring judge Hamilton Hobgood, a giant of judicial rectitude and one of Chief Justice Sharp's most trusted advisers.

The thought of Judge Peoples flouting the Judicial Standards Commission by resigning his district court judgeship only to resurface as a judge of the superior court was untenable. But there was no precedent for dealing with such a situation. If the supreme court did not find its feet and render a solid ruling prohibiting him from taking office, Judge Peoples would be sworn in the following January, vastly complicating the situation. The court heard oral arguments on November 15, 1978. Chief Justice Sharp agreed with the other members of the court that she should be the one to write the opinion. It would be the first time the North Carolina Supreme Court had removed a judge for willful misconduct in office.

Such an opinion, without precedent and with such far-reaching significance, would normally have taken the compulsively thorough chief justice, notoriously slow, a very long time to produce. This time, however, she had a deadline she had to meet. For the first time since her mother died, she missed the family dinner at her sister Florence's house on Christmas Eve, working right through Christmas day. Her loyal staff pitched in on December 26, even though it was a state holiday, and the court held its last conference of the year on December 29. It was even more important than usual that the opinion be unanimous, and there was no time for the usual process of circulating draft after draft in a controversial case. But the court followed the chief justice's lead, and the fifty-eight-page opinion went down unanimously on December 30, just in time to prevent Peoples from being sworn in. In addition to barring him from holding further judicial office (as well as officially removing him as a district court judge), the court also stripped the judge of his retirement benefits, as the statute required.

Reflecting the importance she gave the case and, no doubt, the immensity of her relief, Chief Justice Sharp said, in what might be viewed as an ironic comment, "I felt like [U.S. Supreme Court Chief Justice] Warren must have felt when he got a consensus in the Brown [v. Board of Education] case."[36]

There was a good deal of sympathy for Judge Peoples on the grounds that he was simply trying to help people. He was thought by many to be a decent, kindly man. To his supporters the court's action seemed vindictive and excessive, particularly in light of his acquittals in the related court cases. The loss of his pension, which was automatic under the statute, deeply distressed even those who agreed his conduct had been unacceptable. Rumors abounded that Chief Justice Sharp held a personal dislike for Judge Peoples. It was widely believed that she thought he had maltreated his first wife and that the wife was a relative of hers. It was true that Judge Sharp did not think much of the judge, but she was not related to his first wife.[37] He simply "would not do," as she had written in a note to her files in September 1975, two years before the audit had turned up evidence of his ticket-fixing practices.[38] But the judge was well liked in his part of the state, and many felt he had gotten a raw deal.

The outcome of the case had not been self-evident, particularly given the complete lack of precedent. Even a member of the North Carolina Courts

Commission, which had drafted the legislation establishing the Judicial Standards Commission, said, "As I recall, the entire thrust of [the commission] was to discipline those judges who are sitting as judges. It never dawned on me that the judicial standards commission would be used to discipline a judge after his term had ended by resignation or by his term expiring."[39] Dallas A. Cameron, executive secretary of the commission, had acknowledged at the onset of proceedings that the question of whether the commission had authority over a judge who had resigned was not settled.[40]

Chief Justice Sharp's opinion left nothing but scorched legal earth of Peoples's argument that his resignation had deprived the commission and the court of jurisdiction and had rendered the matter moot. "[I]t would indeed be a travesty if a judge could avoid the full consequences of his misconduct by resigning from office after removal proceedings had been brought against him,"[41] she said. Reviewing the voluminous evidence of the judge's misconduct over a period of more than four years, the chief justice concluded that "it appears beyond any reasonable doubt that Judge Peoples has repeatedly been guilty of wilful misconduct in office and conduct prejudicial to the administration of justice."[42] As for why Judge Peoples should suffer removal from judicial office, past and future, and be deprived of his pension when other judges had merely been censured, she pointed to "a vast difference in the number of cases . . . mishandled and the time during which his misconduct persisted."[43] Moreover, despite the small sums involved and the absence of any financial motive, she said, "It is no part of the business of a judge to receive and handle money to pay a defendant's court costs. . . . Any use or retention of such funds, whether it be inadvertently, forgetfully, or because the judge is short of cash and intends to apply the money eventually to the purpose for which it was received, if not criminal — is wilful misconduct in office. . . ."[44] The nub of the matter was this: "To properly appraise Judge Peoples' judicial conduct we need only ask the question, 'What would be the quality of justice and the reputation of the courts for dispensing impartial justice, if every judge kept a personal file and exercised the duties of his office like Judge Peoples?'"[45]

Despite some hard feelings among Judge Peoples's supporters, knowledgeable observers were gratified. "The strongly worded opinion Chief Justice Susie M. Sharp wrote for the court reclaims for the court system the integrity it lost due to the shocking performance of Peoples as a district judge," the *News and Observer* editorialized.[46] The *Winston-Salem Sentinel* declared, "Peoples' punishment becomes particularly significant in view of the apparent public indifference toward his conduct," reminding its readers that he had been acquitted three times on different charges. "If the public cannot be depended upon to keep judges honest, it is all the more important to have a standards commission and a Supreme Court that will."[47] Albert Coates called his former student to tell her that he thought "that opinion was the finest symbol of all [her] work on the court; that it brought out [her] whole nature; and that it would go down in history as one of the finest works of this court."[48]

Few opinions had meant so much to Judge Sharp. The courts, as an indispensable part of democracy, were sacred and must not be sullied, whether by corruption, carelessness, or incompetence. Writing for the unanimous court, she put teeth in the new judicial standards legislation and gave notice that members of the judiciary would be held to account. As a service to the state, there could be nothing more significant. In a letter to her old friend Janie Sands Smith, Judge Sharp spoke of her relief at having achieved unanimity among her fellow justices: "Had I failed it would have been a sad ending to my career."[49]

The *Peoples* case, five years after Jim Newcomb, the fire extinguisher salesman, had run for chief justice, created another burst of interest in judicial qualifications.

In every legislative session for the past decade, some variant of a merit selection system had been introduced but never passed. Under these plans, a nominating committee would offer several qualified judicial candidates from whom the governor would choose his appointee, who would then face an unopposed retention election at the end of his term. If he was not approved by a specified percentage of voters, another judge would be appointed by the same system.

Although there was widespread agreement that judges ought not to have to engage in partisan politicking and electioneering, many people nonetheless opposed any appointive plan on the grounds that nothing should distance the voters from the election of their public officials, including judges. Democrats liked the status quo because statewide election of judges meant that it was virtually impossible to elect a Republican judge. Even among those who thought that partisan election was not the best means to ensure qualified judges, though, there were differences as to exactly how a merit system should be structured. Who would serve on the nominating committee, for example? Would retention elections be statewide or by district? Supporters of a merit plan acknowledged that it was futile to hope that politics could be eliminated entirely from the process, but they searched for ways to minimize its effect.

By the mid-1970s more than two dozen states had adopted some form of a merit selection system. In North Carolina the same courts commission that in 1971 had recommended legislation for the establishment of the Judicial Standards Commission and for the mandatory retirement of judges had also proposed a modified version of the so-called Missouri Plan as part of a complementary legislative package. The merit plan was the only one of the three proposed constitutional amendments that failed to make it onto the November ballot. In this instance, a major objection was that the judicial nominating committee was too heavily weighted with lawyers.

In 1973, answering a questionnaire put out by the University of North Carolina School of Law, Judge Sharp chose "gubernatorial appointment" as the best method for choosing state judges, out of an array of answers including partisan election, nonpartisan election, election by state legislature, and the Missouri-style merit plan.[50] One year later, just before the chief justice election in which she faced the fire extinguisher salesman, however, she had changed her tune: "A merit selection plan similar to the one introduced in the 1973 General Assembly appears to me to hold the best hope for an appropriate method of selecting judges."[51] While acknowledging that no system was perfect, she noted that the nominating committee system could at least "remove the hazard that totally unqualified persons would be selected for judgeships." She also liked the idea of a nonpartisan retention election in which a judge would "run" on his record. Speaking to the Greensboro Bar Association, she urged further consideration of the merit plan.[52]

The 1974 chief justice race caused many former opponents of a merit system to change their minds. Jim Newcomb had demonstrated that it was possible for a man with no legal training whatever to run for the state's highest judicial office and receive more than a quarter of a million votes. He could have won the race, had it not been an off year for national elections and thus without the coattails of a Republican presidential candidate.

The 1974 General Assembly gave some consideration to an amendment to the state constitution establishing specific requirements for holding judicial office but, reluctant to infringe on the right to run for office, set the proposal aside. As an alternative to legislated judicial standards, a bill was introduced in the 1974 session calling for a constitutional referendum on a merit selection system. Under that bill, a nominating committee made up of both attorneys and laymen would create a list of qualified candidates for judicial positions, from which the governor would fill vacancies caused by death or retirement. Subsequently, the judge would have to win a retention vote at the next general election in order to keep his seat, thus preserving for the voters the right to veto a judicial appointment. The bill failed to win the necessary three-fifths majority, for a variety of familiar reasons, primarily because of the potential for politics to rear its ugly head. Chief Justice Bobbitt, for one, in a speech to the North Carolina State Bar publicly objected to the plan because there was no guarantee that the nominating committee would be nonpartisan or that judicial nominees would represent both parties.[53]

In 1975 legislation was introduced for yet another variant of a judicial merit selection system as well as for a constitutional amendment requiring judges to be licensed attorneys. Despite the renewed catalyst for reform, both failed. As before, opposition to merit selection centered on the "public's right to choose their judges," an argument bolstered by the assertion that, in general, the existing system worked well and provided good judges. Other subterranean factors included the opposition of some rural lawyers who routinely influenced who got on the ballot for judgeships and thus were in a felicitous position when they had a client before a judge. They were not interested in sharing their "nominating" power.[54] But there were other objections to the bill, and, in fact, Chief Justice Sharp herself did not endorse it because, among other things, she did not approve of the method of selecting the nominating committee and did not believe its membership would be "sufficiently representative of the judicial districts."[55]

The failure of the so-called Judge-Be-Lawyer bill, however, distressed her greatly. Opponents of the bill maintained, inter alia, that to say "an elected official must be a member of a particular profession before he can be elected" was a bad precedent.[56] "Just because a man has a law degree don't make his mouth a prayer book," said District Court Judge L. F. "Mule" Faggart, a former Kannapolis policeman then occupying the bench without benefit of law degree.[57] Some commentators believed that the competence of lay judges varied no more or no less than that of judges with legal training.[58] Most people could name one or more judges of both types who should not be on the bench. Of the ten lay judges (out of a total of approximately 120), most were considered "honest, fair and humane."[59] Confidence and common sense could carry a judge a long way in dealing with juvenile and domestic cases, for example.

Matters deteriorated rapidly, however, when a judge untrained in legal issues faced more complicated matters. Bert Montague, director of the Administrative Office of the Courts, commented, "With a little bit of learning, they think they understand everything. They don't have nearly as much doubt about the legally difficult questions as do lawyers."[60] And mistakes were costly. In criminal matters, the defendant had an absolute right to appeal to the superior court for a trial de novo. The case would have to be tried again as if there had never been one in the lower court, contributing to the already severe problem of court congestion. In civil cases, a party's redress was to the court of appeals, an expensive and time-consuming undertaking. In such cases, the only grounds for appeal would be on matters of law, not fact, and no allowance would be made for a lay trial judge's lack of understanding of the law.

Moreover, as Judge Sharp pointed out in a letter to a candidate without legal training who was running for the district court, the tendency of lay judges to avoid civil terms of court put a disproportionate burden on the more qualified judges. In addition, she noted, a lay judge in need of legal advice was likely to seek it from a lawyer he respected. "No doubt that lawyer will give him his honest opinion, but when a judge relies upon a lawyer he will unconsciously become a partisan of that lawyer. . . . When that situation develops although the judge may be unconscious of his bias, others are not; and the result is that the reputation of the courts and the judicial image are impaired."[61]

At the time there were no lay judges on the superior court, but their numbers at the district court level were increasing with every election, and knowledgeable observers believed they would soon appear on the superior court bench, where they would have to handle cases ranging from murder to complicated civil matters far beyond their competence. Judge Sharp warned that when the bench was occupied by someone unfamiliar with the legal system, someone who had never gone to law school and did not understand the judicial reasoning processes or the rules of construction, "[Y]ou run the risk of getting a government of men and not of laws."[62] It was a deep disappointment when the proposed legislation requiring judges to be licensed attorneys did not pass.

Two years later in 1977, the legislature made another major push for a judicial merit selection system. This time Chief Justice Sharp gave it her wholehearted support, believing that the bill corrected her objections to the previous attempt. She even wrote a letter endorsing the proposal and gave permission for bill cosponsor Representative Parks Helms to read it aloud during a public hearing before the House and Senate Courts and Judicial Districts Committees.[63] The new proposed legislation took pains to avoid stacking the nominating committee, with a balanced number of appointments divided among the governor, the chief justice, the Senate president pro tempore, and the Speaker of the House. With 150 members, the committee would be geographically representative, and laymen would have a two-member majority over lawyers. Governor Jim Hunt, however, did not endorse the plan, and it failed once again to achieve the three-fifths majority in the House required for a constitutional amendment.

At this point, the process took an interesting turn. Less than twenty-four hours after the bill was defeated, Governor Hunt "came out foursquare in favor of the proposal."[64] Hunt had indicated that he wished to remain neutral on the issue, and proponents of the legislation had mistakenly believed they had the votes without asking for the governor's active support.[65] After the bill's defeat, it was said in some quarters that the governor had been converted to the idea of a nominating committee when close aides advised him he would be embarrassed if he had to appoint judges from the list compiled by his patronage office. Whatever his reasoning, in March 1977 Hunt issued an executive order establishing a thirty-four-member nominating committee to recommend judges to him when he had a vacancy to fill on the superior court.[66] The governor said that if the system worked after a one-year trial period, he would push for merit selection legislation in the General Assembly.

Under Governor Hunt's plan, the nominating committee would consist of seventeen lawyers and seventeen laymen. The governor would select thirteen laymen; the Speaker of the House of Representatives and the majority leader of the Senate would each choose two laymen and one lawyer; and the supreme court would elect two of their number to serve as chairman and vice chairman. Additionally, Chief Justice Sharp had the responsibility of selecting thirteen lawyers to serve on the committee. In her characteristic way, she surveyed the landscape for individuals she thought would be the best qualified for the job. It happened that they were all white males.

The resulting uproar, particularly among black attorneys, may have surprised her but it did not move her. The North Carolina Association of Black Lawyers issued a statement saying, in part, "We are appalled that N.C. Supreme Court Chief Justice Susie Sharp did not see fit to appoint a single black or female person to the Superior Court Nominating Committee out of the thirteen (13) lawyers she appointed on Monday, August 15. Any assertion that no blacks or women are qualified would be too incredible to warrant refutation. To assert that no blacks or women are available would be contrary to facts within our knowledge."[67]

In response to the torrent of angry letters and phone calls she received, Judge Sharp replied serenely that she believed there was "neither a racist nor a male chauvinist in the group," an answer that rather missed the point.[68] Most likely, her own racial bias would have prevented her from appointing a black lawyer, but it is interesting that she did not make more of an effort to name a female attorney to the committee. Although their numbers were still not large in the state, certainly there were some exceptionally qualified women practicing law who would have been excellent additions. It may be that Judge Sharp had been "the only" for so long, and had worked so long almost exclusively with men, that she saw nothing odd or unbalanced in an all-male committee. The predominance of men was simply something she had internalized, as had most other people of her age and background. Perhaps she felt she would be criticized for giving an unfair boost to female lawyers, whom she had long maintained should not be singled out within the profession. In any event, she saw no reason to take this opportunity to balance the judicial nominating committee's makeup with a female appointee.

Governor Hunt, for his part, had included four women and three blacks among his appointees.[69] Clearly his choices reflected a political awareness that Judge Sharp's did not. She was not in the same position, because she would never have to run for office again. But even if she had been faced with a future election, nothing in her history would indicate that political expedience would override her considered judgment on an issue. Characteristically, she had chosen individuals she believed the best qualified without any effort to be "politically correct."

Although the governor extended the merit selection system for another year and legislation was proposed for the 1979 session of the General Assembly, the measure failed yet again to pass. As Justice James G. Exum Jr. outlined in the draft of a letter, annotated by Chief Justice Sharp, in response to an inquiry from the Merit Selection Project in Columbus, Ohio, Governor Hunt's selection process had had "mixed results."[70] There had been some good appointments, but also some "that might most charitably be described as mediocre." In practice, successful and highly qualified attorneys were reluctant to be appointed because, under the governor's plan, they still had to face partisan elections at the end of their term. Moreover, to be considered for appointment, they had to make their interest public by applying to the committee, which was a deterrent. Salaries, of course, were another issue for a successful attorney, who would take a substantial pay cut to go on the bench.[71]

By the time the issue came up again in the 1979 General Assembly, support had eroded in virtually every sector of the legal community. The state's crime control commission, an advisory board to the governor, voted against supporting the measure, and there was substantial sentiment against it on both the state supreme court and court of appeals. Although Chief Justice Sharp did not comment publicly, there were published reports that both she and Court of Appeals Chief Judge Naomi Morris "were skeptical" of the plan proposed by Governor Hunt, which had increased the membership of the nominating committee to 165, of whom 78 would be appointed by the governor, and which required a 60 percent approval vote in the retention elections. Supreme Court Justice William Copeland and Superior Court Judge Hamilton Hobgood, members of the crime commission, were both vocal in their opposition.

Most people would have agreed with the assessment Chief Justice Sharp made not long after she retired in 1979. "Of course I favor the selection of judges and justices on the basis of merit and merit alone. And surely there must be a better method of selection than our present one which permits any registered voter 21 years of age or older to run for any judgeship from district court judge to chief justice," she said. "*However, no 'merit selection' plan will fulfill its asserted promise unless all persons involved with it are entirely dedicated to the proposition and are firmly resolved that political considerations shall play no part in judicial selection.*"[72]

In 1980 North Carolina voters finally approved a constitutional amendment requiring that all justices and judges of the state courts be licensed lawyers as a condition of election or appointment to the bench. But a quarter of a century after that, merit selection would remain a tantalizing idea that had never found a satisfactory form in North Carolina.

Chief Justice Sharp earned high marks as a strong administrator, but in her role as chief executive of the court she came under fire more than once for blurring the boundaries between the judicial and legislative branches of government. Despite her reverence for the separation of powers, she engaged in actions that some critics denounced as crossing the line. Several episodes in particular caused public concern and even uproar over the court's perceived involvement in the business of the legislature, most of it traceable to the chief justice, acting either personally or in her professional role.

It was true that members of the legislature traditionally had sought advice from supreme court justices during the drafting of legislation. On a formal level, the eighteen-member Judicial Council, made up of judges, district attorneys, and legislators, had provided an avenue for judicial input into the law-making process for nearly three decades. Occasionally, legislators might seek advice on bills in the drafting stage from one or more members of the high court. Court officials might appear before a legislative committee to answer questions about such administrative concerns as personnel, budgets, and salaries. The North Carolina Code of Judicial Conduct permitted a judge to "appear at a public hearing before an executive or legislative body or official on matters concerning the law, the legal system, and the administration of justice, and he may otherwise consult with an executive or legislative body or official."

One line of reasoning held that if technical or constitutional issues could be avoided in the drafting phase by consultation with the judicial branch, it made for a far more efficient process than subjecting an unnecessarily flawed statute to the lengthy and expensive process of judicial review after it had become law. Adherents to stricter interpretations of the separation of powers doctrine regarded this view with alarm. In any event, there was a fine line to be trod by members of the court, who might after all be called upon to rule on the constitutionality of any given statute.

Ironically, one occasion in which Judge Sharp caused controversy in connection with this issue came during the protracted evolution of North Carolina's death penalty law. It will be remembered that she had felt so strongly about the court's lack of authority to "re-write" the capital punishment statute that she had risked political repercussions during the 1974 elections by dissenting to the majority's rulings upholding the death penalty.[73] But, as chief justice, she took an active role in attempting to influence the drafting of new legislation on capital punishment.

After the enactment of the new North Carolina statutes making the death penalty mandatory for first-degree murder or first-degree rape, Justice Sharp wrote the North Carolina Supreme Court's opinion in *State v. Woodson*,[74] the first subsequent capital punishment case to reach the court. Reviewing the case under the new law, the unanimous court found no error in the trial court's imposition of the mandatory death penalty. Justice Exum, in a separate opinion, argued against capital punishment as a matter of public policy but concurred in the case's outcome: "The point is that as a judge I cannot substitute my personal will for that of the Legislature merely because I disagree with its chosen policy."[75]

The case was appealed to the U.S. Supreme Court, which on July 2, 1976, declared the 1974 North Carolina statute unconstitutional.[76] In essence the new law was deemed to have erred too far in the opposite direction from the previous statute. Whereas the old law had been declared invalid because it gave "unbridled discretion" to the jury to decide if a sentence should be death or life imprisonment, the new statute with its mandatory death penalty—eliminating discretion entirely—was held equally unconstitutional.[77] There had to be some way to consider mitigating circumstances before sentencing a person to death. North Carolina had to go back to the drawing board.

In the 1977 session the General Assembly undertook consideration of a new death penalty statute. Opponents of capital punishment seized the opportunity to campaign for its abolition, while supporters debated the circumstances in which it should apply. There was a strong movement to eliminate the death penalty in rape cases, partly in an effort by some to narrow the application of the death penalty, partly on the grounds that such a severe sentence deterred victims from reporting rapes and juries from convicting accused rapists. Many women's groups opposed the death penalty for rape.

Chief Justice Sharp did not agree. Indeed, she felt so strongly that she actively lobbied to keep rape within the category of capital offenses in the proposed legislation.

Among other things, she contacted her state senator, Wesley D. Webster, to express her view that first-degree rape should be punishable by death.[78] Reportedly, she also spoke to her representative in the House of Representatives, Bertha Holt (an unlikely convert, once quoted as saying, "I never could understand how you could teach people not to kill by killing people").[79]

Justice Sharp would argue that she had a right as a citizen to express her views to her own representatives in the General Assembly, but she also held forth to other members of the legislature. She claimed that she never did so unless asked her opinion, but, however the subject arose, she was not reticent, nor was her opinion discounted. When she ran into Representative Richard Wright (D-Columbus) at a Phi Beta Kappa meeting, for example, she bent his ear on her "strong desire to see a death-penalty bill covering rape reach the House floor."[80] Wright was at the time the pivotal swing vote on the House Judiciary II Committee where the bill was under discussion.[81] Asked by a reporter about her activities in connection with the legislation, she said, "I am making no public statement about the matter."[82]

In addition to making her views known to as many legislators as possible, Chief Justice Sharp also composed written arguments for keeping rape as a capital offense, at least one version of which she appears to have sent to Lieutenant Governor James C. Green.[83] Another version went to Representative Myrtle E. ("Lula Belle") Wiseman (D-Avery), with a note on the chief justice's printed "Notations" paper: "Herewith the comments I promised you. Use them as your own if you think they will help keep rape a capital crime."[84] In this version, citing North Carolina cases, Judge Sharp described in explicit detail numerous examples of actual sexual assaults on women. She discounted the notion that most victims were acquainted with their rapists. The courts were not dealing with "the consequences of a petting party which got out of hand," she wrote, but horrific premeditated crimes carried out by predators lying in wait, breaking in, kidnapping, and sometimes hunting in pairs or larger numbers.

Chief Justice Sharp put forth her belief that if capital punishment was a deterrent to murder, as Governor Hunt had recently said in a speech, then it was also a deterrent to rape. As between the victim and the criminal, she had no hesitation. "The constitutional rights of a woman to keep her person inviolate are no less sacred and important than the rights of the rapist, whatever they may be deemed to be after his crime," she wrote. "The danger of rape lurks in every parking lot, on the path a working woman takes to work and in her own bed in the middle of the night, or in the middle of the day if she is at home alone. Frequently the woman is beaten, torn, left with broken bones and worse. Surely this is not the time to minimize the crime of rape by reducing the punishment for it!"[85]

Wiseman, a retired country singer, riveted the House of Representatives when she rose later that spring to recount the story of her rape ten years earlier, in her own home. The issue of capital punishment for rape, however, was unresolved by the time a new statute went into effect on June 1, 1977, limiting the death penalty to first-degree murder or a killing committed during the commission of another felony. Then, on June 29, 1977, the U.S. Supreme Court ruled that the death penalty could not be imposed for rape, at least not when the victim was an adult, effectively ending efforts to pass such a bill in North Carolina.[86]

Chief Justice Sharp had raised some eyebrows with her apparent lobbying on the issue, but those eyebrows might have pierced the roof had it been known that she had gone so far as to draft comments for at least one legislator, Representative Wiseman, to use as her own. If overt advocacy concerning a statute so susceptible to constitutional attack was poor judgment on the part of the sitting head of the state's highest court, how much worse was covert and undisclosed speech writing for members of the General Assembly? Judge Sharp's thin assertion that she was "making no public statement" on the controversy belied her deep involvement.

Judge Sharp, accustomed both by nature and by profession to making decisions, perhaps understandably found it difficult to refrain from offering her thoughts on any given issue. As both a scholar and a pragmatist, she generally made an effort to choose which battles were worth fighting but, despite the protective coloring of a conservative and traditional jurist that she wore, the record reveals a willingness to press against established boundaries, including the notoriously permeable membrane between branches of government.

CHAPTER **18**

EQUAL RIGHTS AMENDMENT

Undoubtedly Justice Sharp's most famous, least understood, and most resented interference in matters of public policy was her opposition to the ratification of the Equal Rights Amendment (ERA) to the U.S. Constitution in North Carolina. Her opposition, largely due to the critical timing of the vote in North Carolina, had a major impact on the failure of the amendment nationally.

The ERA struggle spanned roughly twelve years, from 1970 to 1982, encompassing the last nine years of Justice Sharp's service on the North Carolina Supreme Court, four as chief justice, and continuing past her 1979 retirement. First introduced in Congress in 1923, three years after women achieved the right to vote, the ERA had languished for decades. It boiled to the surface in the late 1960s, and the recently formed National Organization for Women (NOW) vowed to fight for its ratification.

The women's movement of the 1960s and 1970s was a part of the tide of protest and change that surged out of the civil rights movement, Lyndon Johnson's Great Society, and the anti–Vietnam War crusade. This was the era of women activists such as Betty Friedan, Gloria Steinem, and Bella Abzug. Expressions such as "consciousness raising" became part of the language. The first generation of women to benefit from the birth control pill, suddenly able to separate biology from destiny, began pouring into the higher education system and the job market. At the most visible levels, the face of America was changing, as, for example, when Barbara Walters became the first female network news anchor in 1976.

The proposed ERA read: "Equality of rights under the law shall not be denied or abridged by the United States or any State on account of sex. The Congress shall have the power to enforce, by appropriate legislation, the provisions of this article." Such simple language, such a seemingly simple concept.

In 1970 U.S. senator Birch Bayh presided over hearings on the ERA in the Senate Subcommittee on Constitutional Amendments, during which North Carolina's Senator Sam Ervin emerged as the amendment's chief opponent. Among other things, Ervin introduced a string of amendments to narrow the ERA's coverage, which, if passed, would have effectively gutted it. Ervin proposed, ERA notwithstanding, that women should be exempted from compulsory military service and from service in combat units; that protective legislation for women should not be affected; that fathers' responsibility for supporting their children should remain unchanged; that laws based on gender relating to privacy as well as laws dealing with sex offenses should be exempted from ERA coverage. In his own version of the vitiating Hayden Rider introduced by Senator Carl Hayden (D-Ariz.) in 1950,[1] Senator Ervin introduced a proposed exemption permitting legislation intended to enable women "to perform their duties as homemakers and wives." He would later point to the Senate's rejection of his proposed exemptions as an argument that the ERA was intended to affect every aspect of life heretofore protected under gender considerations.

At last, following approval by the House, in 1972 the Senate also passed the ERA. Senator Ervin thereupon spearheaded a successful effort to set a seven-year time limit for the states to ratify the amendment.

Twenty-two states promptly voted their approval, leading proponents to think there would be no difficulty in getting the thirty-eight states required for ratification. But the ERA encountered fierce resistance and ultimately proved one of the most divisive issues in American history. At the end of the seven-year deadline the ERA remained unratified. Supporters managed after great difficulty to get an extension to 1982 through Congress.

The fight over the ERA in North Carolina was brutal. On the face of things, it had appeared that North Carolina was moving along with other parts of the country with respect to women's rights. It was a time, as elsewhere, of raised consciousness and increased social activism. The 1970 report of the North Carolina Citizens' Advisory Council on the Status of Women highlighted numerous areas in which women still suffered discrimination based on gender, with a view to addressing them. Local NOW activists pursued a broad range of antidiscriminatory goals in education, the workplace, and other areas. The newly formed North Carolina Women's Political Caucus, under the leadership of Martha McKay, focused on getting women into government office. Organized women's groups such as the North Carolina Business and Professional Women's Clubs continued their long history of supporting women's issues.

As a comparatively industrialized state, North Carolina had a large percentage of women in its work force. The state boasted a number of high-profile professional women, of whom Chief Justice Sharp was perhaps the most familiar to the average voter, because she held an elective position and her work kept her in the public eye. Well-known North Carolina women included Dr. Ellen Winston, who was appointed commissioner of public welfare in the U.S. Department of Welfare in 1963 and later worked abroad with the United Nations. Another was economist Juanita Kreps, who became vice-president of Duke University in 1977; later appointed secretary of commerce by President Carter, she would become the fourth woman in U.S. history to serve in a cabinet position.

Governor Holshouser, in office from 1973 to 1977, and particularly his successor, Jim Hunt, serving the first two of his four terms as governor, supported the ERA. Major newspapers editorialized in favor of ratification. In the General Assembly, proponents had committed and sensitive leadership in Willis P. Whichard and Herbert L. Hyde as well as others.

But in North Carolina, as in the nation, the proponents' initial flush of confidence faded quickly. In 1973 another eight states ratified, but one state, Nebraska, rescinded its ratification. Between 1974 and 1977 only four new states ratified, while two more rescinded. In 1978 Kentucky also passed a rescission bill, which although vetoed by the acting governor, further indicated the prevailing wind. In North Carolina, supporters waged an unsuccessful struggle to ratify the ERA in every session of the General Assembly between 1973 and the final deadline in 1982.[2]

Perhaps, in retrospect, the failure of the ERA in the Tar Heel State should not have been surprising. When the Nineteenth Amendment to the U.S. Constitution giving women the right to vote was ratified in 1920, North Carolina failed to join the list of states in the yes column. In fact, after Tennessee became the last vote necessary to ratify the woman suffrage amendment, the North Carolina legislature recorded a gratuitous and wholly ineffectual vote of 71–41 against its passage. North Carolina was the state, after all, in which the legislature had sent an 1897 bill for woman suffrage to the Committee on Insane Asylums. When a bill to require equal pay and promotions for women employed in state government was killed in committee in 1963, the *News and Observer* headlined the brief story, "Goody, Goody, Girls! We're Better'n You."[3] It was not until 1971, when the General Assembly voted (unanimously) on a bill to ratify woman suffrage introduced by Representative Whichard, that North Carolina granted its formal approval of the fait accompli of more than half a century before.

Opposition to the ERA in North Carolina was pervasive. The special status accorded southern women was a matter of pride with men and women alike, and anything jeopardizing that delicate balance threatened the most fundamental ways in which men, women, and their families functioned. Women feared losing protections they had in law and custom because of their sex and protested that they did not want "to be like men." Men feared losing their favored status as family heads and in the wider world as well, if women were to be admitted everywhere as their equals. Phyllis Schlafly, national spokesperson for the ultraconservative antifeminist position, took an active role in the North Carolina debate and capitalized heavily on these anxieties. Would women be subject to the military draft? Would public bathrooms have to be unisex? Would men no longer be required to support their families?

Not to be underestimated, too, was the effect of the ongoing struggle of the state with the federal government over a number of issues. Beginning with *Brown v. Board of Education*, U.S. Supreme Court opinions and civil rights legislation had imposed change on what many still referred to as "our way of life." Lingering resentment on the race issue carried over into the debate on the ERA. This resentment was amplified by continuing federal "interference, intervention and intrusion"[4] on a range of other issues. During the decade of the 1970s, while North Carolina debated the ERA, a series of federal mandates on busing, civil rights, environmental protection, and the like repeatedly drilled home the idea that North Carolinians were not free to live their lives according to their own decisions. A case originating in Charlotte, for example, led to the 1971 U.S. Supreme Court ruling in *Swann v. Charlotte-Mecklenburg School Board*, which increased the federal courts' powers over school desegregation. Two years later, *Roe v. Wade* established a woman's right to abortion, ending the debate then taking place in the North Carolina General Assembly. Throughout the 1970s the University of North Carolina fought a battle with the Department of Health, Education, and Welfare, whose efforts to impose a major restructuring of the statewide university system were viewed by a significant number of people as destructive of a proud and progressive institution. Donald G. Mathews and Jane Sherron De Hart, in their in-depth examination of the ERA battle in North Carolina, *Sex, Gender, and the Politics of ERA*, summarize a common attitude: "To businessmen and like-minded lawyers who resented activist judges, affirmative action programs, the Equal Employment Opportunity Commission, federal environmental impact statements, and investigations by the Occupational Safety and Health Administration, a vote against the Equal Rights Amendment seemed a modest but necessary retaliation."[5]

That one of the ERA's most vigorous opponents was North Carolina's own Senator Sam Ervin added considerable weight to arguments against ratification. Even before he gained international fame in 1973 as the chair of the Senate Select Committee to Investigate Campaign Practices, more popularly known as the Watergate Committee, Ervin was a well-known and powerful force in his home state, where he was shrewd enough to downplay his Harvard law degree by declaring himself "just a country lawyer." He had been a member of the North Carolina General Assembly, a superior court judge, a member of the North Carolina Supreme Court, and a U.S. congressman before beginning his twenty-year career in the U.S. Senate in 1954. Known as a strict constructionist constitutional scholar, he was nonpartisan in his interpretation, giving support to liberals on such issues as "no-knock" search laws and prayer in the schools, but opposing most civil rights legislation on the grounds that it infringed on individuals' right to hire whom they wished, sell their homes to whom they chose, and attend school where they wanted.

During the Watergate hearings, televised around the world, Senator Ervin's dancing eyebrows and folksy stories made his unflinching assessment of President Richard Nixon and his aides seem uncomplicated. As the *Washington Post* remarked in the senator's obituary, "At a time when Americans were buffeted by the Vietnam War and Watergate and increasingly distrustful of their leaders, Ervin came across as a stern father figure who was not confused about what was right and wrong, moral and evil, and who took for granted the moral courage to stand up for what was right."[6] When it came to the ERA, confusion was the common condition, and Senator Ervin's adamant opposition went a long way among those who — not without reason — were unsure about the effect the amendment might have.

Susie Sharp was a longtime admirer of "Senator Sam." She had known him since 1936 when he was assigned as a special superior court judge to hold court in Rockingham County. At the time, she was still a relatively new lawyer, and "[b]eing still under the influence of the Law School and its Law Review, [she] frequently deplored the ignorance and deportment of the judiciary," she would write to Ervin in later years. "But when you came we could find no flaw."[7] She shared Ervin's views on civil rights and resonated to his gallant southern attitudes toward women. She heartily approved when he said in a speech before the Senate on August 21, 1970, "It is the better part of wisdom to recognize that discriminations not created by law cannot be abolished by law. They must be abolished by changed attitudes in the society which imposes them."[8] Ervin sent Judge Sharp a copy of his speech, and she replied, expressing her opposition to the amendment. During further ERA hearings before the Senate Committee on the Judiciary in September, Senator Ervin read her letter into the record.[9]

After thanking him for his recent speech to the Senate arguing against the amendment, Judge Sharp had written:

> I am in complete accord with your views on this Amendment and share all your apprehensions about it.
>
> No doubt those sincere and dedicated women who have made a career out of promoting this Amendment will feel that all who oppose it are "against women." That would indeed be a strange posture for me, for it was in high school that I began crusading for equal rights under the law and equal opportunity in every field of endeavor for women. I have worked, "participated," talked and contributed to that end to the utmost of my strength and ability. If this Amendment could do what its proponents believe it would, I would certainly be for it. However, it is my firm conviction that it is not only unnecessary but that it will not accomplish their purpose. On the contrary, I believe that if it is passed the women will have "ambushed themselves," to borrow a phrase.[10]

She based her opposition, first, on her belief that the equal rights clause of the Fourteenth Amendment to the U.S. Constitution protected women as well as men.[11] Moreover, she said, civil rights legislation had been and would continue to be enacted that would provide further barriers to discrimination against women. At the same time, she protested the loss of protective labor legislation such as that nullified by Title VII of the Civil Rights Act of 1964. In fact, her underlying objection to the ERA appeared to rest on a fear that it would deprive women of special protections in the law. "God made men and women different," she said. "He gave her the brains but not the brawn of men, and she bears the children. Because of these differences, in certain situations she is more vulnerable and needs the protection of the law."[12] Despite her firm belief that men and women should be equal in the workplace, she also believed, "There are just some fundamental differences between men and women that the laws won't change."[13] She wrote to Senator Ervin, "[L]aws which bar women from operating saloons, engaging in professional wrestling, and which impose weight-lifting restrictions on them do not offend me. I am satisfied that the majority of women do not feel enslaved by them and that if they are repealed the exploitation of women will result."[14]

These arguments, although widely held by credible ERA opponents such as Professor Paul A. Freund of Harvard Law School and Professor Philip Kurland of the University of Chicago Law School,[15] would not have borne the kind of rigorous examination of which Judge Sharp was capable, had she been inclined to oppose them. Here, however, she was operating from a visceral level and a complicated mind-set that involved her intensely feminine self-image and her lifelong romanticization of the antebellum South, as well as her deeply held belief that the federal government had no right to try to legislate changes in long-standing social attitudes. Had she been disposed to support the ERA, she easily could have argued that the Supreme Court had never interpreted the Fourteenth Amendment to extend the same degree of protection to women that it had given to the suspect categories of race and ethnicity. (Indeed, one commentator in the North Carolina General Assembly said, "The 14th Amendment couldn't pass this body!")[16] Judge Sharp could have noted that antidiscrimination laws such as those embodied in the 1964 and 1965 Civil Rights Acts could be modified or even repealed. A case in point, for example, was Title IX of the Education Amendments of 1972, forbidding sex discrimination in schools receiving federal aid. It took the Department of Health, Education, and Welfare until December 1979 to issue its final policy interpretation of its regulations. Under attack and unenforced for much of its history, Title IX would survive among other things a Supreme Court decision effectively exempting sports programs from the act,[17] but only after Congress overrode President Reagan's veto of the 1988 Civil Rights Restoration Act. Had she favored the ERA, Judge Sharp might have joined those women who viewed so-called protective legislation as outdated and more akin to "protective custody." She might have pointed out that many of the horrors foretold by ERA opponents, such as alimony based on ability to pay, were already the law in North Carolina. Family law statutes affecting divorce, alimony, child custody, and child support had in fact been revised in 1967 to be gender-neutral and would not be substantially altered by the ERA.

But Judge Sharp never wavered in her conviction that the Equal Rights Amendment was a bad idea, a "Pandora's box" better left unopened.

She was at pains to declare her support for women "to make the fullest use of their highest powers and to fulfill themselves in work of their own choosing, equal pay for equal work, the right to participate on equal terms with men in all branches and on all levels of government."[18] She reminded critics that she had been fighting for women's rights since the days when women were not eligible for jury service. "In high school I made equal rights my goal," she said. "From the day I entered law school I have done my utmost to obtain and justify equal rights for women."[19] But she believed there was "a vast difference between equal rights and the so-called equal rights amendment."[20] She was convinced that a constitutional amendment, apart from being unnecessary, would benefit men more than women. "My platform is equal rights for women plus the reasonable protection which the physiological and functional differences between men and women necessitate. Indeed, I am not adverse to a few privileges for women!" she wrote to an anti-ERA member of the North Dakota legislature who requested her views.[21]

In 1970 when Judge Sharp allowed Senator Ervin to read her letter opposing the ERA during congressional hearings, the North Carolina Code of Judicial Conduct had not yet been enacted. Taking a public position on the issue may have given new meaning to the word "injudicious," but there was no formal obstacle to Judge Sharp's action. The code went into effect in September 1973, obliging her to refrain from "becoming involved in controversial issues and making public statements about matters likely to come before the Court for decision."[22] The best that can be said is that she paid lip service to the admonition. She lost no opportunity to let it be known that her views were identical to those of Senator Ervin, even if she was not permitted to speak publicly about the issue. While attempting to adhere to the letter of the code, she in fact exerted every bit of influence she could in opposition to the ERA and can fairly be credited or blamed for playing a significant role in its defeat, not only in North Carolina but also nationally.

When the North Carolina legislature opened its January 1973 session, Representative Whichard introduced a bill to ratify the ERA. In the Senate a resolution in favor of ratification was endorsed by twenty-five out of the fifty members, a positive indication. But by the time the Senate Constitutional Amendments Committee began public hearings in February, supporters were surprised to realize that they had a fight on their hands. An overflow audience of 500 partisans clapped and hissed as a Wake Forest law professor with the apt name of Robert E. Lee, a prominent family law expert, gave extensive testimony against the ERA, even claiming at one point that "women resent men because they have to bear children. And that's something the General Assembly can't change."[23]

Justice Sharp was invited to appear at the hearings, but, after discussing it with Chief Justice Bobbitt, she declined.[24] In reply to a supporter urging her to testify, she said, "I have made my views known to my Senators and Representatives, as well as to those members of the Legislature who have asked me for my private opinion. As a member of the Supreme Court I cannot, with propriety, go beyond that."[25] This was more than a bit disingenuous. She was making her views known to every member of the legislature who crossed her path, whether they asked for her opinion or not. The day before the vote in the Senate, for example, according to her journal she was asking Senator

George Rountree III from New Hanover County whether "he was staked out on ERA." Heaven help those who did inquire about her opinion, like two young men who sat with her at a six o'clock communion service for the legislators on the morning of January 30, 1973. "I tell them while the Chief waits," Judge Sharp recorded.[26]

At the hearings, according to Mathews and De Hart's definitive account, "One witness read aloud a letter from Justice Susie Marshall Sharp that expressed her complete accord with Sam Ervin's views."[27] It is unclear whether Judge Sharp gave permission for her letter to be read. Regardless, ERA opponents made sure her statements were widely publicized. Dorothy M. Slade, a prominent anti-ERA activist, later said that Judge Sharp's letter "provided a weapon that opponents used 'to good advantage.'"[28]

The 1973 debate and vote on the ERA were rife with backroom maneuvering, subterfuge, and reneging on promises. After the House of Representatives resoundingly defeated a bill to submit the ERA to a statewide referendum (calculated to delay the issue and keep the legislators from having to vote), ratificationists believed they were headed for a victory in the House. But just as the House Constitutional Amendments Committee was supposed to send the ratification bill to the floor for a vote, the committee chairman, ERA opponent Claude Kitchin ("Kitch") Josey, suddenly fell "ill." Almost immediately the Senate Constitutional Amendments Committee agreed to send its own ratification bill to the floor, surprising supporters who had concentrated on the House vote. They had only a week to try to organize their forces in the Senate. On February 28, 1973, the Senate defeated the ratification bill 27–23. Two of the votes against the bill were defections. Had those two not changed the votes they had promised, it would have been a 25–25 tie, with Lieutenant Governor Jim Hunt in position to make the deciding vote in favor of ratification. Instead, the bill was dead until the 1975 General Assembly.

It was a heartbreaking defeat for ERA supporters. Had Judge Sharp's well-known opposition to the ERA made any difference in the narrow defeat of the bill? Mathews and De Hart report, "In the postmortem that followed, proponents agreed that Sharp's public opposition and private telephone calls to legislators had been damaging."[29] Martha McKay would later say, "I do think it did hurt . . . because some people hid behind her. That didn't want to come out and were glad to have any straw in the wind. And they used her as an excuse." Senator Ervin himself told Judge Sharp that her comment about women ambushing themselves with the ERA "helped him greatly in his fight against it."[30]

Justice Sharp was on the phone the day after the vote. She called her senator, Wesley Webster, to "commend him for doing right," as well as Senator Gordon Allen (D-Person), one of the defectors, "to thank him for changing his vote."[31] Her involvement in behind-the-scenes machinations deepened when ERA opponent Senator Jack L. Rhyne (D-Gaston) called her later that day.[32] In the effort to persuade the two defecting senators, he had promised that he would introduce an equal rights amendment to the North Carolina constitution. He was "in a state" over the language, and Justice Sharp told him she would have to see it to advise him. "He came dashing over," she recorded in her journal. "I gave him the text of the amendment which was killed several years ago and told him to get Senator [Hamilton C.] Horton [Jr.] to help him write one that would be killed in committee."[33] Later that night, she reported, she heard on the radio that a bill written by Senator Rhyne had been introduced.

The proposed bill was "a joke," according to Martha McKay. Although it declared, "Equality of rights under the law shall not be denied on account of sex," it then stated that "the rights, benefits, or exemptions now conferred by law upon persons of the female sex shall in no way be impaired."[34] In other words, as Senator Charles Deane (D-Richmond), who had sponsored the ratification bill in the Senate, said, the bill was "like an insurance policy. It gives with the big print and takes away with the small print. It doesn't do anything. Under this, we would stay as we are."[35] In any event, nothing came of it.

As she campaigned for chief justice during 1974, it concerned Judge Sharp that she had angered prominent ERA supporters in the state, particularly in Charlotte. But that did not prevent her from expounding on her views, even as she cited the Code of Judicial Conduct and its rule against members of the judiciary becoming involved in controversial issues or making public statements about matters that might come before the court.

In a long letter to a community college teacher who had requested a statement of her position on the ERA for a class she was teaching on Women in Society, Judge Sharp cited the restrictions on her ability to comment and described how her position had become public during the 1973 hearings. Because it "would be improper for me to make any public statement on the ERA," she said, she had declined the invitation of several members of the legislative committee conducting the hearings to appear before it. "I understand, however, that a letter I had written to Senator Ervin back in 1970 'got into the act.' I am not sure how this happened, but I regarded it as unfortunate." Having cleared the ground, she then went on to discuss her reasons for opposing the ERA. She ended helpfully, "You probably already have a complete dossier of Senator Ervin's views on the ERA. However, the enclosed contains some citations which you might like to have if you don't already."[36]

In February 1975 North Dakota became the thirty-fourth state to ratify the ERA. It would be the only state to do so that year. The campaign leading up to the vote was intense on both sides, and the fact that North Carolina Supreme Court chief justice Susie Sharp opposed the ERA was used by those against ratification in their promotional materials. Anti-ERA North Dakota representative Ralph Dotzenrod contacted her in June 1974, asking for confirmation of her quotation about women ambushing themselves with the ERA, along with a short statement of her views on the issue. "It may well be," he wrote, "when our legislature meets in early '75 our state could be the state that decides whether this 27th amendment becomes law."[37] In her response to Representative Dotzenrod, Judge Sharp did not mention the Code of Judicial Conduct before launching into her reasons for opposing the ERA. In closing, she suggested that Senator Ervin's office could supply him with some more material.[38]

Unhappily for Judge Sharp, pro-ERA forces in North Dakota became aware of her evident willingness to be quoted in their ratification battle and contacted their allies in North Carolina. In mid-December an assistant in the office of North Dakota governor Arthur A. Link wrote to Nancy Drum, coordinator of ERA United, Inc., in Winston-Salem: "Some of our legislators have contacted Justice Susie Sharp and have received letters anti-ERA from her. They will be using these letters, of course, in an anti-ratification fight. I understand you have information about Susie Sharp and possibly information about how to counter act her statements."[39] This provoked a letter written the day after Christmas to Judge Sharp from Gladys Tillett, the former suffragist and Democratic national committeewoman from Charlotte who was the titular head of the ERA organization in North Carolina. She included a copy of the North Dakota inquiry and asked Judge Sharp to let her know, before she answered, whether the referenced correspondence dated from 1970 or 1974.[40] In a handwritten note, she extended Judge Sharp the opportunity to clarify whether the North Dakota actions were being taken with or without her knowledge.

Susie Sharp was to be sworn in as chief justice on January 2, 1975. On December 30, the last conference of the Bobbitt court marked the changing of the guard. In addition to the sadness she felt as she participated in the retirement of her "special friend," a terrible cold that augmented her misery, the mountain of business that had to be completed by the court before Chief Justice Bobbitt and Justice Higgins went out of office, and the planning required by the upcoming swearing-in ceremonies, a newspaper article that went out on the United Press International wires all over the country complicated her life enormously. Written by Dollie Smith, a *News and Observer* reporter whom Judge Sharp knew well, it highlighted the new chief justice's "reservations" about the Equal Rights Amendment.[41] Judge Sharp felt obliged to find time in her first days as head of the court to write Gladys Tillett a four-page letter, single-spaced, trying to explain herself.

With respect to the North Dakota fight, Judge Sharp was certain she had not corresponded with anyone other than Representative Dotzenrod, and she quoted for Mrs. Tillett the substantive part of her letter to him. "Regrettably I did not tell Mr. Dotzenrod that my comments to him were 'off the record,'" she admitted. "It was certainly not my intention to become involved in the debate in North Dakota, but, in the light of hindsight, I can now see that I was very shortsighted not to have anticipated that possibility."[42]

"Indeed," one imagines Mrs. Tillett thinking.

As for the UPI story, which had resulted in a deluge of mail, some of it vicious, Judge Sharp defended herself without disclaiming her opinions, which of course were well known to Mrs. Tillett:

> I have been greatly distressed by the UPI feature story, which seems to have blanketed the country during the last days of December. . . . My concern about this story is not that it misrepresents my views, but it leaves the impression that I had just announced them in an interview. That I did not do, have not done, and do not intend to do. However, as you know, on account of that 1970 letter to Sam Ervin, my views are no secret, and any reporter who wants to publicize them apparently feels free to do so, secure in the knowledge that there can be no denial that those are my views. The UPI story was a surprise and disappointment to me. The reporter who wrote that story had long been aware of the 1970 letter but had previously refrained from commenting on me and the ERA. I suppose she felt she could refrain no longer.[43]

The reporter who wrote the story later explained to Judge Sharp that she had been under the impression that the Code of Judicial Conduct only restrained candidates for an election from expressing views on controversies, and that after the election there was no such restraint.[44] But this was not the first time since 1970 that the infamous letter had surfaced. Repeatedly, Judge Sharp managed to have her cake and eat it too by not making any "public statements" but reaffirming the views expressed in the letter and elsewhere. Meanwhile, she continued to express herself "privately."

She had, in fact, made assurances to Gladys Tillett that she would stay out of the ERA fracas. In her letter to Mrs. Tillett on January 7, 1975, she said, "My first reaction to the UPI story was a gasp of dismay and the fear that you might think I had reneged on my statement to you in Charlotte that I would not involve myself in the ERA fight." In Judge Sharp's mind, perhaps she did believe that she had remained above the fray. But others did not agree.

Ratificationists were worried that they were losing momentum. Only three states had ratified the ERA in 1974. Oklahoma and Virginia had both rejected the amendment, and other states were considering rescinding their approval. ERA supporters were watching the 1975 North Carolina General Assembly hopefully, as the 1974 elections had added some pro-ERA legislators to the ranks. In mid-January 1975 the ratification bill was introduced again in the North Carolina House, with hearings scheduled for March. Opponents did their best to drag out the process in the hope that support for the amendment would erode. House Speaker James ("Jimmy") C. Green employed his considerable political expertise to undermine the ratificationists' position. Sam Ervin, who had just retired from the U.S. Senate, performed his usual routine in the hearings, opposed by a Duke law professor, William Van Alstyne. Phyllis Schlafly, who, as the *News and Observer* reported, had "left her fashionable house in Alton, Illinois, her six children, lawyer husband, and two secretaries to tell North Carolina women that their place was in the home,"[45] made a strong impression. The final debate and vote was set for mid-April.

Judge Sharp had tried to keep a low public profile but evidently had not refrained from "educating" anyone who might listen. The week before the vote, ERA supporter Gladys Bullard called "mad as an old wet hen."[46] Judge Sharp's secretary, Virginia Lyon, took down the message. Mrs. Bullard said she had understood that Judge Sharp was "going to stay out of the ERA squabble." But she had learned that Judge Sharp had talked to Senator Benjamin D. Schwartz (D-Wilmington) and because of his conversation with her, he had switched his vote.[47] Mrs. Bullard "seemed quite upset," Virginia wrote. "She said that the ERA backers (including herself) had respected your position and thought that you were going to stay out of the matter."[48] Judge Sharp tried to soothe Mrs. Bullard as best she could, but in her journal she did not deny the charges.[49]

The preliminary vote was a narrow two-vote victory for the ERA proponents. But on the final roll call the next day, after intense lobbying efforts overnight, enough legislators changed their votes to defeat the ERA once again, 62–57.

Both sides spent the interim between the 1975 battle and the next session of the General Assembly in 1977 honing their organizations and strategies. No states ratified the ERA during 1976, but on January 18, 1977, Indiana joined the yes column by one vote, reportedly persuaded by a telephone call from President Carter's wife Rosalynn.[50] In her New Year's message to her supporters, Phyllis Schlafly warned that if North Carolina followed suit the proponents would benefit from "a momentum we cannot match."[51]

With the new year in 1977 Democrats made a triumphant return to the Governor's Mansion and to full command of state government. Judge Sharp took part in all the inaugural events. Her main duty as chief justice was to administer the oath of office to the new governor, thirty-nine-year-old James B. Hunt Jr., but she also attended the inaugural ball, rode in the downtown parade in an open car despite the freezing temperatures, and stood in a receiving line at the public reception for more than four hours without a break. "[T]he receiving line duty this year didn't do me in as badly as the one four years ago—but that was for a Republican Governor; this one is Democratic!" she said.[52]

In January, in what had by now become almost a ritual, ERA supporters and opponents thronged through the corridors of the North Carolina legislature and packed the public hearings. Each side paraded its most persuasive advocates out to the microphones and lobbied individual legislators. Sam Ervin wrote to Judge Sharp, asking her permission for him to read her 1970 letter at his appearance before the Senate committee handling the ERA, but apparently she thought better of it this time.[53]

Meanwhile, both Virginia and Nevada voted down their ERA bills, focusing the national spotlight even more intensely on North Carolina. On February 9, 1977, although two members switched their votes from yes to no, the North Carolina ratification bill passed the House by a vote of 61–55, perhaps thanks in part to telephone calls to several wavering legislators by First Lady Rosalynn Carter. It was the first time the ERA had passed in either chamber of the legislature. Knowledgeable observers believed the chances were good in the Senate.[54]

The anti-ERA forces went into high gear. Phyllis Schlafly and her STOP ERA organization called on conservative mass-mailing expert Richard Viguerie to help them deluge the state with letters containing postcards to be signed and sent to voters' legislators. Anti-ERA members of the Senate reintroduced the old fallback tactic, a statewide referendum instead of a vote in the legislature.

The lobbying and deal making was intense, with Governor Hunt directly involved on the side of the ERA. Four senators announced they would support the anti-ERA referendum tactic, including two who had voted for the ERA in 1973.[55] Among them was Senator Wesley Webster of Rockingham County, although he subsequently changed his mind, having been persuaded that voting for the referendum was "passing the buck."[56] ERA opponents were unable to get enough votes to bring the referendum to the floor. The Senate would vote yes or no on the ERA itself.

In such a tight race Senator Webster's vote was critical. Like most other senators, he was under intense constituent pressure to vote against ratification. He had nonetheless been sufficiently receptive to the pro-ERA forces to agree that in the event of a tie, he would change his no vote to a yes.[57] One of his constituents, of course, was Chief Justice Sharp, who had already called him on February 23, a week before the vote was set in the Senate.[58] Just before the Senate ERA vote on March 1, however, she, like many others, made a last-minute call to press her point of view. Unfortunately for her, a reporter was standing in the office and Senator Webster, apparently in an effort to preserve his hearing, held the receiver away from his ear so that the reporter was able to hear every word the chief justice said.[59] Naturally it made the papers. "I hope you won't let that young governor twist your arm," the reporter heard her tell the senator, along with other admonitions to stand firm.[60] Other reports would quote her as saying, "You don't have to vote the way that boy governor tells you."[61]

Despite phone calls from Governor Hunt and Rosalynn Carter, Senator Webster ultimately voted against the ERA bill.[62] Once again the ERA was defeated, by a margin of two votes.

Judge Sharp's telephone call to Senator Webster, as reported in the newspaper, ignited a storm of criticism. "Many North Carolina legislators are questioning whether growing involvement by the state Supreme Court in legislative matters is proper, legitimate advice or inappropriate lobbying," began a UPI article appearing across the state.[63] Stung, Judge Sharp said, "I didn't realize I was disqualified to talk to my own senator."[64] She cited her refusal to appear before legislative committees and declared she had not "politicked a single soul" except Webster, going on to claim that, although she had answered questions when legislators had asked her, "I didn't initiate the conversation."[65] This was a dubious assertion, based on her own journal entries. She was adamant, however, that she had "no intention of overstepping the bounds" and that she "had no idea I was doing that in a personal call to my senator."

There was a broad contingent, including some editorialists, who agreed with her that she had every right to express her opinion to her own representatives in the legislature. Several of her defenders pointed out that the criticism came primarily from ERA supporters who had suffered defeat. Other people, however, like Representative Patricia Hunt (D-Orange) were of the view that "You can't be a constituent when you hold high office."[66] Although only a few attorney-legislators were willing to comment for the record, Representative James F. Morgan (D-Guilford) spoke for many others who had "expressed concern about the high court's possible influence in other legislation, such as the death penalty and nonjudicial matters." Representative Morgan said that although he appreciated advice and counsel on drafting legislation, it bothered him that a court might have to rule on a law's constitutionality. "If [judges] have been involved in the legislative process, I don't see how they can do it," he said. "I think you've got to work together, but I think you've got to be very careful that neither one of the branches (of government) oversteps its bounds."[67]

The North Carolina defeat was a major loss for the national ERA effort. Only three states needed to ratify the amendment to make it law, but after 1977 the impetus slowed drastically. In the 1979 North Carolina General Assembly, the ratification bill never made it out of committee. In 1981 a "gentlemen's agreement" allowed it to rest dormant in committee rather than be killed outright, in exchange for proponents' promise not to bring it up for debate or vote during the remainder of the session. With the national deadline set for the end of June 1982, proponents managed to get the bill introduced into the 1982 "short session" of the legislature, which met in even-numbered years to deal almost exclusively with the budget. But this last-ditch attempt also failed when the Senate voted to table the measure, and then applied a "clincher" vote that required a two-thirds vote for reconsideration.

With the defeat in North Carolina, the ERA effectively died a national death. Despite the extension of the ratification deadline to 1982, ERA supporters never managed to regain the momentum they had had in the early days of the effort. After Indiana's ratification in 1977, the ERA failed to pass in any other state. Over and over, supporters had pinned their hopes on North Carolina as a key state, believing that a success there could break the logjam in favor of ratification. If North Carolina had succeeded, it is possible that the national outcome might have been different.

Susie Sharp clearly played a role in frustrating the effort in North Carolina, and even in other states. Her prestige, her position as the only woman at the top of the judicial pyramid, and her high visibility as a woman who had transcended her gender to break barriers throughout her lifetime all put her on a par with the tireless Senator Ervin as a powerful voice against the ERA. As a symbol, she vastly magnified her personal viewpoint. Undoubtedly, her opposition was a major factor in the many very close votes that came before the General Assembly. Had she exerted her influence in favor of the ERA instead of against it, her opinion might have swayed enough votes to pass it. As it was, her opposition was felt at every level. In every small town where women discussed the issue and decided whether to work for or against the ERA, in the legislature where her views were heard not only by her own representatives but by the entire body, and even in the nation at large, where her name was used to shore up support against ratification, the fact that the female chief justice of the North Carolina Supreme Court was against the ERA carried enormous weight. It was the most important example of her tendency to "blur the line," overstepping the bounds of her position.

Her opposition was a bitter pill for many women in North Carolina who had previously held her up as an icon of women's rights. To them her position seemed a betrayal of women in general. To pro-ERA activists like Gladys Tillett, Gladys Bullard, and Representative Patricia Hunt (who had beseeched her for an explanation of her opposition, only to be told that the judge felt she "ought to stay out of it"), Judge Sharp's manifest efforts against the ERA seemed a betrayal of a specific promise not to work against ratification, even if she could not agree to work for it. In the perception of the young women who in the 1970s were beginning to become attorneys in increasing numbers, her anti-ERA stance undermined their daily struggles in what was still very much a man's profession. "It is sometimes more difficult (for women lawyers) because of her opposition to things like ERA and her sometimes lack of support for what I would consider women's issues," said one young female attorney in Raleigh after North Carolina had defeated the ERA once again in 1979.[68]

Judge Sharp sincerely believed the ERA to be potentially harmful to women and gave not an inch to those who felt she had betrayed her sex. There is no evidence that she ever dithered for an instant about the wisdom of her position. "Forgive them, Lord, for they know not what they do," she said of the ERA supporters.[69] Regardless of Judge Sharp's reasons for opposing the ERA, the fact of her opposition was what people registered. Many feminists would never understand or forgive her.

CHAPTER 19

STEPPING OFF THE STAGE

In mid-December 1975, almost fourteen years after she took rooms at the Hotel Sir Walter when she came to Raleigh as a new member of the supreme court, Judge Sharp finally moved into an apartment. It was a townhouse on a busy boulevard, a short drive to the Justice Building and not far from the Cameron Village shopping center with its stores and cafeteria. She had resisted the move as long as she could, but the hotel had deteriorated along with the downtown, and she and State Treasurer Edwin Gill were almost the last of the old residents. Gill had lived in the hotel for forty-six years, ever since he came to Raleigh as a member of the 1929 General Assembly, and could not be persuaded to leave. But for Judge Sharp it was time. "The hotel, alas!, has become almost uninhabitable and I no longer felt safe there," she explained.[1] Still, she was reluctant to give up what had been a convenient and happy arrangement.

The new apartment had a living room, dining room, kitchen, and half bath downstairs and two bedrooms with two baths upstairs. A communal laundry room served all the residents. For Judge Sharp, keeping house was a shock. "After fourteen years of having my bed made every morning, linen changed every day, and my tub washed out by someone else, I find being on my own a drastic change," she wrote an old friend.[2] Two weeks after she moved in, Judge Bobbitt found her running the vacuum cleaner and trying to learn how to use the "laundermat [sic]." He said, "If this keeps up, you will have no time to be Chief Justice."[3] Fortunately, she reported, "thanks to my secretary's pull and devotion, I have acquired 'help' twice a week."[4]

She found time to be chief justice, but there were other worries that frayed her attention. She was no less devoted to her responsibilities as head of the family than to her duties as head of the court system, and her family in these years caused her a good deal of concern. Her sister Louise was still living at 629 Lindsey Street in Reidsville. The old place constantly needed work, and Louise continued to hope that Susie might come home. Brother Kits held a terrifyingly responsible job as head of the medical recovery team for the Apollo moon shots at Cape Canaveral, before being posted to Naples, Italy, for three years. Particularly distressing, her sister Florence went through a rough patch in the mid-1970s when her husband, Bob Newsom, was unemployed and, at the age of fifty-five, had a hard time finding another job. For about a year and a half he tried one lead after another, without success. Finally, as their son Rob remembered it, "Mother was convinced they would end up eating Alpo. And they just went into a terrible depressive state."[5]

Judge Sharp sat down and wrote her sister a long letter. "Florence, my dear, dear sister," she began. "I have worried about you until I can neither work nor sleep; and this will not do, for I can no more afford to go to pieces than you can. Each of us is too involved in the lives of too many people who would be hurt beyond repair if we should quit the struggle and give up in despair."[6] Then she told Florence about how their father, Jim Sharp, had failed in his early struggle to support his family, about the harrowing poverty on the Mountain Farm in Virginia, and about his declaration of bankruptcy. It was a story Florence had never heard, so focused was the Sharp family on success, not failure. "The last few nights, for the first time in many years," Judge Sharp wrote, "I have relived times and incidents which occurred before you were born. Better days had pushed them far back into my memory's computer, but they could not erase them altogether. It occurred to me this morning that if you knew about them, and realized what Mamma and Daddy had survived, it might help you to put your present situation in perspective and encourage you to carry on."

She went on to relate in detail what it was like to live in the mountain cabin with no heat or running water. She described the day the appraisers came to inventory the family's meager belongings for the bankruptcy court, and how Annie Sharp "stood very tall" and "used her company manners and voice," her graciousness moving the men to treat her with deference. Judge Sharp told Florence how the family, penniless, had to go live with Annie's sister Susie Garrett and her husband Earle in Reidsville until Jim Sharp got on his feet again. "I reopen this chapter in the family history only because I want to be sure that you realize we have a truly great heritage from our parents to preserve," she wrote. "Mamma too was a proud woman. Remember, she was always a Vance County 'aristocrat!' She proved it the day the appraisers came and many times thereafter."

As the only one of the Sharp children with a memory of this ordeal, Judge Sharp certainly internalized its lessons of endurance, pride, and hope. That neither she nor any other family member ever spoke of it can be seen as an indicator of the degree to which these concepts needed no articulation. An obdurate refusal to accept anything less than ultimate success was a bedrock Sharp family characteristic.

For Florence, it must have been enormously comforting to know that there was no shame in her situation and that her own parents had endured even worse. Judge Sharp's five-page, typewritten, single-spaced letter spoke of all the ways Florence had supported and sustained her husband, and of the need for her to be strong for his sake and the children's. "You must remember that you represent security to Susie and Robby quite apart from financial help." As for financial help, Judge Sharp offered hers, begging Florence not to invade her "rock-bottom savings."

Eventually Bob Newsom began to find work as a consultant and the cloud lifted. But it was not the only cloud in the sky, for the Newsoms' daughter Susie and her husband, Tom Lynch, who now had two little boys, were experiencing marital problems, which would eventually result in their divorce and in family tragedy.

Judge Sharp's natural inclination was to want to fix whatever was wrong. Judge Bobbitt knew this propensity all too well. One day when the two of them were out walking, Judge Sharp noticed that the Eckerd's Drugstore roof was leaking. "I stop to look up," she recorded. "Judge B. says come on, you can't fix the roof and it is not one of your responsibilities."[7] Stress was taking a toll on her. A simple request to Judge Bobbitt to take a package to her friend Lelia Alexander on his next trip to Charlotte irritated him, and his impatient reaction upset Judge Sharp so much that she told her journal that it "ruined her day."[8] She stayed up most of that night reading opinions. The next day Justice Branch—the most cordial and conciliatory of colleagues—brushed her off when she tried to pursue the issues in one of his cases. "I'm not getting enough sleep," she wrote. "Too many people are hurting my feelings."[9] On top of it all, Justice Huskins told her that the secretaries at his end of the hall were afraid of her, that she was "all business" with them and had no small talk.[10] She noted without comment his recommendation that she take more time with them, a commodity of which she had little to spare.

Six months later she experienced a disturbing incident that presaged things to come. One afternoon in May 1978, she wrote, "I get a mental block. I cannot remember writing the speech Va. gives me."[11] It was a short speech she was supposed to deliver that day to 500 students attending a function at Peace College in Raleigh, but she simply could not recognize the typed copy her secretary handed her. "I get terribly upset and finally go to the meeting," she wrote, "but I do not make the speech."[12] The next morning, a Saturday, after a good night's sleep, she went back to the office. "I read the speech and remember it," she wrote, but she marked the journal entry with her symbol for disaster, a skull and crossbones.[13] Perhaps stress contributed to the episode, but certainly her awareness of its potential significance created additional stress.

Life seemed full of irony and poignancy, as was perhaps only natural as she entered her seventies. Her seventieth birthday fell on the seventh day of the seventh month of 1977, a numeric coincidence she noted in her journal. The day began with a seven o'clock phone call from Breck. "He wants to see me," Judge Sharp wrote. "He said, 'I do not want to lose you now!'" This prompted her to muse, "Time brings unforeseen developments!"[14] Occasionally Breck came to North Carolina to visit with his daughter Jean, and Judge Sharp was distressed at his condition. In his mid-eighties and living alone, he was "a sad sight," she wrote. "Mrs. B. would be grief stricken."[15] When he visited in Raleigh in August 1977, Breck conceded that he had come to the conclusion he should not live alone. He was considering proposing marriage to a schoolteacher he had in mind, although he did not know if she would accept. He told Judge Sharp that if she had been practicing law when Venitah died, he would have proposed to her, but not after she became a judge. "Think of this!" Judge Sharp wrote.[16]

She remained in telephone contact with John Kesler, often talking for an hour at a time, but she rarely saw him. When his daughter Frances Sue had her first baby in 1976, it took Judge Sharp by surprise. Frances Sue, in turn, expressed astonishment upon learning that her father apparently had not told Judge Sharp she was expecting a child.[17] Perhaps he had, although it does not seem like a piece of information her mind would have dropped. Her brain circuits were hardwired when it came to John. Still, it was undeniable that nothing was the same. After seeing her on television with other political luminaries he knew, John told her they all looked old. But he ended the call with, "I love you."[18]

On a day-to-day basis, Judge Bobbitt was her constant companion. When he retired as chief justice, the court found space in a small unused room for him to keep an office of sorts, a place to come and read the paper or recent opinions, so in some ways her contact with him remained unchanged. He was no longer on the court, but he had not left the building. It was a situation fraught with the potential for upsetting the balance of their relationship, as Judge Sharp took his place as chief justice and he was forced off stage. In the days shortly after her swearing-in, she referred to Bobbitt as "my chief"[19] in an acknowledgment that although the official titles had changed she would always look up to him, and she was exquisitely aware of his sensitivities. She never seemed to mind that he was still coming to the Justice Building every day, and in fact seemed to welcome it, never hesitating to ask his advice if she felt he could offer insight into a situation. Judge Bobbitt mostly took his changed status with humor, telling people who asked what he was doing in retirement that he was "a law clerk without pay."[20] Judge Sharp would add that he had a job as a consultant but that she was having a hard time keeping him interested.

The fact that he was no longer officially on the court, however, meant that Judge Bobbitt did not receive invitations to many of the functions Judge Sharp attended as a matter of course, socially and professionally. Both in order to have an escort and to afford Judge Bobbitt the pleasure, she often conspired behind the scenes to get him invited when he otherwise would not have received an invitation. This she did with the utmost discretion, careful not to let him know she was responsible for his undiminished popularity. Her journal is full of remarks like "Black tie–long dress dinner at Angus Barn for Shearon Harris. (Judge asks the blessing and then comes back to sit by me. He does not know that I told the man to ask him.)"[21] It was not in her to let a situation go unaddressed, and like the drugstore roof, Judge Bobbitt's situation needed attention. Unlike the roof, however, his happiness was something she viewed as well within her realm of responsibilities.

There were times, however, that whatever buried resentment Judge Bobbitt had would work its way to the surface. Judge Sharp's attention, no matter how well meaning, could be suffocating. When her all-enveloping focus combined with her superior star power as the sitting chief justice, her presence could become overmuch for her companion, who continued to relish his own share of the limelight. There was, for example, the time Judge Bobbitt pointedly excluded her from what could have been a pleasant springtime excursion down East, where the retired chief justice was to preside over a small but meaningful and interesting ceremony.

In April 1979 the local chapter of the Daughters of the American Revolution planned to honor James Iredell, appointed to the first United States Supreme Court by George Washington in 1790, by placing a plaque on his grave, which was in the cemetery on Hayes Plantation just outside the historic town of Edenton, North Carolina.[22] Established in the late 1600s, Edenton was known as one of the loveliest towns in the South. It had been an important colonial town, home to signers of the Declaration of Independence and the United States Constitution. Beautifully situated on the Albemarle Sound, it was full of lovely old houses and was graced with a magnificent Georgian courthouse on the waterfront. Judge Bobbitt had been invited to make the principal address at the graveyard ceremony, which would be attended by James Iredell's descendants, members of the DAR, and other dignitaries.

The prospect of such an interesting ceremony in such a beautiful old town on a day in April, presided over by her dear friend, Judge Bobbitt, was intensely appealing to Judge Sharp. Judge Bobbitt, however, did not suggest that she accompany him, even though she had been requested by event organizers to supply material for his introduction. "At the present time I do not know whether I can come to Edenton with the Judge or not," she wrote when she complied with this request a couple of weeks beforehand. "I hope very much I can come."[23]

The week of the event, Judge Sharp could stand it no longer. "After supper I ask him if he wants me to come to Edenton." This precipitated a blowup. "He says he knew something like this would happen and he says he will give me his research and I can make the speech," she reported. When a participant later expressed disappointment that Judge Sharp had not accompanied Judge Bobbitt for the occasion, Judge Sharp confided to her journal, "I could not tell [him] that I wanted to come but he made it very plain he did not want me."[24] Thus, on that Saturday when Judge Bobbitt was in Edenton as the featured guest speaker under the trees in the old graveyard, Judge Sharp remained in Raleigh, where she bought Judge Bobbitt "a $5 handkerchief which he in no wise deserves."[25]

Despite such eruptions, however, the relationship between the two justices was for the most part unruffled, and they continued to enjoy the steady routine of companionship they had maintained for so many years. It would be hard to overstate the affection people felt for them as a couple, among the general public as well as their close acquaintances. Complete strangers felt free to make comments to Chief Justice Sharp about her marital status, like the woman she encountered one morning when she went to renew her driver's license. "As I leave with my license and a fair picture, some unknown lady asks me when I have to retire," she recorded. "I tell her and she said, 'They say that there will be no reason in the world why you all can't get married then.'"[26] Another time a distinguished federal judge, having had too much to drink, said that "more people are hoping that Bill B. and I will get married as soon as I retire; that the whole state has watched that wonderful romance and wishes it to continue."[27]

Judge Sharp and Judge Bobbitt had first discussed marriage in 1967, but over the years when they were on the court they had found neither the necessity nor the rationale to bring them to the altar. Some indication that Judge Sharp kept the possibility in the back of her mind can be found in a journal entry dated August 9, 1979, just a few days after her retirement. "Now I know—" it begins without preamble. "[H]e was telling me about a conversation with Fred Helms who told him that he and I ought to get married. He said he started to say, 'Why should I be that stupid?'" Instead he moderated his words to say, "Why destroy a beautiful friendship?"[28] Judge Sharp's only comment is, "I said nothing." The issue is never mentioned again in her journals.

Judge Bobbitt's recounting of his conversation with Fred Helms seems an unnecessarily harsh announcement, if that is what it was, that Judge Bobbitt no longer entertained the idea of marriage. In her deepest heart, however, Judge Sharp may have recognized that they were better off with their separate-yet-inseparable modus operandi. Why destroy a beautiful friendship, indeed. They continued as before, devoted to each other and constantly together. A childhood friend from Reidsville, fully aware that Judge Sharp never married, would one day remark that of all the Sharp brothers and sisters, "Susie had the most successful marriage of any girl in the family."[29]

As the time drew closer for her mandatory retirement, Chief Justice Sharp thought longingly of a life with fewer responsibilities. In March 1978, declining an invitation to attend a party in Asheville, she remarked, "My retirement date is 31 July 1979, and I look forward 'to running at large in an unfenced field,' as my former colleague, Justice Higgins, was wont to say."[30] The preceding year had been particularly arduous, which no doubt contributed to her sense of beleaguered confinement.

In February 1977 Vice President Walter F. Mondale had asked her to serve on a nine-member presidential commission to select the new head of the Federal Bureau of Investigation.[31] Legendary FBI director J. Edgar Hoover had reigned from 1924 until his death in 1972, just before burglars broke into the Democratic Party National Committee office and precipitated the Watergate scandal, which unfolded over the next two years. In the five years since Hoover's death, the FBI's image had been badly soiled, with numerous disclosures of, inter alia, political spying, illegal break-ins, alleged kickbacks, and pension fund irregularities during Hoover's tenure.[32] The Watergate scandal added its own layer of dirt, most notably when interim director L. Patrick Gray admitted that he had burned key Watergate papers on orders from the Nixon White House. President Richard Nixon appointed Clarence M. Kelley as director in 1973, on the heels of the Watergate revelations and Gray's subsequent resignation. When President Jimmy Carter took office in January

1977, he wasted no time in disassociating his administration from any Watergate taint. One of his first actions was to instigate the search for a new director of the FBI.

Judge Sharp initially declined the search committee assignment, telling Mondale "it didn't look sensible" due to her heavy work load at home. But her old friend Griffin B. Bell, recently appointed U.S. attorney general, called and put the pressure on her, and she felt she could not refuse. "Susie Succumbs," one paper reported the next day, leading some jokesters to remark on her apparent demise à la Mark Twain.[33] It was probably Griffin Bell who suggested her name. The presence of the highly regarded female chief justice from North Carolina would contribute to the commission's credibility. Other commission members were a sampling of distinguished politicians and members of the legal profession, as well as the former head of the American Civil Liberties Union. The chairman, Irving S. Shapiro, was head of E. I. DuPont de Nemours and Co. That Attorney General Bell wanted Judge Sharp on the commission was an indication of her national stature.

The search committee turned out to be even more of a burden than she had expected, and far more frustrating. In the end she had very little to show for it. She made repeated trips to Washington, D.C., for the commission meetings, which in terms of time away from her own work and the extra weariness of travel severely eroded the energies she needed to conduct the business of the court. In February the nine members of the committee met with the president, vice president, and attorney general in the White House, then reconvened in April to narrow their choices from an initial list of some 235 applicants. The *News and Observer* reported that Chief Justice Sharp was unaware if there were any women on the preliminary list of candidates, but she herself had not nominated any. "I don't know of any woman at this point who is qualified to take it," she said.[34] That this impolitic statement did not make a ripple was a reflection of public opinion in 1977, when it would have been difficult to find someone to argue that a woman should run the nation's most famously macho agency.

In May Judge Sharp made four trips to the capital, spending a total of ten days.[35] Under severe time constraints from the president, who refused Chairman Shapiro's request for an additional thirty days, and concerned about the potential for too much FBI influence in the selection process, the committee sought approval from Attorney General Bell to rely on "name checks" run by the Secret Service as opposed to in-depth background checks normally done by the FBI. Working straight through until six o'clock or later each day, sending out for lunch, the committee interviewed the forty-eight top applicants.

In the evenings the members reviewed their notes for the day and compared the candidates.[36]

The commission issued its final report in June 1977, listing five names as candidates for the president's consideration.[37] They included a judge from Massachusetts, a prosecutor from Los Angeles, a director of an FBI office in Pennsylvania, a federal appellate judge from Illinois, and a black sheriff from Detroit.[38] None were household names, and questions soon arose as to whether any of them had the stature necessary to redeem the bureau from its tattered condition. Moreover, the press, which conducted significantly more thorough investigations than had the commission, uncovered serious issues in the backgrounds of four of the candidates. The fifth they declared unbesmirched but possessing virtually no administrative experience.[39] The *Los Angeles Times* reported that the search committee had "settled for short-cut investigation methods, bowed to White House demands for quick action, and ultimately leaned heavily on committee members' 'gut judgment' about candidates who were interviewed."[40]

President Carter promptly indicated his dissatisfaction with the commission's list and began interviewing additional candidates. Finally, on August 16, 1977, the president announced he had chosen a federal judge from Alabama, Frank M. Johnson Jr., a registered Republican known for his tough desegregation rulings in the 1960s, to head the bureau. It was a well-received appointment, but unfortunately Johnson had to withdraw his name for health reasons before he could take office. Finally, in February 1978, William H. Webster of St. Louis, a federal judge on the Eighth U.S. Circuit Court of Appeals, was sworn in as the new director of the FBI.

In a letter to Clarence Kelley, Judge Sharp declared, "I regard my inclusion on the FBI Committee as one of the most frustrating and disappointing experiences of my life."[41] It was doubly frustrating to have spent so much time on the effort only to have the committee's work nullified, because, at the time that she was required to be in Washington so much, she also had a battle on her hands in the North Carolina General Assembly, where the judicial budget was on the chopping block.

The main bone of contention was judicial salaries.

In years past, the various groups within the judicial system had each lobbied the legislature for salary increases or other additions to their budgets. Superior court judges, for example, matched their political clout against that of district court judges, district attorneys, clerks of court, and other members of the system. It was a dog-eat-dog, piecemeal approach that resulted in inequities and inconsistencies. Chief Justice Sharp made it one of the major goals of her administration to present a unified budget request to the legislature for the entire judicial system over which she presided.

The issue was of special concern to the members of the judiciary, who had had no substantial salary increase since 1973, during a time of high inflation and a sharply rising cost-of-living index.[42] The quality of the judiciary was threatened. The opportunity to become a superior court judge, for example, generally came to a lawyer at the peak of his career and earning power. The disparity between a judge's salary and the income of a top attorney was not conducive to improving the caliber of judges.

Chief Justice Sharp undertook to hammer out a unified proposal for salary increases across the entire judicial department, from clerk's offices to the supreme court. Her first task was to work with all the different groups to get them to agree to a reasonable request, which then could be put forward convincingly as part of the overall package. During the summer of 1976, she organized an advisory committee made up of representatives of the court of appeals, superior court judges, district court judges, district attorneys, public defenders, and clerks of superior court.

Chief District Court Judge J. Phil Carlton wrote in a letter to all the district court judges, "It should be noted that this was an advisory committee formed by the Chief Justice on her own initiative. As the chief administrative officer of the judicial system for the State, she is charged with the responsibility of submitting budgetary recommendations for the judicial department. She certainly had no obligation to call the various groups within the system together." He added, "No Chief Justice, to my knowledge, has taken such a personal interest in adequate compensation for all components of the system in the past."[43]

Each representative on the advisory committee, having first achieved agreement within his group on its goals, bargained intensely with the other representatives and with the chief justice. The proposals needed to reflect not only the justifiable demands of each group but also a sense of proportionality among the different groups. Superior court judges' salaries, for example, needed to be in proportion to those of district court judges. District court judges felt that they should have somewhat higher salaries than district attorneys, a view the district attorneys contested. And so forth. Most important, however, it was essential to remain united and not allow the old "devil take the hindmost" system to take over again. In the end, keeping in mind the adage that politics is the art of the possible, everyone gave up something, and Chief Justice Sharp put together a package she could present to the General Assembly.

Throughout, Judge Sharp proceeded with the guidance and assistance of political experts like Superior Court Judge Hamilton Hobgood. She spoke out on the necessity for adequate judicial salaries in an effort to educate the public. She held private conferences with Governor Jim Hunt, Lieutenant Governor Jimmy Green, House Speaker Carl Stewart, and other key legislative leaders, obtaining their support. It was a shock, therefore, when the package came under fire and looked as if it were headed for defeat.

There were several issues creating opposition, among them the steep rise in the salaries requested. Although scaled back, the initial requests nonetheless ranged up to increases of over 29 percent.[44] This was in contrast to the 6.5 percent increase proposed for other state employees.[45] Although North Carolina ranked twenty-eighth among the states in the salaries paid to superior court judges,[46] this and other sharp increases raised eyebrows and hackles. There was an outcry about the judiciary's demands as compared to salaries for schoolteachers. As always, there was a vocal contingent that felt the courts were needlessly inefficient and that measures should be taken to improve that situation instead of raising salaries for court personnel. Judges in particular were condemned for apparently not working more than a few days a week, as it sometimes seemed when a court calendar broke down, leaving the court with no cases to try until the following week. Members of the judiciary pointed out that much of this sort of thing was unavoidable and an integral part of the trial system. There was no way to predict how many cases on the week's docket might settle at the last minute, for example. Moreover, when not holding court, judges had other chores to do outside of the public eye. But the perception persisted. Finally, a recent flap about judges' expense accounts also lingered in the public's mind. The result was a sharp reaction against the proposed judicial budget package.

"I had not expected to encounter so much overt hostility," wrote Judge Sharp.[47] She was unaccustomed to having her views disregarded. Having analyzed a problem and arrived at a reasonable solution, she expected others to see her point of view. It was obvious to her that salaries were too low to attract good judges and other court personnel and that the solution was to raise them as much as possible within the constraints of the state budget, especially because it had been four years since there had been any meaningful raises in the judicial department. For example, as she noted when she appeared before one legislative committee, she estimated that she spent at least half of her "administrative time" dealing with problems created by district court judges who did not measure up to the required standards.[48] When a chief district court judge was not performing satisfactorily, she sometimes found it difficult to remove him because there was no competent person available to take his place, a situation directly related to judicial compensation.[49]

It went without saying that the quality of the state's judicial system had a real and important impact on the lives of the state's citizens. She did not understand how anyone could oppose reasonable salary increases for court personnel.

Judge Sharp's entire mind-set was at the other end of the spectrum from that of the typical legislator. Her law clerk, Joe Eason, who came to work for her the following fall and whose uncle had been on one of the legislative committees involved in the budget battle, observed that her pattern of deliberating over an issue, then reaching a decision she believed both right and correct, and thereafter never having to retreat was not well suited to the legislative process.[50] "A firm conviction of one's correctness" might work well for a chief justice but not for a legislator. As a judge, she was right unless and until she was reviewed and reversed by a higher court. Eason said, "She would look for what was the right solution and then try to convince people that was right." This was in contrast to the typical legislator, who, he said, would start with, "What can I pass? Or, what's the lay of the land?" Another difference was that in general every legal case was decided on its own merits, whereas, Eason said, "There's no such thing as a single issue in the General Assembly. Every issue is interrelated with every other piece of legislation that's in there."[51]

In the end, the 1977 legislative session passed the requested salary increases for appellate judges, superior court judges, district court judges, and district attorneys, to be phased in over two years. But public defenders, assistant district attorneys, and clerks of court were limited to the 6.5 percent increase allowed all state employees (a situation remedied in the 1978 legislative session).[52]

The budget battle was a humbling experience for Chief Justice Sharp. In the aftermath, she wrote to thank those who had stood by her through the process, like Lieutenant Governor Green, to whom she said, "The 1977 Legislature was the first with which I ever had 'official business,' and I soon learned that inexperience was NO asset and that our package plan for judicial salaries had formidable opposition. Having sold the judges and solicitors on the idea that judicial salaries should be fixed and maintained in relation to each other and in accordance with a unified plan worked out by the Administrative Office of the Courts, I trembled to think of the consequences if our judicial budget went down in ignominious defeat—for surely it would have meant a reversion to the policy of 'Every man for himself, and the Devil take the hindmost.'"[53]

Nonetheless, she had modernized the budget process for the judiciary by initiating and shepherding a unified budget proposal through the legislature, doing the tough groundwork to make it happen. It was the act of a modern administrator, an activist, and a pragmatist. Bringing judicial salaries up to a more attractive level was in itself a contribution to the quality of justice dispensed by the state's judges, but by unifying and organizing the needs of the various groups within the department, she also paved the way for more efficient negotiations with the legislature in the future. Like her leadership in the area of judicial standards, this was one of the ways in which she transformed the office of chief justice and improved the quality of the state's court system.

On another question, Judge Sharp was resolutely conservative. She was adamant in her opposition to cameras in the courtroom, an issue that attracted a good deal of attention in the mid-1970s, during her years as chief justice. As one aspect of the fair trial–free press balance, the use of photographic and broadcasting equipment of all kinds was generally barred in American courtrooms, largely as a result of the media circus that had overwhelmed the 1935 Lindberg baby kidnap-murder trial. Since that time, technical advances had minimized the disruptive effect of broadcasting equipment, one of the strongest early arguments against allowing cameras. Many observers felt that cameras in the courtroom would serve the public interest. The issue was whether allowing cameras in the courtroom would infringe upon the constitutional guarantee of a fair trial and the orderly administration of justice. On the plus side, supporters argued, inter alia, that courtroom proceedings were public business, and that the scrutiny of the camera would result in a higher standard of justice. On the negative side, opponents feared an adverse impact on the willingness of witnesses to testify and, conversely, the tendency of lawyers' and judges' prima donna temperaments to bloom in the eye of the camera. The press inevitably would gravitate to the most sensational aspects of court proceedings. In addition, some believed that the exposure produced by the camera would constitute an excessively cruel addition to the pain of a defendant—not guilty unless and until so found in trial—and his family. As Judge Sharp once said, "To publish the fact that John Doe is being tried for murder is one thing. To take his picture in court as he sits by his frightened, sorrowing and embarrassed wife, mother or children is another."[54]

The year of her retirement would mark half a century since she began practicing law with her father in Reidsville in 1929. No one had worked more tirelessly for the courts of North Carolina. But before she surrendered her position as chief justice, she had one more service to perform: heading off yet another gubernatorial attack on the traditional succession of the senior associate justice to chief justice.

Governor James B. Hunt was elected to his first term as governor in 1976, and promptly set about getting a constitutional amendment passed that would permit the governor to serve two consecutive terms. Hunt would go on to be reelected in 1980, becoming the first governor in North Carolina history to serve two consecutive four-year terms. He would serve two more terms back-to-back between 1993 and 2001. For an entire generation, Jim Hunt was the face of North Carolina government almost to the extent that Franklin Delano Roosevelt embodied the national government over his three-plus terms in office. In 1979, however, Hunt was just a very young and very ambitious governor in his first term, and he had not only new ideas but also political debts to pay.

One of Hunt's closest advisers was J. Phil Carlton, a good friend since college days, a former district court judge, and a member of Hunt's cabinet before his appointment to the North Carolina Court of Appeals. Rumors were rampant that Governor Hunt intended to appoint the forty-one-year-old Carlton as chief justice upon Judge Sharp's retirement, partly because the governor was of the opinion that "the court system was being run by a bunch of antediluvians,"[55] partly to reward his longtime political ally. Such an appointment would derail the normal succession of the most senior associate justice, Joe Branch. Branch, like others, had arrived on the high court by way of politics. He had served four terms in the legislature, and had been legislative counsel to two former governors, Luther Hodges and Dan K. Moore. It was Dan Moore who had appointed him to the bench in 1966, after Branch had managed his gubernatorial campaign. Politics aside, however, he was considered eminently fitted for the post. He was a much-respected and admired member of the court, adept at bridging differences. Members of the court were unanimously in favor of his ascending to the position of chief justice.

The suggestion that Hunt might break with tradition to become the first governor in the twentieth century to appoint someone other than the senior associate justice to the top position on the court provoked a sharp response. Members of the court expressed concern that Carlton's appointment "would inject internal politics into the court and disrupt its inner workings by creating competition" to head the court.[56] Justice Lake declared that "it would be a tragic mistake" to change the time-honored method of succession. Among other things, he noted that because of the chief justice's power to appoint chief district court judges and to control patronage within the Administrative Office of the Courts, which had seventy employees, Hunt "would certainly be open to suspicion that the governor was seeking to control those appointments for the advantage of his own political fortunes."[57] Chief Justice Sharp said, "I just can't think of anything worse than having this court involved in state politics."[58]

At least as early as January 1979, Judge Sharp was talking to sources who were in a position to advise her, like former governor Terry Sanford, whom she called to have a long talk about the rumors. "He says the trouble is that Carlton has been promised the CJ job and Joe [Branch] will not have to retire before Hunt's second term is over."[59] Part of the problem, too, was that Branch had not supported Hunt in the gubernatorial primary, having preferred Charlotte businessman Ed O'Herron.[60] Branch let it be known he would run for the position if the governor appointed Carlton, a disruptive and undesirable situation.[61]

Finally, Chief Justice Sharp took the bull by the horns and composed a lengthy letter to the governor.[62] Signed by every member of the court as well as by retired chief justice Bobbitt and retired associate justices Carlisle W. Higgins, I. Beverly Lake, Dan K. Moore, and J. Will Pless Jr., the letter urged Governor Hunt to appoint Senior Associate Justice Branch as chief justice, keeping intact a tradition unbroken for more than three-quarters of a century. This "antediluvian" preference was not based on sentiment but rather on such major considerations as the importance of experience on the court to a new chief justice. The most important function of the traditional method of succession, however, was to shield the court from politicking by hopefuls not currently on the court, as well as from "internal conniving and plots." This safeguard was not in place in other jurisdictions. "To realize how fortunate we have been in North Carolina, one has only to attend a meeting of the Conference of Chief Justices to learn what happens to the work and decision-making processes in Supreme Courts of other states when there is internal friction, political or otherwise," the justices warned.

Judge Sharp sent the letter off with an accompanying note on March 7, 1979. Two months later at the end of the spring term, when she presided over the court for the last time, there still had been no response from the governor.[63] Not until May 23 did Hunt schedule a meeting to let her know that he was going to appoint Justice Branch to be chief justice.[64]

The announcement was well received. Although some observers suggested that Hunt had missed an opportunity to inject more innovation into the court system, most viewed the sixty-three-year-old Branch as open to new ideas despite his conservative beliefs.[65] The issue of cameras in the courtroom, for example, steadfastly opposed by Chief Justice Sharp, might be reexamined. The general feeling was that the new regime would continue on an evolutionary path, without the disruption that a more revolutionary administration might provoke. As a *Raleigh Times* editorial put it, "[C]hoosing Branch assuaged some real fears among his Supreme Court peers and in the state bar. The fear was not that Carlton would be a bad justice, but that putting a strong-minded young newcomer straight into the top job would inject too potent a jolt of change and politics into the court's atmosphere and strain the delicate web of continuity and collegiality that holds any such court together." The editorial concluded, "These intangibles' importance can't be measured, but it exists. Hunt was wise to recognize it."[66]

Judge Carlton, who had graciously let it be said that he had withdrawn from consideration and recommended Justice Branch to the governor, was in the audience when Hunt made the formal announcement of his choice.[67] Three weeks later, Governor Hunt named Carlton to the seat on the supreme court to be vacated when Branch became chief justice.[68]

Chief Justice Sharp's vigorous leadership in forestalling the governor's contemplated assault on the traditional succession of the chief justice had kept the lid on Pandora's Box.

During this time, the top position on the North Carolina Court of Appeals was also in the news. For a period of eight months, from December 1, 1978, until Chief Justice Sharp's retirement on July 31, 1979, North Carolina had the distinction of being the first and only state in the union whose supreme court and court of appeals were both headed by women.

When Judge Walter E. Brock resigned his position as chief judge of the court of appeals upon his appointment to the North Carolina Supreme Court, Chief Justice Susie Sharp appointed Judge Naomi Elizabeth Morris to take his place.[69] Years before, Judge Morris, known as "Peanut," had so impressed W. A. Rand, the attorney for whom she worked as a legal secretary in Wilson, North Carolina, that he had encouraged her to attend law school. If she did well, he told her, she could have a job in the law firm when she finished. In the mid-1950s, such an offer was rare indeed. It was in 1952, for example, that future U.S. Supreme Court justice Sandra Day O'Connor graduated with high honors from Stanford Law School and was unable to get a job in a law firm except as a stenographer. More than a quarter century after Susie Sharp graduated from law school, little had changed with respect to opportunities for women in the profession. Like Susie Sharp, Naomi Morris had the exceptional opportunity of entering a general law practice when she received her law degree.

At the University of North Carolina School of Law, Naomi Morris served as an associate editor of the *Law Review* and in 1955 graduated fourth in her class, at the age of thirty-four.[70] She then embarked on a successful career in Mr. Rand's firm, soon known as Lucas, Rand, Rose, Morris & Meyer. Immersed in her practice, when Governor Dan K. Moore asked if she would accept an appointment as one of the first six judges on the newly created court of appeals in 1967, she was taken by surprise.

As Naomi Morris told the story, "I told him that . . . it never entered my mind . . . and I would certainly have to think about that."[71] She asked if she could have some time to think it over, and the governor granted her twenty-four hours. "I left his office and went straight to Judge Sharp's office."[72]

With encouragement from Judge Sharp, "Peanut" Morris began what would be a fifteen-year career on the court of appeals, where she served with distinction as the number of judges on the court increased from six to twelve. Judge Morris would have liked to have gone on to the North Carolina Supreme Court, but a poor relationship with Governor Hunt thwarted her hopes for an appointment, despite support from Judge Sharp and many others. When Justice Walter E. Brock announced his resignation from the supreme court in 1980, the recently retired chief justice Sharp wrote the governor to urge him to appoint Naomi Morris. "There is presently no other woman in the State who has her background, experience, and qualifications for a seat on the Court. In the nature of things there can be no other woman so well qualified for some years to come." Judge Sharp even indulged in the argument that while she was sure that there were "several" gentlemen who sought to succeed Justice Brock, it occurred to her that "if you appoint Judge Morris they will all understand why you chose her, but no disappointed gentleman will ever be able to understand you preferred Mr. X to him!"[73] Governor Hunt was not moved and circumvented the problem by appointing another candidate from Wilson, Louis B. Meyer, Judge Morris's former law partner.

Judge Sharp's letter, however, pointed up the scarcity of women with the credentials to take a seat on the supreme court in 1980. Her letter, in fact, went on to discuss the shortage of women with the experience to become superior court judges as well, a factor she argued as an additional consideration in favor of Judge Morris's appointment to the high court. Although there were a number of outstanding women attorneys who were specialists in taxation, real estate transactions, corporate organization, Securities and Exchange practice, and the like, Judge Sharp said, "[f]ew, however, if any, have had the varied and considerable trial experience which, in my view, is an essential qualification for a superior court judge. In due course I have no doubt that many women will become skilled trial lawyers, but it will be a while yet."[74]

Given the political nature of judgeships and the historically small numbers of women in the legal profession, it was not surprising that few judicial plums had gone to women. Although the numbers of female law students were increasing sharply, graduates were still relatively young and inexperienced, and had yet to gain the connections and clout that their male counterparts routinely used to further their ambitions. Women attorneys previously had not been organized to lobby for their interests or to increase their visibility within the profession. That began to change with the formation of such groups as the North Carolina Association of Women Attorneys, which, among other things, gathered information about the availability of judgeships and recruited, screened, and endorsed women candidates. Judge Sharp, however, took a dim view of such women-only associations, believing it offered men the opportunity to let women rise within their own organization, defusing the demand for positions in the wider legal community.[75] She never deviated from her belief that "work has no sex" and that to set yourself apart was a mistake. A good lawyer was a good lawyer, and that was all that should be considered.

In a lengthy article for the North Carolina Bar Association publication, *BarNotes*, entitled "The Changing Status of Women Lawyers," Joslin Davis, herself a lawyer, noted that in North Carolina the distribution of female judges followed an "inverted bell pattern," with women represented at the highest and lowest levels of the judiciary but not in the middle, at the important superior court level.[76] In 1980 North Carolina had four women judges out of a total of approximately 200. After Chief Justice Sharp retired in July 1979, Judge Morris was the only woman at the appellate level, while the other three women judges were on the district court. The high visibility of a few token women, whether at the highest appellate level or in the "everyday" district courts where the vast majority of citizens experienced the judicial system, nourished the idea that there were few women with the qualifications to be judges.

North Carolina, the only state whose two appellate courts were headed by women, might have appeared to be an Amazonian stronghold on the cutting edge of society. But fifty years after Susie Sharp began practicing law in Reidsville, arguing cases to all-male juries, there were still so few women attorneys with trial experience in the state that the landscape was all but bare of potential female judges. It had been more than a decade since the Apollo spacecraft had landed on the moon, and two years since the birth of the first test tube baby, but in 1980 Susie Sharp and Naomi Morris were still exceptions to the rule.

Judge Sharp was fond of quoting Kierkegaard's remark that "life must be lived forward, but can only be understood backward." Looking back, there were some things she would never understand, but she had lived her life forward in every way, creating a new kind of individual on the scene, a woman whose accomplishments would have been exceptional for a man, let alone a flower of southern womanhood. She had made a place for herself in a man's world and ultimately had attained the highest position in the state's legal system. That she crowned her career by serving as chief justice was even more remarkable in that it was a position bestowed on her, not by a governor or her colleagues, but by a statewide election, a powerful validation of what had been by any measure an extraordinary journey.

One observer described the chief justice on the eve of her retirement: "At 72, she's a small and frail-looking spinster, standing only 5-foot-2. Her blue-gray hair is coiffed every week. She takes pride in her virtually unlined complexion.

"She wears glasses, and the collar of her black robe is lined with a bit of lace to soften its judicial severity.

"Yet, her frail appearance is deceiving, according to associates and friends who say her strong will and singlemindedness have enabled her to prosper in a legal world dominated by men."[77] Judge Sharp herself, ever conscious of her image and the toll extracted by her many worries, admonished the Winston-Salem artist who did a portrait of her to hang in the Wentworth Courthouse to paint her "as she looked when she went on the Supreme Court, not the way she looked when she came off."[78]

From the vantage point of 1979, it was hard even to recall the scared law student, the unwanted lady lawyer, the unanticipated trial court judge, the overwhelmed supreme court justice. She had been all these things, but had persevered to transform the common perception of each category. As a lawyer, she had been one of the very few women who undertook to study law, one of even fewer who entered practice, and almost if not entirely alone as a woman with an active courtroom practice. In her thirteen years on the trial court bench, she confounded expectations and made a reputation any man could envy. Who could measure the impact she had, first, by her mere presence at the bar and on the bench and, second, by the superior performance she had turned in at every level? She would never know how many people were influenced by her ceaseless proselytizing for active participation in democracy and her exhortations on jury service or the responsibility to be an educated voter. How many citizens, male and female, saw and heard her in the courtroom and were moved in some way, large or small, toward a broader understanding of the capabilities of women in society? To the end of her life, apparent strangers would approach her in the street or a shop or restaurant to recount the time they served on a jury in her court, and what a difference it made in their lives.

Susie Sharp served seventeen years on the North Carolina Supreme Court, during the turbulent 1960s and 1970s. There, she made her mark both as a fine legal mind and as an administrator. As the author of more than 600 opinions, some of them among the most thoughtful to come out of the court in its history, she elevated the level of discourse on the issues and established a benchmark for careful but innovative jurisprudence.[79] Considered "easily the most meticulous, thorough scholar on the bench"[80] during her tenure, she eased the way forward for the state's judges, attorneys, and litigants with her lucid and instructive opinions. At the time of her retirement, editorials across the state echoed the sentiment expressed by the *Winston-Salem Journal*: "She must be numbered among the most influential North Carolina jurists of this century. Her impact upon the state's legal and court systems can permit no lesser assessment."[81] According to another observer, "Her colleagues speak admiringly of her tenacity in pursuing an argument, and say she gave the court a spirit it is not likely to have again soon. They credit her with giving the court a greater reputation nationally and with pointing it in some new directions legally." The writer quoted one legal observer, who said, "There's no doubt about it, she did things very few justices could have done, and she did it because she knew the law better than anyone else and had absolute certainty of her convictions."[82]

That commentators could, and did, with equal certitude characterize Justice Sharp as a traditionalist who took few risks and as one of the most liberal members of the court is the key to understanding much about her success. She was both. Even her most "activist" opinions were deeply rooted in precedent from *somewhere* and exhaustively traced the legal reasoning as it applied to the North Carolina situation. By adhering to traditional—and rigorous—legal scholarship, she freed herself to search out new paths through law and public policy. She was a rule breaker but always careful to appear the opposite. Just as she camouflaged her private life with the appearance of a proper southern spinster, in some of her most important supreme court opinions she accomplished progressive results by being the scholar's scholar.

As chief justice, she made it her business to improve the quality of the state's judiciary in every way she could. Setting high standards for judicial conduct, she demanded the best from North Carolina's judges at every level. One commentator said, "If nothing else endures from her tenure on the Supreme Court her insistence on honest judges will be a mighty monument. More than any other public servant during the past decade, Susie Sharp fought to make state judges responsible for their actions and inactions. . . . Without that kind of leadership, the state judiciary can fall into traps leading to injustice and corruption."[83] As an administrator, she went the extra mile to see that judges and court personnel were compensated fairly, an effort that benefited the average citizen at least as much as those on the judicial payroll.

Nothing would have pleased Susie Sharp more than to be remembered without any mention of the fact that she was a woman. She had always wanted to be judged on her merits, ever hoping for the day that gender would be irrelevant. Dismissing the view that her gender had impeded her, she said, "If I had been a man, I just would have been one of many. My sex hasn't been a handicap to me."[84] To her, an obstacle was not to be confused with a handicap. She had liked being the first. "I broke the ice," she said. "I hope I made it a little easier for women who want to be lawyers and judges. But no one else can have the fun, the pleasure and the shock of being first."[85] It was ironic that her opposition to the Equal Rights Amendment would blur her image as an advocate for women's rights, an impeachment she never accepted.

Certainly she was an advocate for women's rights, both by word and by example. Her own life, however, as she perceived it, was not really about the struggle to be a successful woman in a man's world. She had achieved that success, and not without struggle, but she did not feel that her gender had hindered her. Her success was due to her extraordinary ability combined with fortuitous circumstances and, if anything, she would say that being a woman had been a benefit. In that sense, she did not experience in the same way the struggle most other women had endured. By the time of the ERA battle, therefore, Susie Sharp was far beyond grappling with the gender issue, even as many women were confronting it for the first time. Her personal response to the issue had been to work hard and ignore it. Thus she basically transcended the struggle in which so many women were mired.

Judge Sharp's opposition to the ERA, not to be confused with opposition to women's rights, can be attributed to an intellectual disagreement about the means to an end. The racist attitudes that she harbored during her life, however, do not support a similar justification. It can be said that she had been indoctrinated from infancy in these attitudes, perhaps more so than most people, and that she was far from the worst. Still, her failure to grow into a broader understanding on race was perhaps her greatest personal failing, viewed across her lifetime.

It should be remembered that, in the context of her times, her attitudes were not unusual. In fact, at the time it was the proponents of integration who were conspicuous. It was not until 1971 that the U.S. Supreme Court invalidated North Carolina's antibusing statute in *Swann*, a case originating in Charlotte,[86] and well into the 1970s before schools were truly integrated. The state's ban on interracial marriage remained on the books until invalidated by the U.S. Supreme Court in 1967.[87] The notorious Wilmington 10 case, arising out of race riots in Wilmington, North Carolina, dragged out for a decade, providing fodder for Amnesty International and other human rights activists until the state finally dropped its case in 1981. It would in fact be many years after *Brown* and the civil rights legislation passed in the mid-1960s before racism became politically incorrect. If Judge Sharp did not evolve in her views on race, she was not alone. And by the time real societal changes began to be manifested and—even more important—felt in the zeitgeist, Judge Sharp was in her seventies and unlikely to undergo a dramatic transformation.

In fact, it is the very prevalence of racism during her times that illuminates Judge Sharp's ability to rise above her own racism in her political and judicial roles. Her steadfast belief in the rule of law and her comprehension of the imperatives of North Carolina's future outweighed her racial prejudice. In her unhesitating rejection of I. Beverly Lake's segregationist gubernatorial campaign and her embrace of Terry Sanford's moderate approach to racial issues, as well as in her judicial decisions in which she ruled against proponents of segregation, she surmounted her deeply felt aversions and her opposition to the role of the federal government on the issue. To her, the rule of law, however much one disagreed with a particular law, was sacrosanct. And her understanding of the destructive effect of massive resistance, adopted by some other southern states, compelled her to support policies that would keep North Carolina's schools open and its businesses prosperous. A devout daughter of the Old South, she cast her lot with the New South. If the unvanquished tenacity of her racial prejudice was her greatest failure, her ability to overcome her basest feelings in the political and judicial domain was among her greatest triumphs.

As a woman, she had lived as she pleased, shouldering responsibilities both personal and professional without hesitation. "Actions have consequences," she wrote, and she was willing to accept both the satisfactions and the disappointments of hers. Perhaps it was no accident that her lovers were with one exception married and therefore "unavailable," leaving her free to pursue her career. She never swerved in her belief that a woman could not do justice to both marriage and a demanding career, her conviction that, "You have got to choose. When you get old and decrepit, you might rather have grandchildren than a lot of honorary degrees. You can't have both."[88]

Susie Sharp's affairs with married men, sometimes overlapping, are perhaps the most opaque aspect of her life, and constitute one of the most significant examples of contradictions in her character. On the one hand, she had determined at a young age that she did not wish to marry, a determination only temporarily derailed in law school when for a moment it seemed possible she might marry John Kesler, who without question was the love of her life. This preference for remaining single can be viewed as a desire to retain control over her life, her profession, her emotions.

On the other hand, her recklessness seems more like an invitation to chaos, not control. As a public person, she risked losing everything she had worked for. Had she been a man, it is possible that extramarital affairs, even had they become public, would have had no adverse effect on her career, especially in those pre-Clintonian years. One has only to think of President John F. Kennedy's widely known sexual exploits, which were protected by the press, to imagine how a man in her position could have kept his public and private lives completely separate. As a woman, it seems highly unlikely that she would have been granted this option. That she carried it off without disastrous results says something about her self-discipline and her focus on goals, as well as the deep affection in which she was held not only by her lovers, past and present, but even by their wives. She was not perfect, and would have been the first to say so. She would have argued, however, that she had enriched the lives of the men she loved without taking anything away from their separate families.

In her public role, particularly as a judge, she adhered to the strictest formalities. She was properly dressed, she went by the book, and she did not indulge familiarities. As one of her former clerks remarked, if her colleagues expected her to chitchat and comment off the record on the courthouse steps, for example, they would be disappointed. "She was on record from the moment she stepped out of the car," he declared.[89] The average citizen, knowing nothing of Judge Sharp's hidden private life, evaluated her on her performance as a public servant and a personage. As for Judge Sharp, she felt at ease with herself. "I find some comfort in a pronouncement of the Mississippi Supreme Court," she would remark. "'Judges,' said that august tribunal, 'are but men, encompassed by error, seasoned with sin, and fettered by falli-bility.' What woman couldn't meet those expectations!"[90]

There are no simple answers to the questions "Why her? Why then?" Judge Sharp herself liked to say that she was simply in the right place at the right time. Obviously, she was a rare intellect and a gifted politician. She had the inestimable advantage of a lawyer father who put her to work when she would otherwise not likely have found a job practicing law. "Had I hung out my shingle as a sole practitioner in 1929, I have little doubt that I would have starved," she once said.[91] She herself considered her father's openness to the idea that she might pursue the law as a profession to be "quite remarkable because he was a traditionalist, if there ever was one."[92]

Given the times, it is possible that she benefited from her sex as much she was hindered by it, as she always said. Perhaps it was true, for example, that "the jury listened to what [she] had to say—out of curiosity if nothing else."[93] Perhaps Governor Kerr Scott would never have thought to appoint a Reids-ville lawyer to the superior court bench, despite his or her political support, had the lawyer not been a woman. Certainly Governor Terry Sanford was de-lighted to have the opportunity to put the first woman on the North Carolina Supreme Court. But the rest was hers, forged out of hard work and conscien-tiousness and sheer brilliance. No one ever regretted appointing Susie Sharp to anything.

After fifty years in the legal profession, she was an institution. She had blazed a trail for other women to follow and made their way easier. Nonethe-less, it was decades after her appointment to the superior court in 1949 before women began applying to law schools in any substantial numbers. In 1960, more than ten years after Governor Kerr Scott put her on the bench, women made up only 4 percent of all law students nationwide, according to the *U.S. News and World Report*.[94] It was not until the mid-1970s that women began to be a significant presence at the entry level of the profession. By 1974, the year Susie Sharp was elected chief justice, 19 percent of all law students were women.[95] The numbers rose markedly between 1974 and 1979, the year she retired. During the 1979–80 school year, in North Carolina women composed about 28 percent of the law students in the state's five law schools.[96] Percent-ages for practicing female lawyers and women on the bench trailed behind, reflecting a similar curve. At the time Susie Sharp retired, approximately 550 of North Carolina's 8,000 lawyers were women, or about 6.5 percent.[97] Out of approximately 200 judgeships, North Carolina had four female judges, of whom only one, Naomi Morris, served on an appellate court. There were no women on the superior court.[98] The profession remained resistant to women in the ranks well into the 1980s. Some would say that even today the legal profession presents more obstacles for women than for men, despite great progress. But one wonders how much longer the improvements might have taken had it not been for Susie Sharp's example.

When she finally stepped down on July 31, 1979, Chief Justice Susie Marshall Sharp could do so with a sense of achievement and satisfaction. Her legacy, without regard to her gender, was assured in the annals of North Carolina jurisprudence.

EPILOGUE

It seemed right that, after half a century of hard work and sacrifice, Judge Sharp should have years of pleasure and enjoyment ahead of her. She looked forward to having time to travel, to indulge her thwarted interest in cooking, to relax for the first time in her life without the pressure of an all-consuming job. But her later years were to be filled with misfortune and tragedy on an epic scale.

She did have an opportunity to do some foreign traveling with Judge Bobbitt during the first few years after her retirement. With various groups, they visited England and Scotland, Scandinavia, Greece, and the Canadian Rockies and enjoyed themselves immensely despite some physical challenges. After their first trip, five weeks in the United Kingdom, Judge Sharp told one correspondent that her only regret was that she could not have gone sooner. Among other things, "It brought the realization that my increasing deafness is a real handicap, and something of a hazard, to travel."[1]

In Raleigh, she and Judge Bobbitt continued to go to the Justice Building every day, where the court provided them with makeshift office space. Judge Sharp described her routine in her new "chambers," a seven-by-seventeen-foot cubbyhole that she had formerly used as an overflow file room: "It has no 'phone, no push buttons—only files, a desk, a chair, and my faithful old manual typewriter. With the permission of the present C.J. I'm a tenant-at-will in order to sort, evaluate, and dispose of the 'papers' I accumulated during the 17 years I was on the Court. I'm not making very satisfactory progress because I want to keep more 'stuff' than I have space to warehouse. I'm finding it very hard to 'throw my life away.'"[2] She sorely missed having her faithful secretary, Virginia Lyon, to type her letters, in most of which she apologized for their unprofessional appearance.

She continued to be in contact with John Kesler by way of long phone calls and very occasional visits. In his eighties, he was acutely conscious that they were nearing the end. When Judge Sharp visited him one weekend, after putting Judge Bobbitt on the plane to Charlotte, he told her that the visit had "an aura of finality about it," and she went home with a heavy heart.[3] More and more his daughter Frances Sue took care of staying in touch on her father's behalf with cards and letters. Several times she brought her children along with her father to see Judge Sharp in Raleigh, where they took in exhibits at the Museum of Natural History and went to ride the carousel and miniature train at Pullen Park. In 1983 Judge Sharp went to see him in Salisbury and recorded a heartfelt conversation in which he told her that she had never understood his situation, "that in '28 he had no prospects . . . that his father was a tenant farmer on Judge Hairston's place." Judge Sharp told him, "It would not have made any difference to me if it had been the dismal swamp." He said he had always loved her. Finally, he asked, "Have we about covered it?" Judge Sharp responded, "No, we will never do that." She wrote, "We were then sitting on the foot of the bed and he said, 'Should I go?' I said, 'It is for you to say.' He stays."[4]

They remained in contact, but time was taking a toll on them both.

At her age, losses of all sorts were inevitable. Breck died in 1982, just a couple of months short of his ninety-first birthday. Judge Sharp fell and broke off two front teeth at the gum line, as well as hurting her knee and her arthritic shoulder. She was becoming forgetful, which upset her. But it was a series of family tragedies that defined her later years and from which she would never recover.

One May night in 1983 she was pecking away at her typewriter on the card table in her apartment when her sister Annie Hill called to tell her that their first cousin in Danville, Virginia, Alice Marie Garrett Anderson, had shot and killed her husband George, shot the young woman who was with him in the back as she fled, and then turned the gun on herself and blown her brains out. Alice Marie was the daughter of Annie Sharp's beloved sister Susie Garrett and Early Garrett, with whom the Sharps had shared a home in times of financial stress. Alice Marie and her husband, who was a lawyer, civic leader, and member of the Virginia House of Delegates, had been married for thirty-three years before they divorced in December 1982. The young woman was George's secretary, whom he had been dating seriously; there had been talk of marriage. The secretary was expected to live, but that mattered little to either Alice Marie or George, both dead. Susie wrote an old friend, "This affair is the worst thing which ever happened to our family."[5] She could not have imagined what was yet to come.

Her niece Susie Newsom Lynch, separated from her husband Tom, had taken her two small boys, Jim and John, to Taiwan just after Christmas 1979 in an ill-considered effort to study Chinese, against all advice of family and friends. The trip had been a disaster during which all three had had pneumonia, and Susie accomplished little if anything with her studies. In six months, they were back in Greensboro.

When she returned, Susie Lynch was so haggard and frail that her mother told her to get Dr. Klenner to give her a checkup. Diagnosing multiple sclerosis, he began a course of weekly intravenous treatment with massive doses of B complex vitamins. That summer Susie enrolled at Wake Forest University in anthropology, but quit after one semester and signed up for courses in business at the University of North Carolina at Greensboro. Living at home with her parents caused friction. Susie was unrelenting in her diatribes against the boys' father, Tom, especially after she learned he was seeing his dental assistant, Kathy Anderson, who soon moved in with him.[6] A North Carolina judge set up a visitation schedule giving Tom roughly a month with Jim and John in the summers, plus Christmas and spring vacation every other year, in addition to any visits he wished to make in North Carolina with two weeks' notice. Living in New Mexico made it extremely tough for him to see his children, and Susie fought him at every turn to make it as difficult as possible. Tom's mother, Delores Lynch, who was helping Tom pay the legal bills, was particularly vociferous about her unhappiness with the arrangements.

When Susie Lynch began taking "treatments" from Dr. Klenner for her purported multiple sclerosis, she struck up a renewed friendship with her first cousin Fritz, who was helping his father in the clinic. Soon Fritz was spending a lot of time at the Newsoms' with Susie and the two boys. Supposedly he was merely trying to support and protect his cousin during her time of trouble, but Florence soon suspected that the relationship was more than that, which was deeply distressing. Fritz's marriage had fallen apart in 1981. He had an apartment in Durham and told his family and others that he was in medical school at Duke. Weekends, he was working at his father's office as a physician's assistant. In fact, however, he was spending most of his time indulging paranoid fantasies and buying guns, ammunition, explosives, and military paraphernalia. To the guys he hung out with at the gun shop or his auto mechanic's, he spun chillingly convincing tales of exploits as an intelligence officer for Special Forces in Vietnam or as a clandestine agent for the army's antiterrorist Delta Force. Susie Lynch began telling her divorce lawyer, Sandy Sands, stories about Tom being involved with drugs, gambling, and underworld activities, stories that must have been invented or at least encouraged by Fritz.

In December 1982 Susie and Tom's divorce became final. In January Susie and her mother had a confrontation, and Susie moved out into an apartment. To her mother's pain and mystification, Susie seemed determined to cut all ties, communicating only with Fritz and the Klenners, who had always been the family outcasts. Susie's formerly beloved aunt, the chief justice of whom she had been extremely proud, tried in vain to have a conversation with her and was deeply troubled. Everyone was worried about the two little boys.

In July 1983 someone broke into 629 Lindsey Street in Reidsville and stole all the silver and jewelry in the house. Whoever did it knew exactly where the valuables were. Deep down, some family members feared that Fritz was the perpetrator, but there was no evidence. The following spring Dr. Klenner died. Judge Sharp made a point of warning Annie Hill about Fritz practicing medicine without a license,[7] and the clinic closed soon thereafter, but Fritz continued to see patients at the house.[8]

On July 22, 1984, Delores Lynch and her daughter Janie were brutally murdered at their home in Kentucky. Although the police said robbery appeared to be the motive, there were few clues and the crime went unsolved. Susie Lynch told several people, including her brother Rob and her lawyer, Sandy Sands, that it was a gangland killing resulting from Tom's debts to the mob. Rob, who was having his own struggles at this time, thought she was crazy. He thought about his cousin Alice Marie and wondered if there was a strain of madness in the family.[9]

At the time of the Kentucky murders, Jim and John were visiting their father in New Mexico. Tom, increasingly concerned about the boys, determined to try once again to get increased visitation rights, and he made overtures to Susie's parents in an effort to improve his relationship with them. Florence and Bob were so worried about Susie's strange behavior and about Fritz's increasing influence that they were receptive. Worries increased when Judge Sharp found out from her old friend Terry Sanford, who was then president of Duke University, that Fritz had never been enrolled at Duke.[10]

In early March 1985 Fritz moved in with Susie Lynch and the boys; he introduced her to several people as his wife. In mid-March, Jim and John assisted at a ceremony in the Rockingham County courthouse when Judge Sharp's portrait joined her father's on the courtroom wall. Soon after, Tom and Kathy took the boys to Disneyland, where they had a wonderful time. Yearning to see more of his children, Tom called Bob Newsom to ask if Bob would support him if he went back to court to request an additional two weeks' visitation per year. Specifically, would Bob testify that it would be beneficial for the boys to spend more time with their father? Bob agreed. The court hearing was set for May 23, 1985. The news that her father would be testifying for Tom was not well received by Susie and Fritz.

On the night of May 18, Bob and Florence were at Bob's mother's house in Winston-Salem. After Bob's father had died, he and Florence had spent many weekends with Nanna, who wanted to stay in her house but who was gradually declining. Bob and Florence had decided to move in with her, and the renovation undertaken to accommodate them was almost finished. But on that night someone entered the house and murdered all three of them. Bob and Nanna had each been shot three times. Florence had been shot twice; in addition, she had multiple stab wounds and her throat had been slit.

Apprised of the recent murders of Tom Lynch's mother and sister in Kentucky, the authorities began to piece together a theory implicating Fritz Klenner and possibly Susie Lynch in all the killings. Finally, on June 3, 1985, as law enforcement officers were organizing to arrest Fritz at the apartment, they saw him, Susie, and the two boys get into Fritz's heavily customized black Chevy Blazer and drive off. An attempt to get Fritz to stop at the apartment entrance failed and he drove away, followed by five law enforcement vehicles and monitored by a State Bureau of Investigation helicopter above. Firing an Uzi 9-millimeter submachine gun out the driver's window, Fritz wounded three officers as the bizarre caravan made its way at a stately pace through Greensboro, innocent bystanders diving for cover in every direction. Finally, just north of Greensboro near the community of Summerfield, the Blazer slowed almost to a stop and then exploded. There were no survivors. Evidence later revealed that before the bomb under Susie Lynch's seat was detonated, little Jim and John had ingested cyanide before they were shot, probably by their mother. As Jerry Bledsoe, a reporter for the *Greensboro News and Record*, meticulously documented in his newspaper coverage and later in his book, *Bitter Blood*, the evidence led to the conclusion that Fritz had been primarily responsible for the murders, while a question remained as to whether Susie Lynch herself had participated in the killings of Delores and Janie Lynch, in addition to those of her sons.

Judge Sharp, like other family members, was devastated. The series of tragedies was simply incomprehensible. Susie, her namesake, had been the apple of her eye. It was hard for her to accept that she might have been a willing partner with Fritz in the homicides, or even, as some thought, the manipulator behind it all. Looking back through her journal, Judge Sharp was appalled to find an entry for July 22, 1984, the day Delores and Janie Lynch were murdered, that said, "Fritz has not been home for 2 weeks and A. Hill has heard nothing from him. She knows nothing about him." Moreover, the entry continued, Fritz's sister Gertrude said "he is engaged in something big and bad."[11] According to Fritz, of course, he was always engaged in something "big and bad," but Judge Sharp must have asked herself what if anything could have been done to understand his and Susie Lynch's spiraling madness, and to avert the catastrophe. "After my best-beloved, youngest sister, her husband, whom I loved as a brother, and his saintly mother were killed, I thought I could never know peace until their murderer was identified and brought to justice. However, the subsequent events which identified him have shattered all hopes of peace," she wrote.[12]

The effect on Judge Sharp was desolating. The killings were certainly among the most important things that ever happened to her, even though they came so late in her life. She never fully regained her emotional equilibrium. Her sense of obligation to others was a powerful incentive to "keep up appearances," but she was deeply depressed.[13] A year later she was still struggling. Her doctor said her chronic fatigue and weariness were not due to any physical cause that he could find, but that she was suffering from depression.[14] "He says that I am trying hard but I am grieving and that is the trouble."[15] Perhaps the most telling sign of her incapacitation was her admission that she was uninformed about the candidates running in the spring 1986 primaries. "Get Franklin [Freeman] to tell me who to vote for and mark my absentee ballot," she recorded.[16] Also, she acknowledged that she was unlikely ever to write the book she had planned for so long.[17]

She found little comfort in her faith. Writing about her sister Florence's death, she said that it reminded her "of something Mamma said once: She did not believe that when we died we could look down and see what was happening on earth; that there could be no joy in heaven if those who went before could see the suffering of loved ones below."[18]

Adhering to her routine was one way of getting through the days. Her daily two-mile walk, however, led to another disastrous event. On October 23, 1986, she was at the intersection of St. Mary's and Peace streets in Raleigh, crossing with the light, when she was hit by a car turning left. Her injuries included a leg broken in two places, a broken shoulder, and a cervical fracture. She was in the hospital for two weeks, then spent almost two months in a rehab facility. Complicating matters, her leg did not heal straight, which threw her off balance. It was a slow process but with her indomitable will, she gradually regained her ability to walk, something the doctors confessed they had not expected to see her do.[19] Eventually, she was even able to drive again. And her vanity remained intact, as evidenced by her letter to the *Winston-Salem Journal* continuing her lifelong efforts to purge the files of unflattering photographs: "[A] dismal thought has just occurred to me: I will be 80 years old in July and if you don't have a better picture of me in your morgue, I'd better presume to offer to send you one."[20] When a visitor came to call in June 1988, she found Judge Sharp "beautifully dressed in a solid rose colored dress, hair coiffeured to perfection, and neck collar in place."[21]

Judge Bobbitt continued to be her daily companion, and she his. Until the late 1980s, local citizens could count on seeing the pair walking to the Mecca, a venerable Raleigh restaurant favored by the legal profession, for breakfast. After buying the morning papers, they would repair to their makeshift quarters in the Justice Building until time for lunch. In the evening they might attend a social function or share a light supper at home, her place or his. Their mutual support and devotion was lovely to behold. In 1984 Judge Sharp's former secretary, Virginia Lyon, remarked to Judge Sharp that she well remembered when the two had started going out together, seventeen years before. Judge Sharp's journal records her subsequent conversation with Judge Bobbitt the next night, when she took him home to his apartment after they had watched the news together. "When he tells me that he hates to take up so much of my time I tell him that the past 17 years have been the happiest of my life; that the loner was no longer lonesome; that I loved him dearly."[22]

Toward the end of the 1980s Judge Bobbitt's daughter, Sarah Carter, took the leading role in caring for her father, who, although his mind remained sharp, suffered from congestive heart failure. Sarah also did what she could to help Judge Sharp, who, despite her best efforts, was not coping well. Forgetfulness had become more than an occasional problem. Around 1990 Franklin Freeman among others noticed that Judge Sharp's mind was slipping. On one occasion, for example, a friend with a child in the fourth grade asked if she could arrange for the class to come down to the supreme court and get a little tour from the retired chief justice. Most uncharacteristically, as Freeman recalled, Judge Sharp was extremely worried about what questions they might ask and generally agonized over the prospect.[23] By Christmas 1990 Judge Bobbitt was trying, unsuccessfully, to convince her that she needed an assistant to help her with housework, meals, driving, and the like.[24] Judge Sharp's neighbor, Rebecca Gill, also realized that matters had gone downhill. The apartment was so full of old magazines, catalogs, newspapers, and mail that there was nowhere to sit and scarcely room to walk. As Mrs. Gill recalled, "There was not one spot where you could sit down or move or anything else except a couch where she kept a place where Judge Bobbitt and she would sit and one chair for a visitor."[25] Once Mrs. Gill found a stock certificate for 800 shares of General Motors mixed up with all the newspapers and had to wonder what might have disappeared in the morass. Mrs. Gill told Sarah Carter that something needed to be done and contacted Norwood Robinson, who was still practicing law in Reidsville.[26] As a result, Robinson took over Judge Sharp's financial matters and in coordination with Judge Sharp's siblings arranged for her to have the help she needed at home.

In 1991, at the age of ninety-one, Judge Bobbitt wrote Judge Sharp's brother Tom in Florida, to give him some idea of how matters stood.[27] He telephoned Judge Sharp every morning and every evening to chat and see that all was well, he said, and to make sure her assistant was nearby. At lunchtime one of the assistants would drive her to meet Judge Bobbitt and, often, his daughter Sarah, for lunch at the K&W Cafeteria. Then again at night, Judge Sharp would be taken to Judge Bobbitt's apartment for dinner. Inevitably, despite such loving care, she continued to fail, her great mind disintegrating and finally ceasing, for any practical purpose, to exist. Perhaps it was a mercy, for when John Kesler died in July 1992, followed by Judge Bobbitt the following September, she never knew it.

Susie Marshall Sharp died March 1, 1996. The *New York Times* headlined her obituary with the words "Trail-Blazing Judge." Her funeral in the Main Street United Methodist Church in Reidsville was attended by all the sitting justices of the North Carolina Supreme Court as well as most of the former justices. As her coffin was borne out the church door to be transported to the Sharp family plot in Greenview cemetery, the many members of the legal profession who had attended the service lined the walkway to the street while the rest of the congregation followed behind. She would have liked the summation offered by one superior court judge, who said, "Chief Justice Susie Sharp was to the trial court bench in North Carolina as the North Star is to sailors."[28]

A NOTE ON SOURCES

In addition to the letters and journals described in the preface, Susie Sharp's papers included a group of seven volumes, an assortment of desk book calendars and blank-paged books, into which Susie Sharp had copied letters from Breck and John Kesler, in shorthand. The four volumes containing Breck's correspondence covered thirty years, from 1928 to 1958. There were three volumes of John's letters, dating roughly from 1947 to 1966, with a few early letters from 1928 also included. Here I was forced to be selective if I hoped to live long enough to finish the biography. I have translated letters around key dates, but these volumes remain a largely untapped source for a future researcher.

Yet another category of material was the scrapbooks that Susie Sharp kept up throughout her life. This collection of newspaper clippings, memorabilia, and correspondence was extremely useful. In addition, the family had many photograph albums, and Louise Sharp could identify most of the people not otherwise identified.

Other sources will be found in the endnotes and acknowledgments. Unless otherwise identified, materials referenced are now in the Susie Marshall Sharp Papers in the Southern Historical Collection, housed in Wilson Library on the campus of the University of North Carolina at Chapel Hill.

NOTES

Abbreviations

ABS	Annie Blackwell Sharp
AHG	Allen H. Gwyn
JCK	John C. Kesler
JMS	James Merritt Sharp
MSB	Millard Sheridan Breckenridge
NCC	North Carolina Collection, Louis Round Wilson Library, University of North Carolina at Chapel Hill
NCSA	North Carolina State Archives, Raleigh, North Carolina
RCC	Rockingham Community College, Historical Collections Room, Gerald B. James Library, Wentworth, North Carolina
SHC	Southern Historical Collection, Louis Round Wilson Library, University of North Carolina at Chapel Hill
SMS	Susie Marshall Sharp
UNC-G	University Archives and Manuscripts, Walter C. Jackson Library, University of North Carolina at Greensboro

Introduction

1. Fitzgerald, *The Crack-Up*, 69.

2. As one scholar has noted, "Radical individualism, amounting at times to broad tolerance of extreme personal eccentricity, is set off against a social conformity so stultifying that it has sometimes been equated with paranoia and has been described in terms ranging from 'garrison psychology' to totalitarianism." Havard, *The Changing Politics of the South*, 5–6.

Chapter 1

1. "Upton G. Wilson Draws Parallels in Lives of Two Families of Sharpes [*sic*] in Rockingham," *Winston-Salem Journal and Sentinel*, September 14, 1930. Jim Sharp's father, James Marshall Sharp, married Eliza Merritt Garrett from Huntsville Township.

2. Louise Sharp, interview with author, November 8, 1994.

3. Rodenbough, *Heritage of Rockingham County*, 556.

4. Mildred Reed, "War Finance and Fraternalism Sort of Pastime for Reidsville Lawyer," *Greensboro News-Record*, November 18, 1945.

5. Louise Sharp, interview with author, November 8, 1994.

6. SMS to Sallie Sharp (James V.["Kits"] Sharp's daughter), June 22, 1982.

7. Sharp Institute, 1903–4 brochure, copy in SMS Papers.

8. See *Reidsville Review*, April 8, 1904; April 19, 1904.

9. Sharp Institute, 1905–6 [*sic*] brochure, copy in SMS Papers.

10. List of Taxables for Nutbush District, Granville County, N.C., for the years 1855 through 1860, NCSA.

11. According to the 1860 Granville County census, John Pomfret Blackwell Sr. owned thirty-nine or forty slaves, while contemporaneous tax records show between seventeen and twenty-two slaves for the five-year period 1855–60. 1860 Granville County (Nutbush District) Census, Slave Schedule; List of Taxables for Nutbush District, Granville County, N.C., for the years 1855 through 1860, NCSA. Because only adult male slaves were subject to tax, the two figures are not inconsistent. Annie Blackwell's older sister Blanche, in her later years, estimated their grandfather's holdings to be even larger, recalling that he owned about 2,000 acres and around seventy-five slaves. Blanche Blackwell Smith, "Reminiscences." Susie Sharp, in a journal entry dated August 6, 1964, declared that *her* grandfather, John P. Blackwell Jr., also owned 1,000 acres and slaves. This is certainly possible because children and adolescents often did have their own slaves. The younger Blackwell was about fifteen years old when the Civil War began. But Susie Sharp's remark that her grandfather owned 1,000 acres and slaves sounds like a conflation of chronology and ownership data.

12. Blackwell enlisted as a private at Yellow Tavern, near Richmond, on June 2, 1864. See Compiled Military Service Record for John P. Blackwell, Company E, North Carolina Cavalry (Ninth State Troops) (Confederate), National Archives Microcopy No. 270, roll 2 (NCSA F.6.57P), NCSA (indicating a payment of thirty-five dollars to Private Blackwell for "private horse"). In an interview with the author, Louise Sharp said that her grandfather Sharp had joined the cavalry because his father could give him a horse. However, in light of the referenced Confederate Army documentation as well as knowledge of the less privileged position of the Sharp family, I suspect she confused him with Grandfather Blackwell. See Louise Sharp, interview with author, November 8, 1994.

13. Smith, "Reminiscences."

14. Grandfather Blackwell then went to live with his namesake son, Annie's father, and his family. He died five years later in his eighties, still able to read his Bible without his glasses until the week of his death. Ibid.

15. ABS to Frances Garrett, January 6, 1964, courtesy of Clara Garrett Fountain.

16. Ibid.

17. Smith, "Reminiscences."

18. Ibid.

19. Carlson, "Homeplace and Tobaccoland," 63.

20. Dodd, *Reminiscences, 1811–1911*.

21. Register of Deeds, Granville County, Oxford, N.C., book 23, p. 155.

22. Edwards, *Gendered Strife*, 219–20.

23. Peace, "Zebulon Baird Vance," in *Zeb's Black Baby*, unnumbered page.

24. Ibid.

25. SMS to Mrs. Frank Gibbs, January 24, 1964 (thanking her for her book, *This Is*

the Way We Were [*sic*]). This book is actually called *The Way We Were* and was written by Mrs. Gibbs under her maiden name, Mary Polk, published by J. F. Blair (Winston-Salem, N.C., 1962).

26. Sallie Wortham Blackwell died when Annie Blackwell was nine years old. About six years later, John P. Blackwell remarried. The bride was a widow named Sallie Royster Pittard, who became a beloved stepmother to the Blackwell children, and who also emphasized the importance of their education.

27. ABS to Frances Garrett, January 6, 1964, courtesy of Clara Garrett Fountain.

28. Minutes, The Know North Carolina Book Club, March 14, 1967; *Reidsville Review*, March 26, 1948.

29. SMS, photograph album.

30. *Reidsville Review*, January 25, 1907.

31. Ibid., February 1, 1907.

32. Residents of Reidsville offered such inducements as "a free site, water protection and a glad welcome and cooperation on the part of all our people." *Reidsville Review*, January 25, 1907.

33. *Reidsville Review*, March 15, 1907; *Webster's Weekly* (Reidsville, N.C.), March 14, 1907. Rocky Mount had been incorporated as a city only the preceding February. Somewhat unusually, it straddled the county line between Nash and Edgecombe counties. The Sharps lived in a house at the intersection of Western Avenue and Nash Street. SMS to Mrs. S. B. Dominick, June 11, 1962 (based on information in letter with hand-drawn map from Annie B. Sharp, n.d.). Susie was born in Nash County.

34. Marshall was a family name on the Blackwell side as well. John Pomfret Blackwell Sr.'s mother was named Mary Marshall. See, e.g., Louise Sharp, notes to Commander Clark C. Tothrow, USN, for his introduction of Justice Susie Sharp at Cherry Point, N.C., May 1, 1962.

35. See Bledsoe, *Bitter Blood*, 106. According to Louise Sharp, the family "went bankrupt" twice, but I have been unable to document a bankruptcy filing for the Rocky Mount period.

36. James V. ("Kits") Sharp, interview with author, March 22, 1995; Mildred Reed, "War Finance and Fraternalism Sort of Pastime for Reidsville Lawyer," *Greensboro News-Record*, November 18, 1945.

37. Although a Wake Forest Alumni Directory published in 1961 shows that "James Muritte Sharpe [*sic*]" attended the law school in 1907–8, family history and other evidence indicate that he attended only a shorter review course designed to prepare students for the bar exam. E.g., JMS to ABS, January 19, [1908], courtesy of James V. ("Kits") Sharp. The letter is dated 1907 but undoubtedly was written in January 1908. Apart from the fact that the Sharps were still at Sharp Institute until it burned on January 22, 1907, the letter speaks of "baby," who is cutting a new tooth, a reference to Susie, born July 7, 1907, in Rocky Mount. Further confusing the issue, in a speech to the Chi Omega sorority in Chapel Hill on April 3, 1959, Susie Sharp mistakenly indicated that her father had passed the bar and received his law license in August 1907, probably because Professor Gulley's August bar review course was well established, whereas a winter course apparently was not as widely known. Author's telephone conversation with J. Edwin Hendricks, author of a history of the Wake Forest

University law school, October 26, 2004. Jim Sharp's letter to his wife clearly states that the term lasted about four weeks, but in a newspaper interview Susie Sharp once said he attended for six weeks. Mamie H. Braddy, "Your Honor—Judge Sharp!" *Twin City Sentinel* (Winston-Salem, N.C.), July 1, 1949.

38. A notice in the February 11, 1908, *Reidsville Review* states, "Mr. James A. Sharpe, Jr. [*sic*] of this county has been granted license to practice law." By May 26, 1908, he must have been established in practice because the *Review* noted that "Attorney J. M. Sharp, of Stoneville, was in town yesterday and gave us a pleasant little call." *Reidsville Review*, May 26, 1908.

39. Sharp joined the Masons in 1908, according to the *Greensboro Daily News* obituary, August 3, 1952.

40. Louise Sharp, author's interview with James V. ("Kits") Sharp and Louise Sharp, March 22–23, 1995.

41. Powell, *North Carolina through Four Centuries*, 411.

42. Case No. 374, filed September 8, 1914, Docket Book C, Page 166, in the District Court of the United States for the Western District of Virginia. The modern bankruptcy court came into existence in 1978.

43. SMS to Florence Newsom, February 15, 1976, courtesy of Robert W. Newsom III.

44. The family lore is that Ira Humphreys knew Jim Sharp, asked him to join his law firm, and the two were partners until Humphreys got elected recorder's court judge, but this is not supported by the *Reidsville Review*. Humphreys was already a judge in the recorder's court when Sharp arrived, and appears to have continued his practice as a lawyer as well. Sharp had his own separate ad for his solo practice from the earliest days in Reidsville.

45. Van Buren Humphreys, b. April 28, 1842, belonged to Company H of the 45th North Carolina Regiment. Henderson, *North Carolina: The Old North State and the New*, 397.

46. *Reidsville Review*, September 18, 1914.

47. Susie's second-grade teacher was Miss Dora Coates, sister of Albert Coates, who founded the North Carolina Institute of Government in Chapel Hill. Louise Sharp, interview with author, November 21, 1994.

48. SMS to Florence Newsom, February 15, 1976, courtesy of Robert W. Newsom III.

49. "Reminiscences of Local Businessman Francis Womack," *Reidsville Review*, April 21, 1988 (reprint of address given to Rotary Club in 1930s).

50. Ibid.

51. Butler, *Rockingham County*, 54.

52. "Death Claims J. M. Sharp of Reidsville," *Greensboro Daily News*, August 3, 1952; "President J. M. Sharp Names Committees," *Reidsville Review*, July 20, 1915; "Reidsville Boosters Down to Business," *Reidsville Review*, July 27, 1915.

53. Official Proceedings of the Twenty-fifth Annual Session of the North Carolina State Council Jr. O.U.A.M., 1915, 14, NCC.

54. Bureau of the Census, *Abstract of the Twelfth Census of the United States 1900*, 3d ed. (Washington, D.C.: Government Printing Office, 1904).

55. See Margaret Fillman Chaney, interview with author, January 18, 1995.

56. Annie Hill Sharp Klenner, author's interview with Annie Hill Sharp Klenner and Louise Sharp, January 23, 1995.

57. ABS, "History of Chatter Box," 1938, photocopy, courtesy Dr. Lawrence A. Taylor. The house had a different street number (255) at this time. SMS to MSB, April 25, 1955.

58. See Louise Sharp, drafts of autobiography written as part of her application to the navy, January 24, 1947. See also Evelyn Balsley and Dorothy Snodgrass, interview with author, January 9, 1995.

59. Annie B. Sharp, Inheritance and Estate Tax Return and accompanying appraisal of property at 629 Lindsey Street, Reidsville, N.C., by William C. Stokes, October 29, 1971.

60. SMS to W. C. ("Mutt") Burton, June 21, 1982.

61. Louise Sharp, interview with author, November 8, 1994.

62. Josephine T. Wilson, interview with author, May 31, 1995.

63. The Primitive Baptists, a group of ultraconservative Baptist churches found mainly in the South, broke away from the mainstream Baptist Church in America in the mid-nineteenth century. They are strict Calvinists, "believe in the total depravity of man, . . . practice immersion . . . and foot washing." Ferm, *An Encyclopedia of Religion*, 608. They oppose religious education for their preachers and Sunday School for their children, as well as any missionary society, "benevolent" organization, fraternal order, and the like.

64. ABS journal, February 15, 1923; December 25, 1922 (photocopy of handwritten original), courtesy of James V. ("Kits") Sharp, copy in SMS Papers.

65. Ibid., February 15, 1923.

66. Ibid., August 29, 1923.

67. Louise Sharp, interview with author, November 8, 1994.

68. ABS journal, November 19, 1922 (photocopy of handwritten original), courtesy of James V. ("Kits") Sharp, copy in SMS Papers.

69. SMS, speech at Caswell County Courthouse Dedication, July 18, 1976, Yanceyville, N.C.

Chapter 2

1. Female teachers had attended Randolph-Macon Woman's College in Lynchburg, Va.; Oxford College in Oxford, N.C.; Peace Institute in Raleigh, N.C.; and Winthrop College in South Carolina.

2. Among Susie Sharp's papers were a sizable number of folded-up schoolgirl notes.

3. Conversation with W. C. ("Mutt") Burton, December 1, 1994 (visit with Gladys Coates).

4. Tom Sieg, "Susie Sharp—She Broke New Ground Gently to Become N.C.'s Chief Justice," *Winston-Salem Journal*, May 17, 1987.

5. See Donie Counts to SMS, February 1929, concerning her prediction that Susie would marry Dillard Gardner.

6. Donie Counts to SMS, [summer 1924].

7. *Reidsville Review*, November 5, 1920.

8. Leslie Wayne, "Why, Susie, You Ought to Be Chief Justice," *Philadelphia Inquirer*, April 17, 1978.

9. SMS to Mr. E. R. Rankin, April 25, 1962.

10. Ibid.

11. W. C. ("Mutt") Burton, "No. 7 Is Significant in Miss Susie's Life," *Greensboro Daily News*, March 11, 1962.

12. Albright, "The Senator and the Simmons Machine," *The State*, December 1982, 18.

13. *Reidsville Review*, August 20, 1920.

14. Ibid., October 19, 1920.

15. Susie M. Sharp, interview by Jane L. Sharpe, 1982, audiocassette, AHG Papers, RCC.

16. SMS to JCK, October 20, 1957.

17. "Susie Sharp—Seeks High Post," *Wilmington Star*, November 3, 1974; see also Janie Sands Smith, author's interview with Louise Sharp and Janie Sands Smith, November 21, 1994, as well as author interviews with other family members.

18. *Reidsville Review*, August 12, 1921.

19. Louise Sharp, interview with author, November 8, 1994.

20. Ibid.

21. ABS journal, September 23, 1922 (photocopy of handwritten original), courtesy of James V. ("Kits") Sharp, copy in SMS Papers.

22. Ibid.

23. The twins developed bloody diarrhea accompanied by high fever. Subsequently, meningitis developed and death followed. Family recollection attributes the cause to tainted milk, bought from the local dairy. Ironically, the Sharps had gotten rid of the family milk cow in favor of commercial milk based on the theory that it would be safer because it had to be inspected.

24. *Reidsville Review*, November 20, 1922; August 31, 1923.

25. ABS journal, September 10, 1923 (photocopy of handwritten original), courtesy of James V. ("Kits") Sharp, copy in SMS Papers.

26. Family legend has it that the black woman who was doing the family's laundry, Matilda Purcell, jolted Annie back to life by telling her that it was not right for her to grieve so. The Lord would punish her by taking another of her children if she did not snap out of it, she told Annie. Louise Sharp, interview with author, February 13, 1995.

27. Ibid.

28. SMS to Allen Garrett, November 11, 1974.

29. *Reidsville Review*, June 4, 1924. Susie Sharp later claimed, "They never did announce at commencement which one of us was valedictorian. . . . They just didn't have it that year." Sieg, "Susie Sharp—She Broke New Ground Gently To Become N.C.'s Chief Justice." But the newspaper did publish their grade averages, and in her "Commencement Memories" book Susie wrote Dillard's name next to "Valedictorian." See also ABS journal, June 2, 1924 (photocopy of handwritten original),

courtesy of James V. ("Kits") Sharp, copy in SMS Papers. It is difficult to believe the valedictorian and salutatorian were not announced.

30. *Renocahi*, Senior Number, 1924, courtesy of Margaret Fillman Chaney.

31. See Colin and Roundtree, *The Changing Face of Justice.*

32. Ann Bach, "Justice Sharp's Advice: Strive for Excellence," *Asheville Times*, July 26, 1974.

33. "Susie Sharp—Seeks High Post."

34. E.g., ibid.

35. James V. ("Kits") Sharp, interview with author, March 22–23, 1995.

36. Ibid.

37. SMS to Laura Callis, February 1, 1975.

38. James V. ("Kits") Sharp, interview with author, March 22–23, 1995.

39. P. Dean, "Learning to Be New Women," 286.

40. See ibid., 289.

41. Ibid., 299. Born in 1884 in Carbondale, Illinois, Elliott graduated from Hanover College in Indiana in 1910 before undertaking graduate studies in history and political science at Columbia University in New York City, receiving her master's degree in 1913.

42. Harriet Elliot would eventually serve as dean of women at NCCW. Susie Sharp was very familiar with her achievements and views.

43. Bowles, *A Good Beginning*, 58.

44. A graduate of Mercer University in Macon, Georgia, Jackson came to the State Normal in 1909, becoming chairman of the faculty of social science and vice president of the college in 1921. It may be worth noting, in the context of NCCW's role with respect to women's rights, that Jackson, who had come to the State Normal only four years before Elliott, and who unlike Elliott did not have a master's degree, made $5,200 (plus $200 for his duties as vice president) in 1925, whereas Elliott, also a department chair just as Jackson was, made only $3,000. Department of Social Sciences faculty salaries (1925), General Correspondence Faculty 1925, Julius Isaac Foust Papers, UNC-G.

45. Bowles, *A Good Beginning*, 54. Walter C. Jackson became the third president of the college in 1934 and served until his retirement in 1950.

46. In 1939, when she was on the Sixth Circuit U.S. Court of Appeals, Judge Florence Allen received the first honorary degree awarded by NCCW.

47. Bowles, *A Good Beginning*, 119.

48. NCCW received its accreditation from the Association of Secondary Schools and Colleges of the Southern States in 1921, joined by Wake Forest and Meredith in that year; in the state, only the University of North Carolina, Trinity College (later Duke University), and Davidson College had previously been accredited. Bowles, *A Good Beginning*, 108. By 1930 NCCW would be the second largest woman's college in the nation, with 1,900 students and 170 faculty members. P. Dean, "Learning to Be New Women," 303.

49. See Chafe, *Paradox of Change*, 99–118.

50. Ibid., 107.

51. Ibid., 109.

52. Brown, "The College Girl's Attitude."

53. "Miss Byrd Talks on Women of the State," *The Carolinian*, April 29, 1926, 1, UNC-G.

The issue surfaced in the press as well, with one local paper devoting at least one article in 1925 to disproving the "Idea That College Women Do Not Study Matrimony," extrapolating from the class of 1897's statistics to suggest that of the 259 members of the class of 1926, 131 would marry. *Greensboro Daily News*, 1925, copy in Clipping File, "Woman's College of the University," 355, NCC.

54. *Alumnae News*, Woman's College of the University of North Carolina (August 1949), UNC-G. Mary Macy Petty, the chairman of the chemistry department, was a Wellesley graduate and had done advanced work at Harvard, Columbia, Cornell, and the University of California. Bowles, *A Good Beginning*, 41. See also newspaper articles in which SMS refers to this decision, e.g., Ellen Betts, "Judge Susie Sharp — Father Inspired Her Legal Career," *Raleigh Times*, January 15, 1974. Interestingly, however, her brother Tommy, a chemistry major at the University of North Carolina who became a chemical engineer, never discussed this turning point with her, in retrospect or otherwise, and was never even aware of her flirtation with chemistry. Thomas A. Sharp, interview with author, March 5, 1996.

55. Ringer, "Law as a Profession for Women," 12–13.

56. Ibid., 12.

57. In 1926 Kathrine Robinson married a fellow lawyer, Reuben Oscar Everett, and moved to Durham, where the two of them practiced together. Kathrine Robinson Everett practiced law well into her nineties, and died in 1992 at the age of ninety-eight.

58. *Alumnae News*, NCCW (October 1924), NCC.

59. *Philadelphia Inquirer*, April 17, 1978.

60. "Personalities of the Northwest," *Winston-Salem Journal and Sentinel*, October 15, 1939.

61. See Margaret Fillman (later Chaney) to SMS, March 1926 ("I presume you will be something of a sylph").

62. Margaret Fillman (later Chaney) to SMS, March 30, 1926. See also Janie Sands (later Smith) to SMS, September 8, 1926 (writing of a teacher, "My crush is just as violent as yours on Mr. Jackson"); Lena Keller to SMS, September 21, 1926 (reporting on visit to the Jacksons' house).

63. Frances Sharp to SMS, July 14, 1926.

64. SMS, interview by Jane L. Sharpe, 1982. At the time, students could apply to law school after only one year of college.

65. Raymond Mason Taylor, interview with author, July 23, 1996.

Chapter 3

1. Unless otherwise noted, historical information on the UNC School of Law comes from Wettach, *A Century of Legal Education*.

2. Hartig, "205 Years and Counting," 11.

3. At this time North Carolina was one of nineteen states requiring less than three

years of law school for admission to the bar, and one of only five states in which the state supreme court conducted the bar examinations rather than a board of commissioners appointed for that purpose.

4. Wettach, *A Century of Legal Education*, 57–58.

5. Ibid., 62.

6. Two years of college were required for admission after 1925, making Susie Sharp a member of the first class for whom two years of college were a prerequisite. Ibid., 51.

7. The cornerstone for Old East was laid in 1793, and it opened to students in 1795; Person Hall was begun in 1796. South Building was begun in 1798 but not finished for another decade.

8. Edy, "Excuses, Excuses," 32.

9. SMS, "Breaking the Barriers Which Face Women in Public Affairs," speech to Business and Professional Women's Club, Salisbury, November 9, 1957.

10. *Bradwell v. Illinois*, 83 U.S. (16 Wall.) 130 (1872).

11. Gasaway and Wegner, "Women at UNC," 706.

12. Mrs. Lilian Rowe Fry was admitted to UNC law school in 1911 and, although she did not graduate, she obtained her law license, becoming the second woman in North Carolina to do so.

13. In a 1996 *New York Times* article, Elizabeth Dole "acidly describes being one of five women in a class of 150 on property law at Harvard. They were called on only once, on 'Ladies Day,' when 'they were summoned to the front of the room to read a poem of their own composition.'" James Bennet, "The Doles Tell Their Two Tales, and Hope for One Happy Ending," *New York Times*, July 7, 1996.

14. It would not be until 1955, however, that the first woman joined the UNC law school faculty. Gasaway and Wegner, "Women at UNC," 708.

15. Ibid., 707. By 1920 North Carolina had licensed only twelve women to practice law.

16. According to the UNC General Alumni Association, there were no female graduates in the classes of 1927 or 1928.

17. Kerry Derochi, "The Carolina Woman," *Daily Tar Heel*, September 25, 1980.

18. SMS, speech to UNC law school banquet, n.d.

19. Ellen Betts, "Judge Susie Sharp—Father Inspired Her Legal Career," *Raleigh Times*, January 15, 1974.

20. Janie Sands (later Smith) to SMS [1926].

21. SMS, "The Law as Seen from the Distaff Side," speech to Georgia Association of Women Lawyers, Atlanta, November 5, 1949.

22. Ibid.

23. SMS, "Experiences in the Law," speech, [1950s?].

24. SMS to JCK, July 25, 1963.

25. JMS to SMS, January 12, 1927.

26. Ibid.

27. Derochi, "The Carolina Woman."

28. *Tar Heel*, October 2, 1926. Susie Sharp was defeated by Charlie McAnally. After 1929 the student newspaper was known as the *Daily Tar Heel*.

29. Derochi, "The Carolina Woman."

30. P. Dean, "Women on the Hill," 7.

31. *Tar Heel*, January 29, 1927.

32. P. Dean, "Women on the Hill," 9.

33. SMS, preface to *Fifty Years with Albert Coates*, by Gladys Hall Coates (Chapel Hill: North Caroliniana Society, 1979), iv.

34. Ibid.

35. Ibid., iii–iv.

36. ABS to SMS, September 29, 1926.

37. ABS to SMS, October 19, 1926.

38. JMS to SMS, November 5, 1926.

39. *Tar Heel*, February 26, 1927.

40. JMS to SMS, March 1, 1927.

41. JMS to SMS, May 30, 1927.

42. JMS to SMS, January 12, 1927.

43. *Tar Heel*, August 18, 1927.

44. E.g., Lee Kennett, July 26, 1927.

45. Constance Gwaltney to SMS, October 1, 1926.

46. Janie Sands (later Smith) to SMS, February 3, [1927].

47. Janie Sands (later Smith) to SMS, May 4, 1927.

48. SMS Journal Abstract, June 24, 1927.

49. *Tar Heel*, September 29, 1927.

50. Ibid. The faculty in 1927 consisted of the following professors: Dean Charles T. McCormick, M. T. Van Hecke, P. H. Winston, Albert Coates, E. Karl McGinnis, William Ney Evans, and Millard Sheridan Breckenridge. (A. C. McIntosh was on leave.)

51. Ibid.

52. Ibid.

53. Ibid., October 8, 1927.

54. Western Reserve University later joined with Case Institute of Technology to become Case Western Reserve University.

55. Unidentified "award citation" in SMS scrapbook, n.d.

56. Tribute to Millard Sheridan Breckenridge at the time of his death (August 24, 1982), signed by William B. Aycock, Frank R. Strong, and Henry Brandis Jr., two of whom were former students. The tribute was read in the Faculty Council meeting in October 1982, according to a letter from Jean Breckenridge to SMS, dated November 5, 1982.

57. Jean Breckenridge, interview with author, January 11, 1995.

58. SMS Journal Abstract, November 5, 1927.

59. Nuion Bouillat to SMS, September 26, 1927.

60. Janie Sands (later Smith) to SMS, November 10, 1927.

61. Donie Counts to SMS, January 1927.

62. Frances Sharp to SMS, November 8, 1927.

63. Frances Sharp to SMS, November 11, 1927.

64. Margaret Fillman (later Chaney) to SMS, October 5, 1927.

65. In December, Margaret Fillman (later Chaney) registered her astonishment at the turn of events in Chapel Hill, writing, "My curiosity is fairly burning me up — who is the male of whom you speak so lovingly? This is so sudden and to think you haven't confided in 'Grandma.' I'm surprised at my sheep gone astray. . . . You seem to be not in favor of practicing law — I'm more surprised every minute. Naturally it's hard to conceal your true feelings from your father. If the man were 'financially able' or 'sufficiently interested' to ask you to — ahem, er, er, a — be his bride, would you, Susie? I almost think not." Margaret Fillman (later Chaney) to SMS, December 13, 1927.

66. Helen Henry to SMS, January 21, 1928.

67. See Janie Sands (later Smith) to SMS, April 12, 1928.

68. SMS to JCK, October 25, 1953.

69. SMS Journal Abstract, February 1928.

70. Ibid., March 15, 1928.

71. Ibid., February 7, 1928.

72. Ibid., February 7, 1928; April 4, 1928.

73. Wettach, *A Century of Legal Education*, 92.

74. Ibid.

75. JMS to SMS, February 1, 1927.

76. Sallie Sharp to SMS, August 14, 1928.

77. JMS to SMS, August 7, 1928.

78. "Out of 181 Candidates for Bar 104 Pass Test and 77 Fail to Survive," *Greensboro Daily News*, dateline August 24, 1928.

79. SMS to JCK, September 14, 1951.

80. "Out of 181 Candidates for Bar 104 Pass Test and 77 Fail to Survive."

81. Edith Averitt to SMS, September 8, 1928 ("I wish J. K. had sent you one line").

82. Edith Averitt to SMS, September 17, 1928. For reference to Edith Averitt's status, see notes prepared by SMS for class reunion in 1965 on three typescript sheets beginning, "The following is a list of first-year law students who entered Law School in September 1926," SMS scrapbook.

83. Frances Sharp to SMS, November 23, 1928.

84. Order signed by Superior Court Judge J. H. Clement, November 30, 1928.

85. SMS, draft of speech to the American Academy of Achievement on occasion of Golden Plate Award, circa 1982.

86. Ibid.

87. Ibid.

88. *Tar Heel*, September 27, 1928.

89. Ibid., October 6, 1928.

90. Ibid., September 22, 1928.

91. AHG to SMS, October 3, 1928.

92. "Still Another Letter from Senator Sharp," *Reidsville Review*, May 18, 1928.

93. "To the Members of the Junior Order," *Reidsville Review*, October 5, 1928; letter to the editor, *Reidsville Review*, October 19, 1928.

94. Sallie Sharp to SMS, November 11, 1928.

95. JMS to SMS, October 31, 1928.

96. JMS to SMS, November 19, 1928.

97. *Tar Heel*, December 13, 1928.

98. Ina Young to SMS, July 30, 1929.

99. See Earle Garrett to SMS, October 7, 1944 ("the diaries you burned"); Gladys Morgan Happer, October 9, 1944.

100. Hereafter, "Breck Record."

101. Breck Record, August 21, 1928.

102. Ibid., August 29, 1928.

103. SMS Journal Abstract, February 7, 1929.

Chapter 4

1. Jim Sharp actually transferred title to the office furniture, filing cabinets, and books to Susie, subject to his right to use the property for the practice of law so long as he desired. Instrument dated January 1, 1929. Courtesy of James V. ("Kits") Sharp.

2. *Reidsville Review*, March 8, 1929.

3. Drachman, *Sisters in Law*, 174.

4. *Tar Heel*, February 23, 1929; March 2, 1929.

5. The photo was of Belle Doub, in the Wilmington newspaper. Edith Averitt to SMS, March 15, 1929. Alas, there is no evidence that Susie Sharp herself supplied the erroneous photograph, although such mischief might not have been beyond her.

6. SMS to Sallie Sharp (James V. ["Kits"] Sharp's daughter), June 22, 1982.

7. Ibid.

8. Ibid.

9. Mabel Bacon to SMS, February 2, 1929 [dated by SMS].

10. MSB to SMS, n.d. ("Fri. 3 p.m."); Breck Record, February 25, 1929.

11. Ruby Ross to SMS, February 11, 1929.

12. Program, Fourth Annual Dinner, The Law School Association, May 18, 1929, SMS scrapbook; *Tar Heel*, May 23, 1929.

13. Jefferson Fordham, who became the dean of the University of Pennsylvania Law School, was the uncle of University of North Carolina chancellor Christopher Fordham (1980-88).

14. Ruby Ross to SMS, April 4, 1929.

15. SMS to Mrs. May Thompson Evans, August 8, 1932.

16. Velma Jean Clary, "Susie's a Sharp Cookie," *Winston-Salem Sentinel*, October 24, 1974.

17. SMS, "Experiences in the Law," speech, n.d. She gave some variant of this speech on a number of occasions.

18. Ibid.

19. Maude Brown to SMS, September 17, 1929.

20. Howard Godwin to SMS, July 18, 1929.

21. SMS to J. S. Bourne, May 28, 1929.

22. JMS to J. S. Bourne, June 6, 1929.

23. The judge averred that her client "could no more acquire a good title to a stolen check made payable to cash which he himself had taken in good faith and for which he had given value than he could get title to a stolen horse or cow." SMS, "Experiences in the Law."

24. SMS Journal Abstract, April 2, 1929.

25. *News and Observer*, April 25, 1929.

26. *Raleigh Times*, April 25, 1929.

27. *Greensboro Daily News*, April 26, 1929.

28. Ibid.

29. MSB to SMS, April 26, 1929.

30. *Reidsville Review*, September 30, 1929.

31. Dorothy Fahs (later Beck) to SMS, September 26, 1929.

32. Ibid.

33. *Ware v. Knight*, 199 N.C. 251 (1930), argued in Surry County in October 1929.

34. SMS, speech at Swearing-in Ceremony for Melzer A. ("Pat") Morgan Jr. as superior court judge, Judicial District 17-A, Wentworth, N.C., September 1, 1981.

35. Ruby Ross to SMS, March 11, 1930.

36. *Reidsville Review*, February 28, 1930.

37. SMS, speech to UNC law school banquet, [May 10, 1940]. See "Law Students Given Awards at Carolina," *Greensboro Daily News*, May 11, 1940 ("The banquet program was featured by addresses by Miss Susie Sharp, attorney of Reidsville, and Prof. J. Douglass Poteat, of the Duke University law school").

38. Andy Vanore, who was one of Justice Sharp's law clerks, recalled her telling him about the quirk in the courthouse that allowed the jury to be overheard from "a room nearby." She told him that "although her daddy from time to time would visit that room, and although she was tempted from time to time to visit that room, she never did." Vanore recalled that out of concern for her father's reputation she admonished him, "Don't you ever tell anybody that now!" Andrew A. Vanore Jr., interview with author, July 31, 1998. See also William H. Sturges, interview with author, December 14, 1998 (denial).

39. Ruby Ross to SMS, March 11, 1930.

40. Hugh P. Griffin, interview with author, March 25, 1998.

41. SMS, speech to UNC law school banquet, [May 10, 1940].

42. Allen Langston to SMS, March 13, 1933. This practice apparently existed in other courthouses as well. Raymond Mason Taylor describes a similar situation in the Beaufort County Courthouse. Interview with author, July 23, 1996. The Reidsville attorney who heard Susie Sharp tell the tale on herself believes that she continued the practice even when she was a judge. Hugh P. Griffin, interview with author, March 25, 1998.

43. See SMS Journal Abstract, August 13, 1930.

44. [*Reidsville Review*], March 1930, SMS scrapbook.

45. Grady M. Hood to SMS, May 14, 1930. Hood graduated from the law school in 1928; he was a student editor of the law review.

46. SMS, speech to Cobb's School House PTA, July 6, 1929. This was a line she took directly from a cartoon she had carefully pasted into her scrapbook; like a num-

ber of her favorite sayings, she would repeat it many times over the years. The cartoon clipping has no visible signature or other identifying information.

47. Ibid.

48. "Susie Sharp — Seeks High Post," *Wilmington Star*, November 3, 1974.

49. Ibid.

50. "Supreme Court Stops a Woman's Talk; Miss Susie Sharp Has to Come Again," *Greensboro Daily News*, April 2, 1930.

51. Ibid.

52. *Ware v. Knight*.

53. See, e.g., MSB to SMS, [August 31, 1930] ("Labor Evening").

54. Butler, *Rockingham County*, 89.

55. His name was Jack Massey. See Maude Brown to SMS, July 1929, and other references to "Jack" or "JM."

56. Maude Brown to SMS, July 1929.

57. Maude Brown to SMS, November 3, 1929.

58. SMS Journal Abstract, April 20, 1929.

59. See, e.g., Maude Brown to SMS, April 28, 1930 ("I was sorry to hear about Mr. Jim's ultimatum in regard to the lawyer friend"). In later years, when asked the inevitable question as to why she had not married, Susie Sharp occasionally claimed that she had been "very fond" of a young man when she was first practicing law with her father, but that her father had disapproved of her suitor, and she had thereafter been "married to the law." See, e.g., Andrew A. Vanore Jr., interview with author, July 31, 1998. This was a convenient story that played into the common assumptions about the spinster judge and served to satisfy the listener without further explanation.

60. Ruby Ross to SMS, May 1930.

61. Arlene Edwards, "A Life Well Lived," *Winston-Salem Journal*, January 8, 1978.

62. *Reidsville Review*, June 11, 1930.

63. Louise Sharp, interview with author, November 21, 1994.

64. Louise Sharp, conversation with author, n.d.

65. JMS to SMS, September 24, 1930.

66. Louise Sharp, conversation with author, n.d.

67. Charles T. McCormick to SMS, August 18, 1930.

68. Ruby Ross to SMS, August 24, 1930.

69. Ruby Ross to SMS, [August 1930] (hand-dated by SMS).

70. Charles T. McCormick to SMS, August 27, 1930.

71. Ibid.

72. Ibid.

73. SMS to Charles T. McCormick, September 4, 1930.

74. MSB to SMS, [August 31, 1930] ("Labor Evening").

75. Ibid.

76. Ibid.

77. Ibid.

78. The camp was "hidden back in the hills" about six miles northwest of Reidsville, just off N.C. Highway 65. *Reidsville Review*, July 2, 1930. Called Camp Cherokee, it was begun in 1924. *Reidsville Review*, July 2, 1930; July 15, 1931.

79. SMS Journal Abstract, July 7, 1930; July 8, 1930.

80. Ibid., July 20–22, 1930.

81. Venitah Breckenridge's obituary in the *News and Observer*, January 22, 1966, said she was a native of Bath, South Dakota, who died at the age of seventy-four, which would make her a year younger than Breck, who was born in 1891.

82. Jean Breckenridge, interview with author, January 11, 1995.

83. Jean Breckenridge, conversation with author, May 10, 2000.

84. Breck Record, June 9, 1929.

85. Ibid., December 6, 1929.

86. Ibid., May 10, 1930.

87. Ibid., June 1, 1930.

88. JMS to SMS, September 24, 1930.

89. After an initial, unhappy experience with an unnamed landlady, Susie Sharp moved into a room rented by Dr. and Mrs. Henry Roland Totten. Dr. Totten was a professor of botany at the university, and his wife Addie was known as "Mrs. Garden Club of North Carolina." Childless, the two were generous with their time and expertise, contributing greatly to the natural beauty of Chapel Hill and beyond. Mrs. Totten and Mrs. Sharp, sharing their passion for growing things, were soon sending each other plants from their gardens. The warmth of the Tottens' home went a long way to alleviate Susie Sharp's unhappiness with her situation.

90. "Salesman Sharpe [*sic*]," newspaper clipping, n.p., n.d.; "Jus? — Lux?" [*Daily Tar Heel?*], [1931], SMS scrapbook.

91. See reference in *Daily Tar Heel*, October 25, 1930, to review of *An American Epoch* in preceding Sunday's *New York Times*.

92. *Daily Tar Heel*, November 2, 1930; SMS Journal Abstract, January 8, 1931.

93. ABS to SMS, November 15, 1930 (note appended to letter from Sallie Sharp to ABS, forwarded to SMS).

94. Sallie Sharp to Arthur Taylor, March 28, 1934, courtesy of Dr. Lawrence A. Taylor.

95. SMS to Sallie Sharp (James V. ["Kits"] Sharp's daughter), June 22, 1982.

96. Margaret Fillman (later Chaney) to SMS, September 26, 1930.

97. ABS to SMS, September 26, 1930.

98. Ibid.

99. JMS to SMS, October 22, 1930.

100. See, e.g., Sallie Sharp to ABS, November 15, 1930; March 6, 1931; JMS to SMS, September 18, 1931.

101. SMS Journal Abstract, March 3, 1932. See also ibid., November 9, 1931; February 27, 1932.

102. ABS to SMS, n.d. ("Friday p.m."). See also SMS Journal Abstract, May 9, 1931 ("Buy radio") and other contemporaneous correspondence.

103. Sallie Sharp to ABS, November 15, 1930.

104. ABS to SMS, June 18, 1931; Louise Sharp, interview with author, November 21, 1994.

105. Annie Hill Sharp (later Klenner) to ABS, [1931] (fragment, "be a nurse, as best I can"), signed "Higgy," Annie Hill's nickname.

106. JMS to SMS, January 21, 1931.

107. Ibid.

108. Margaret Fillman (later Chaney) to SMS, October 15, 1930.

109. The spelling was changed in later years to Hillsborough.

110. Breck Record, December 16, 1930.

111. Ibid., January 8, 1931.

112. Ibid., January 27, 1931.

113. Ibid., March 26, 1931.

114. SMS Journal Abstract, July 20, 1931; September 1, 1931.

115. Ibid., September 30, 1931; November 5, 1931.

116. Breck Record, June 9, 1931.

117. Ibid., June 26, 1931.

118. Ibid., July 7, 1931.

119. Ibid., October 31, 1931.

120. E.g., SMS Journal Abstract, June 22, 1931.

121. Dorothy Fahs Beck to SMS, October 29, 1930.

122. Dorothy Fahs Beck to SMS, April 13, 1931.

123. Dorothy Fahs Beck to SMS, May 10, 1931.

124. E. C. Hamblen, M.D., Associate Professor of Obstetrics and Gynecology, Duke University School of Medicine, to SMS, July 18, 1932. By way of second opinion, Susie Sharp wrote her dear friend Gladys Morgan, whom she had met when Gladys was in medical school at UNC. Gladys's advice was not much help. "The only thing that I have heard suggested for such conditions that you did not mention — is to get married. Anyway I believe in Birth Control." Gladys Morgan (later Happer) to SMS, July 29, 1932.

125. Breck Record, June 15, 1931.

126. Ibid., July 14, 1931.

127. Ibid., February 23, 1932.

128. SMS Journal Abstract, December 24, 1931; Breck Record, December 24, 1931.

129. Breck Record, July 18, 1931.

130. Ibid., February 2, 1932. In fact, there is evidence in later entries that Venitah knew of more than one other extramarital affair, when Susie Sharp quotes her referring to the "others."

131. Ibid., February 9, 1932.

132. Ibid., February 2, 1932.

133. Ibid., June 11, 1932.

134. *In re Beale's Will*, 202 N.C. 618 (1932) (caveat to will of Eva R. Beale upheld). Allen Gwyn was opposing counsel. See "Court Impressed by Miss Sharp's Speech," *Greensboro Daily News*, April 5, 1932.

135. Breck Record, August 12, 1932.

136. JMS to SMS, February 3, 1932.

137. Sallie Sharp to SMS, June 30, 1932.

138. Margaret Fillman (later Chaney) to SMS, June 13, 1932.

139. Margaret Fillman (later Chaney) to SMS, July 11, 1932.

140. Breck Record, February 23, 1932.

141. Ibid., May 9, 1932.

142. Ibid., June 4–6, 1932.

143. SMS Journal Abstract, June 6, 1932.

144. Allen Langston to SMS, July 20, 1932.

145. Maude Brown to SMS, January 29, 1933.

146. Allen Langston to SMS, July 4, 1933. She did not attend, however, pleading the press of work. The guests apparently included only the Elliotts, the Carrolls, the McIntoshes, and the Van Heckes. Allen Langston to SMS, August 12, 1933.

147. Breck Record, July 23, 1932.

148. Ibid., August 12, 1932.

Chapter 5

1. SMS, interview by Jane L. Sharpe, 1982, audiocassette, AHG Papers, RCC.

2. JMS to Fred P. Parker Jr., August 17, 1935.

3. JMS to Greensboro Travelers claim adjuster, March 26, 1936.

4. Louise Sharp, author's interview with Louise Sharp and Annie Hill Sharp Klenner, January 23, 1995.

5. Ibid.

6. SMS, interview by Jane L. Sharpe, 1982. See also SMS to Judge Johnson J. Hayes, April 3, 1962.

7. SMS, interview by Jane L. Sharpe, 1982.

8. SMS Journal Abstract, September 22, 1932.

9. *Reidsville Review*, December 8, 1933.

10. Ibid.

11. Davis, "The Changing Status," 8.

12. Ibid.

13. Ibid., 9.

14. Ibid.

15. Kay Miller, "Susie Sharp: The Law's Been Her Life," *Winston-Salem Journal*, July 3, 1977.

16. SMS, "The Law as Seen from the Distaff Side," speech to Georgia Association of Women Lawyers, Atlanta, November 5, 1949.

17. SMS to JCK, October 9, 1952.

18. Miller, "Susie Sharp: The Law's Been Her Life."

19. Tom Sieg, "Susie Sharp—She Broke New Ground Gently to Become N.C.'s Chief Justice," *Winston-Salem Journal*, May 17, 1987.

20. Allen Langston to SMS, February 22, 1934.

21. SMS remarks on the occasion of the presentation of the portrait of J. Hampton Price in the Rockingham County Courthouse, July 10, 1972 (quoting Arthur Train's fictional lawyer, Old Mr. Tutt) ("Friends, Associates Gather for Price," *Eden News*, July 12, 1972).

22. Allen H. Gwyn Jr., interview with author, January 27, 1995.

23. SMS Journal Abstract, September 19, 1932.

24. "Temporary Order in Child Custody Case," [*Reidsville Review*], [1933], SMS scrapbook.

25. Ibid.

26. SMS to MSB, January 15, 1965.

27. Nina Tyner to JMS, handwritten note [1934] (emphasis in original), SMS scrapbook.

28. *Tyner v. Tyner*, 206 N.C. 776 (1934). At the time, the common-law presumption was that the father had the right of custody of minor children, not the mother, although the general rule had been relaxed in recent years. The trial court heard forty-three affidavits on behalf of the mother and forty-eight on behalf of the father. Chief Justice Stacy, Justice Brogden, and Justice Clarkson dissented, noting among other things that it did not appear that an injustice would be done to anyone by allowing Mrs. Tyner partial custody. Ibid. at 782.

29. SMS to MSB, January 16, 1965.

30. W. C. ("Mutt") Burton, "Allen Gwyn, An Introduction" (campaign brochure for North Carolina Supreme Court election), 1952.

31. *Reidsville Review*, August 4, 1933.

32. Allen Langston to SMS, August 12, 1933.

33. Sallie Sharp to Arthur Taylor, August 7, 1933, courtesy of Dr. Lawrence A. Taylor.

34. SMS, speech to law students, [1951].

35. E.g., SMS, "Experiences in the Law," speech, n.d. See also W. C. ("Mutt") Burton, "Reidsville Negro Woman Wins 'Separation,'" *Greensboro Record*, November 26, [c. 1933], SMS scrapbook; author's telephone conversation with W. C. ("Mutt") Burton, February 16, 1995.

36. Thomas A. Sharp to author, August 24, 1995.

37. JMS to Mrs. Lula Reid, May 11, 1934.

38. Thomas A. Sharp to author, August 24, 1995.

39. Miller, "Susie Sharp: The Law's Been Her Life."

40. Background on this subject is from Salmond, "'The Burlington Dynamite Plot,'" 398–434.

41. SMS Journal Abstract, March 4–5, 1935; Paul Green to SMS, April 7, 1935, Paul Green Papers, SHC.

42. Canceled check, Paul Green to Susie Sharp, March 4, 1935; "Report of the Chapel Hill Defense Committee for the Burlington Workers" (statement of expenses), Paul Green Papers, SHC.

43. Paul Green to Mr. Powell, May 18, 1954, Paul Green Papers, SHC.

44. Ruby Ross to SMS, May 16, 1935 (enclosing May 14, 1935, *Tar Heel* clipping, "For a Fair Trial," letter to the editor, asking for donations for the defense). The appeal was heard in the North Carolina Supreme Court the following August, without Susie Sharp's participation.

45. SMS to Annie Hill Sharp Klenner, December 11, 1937.

46. SMS Journal Abstract, June 4, 1934; "Just among Friends," [*Reidsville Review*], September 14, 1939.

47. SMS Journal Abstract, June 10, 1937.

48. The company was extraordinarily generous. For the first five months of their lives, the quads remained in the hospital. When they did go home, it was to a 148-acre farm Pet Milk had purchased for the family from none other than Jim Sharp, near his old home place at Intelligence. The company paid to add a room onto the little house there, and hired a nurse named Elma Pearl Saylor to care for the quads around the clock. The Fultzes had six other children born before the quads and one born soon after, however, and the circumstances were so difficult that in 1952 Mrs. Saylor and her husband Charles legally adopted the four girls, who went to live with them in nearby Caswell County.

Pet Milk took a personal interest in the well-being of the quads far beyond any commercial benefit received, and Susie Sharp thought very highly of the representatives with whom she dealt over the years. The Fultz quads, however, were bitter in later years about what they perceived as exploitation by the company and resented the termination of their support. Three of the quads, Mary Louise, Mary Ann, and Mary Alice died of breast cancer at the ages of 45, 50, and 55, respectively, a disease which the surviving quad, Mary Catherine, believed may have been related to the massive vitamin doses they were given by Dr. Fred Klenner. See, e.g., Lorraine Ahearn, "And Then There Was One," *Greensboro News-Record*, six-part series, August 4–9, 2002.

49. SMS to "Laurie," July 13, 1982.

50. AHG to Governor Terry Sanford, February 11, 1962, AHG Papers, RCC.

51. SMS, interview by Jane L. Sharpe, 1982.

52. Among the papers found in the old Sharp & Sharp office safe when it was cleaned out in 2004 were the letters of authorization and the contract retaining Susie Sharp as attorney for the plaintiffs. Estella Harmel Wilkins, Attorney, to SMS, August 8–18, 1944.

53. SMS, "The Law as Seen from the Distaff Side."

54. W. C. ("Mutt") Burton, "Six Tar Heels Almost Marooned When Barristers' Ship Sails," *Greensboro Record*, August 23, 1935.

55. SMS to Fred P. Parker Jr., August 28, 1935.

56. Louise Tesh Wyrick, interview with author, February 13, 1995. See also correspondence between SMS and Margaret Newnam discussing the legalities of the abdication and marriage, etc., attached to clipping dated December 5, [1936]. (The abdication was December 11, 1936.)

57. During the summers of 1930, 1932, and 1933, and during the winter of 1934–35, Professor Breckenridge worked in Washington, D.C., "as a legal advisor to the House Interstate and Foreign Commerce Committee, which was engaged in an effort to regulate holding companies through direct legislation and through the taxing power. . . . [H]e contributed to recommendations and proposed legislation which formed the basis of reports to both the 71st and 73rd Congresses." He was a member of the National Conference on Uniform Laws (1934–35). In 1935 he and Emmitt C.

Willis initiated annotations to the North Carolina Workmen's Compensation Act, editing succeeding revisions of the statute. In 1952 this work was taken over by the North Carolina General Statutes Commission, on which Breckenridge had served as a member from 1943 to 1945. "Service to the Profession Typifies Career of Professor Millard Sheridan Breckenridge," *Tar Heel Barrister*, May 1960, 6.

58. Breck Record, November 12, 1932.

59. Ibid., January 29, 1933.

60. Jean Breckenridge, interview with author, January 11, 1995.

61. SMS Journal Abstract, October 1, 1935.

62. Ibid., August 31, 1936.

63. Ibid., April 7, 1939.

64. Sieg, "Susie Sharp—She Broke New Ground Gently to Become N.C.'s Chief Justice."

65. Louise Sharp, draft introduction for Susie Sharp's appearance at Cherry Point, N.C., on May 1, 1962.

66. Ibid.

67. Sallie Sharp to Arthur Taylor, April 3, 1933, courtesy of Dr. Lawrence A. Taylor.

68. Sallie Sharp to SMS, November 7, 1936.

69. Sallie Sharp to Arthur Taylor, February 24, 1934, courtesy of Dr. Lawrence A. Taylor.

70. Sallie Sharp to Arthur Taylor, April 5, 1934, courtesy of Dr. Lawrence A. Taylor.

71. Louise Sharp, interview with author, November 14, 1994.

72. JMS to Fred Klenner, February 15, 1942. One notes that this was the day after Valentine's Day.

73. James V. ("Kits") Sharp, interview with author, March 22, 1995.

74. Like Susie and Annie Hill, Tommy was salutatorian of his high school class.

75. Louise Sharp, draft of autobiography for application to the navy, January 24, 1947.

76. Louise Sharp to SMS, March 11, 1948.

77. SMS to Florence Sharp Newsom, February 15, 1976, courtesy of Robert W. Newsom III.

78. Ibid.

79. Florence Sharp to SMS, September 24, 1942.

80. James V. ("Kits") Sharp to SMS, July 7, 1985; James V. ("Kits") Sharp, interview with author, March 22–23, 1995.

81. Rose Post, "Justice Corrected Errors," *Salisbury Post*, March 7, 1996.

82. Gladys Morgan Happer to SMS, June 21, 1948.

Chapter 6

1. SMS campaign speech, chief justice election, Winston-Salem, N.C., 1974.

2. SMS to Mrs. Frank Gibbs, January 24, 1964.

3. JMS, "J. M. Sharp Says Let the Truth Speak for Itself," *Reidsville Review*, May

14, 1946 (article by Sharp in support of John Folger's election to the U.S. House of Representatives).

4. SMS Journal Abstract, January 31, 1933; JMS to U.S. Representative William B. Umstead, February 18, 1933.

5. JMS to Attorney General of the United States, Endorsements of J. M. Sharp of Reidsville, North Carolina, for the Position of District Attorney for the Middle District of North Carolina, courtesy of James V. ("Kits") Sharp. This black binder containing a thick collection of endorsements for Jim Sharp was among the materials found in the safe of the former Sharp & Sharp law offices in October 2004. See also JMS to U.S. Representative William B. Umstead, February 18, 1933 (listing supporters, including "practically all of the judges in or who border on the middle district, the Attorney General of the State, the Secretary of State . . . Mrs. Palmer Jerman, National Committee woman of North Carolina, practically a complete list of all the attorneys of Orange County, including the faculty of the University Law School, the attorneys of Person County, Caswell County").

6. Theodore C. Bethea to Governor Clyde R. Hoey, June 4, 1937, AHG Papers, RCC. After winning the election, Gwyn wrote to Governor Hoey, thanking him for "the fair deal" given him during the contest. "I am satisfied that the power of your office was not thrown in the scales against me." AHG to Governor Clyde R. Hoey, July 12, 1938, AHG Papers, RCC.

7. "Mr. Glidewell Says He Was Joking with Newspaper Man," *Reidsville Review*, February 4, 1928.

8. See, e.g., SMS, speech draft fragment ("I got into politics in the early thirties"), [1974].

9. SMS to May Thompson Evans, August 8, 1932.

10. *Reidsville Review*, August 31, 1932.

11. Ibid., September 2, 1932. Rockingham County historically had been a particularly political county. In a modern example of this tradition, in 1976 longtime Rockingham County sheriff Carl H. Axsom was inaugurated in Chicago as the president of the National Sheriffs' Association, an honor indicating his political prowess on both a local and national level. June Milby, *Reidsville Review*, June 21, 1976. In 1932 a county sheriff was arguably one of the most political and powerful officials in the state.

12. SMS, speech draft fragment ("I got into politics in the early thirties"), [1974].

13. SMS, "Women in Politics," speech draft, [c. 1948].

14. *State v. Knight*, 169 N.C. 333 (1915).

15. *Bank v. Redwine*, 171 N.C. 559 (1916). In this case the majority did not reach the question of whether a woman could be a deputy clerk of court but elaborated at length on the legal reasons why it was impermissible, "lest citizens might be misled by our silence." Ibid. at 569. Chief Justice Walter Clark, however, filed a lengthy dissent addressing this issue.

16. Lillian Exum Clement (who married Elias Eller Stafford three months into her legislative term) was a lawyer and, according to one newspaper article, a former sheriff's deputy. Jena Heath, "Marshal Reflects Rise of Women," *News and Observer*, January 12, 1997. She was the second woman in North Carolina, after Julia M. Alexan-

der, to practice law without a male partner. Colin and Roundtree, *The Changing Face of Justice*, 18.

17. Gertrude Dills McKee died in 1948 just before entering her fourth term. Marjorie Hunter, "Few N.C. Women Have Made Political History," *Winston-Salem Journal and Sentinel*, January 7, 1951.

18. "Bailey and Hancock Speak at Reidsville," *Greensboro Daily News*, November 18, 1933.

19. Jackson Day Dinner program, January 8, 1936, SMS scrapbook.

20. "Managers for Gregg Cherry Are Announced," *Reidsville Review*, March 20, 1944. He chose county coroner and civic leader George Hunt to be his Rockingham County campaign manager.

21. Cheney, *North Carolina Government, 1585–1974*, 1371.

22. Ibid.

23. Margarette Smethurst, "More Than Jury Duty Hangs on Adoption of Amendment," *News and Observer*, November 3, 1946.

24. See Key, *Southern Politics*, 213.

25. Ibid.

26. She replaced another woman, Mrs. J. R. Page of Aberdeen, who had died. Governor Cherry reappointed three existing members of the board, and named one new member, H. P. Taylor of Wadesboro, to fill the unexpired term of Herman Cone of Greensboro, who had resigned. Susie Sharp's term was to expire July 1, 1948. "Miss Susie Sharp Is Named to State Board," n.p., n.d., SMS scrapbook.

27. *State v. Emery*, 224 N.C. 581 (1944).

28. Pat Borden, "Women Show Strength on Political Scene," *Charlotte Observer*, October 31, 1974. Neither Susie Sharp's papers nor newspaper accounts, however, provide a record of her precise activities.

29. "Under the Dome," *News and Observer*, November 11, 1944.

30. Margarette Smethurst, "Women Don't Have to Serve on Juries to Cast Ballots," *News and Observer*, November 12, 1944.

31. "Turning the Clock Back," *News and Observer*, November 10, 1944.

32. Ibid.

33. *Emery*, 224 N.C. at 591.

34. "Turning the Clock Back."

35. *Emery*, 224 N.C. at 587.

36. Ibid. (emphasis added).

37. Levy, Note, "Constitutional Law—Right of Women to Serve on Juries," 152; see also Grossman, "Women's Jury Service," 1137–38 (as of 1938, women remained ineligible for jury service in twenty-three states).

38. *Strauder v. West Virginia*, 100 U.S. 303 (1880).

39. It would not be until 1968 that women could serve on juries in all fifty states. In 1975, in *Taylor v. Louisiana*, 419 U.S. 522, the U.S. Supreme Court recognized a constitutional issue in the systematic exclusion of women from juries, based on the defendant's right to a jury drawn from a fair cross section of the community. Finally, in 1994, the Court in *J. E. B. v. Alabama ex rel. T. B.*, 511 U.S. 127, acknowledged a link

between women's citizenship and jury service, holding that peremptory challenges based solely on sex violated the equal protection clause of the Fourteenth Amendment. For discussions of the legal history of women's jury service, see, e.g., Kerber, *No Constitutional Right to Be Ladies*; Grossman, "Woman's Jury Service."

40. Kerber, *No Constitutional Right to Be Ladies*, 138.

41. Mrs. Charles G. Doak, "Federated Club Women Demand Clarification of Jury Clause," *News and Observer*, November 19, 1944.

42. Ibid.

43. "Under the Dome," *News and Observer*, November 23, 1944.

44. Ibid., November 18, 1944.

45. Jane Keane, "Tar Heel Voters to Act on Jury Duty Amendments," *News and Observer*, November 3, 1946.

46. Gertrude Carraway, "Tar Heel Women Get Around, Regardless of Constitution," *News and Observer*, November 3, 1946.

47. Lynn Nisbet, "Around Capitol Square," *Reidsville Review*, October 23, 1946.

48. "Party Leaders Give Approval to Amendments," *Charlotte Observer*, November 4, 1946.

49. Cheney, *North Carolina Government, 1585–1974*, 933.

50. *North Carolina Manual, 1947*, 232.

51. "Amendment Raises New Problems for County," *Charlotte Observer*, November 10, 1946.

52. Martha Varner Clontz, "North Carolina Women Have Been Slow to Exercise Their Jury Privilege," *Greensboro Daily News*, December 2, 1951.

53. SMS, speech at High Point, typed index cards, n.d.

54. The story of the Institute of Government, which was established in 1931 with Coates's initiative and tenacity, the help of his wife Gladys, and his own funds, is one of the great sagas of North Carolina public service. The institute, now a part of the University of North Carolina School of Government, has made untold contributions to state and local government in North Carolina and has served as a model to other states.

55. SMS to Ingrid W. Reed, Administrative Director, Rockefeller Public Service Awards, Woodrow Wilson School of Public and International Affairs, Princeton University, June 30, 1980.

56. Ibid.

57. *J. E. B. v. Alabama ex rel. T. B.*

58. The other two were Dr. M. P. Cummings of Reidsville and Floyd Osborne, a politically powerful attorney from Leaksville.

59. SMS, "An Unlikely Jurist," typescript, [1974].

60. It began with either a misunderstanding or a double cross, depending on whose side one took. Chatham had returned from his service in World War II with the notion of running for the Fifth District congressional seat and found encouragement in indications from Folger that he did not intend to run again if he were opposed. On March 7, 1946, Folger filed for reelection. Four days later a delegation of Chatham supporters consisting of Robert M. Hanes and W. L. Ferrell of Winston-Salem and

W. A. Neaves of Elkin pressed a call on Congressman Folger in Washington. They reminded Folger of what they termed his decision not to run if opposed and informed him that he would have opposition from Thurmond Chatham. Chatham supporters alleged that, upon the suggestion that he step aside, Folger agreed to do so. Folger, however, denied making any such agreement and claimed to have suggested instead that Chatham put his congressional ambitions on hold. Whatever the actual conversation, Chatham filed as a candidate the afternoon of the morning on which his supporters met with Folger in Washington. Chester Davis, "Chatham-Folger Race Was Bitter," *Winston-Salem Journal and Sentinel,* June 19, 1966.

61. Ibid.

62. Ibid. The Congress of Industrial Organizations later merged with the American Federation of Labor to form the AFL-CIO.

63. Campaign flyer, SMS scrapbook.

64. "Fifth District Speakers Blast Politics of Other," n.p., dateline Elkin, May 20, [1946], SMS scrapbook.

65. Davis, "Chatham-Folger Race Was Bitter."

66. Ibid.

67. Ibid.

68. Ibid.

69. SMS, "An Unlikely Jurist," typescript, [1974] (emphasis in original).

70. Davis, "Chatham-Folger Race Was Bitter."

71. For the detailed reports of this campaign and election, I have drawn on two articles by Chester Davis, the June 19, 1966, "Chatham-Folger Race Was Bitter" article, already cited, and one dated August 2, 1962, "Memories of a Wild Election in 1946," from the *Winston-Salem Journal.*

72. Davis, "Chatham-Folger Race Was Bitter."

73. A third candidate, Joe Harris, had 805 votes. Ibid.

74. Ibid.

75. Davis, "Memories of a Wild Election in 1946."

76. William T. Joyner to W. Benton Pipkin, June 24, 1946, *Reidsville Review,* n.d., SMS scrapbook.

77. Lynn Nisbet, "Around Capitol Square," *Reidsville Review,* n.d., SMS scrapbook.

78. Ibid.

79. Newspaper clipping, "Stop! Look! Marvel!" n.p., n.d., SMS scrapbook.

80. Newspaper clipping, n.p., n.d., SMS scrapbook.

Chapter 7

1. W. T. Bost, "Among Us Tar Heels," *Greensboro Daily News,* July 16, 1949.

2. Key, *Southern Politics,* 205.

3. Ibid., 211.

4. Ibid.

5. Edsall and Williams, "North Carolina: Bipartisan Paradox," 368.

6. Ibid.

7. Robert E. Williams, "Kerr Scott Disperses Old Political Machine," *News and Observer*, July 4, 1948.

8. Bennett and Wegner, "Lawyers Talking," 855.

9. Corbitt, *Public Addresses, Letters and Papers of William Kerr Scott*, xvii–xviii.

10. Terry Sanford, interview with author, June 12, 1995.

11. Ibid.

12. Other candidates were Oscar Barker, Olla Ray Boyd, and W. F. Stanly.

13. Corbitt, *Public Addresses, Letters and Papers of William Kerr Scott*, xvii.

14. *Reidsville Review*, February 25, 1948. It is worth noting that his first campaign speech was to the Business and Professional Women's Club of Durham.

15. Ibid.

16. Corbitt, *Public Addresses, Letters and Papers of William Kerr Scott*, xvi.

17. *Reidsville Review*, May 5, 1948.

18. Albright, "O. Max Gardner and the Shelby Dynasty," *The State*, August 1983, 10.

19. Rob Christensen, "The Scotts of Haw River," *News and Observer*, January 17, 1999; Covington and Ellis, *Terry Sanford*, 110.

20. Simmons Fentress, "Kerr Scott: Man of Surprise, Controversy," *News and Observer*, January 4, 1953.

21. Christensen, "The Scotts of Haw River." Sanford supported Mayne Albright, like himself a young liberal lawyer and returned veteran, in the first primary. In 1949 Sanford was elected president of the statewide Young Democrats Club.

22. See ibid.

23. Fentress, "Kerr Scott: Man of Surprise, Controversy."

24. Allen H. Gwyn Jr., interview with author, January 27, 1995.

25. Terry Sanford, interview with author, June 12, 1995.

26. Dewey H. Huffines Jr., interview with author, December 30, 1994 (stating that his father was one who declined the job of campaign manager for Kerr Scott). Stokes County clerk of superior court J. Watt Tuttle recommended two names to Scott, R. P. Richardson and P. D. McMichael, both of Reidsville. J. Watt Tuttle to Kerr Scott, March 31, 1948, AHG Papers, RCC. At the end of March 1948, the *News and Observer*'s "Under the Dome" column reported that Scott had announced only one of his county managers. During the remaining time up until the first primary, the paper routinely announced the candidate's choices for county campaign managers, but did not name anyone for Rockingham County. Nor did a search of the *Greensboro Daily News* and the *Reidsville Review* turn up a name. It is possible that Scott did not have a Rockingham County manager for the first primary.

27. Cheney, *North Carolina Government*, 1371.

28. Havard, *The Changing Politics of the South*, 370. The remaining small percentage was divided among the three minor candidates, Oscar Barker, Olla Ray Boyd, and W. F. Stanly.

29. SMS, "An Unplanned Judicial Career," typescript, n.d.

30. Allen H. Gwyn Jr., interview with author, January 27, 1995.

31. "Under the Dome," *News and Observer*, March 19, 1948.

32. Ibid. In the Senate race, J. Melville Broughton chose women to manage his

campaign in two counties, Mrs. J. Foust Lane in Chatham and Mrs. C. P. Rogers Jr. in Yancey. "Under the Dome," *News and Observer*, May 6, 1948.

33. SMS, "An Unplanned Judicial Career," typescript, n.d. She resigned her position as vice chairman of the Rockingham County Democratic Party to head the Scott campaign in the county.

34. SMS, radio address, WFRC Radio [Danville, Va.], June 24, 1948, text printed in *Reidsville Review*, June 25, 1948.

35. Ibid.

36. Herbert Foster, "Scott Takes Rest after Victory," *Reidsville Review*, June 28, 1948.

37. Cheney, *North Carolina Government*, 1371.

38. Foster, "Scott Takes Rest after Victory." Only 3 of North Carolina's 100 counties switched from Scott to Johnson. Ibid.

39. Ibid.

40. Cheney, *North Carolina Government*, 1371; "Scott Takes County by 5–3 Margin," *Reidsville Review*, June 28, 1948. In November, against the Republican candidate, George M. Pritchard, Kerr Scott totaled 570,995 to Pritchard's 206,166 votes, a margin of less than 3-to-1. In Rockingham County Scott prevailed by a margin of nearly 5-to-1 (10,040 to 2,134). Cheney, *North Carolina Government*, 1401.

41. SMS, "An Unplanned Judicial Career," typescript, n.d.

42. "Woman and Raleigh Man among Five Appointed as Superior Court Judges," *News and Observer*, June 22, 1949.

43. SMS, remarks at presentation of Hamp Price portrait [Wentworth, N.C.], July 10, 1972.

44. SMS, "An Unplanned Judicial Career," typescript, n.d.

45. SMS, remarks at presentation of Hamp Price portrait.

46. SMS, "An Unplanned Judicial Career," typescript, n.d. One report gave Scott's response as, "How's her health?"

47. SMS, remarks at presentation of Hamp Price portrait.

48. SMS, "An Unplanned Judicial Career," typescript, n.d.

49. Ibid.

50. Havard, *The Changing Politics of the South*, 371.

51. W. T. Bost, "Miss Susie Sharp May Become Special Superior-Court Jurist," *Greensboro Daily News*, dateline February 6, 1949, SMS scrapbook.

52. A. P. Sands to Governor Kerr Scott, February 14, 1949, Governor W. Kerr Scott Papers, Special Judges, NCSA.

53. W. H. Nelson to Governor Kerr Scott, February 14, 1949, Governor W. Kerr Scott Papers, Special Judges, NCSA.

54. "Under the Dome," *News and Observer*, n.d., SMS scrapbook. The following year, Governor Scott proudly stated, "I believe in women in government. I appointed the first woman judge in the state and the first women members of the boards of Health and Conservation and Development. I have placed forty-six women on committees and commissions, and they are doing a good job." Governor Kerr Scott, Address before 66th Annual Convention of the North Carolina Education Association

in Raleigh, March 9, 1950, in Corbitt, *Public Addresses, Letters and Papers of William Kerr Scott*, 163.

55. Eula Nixon Greenwood, "Raleigh Roundup," *Leaksville News*, February 10, 1949.

56. Senator J. Hampton Price to Governor Kerr Scott, March 25, 1949, Governor W. Kerr Scott Papers, Special Judges, NCSA.

57. Senator J. Hampton Price to AHG, March 3, 1949, AHG Papers, RCC.

58. AHG to Governor W. Kerr Scott, March 5, 1949, AHG Papers, RCC.

59. AHG to John M. Johns, unsent draft of letter recommending SMS for vice chairman of the North Carolina Democratic Executive Committee, n.d., AHG Papers, RCC.

60. SMS journal, March 6, 1949.

61. *Leaksville News*, n.d., SMS scrapbook. The roads issue also contained a proposal to boost the state gasoline tax by one cent. A $25 million bond issue for school construction was on the ballot as well.

62. SMS to Governor Kerr Scott, June 4, 1949, Governor W. Kerr Scott Papers, Special Judges, NCSA.

63. Ibid.

64. Ibid.

65. SMS, interview by Jane L. Sharpe, 1982, audiocassette, AHG Papers, RCC.

66. "Our Lady Chief Justice," *North Carolina Magazine*, February 1975, 25.

67. SMS, "The Law as Seen from the Distaff Side," speech to Georgia Association of Women Lawyers, Atlanta, November 5, 1949; Doris Lockerman, "Judge (Miss) Susie Sharp Knows Her Governor," *Atlanta Constitution*, November 6, 1949.

68. SMS, interview by Jane L. Sharpe, 1982.

69. SMS, draft fragments ("Tuesday was quite a day"), [June 1949]; see also SMS journal, June 21, 1949.

70. W. C. ("Mutt") Burton, "Her Honor Gives Interview While Hair Is Shampooed," *Greensboro Daily News*, June 22, 1949.

71. SMS, draft fragments ("Tuesday was quite a day"), [June 1949].

72. Ibid.

73. Bernadette W. Hoyle, "'To Me — She's Still Sue,' Says Father," *Durham Morning Herald*, July 3, 1949.

74. P. Dean, "Women on the Hill," 16.

75. SMS, draft fragments ("Tuesday was quite a day"), [June 1949].

76. SMS, "Why I Ran for Chief Justice," typescript, n.d.

77. W. C. ("Mutt") Burton, "Typist Had Gender Mixed Up in Miss Sharp's Commission," *Greensboro Daily News*, dateline June 22, 1949, SMS scrapbook.

78. Editorial, *Reidsville Review*, June 24, 1949; "Miss Sharp to Be Sworn in on July 1," *Reidsville Review*, June 22, 1949.

79. Mamie H. Braddy, "Charming Judge Sharp Wears Her New Honors Becomingly," *Twin City Sentinel* (Winston-Salem, N.C.), June 22, 1949.

80. Kay Miller, "Susie Sharp: The Law's Been Her Life," *Winston-Salem Journal*, July 3, 1977.

81. Bost, "Among Us Tar Heels."

82. This address was later printed in the March 1948 issue of *Popular Government*, published by the Institute of Government in Chapel Hill.

83. Bost, "Among Us Tar Heels" (quoting from SMS, "Ladies of the Jury").

84. Ibid.

85. SMS to Governor Kerr Scott, June 26, 1949, Governor W. Kerr Scott Papers, Special Judges, NCSA.

86. SMS journal, July 1, 1949.

87. Scott appointed a total of five new special judges at this time, all of whom had supported him in the primaries or worked for his program in the 1949 General Assembly. The other four were State Representative William T. Hatch of Raleigh; State Senator William Halstead of Camden; A. R. Crisp of Lenoir, attorney and judge of Caldwell County Recorder's Court; and Harold Bennett of Asheville, a young returning-vet attorney. He also reappointed two special judges, W. H. S. Burgwyn of Woodland and George B. Patton of Franklin. Newspaper reports said Patton kept his seat because "Scott considered him a sport." "Woman and Raleigh Man among Five Appointed as Superior Court Judges," *News and Observer*, June 22, 1949.

88. "State Swears in 13 New Officials as Scott Hits at 'Slow Courts,'" *Raleigh Times*, July 1, 1949; *Reidsville Review*, dateline July 1, 1949, SMS scrapbook.

Chapter 8

1. Kay Miller, "Susie Sharp: The Law's Been Her Life," *Winston-Salem Journal*, July 3, 1977.

2. "But man, proud man / Drest in a little brief authority / Most ignorant of what he's most assured . . . / Plays such fantastic tricks before high heaven / As make the angels weep." SMS, notes for Allen H. Gwyn's eulogy.

3. SMS, "Why I Ran for Chief Justice," typescript, n.d.

4. Consequently, the governor's office, which was then in charge of assigning superior court judges, never issued a commission to Judge Sharp for that term of court.

5. "Judge Susie Sharp Gets 'Cold Feet' and Fails to Appear in Court Here," *Stanley News & Press*, July 12, 1949.

6. W. C. ("Mutt") Burton, "It Was All A Mistake When Lady Judge Failed to Show Up for Albemarle Court," *Greensboro Daily News*, dateline July 11, 1949, SMS scrapbook.

7. "Judge Susie Sharp Gets 'Cold Feet' and Fails to Appear in Court Here."

8. Ibid.

9. Editorial, "Disappointment," *Stanly News and Press*, July 15, 1949, SMS scrapbook.

10. Lynn Nisbet, "19 Men Have Served as Special Judges," *Reidsville Review*, January 7, 1944.

11. SMS, speech to Sheriffs' Association, July 30, 1974.

12. Unless otherwise noted, this account is taken primarily from SMS's letter to Professor Breckenridge dated July 30, 1949.

13. Other help came in the form of a note the clerk handed to her. In an undated fragment found among the "lace letters" to John Kesler in Susie Sharp's effects, she wrote, "It gave me a shot in the arm—as well as a lump in the throat—just as my knees were beginning to buckle." It is unclear, however, whether the note was from Breck or from John. On the paper itself she noted in shorthand, "Wrote to Breck about my first week on the court." Because her mention of the supportive note would logically have been included in her lengthy letter to Breck if he were the author, her handwritten notation is likely a reminder to herself that the complete recitation of events is in her report to Breck, and the fragment was actually written to John.

14. SMS, speech to Sheriffs' Association, July 30, 1974.

15. Mary Lib Wilson, "Judge Sharp Metes Out Justice Coolly in Humid Courtroom," *Greensboro Daily News*, July 26, 1949.

16. *State v. Carpenter*, 231 N.C. 229, 231 (1949).

17. SMS, speech to North Carolina Bar Association, Asheville, N.C., July 2, 1975.

18. Counsel for the defendant comprised A. P. Kitchin, W. G. Pittman, R. Brookes Peters, and E. O. Brogden Jr.

19. Isaac S. London, "Prison Punishment Method Draws Rebuke from Judge," n.p., July 30, 1949, SMS scrapbook.

20. Judge Sharp had instructed the jury, "If you do not believe the evidence of the defendant beyond a reasonable doubt, then in that event only, would you return a verdict of not guilty." This backhanded reference to the defendant's admissions of culpable behavior effectively shifted the burden of proof from the prosecution to the defendant. In other words, only if the jury did not believe Carpenter's self-incriminating statements should he be acquitted. The supreme court found that the instruction, phrased in the negative, confused the jury, and that it pinned too much emphasis on the defendant's testimony alone in relation to the critical issue of guilt or innocence. *Carpenter*, 231 N.C. at 242.

21. *Carpenter*, 231 N.C. at 241.

22. "Handcuffing Case Brought to Quick End," n.p., dateline January 10, 1950, SMS scrapbook.

23. Flogging, for example, did not disappear, but stricter guidelines were put in place.

24. "Disappointed but Encouraged," *Greensboro Record*, December 1, 1949.

25. SMS, speech to superior court judges, Raleigh, N.C., March 17, 1978.

26. Editorial, *Daily News* (Washington, N.C.), August 25, 1951; SMS to JCK, January 27, 1956.

27. J. Frank Huskins, interview with author, December 2, 1994.

28. SMS to JCK, February 24, 1952.

29. SMS to Superior Court Judge Hamilton H. Hobgood, February 21, 1979.

30. "Judge Sharp Opens Court," *Fayetteville Observer*, October 10, 1949.

31. Blonnie Pittman, "Beauty and the Bench Little Confusing to Lincoln Lawyers," *Gastonia Gazette*, January 23, 1951.

32. Essie Cofield, "Glancing at Graham," [*Daily Times-News* (Burlington, N.C.)], November 14, 1949.

33. Ibid.

34. Ibid.

35. SMS to JCK, November 23, 1952.

36. James G. Exum, former North Carolina Supreme Court chief justice, interview with author, April 16, 1999.

37. Samuel F. Wells Jr., interview with author, December 4, 1998. Wells was a neighbor who as a child spent much time in the Sharp household on Lindsey Street; as a teenager, he once had the job of chauffeur to Jim Sharp, recovering from a not very serious stroke. Wells went on to acquire his Ph.D. from Harvard along with many other prestigious markers of a brilliant academic career, including the position of deputy director of the Woodrow Wilson International Center for Scholars in Washington, D.C.

38. I have seen this consistently attributed by Susie Sharp to Will A. Lucas, of the old Wilson firm Lucas & Rand, in a number of newspaper articles as well as at least one speech she made (Naomi Morris Day, Wilson, N.C., August 7, 1967), but in an undated letter (shortly before Labor Day 1951) to JCK, she states that it was Mr. W. A. Rand who paid her the compliment.

39. SMS, "The Law as Seen from the Distaff Side," speech to the Georgia Association of Women Lawyers, Atlanta, November 5, 1949; Doris Lockerman, "Judge (Miss) Sharp Knows Her Governor," *Atlanta Constitution*, November 6, 1949.

40. Jean Breckenridge, interview with author, January 11, 1995.

41. James M. Taylor, telephone interview with author, November 1, 1997.

42. Venitah Breckenridge to SMS, August 23, 1949.

43. Gwyn, *Work, Earn and Save.*

44. At least one probation officer told Judge Sharp that "the boys who get in trouble . . . can't afford to make those payments and live; that when the first emergency arises and they have to miss a payment they get scared and abscond." Susie Sharp was not sure whether she would include this in her report to Judge Gwyn. SMS to JCK, September 9, 1955.

45. Allen H. Gwyn Jr., interview with author, January 27, 1995; "Judge Declares Jury No Place for Klansmen," *Greensboro Daily News*, November 22, 1966.

46. Hugh P. Griffin, interview with author, March 25, 1998. This general view of Judge Gwyn's propensities was also voiced in an interview with the author by a Greensboro attorney of the period, who wished to remain off the record.

47. SMS to JCK, April 1952 ("I have never quite been able to make myself believe that my fellow townsman, with all his faults, is quite the wolf you suspect him of being or that he could qualify as a first-class menace"); SMS to her parents, April 4, 1952 (tying Judge Gwyn by name to story referenced in letter to JCK); SMS journal, March 23, 1958.

48. SMS Journal Abstract, March 10, 1937. Susie Sharp had noted in her journal four years earlier that "people are talking" about the pair. SMS journal, August 25, 1933.

49. Louise Sharp, conversation with author, February 21, 1995.

50. "JCK Record." She continued to write about John Kesler in her everyday journal, while maintaining an unbroken listing of their encounters in the separate notebook, with occasional scattered comments.

51. On the end page of Susie Sharp's Journal Abstract is a list consisting solely of the birthdays of Breck, John Kesler, and Allen Gwyn, along with the date that she and Breck first became lovers.

52. SMS journal, May 26–27, 1948.

53. Ibid., February 10, 1952.

54. Rose Post, "Great July 4th Parade on Liberty St.," [*Salisbury Post?*], n.d., SMS scrapbook.

55. SMS journal, August 4, 1949.

56. Ibid., February 17, 1950; March 3, 1950.

57. Ibid., January 20, 1951.

58. Ibid., February 7, 1951.

59. Ibid., April 25, 1951.

60. Ibid.

61. Ibid., June 30, 1951.

62. Ibid., July 11, 1951.

63. Ibid., July 16, 1951.

64. SMS, interview by Jane L. Sharpe, 1982, audiocassette, AHG Papers, RCC.

65. Ibid.

66. SMS journal, June 20, 1951.

67. Ibid., December 29, 1951.

68. Ibid., January 13, 1952.

Chapter 9

1. MSB to SMS, September 29, 1949 (SMS handwritten copy). For thirty years, from December 1928 to August 1958, Susie Sharp copied Breck's letters, in shorthand, into four bound volumes.

2. Eula Nixon Greenwood, "Raleigh Roundup," *Leaksville News*, February 10, 1949.

3. W. T. Bost, "Miss Susie Sharp May Become Special Superior Court Jurist," *Greensboro Daily News*, dateline February 6, 1949, SMS scrapbook.

4. Governor W. Kerr Scott Papers, Judges, Endorsements, NCSA.

5. SMS to Kerr Scott, October 15, 1950, Governor W. Kerr Scott Papers, Judges, Endorsements, NCSA.

6. "Jeff Johnson had been Frank Graham's campaign manager, so he was more or less in the Scott camp." Terry Sanford, interview with author, June 12, 1995.

7. SMS to JCK, September 13, 1951.

8. In 1944 Helen Brooke Taussig, with Alfred Blalock, developed a surgical technique to alleviate the "blue-baby" condition, or cyanosis, caused by a congenital heart defect that prevented complete blood circulation to the lungs. The operation saved many babies from invalidism or death.

9. SMS to UNC-G Chancellor William H. Moran, May 13, 1985.

10. SMS journal, February 11, 1950.

11. SMS to UNC-G Chancellor William H. Moran, May 13, 1985.

12. SMS, speech on Naomi Morris Day, Wilson, N.C., August 7, 1967.

13. See Jim Chaney, "Six Seeking Court Post," *News and Observer*, May 25, 1952.

14. "Scott Explains His Selection of Valentine," *Greensboro Daily News*, September 19, 1951.

15. Ibid.; "Under the Dome," *News and Observer*, September 19, 1951.

16. SMS journal, September 28, 1951.

17. Editorial, "Advice from Judge Susie," *Greensboro Daily News*, November 12, 1951.

18. SMS journal, November 11, 1951.

19. AHG to Kerr Scott, November 16, 1951, Governor W. Kerr Scott Papers, Judges, Supreme Court, NCSA.

20. Kerr Scott to AHG, November 27, 1951, Governor W. Kerr Scott Papers, Judges, Supreme Court, NCSA.

21. SMS journal, November 16, 1951.

22. Ibid.

23. Ibid., November 17, 1951.

24. Ibid., December 8, 1951.

25. Ibid., December 15, 1951.

26. Chaney, "Six Seeking Court Post."

27. Ibid.

28. SMS to MSB, February 16, 1952.

29. Ibid.

30. SMS journal, February 29, 1952.

31. H. F. ("Chub") Seawell Jr. was the Republican candidate in November.

32. A prominent North Carolina Republican, John J. Parker, had the distinction of being the first nominee to be rejected by the U.S. Senate in the twentieth century. He was heavily opposed by labor organizations and the NAACP and lost by two votes on May 7, 1930.

33. SMS to AHG, June 2, 1952, AHG Papers, RCC.

34. SMS to Mr. and Mrs. Breckenridge, July 16, 1952.

35. AHG to William B. Umstead, September 8, 1952, copy in SMS Papers.

36. AHG to William B. Umstead, May 4, 1953, AHG Papers, RCC.

37. Norwood E. Robinson, interview with author, November 16, 1994.

38. JMS to ABS, September 15, 1949.

39. SMS to JCK, October 1, 1954.

40. SMS to MSB, [May 1950].

41. SMS to JCK, January 18, 1952.

42. Ibid.

43. SMS to Mr. and Mrs. Breckenridge, July 3, 1952.

44. Ibid.

45. SMS to JCK, July 11, 1952.

46. SMS to Mr. and Mrs. Breckenridge, July 16, 1952.

47. Ibid.

48. SMS to JCK, July 17, 1952.

49. Ibid.

50. James V. ("Kits") Sharp, interview with author, March 22–23, 1995.

51. SMS to JCK, September 1, 1952.

52. SMS to JCK, October 5, 1952.

53. Ibid.

54. SMS to JCK, October 24, 1952.

55. SMS to JCK, September 14, 1952.

56. Ibid.

57. SMS to JCK, October 24, 1952.

58. Sallie Sharp Taylor died September 2, 1953.

59. The death certificate cites "pulmonary embolus" as the ultimate cause of death.

60. SMS to JCK, September 7, 1953.

61. Ibid.

Chapter 10

1. "Miss Susie," *News and Observer*, March 10, 1954.

2. Margaret Turner, "Her Honor, Judge Susie, to Ornament Banquet of Local Lawyers Nov. 5," *Atlanta Journal*, October 30, 1949.

3. "Judge Susie Goes Home to Preside over Court," *Greensboro Record*, March 9, 1954; W. C. ("Mutt") Burton, "Judge Sharp Presides First Time at Home," *Greensboro Daily News*, March 9, 1954.

4. Burton, "Judge Sharp Presides First Time at Home."

5. *Greensboro Daily News*, dateline March 25, 1962, SMS scrapbook.

6. Norwood E. Robinson, interview with author, November 8, 1994; see also Norwood Robinson, Dallas Cameron, A. C. Snow, and Danny Moody, video filmed prior to the presentation of Justice Susie M. Sharp's portrait to the North Carolina Supreme Court, June 11, 1996, North Carolina Supreme Court Library, Raleigh, North Carolina.

7. SMS to JCK, October 6, 1961.

8. SMS journal, May 23, 1956.

9. Johnny Corey, "When Judge Susie Sharp Presides, How Do Lawyers, Jurors React?" *Greensboro Daily News*, January 25, 1955.

10. Katharine Halyburton, "First Woman Judge of N.C. Holds High Place in Associates' Hearts," *Charlotte Observer*, January 27, 1950.

11. Blonnie Pittman, "Beauty and the Bench Little Confusing to Lincoln Lawyers," *Gastonia Gazette*, January 23, 1951.

12. Pat Rees, "First Death Sentence," *Fayetteville Observer*, April 8, 1960.

13. SMS, speech to North Carolina Sheriffs' Association, Wrightsville Beach, N.C., July 30, 1974.

14. David R. Nelsen, "Armed Judges Say Guns Are Needed," *News and Observer*, June 1, 1975. Susie Sharp had owned more than one gun in her life, including a .32 Smith & Wesson given her by her local sheriff in 1957. SMS to JCK, October 25, 1957. As an associate supreme court justice, she bought a pistol for which she obtained a gun permit, duly reported in the *News and Observer*. "Justice Sharp Gets Permit for Pistol," [August 1967], SMS scrapbook; J. Will Pless to SMS, August 5, 1967. After her

death, I had an unsettling experience while examining the contents of Susie Sharp's Reidsville bedroom with her brother, Kits Sharp. From a bookshelf, I pulled off one of those hollowed-out fake books used to conceal valuables and discovered a .38 revolver inside. It was fully loaded with flat-nosed bullets, which Kits Sharp carefully removed.

15. SMS, speech to Sheriffs' Association, July 30, 1974.

16. Hendricks, *Seeking Liberty and Justice*, 46; "Curia Passim, a Brief History of the Sites of the North Carolina Supreme Court," brochure published for the North Carolina Supreme Court's Diamond Centennial (175th anniversary) (Raleigh, N.C., 1993).

17. See, e.g., Christie S. Cameron, interview with author, January 26, 1999.

18. SMS to Albert Coates, January 3, 1958.

19. Shirley Mudge, "State's Only Lady Judge Loves Court and Kitchen, Too," *The Herald* (Sanford, N.C.), May 10, 1958.

20. SMS to JCK, May 19, 1959.

21. Ibid. See also "Judicial Robes Made by Marion Woman," *Winston-Salem Journal*, July 7, 1965.

22. SMS, speech to Young Democrats, Reidsville, 1958.

23. Ibid.

24. SMS to JCK, August 20, 1959.

25. SMS, speech to Young Democrats, Reidsville, 1958.

26. SMS, speech at Peace Institute commencement, May 28, 1951.

27. SMS, "Believe in God and Do Something: A Plea for Intelligent Participation in Public Affairs," speech at Greensboro College (commencement exercises), May 26, 1952, *Greensboro College Bulletin* 39 (June 1952).

28. SMS, "Breaking the Barriers Which Face Women in Public Affairs," speech to Business and Professional Women's Club, Salisbury, November 9, 1957.

29. Ibid.

30. SMS, speech to Kiwanis Club, Reidsville, July 1953.

31. SMS, speech to UNC-G Alumnae Association, December 10, 1955.

32. SMS, speech to Kiwanis Club, Reidsville, July 1953.

33. Ibid.

34. SMS, speech to UNC-G Alumnae Association, December 10, 1955.

35. Ibid. Obviously, some African Americans or other minorities might take a different view of this argument, but they would not necessarily be better off with the juryless court.

36. Mudge, "State's Only Lady Judge Loves Court and Kitchen, Too." Jury nullification is the term used when a jury ignores the law to reach a result it deems more just or appropriate.

37. SMS, speech to UNC-G Alumnae Association, December 10, 1955.

38. SMS, "The Task of Womanhood in Our Time," speech at Pinehurst, N.C., n.d.

39. Mudge, "State's Only Lady Judge Loves Court and Kitchen, Too."

40. SMS to JCK, September 3, 1952.

41. Pressly, "Monday Is Ladies' Day in Our Courts," 4.

42. SMS, "The Task of Womanhood in Our Time."

43. SMS, speech to UNC-G Alumnae Association, December 10, 1955, *Alumnae News*, January 1956.

44. SMS to JCK, March 24, 1953.

45. "Women Play Inactive Role in State Politics," *Statesville Daily Record*, October 7, 1950.

46. SMS, "Breaking the Barriers Which Face Women in Public Affairs."

47. Ibid.

48. Ibid.

49. Ibid.

50. SMS, "The Law as Seen from the Distaff Side," speech to Georgia Association of Women Lawyers, Atlanta, November 5, 1949.

51. Ibid.

52. Ibid.

53. SMS, "Breaking the Barriers Which Face Women in Public Affairs."

54. SMS, "The Law as Seen from the Distaff Side."

55. SMS, "Breaking the Barriers Which Face Women in Public Affairs."

56. SMS, "The Task of Womanhood in Our Time."

57. SMS, "Breaking the Barriers Which Face Women in Public Affairs."

58. SMS, speech at Flora McDonald College, November 7, 1953. She added, "But note well, I did not say feminine wiles; there is a vast, qualitative difference!"

59. SMS, speech, unidentified audience, [1948] ("I have been asked to talk to you on the general subject of race relations").

60. Ibid.

61. Ibid.

62. In fact, the Pearsall Plan functioned as a safety valve, offering options that went all but unused by segregationists.

63. Larry Jinks, "Segregation Is Ended on City's Golf Course," *Charlotte Observer*, December 5, 1956.

64. Ibid.

65. SMS to MSB, December 11, 1956.

66. Ibid.

67. SMS to Mr. and Mrs. Breckenridge, March 13, 1958.

68. SMS to JCK, November 21, 1961.

69. SMS, commencement address, Stratford College, Danville, Virginia, June 2, 1956.

70. SMS, speech to Raleigh Women's Club, September 1950.

71. SMS to JCK, February 21, 1961.

72. Ed Kemp, "Shackleford Trial Draws Huge Crowds," *Greensboro Daily News*, dateline September 25, 1949, SMS scrapbook.

73. Ibid.

74. *State v. Shackleford*, 232 N.C. 299 (1950).

75. "Shackleford's Execution Is Set Today," *Greensboro Daily News*, June 30, 1950.

76. Ibid.

77. "Police Probing New Statement in Rape Case," n.p., dateline July 6, 1950, SMS scrapbook.

78. Pittman, "Beauty and the Bench Little Confusing to Lincoln Lawyers."

79. Pat Reese, "First Death Sentence 'Numbed' Lady Judge," *Fayetteville Observer*, April 8, 1960.

80. James Earl Hester, "Woman Judge Likes Job but Is Stranger at Home," *Roxboro Courier-Times*, November 3, 1952.

81. Ibid.

82. Lane Kerr, "Scales Sentenced to Die for Slaying," *Greensboro Daily News*, March 12, 1955.

83. Ibid.

84. "Roy Oakes Sentenced to Death," *Greensboro Daily News*, April 25, 1958.

85. The appellate court found error in the judge's charge to the jury, although according to Susie Sharp it was identical to the charge she had used in the Shackleford trial. SMS to JCK, March 31, 1961.

86. SMS to JCK, October 26, 1956.

87. William D. Snider, "State's Court System Untouched by Major Reform in Forty Years, Needs Overhauling," *Greensboro Daily News*, May 18, 1952.

88. Ibid.

89. SMS, "A New Judge Looks at the Bar," speech at 18th annual meeting of the North Carolina State Bar, Raleigh, N.C., October 26, 1951.

90. Ibid.

91. Chief Justice M. V. Barnhill, "Chief Justice Raps 'Political' Special Judgeships," letter to the editor, *Asheville Citizen*, August 9, 1954.

92. SMS to Mr. and Mrs. Breckenridge, April 17, 1955. See also, SMS journal, April 17, 1955.

93. MSB to SMS, May 21, 1955. This was a reference to Carlisle Higgins's 1933 appointment as U.S. district attorney for the Middle District.

94. Ibid. Chief Justice Barnhill later recounted the same version of events to attendees at the North Carolina Bar Association meeting in Asheville. "Under the Dome," *News and Observer*, June 21, 1955.

95. MSB to SMS, May 21, 1955.

96. Joe Doster, "Her Honor Susie: Real Sharp Judge," *Charlotte Observer*, June 28, 1957.

97. Hugh P. Griffin, interview with author, March 25, 1998.

98. Marjorie Hunter, "Only North Carolina Woman Judge Expected to Keep Seat on Bench," *Winston-Salem Journal*, March 9, 1955.

Chapter 11

1. SMS journal, January 17, 1952.

2. Ibid., January 22, 1958.

3. Ibid., July 15, 1954.

4. Ibid., July 18, 1954.

5. Ibid., February 10, 1952.

6. Ibid., February 6, 1952.

7. Ibid., June 15, 1952.

8. SMS 1958 journal, cover pages (quoting Elbert Hubbard).

9. W. C. "Mutt" Burton, "No. 7 Is Significant in Miss Susie's Life," *Greensboro Daily News*, March 11, 1962.

10. SMS to JCK, February 2, 1953.

11. He wanted to bequeath Susie Sharp the contents of his law office, but worried that people might infer from this that they had been more than professional colleagues. SMS journal, May 21, 1952.

12. Ibid., June 18, 1954.

13. Ibid., June 25, 1954.

14. Susie Sharp also copied out long sections of John Kesler's letters in shorthand, as she did for Breck's.

15. SMS journal, February 17, 1955.

16. Ibid., February 21, 1955.

17. Ibid.

18. Ibid.

19. Ibid., November 14, 1956; SMS to JCK, September 18, 1959.

20. SMS journal, June 4, 1959.

21. See, e.g., SMS journal, November 1, 1955; SMS to JCK, November 2, 1955.

22. SMS to JCK, November 2, 1956.

23. SMS journal, March 11, 1959. In an interview on the eve of her retirement, Susie Sharp mentioned the Depression as one reason she had never married. Henry Scott, "Strong-Willed Sharp Prospered in Legal World," *Charlotte Observer*, July 29, 1979.

24. SMS journal, December 29, 1955.

25. SMS to JCK, March 16, 1956; see also, e.g., H. E. O. Heineman, Vice President, Pet Milk Company, to SMS, March 16, 1964; SMS to Mr. and Mrs. Charles A. Saylor, May 25, 1964; SMS to H. E. O. Heineman, May 25, 1964; SMS to G. H. Taylor, July 2, 1964.

26. SMS to JCK, October 9, 1955.

27. SMS to MSB, May 28, 1955.

28. Larry started medical school at UNC in the fall of 1959.

29. SMS to JCK, January 11, 1959.

30. Dr. and Mrs. Lawrence A. Taylor, interview with author, June 10, 1996.

31. SMS to JCK, January 10, 1960.

32. SMS to JCK, April 2, 1961.

33. SMS to JCK, June 26, 1959.

34. SMS to JCK, July 10, 1959.

35. SMS to JCK, [1960].

36. SMS to JCK, July 17, 1959.

37. SMS to Evelyn Ripple, November 25, 1961.

38. J. Gaskill McDaniel, "Judge Sharp Worries over Court Decisions," *News and Observer*, September 21, 1952.

39. Ibid.

40. Louise Sharp, interview with author, December 5, 1994.

41. AHG to William B. Umstead, January 11, 1954, AHG Papers, RCC.

42. AHG to William B. Umstead, January 28, 1954, AHG Papers, RCC.

43. SMS to JCK, April 12, 1959.

44. SMS journal, June 5, 1954.

45. Judge Gwyn wrote Justice Higgins a gracious note at the end of August, congratulating him on his appointment and wishing him well. "I am much more interested in the direction in which one travels than the speed with which he travels," he wrote. "I am satisfied with your speed and also the direction of your travel." AHG to Carlisle W. Higgins, August 30, 1954, AHG Papers, RCC.

46. SMS to Mr. and Mrs. Breckenridge, August 11, 1956.

47. SMS to Lucille Elliott, November 13, 1956.

48. SMS to Leonard S. Powers, March 30, 1962. It is interesting to note that in June 1956 Powers announced that he would resign his position as administrative assistant to the chief justice to accept a position teaching law at the University of North Carolina, effective in September — an indication that he may have been well aware of Chief Justice Barnhill's timetable for resignation.

49. Marjorie Hunter, "Judge Sharp Is Backed for N.C. Supreme Court," *Winston-Salem Journal*, October 3, 1957.

50. SMS journal, February 7, 1957. Susie Sharp's former law school professor and founder of the Institute of Government, Albert Coates, told her he thought her chances were best in the next four years. Ibid., June 2, 1957.

51. Ibid., February 21, 1958. See also SMS to Lennox P. McLendon of Greensboro, April 3, 1962.

52. "Under the Dome," *News and Observer*, January 29, 1959.

53. Luther Hodges had never run for office before running for lieutenant governor, and particularly in the beginning of his tenure as governor he ran things more like a chief executive officer than a politician, making appointments without the customary consultation with party chairmen in the counties and even without determining an appointee's party loyalty. See Jay Jenkins, "Sanford to Bring a New Look," *Virginian-Pilot and the Portsmouth Star*, July 17, 1960.

54. "Moore Gets High Court Seat; Mintz New Judge," *News and Observer*, January 30, 1959.

55. "Under the Dome" assigned the following geographical designations: Chief Justice Winborne and Justices Bobbitt, Denny, and Higgins were from the West, while Justices Johnson, Parker, and Rodman were easterners. "Under the Dome," *News and Observer*, January 29, 1959.

56. Telegram (copy), Francis E. Winslow to Luther B. Hodges, January 29, 1959, sent to SMS by Mr. Winslow, with note, "This is for your scrap book now!" January 30, 1959, SMS scrapbook.

57. Luther B. Hodges to Francis E. Winslow, February 2, 1959, original sent to SMS by Mr. Winslow, January 30, 1959, SMS scrapbook.

58. SMS to MSB, February 12, 1959.

59. SMS to JCK, January 29, 1959.

60. SMS journal, March 7, 1959.

61. SMS to Paul Ervin, October 8, 1959.

62. SMS journal, January 7, 1960.

63. Ibid.

64. SMS to JCK, January 31, 1960. Born November 12, 1893, Judge Gwyn was sixty-six years old at this time.

65. Allen H. Gwyn Jr., interview with author, January 27, 1995. It did not appear, however, that she had much hope of being appointed by the sitting governor, Luther Hodges. One of Judge Sharp's supporters, prominent Winston-Salem attorney Irving Carlyle, told her that he had had dinner with the governor and that, although Mrs. Hodges was very enthusiastic about the idea of Susie Sharp on the supreme court, "he could not get any response out of His Ex." Carlyle said they would just have to not let anybody on the court die "before TS got in." SMS journal, January 27, 1960.

66. Judge Sharp was presiding in August 1960 when trespass cases against "45 A&T and Bennett College students, which resulted from sit-in demonstrations in local variety stores last spring, were continued in Guilford Superior Court." According to a newspaper account, "The attorney for the students asked for the continuance since they have all 'scattered hither and yon' after the colleges closed. Judge Susie Sharp ruled that the cases be continued until a later term of court." Dorothy Benjamin, "Store 'Sit-Down' Trespass Cases Postponed Here," *Greensboro Record*, August 8, 1960.

67. Woodrow Price, "Sanford Slaps Back at Racist Campaign of Candidate Lake," *News and Observer*, June 1, 1960.

68. Ibid.

69. See SMS journal, May 15, 1960.

70. Ibid., May 29, 1960; June 3, 1960.

71. SMS to JCK, June 30, 1960.

72. Covington and Ellis, *Terry Sanford*, 239.

73. Ibid., 240.

74. Ibid.

75. Ibid.

76. Ibid.

77. Terry Sanford, interview, UNC-TV broadcast, May 27, 1998.

78. Covington and Ellis, *Terry Sanford*, 240.

79. Rob Christensen, "Sanford Answered History's Knock, Changed Course of RTP," *News and Observer*, April 27, 1998.

80. Drew Pearson, "Merry-Go-Round," [*Charlotte Observer*], July 13, 1960.

81. Covington and Ellis, *Terry Sanford*, 241.

82. William D. Snider, "November Issues: Race, Romanism and Rebellion," *Greensboro Daily News*, July 17, 1960.

83. Drescher, *Triumph of Good Will*, 241.

84. For a discussion of these factors, see Snider, "November Issues: Race, Romanism and Rebellion."

85. SMS to JCK, July 15, 1960.

86. SMS to JCK, July 17, 1960.

87. Ibid.

88. Ibid.

89. Ibid.

90. Ibid.

91. SMS to JCK, December 4, 1964.

92. Ibid.

93. Ibid.

94. Ibid.

95. SMS journal, October 18–19, 1961.

96. Drew Pearson, "Pearson Discounts Jack-Terry Deal," *Charlotte News*, August 22, 1960.

97. SMS to JCK, August 5, 1960.

98. SMS to JCK, September 28, 1960.

99. SMS journal, August 31, 1960.

100. E.g., Ragan, *The New Day*, 87.

101. SMS journal, January 17, 1961; January 22, 1961.

102. Her childhood friend Margaret Fillman Chaney would later say, "Religion didn't appeal to her a-tall." Interview with author, January 18, 1995.

103. Florence Sharp Newsom to SMS, April 4, 1952.

104. SMS to JCK, September 3, 1952. In 1965 Susie Sharp's sister Florence and her husband, Bob Newsom, formally expressed in writing their desire that in the event of their death their daughter Susie Newsom would go to live with her aunt, Susie Sharp. Florence and Robert W. Newsom Jr. to SMS, September 19, 1965 (formal statement of their wishes); Florence Newsom to SMS, September 19, 1965 (personal letter accompanying statement, also expressing her and Bob's wishes); Robert W. Newsom Jr., September 20, 1965 (handwritten codicil to his will).

105. SMS to JCK, April 26, 1954.

106. SMS to JCK, December 4, 1964.

107. SMS journal, April 21, 1961.

108. John Kesler introduced the "Extra Judges" bill, which had been proposed by the Judicial Council and endorsed by Sanford as "necessary to keep the court dockets from getting behind." Roy Parker Jr., "Extra Judges Bill Passed by Senate," *News and Observer*, February 28, 1961.

109. SMS to JCK, October 29, 1961.

110. SMS to Bert Bennett, April 1, 1962.

111. SMS journal, January 9, 1962.

112. Ibid., January 10, 1962.

113. Ibid.

114. Terry Sanford, interview with author, June 12, 1995.

115. SMS journal, January 21, 1962; January 26, 1962; Allen H. Gwyn Jr. to author, June 25, 1996; SMS to Vera B. (Mrs. G. V.) Lawrence (president, North Carolina Council of Women's Organizations), April 4, 1962.

116. Allen H. Gwyn Jr. to author, June 25, 1996.

117. Allen H. Gwyn Jr. to Terry Sanford, January 19, 1962, Governor Terry Sanford Papers, Appointments 1961–65, Judges, Supreme Court, Recommendations, NCSA.

118. "Under the Dome," *News and Observer*, February 4, 1962.

119. Ibid., February 7, 1962.

120. SMS journal, February 11, 1962.

121. AHG to Terry Sanford, February 11, 1962, Governor Terry Sanford Papers, Appointments 1961–65, Judges, Supreme Court, Recommendations, NCSA; AHG Papers, RCC (copy).

122. SMS journal, February 11, 1962.

123. SMS to Evelyn Ripple, March 5, 1962.

124. Ibid.

125. SMS to Evelyn Ripple, March 8, 1962.

126. SMS journal, March 8, 1962.

127. Thomas W. Lambeth, interview with author, June 10, 1998; Terry Sanford, interview with author, June 12, 1995.

128. Terry Sanford, interview with author, June 12, 1995.

129. Ibid.

130. Press release from the Governor's Office, June 22, 1961, Governor Terry Sanford Papers, Appointments, Women Appointees, SHC; list of women appointed by Governor Sanford through March 1962, Governor Terry Sanford Papers, General Correspondence 1962, Press Secretary's Files, Women Appointed, NCSA.

131. Terry Sanford, interview with author, June 12, 1995.

132. Ibid.

133. Ibid.

134. Tom Lambeth, interview with author, June 10, 1998.

135. Ibid.

136. Ibid. Ben Roney, for example, would likely tell him he could not appoint a woman justice.

137. Governor Terry Sanford Papers, Appointments 1961–65, Judges, Supreme Court, Recommendations, NCSA.

138. SMS to Eunice Ayers, April 4, 1962.

139. Martha C. McKay, interview with author, June 25, 1998. Terry Sanford said in his interview with me that he had consulted Martha McKay, but she was adamant in her recollection that he did not do so, and I believe Sanford was simply assuming that he would have consulted her. McKay did recall that when reporters asked Sanford about the new associate justice's alleged remarks on "woman's place," he told them to ask McKay to comment, but this was after Susie Sharp had been appointed.

140. See Thomas W. Lambeth, interview with author, June 10, 1998.

141. See, e.g., ibid.

142. Terry Sanford to Philip R. Hedrick, April 4, 1962, Governor Terry Sanford Papers, Appointments 1961–65, Judges, Supreme Court, Recommendations, NCSA.

143. SMS journal, October 7, 1980.

144. Professors Herbert R. Baer, M. S. Breckenridge, Frank W. Hanft, Fred B. Mc-Call, M. T. Van Hecke, and R. H. Wettach.

145. MSB to SMS, March 9, 1962.

146. E.g., SMS to Mrs. W. Kerr Scott, March 26, 1962; SMS to Mr. Lennox P. McLendon, April 3, 1962.

147. There are ten letters in support of Don Phillips from West Jefferson (Ashe County) in the governor's recommendations file, and two for Frank Huskins. Governor Terry Sanford Papers, Appointments 1961–65, Judges, Supreme Court, Recommendations, NCSA.

148. Ibid.

149. Terry Sanford, interview with author, June 12, 1995.

150. SMS journal, March 9, 1962.

151. Terry Sanford, interview with author, June 12, 1995.

152. SMS journal, March 9, 1962.

153. Ibid.

154. Ibid.

155. Ibid.

156. Ibid.

157. Ibid., March 10, 1962.

158. Ibid., March 13, 1962.

159. Bette Elliott and Linda Sherrill, "This Town of Ours," *Raleigh Times*, March 14, 1962.

160. Ibid.

161. SMS journal, March 14, 1962.

162. JCK to SMS, March 13, 1962, SMS shorthand copy.

163. Jay Jenkins, "New Chief Justice, Associate Installed," *Charlotte Observer*, March 15, 1962. Additional seating supplemented the leather armchairs.

164. For a description of the justices' seat switching during the swearing-in ceremony, see "Under the Dome," *News and Observer*, March 15, 1962. At the time Susie Sharp joined the supreme court bench, seniority was as follows: Denny (1942), Parker (1952), Bobbitt (1954), Higgins (1954), Rodman (1956), Moore (1959), Sharp (1962).

165. SMS, address, North Carolina State Bar, Annual Meeting, November 1962; SMS, speech to Sheriffs' Association, July 30, 1974.

166. "Our Lady Chief Justice," *North Carolina Magazine*, February 1975; "Judge Susie Sharp Started Career as School Debater," *Durham Morning Herald*, March 11, 1962.

167. SMS to Terry Sanford, May 18, 1985.

168. SMS to Vera Lawrence, April 4, 1962.

169. SMS journal, April 7, 1962. Margaret Fillman Chaney remarked, "She probably said, 'Yes, I believe in this and I believe in that and I'll go ahead and join, but I don't'—Somehow you never thought she meant it. Really and truly." Interview with author, January 18, 1995. See also Louise Sharp, "Note to Sandra Apple, Sec. Main St. United Methodist Church," June 14, 1990 ("Susie M. Sharp . . . Joined church in April (4), 1962").

Chapter 12

1. Roy Parker Jr., "Courtroom Is Home for Woman Jurist," *News and Observer*, March 10, 1962.

2. "Woman Judge Gets Appointment to North Carolina's High Court," *New York Times*, March 10, 1962.

3. SMS to JCK, March 11, 1962.

4. J. Gaskill McDaniel, "Judge Sharp Worries over Court Decisions," *News and Observer*, September 21, 1952 (dateline New Bern). Interestingly, the 1952 article was the one that quoted Judge Sharp to the effect that her appointment to the superior court had taken her completely by surprise.

5. Joan Brock, "Feminine Touch Pervades Justice Building," *News and Observer*, March 17, 1962.

6. Ibid.

7. SMS to JCK, March 11, 1962.

8. Martha C. (Mrs. Herbert S.) McKay to SMS, March 13, 1962.

9. SMS to JCK, March 11, 1962.

10. SMS to Martha C. McKay, March 18, 1962.

11. SMS to Doris Cromartie, May 10, 1962; SMS to Martha C. McKay, May 10, 1962.

12. Ibid.

13. Ibid.

14. SMS to Martha C. McKay, March 18, 1962.

15. *Asheville Citizen-Times*, March 11, 1962.

16. Editorial, *Asheville Times*, March 14, 1962.

17. Ibid. The editorial also said, "Kerr Scott was the last man to occupy the Governor's office to give Western North Carolina anything like a fair shake. It may be indicative of something, that since his tenure the Republican vote in the 12th Congressional district has increased from 26,710 in 1950 to 56,368 in 1960. In Buncombe it's jumped from 8,746 in 1948 to 24,636 in 1960."

18. SMS journal, March 19, 1962.

19. E.g., Hugh Lobdell to Terry Sanford, March 14, 1962; Henry E. Fisher to Terry Sanford, March 15, 1962, Governor Terry Sanford Papers, Appointments 1961–65, Judges, Supreme Court, Recommendations, NCSA.

20. Joseph Grier Jr. to Terry Sanford, March 13, 1962, Governor Terry Sanford Papers, Appointments 1961–65, Judges, Supreme Court, Recommendations, NCSA.

21. Terry Sanford to Philip R. Hedrick, April 4, 1962, Governor Terry Sanford Papers, Appointments 1961–65, Judges, Supreme Court, Recommendations, NCSA.

22. W. C. Burton, "Reidsville Scene," *Greensboro Daily News*, March 26, 1962.

23. Albert Coates to SMS, April 16, 1962.

24. SMS to JCK, March 11, 1962.

25. SMS to Evelyn Ripple, April 4, 1962; SMS to W. Cirt Aldred, April 4, 1962.

26. SMS to JCK, n.d. ("They were even less satisfactory than the reduction in pay I have taken"). According to the *Charlotte Observer*, her salary was $19,000 per year. "Class Valedictorian Escorted Salutatorian Susie Around," *Charlotte Observer*, March 15, 1962.

27. Memo to SMS from Dillard Gardner, May 30, 1962; letter, Gus K. Sproat, Chief Clerk, Supreme Court of Hawaii, to Adrian Newton, Clerk of the Supreme Court of North Carolina, June 15, 1962; Anna O. Blum, President, National Association

of Women Lawyers, to Dillard Gardner, July 23, 1962; September 10, 1962; W. C. ("Mutt") Burton, "No. 7 Is Significant in Miss Susie's Life," *Greensboro Daily News*, March 11, 1962.

28. SMS to JCK, [March 1962].

29. Bert L. Bennett to SMS, March 28, 1962, enclosing copy of letter from Mrs. Herman Halpern, Program Chairman, and Mrs. Julia Rumph, President, Democratic Women of Forsyth County, March 23, 1962.

30. SMS to Mrs. Julia M. Rumph, President, Democratic Women of Forsyth County, April 1, 1962.

31. SMS to Bert L. Bennett, Chairman, State Democratic Executive Committee, April 1, 1962.

32. Ibid.

33. See, e.g., SMS to Superior Court Judge Frank M. Armstrong, April 2, 1962.

34. SMS to Bill and Winona Covington, April 2, 1962.

35. Ibid.

36. SMS to JCK, n.d. (referencing letter from Governor Terry Sanford to SMS, April 10, 1962). Another situation arising upon her appointment was easier to deal with. An attorney and party activist from Monroe, Robert L. Huffman, wrote to Tom I. Davis, executive director of the North Carolina Democratic Executive Committee, about an intimation reportedly seen in the *Charlotte Observer* to the effect that Susie Sharp was a Republican. "If I am to be falsely accused," Justice Sharp wrote to Davis, "the charge of being a Republican is the one I can refute quickest." She laid out her case, citing chapter and verse of her and her father's participation in the Democratic Party, concluding: "I have voted the straight Democratic ticket since the day I became twenty one [sic] without any deviation whatever. I even voted for Al Smith. I would have been disinherited had I shown any signs of defection—which I never did. The nearest I ever came to it was in the sixth grade when I 'took up' with a little Republican named Margaret at school." SMS to Tom I. Davis, April 4, 1962.

37. Louise Sharp, interview with author, December 5, 1994. Louise admonished the officer in charge of Justice Sharp's visit not to "say anything that would embarrass her and don't get me in trouble with her." Louise Sharp to Commander Clark C. Totherow, USN, note accompanying biographical notes for introduction of Justice Sharp. See also SMS to JCK, May 4, 1962.

38. SMS to Evelyn Ripple, May 2, 1962; SMS to JCK, May 4, 1962. Judge Sharp typically characterized herself as a "girl." See, e.g., SMS to JCK, July 26, 1954 ("It seems that nobody but you and I knows that I am just a girl!").

39. Justice Sharp moved into room 314 in 1970, where she remained until occupying the chief justice's chambers in 1975. Louise Stafford, North Carolina Supreme Court Librarian (retired), memo to author, October 22, 1997.

40. Brock, "Feminine Touch Pervades Justice Building."

41. SMS to Dr. Justus Bier, May 29, 1962.

42. Raymond Mason Taylor, interview with author, July 23, 1996.

43. Raymond Mason Taylor, interview with author, August 6, 1996.

44. James G. Billings, interview with author, September 2, 1998.

45. Raymond Mason Taylor, interview with author, July 23, 1996.

46. Ibid.

47. SMS journal, December 10, 1962. Prudently, she waited until after the November election before making the "purchase."

48. Ibid., December 11, 1962.

49. Justice Carlisle W. Higgins to R. D. McMillan Jr., August 24, 1970, copy in SMS Papers.

50. Minutes of the Conference Held 14 September 1971, North Carolina Supreme Court, by permission of Chief Justice Burley Mitchell.

51. SMS journal, September 14, 1971.

52. Raymond Mason Taylor, interview with author, July 23, 1996. When Justice Sharp first joined the supreme court, the marshal-librarian was her childhood friend, Dillard Gardner. After his death in 1964, Raymond Mason Taylor took the position.

53. Billy Arthur, "When the Sir Walter Was 'The Third House of the Legislature,'" *Chapel Hill News*, April 26, 1998.

54. Annie B. Sharp to Mrs. Hoyle, May 27, 1962.

55. Louise Sharp, interview with author, December 5, 1994.

56. SMS to JCK, May 5, 1962.

57. SMS to JCK, May 26, 1962.

58. Thomas W. Lambeth, interview with author, June 10, 1998.

59. SMS journal, March 19, 1962.

60. J. A. C. Dunn, "Clock Ticks, Judges Listen, Rinaldi Waits," *Charlotte Observer*, May 20, 1965.

61. Raymond Mason Taylor, interview with author, August 6, 1996.

62. Henry S. Manning, interview with author, August 12, 1998.

63. SMS to JCK, [week of April 10, 1962] ("I had a nice letter from No. 1 this week—").

64. SMS to JCK, November 13, [1962].

65. Andrew A. Vanore Jr., interview with author, July 31, 1998.

66. SMS to JCK, May 5, 1962.

67. Ibid.

68. SMS to Evelyn Ripple, May 8, 1962.

69. Ibid.

70. SMS to Evelyn Ripple, June 11, 1962.

71. SMS to Lelia Alexander, November 23, 1962. Writing to John Kesler, the new justice described how her life was different from the days when she was "on the circuit" as a superior court judge: "Then every week was bound to bring some human interest story, some 'bon mot,' some amusing incident which I saved for you and could hardly wait to write. But how changed it all is in the Cloisters where little ever happens that is worth reporting—and if it is worth reporting, I can't!" SMS to JCK, November 13, [1962].

72. SMS to JCK, [week of April 10, 1962].

73. Ibid.

74. Ibid.

75. SMS to Mrs. Marie H. Wiley, April 24, 1962.

76. William C. Myers, interview with author, August 17, 1998.

77. E. Richard Jones Jr., interview with author, July 1, 1998.

78. See Dunn, "Clock Ticks, Judges Listen, Rinaldi Waits"; Matthew Eisley, "Time Doesn't March until the Justices File In," *News and Observer*, November 5, 2002.

79. Raymond Mason Taylor, interview with author, July 23, 1996.

80. Louise Sharp, interview with author, December 5, 1994.

81. For descriptions of courtroom procedure, see, e.g., "Ceremony upon the Opening of Court," Raymond Mason Taylor, memo, February 8, 1966; Kay Miller, "Everything from Orange Juice to Races," *News and Observer*, March 30, 1976; Dunn, "Clock Ticks, Judges Listen, Rinaldi Waits."

82. SMS, "Common Errors in Appellate Practice—The Mechanism by Which the Court Hears Appeals," speech at Institute on North Carolina Appellate Practice and Procedure, North Carolina Bar Foundation, October 1965.

83. Ibid.

84. Writing in 1975, Chief Justice Sharp remarked, "I find it very unsatisfactory to have to depend on a law clerk for my preliminary investigation. These 'young'uns' come out of law school with the idea that every person who has been convicted has been denied his constitutional rights. . . .

". . . I find their preliminary reports helpful but no substitute for my own examination of the record. . . . Someday I am going to find a law clerk who will be able to write a statement of facts which I can lift from his report and use in an opinion, but today I have never had one which suited me exactly." SMS to Professor Robert A. Leflar, University of Arkansas School of Law, May 8, 1975.

85. E. Richard Jones Jr., interview with author, July 1, 1998; SMS letter to JCK, June 15, 1962.

86. E. Richard Jones Jr., interview with author, July 1, 1998. At least one subsequent clerk employed this same technique.

87. Ibid.

88. Henry S. Manning, interview with author, August 12, 1998.

89. SMS to JCK, June 20–21, 1962.

90. "Conference Rules," n.d., typescript, photocopy.

91. Henry Scott, "Judge Sharp—a Court's Order: Rock of Tradition, Seldom Jarred by Judicious Dissent," *Charlotte Observer*, July 29, 1979.

92. SMS journal, September 13, 1962.

93. The expression "Hobson's choice" is said to have originated with a livery stable owner in Cambridge, England, who would provide a customer with the horse nearest the door or no horse at all.

94. SMS, "Greetings from Chief Justice Sharp," speech to North Carolina State Bar, Charlotte, October 28, 1977.

95. William A. Shires, "A Touch of Lavender in Basket," *Raleigh Times*, December 3, 1966. For general background on the voting and drafting process, see Miller, "Everything from Orange Juice to Races."

96. Henry Belk, "Justices Brush Elbows with Ordinary Folk," *Greensboro Daily News*, September 20, 1965. See also Charles Craven, "State's Top Judges Unwind over Lunch," *News and Observer*, November 25, 1977.

97. SMS to Robert A. Leflar, May 8, 1975. Justice Sharp was also quoted publicly

as saying that the justices were not above discussing cases at lunch (Craven, "State's Top Judges Unwind over Lunch").

98. Craven,"State's Top Judges Unwind over Lunch" (quoting Justice William J. Copeland).

99. SMS journal, May 15, 1962.

100. SMS to JCK, December 1964.

101. Bert Bennett, State Chairman, to Dave McConnell, Chairman, North Carolina Board of Elections, June 6, 1962, copy in SMS Papers.

102. See Bert M. Montague, Administrative Assistant to the Chief Justice, "Courts of North Carolina," typescript pamphlet, n.d. [pre–court reform].

103. "Historical Development of the North Carolina Court System," in *North Carolina Courts, 1991–92: Annual Report of the Administrative Office of the Courts*; "Judge Calls J. P. System Scandalous," *Charlotte Observer*, November 4, 1962.

104. J. Spencer Bell, Chairman, "Report of the Committee on Improving and Expediting the Administration of Justice to the 1958 Conference of the North Carolina Bar Association" (speech prepared for delivery June 13, 1958, at the annual meeting of the North Carolina Bar Association at Myrtle Beach, S.C.), copy in SMS Papers; John Sanders, Assistant Director, Institute of Government, "Court Reform: Where Shall the Power Lie?" *Greensboro Daily News*, April 26, 1959.

105. Jay Jenkins, "Study Unit Nips Section of Bell's Court Proposal," *Charlotte Observer*, January 24, 1959. This article created consternation within the commission, whose members had agreed not to discuss their conclusions publicly before delivering their report to the governor. In a letter to John Kesler, Justice Sharp puzzled over the source of the leak, even speculating that the meeting might have been "bugged." SMS to JCK, January [25], 1959. Although she disclaimed the reference to her role, she said the article was "deadly accurate and contained information that only one on the inside could have supplied." She wondered if the reporter's reference to her as having had "the key role" could be traced to a comment by commission member Ed Yarborough, who cracked, as the group adjourned the night before the article appeared, "This plan is Sharp wine in Bell bottles." According to Justice Sharp, it was Yarborough who had come up with the proposal that broke the impasse between her plan and the Bell plan.

106. Sanders, "Court Reform: Where Shall the Power Lie?"

107. One result of court reform was that, before coming into the state system, some counties replaced all their good typewriters, desks, and other equipment with worthless substitutions scrounged from abused and neglected corners of county buildings. The state, forced to declare such furnishings surplus junk, bought new replacements paid for by the state taxpayers. Raymond Mason Taylor, interview with author, November 4, 1996.

108. Ibid.

109. See ibid.

110. See ibid.

111. Terry Sanford to SMS, handwritten note on Governor's Office notepad, n.d.; SMS journal, October 31, 1962.

112. SMS journal, October 31, 1962.

113. Ibid., November 1, 1962.

114. Several months earlier, Justice Bobbitt had been heard to comment that Judge Pless supported court reform in the hope that the number of supreme court justices would be increased from seven to nine. SMS journal, August 27, 1962. Whatever his reasoning, Bobbitt's opposition upset some of his old Charlotte colleagues, who claimed that the last time they talked to him he had not read the bill and they did not think he had yet. SMS to JCK, [1962] ("I know you were kidding me").

115. "3 Justices Are against Amendment," *Greensboro Daily News*, November 2, 1962.

116. "High Court Justices Split on Court Plan," *News and Observer*, November 2, 1962.

117. SMS journal, November 1–2, 1962.

118. SMS, "Judge Susie's Speech," typescript; "Judge Calls J. P. System Scandalous."

119. SMS, "Judge Susie's Speech," typescript.

120. SMS to JCK, November 9, 1962.

121. See, e.g., SMS to Judge Martha C. Daughtrey, November 16, 1982. The General Assembly passed the Judicial Department Act of 1965 to implement the new judicial article in the North Carolina Constitution. The newly created Administrative Office of the Courts was established effective on July 1, 1965.

122. SMS to JCK, November 16, 1962.

123. "Under the Dome," *News and Observer*, December 8, 1962.

124. SMS to JCK, December 14, 1962.

125. SMS journal, December 27, 1962.

Chapter 13

1. Judge Sharp wrote to John Kesler about JFK's assassination: "The news of the President's assassination stunned me so that I was about to start home without writing this letter. . . . I was dictating when we got the news. Mrs. #4 called him, and he buzzed all of us on the intercom." SMS to JCK, [November 1963].

2. Judge Hughes was one of three women on the federal bench at the time. The other two were Florence E. Allen, U.S. Court of Appeals for the Sixth Circuit, and Burnita Shelton Matthews, U.S. District Court for the District of Columbia. In 1970, when Judge Hughes was the featured guest at an informal luncheon discussion at Wake Forest University, Judge Sharp contrived to get herself invited. Writing to the dean of women after the event, Judge Sharp expressed her gratitude for being absolved "from the presumption of having invited myself!" She told the dean, "I had wanted to meet Judge Sarah Hughes for twenty years; so when Mr. Hays told me she was coming to Wake Forest, I just 'made bold.'" SMS to Lu Leake, May 4, 1970. A local newspaper reported, "One of the most interested listeners at the session yesterday was another jurist—Associate Justice Susie Sharp of the N.C. Supreme Court. The two petite judges had plenty to say to each other and each looked her feminine best—Judge Sharp in white linen and Judge Hughes in a pale blue dress, each proving

that you can be a successful judge and a lady, too." Annie Lee Singletary, "Judge Sarah Hughes' Career: From Beat to Bench," *Winston-Salem Journal*, May 1, 1970. Judge Hughes had a Winston-Salem connection, having taught science at Salem Academy for two years after her graduation from Goucher College. Ibid.

3. SMS to JCK, [November 1963].

4. SMS journal, November 24, 1963.

5. Ibid., November 25, 1963.

6. SMS to President Lyndon Baines Johnson, July 9, 1964.

7. Editorial, "Speaker Ban: Study in Contrasts," *Greensboro Daily News*, August 13, 1965.

8. Jefferson B. Fordham to Governor Dan K. Moore, June 10, 1965 (copy forwarded to SMS by Governor Moore).

9. SMS to Jefferson B. Fordham, July 7, 1965. She also included her analysis of the situation: "Because his constituents regard it as a weapon against communism many a legislator who knows better would have voted for the ban notwithstanding. Furthermore, the sad truth is that the acceptance of the ban also evidences a deep seated resentment against the University throughout the state. This resentment includes Junius Scales; it is a part of the desegregation trauma; it is fanned by the reports which students take home of the breakdown of student government, drunken orgies and immorality both on the campus and in the fraternities."

10. *Dickson v. Sitterson*, 280 F. Supp. 486 (M.D.N.C. 1968). The law was not officially taken off the books until 1994, however.

11. Douglas, *Reading, Writing and Race*, 49.

12. 402 U.S. 1 (1971).

13. SMS to JCK, March 9, 1963.

14. SMS to JCK, April 30, 1963.

15. SMS to Evelyn Ripple, July 4, 1964.

16. SMS to Jessie Mebane, September 2, 1964.

17. Ibid.

18. Ibid.

19. Ibid.

20. Ibid.

21. *State v. Cobb*, 262 N.C. 262 (1964).

22. Ibid. at 266.

23. Ibid.

24. *Robinson v. Florida*, 378 U.S. 153, 156 (1964).

25. *Fox v. North Carolina*, 378 U.S. 587 (1964); *Williams v. North Carolina*, 378 U.S. 548 (1964).

26. *Dilday v. Beaufort Co. Bd. of Educ.*, 267 N.C. 438 (1966).

27. Ibid. at 451.

28. Ibid. at 452.

29. Ibid. at 455 (Lake, J., concurring).

30. Ibid. at 456 (Lake, J., concurring).

31. Ibid. at 452.

32. Ibid.

33. "Justice Susie Sharp Leading Vote-Getter," *News and Observer*, November 30, 1966.

34. Revealingly, Justice Sharp's opinions adhered closely to precedent on the law of evidence. Many of these cases were late in her career after she had become chief justice, but her appreciation for predictability on evidence issues, so often raised and answered in the heat of trial, was deep and long-lasting. See, e.g., *Woods v. Ins. Co.*, 295 N.C. 500 (1978); *Duggins v. Bd. of CPA Examiners*, 294 N.C. 120 (1978); *State v. Foddrell*, 291 N.C. 546 (1977).

35. *Rabon v. Hosp.*, 269 N.C. 1 (1967).

36. Ibid. at 3 (citation omitted).

37. Ibid.

38. Ibid. at 5.

39. Ibid.

40. Ibid. at 7.

41. Ibid.

42. Henry S. Manning, interview with author, August 12, 1998.

43. Ibid.

44. *Rabon*, 269 N.C. at 12. Justice Sharp made a distinction between hospitals and legitimate charities such as churches, orphanages, rescue missions, transient homes for the indigent, and the like, which would retain the protection of the charitable immunity doctrine. Ibid. at 21.

45. Ibid. at 16–20.

46. Ibid. at 13 (citation omitted).

47. SMS to Justice Hunt Parker, "Spring Term 1963," re: *Gaskins v. Ins. Co.*, 260 N.C. 122 (1963).

48. SMS to W. Kerr Scott, October 15, 1950, Governor W. Kerr Scott Papers, Judges, Endorsements, NCSA.

49. SMS journal, August 5, 1966.

50. Governor Dan K. Moore appointed Pless to Justice Parker's seat when Parker succeeded Chief Justice Denny. According to Henry Manning, Governor Moore allowed Pless to cap his career with a position on the court, but he made it clear that Pless was to resign in short order to make room for Frank Huskins, director of the newly created Administrative Office of the Courts. Moore allegedly told Pless, "I'm going to put you on the court but I want your letter of resignation right now. I'm going to put Frank Huskins in that spot before I go out of the governor's office. . . . He's going to take your seat. And I'm going to have your letter of resignation before I even appoint you." Henry S. Manning, interview with author, August 12, 1998.

51. Such a hybrid prospective application was more problematic than a pure prospective application, because it required Rowan Memorial Hospital to pay damages even though the law had been otherwise when the case arose, and yet excluded any other plaintiffs negligently injured prior to the decision. However, she had substantial authority to support her. The court denied a petition for rehearing based on this point, alleging violation of the U.S. Constitution's equal protection provisions.

52. Raymond Mason Taylor, interview with author, August 6, 1996.

53. "When our newest Justice arrived the Court stood three to three, and it appeared for a while that Rabon v. Hospital would be 'an advisare vult indefinitely.' However, he finally broke the tie; so you should really credit him with getting the decision down." SMS to William T. Covington, January 25, 1967.

54. SMS to Jefferson B. Fordham, February 28, 1967.

55. "Powers of Judiciary Are Issue in Ruling," [*Winston-Salem Journal?*], January 21, 1967, SMS scrapbook.

56. SMS, interview by Jane L. Sharpe, 1982, audiocassette, AHG Papers, RCC.

57. *Plessy v. Ferguson*, 163 U.S. 537 (1896).

58. John Leo, "Sad Affair with 'Romantic Judging,'" *News and Observer*, January 17, 1995.

59. *Rabon*, 269 N.C. at 20.

60. Ibid.

61. Editorial, "Making Law," *News and Observer*, January 23, 1967. There are some who trace the current crisis in health care back to the rationale in *Rabon*, because it opened up the hospital to malpractice litigation and thus could be said to be responsible for the increase in medical costs and insurance premiums. E.g., Hugh P. Griffin, interview with author, March 25, 1998. As Justice Sharp had gone to great lengths to point out in her opinion, however, North Carolina was if anything bringing up the rear with respect to the national trend on charitable immunity.

62. Michael Skube, "As Justice Sharp Leaves," *Winston-Salem Journal*, August 5, 1979 (quoting unnamed source). In 1976 Justice Sharp addressed the immunity issue as it applied to contracts entered into by the state. *Smith v. State*, 289 N.C. 303 (1976).

63. Questionnaire from the University of Connecticut, November 25, 1973.

64. Ibid., quoting Karl Llewellyn, *Jurisprudence: Realism in Theory and Practice* (Chicago: University of Chicago Press, 1962).

65. SMS to MSB, January 15–17, 1965.

66. *Terry v. Double Cola Bottling Co.*, 263 N.C. 1 (1964).

67. Ibid. at 7 (Sharp, J., concurring).

68. Ibid. Justice Sharp wrote: "Whether we call the rule for which I contend strict liability in tort, as the professors and chaste logic might require, or an implied warranty of fitness imposed by law, makes no difference. It seems to me that reason and justice should now impel this Court to hold that, under modern merchandising conditions, a manufacturer of food products in sealed containers represents to all who acquire them in legitimate channels of trade that his goods are wholesome and fit for human consumption; and that, if they are not, and injury results to the ultimate consumer, he may recover as well against the manufacturer as against his immediate vendor." Ibid. at 13.

69. Ibid. at 4.

70. Her interest may have been stimulated initially by cases that Sharp & Sharp handled in the 1930s. In one case their client had discovered "a tiny mouse" in a bottle of Coca-Cola. The bottle was traced back to the bottling plant "where it was secured sealed until it was delivered to the party with the mouse in it," according to a letter to the bottler signed by Jim Sharp. The client had drunk some of the cola "and was

made deathly sick." Mr. Sharp wrote, "[I]f we can settle it without going into court we would be glad to do so." JMS to Coca-Cola Bottling Co., Reidsville, May 19, 1934. Another case alleged the discovery of "a variety of insects, several flies and other larger winged insects" in a Coke bottle. Complaint in suit by D. C. Gammon against the Reidsville Coca-Cola Bottling Company in Reidsville Recorder's Court, 1935, Sharp & Sharp files.

71. *Terry*, 263 N.C. at 13 (Sharp, J., concurring).

72. Ibid.

73. *Tedder v. Pepsi-Cola Bottling Co. of Raleigh*, 270 N.C. 301 (1967).

74. N.C. Gen. Stat. § 99B-2(b) (1979).

75. *Leatherman v. Leatherman*, 297 N.C. 618 (1979).

76. N.C. Gen. Stat. §§ 50-20, 50-21 (1981).

77. *Leatherman*, 297 N.C. at 628 (Sharp, C.J., dissenting, joined by Huskins, J.).

78. Ibid. at 624.

79. "Two classes of trusts arise by operation of law; resulting trusts and constructive trusts. '[T]he creation of a resulting trust involves the application of the doctrine that valuable consideration rather than legal title determines the equitable title resulting from a transaction; whereas a constructive trust ordinarily arises out of the existence of fraud, actual or presumptive—usually involving the violation of a confidential or fiduciary relation—in view of which equity transfers the beneficial title to some person other than the holder of the legal title.'" Ibid. at 621.

80. Ibid. at 636 (Sharp, C.J., dissenting, joined by Huskins, J.).

81. *Booker v. Medical Center*, 297 N.C. 458 (1979).

82. N.C. Gen. Stat. § 97-53 (13) (1971).

83. *Booker*, 297 N.C. at 470.

84. This issue was not raised on appeal to the North Carolina Supreme Court. Ibid. at 465.

85. Ibid. at 469.

86. Ibid. at 466–67.

87. Ibid. at 472.

88. Ibid. at 475.

89. 297 N.C. 636 (1979).

90. Plaintiffs' lawyers attributed much of the liberalization of worker's compensation cases in the 1980s to the departure from the court of Justice Frank Huskins in February 1982. Huskins, who had served as chairman of the Industrial Commission before joining the court, was considered to have exerted an influence on the court against finding in favor of the worker. Jack Betts, "A Court in Transition," *Greensboro Daily News*, September 19, 1982.

91. *Sutton v. Duke*, 277 N.C. 94 (1970).

92. *D&W, Inc. v. City of Charlotte*, 268 N.C. 577 (1966).

93. Kenneth G. Slocum, "The Brown-Bag Blues: North Carolina Has Wets Crying in Beer," *Wall Street Journal*, January 30, 1967.

94. Porter Munn, "Brown-Bag Ban Is Effective Now, N.C. Supreme Court Says Sharply," *Charlotte Observer*, December 20, 1966; SMS journal, December 19, 1966.

95. Henry S. Manning, interview with author, August 12, 1998.

96. Slocum, "The Brown-Bag Blues: North Carolina Has Wets Crying in Beer."

97. SMS journal, December 5, 1966.

98. Ibid.

99. SMS journal, December 6, 1966.

100. SMS to JCK, July 17, [1964].

101. *Toone v. Adams*, 262 N.C. 403 (1964).

102. *Time*, October 2, 1964.

103. *Toone*, 262 N.C. at 408.

104. Jack Betts, "Susie Marshall Sharp, Straight Shooter," *News and Observer*, March 3, 1996.

105. SMS to JCK, July 27, 1964 (quoting Breck).

106. SMS to MSB, October 10, 1964.

107. SMS journal, July 2, 1964; Kay Miller, "Biographical Profile, Chief Justice Susie Sharp," typescript, n.d.

108. SMS to JCK, July 17, [1964]; May 12, 1955.

109. SMS journal, July 2, 1964.

110. Jack Betts, "Sympathy for the Officials? Never!" *Charlotte Observer*, June 26, 1993.

111. Joe Doster, "Appeals Court Has Speeded Up Process of Justice in N.C.," *Winston-Salem Journal-Sentinel*, August 2, 1970; handwritten tally attached to "Information on Intermediate Court of Appeals," [1965] (showing 379 written opinions for fiscal year 1962–63, and 181 motions).

112. Untitled, undated typescript, labeled "Montague" by hand ("An appeal may be taken"), [1965]. Bert Montague was administrative assistant to the chief justice. The typed manuscript shows 462 as the number of opinions written in fiscal 1964–65, with that number crossed out and corrected by hand to read 473. See also handwritten tally attached to "Information on Intermediate Court of Appeals," [1965] (showing 473 written opinions for fiscal year 1964–65).

113. *Raleigh Times*, September 10, 1966.

114. Untitled, undated typescript, labeled "Montague" by hand ("An appeal may be taken"), [1965].

115. *Gideon v. Wainwright*, 372 U.S. 335 (1963); *Miranda v. Arizona*, 384 U.S. 436 (1966).

116. SMS to MSB, October 10, 1964.

117. As of August 2007, the court of appeals had increased to fifteen judges.

118. Doster, "Appeals Court Has Speeded Up Process."

Chapter 14

1. Terry Sanford, interview with author, June 12, 1995.

2. Terry Sanford, interview, UNC-TV broadcast, May 28, 1998. Henry Hall Wilson Jr., a North Carolinian who had worked for both Sanford and Kennedy during the campaign, became a special assistant in the White House, a legislative liaison with an office three doors from the Oval Office. Ibid. Charged primarily with moving the Kennedy legislative initiatives through Congress, he also served as Governor San-

ford's conduit to federal appointments and favors. Covington and Ellis, *Terry Sanford*, 268. If Sanford needed anything, all he had to do was pick up the phone and call Wilson. Terry Sanford, interview, UNC-TV broadcast, May 28, 1998.

3. Rob Christensen, "Sanford Answered History's Knock, Changed Course of RTP," *News and Observer*, April 27, 1998.

4. See, e.g., Ragan, *The New Day*, 87; Christensen, "Sanford Answered History's Knock, Changed Course of RTP."

5. Terry Sanford to John F. Kennedy, October 29, 1962. A blind carbon copy went to Henry Hall Wilson. The White House acknowledged the request November 7, 1962. Governor Terry Sanford Papers, Government, Federal Appointments, NCSA.

6. Terry Sanford to John F. Kennedy, October 29, 1962, Governor Terry Sanford Papers, Government, Federal Appointments, NCSA.

7. Resolution and accompanying correspondence, June 22, 1962, Governor Terry Sanford Papers, Appointments 1961–65, Judges, Supreme Court, NCSA.

8. Superior Court Judge J. William Copeland to Terry Sanford, n.d. [probably late September or October 1962], Governor Terry Sanford Papers, Government, Federal Appointments, NCSA.

9. SMS to Terry Sanford, January 24, 1963.

10. SMS journal, January 31, 1963.

11. SMS to Evelyn Ripple, September 18, 1963.

12. SMS to Terry Sanford, January 24, 1963.

13. Eudora Garrison, "Susie Sharp: Every Inch a Judge and a Lady," *Charlotte Observer*, March 13, 1962.

14. Ibid.

15. SMS to JCK, August 22, 1963. This apparently refers to the conversation SMS had with Terry Sanford, noted in her journal on January 31, 1963: "[The governor] says he told 'Henry' [Hall Wilson] in Washington and he wanted to know if she meant it. I said, 'She's an honest woman.'"

16. SMS journal, November 22, 1961.

17. Ibid., November 26, 1961.

18. Ibid., December 6, 1961; December 17, 1961.

19. Ibid., January 5, 1962.

20. Ibid., February 4, 1962.

21. Ibid., March 16, 1962; JCK to SMS, n.d., SMS's shorthand copy.

22. SMS journal, April 20, 1962.

23. Ibid., May 27, 1962.

24. Ibid., September 21, 1962.

25. Ibid., October 28, 1962.

26. Ibid., March 17, 1963.

27. "5 Justices File for New Terms," *Durham Morning Herald*, February 10, 1966.

28. The woman was Marjorie Pless. SMS journal, February 10, 1966.

29. ABS to Susie Garrett, February 14, 1966, courtesy of Clara Garrett Fountain.

30. SMS to William Snider, February 18, 1966.

31. SMS to William Blackwell, February 17, 1966.

32. Ibid.

33. SMS to William Snider, February 18, 1966.

34. Ibid.

35. Ibid.

36. Ibid.

37. Ibid.

38. Ibid.

39. SMS to William Blackwell, February 17, 1966.

40. SMS journal, February 16, 1966.

41. ABS to Susie Garrett, February 14, 1966, courtesy of Clara Garrett Fountain.

42. Newman, *Hugo Black*, 566.

43. SMS to Charles B. Wade Jr., Vice President, R. J. Reynolds Tobacco Co., August 14, 1965.

44. SMS to Marjorie Hunter, September 23, 1965.

45. Ibid.

46. SMS to William Snider, February 18, 1966.

47. Ward, "An Extraconstitutional Arrangement."

48. Ibid.

49. Ibid., citing Williams, *Thurgood Marshall*, 329.

50. U.S. senators Sam Ervin Jr. and B. Everett Jordan to President Lyndon B. Johnson, March 2, 1967, copy in SMS Papers.

51. SMS to Miss Marjorie Yokley, President, North Carolina Federation of Women's Clubs, Inc., March 6, 1967.

52. SMS to U.S. senators Sam Ervin Jr. and B. Everett Jordan, March 6, 1967.

53. Dan K. Moore to Lyndon B. Johnson, March 8, 1967 (copy sent to SMS by Dan Moore); SMS to ABS, March 9, 1967.

54. Dan K. Moore to SMS, March 8, 1967.

55. Congressman David N. Henderson to Allen H. Gwynn [*sic*] Jr., March 14, 1967, copy in SMS Papers.

56. *A Joint Resolution Memorializing the President of the United States to Appoint Associate Justice Susie Marshall Sharp to the Supreme Court of the United States*, North Carolina General Assembly, Session 1967, Resolution # 21, H.R. 203, Session Laws of 1967, p. 1926, ratified March 10, 1967.

57. AHG to Senator Sam J. Ervin, March 10, 1967; AHG to Senator Everett Jordan, March 10, 1967, AHG Papers, RCC.

58. James A. Webster Jr. to Lyndon B. Johnson, March 13, 1967 (cc to SMS).

59. William M. Storey, Secretary-Treasurer, North Carolina Bar Association, to Lyndon B. Johnson, May 9, 1967 (bcc to SMS).

60. SMS journal, March 29, 1967; Thomas J. Bolch, interview with author, August 7, 1998.

61. Thomas J. Bolch, interview with author, August 7, 1998.

62. Henry S. Manning, interview with author, August 12, 1998. Manning had become very close to Justice Sharp during his year of clerkship. She had even agreed to be godmother to his baby son, and she would continue a close relationship with

him and his family over the years. After her name was put forward as a prominent possibility for Justice Clark's seat, she shared thoughts with Manning that she might not have shared with others. His recollections merit, therefore, particular weight.

63. SMS to Joseph W. Grier, March 22, 1967. See also SMS to Mrs. J. E. (Mary) Whitfield, March 20, 1967.

64. SMS to Mrs. J. E. (Mary) Whitfield, March 20, 1967.

65. SMS journal, January 18, 1963.

66. Ibid., June 18, 1963.

67. Ibid., January 13, 1964.

68. Ibid., August 9, 1964.

69. Ibid., September 15, 1965.

70. Henry S. Manning, interview with author, August 12, 1998.

71. Chief Justice Warren Burger, confirmed, 1969; Clement Haynsworth and G. Harrold Carswell, not confirmed, 1970; Justice Harry A. Blackmun, confirmed, 1970; William H. Rehnquist, confirmed, 1972; Lewis F. Powell Jr., confirmed, 1972.

72. Strom Thurmond switched to the Republican Party in 1964.

73. SMS to U.S. representative Richardson Preyer, May 29, 1969.

74. SMS to Dr. Rachael Davis, December 5, 1969.

75. SMS to Judge Francis O. Clarkson, December 4, 1969.

76. J. Dean, *The Rehnquist Choice*, 21, citing Jacobstein and Mersky, *The Rejected: Sketches of the 26 Men Named for the Supreme Court But Not Confirmed by the Senate* (Milpitas, Calif.: Toucan Valley Publications, 1993), 152.

77. SMS to Carol F. Boisseau, March 24, 1970.

78. J. Dean, *The Rehnquist Choice*, 155, quoting National Archives and Records Administration (NARA) transcript.

79. See ibid., 63, 89.

80. See ibid., 104–5.

81. Dobbins, cartoon, *Boston Herald Traveler* (Ben Roth Agency), n.d., SMS scrapbook.

82. J. Dean, *The Rehnquist Choice*, 104, quoting NARA transcript.

83. Ibid., 178–85, quoting NARA transcript.

84. Ibid., 113, quoting NARA transcript.

85. Ibid.

86. Senators Sam J. Ervin Jr. and B. Everett Jordan to Richard M. Nixon, September 23, 1971, copy in SMS Papers.

87. Petition to President Nixon signed by twenty-six members of the UNC School of Law faculty, September 27, 1971, copy in SMS Papers.

88. See David Lawrence, "Pressure for Woman on the Court," *Washington Star*, September 28, 1971.

89. J. Dean, *The Rehnquist Choice*, 303 n. 4.

90. Ibid., 113, quoting NARA transcript.

91. See ibid., 110.

92. SMS to Mrs. Hattie D. Clinton, October 4, 1971.

93. Ibid.

94. SMS to William Friday, October 15, 1971.

95. The twelfth vote was "not opposed," rather than "qualified."

96. J. Dean, *The Rehnquist Choice*, 235, quoting NARA transcript.

97. Ibid., 247–48, quoting NARA transcript.

98. See ibid., 247–49.

99. Jack Betts, "N.C. Delegation Proposes Sharp for Court Seat," *Greensboro Daily News*, November 14, 1975.

100. Ibid.

101. O'Brien, "Filling Justice William O. Douglas' Seat."

102. SMS to Mrs. Thomas A. ("Bobbie") Sharp, December 1, 1975.

103. Terry Sanford, interview with author, June 12, 1995. ("I could have probably put her on the Supreme Court of the United States when Kennedy was president. And I raised that question with her. . . . But I remember specifically [her] telling me that she wasn't interested in that. . . . [A]t that time, I was in a position, probably, to have been able to have considerable influence on that particular appointment.") Kennedy thought so highly of Sanford that three days before he was assassinated, Kennedy told his secretary, Evelyn Lincoln, that he planned to jettison Johnson as his vice-presidential running mate and was considering replacing him with Sanford. Lincoln, *Kennedy and Johnson*, 205.

104. Grossman, "The Role of the American Bar Association in the Selection of Federal Judges," 805.

105. Ross, "Participation by the Public in the Federal Judicial Selection Process," 37.

106. Report of the Standing Committee on Federal Judiciary, Annual Report of the American Bar Association, vol. 87 (Chicago: Headquarters Office, 1963), 605.

107. Ibid., 607.

108. Ibid., vol. 92 (1968), 434; vol. 93 (1968), 419.

109. Ibid., vol. 94 (1970), 459.

110. Exhibit C-2, John W. Mitchell to Leon Jaworski, President of the ABA, and Lawrence E. Walsh, Chairman, Standing Committee on Federal Judiciary, *A.B.A. Reporter* 97 (1973): 229.

111. Exhibit C, Special Report by the Standing Committee on Federal Judiciary to the House of Delegates, October 31, 1971, *A.B.A. Reporter* 97 (1973): 224–25.

112. See J. Dean, *The Rehnquist Choice*, 157. The other candidates were Senate Majority Whip Robert Byrd of West Virginia, Fifth Circuit U.S. Court of Appeals judge Charles Clark, and Fifth Circuit U.S. Court of Appeals judge Paul H. Roney.

113. Ibid., 189.

114. SMS to Thomas A. Sharp, October 28, 1971.

115. Covington and Ellis, *Terry Sanford*, 359–63.

Chapter 15

1. Governor Luther Hodges initially appointed John Kesler to the Judicial Council in 1959 for a two-year term, subsequently renewed. This appointment was con-

sidered a much-coveted honor. The council, consisting of supreme court members, attorneys, superior court judges, and representatives of the General Assembly, made recommendations to the legislature regarding statutory improvements in the judicial system.

2. SMS journal, March 29, 1966.

3. SMS to JCK, June 21, 1965.

4. Ibid.

5. See, e.g., SMS journal, October 31, 1964; February 6, 1965.

6. SMS to JCK, October 29, 1965.

7. SMS to Jessie Mebane, September 2, 1964.

8. ABS to Susie Garrett, May 5, 1965, courtesy of Clara Garrett Fountain.

9. Ibid.

10. Norwood E. Robinson, interview with author, November 16, 1994.

11. SMS to Marion Allen, August 16, 1967.

12. SMS to Mrs. Floyd Angel, August 30, 1967.

13. Ibid.

14. SMS to Bertha Thompson, September 6, 1967.

15. SMS to Mrs. Thomas A. ("Bobbie") Sharp, September 11, 1967.

16. SMS to Jimmy Taylor, October 17, 1967.

17. Ibid.

18. SMS to Mrs. Zillie Cole, November 28, 1967.

19. SMS to Thomas A. Sharp, June 17, 1971; SMS to Barbara Taylor, October 22, 1972.

20. SMS to Charles W. Campbell, August 26, 1969; Charles W. Campbell to SMS, October 3, 1969; SMS to Thomas A. Sharp, June 17, 1971.

21. Louise Sharp to Evelyn Garrett, June 1, 1968, courtesy of Clara Garrett Fountain.

22. "Engineer Gets Food Firm Job," *Winston-Salem Sentinel*, August 2, 1968.

23. SMS to J. Patrick Kelly, Executive News Editor, *Winston-Salem Journal*, May 26, 1969.

24. Thomas A. Sharp to author, February 18, 1995.

25. SMS to Velma Jean Clary, *Winston-Salem Journal and Sentinel*, May 4, 1970.

26. SMS to Susie Newsom Lynch, February 15, 1972.

27. SMS to Lieutenant Governor Pat Taylor, March 26, 1969.

28. Ibid.

29. Editorial, "A Great Mind, A Merry Twinkle," *News and Observer*, September 29, 1992.

30. Louise Sharp, interview with author, December 5, 1994.

31. Background material on Justice Bobbitt is drawn primarily from Willis P. Whichard, "Presentation Address," given upon the presentation of Chief Justice William H. Bobbitt's portrait to the North Carolina Supreme Court, March 10, 1993, and Joseph W. Grier Jr., "William Haywood Bobbitt, His Legal and Judicial Career, 1922–1974," November 12, 1976, copy in SMS Papers.

32. Whichard, "Presentation Address," March 10, 1993.

33. See Teri Crook, "W. H. Bobbitt, Retired N.C. Chief Justice, Dies," *News and*

Observer, September 28, 1992; Bob Wilson, "A Reverence for the Law and a Twinkle in the Eye" ("Tar Heel of the Week"), *News and Observer*, May 9, 1971.

34. Willis P. Whichard, interview with author, October 18, 1994.

35. SMS to JCK, October 29, 1965.

36. SMS journal, April 15, 1967.

37. Ibid., May 26, 1967.

38. Ibid., July 25, 1967.

39. Ibid., August 3, 1967.

40. Ibid., August 8, 1967.

41. Ibid.

42. Ibid., August 12, 1967.

43. Ibid.

44. Ibid., August 18, 1967.

45. Ibid., August 22, 1967.

46. Ibid., August 27, 1967.

47. Ibid., September 5, 1967.

48. Ibid., September 1, 1967. Presumably, it would be just as unseemly for a wife to succeed her husband as chief justice as it would be for a husband and wife to serve on the court simultaneously.

49. Ibid.

50. Ibid., October 11, 1967.

51. Ibid., October 22, 1967.

52. Mary Regan, "Four Women, Four Views," *News and Observer*, August 23, 1970.

53. SMS journal, October 13, 1967.

54. James C. Fuller, interview with author, October 20, 1998.

55. SMS journal, October 28, 1967.

56. Ibid.

57. Ibid., November 9, 1967.

58. Ibid.

59. Ibid., March 6, 1968.

60. Ibid., November 9, 1967.

61. Ibid., January 11, 1968.

62. Ibid., January 7, 1968.

63. Ibid., December 3, 1967.

64. Ibid., March 15, 1968.

65. Ibid., May 5, 1968.

66. Ibid., June 25, 1968.

67. Ibid., June 22, 1968.

68. Ibid.

69. Ibid.

70. Ibid., October 19, 1967.

71. Ibid., September 21, 1969.

72. Ibid., September 22, 1969.

73. See Ned Cline, "Lake's Rocky Road Takes New Direction," *Charlotte Observer*,

August 14, 1978: "In Lake's 13 years on the supreme court he has been a diligent worker and a jurist highly regarded by his colleagues, even when they disagreed with his opinions. . . . 'Sometimes we'd like to shake him because he's certainly conservative,' Chief Justice Susie Sharp said. 'His philosophy is not much different from some of the rest of us, but his style is. There has never been any lack of respect for his opinions because even if he's arguing against you, he's strengthening your knowledge of the situation.'"

74. "No. 1 Waitress Becomes U.S. Citizen," *News and Observer*, March 27, 1970.

75. SMS journal, January 5, 1969.

76. Ibid., October 10, 1968; October 11, 1968.

77. Ibid., January 8, 1969.

78. Sherry McCullough, "Chief Justice Sworn," *Raleigh Times*, November 17, 1969.

79. See, e.g., SMS to siblings, May 11, 1973.

80. SMS to Janie Sands Smith and her mother (Mrs. A. P. Sands), May 14, 1971.

81. See, e.g., SMS journal, March 9, 1972.

82. Florence Newsom to SMS, March 20, 1972.

83. SMS journal, July 20, 1970.

84. Ibid., December 31, 1970.

85. Ibid., May 26, 1971.

86. SMS to Caroline Earnhardt, August 24, 1972.

87. SMS journal, September 9, 1972.

88. Ibid.

89. Ibid., December 22, 1972.

90. Ibid.

91. Eleanor Dare Kennedy, "Susie Sharp: Her Election as Chief Justice 'Happy Combination of Circumstances,'" *Greensboro Daily News*, December 29, 1974.

92. SMS to Lucy Haynes, December 6, 1972.

93. SMS journal, December 31, 1972.

94. JCK to SMS, [fragment hand-dated by SMS "173"].

95. SMS to JCK, [fragment hand-dated by SMS "173"].

96. Ibid.

97. SMS journal, January 24, 1973.

98. Ibid., February 6, 1973.

99. Ibid., February 24, 1973.

100. Ibid., February 25, 1973.

Chapter 16

1. Since Reconstruction only one Republican, Daniel L. Russell, had served as governor (1897–1901).

2. Ned Cline, "Holshouser Can Alter Political Complexion of N.C. Judiciary," *Greensboro Daily News*, December 3, 1972.

3. Robert Morgan served as North Carolina state senator before becoming attor-

ney general (1969–74) and U.S. senator (1975–81). As it happened, Lake and Morgan came to a parting of the ways in 1974 when Morgan, running for the U.S. Senate, attempted to distance himself from Lake as he sought to broaden his appeal to black voters. Lake publicly withdrew his support for Morgan.

4. See, e.g., Cline, "Holshouser Can Alter Political Complexion of N.C. Judiciary."

5. SMS journal, November 30, 1972. Francis M. Parker was a judge on the North Carolina Court of Appeals (1967–80).

6. Ibid., December 1, 1972.

7. Ibid., December 1, 1972; June 13, 1973; September 6, 1973.

8. Ibid., January 2, 1973.

9. The terms of the other four justices did not expire until after Governor Holshouser's only term in office; at that time, the North Carolina Constitution did not allow governors to succeed themselves.

10. There is some confusion about Higgins's date of birth, which is given as October 17, 1889, by Emergency Justice Emery B. Denny, in "History of the Supreme Court of North Carolina From January 1, 1919, Until January 1, 1969," 274 N.C. 611, 621 (1968). In his address at the presentation of Justice Higgins's portrait to the North Carolina Supreme Court on May 7, 1981, however, the Honorable Francis M. Parker gave Higgins's birth year as 1887. In the printed copy of the address, this date is accompanied by a note stating that the date was obtained from original entries in the Higgins family Bible and was verified by Higgins's younger sister, Mrs. Clyde Carico. Parker Address, 302 N.C. 647 (1981). Justice Sharp's journal has the following entry dated January 3, 1975 (swearing-in ceremony for Justice James G. Exum Jr. and Justice James William Copeland), referring to a statement by Higgins's daughter "Flip" (Mrs. Robert T. Bridges): "Flip tells Sarah that Judge Higgins is 87 years old; that he was sick as a child and lost 2 years. That he did not want to be older than others and 'lost' two years." ("Sarah" is probably Judge Bobbitt's daughter, Sarah Carter.)

11. Paul Bernish, "N.C.'s 2 Highest Courts to Have Vacancies," *Charlotte Observer*, September 4, 1973.

12. Judge Gwyn died December 16, 1969, at the age of seventy-six, after suffering a heart attack on December 1 at a Duke-Carolina basketball game in the Greensboro Coliseum. Justice Sharp delivered the eulogy at a special memorial service in Reidsville on June 22, 1970. Judge Gwyn's wife, Miss Janie, wrote Justice Sharp to thank her for the "beautiful tribute" and said, "Remember, Susie, we all love you and any time we can serve you in any way please call on us." Mrs. Allen H. Gwyn to SMS, n.d.

13. SMS journal, January 2, 1973.

14. Ibid., May 22, 1973.

15. Ibid., June 11, 1973.

16. Ibid.

17. Ibid.

18. Chief Justice Bobbitt, as it happened, had been in the hospital since June 3 for some surgery, but Justice Sharp visited him regularly during his stay. SMS journal, June 1973.

19. Ibid., June 12, 1973.

20. Ibid.

21. Ibid., June 13, 1973.

22. Ibid., June 14, 1973.

23. Ibid., June 13, 1973.

24. Bobbitt himself apparently never dismissed the idea out of hand. In December 1972, just before Holshouser's inauguration, he informed her that he had decided to remain on the court at least through the following spring. Ibid., December 9, 1972. It is not likely he would ever even have considered resigning before his term expired at the end of 1974, assuming his health permitted him to stay, unless Judge Sharp received what he certainly felt was her due, the chief justice's chair. He had earlier lamented to her that he had made a bad mistake by not stepping down while Scott was in office. (Justice Sharp replied that Higgins was the culprit because he refused to resign in favor of Frank Parker.) SMS journal, September 6, 1973. In August 1974 he told her he would quit but for the political situation, and to be sure it was far too late by then. Ibid. Chief Justice Bobbitt did not want to retire. In the view of his former law clerk, later Supreme Court Justice Willis P. Whichard, the stress surrounding his impending forced retirement may have precipitated Bobbitt's heart attack in the fall of 1974. Willis P. Whichard, interview with author, October 18, 1994.

25. SMS journal, June 13, 1973; June 18, 1973; June 20, 1973; July 3, 1973; July 12, 1973.

26. Ned Cline, "Susie Sharp to Seek Top Chair," *Greensboro Daily News*, July 1, 1973.

27. SMS, "Why I Ran for Chief Justice," typescript, n.d. See also SMS, typed remarks ("With all deference to the author . . ."), attached to draft copy of "The Changing Status of Women Lawyers" by Joslin Davis, to be published in *BarNotes* (April 1980).

28. SMS to Caroline Earnhardt, June 21, 1973.

29. SMS, "Why I Ran for Chief Justice," typescript, n.d. See also SMS, typed remarks ("With all deference to the author . . .").

30. SMS, typed remarks ("With all deference to the author . . ."). See also SMS, "Why I ran for Chief Justice," typescript, n.d. Eleven years later, in 1985, North Carolina elected another Republican governor, James G. Martin. He served two terms in the interregnum between Democrat James B. Hunt's double set of double terms as governor (1977–1985; 1993–2001), which was now possible because Hunt had gotten the law changed to allow a governor to succeed himself. In 1985 Martin appointed Wake Forest law professor Rhoda Billings to the supreme court. She was the first Republican to serve on the court since the turn of the century. The following year when Chief Justice Joe Branch resigned, Governor Martin broke the long-standing tradition of appointing the senior associate justice to become chief justice, naming Billings to that position instead of Justice James G. Exum Jr. When he was passed over, Exum retired from the court and ran successfully for chief justice in the next election. Thus Billings served only a matter of months as chief justice.

31. SMS to retired North Carolina Supreme Court justice W. B. Rodman Jr., August 13, 1973.

32. SMS journal, December 27, 1973 ("Call Bob Farrington at night and get sound advice").

33. Ibid., December 28, 1973.

34. Ibid., December 29, 1973.

35. Alex K. Brock, Director of Elections, to SMS, January 3, 1974 (acknowledging receipt of check for $390).

36. See, e.g., Ginny Carroll, "Sharp Seeks Election as Chief Justice," *News and Observer*, January 4, 1974.

37. Bill Gormley, "Justice Sharp Eyes Race for Chief State Justice," n.p., n.d., SMS scrapbook. As with other efforts to change the process, however, talk of nonpartisan judicial elections led nowhere. Nonetheless, the reality of contested races where before there had been none, requiring candidates to spend more time and money and possibly to incur political debts as well, would lead to renewed consideration of some sort of merit selection plan. Rip Woodin, "Newcomb Victory Revives Judicial Standards Issue," *Greensboro Daily News*, May 19, 1974.

38. In 1974 North Carolina had only two Republican judges above the district court level, Court of Appeals Judge James M. Baley (running for Justice Sharp's associate justice seat) and Superior Court Judge Donald L. Smith. Previously most low-level judges had been appointed by county commissioners, but in 1968 the Uniform Courts legislation mandated judicial elections at the lower level of the system. In 1974 there were 169 elected judges in the state, many of whom were "young, bright and ambitious." Woodin, "Newcomb Victory Revives Judicial Standards Issue." Once they served their apprenticeship at the district court level, they were apt to run for the superior court or an appellate court seat. Because of the rapidly growing strength of the Republican Party in the state, the result was an increase in the number of contested races.

39. See, e.g., Carroll, "Sharp Seeks Election."

40. The *Charlotte Observer* took her to task for the photo, suggesting that it was "less than judicious" if not an outright violation of the newly drafted code of judicial conduct (written and distributed the year before by the North Carolina Supreme Court). *Charlotte Observer*, February 24, 1974.

41. Jack Scism, "Susie Sharp Files for Chief Justice," *Greensboro Daily News*, January 4, 1974.

42. SMS to retired North Carolina Supreme Court justice W. B. Rodman Jr., August 13, 1973.

43. *Wall Street Journal*, January 7, 1974.

44. Reese Hart, "Jurist Appears Shoo-In for Top Court Post," *Durham Herald*, January 7, 1974.

45. SMS to Bailey Webb, December 22, 1973.

46. Judge Frank Armstrong to SMS, September 13, 1973.

47. SMS journal, January 25, 1974.

48. Ibid., January 28, 1974.

49. Ibid., January 26, 1974.

50. These efforts included a letter ("brutally frank") from Superior Court Judge James H. Pou Bailey as well as personal visits from Sam Ervin III and Jim Exum (who

would run in November and win the seat Justice Sharp vacated), Harry Martin, Tom Seay, Judge Robert Rouse, and Lacy Thornburg. SMS journal, February 3, 1974; February 5, 1974. George Ragsdale also was busy in the background.

51. Form letter from Judge Robert A. Collier Jr., January 25, 1974. See also SMS to Superior Court Judge Hamilton H. Hobgood, February 6, 1974, concerning recipients; SMS to William D. Caffrey, February 9, 1974, concerning lawyer recipients.

52. SMS to Judge Hamilton H. Hobgood, September 4, 1974.

53. James G. Exum, interview with author, April 16, 1999; Robert A. Collier Jr., interview with author, April 29, 1999.

54. Jim Schlosser, "Justice, at 66, Trying for Another First," *Greensboro Record*, February 11, 1974. For complete list, see SMS to Bill Caffrey, February 9, 1974. The last chief justice to serve more than six years was Judge Stacy, who died in 1951. See also SMS-annotated list made in November 1978, attached to clipping, Daniel C. Hoover and Nadine Cohodas, "Hunt Reported Eyeing Carlton for Chief Justice," *News and Observer*, November 10, 1978.

55. SMS journal, February 18, 1974.

56. SMS to Rose Senn, February 14, 1974.

57. Robert A. Collier Jr., form letter, February 22, 1974.

58. "Under the Dome," *News and Observer*, February 25, 1974.

59. Ibid.

60. "Jurists Found Guilty in Mad Dash for Office," *Salisbury Evening Post*, February 26, 1974.

61. Ibid.

62. "Late Flight," *Salisbury Evening Post*, February 25, 1974. See also Robert A. Collier Jr., interview with author, April 29, 1999.

63. Ginny Carroll, "Many Candidates Seek Court Seats," *News and Observer*, February 26, 1974.

64. J. Will Pless Jr. to SMS, February 25, 1974.

65. GOP state chairman Thomas Bennett said that its judicial candidates committee had been unable to recruit anyone to run against Justice Sharp because "no attorney was interested in filing due to the fact it would require a statewide race and an expensive campaign with the odds stacked against him." Woodin, "Newcomb Victory Revives Judicial Standards Issue."

66. Doug Waller, "'I'm Not Trying to Be a First,'" *Greensboro Record*, March 7, 1974.

67. "Profile: Judge Elreta Alexander—Minister of Justice," *North Carolina Association of Women Attorneys Newsletter* 2 (November 1979).

68. Ibid.

69. Ibid.

70. SMS to Kate (Mrs. Robert H.) Williamson, April 22, 1960.

71. Colin and Roundtree, *The Changing Face of Justice*, 84. According to Colin and Roundtree, Alexander was the second African American to be elected to a judgeship of any kind in the country. See also Statement of Elreta Melton Alexander, District Court Judge, Eighteenth Judicial District, The General Court of Justice of North Carolina, Regarding Filing for Election to the Office of Chief Justice of the Supreme

Court of North Carolina, copy in SMS Papers; Ginny Carroll, "Judge, Executive Vie in Race," *News and Observer*, April 21, 1974.

72. Bill Lee, "Judges in Guilford: How Bar Ranks Them," *Greensboro Daily News*, January 4, 1976. See also "Profile: Judge Elreta Alexander—Minister of Justice."

73. Lee, "Judges in Guilford: How Bar Ranks Them."

74. James G. Exum, interview with author, April 16, 1999.

75. Carroll, "Judge, Executive Vie in Race."

76. Ibid.

77. James G. Exum, interview with author, April 16, 1999.

78. Robert B. Cullen, "Candidate Looks to Lincoln," *Raleigh Times*, May 31, 1974.

79. Ibid.

80. Ibid.

81. The only requirements were to be twenty-one years old and a qualified, registered voter of the state. See Mark Brock, "Supreme Court Justice Race Quiet, Historic," *Charlotte News*, October 15, 1974, attached to letter from Lelia Alexander to SMS, October 19, 1974.

82. SMS to Jefferson B. Fordham, November 20, 1974.

83. Cullen, "Candidate Looks to Lincoln."

84. Ginny Carroll, "Newcomb Brings Unique Record to Court Race," *News and Observer*, October 10, 1974.

85. Harry Stapleton, "Newcomb Sees Victory in N.C. Justice Race," *Greensboro Daily News*, May 13, 1974.

86. Cullen, "Candidate Looks to Lincoln."

87. Paul Bernish, "Nonlawyer 'Trusts in God,'" *Charlotte Observer*, May 15, 1974.

88. SMS to Mrs. W. T. Duckworth, President, Buncombe County Democratic Women, and Mrs. Charles Frank, Chairman, Eleventh District Democratic Women, Asheville, N.C., April 13, 1974.

89. SMS to Mary Ruth Nelms, Clerk, Superior Court of Granville County, February 25, 1974. As of the day before the filing deadline, Justice Sharp believed she would have no Democratic opposition.

90. SMS to Dr. and Mrs. Lawrence A. Taylor, April 28–29, 1974, courtesy of Dr. and Mrs. Lawrence A. Taylor.

91. Ibid.

92. June Milby, "Fish, Politics and Fellowship," *Reidsville Review*, April 29, 1974.

93. SMS to Dr. and Mrs. Lawrence A. Taylor, April 28–29, 1974, courtesy of Dr. and Mrs. Lawrence A. Taylor.

94. SMS to Horace E. Stacy Jr., May 2, 1974.

95. SMS to T. A. Williams, April 23, 1974.

96. SMS to Dr. Bayard Carter, October 2, 1974.

97. SMS to Dr. and Mrs. Lawrence A. Taylor, April 28–29, 1974, courtesy of Dr. and Mrs. Lawrence A. Taylor.

98. Ibid.

99. Ibid.

100. Ibid.

101. SMS to William C. Stokes, January 23, 1974.

102. Editorial, "Three Choices for Supreme Court," *News and Observer*, April 28, 1974.

103. SMS to William D. Caffrey, May 23, 1974.

104. Ann Bach, "Justice Sharp's Advice: Strive for Excellence," *Asheville Times*, July 26, 1974.

105. Ginny Carroll, "Holshouser, Bennett Shun GOP Nominee," *News and Observer*, May 14, 1974.

106. "Women of the Year," *Time*, January 5, 1976, 14.

107. SMS, speech draft fragment ("I got into politics in the early thirties"), [1974]: "At least 44 women will run for congress this year on the Democratic and Republican tickets — 26 of them are Democrats."

108. SMS to William C. Stokes, May 15, 1974.

109. Carroll, "Holshouser, Bennett Shun GOP Nominee."

110. Bernish, "Nonlawyer 'Trusts in God.'"

111. Ibid.

112. Ibid.

113. Ned Cline, "Tar Heel Republicans Face a Ballot Dilemma," *Greensboro Daily News*, October 13, 1974.

114. Ibid.

115. SMS to Ralph H. Ramsey Jr., May 22, 1974.

116. Bill Lee, "Labor Party Men Campaign in City for Voter Support," *Greensboro Daily News*, July 13, 1974.

117. J. A. C. Dunn, "Yes, North Carolina, Chief Justice Is Elected," *Winston-Salem Journal and Sentinel*, October 6, 1974.

118. SMS, speech to Buncombe County Bar Association, Asheville, N.C., July 25, 1974.

119. "Judge Sharp Elected Chief Justice," *Durham Morning Herald*, November 6, 1974.

120. SMS to Hugh L. Key Jr., September 2, 1974.

121. SMS to former governor Luther H. Hodges, September 4, 1974.

122. SMS to Gladys Poindexter, November 3, 1974.

123. Ibid.

124. "Justice Sharp Never Had to Campaign until Now," *Chapel Hill Newspaper*, September 18, 1974.

125. Questionnaire from Sandra Jean Leechford (a student in Fayetteville, North Carolina) to SMS, October 31, 1973.

126. *State v. Jarrette*, 284 N.C. 625, 653 (1974).

127. 408 U.S. 238 (1972).

128. The essence of the Court's patchwork opinion was that the arbitrariness of such discretion rendered the imposition of the death sentence "cruel and unusual" in violation of the Eighth and Fourteenth amendments to the U.S. Constitution. What *Furman* did not do was to declare the death penalty in and of itself unconstitutional, but with each of the nine justices writing a separate opinion and unable to agree on the basis of their decision, the states were left to flounder. The chief justice of the Utah Supreme Court expressed the prevailing level of frustration in a post-*Furman*

opinion: "To say that *Furman* has created a (expletive deleted) quandary for state legislatures and courts is to put it mildly." *State v. Winkle*, 528 P.2d 467 (1974). Inmates on death row in North Carolina as elsewhere had their sentences vacated and their cases remanded to the superior court for the imposition of life imprisonment.

129. *State v. Waddell*, 282 N.C. 431 (1973).

130. Ibid. (Bobbitt, C.J., Higgins, J., and Sharp, J., dissenting).

131. *State v. Jarrette*, 284 N.C. 625, 668–69 (1974) (Bobbitt, C.J., dissenting, joined by Higgins, J., and Sharp, J.).

132. N.C. Gen. Stat. §§ 14-17, 14-21 (1975).

133. *State v. Williams*, 286 N.C. 422 (1975) (Sharp, C.J., Exum, J., and Copeland, J., dissenting).

134. Ibid. at 437 (Sharp, C.J., dissenting as to the death penalty).

135. *State v. Jarrette*, 284 N.C. 625, 670 (1974) (Sharp, J., concurring further in the dissenting opinion of Chief Justice Bobbitt).

136. An exception would be her decision to join the church despite her views on organized religion. Most people, however, probably already thought she was a member.

137. SMS, speech to Greensboro Bar Association, September 19, 1974.

138. Form letter, typescript, n.d., apparently to be sent out by the Administrative Office of the Courts in response to letters questioning Justice Sharp's position on the death penalty ("Ordinarily a member of the Supreme Court does not reply to a letter such as yours . . .").

139. Judge Hamilton H. Hobgood to SMS, March 26, 1974.

140. William D. Kenerly, interview with author, November 3, 1998.

141. SMS to Allan R. Gitter, May 31, 1974.

142. SMS to Gladys S. Britt, June 1, 1974.

143. SMS to Joseph M. Hunt Jr., June 1, 1974.

144. Mrs. Carl Glenn Pickard to SMS, August 17, 1974.

145. Joe Junod, "The GOP Primary: Qualifications Didn't Count," Post Scripts [*Salisbury Post*, May 1974 (see SMS to Dr. George Johnson Jr., June 4, 1974, quoting the column from "last week")], SMS scrapbook. See also SMS to Evelyn Ripple, June 17, 1974; SMS to Albert Coates, June 28, 1978.

146. James G. Exum, interview with author, April 16, 1999.

147. SMS to William D. Caffrey, May 23, 1974.

148. SMS to Eugene T. Bost Jr., October 21, 1974.

149. SMS, speech fragment or notes ("In the last 23 years we have had 6 chief justices"); see also Carroll, "Sharp Seeks Election as Chief Justice."

150. SMS to Mrs. Joseph M. Hunt Jr., October 15, 1974.

151. SMS to Mrs. George F. Hundley, September 2, 1974.

152. Judge Hamilton H. Hobgood to SMS, February 5, 1974.

153. SMS, press release, September 25, 1974. In her oral statement, she named her campaign managers: Dan E. Stewart, retired vice president of Carolina Power and Light Company and director of conservation and development under Governor Dan K. Moore, and Mrs. L. Y. (Bess) Ballentine, former executive secretary of the North Carolina Automobile Dealers Association, a fixture in state politics who

had served as state president of the North Carolina Young Democrats, secretary to the North Carolina Democratic Executive Committee, and delegate to the National Democratic Convention.

154. Charles T. Boyd to Justice Bobbitt, September 20, 1974 (copy).

155. E.g., SMS to Eugene T. Bost Jr., October 11, 1974.

156. Florence Newsom to SMS, September 21, 1974.

157. Ibid.

158. SMS to Richardson Preyer, August 26, 1974.

159. SMS to James Mullen, September 9, 1974.

160. SMS to Miriam Cox, October 29, 1974.

161. SMS to MSB, October 31, 1974.

162. SMS to William C. Stokes, October 31, 1974.

163. Judge Alexander sent a gracious telegram to the new chief justice the day after the election: "Congratulations to you and the voters of our state for their good judgment. Best wishes, Elreta Melton Alexander."

164. SMS to Robert B. Byrd, November 21, 1974.

165. John Sink, *Durham Morning Herald*, November 10, 1974.

166. SMS, "An Unlikely Jurist," typescript, n.d. This number varied somewhat in Justice Sharp's recollection. See, e.g., "Statement by Chief Justice Susie Sharp: Courthouse Study Report, September 20, 1978"; SMS to JCK, February 29, 1960 ("It would be fun to make all 100 of them").

167. These numbers come from a sheet in SMS's files, "County Check List" with handwritten heading, "Results of November 5, 1974 General Election." There is a separate sheet for SMS and for Newcomb but none for Ezrol (who got approximately 1 percent or 10,000 votes). See also Ferrel Guillory, "A Paradoxical Southern Lady," *South Magazine*, May–June 1975, 46.

168. "Women of the Year," *Time*, January 5, 1976. Judge Sharp took exception to the magazine's characterization of her position on the death penalty and of her opinion in a case approving the use of state funds for the busing of inner-city school children (*Styers v. Phillips*, 277 N.C. 460 [1971]). She said the bus case was strictly a taxation matter, a question of who should pay for busing children, the state or the counties. See Kay Miller, Information Officer for the North Carolina Supreme Court, to Mrs. M. A. Silver, February 4, 1976. Some opponents of school desegregation plans involving busing of city children nonetheless viewed the case as a possible barrier to such busing.

169. The others were author Susan Brownmiller, labor activist Addie Wyatt, navy lieutenant commander Kathleen Byerly, journalist Carol Sutton, and Episcopal priest Alison Cheek.

170. See SMS, speech to Democratic Women's Banquet, Charlotte, September 27, 1974.

Chapter 17

1. One of her innovations as chief justice was to change the time for oral arguments. Rather than beginning at ten o'clock and continuing straight through until

two o'clock with unfinished arguments held over until the following day, arguments under Chief Justice Sharp's regime began at nine thirty and continued until a lunch break at twelve thirty, resuming at two o'clock and continuing until conclusion. "Under the Dome," *News and Observer*, October 6, 1975.

2. SMS to MSB, December 30, 1977.

3. A constitutional amendment establishing the Judicial Standards Commission was approved by the voters in the November 1972 elections.

4. SMS journal, October 15, 1973.

5. Ibid.

6. Ibid.

7. Elizabeth Cochrane Bunting, interview with author, November 30, 1998.

8. Ibid.

9. SMS, speech to North Carolina Bar Association, Asheville, N.C., July 2, 1975.

10. Franklin Freeman, interview with author, April 25, 1996.

11. Ibid.

12. See, e.g., *Small v. Martin*, 85-987-CRT (E.D.N.C. 1985).

13. Franklin Freeman, interview with author, April 25, 1996.

14. Franklin Freeman, "Presentation Address of the late Chief Justice Susie Sharp's Portrait," June 11, 1996.

15. Franklin Freeman, interview with author, April 25, 1996.

16. Norwood E. Robinson, interview with author, November 16, 1994.

17. Nadine Cohodas, "Chief Justice Has Considerable Clout," *News and Observer*, November 26, 1978.

18. Ibid.

19. Nadine Cohodas, "Court Adjourns for Susie Sharp," *News and Observer*, July 15, 1979.

20. Transcript of editorial broadcast by WRAL-TV on November 20, 1974, and November 21, 1974, attached to letter from William P. Cheshire, editorial director, to SMS, November 21, 1974.

21. Bert M. Montague, Director, Administrative Office of the Courts, "Assignment of Judges," memorandum to chief district judges, October 28, 1975, copy in SMS Papers.

22. Ibid.

23. Franklin Freeman, interview with author, April 25, 1996. The judge removed as chief was W. Milton Nowell, whom Judge Sharp replaced with Judge Pat Exum. Ibid. Judge Nowell was the respondent in a Judicial Standards Commission proceeding in 1977.

24. N.C. Const. art. IV, § 17 (1).

25. Arnold, "The Judicial Standards Commission," 17.

26. N.C. Const. art. IV, § 17 (2) and implementing legislation, N.C. Gen. Stat. Ch. 7A, Art. 30 (1973). The commission, established January 1, 1973, was made up of a court of appeals judge, a superior court judge, and a district court judge, all appointed by the chief justice; two lawyers with at least ten years in practice, appointed by the state bar council; and two laymen, appointed by the governor.

27. The grounds listed by the statute were (1) Willful misconduct in office; (2)

Willful and persistent failure to perform his duties; (3) Habitual intemperance; (4) Conviction of a crime involving moral turpitude; (5) Conduct prejudicial to the administration of justice that brings the judicial office into disrepute; (6) Mental or physical incapacity interfering with the performance of the judge's duties that is, or is likely to become, permanent. N.C. Gen. Stat. § 7A-376 (1973). Censure of a judge is a public reprimand issued by the supreme court. The commission may, on its own, deliver a private reprimand. See Arnold, "The Judicial Standards Commission," 18.

28. N.C. Gen. Stat. § 7A-376 (1973).

29. Franklin Freeman, interview with author, April 25, 1996.

30. *In re Nowell*, 293 N.C. 235, 245 (1977).

31. Only the state of Alaska had initially followed the "substantial evidence" test, which required the state supreme court to be bound by the Judicial Standards Commission's findings if they were supported by substantial evidence, even if other record evidence supported findings to the contrary. Ibid. at 246–47.

32. Ibid. at 246–47.

33. *In re Hardy*, 294 N.C. 90 (1978).

34. *In re Nowell*, 293 N.C. at 247.

35. Franklin Freeman, interview with author, April 25, 1996.

36. SMS to Janie Sands Smith, January 20, 1979.

37. See Bailey Webb, "Glimpses of Susie Marshall Sharp," n.d., copy in SMS Papers. Bailey Webb was Justice Sharp's cousin, a physician, who often documented her visits with the judge.

38. SMS, note to file, September 8, 1975.

39. Sneed High, Fayetteville attorney and former courts commission member, quoted in Nadine Cohodas, "Panel Founders Differ over Hold on Peoples," *News and Observer*, April 27, 1978.

40. Ibid.

41. *In re Peoples*, 296 N.C. 109, 150–51 (1978), *cert. denied*, 442 U.S. 929 (1979).

42. *In re Peoples*, 296 N.C. at 155.

43. Ibid. at 158.

44. Ibid. at 156.

45. Ibid.

46. Editorial, "Peoples Ruling Justified," *News and Observer*, January 3, 1979.

47. Editorial, "Judging a Judge," *Winston-Salem Sentinel*, January 3, 1979.

48. Albert Coates, phone message taken by Virginia Lyon for SMS, [January 1979].

49. SMS to Janie Sands Smith, January 20, 1979. Judge Peoples petitioned unsuccessfully for certiorari to the U.S. Supreme Court. *In re Peoples*, 296 N.C. 109 (1978), *cert. denied*, 442 U.S. 929 (1979). Supporters in the legislature made two attempts, in 1979 and 1981, to enact bills to restore the judge's pension, but without success. Mark Murrell, "Fund-Raising Barbecue Held to Fete Peoples," *News and Observer*, March 14, 1982. In 1982 friends sponsored a fund-raising barbecue for him, attended by more than 4,000 people from the Ninth Judicial District. The judge, suffering from cancer and the effects of a stroke in November 1981, was said to be "in bad financial shape."

Several political figures, including Lieutenant Governor James C. Green and Insurance Commissioner John R. Ingram, were among the guests. Ibid.

50. Study of Women in State Judicial Systems questionnaire, University of North Carolina School of Law, Katherine Hall, Research Analyst, September 30, 1973.

51. *News and Observer* questionnaire to candidates in contested judicial races, October 16, 1974.

52. SMS, speech to Greensboro Bar Association, September 19, 1974.

53. Rip Woodin, "Newcomb Victory Revives Judicial Standards Issue," *Greensboro Daily News*, May 19, 1974.

54. See, e.g., Robert B. Cullen, "Judicial Reform at Standstill," *Raleigh Times*, May 12, 1975.

55. SMS to Hon. H. Parks Helms, March 9, 1977.

56. Daniel C. Hoover, "Senate Kills Rule for Judges," *News and Observer*, May 8, 1975.

57. Susan Jetton, "Must Judge Have Legal Training to Do Good Job?" *Charlotte Observer*, May 4, 1975.

58. Ginny Carroll, "Non-Lawyer Judges Stir Legal Training Debate," *News and Observer*, January 13, 1975.

59. Jetton, "Must Judge Have Legal Training to Do Good Job?"

60. Ibid.

61. SMS to Jim Miles, June 1, 1976 (discussing her objections to nonlawyers on the bench).

62. Ferrel Guillory, "A Paradoxical Southern Lady," *South Magazine*, May–June 1975, 46. See also SMS to Jim Miles, June 1, 1976.

63. SMS to Hon. H. Parks Helms, March 9, 1977; "Courts: Select Judges by Merit, Sharp Urges," n.p., March 10, 1977, SMS scrapbook.

64. Jack Betts, "Hunt Backs Merit Selection Plan Day after Defeat," *Greensboro Daily News*, March 31, 1977.

65. Ibid.

66. Appellate judges would not be appointed through the new system. At this point, the governor was required by law to appoint district court judges from a list of recommendations made by district bars. Martin Donsky, "Merit Judge Panel Is Set Up by Hunt," *News and Observer*, July 29, 1977.

67. Charles E. Daye, Statement of the North Carolina Association of Black Lawyers Regarding Justice Sharp's Appointments to the N.C. Superior Court Nominating Committee, August 16, 1977.

68. See, e.g., SMS to Charles E. Daye, August 15, 1977; SMS to Kenneth B. Spaulding, August 16, 1977.

69. "Hunt Names 13 to Judicial Nominating Committee," *Raleigh Times*, August 10, 1977.

70. Justice James G. Exum Jr. to Robin Grossman, September 20, 1978, copy in SMS Papers.

71. Chief Justice Sharp added a comment to Justice Exum's draft. Merit selection, she said, "can be converted into a façade for purely political appointments unless it is

administered by persons who are dedicated to the principles of merit selection and who, in good faith, fearlessly seek to implement them."

72. Questionnaire from North Carolina Center for Public Policy Research, Inc., August 27, 1979.

73. Justice Sharp, criticized for what was perceived as her opposition to the death penalty, asked Franklin Freeman to respond to citizens who expressed their dismay, explaining that she was not opposed to capital punishment. E.g., Franklin Freeman to Mrs. Paul McAllister, May 18, 1976.

74. *State v. Woodson*, 287 N.C. 578 (1975), *rev'd*, 428 U.S. 280 (1976). Chief Justice Sharp devoted two paragraphs to an explanation of why she and the other justices who had dissented in the capital punishment cases decided between the time the U.S. Supreme Court's ruling in *Furman* declared the North Carolina statute unconstitutional and the legislature's enactment of the new statute in 1974 now voted to uphold the death sentence.

75. *Woodson*, 287 N.C. at 600 (Exum, J., concurring), *rev'd*, 428 U.S. 280 (1976).

76. *Woodson*, 428 U.S. 280 (1976).

77. The U.S. Supreme Court found three major objections to the North Carolina statute: (1) it departed markedly from contemporary standards of decency, (2) it failed to establish objective standards to guide the jury or to aid an appellate court in determining whether the imposition of the death penalty was unconstitutionally arbitrary or capricious, and (3) it failed to allow the "particularized consideration of relevant aspects of the character and record of each convicted defendant" before he was sentenced to death. Ibid. at 301–4.

78. SMS journal, February 23, 1977.

79. Bill Gilkeson, "Limited Victory Won by Capital Punishment Foes," *Durham Morning Herald*, April 21, 1977; "N.C. House Aims at Death Penalty," *Greensboro Daily News*, May 4, 1977.

80. Gilkeson, "Limited Victory Won by Capital Punishment Foes."

81. Ibid.

82. Ibid.

83. SMS, typescript ("The Fourth Quarter Report on Crime in North Carolina …") annotated "3/18/77 (Green)"; SMS, typescript (one paragraph) annotated "This information was transmitted to Lieut-Gov. Greene [*sic*] 3-30-77."

84. SMS to Lula Belle Wiseman, February 7, 1977. Representative Wiseman argued for the death penalty for rapists who mutilate their victims or who rape children when she addressed the House on May 3, 1977.

85. SMS to Lula Belle Wiseman, February 7, 1977 ("The Governor in his speech on law and order …").

86. *Coker v. Georgia*, 433 U.S. 584 (1977).

Chapter 18

1. The Hayden Rider provided: "The provisions of this article shall not be construed to impair any rights, benefits, or exemptions now or hereafter conferred by law upon persons of the female sex." U.S. Congress, Senate, 81st Cong., 2d sess., January

23, 24, 25, 1950, *Congressional Record* 96 (1950):738–44, 758–62, 809–13, 861, 873. The Hayden Rider passed the Senate by a vote of 51–31 in 1950, and by 58–25 when the strategy was repeated in July 1953.

2. For a comprehensive account of the battle for the ERA in North Carolina, see Mathews and De Hart, *Sex, Gender, and the Politics of ERA.*

3. "Goody, Goody, Girls! We're Better'n You," *News and Observer*, June 5, 1963.

4. Mathews and De Hart, *Sex, Gender, and the Politics of ERA*, 206.

5. Ibid.

6. James R. Dickenson, "Sen. Sam Ervin, Key Figure in Watergate Probe, Dies," *Washington Post*, April 24, 1985.

7. SMS to Sam J. Ervin Jr., October 13, 1984; see also SMS to Richard L. Dabney, November 7, 1975.

8. Remarks prepared by Senator Sam J. Ervin Jr. (D-N.C.) for delivery to the Senate on August 21, 1970, attached to letter from Senator Ervin to SMS, August 21, 1970.

9. U.S. Congress, Senate, *Equal Rights, 1970*, Hearings before the Committee on the Judiciary, U.S. Congress, Senate, 91st Cong., 2d sess., September 9, 10, 11, 15, 1970 (Washington, D.C.: Government Printing Office, 1970).

10. SMS to Senator Sam J. Ervin Jr., August 28, 1970.

11. "All persons born or naturalized in the United States, and subject to the jurisdiction thereof, are citizens of the United States and of the state wherein they reside. No state shall make or enforce any law which shall abridge the privileges or immunities of citizens of the United States; nor shall any state deprive any person of life, liberty, or property, without due process of law; nor deny to any person within its jurisdiction the equal protection of the laws." U.S. Const. amend. XIV, § 1.

12. SMS, typescript, n.d. ("My views on equal rights for women — Surely you don't need to ask me that question!").

13. Leslie Wayne, "'Why, Susie, You Ought to be Chief Justice,'" *Philadelphia Inquirer*, April 17, 1978.

14. SMS to Senator Sam J. Ervin Jr., August 28, 1970.

15. Sam J. Ervin Jr. to SMS, February 14, 1977; Mathews and De Hart, *Sex, Gender, and the Politics of ERA*, 30, 34, 37.

16. Mathews and De Hart, *Sex, Gender, and the Politics of ERA*, 64.

17. *Grove City v. Bell*, 465 U.S. 555 (1984) (holding that Title IX applied only to discrimination in admissions or in federally funded programs, which generally did not include sports programs).

18. SMS, typescript, n.d. ("My views on equal rights for women — Surely you don't need to ask me that question!").

19. Ibid. See also SMS to Susan Phifer, June 7, 1974.

20. SMS, typescript ("Equal Rights"), n.d. ("In my view there is a vast difference between equal rights and the so-called equal rights amendment").

21. SMS to Rep. Ralph Dotzenrod, July 1, 1974.

22. SMS to Susan Phifer, June 7, 1974.

23. Leslie Wayne, "Equal Rights Amendment Argued in the Assembly," *News and Observer*, February 2, 1973.

24. SMS journal, February 2, 1973 ("Call Senator Rhyne to tell him that I can not testify before his committee on the ERA"). See also SMS to Vivian Reid, February 1, 1973.

25. SMS to Vivian Reid, February 1, 1973. See also SMS journal, January 24, 1973 ("Call David Blackwell and Senator Webster re the Equal Rights Amendment").

26. SMS journal, January 30, 1973.

27. Mathews and De Hart, *Sex, Gender, and the Politics of ERA*, 61.

28. Ibid.

29. Ibid., 64.

30. SMS journal, May 13, 1973.

31. Ibid., March 1, 1973. The other "turncoat" was Senator Mike Mullins (R-Mecklenburg), who was defeated in his next bid for reelection.

32. Ibid.

33. Ibid.

34. "ERA Opponents Offer Measure," *News and Observer*, March 2, 1973; Mathews and De Hart, *Sex, Gender, and the Politics of ERA*, 241 n. 25.

35. "ERA Opponents Offer Measure."

36. SMS to Susan Phifer, June 7, 1974.

37. North Dakota Rep. Ralph Dotzenrod to SMS, June 10, 1974.

38. SMS to North Dakota Rep. Ralph Dotzenrod, July 1, 1974.

39. Katherine M. Satrom to Nancy Drum, December 13, 1974 (copy).

40. Gladys Tillett to SMS, December 26, 1974.

41. Dollie L. Smith, "Woman Judge Fears Losses under ERA," *Richmond Times-Dispatch*, January 5, 1975.

42. SMS to Gladys Tillett, January 7, 1975. Apparently there had been some other fracas involving Representative Rhyne because she said, "In fairness to Mr. Dotzenrod I have to say that this situation is not comparable to the one with Mr. Rhyne."

43. Ibid. The incident seemed like a replay of the furor over the newspaper article when she first went on the supreme court, in which she was quoted as saying the average woman's place was in the home. In both cases, the article appeared to be based on an interview. In fact, however, the Dollie Smith story's quotations do not come from the 1970 letter; it is not clear where they came from if not in conversation with Judge Sharp.

44. SMS to Edith Alley, February 17, 1975.

45. Mathews and De Hart, *Sex, Gender, and the Politics of ERA*, 68.

46. SMS journal, April 9, 1975.

47. Virginia Lyon to SMS, n.d. ("Gladys Bullard called . . ."); SMS journal, April 9, 1975. See also SMS to Senator Schwartz, July 31, 1975. Gladys Bullard also accused Judge Sharp of talking to Coy Privette, a Baptist minister and vocal conservative activist.

48. Virginia Lyon to SMS, n.d.; see also SMS journal, April 9, 1975.

49. SMS journal, April 9, 1975.

50. Mathews and De Hart, *Sex, Gender, and the Politics of ERA*, 87.

51. Ibid., 79.

52. SMS to Mrs. T. W. Snodgrass, January 10, 1977.

53. Senator Sam J. Ervin Jr. to SMS, February 14, 1977. The only indication of her response is the phone number of his residence written in her hand on the top of the letter. Presumably she telephoned him to decline.

54. David R. Nelsen, "ERA Adversaries Not Letting Up," *Raleigh Times*, February 10, 1977.

55. Mathews and De Hart, *Sex, Gender, and the Politics of ERA*, 88.

56. Martin Donsky, "ERA Factions Held Senators in Tug-of-War," *News and Observer*, March 2, 1977. Mathews and De Hart say Wesley Webster announced he would vote for the referendum; Martin Donsky's article, "ERA Factions Held Senators in Tug-of-War," says Webster later agreed to vote against it even though he was anti-ERA. Webster subsequently voted against the ERA. The referendum did not come up for a vote because supporters lacked the votes at the end.

57. Dollie L. Smith, "Sharp's Call Stirs Up Storm," *Raleigh Times*, March 7, 1977.

58. On that occasion she talked with him not only about the ERA but also about another concern she had—as a private citizen, of course—capital punishment for rape (then under consideration in the legislature, prior to the U.S. Supreme Court ruling declaring it unconstitutional). SMS journal, February 23, 1977.

59. SMS journal, March 14, 1977; Martin Donsky, "Susie Sharp Calls to Protest ERA," *News and Observer*, March 2, 1977; Dollie L. Smith, "Justice Sharp's Call to Senator on ERA Issue Bring[s] Criticism," [*Reidsville Review*], March 7, 1977, SMS scrapbook.

60. Donsky, "Susie Sharp Calls to Protest ERA."

61. E.g., Jack Betts, "Justice Susie Sharp Retiring after Many Years of Firsts," *News and Observer*, July 29, 1979.

62. See Donsky, "ERA Factions Held Senators in Tug-of-War."

63. Smith, "Justice Sharp's Call to Senator on ERA Issue Bring[s] Criticism."

64. Ibid.

65. Ibid.

66. Editorial, "Justice Sharp Not Guilty," *Raleigh Times*, March 9, 1977.

67. Smith, "Justice Sharp's Call to Senator on ERA Issue Bring[s] Criticism."

68. Henry Scott, "Strong-Willed Sharp Prospered in Legal World," *Charlotte Observer*, July 29, 1979.

69. Ibid.

Chapter 19

1. SMS to Caroline Earnhardt, December 8, 1975.

2. SMS to Mary Snell, January 3, 1976.

3. SMS journal, December 28, 1975.

4. SMS to Mary Snell, January 3, 1976.

5. Robert W. Newsom III, interview with author, January 14, 1998.

6. SMS to Florence Newsom, February 15, 1976, courtesy of Robert W. Newsom III.

7. SMS journal, May 23, 1977.

8. Ibid., November 10, 1977.

9. Ibid., November 11, 1977.

10. Ibid.

11. Ibid., May 19, 1978.

12. See speech draft, May 19, 1978, with an annotation about the occasion and marked "undelivered."

13. SMS journal, May 20, 1978.

14. Ibid., July 7, 1977.

15. Ibid., June 27, 1977.

16. Ibid., August 13, 1977.

17. Frances Sue Kesler Driscoll to SMS, October 1976 ("I have come to plead my case").

18. SMS journal, February 4, 1977.

19. Ibid., January 3, 1975.

20. Ibid., September 19, 1975.

21. Ibid., August 30, 1978.

22. See "James Iredell Association Newsletter," September 1979.

23. SMS to Lloyd Griffin, March 28, 1979.

24. SMS journal, March 26, 1980.

25. Ibid., April 21, 1979.

26. Ibid., June 29, 1978.

27. Ibid., October 19, 1978.

28. Ibid., August 9, 1979.

29. W. C. ("Mutt") Burton, interview with author, January 19, 1995.

30. SMS to Dr. Eugenia Hunter, March 20, 1978.

31. The other members of the commission were Irving S. Shapiro, chairman of E. I. DuPont de Nemours and Co.; Los Angeles mayor Thomas Bradley; Frederick August Otto Schwarz, former chief counsel to the Senate Select Committee on Intelligence; Charles Morgan Jr., former head of the Washington legislative office of the American Civil Liberties Union; Cruz Reynoso, associate judge on California's Third District Court of Appeals in Sacramento; Joseph Timilty, Massachusetts state senator; Mary Eleanore Wall, member of the Dupage County (Illinois) board and wife of Rev. James Wall, who directed President Carter's Illinois campaign. Outgoing director Clarence Kelley also served on the commission. Raymond M. Taylor to SMS, memorandum, February 21, 1977 (background on other committee members); "Kelley Joins Search for Successor," *Raleigh Times*, February 18, 1977.

32. "The F.B.I. List Narrows Down to Just Five," *New York Times*, June 19, 1977.

33. When his premature obituary appeared in the *New York Journal*, Mark Twain remarked, "Reports of my death are greatly exaggerated."

34. "No Women on FBI Chief List," *News and Observer*, April 11, 1977.

35. Each time she got on the plane to Washington, she took out life insurance, naming all her siblings plus Virginia Lyon as beneficiaries. SMS, list of beneficiaries, n.d. (FBI committee file).

36. SMS to Jane Edmisten, June 1, 1977.

37. Final Report of the Committee on Selection of the Director of the Federal

Bureau of Investigation, submitted to the president by Irving S. Shapiro, Chairman, June 10, 1977. The five were: Los Angeles County district attorney John K. Van de Kamp; Wayne County (Detroit, Michigan) sheriff William Lucas; federal circuit court judge Harlington A. Wood Jr.; veteran FBI official Neil J. Welch; and Massachusetts state court judge John J. Irwin Jr.

38. Editorial, "Wanted for the F.B.I.," *New York Times*, June 20, 1977.

39. See, e.g., "The F.B.I. Five: A Closer Look," *Newsweek*, July 11, 1977; Norman Kempster and Ronald J. Ostrow, "Doubts Raised about Selection Process for FBI 'Finalists,'" *Los Angeles Times* (reprinted in the *Washington Post*), July 5, 1977.

40. Kempster and Ostrow, "Doubts Raised about Selection Process for FBI 'Finalists.'"

41. SMS to Clarence E. Kelley, July 15, 1977.

42. SMS, typescript ("All of you, I am sure, will recall that in 1975 we had a recession"), [July 1, 1977]; SMS, typescript ("No. 1. Salary Increase for Judicial Officials") (remarks for her appearance before Advisory Budget Commission, fall 1976).

43. J. Phil Carlton to All District Court Judges, memorandum, "Judicial Compensation," September 30, 1976.

44. Ibid.; SMS, typescript ("All of you, I am sure, will recall that in 1975 we had a recession"), [July 1, 1977], Exhibit 1, "Proposed Salaries."

45. See Bert M. Montague to Judges of the Court of Appeals, Superior Court and District Court, District Attorneys, Public Defenders, Clerks of Superior Court, memorandum, "Judicial Salaries," April 29, 1977.

46. SMS, "No. 1. Salary Increase for Judicial Officials," typescript (remarks for her appearance before Advisory Budget Commission), fall 1976.

47. SMS to North Carolina Superior Court Judge John Webb, July 11, 1977.

48. SMS, typescript ("All of you, I am sure, will recall that in 1975 we had a recession"), [July 1, 1977]. Chief Justice Sharp made three appearances before official committees: the Advisory Budget Commission, a subcommittee of the Joint Appropriations Committee, and the Joint Appropriations Committee. SMS to Ed Williams, June 20, 1977.

49. SMS, typescript ("All of you, I am sure, will recall that in 1975 we had a recession"), [July 1, 1977].

50. Joseph W. Eason, interview with author, November 24, 1998.

51. Ibid.

52. Justice Sharp was "surprised, disappointed, and chagrined" that public defenders were not treated the same as district attorneys in the 1977 budget. "I explained to every committee before which I appeared, and to every group to which I explained our package plan for salaries, that the law requires the State to provide every indigent with competent counsel, equal in ability to the State's attorney," she lamented. SMS to North Carolina Representative Lura S. Tally, July 22, 1977.

53. SMS to Lieutenant Governor James Green, July 26, 1977.

54. SMS, speech draft, typescript ("It has been pointed out many times that the press must rely on the judiciary to maintain its constitutional right of freedom of the press"), n.d.

55. SMS journal, March 8, 1979.

56. Daniel C. Hoover and Nadine Cohodas, "Hunt Reported Eyeing Carlton for Chief Justice," *News and Observer*, November 10, 1978.

57. Ibid.

58. Ibid.

59. SMS journal, January 14, 1979.

60. Editorial, "The New Chief Justice," *Greensboro Daily News*, May 26, 1979.

61. Henry Scott, "Judge Sharp—A Court's Order: Rock of Tradition, Seldom Jarred by Judicious Dissent," *Charlotte Observer*, July 29, 1979.

62. Letter to Governor James B. Hunt, March 7, 1979, signed by all members of the supreme court as well as all retired justices.

63. SMS journal, May 9, 1979.

64. Ibid., May 23, 1979; SMS to Chief Justice James Duke Cameron, Supreme Court of Arizona, June 4, 1979.

65. Tom Ayres, "Branch Called a Conservative Open to New Ideas," *Raleigh Times*, May 24, 1979.

66. Editorial, "Joe Branch Right Choice," *Raleigh Times*, May 28, 1979.

67. Jack Betts, "Branch to Replace Sharp," *Greensboro Daily News*, May 25, 1979.

68. Phil Carlton served on the North Carolina Supreme Court until 1983. In the 1992 gubernatorial election when Jim Hunt ran for his third term as governor, Carlton was implicated in a controversy known as "scannergate," when Republican gubernatorial nominee Jim Gardner learned Hunt supporters were listening in on his cellular phone conversations.

69. The appointment was effective December 1, 1978. Franklin Freeman, News Release, November 20, 1978.

70. Interview with Naomi Morris by Pat DeVine, November 11 and 16, and March 29, 1983 (B-0050), in the Southern Oral History Program Collection (#4007), Southern Historical Collection, Wilson Library, University of North Carolina at Chapel Hill.

71. Ibid.

72. Ibid.

73. SMS to Governor James B. Hunt, November 13, 1980.

74. Ibid.

75. See, e.g., Davis, "The Changing Status," 12.

76. Ibid., 11.

77. Henry Scott, "Strong-Willed Sharp Prospered in Legal World," *Charlotte Observer*, July 29, 1979.

78. Louise Sharp, interview with author, November 8, 1994.

79. She was the author of 459 majority opinions, 124 concurring opinions, and 45 dissenting opinions, a total of 628 written opinions. Franklin Freeman, "Presentation Address of the Late Chief Justice Susie Sharp's Portrait," June 11, 1996. But see SMS journal, March 7, 1980: "Call Va. who comes down and we find my bound opinions in the basement. Count them all as 639."

80. Michael Skube, "As Justice Sharp Leaves," *Winston-Salem Journal*, August 5, 1979.

81. Editorial, "End of an Era," *Winston-Salem Journal*, August 1, 1979.

82. Skube, "As Justice Sharp Leaves."

83. Editorial, "Salute to Susie Sharp," *Asheville Citizen*, reprinted in *News and Observer*, August 16, 1979.

84. Scott, "Strong-Willed Sharp Prospered in Legal World."

85. Nadine Cohodas, "Court Adjourns for Susie Sharp," *News and Observer*, July 15, 1979.

86. *Bd. of Educ. v. Swann*, 402 U.S. 43 (1971).

87. *Loving v. Virginia*, 388 U.S. 1 (1967).

88. Elizabeth Shelton, "Are the Scales Weighted against Women Judges?" *Washington Post*, September 19, 1965.

89. Joseph W. Eason, interview with author, November 24, 1998.

90. SMS, speech to UNC law school banquet, n.d.; SMS, speech on Naomi Morris Day, Wilson, N.C., August 7, 1967, quoting *State v. Metts*, 125 Miss. 819, 836 (1921) (Etheridge, J., dissenting). The exact quotation in the original is, "Judges at last are but men subject to the imperfections and frailties of other men, encompassed by error, seasoned with sin, and fettered by fallibility."

91. Davis, "The Changing Status," 6.

92. Scott, "Strong-Willed Sharp Prospered in Legal World."

93. Davis, "The Changing Status," 9.

94. "A Close-Up of Women in U.S. . . . . And Ways Their Status Is Changing," *U.S. News and World Report*, December 8, 1975.

95. Ibid.

96. Davis, "The Changing Status," 13.

97. Ibid.

98. Ibid., 11.

Epilogue

1. SMS to George D. Jackson, September 7, 1980.

2. SMS, typescript ("I no longer have an office . . ."), n.d.

3. SMS journal, June 13–14, 1980.

4. Ibid., May 14, 1983.

5. SMS to Evelyn Ripple, August 4, 1983.

6. Tom and Kathy later married.

7. SMS journal, May 23, 1984.

8. Ibid., August 15, 1984.

9. Bledsoe, *Bitter Blood*, 331.

10. SMS journal, April 29, 1985.

11. Ibid., July 22, 1984; June 20, 1985.

12. SMS, handwritten draft ("I have not had the stamina to write . . ."), n.d.

13. Ibid.

14. SMS journal, May 1, 1986; May 29, 1986; SMS, typescript ("I am doing my best to cope . . ."), [July 1986].

15. SMS journal, May 29, 1986.

16. Ibid., April 29, 1986.

17. SMS, typescript ("I am doing my best to cope . . ."), [July 1986]. See also SMS to Jean Breckenridge, December 23, 1980 (lamenting the loss of Jean's book manuscript to fire: "It doesn't look like I shall ever start mine!").

18. SMS to Earle and Evelyn Garrett, August 27, 1985, courtesy of Clara Garrett Fountain.

19. See, e.g., SMS to Wade Brown, May 24, 1987.

20. SMS to Joe Goodman, managing editor, *Winston-Salem Journal*, June 1, 1987.

21. Bailey Webb, "Justice Susie Marshall Sharp (ret.)," Notes for the Book Club of Mrs. Louise Efird Davidson, Brevard, N.C., June 12, 1988, copy in SMS Papers.

22. SMS journal, May 9, 1984.

23. Franklin Freeman, conversation with author, March 4, 1996.

24. William H. Bobbitt to Bailey Webb, December 1990, copy in SMS Papers.

25. Rebecca O. Gill, interview with author, November 3, 1994.

26. Ibid.

27. William H. Bobbitt to Thomas A. Sharp, February 10, 1991, courtesy of Thomas A. Sharp.

28. Debra Hadley, "'Judge Susie' Fondly Remembered," *Hickory Daily Record*, [1996] (quoting Forrest Ferrell, senior resident superior court judge for Catawba County).

SELECTED BIBLIOGRAPHY

This is necessarily a condensed listing of sources consulted over a period of more than a dozen years. I cannot recommend too highly the rich resources in the Southern Historical Collection, including its Southern Oral History Program Collection, and in the North Carolina Collection at the University of North Carolina at Chapel Hill. The North Carolina State Archives in Raleigh are another extraordinarily rich source. Among the individuals listed under interviews, there were a number who graciously met with me numerous times; for that reason, I have not listed the specific interview dates below, though I have cited specific dates in the notes. Where newspaper names changed over the period covered, I have listed the different names.

Archives and Manuscript Collections

Chapel Hill, North Carolina
 North Carolina Collection, Louis Round Wilson Library, University of North
   Carolina at Chapel Hill
 Southern Historical Collection, Louis Round Wilson Library, University of
   North Carolina at Chapel Hill
  Paul Green Papers
  Martha C. McKay Papers
  Terry Sanford Papers
  Susie Marshall Sharp Papers
  Southern Oral History Program Collection
  Capus Waynick Papers
 University of North Carolina Alumni Office
Greensboro, North Carolina
 University Archives and Manuscripts, Walter C. Jackson Library, University of
   North Carolina at Greensboro
  Julius Isaac Foust Papers
  W. C. Jackson Papers
Oxford, North Carolina
 Richard H. Thornton Library
Raleigh, North Carolina
 North Carolina State Archives
  Compiled Military Service Records (Confederate Army)
  Granville County census, land, and tax records
  Governor Terry Sanford Papers
  Governor W. Kerr Scott Papers
 North Carolina Supreme Court Library

Washington, D.C.
　　National Archives
Wentworth, North Carolina
　　Historical Collections Room, Gerald B. James Library, Rockingham
　　　　Community College
　　　　Allen Hatchett Gwyn Papers
Winston-Salem, North Carolina
　　Special Collection Archives, Z. Smith Reynolds Library, Wake Forest University

Interviews Conducted by the Author

Elreta Alexander
Eunice Ayers
Evelyn Balsley
Virginia Douglas Bell
Bert L. Bennett
James G. Billings
R. Max Blackburn
Robert R. Blackwell
Thomas J. Bolch
Jean Breckenridge
Elizabeth Cochrane Bunting
W. C. Burton
Peggy Byrd
Christie S. Cameron
Robert W. Carter Jr.
Gary D. Chamblee
Margaret Fillman Chaney
Gladys Coates
Robert A. Collier Jr.
S. V. ("Peaches") Dunlap
Caroline Earnhardt
Joseph W. Eason
James G. Exum
Lon Folger
Franklin Freeman
James C. Fuller
A. Earle and Evelyn Garrett Jr.
Rebecca O. Gill
Mary Garrett Glidewell
Hugh P. Griffin
Allen H. Gwyn Jr.
Julius J. Gwyn
Trish Gwyn
John W. Hardy

Perry Henson
Cecilia (Mrs. William Scott) Hester
Dewey H. Huffines Jr.
J. Frank Huskins
E. Richard Jones
Allen T. Joyner
William D. Kenerly
Annie Hill Sharp Klenner
Horace R. Kornegay
Thomas W. Lambeth
Phil Link
Henry S. Manning
Harry C. Martin
Martha C. McKay
William C. Myers
Ab and Rachael Newnam
Robert W. Newsom III
David S. Orcutt
Frank Penn
C. H. Pope
Norwood E. Robinson
John L. Sanders
Terry Sanford
James V. ("Kits") and Gwen Sharp
Louise Sharp
Thomas A. Sharp
Houston P. Sharpe
Janie Sands Smith
Dorothy Snodgrass
William H. Sturges
Robert W. Sumner
James M. Taylor
Lawrence A. and Barbara Taylor
Raymond Mason Taylor

Andrew A. Vanore Jr.
E. Garrett Walker
E. Thomas Watson
Bailey D. Webb
Samuel F. Wells Jr.
Willis P. Whichard

Frances Watlington Wilson
Josephine T. Wilson
Myrtle W. Wilson
Louise Tesh Wyrick
Noel Yancey

Other Interviews

Interview with Susie M. Sharp by William C. Friday, UNC-TV, "Carolina People,"
    January 22, 1981
Interview with Susie M. Sharp by Jane L. Sharpe, 1982, Allen Hatchett Gwyn
    Papers, Historical Collections Room, Gerald B. James Library, Rockingham
    Community College, Wentworth, North Carolina
Interviews with Terry Sanford, UNC-TV, May 26, 27, and 28, 1998
Southern Oral History Program Collection (#4007), Southern Historical
    Collection, Wilson Library, UNC-Chapel Hill
    Series A, Southern Politics
    Series B, Individual Biographies
    Series C, Notable North Carolinians
    Series G, Southern Women
    Series J, Legal Professions, including, in particular, interviews with
        Bert Bennett (A-118)
        Joel Fleishman (A-121)
        I. Beverly Lake Sr. (C-0043)
        Tom Lambeth (A-131)
        Martha McKay (A-324, A-133)
        Naomi Morris (B-0050)
        Elreta Alexander Ralston (J-0018)
        Terry Sanford (A-327-1, A-327-2, A328-2, A-140)
        Susie Sharp (B-0053)
Video, Norwood E. Robinson, Dallas Cameron, A. C. Snow, and Danny Moody
    reminiscing, filmed prior to the presentation of Chief Justice Susie M.
    Sharp's portrait to the North Carolina Supreme Court, June 11, 1996, North
    Carolina Supreme Court Library, Raleigh, North Carolina

Newspapers

Charlotte Observer
Durham Morning Herald
Greensboro Daily News; Greensboro Record; Greensboro News-Record
News and Observer
Raleigh Times
Reidsville Review
Salisbury Post

Tar Heel; Daily Tar Heel

Winston-Salem Journal; Winston-Salem Sentinel; Winston-Salem Journal and Sentinel

Books and Articles

Administrative Office of the Courts. State of North Carolina. *100 Courthouses: A Report on North Carolina Judicial Facilities*. Vol. 2. Raleigh: School of Design, North Carolina State University at Raleigh, 1978.

Albright, Mayne. "O. Max Gardner and the Shelby Dynasty." *The State*, April 1983, 8–11, 27; July 1983, 10–13; August 1983, 8–11, 26; January 1984, 14–17.

———. "The Senator and the Simmons Machine." *The State*, November 1982, 8–12, 31; December 1982, 17–20, 28–29.

Almeida, Ava De. "Lifting the Veil of Sisterhood: Women's Culture and Student Activism at a Southern College, 1920–1940." Master's thesis, University of North Carolina at Chapel Hill, 1989.

Angley, Wilson, Jerry L. Cross, and Michael Hill. *Sherman's March through North Carolina, a Chronology*. Raleigh: North Carolina Division of Archives and History, 1995.

Arnold, Gerald. "The Judicial Standards Commission—Assuring the Competence and Integrity of North Carolina Judges." *Popular Government*, Fall 1983, 17–20.

Ayers, Edward L. *The Promise of the New South: Life after Reconstruction*. New York: Oxford University Press, 1992.

Baker, Debra. "The Fight Ain't Over." *ABA Journal*, August 1999, <http://www.wellesley.edu/Polisci/wj/100/baker-era.html>. September 7, 2005.

Bardolph, Richard. "NCCW and Woman's Suffrage." *Alumni News*, University of North Carolina at Greensboro, Fall 1984, 8–11.

Barrett, John G. "North Carolina in the Service of the Confederacy." In *North Carolina Government: 1585–1974*, edited by John L. Cheney, 375–85. Raleigh: North Carolina Department of the Secretary of State, 1975.

Bennett, David H. *The Party of Fear: From Nativist Movements to the New Right in American History*. Chapel Hill: University of North Carolina Press, 1988.

Bennett, Walter H., Jr., and Judith Welch Wegner. "Lawyers Talking: UNC Law Graduates and Their Service to the State." 73 *North Carolina Law Review* 846–938 (1995).

Blackburn, George T., II, general chairman. *The Heritage of Vance County, North Carolina*. Winston-Salem: Vance County Historical Society, 1984.

Bledsoe, Jerry. *Bitter Blood*. New York: Penguin Group, New American Library, Onyx, 1989.

Bowles, Elisabeth Ann. *A Good Beginning: The First Four Decades of the University of North Carolina at Greensboro*. Chapel Hill: University of North Carolina Press, 1967.

Brown, Harriet. "The College Girl's Attitude toward Changing Social Conditions." *Alumnae News*, North Carolina College for Women, July 1926, 22–25. North Carolina Collection, Wilson Library, University of North Carolina at Chapel Hill.

Butler, Lindley S. *Rockingham County: A Brief History*. Raleigh: North Carolina
Division of Archives and History, 1982.

Butler, Lindley S., and Alan D. Watson, eds. *The North Carolina Experience: An
Interpretive and Documentary History*. Chapel Hill: University of North Carolina
Press, 1984.

Carlson, Andrew J. "Homeplace and Tobaccoland: A History of Granville County."
In *Heritage and Homesteads: The History and Architecture of Granville County,
North Carolina*, 1–162. Oxford: Granville County Historical Society, 1988.

Chafe, William H. *The Paradox of Change: American Women in the 20th Century*.
New York: Oxford University Press, 1991.

Cheney, John L., ed. *North Carolina Government, 1585–1974: A Narrative and
Statistical History*. Raleigh: North Carolina Department of the Secretary of
State, 1975.

Colin, Emily, and Lynn P. Roundtree. *The Changing Face of Justice: A Look at the
First 100 Women Attorneys in North Carolina*. [Raleigh]: North Carolina Bar
Association, 2004.

Corbitt, D. L., ed. *Public Addresses, Letters and Papers of William Kerr Scott, Governor
of North Carolina, 1949–1953*. Raleigh: Council of State, State of North Carolina,
1957.

Covington, Howard E., Jr., and Marion A. Ellis. *Terry Sanford: Politics, Progress and
Outrageous Ambitions*. Durham, N.C.: Duke University Press, 1999.

Crow, Jeffrey J. "The Civil War in Eastern North Carolina: A New Opportunity for
Interpretation." *Carolina Comments* (North Carolina Division of Archives and
History, Raleigh) 47, no. 4 (July 1999): 88–95.

———. "Cracking the Solid South: Populism and the Fusionist Interlude." In *The
North Carolina Experience: An Interpretive and Documentary History*, edited by
Lindley S. Butler and Alan D. Watson, 333–54. Chapel Hill: University of North
Carolina Press, 1984.

Davis, Joslin. "The Changing Status of Women Lawyers." *BarNotes* (North Carolina
Bar Association), April 1980, 5–13. North Carolina Collection, Wilson Library,
University of North Carolina at Chapel Hill.

Dean, John. *The Rehnquist Choice*. New York: Simon & Schuster, 2001.

Dean, Pamela. "Learning to Be New Women: Campus Culture at the North
Carolina Normal and Industrial College." *North Carolina Historical Review* 68,
no. 3 (July 1991): 286–306.

———. "Women on the Hill: A History of Women at the University of North
Carolina." Chapel Hill: Division of Student Affairs, University of North Carolina
at Chapel Hill, printed on the occasion of the dedication of the Katherine
Kennedy Carmichael Residence Hall, November 5, 6, and 7, 1987.

Dodd, Rebekah Y. *Reminiscences, 1811–1911*. [Henderson(?), N.C.: Author(?)], 1941.
North Carolina Collection, Wilson Library, University of North Carolina at
Chapel Hill.

Douglas, Davison M. *Reading, Writing and Race: The Desegregation of the Charlotte
Schools*. Chapel Hill: University of North Carolina Press, 1995.

Drachman, Virginia G. *Sisters in Law: Women Lawyers in Modern American History.* Cambridge, Mass.: Harvard University Press, 1998.

Drescher, John. *Triumph of Good Will.* Jackson: University Press of Mississippi, 2000.

Durden, Robert F. "North Carolina in the New South." In *The North Carolina Experience*, edited by Lindley S. Butler and Alan D. Watson, 309–32. Chapel Hill: University of North Carolina Press, 1984.

Edsall, Preston W., and J. Oliver Williams. "North Carolina: Bipartisan Paradox." In *The Changing Politics of the South*, edited by William C. Havard. Baton Rouge: Louisiana State University Press, 1972.

Edwards, Laura F. *Gendered Strife and Confusion: The Political Culture of Reconstruction.* Urbana: University of Illinois Press, 1997.

Edy, Carolyn. "Excuses, Excuses." *Carolina Alumni Review* 86, no. 4 (July–August 1997): 28–33.

Escott, Paul D. "Unwilling Hercules: North Carolina in the Confederacy." In *The North Carolina Experience: An Interpretive and Documentary History*, edited by Lindley S. Butler and Alan D. Watson, 265–83. Chapel Hill: University of North Carolina Press, 1984.

Ferm, Vergilius, ed. *An Encyclopedia of Religion.* Paterson, N.J.: Littlefield, Adams, 1964.

Fitzgerald, F. Scott. *The Crack-Up.* Edited by Edmund Wilson. New York: New Directions, 1993.

Franklin, John Hope. *Reconstruction after the Civil War.* Chicago: University of Chicago Press, 1994.

Gardner, Bettie Sue. *Rambles through the County of Rockingham.* Reidsville, N.C., 1950. North Carolina Collection, Wilson Library, University of North Carolina at Chapel Hill. Typescript.

Gasaway, Laura N., and Judith W. Wegner. "Women at UNC and in the Practice of Law." 73 *North Carolina Law Review* 705–24 (1995).

Gilmore, Glenda Elizabeth. *Gender and Jim Crow: Women and the Politics of White Supremacy in North Carolina, 1896–1920.* Chapel Hill: University of North Carolina Press, 1996.

Grossman, Joanna L. "Women's Jury Service: Right of Citizenship or Privilege of Difference?" 46 *Stanford Law Review* 1115–60 (1994).

Grossman, Joel B. "The Role of the American Bar Association in the Selection of Federal Judges: Episodic Involvement to Institutionalized Power." 17 *Vanderbilt Law Review* 785–814 (1964).

Guillory, Ferrel. "A Paradoxical Southern Lady." *South Magazine*, May–June 1975.

Gwyn, Allen H. *Work, Earn and Save.* Chapel Hill: Institutes for Civic Education, Extension Division, University of North Carolina, 1963. School of Government Library, University of North Carolina at Chapel Hill.

Hartig, Kate. "205 Years and Counting." *Blue & White Magazine*, December 1998. North Carolina Collection, Wilson Library, University of North Carolina at Chapel Hill.

Harvey, Edna. "What Present Day College Girls Are Thinking." *Alumnae*

News, North Carolina College for Women, July 1925, 30–32. North Carolina Collection, Wilson Library, University of North Carolina at Chapel Hill.

Havard, William C., ed. *The Changing Politics of the South*. Baton Rouge: Louisiana State University Press, 1972.

Henderson, Archibald. *North Carolina: The Old North State and the New*. Chicago: Lewis Publishing, 1941.

Hendricks, J. Edwin. *Seeking Liberty and Justice: A History of the North Carolina Bar Association, 1899–1999*. Edited by Lynn P. Roundtree. Raleigh: North Carolina Bar Association, 1999.

————. *Wake Forest University School of Law: 100 Years of Legal Education, 1894– 1994*. Winston-Salem: Wake Forest University, 1994.

History of North Carolina. Vol. 6. North Carolina Biography. Chicago: Lewis Publishing Company, 1919.

Hoffman, Philip. "Does the U.S. Supreme Court Need a Female Justice?" *Parade*, December 11, 1966.

Ireland, Robert E. *Entering the Auto Age: The Early Automobile in North Carolina, 1900–1930*. Raleigh: North Carolina Division of Archives and History, 1990.

Kerber, Linda K. *No Constitutional Right to Be Ladies: Women and the Obligations of Citizenship*. New York: Hill and Wang, 1998.

Key, V. O., Jr. *Southern Politics in State and Nation*. 1949. Reprint, Knoxville: University of Tennessee Press, 1984.

Lathrop, Virginia Terrell. *Educate a Woman: Fifty Years of Life at the Woman's College of the University of North Carolina*. Chapel Hill: University of North Carolina Press, 1942.

Leary, Helen F. M., ed. *North Carolina Research: Genealogy and Local History*. 2d ed. Raleigh: North Carolina Genealogical Society, 1996.

Lefler, Hugh Talmage, and Albert Ray Newsome. *The History of a Southern State: North Carolina*. Chapel Hill: University of North Carolina Press, 1973.

Leloudis, James L. *Schooling the New South: Pedagogy, Self, and Society in North Carolina, 1880–1920*. Chapel Hill: University of North Carolina Press, 1996.

Levy, Idrienne E. Note, "Constitutional Law—Right of Women to Serve on Juries." 23 *North Carolina Law Review* 152–58 (1945).

Lincoln, Evelyn. *Kennedy and Johnson*. New York: Holt, Rinehart and Winston, 1968.

Little, M. Ruth. *Sticks and Stones: Three Centuries of North Carolina Gravemarkers*. Chapel Hill: University of North Carolina Press, 1998.

Louis, Martin B. "A Survey of Decisions under the New North Carolina Rules of Civil Procedure." 50 *North Carolina Law Review* 729–60 (1972).

Luebke, Paul. *Tar Heel Politics: Myths and Realities*. Chapel Hill: University of North Carolina Press, 1990.

Manarin, Louis H., comp. *North Carolina Troops, 1861–1865: A Roster*. Raleigh: North Carolina Division of Archives and History, 1966-[98].

Mathews, Donald G., and Jane Sherron De Hart. *Sex, Gender, and the Politics of ERA*. New York: Oxford University Press, 1990.

Moore, John C., comp. *Roster of North Carolina Troops in the War between the States*. Raleigh: Ashe & Gatling, 1882.

Morris, Naomi E. "An Interview with Judge Naomi Elizabeth Morris (1921–1986)," by Pat DeVine. *Juridicus, the Journal of the North Carolina Supreme Court Historical Society,* October 2001, 1–20.

Newman, Roger K. *Hugo Black: A Biography.* New York: Pantheon Books, 1994.

North Carolina Manual, 1947. Raleigh: North Carolina Secretary of State.

O'Brien, David M. "Filling Justice William O. Douglas' Seat: President Gerald R. Ford's Appointment of Justice John Paul Stevens." Paper presented at the Seventh Presidential Conference, "Gerald R. Ford: Restoring the Presidency," Hofstra University, April 6–9, 1989. <http://www.supremecourthistory.org/04_library/subs_volumes/04_c11_f.html>. March 23, 2005.

Paschal, George Washington. *History of Wake Forest College, 1905–1943.* Vol. 3. Wake Forest: Wake Forest College, 1943.

Peace, Samuel Thomas, Sr. *Zeb's Black Baby.* Henderson, N.C., 1955. North Carolina Collection, Wilson Library, University of North Carolina at Chapel Hill.

Pleasants, Paul. "The Eight Towns of Rockingham." *State Magazine,* March 28, 1953, 16–20, 26–28.

Polk, Mary. *The Way We Were.* Winston-Salem: J. F. Blair, 1962.

Powell, William S. *Higher Education in North Carolina.* Raleigh: State Department of Archives and History, 1970.

———. *North Carolina: A History.* Chapel Hill: University of North Carolina Press, 1988.

———. *North Carolina through Four Centuries.* Chapel Hill: University of North Carolina Press, 1989.

———, ed. *Dictionary of North Carolina Biography.* Chapel Hill: University of North Carolina Press, 1979–96.

Pressly, Harriet. "Monday Is Ladies' Day in Our Courts." *State Magazine,* March 1, 1952, 3–4.

Ragan, Sam, ed. *The New Day.* Zebulon, N.C.: Record Publishing Company, 1964.

Ringer, Gladys Wells. "Law as a Profession for Women." *Alumnae News,* North Carolina College for Women (October 1925), 11–14. North Carolina Collection, Wilson Library, University of North Carolina at Chapel Hill.

Rodenbough, Charles Dyson, ed. *The Heritage of Rockingham County, North Carolina.* Winston-Salem: Rockingham Historical Society, in cooperation with Hunter Publishing, 1983.

Ross, William G. "Participation by the Public in the Federal Judicial Selection Process." 43 *Vanderbilt Law Review* 1–84 (1990).

Salmond, John A. "'The Burlington Dynamite Plot': The 1934 Textile Strike and Its Aftermath in Burlington, North Carolina." *North Carolina Historical Review* 75, no. 4 (October 1998): 398–434.

Scott, Anne Firor. *The Southern Lady: From Pedestal to Politics, 1830–1930.* Charlottesville: University of Virginia Press, 1995.

Scott, William Kerr. *Public Addresses, Letters and Papers of William Kerr Scott, Governor of North Carolina, 1949–1953.* Edited by D. L. Corbitt. Raleigh: Council of State, State of North Carolina, 1957.

Sharpe, Bill. "The Gem of the Piedmont." *State Magazine,* March 28, 1953, 3–5, 13–15.

"Sketches of the County of Rockingham, N.C." Reprinted in the *Journal of Rockingham County History and Genealogy* 6, no. 1 (June 1981): 1–31.

Smith, Blanche Blackwell. "Reminiscences." N.d. North Carolina Collection, Wilson Library, University of North Carolina at Chapel Hill. Typescript, photocopy.

Strouse, Jean. *Morgan: American Financier*. New York: Random House, 1999.

Tise, Larry E. "Confronting the Issue of Slavery." In *The North Carolina Experience*, edited by Lindley S. Butler and Alan D. Watson, 193–216. Chapel Hill: University of North Carolina Press, 1984.

Trelease, Allen W. "Reconstruction: The Halfway Revolution." In *The North Carolina Experience*, edited by Lindley S. Butler and Alan D. Watson, 285–307. Chapel Hill: University of North Carolina Press, 1984.

Ward, Artemus. "An Extraconstitutional Arrangement: Lyndon Johnson and the Fall of the Warren Court." White House Studies, Spring 2002. <http://www.findarticles.com/p/articles/mi_m0KVD/is_2_2/ai_93792508>. March 23, 2005.

Wettach, Robert H. *A Century of Legal Education*. Chapel Hill: University of North Carolina Press, 1947.

Williams, Juan. *Thurgood Marshall: American Revolutionary*. New York: Times Books, 1998.

Zuber, Richard L. *North Carolina during Reconstruction*. Raleigh: North Carolina Division of Archives and History, North Carolina Department of Cultural Resources, 1996.

ACKNOWLEDGMENTS

I owe an everlasting debt of gratitude to the countless individuals who helped me, over a period of more than a decade, to document the life of Susie Marshall Sharp. It is impossible to list them all, but there are some without whom this book would not exist, and I would like to acknowledge them here in an effort to express some small portion of my appreciation.

Grants from several organizations, early in the project, gave me critical moral support as well as financial assistance. I am deeply grateful to the Z. Smith Reynolds Foundation, the Mary Duke Biddle Foundation, and the North Caroliniana Society (Archie K. Davis Fellowship).

Members of Susie Sharp's family, ranging from her siblings to distant cousins, were uniformly generous and helpful to me. A special word, however, must be said about her sister Louise Sharp and her brother James V. ("Kits") Sharp. Louise went out of her way not only to give me the benefit of her retentive mind but also to pave the way for me to interview numerous other relatives and friends. Kits and his wife Gwen also went out of their way, making sure I had access to Susie Sharp's papers and other materials, right up until 2004, when the successor to the old Sharp & Sharp law firm closed its doors and Kits discovered a number of interesting items that Susie or her father had placed in the firm's safe, including several family letters dating from the late 1800s. I am also indebted to Susie Sharp's nephew and his wife, Dr. and Mrs. Lawrence A. Taylor, for copies of family letters and papers. To Susie Sharp's nephew Robert W. Newsom III, I am grateful for the copy of her February 15, 1976, letter to her sister Florence, recounting the untold history of the failed Mountain Farm and Jim Sharp's bankruptcy. Clara Garrett Fountain, the daughter of Susie Sharp's cousin A. Earle Garrett Jr., generously shared with me her meticulously tended archive of family papers.

None of Susie Sharp's family members ever suggested that I tailor or censor the material in this biography in any way.

Librarians and archivists are a special breed, and I have been the beneficiary of their perseverance, ingenuity, and expertise. I would like to thank H. G. Jones and Robert G. Anthony Jr. for particular help and encouragement, along with the dedicated staffs of the North Carolina Collection, the Southern Historical Collection, and the Kathrine R. Everett Law Library at the University of North Carolina at Chapel Hill. Louise Stafford, in her position as librarian of the North Carolina Supreme Court Library, offered indispensable guidance and assistance, as did her successor, Thomas P. Davis. The staffs of the North Carolina State Archives in Raleigh, the Walter Clinton Jackson Library at the University of North Carolina at Greensboro, and the Special Collection Archives of the Z. Smith Reynolds Library at Wake Forest University were also unfailingly helpful, as was the staff in the University of North

Carolina Alumni Office. Fann Montague helped me with Blackwell family genealogy at the Richard H. Thornton Library in Oxford, North Carolina, a superb resource for Granville County history. In addition, I am grateful to Robert W. ("Bob") Carter Jr. and Michael Perdue, who facilitated my access to papers donated to the Rockingham County Historical Collections at the Rockingham Community College by the Allen H. Gwyn family, as well as to other items in the library's collection. Bob Carter also supplied me with some of the fruits of his research about the Sharp family in Rockingham County, and accompanied me on a most interesting excursion in the area around Intelligence, North Carolina, during which I was able to interview some longtime residents.

Susie Sharp's friends and professional colleagues, far too numerous to list here, provided me with hours of interviews and insights, for which I am deeply appreciative. Her law clerks were tremendously helpful in their recollections of Justice Sharp as a person as well as a member of the North Carolina Supreme Court, and added greatly to the background on important cases. Norwood E. Robinson, who practiced law with Susie Sharp's father and who was a devoted adviser to the Sharp family, allowed me access to the files documenting Judge Sharp's seventeen years on the supreme court, which had been stored in his basement.

Among those individuals who knew her well, Willis P. Whichard deserves special mention. In addition to sharing his recollections with me in an interview, he read the book in manuscript and gave me valuable suggestions, which he was in a unique position to offer, having known Susie Sharp since the days he clerked for Justice William H. Bobbitt and having served on the North Carolina Supreme Court himself, as well as having served in the legislature during the period it was occupied with the Equal Rights Amendment, just to name a few examples of the breadth of his background knowledge. Angela Williams also read the manuscript and provided me with her editorial expertise.

Others who gave me encouragement, advice, or assistance beyond any duty to do so include Walter Bennett, William H. Chafe, Gladys Coates, W. Robert Connor, Leonard F. Dean, Anne Dellinger, Patricia DeVine, Nancy Donald, Susan Ehringhaus, Dirk Frankenberg, William C. Friday, Jacquelyn Dowd Hall, Watts Hill Jr., John Mabe, Bill and Sally Massengale, Melzer A. Morgan Jr., Roger K. Newman, Wyndham Robertson, Sarah Schroth, Anne Firor Scott, Julia Ann and Dick Taylor, Linda C. Vernon, Fran Weaver, and Judith Wegner.

Susie Sharp's family members, friends, professional colleagues, and former law clerks all added immeasurably to the portrait of Susie Sharp in both her public and private life. I am profoundly grateful to each and every one. Any errors, of course, are mine alone.

Acknowledgments

INDEX

Note: Page numbers in *italic* indicate photographs; SMS = Susie Marshall Sharp.

Beck, Dorothy Fahs, 59–60, 75–76
Bell, Griffin B., 413
Bell, J. Spencer, 268, 269
Bennett, Bert: in 1960 gubernatorial election, 221, 223; and SMS's comments on women's roles, 250; and SMS's speeches, 253–54; and SMS's supreme court appointment, 229, 232, 253
Bennett, Harold, 468 (n. 87)
Bennett, Thomas, 354, 355, 504 (n. 65)
Berry, Margaret, 39
Bier, Justus, 255
Billings, Rhoda, 502 (n. 30)
Birth control, 76, 275, 389
Black, Hugo L., 310, 316
Blackmun, Harry A., 310, 315
Blacks: in 1946 congressional elections, 110; limits on opportunities for, 130; Jim Sharp's treatment of, as clients; 19; SMS's treatment of, as clients, 86–88; SMS's views on, 195–200, 275; as lawyers and judges, 347–48, 383–84, 504 (n. 71). *See also* Civil rights movement; Race; Racism; Segregation
Blackwell, Annie Britt. *See* Sharp, Annie Britt Blackwell
Blackwell, Blanche, 11, 90, 442 (n. 11)
Blackwell, John Pomfret, Jr., 9–10, 442 (nn. 11–12), 443 (n. 26)
Blackwell, John Pomfret "Marse Johnnie," Sr., 8–10, 442 (nn. 11, 14)
Blackwell, Mary Ann Webb, 9–10
Blackwell, Sallie Green Wortham, 9, 443 (n. 26)
Blackwell, Sallie Royster Pittard, 443 (n. 26)
Blackwell, Susie. *See* Garrett, Susie Blackwell
Blackwell, William, 303, 304
Blackwell family, 8–11; aristocratic origins of, 8, 10–11, 14, 407; slave ownership by, 9, 442 (n. 11)

Bledsoe, Jerry: *Bitter Blood*, 435
Board of Corrections and Training, 104, 462 (n. 26)
Bobbitt, Sarah Buford Dunlap, 325
Bobbitt, William Haywood, 246; associate justice appointment of, 216, 323; as associate justice candidate, 168, 173–76, 216; career of, 259, 323–25; on charitable immunity, 284; chief justice appointment of, 331–32, 337; children of, 325, 437–38; death of, 438; on death penalty, 359; education of, 324; and ERA, 396; and geographic composition of court, 233, 478 (n. 55); Gwyn on, 216, 326–27; health problems of, 364, 437, 501 (n. 18); on housekeeping by SMS, 406; on judicial reform, 270, 488 (n. 114); marriage of, 325; on merit selection system, 381; opinions written by, 324–25; personality of, 259, 323–24; retirement of, 336–37, 339, 399–400, 409–10, 502 (n. 24); SMS's collaborative work with, 330–31; on succession in supreme court, 420; on 1974 supreme court election, 340, 341, 363–64, 502 (n. 24); at swearing-in ceremonies, 367; on women law clerks, 368–69
—SMS's affair with, 323–35; careers threatened by, 326–27, 330; constant companionship in, xvi, 332, 409–10, 412, 437; correspondence in, xvi; development of, 323–31; duration of, 437; end of, 438; happiness in, 437; Kesler and, 325–26, 328, 329, 331, 333, 335; love in, 326, 328–29, 437; marriage discussed in, 326–27, 329–30, 409, 411–12; physical aspect of, 330; public awareness of, 329–31, 411; resentment in, 410–11; after retirement of Bobbitt, 409–12; after retirement of SMS, 431–32, 437–38; start of, 323, 325–26; stress in, 408; travels in, 431

Criminal Code by, 57, 101; on bar exam, 49; classes taught by, 41–43; correspondence with SMS, 188; in Institute of Government, 108–9, 463 (n. 54); on judicial misconduct, 379; relationship with SMS, 43; sister of, 444 (n. 47); on SMS as associate justice, 478 (n. 50); on SMS as chief justice, 252; at swearing-in ceremonies, 236; travels with, 90; on women jurors, 108–9

Coates, Dora, 444 (n. 47)

Coates, Gladys, 90, 236, 252, 463 (n. 54)

Cochrane, Elizabeth, 368–69

Code, Criminal, 57, 101

Collier, Robert A., Jr., 344–47

Columbia University School of Law, 347–48

Communist Party, 87, 159, 275

Congress, U.S.: ERA in, 389, 390, 394; on segregation, 196; and U.S. Supreme Court appointments, 315, 317

Congressional elections: of 1946, 109–15, 463 (n. 60); of 1950, 109, 179; of 1972, 339; of 1974, 354, 365

Congress of Industrial Organizations (CIO), 110–11, 464 (n. 62)

Connor, George W., 43, 49

Conservatism, judicial: of R. Hunt Parker, 258–59; of SMS, 286–87, 425

Constitution, N.C.: on appellate courts, 296–97; commissions on, 218, 268–69, 487 (n. 105); on court reform, 268–72; and judicial qualifications, 380, 381, 385; on judicial standards, 373–74, 509 (n. 3); on juries, 104, 107–8, 192; on racial intermarriage, 195

Constitution, U.S.: Fourteenth Amendment to, 106, 109, 197, 278–79, 363, 394, 395, 513 (n. 11); Nineteenth Amendment to, 23, 102, 105, 391

Contraception, 76, 275, 389

Conway, Jill Ker, 366

Coolidge, Calvin, 52

Copeland, J. William, 245, 299, 346, 365, 385

Couch, William T., 87

Counts, Donie, 21–22, 46

Court reform. *See* Judicial system, N.C.

Court system. *See* Judicial system, N.C.

Covington, William T., 70–71, 254, 367

Covington, Winona, 254

Crisp, A. R., 468 (n. 87)

Cromartie, Doris, 221, 250

Cromer, Elmo, 112

Crutchfield, Harry L., 42, 47

Daily Tar Heel. See Tar Heel/Daily Tar Heel

Daughters of the American Revolution (DAR), 410–11

Davis, Joslin, 423

Davis, Robert M., 346–47

Davis, Tom I., 253–54, 484 (n. 36)

Dean, John W., 311–12, 316

Deane, Charles, 398

Death penalty: Gwyn and, 85; judicial input on, 386–88; supreme court opinions on, 201, 202, 203, 359–60, 386, 512 (n. 74); for rape, 358, 359, 387–88, 512 (n. 84); SMS's first experiences with, 85, 185; SMS's views on, 85, 141–42, 203, 358, 360–61; statutes on, 358–59, 386–88; in 1974 supreme court election, 358–61; U.S. Supreme Court on, 358–59, 386, 388, 506 (n. 128), 512 (n. 77)

Democracy, SMS's beliefs about, 189–90

Democratic Party: ABA and, 314; conflict within, 130–31; gerrymandering by, 10, 204; Jim Sharp in, 52–53, 100, 101; judicial appointments by, 336; political machine of, 104, 130, 135; and Republican Party's rise, 224, 333–34; Sharp family in, 189; SMS's alienation from, 274–75; SMS's involvement in, 101–4, 466 (n. 33),

484 (n. 36); on women jurors, 108; women's votes and, 23, 104

Democratic Women of Forsyth County, 253–54

Denny, Emery B.: age of, 218; career of, 259; chief justice appointment of, 232; and geographic composition of court, 233, 478 (n. 55); on judicial reform, 270, 271; on power of justices, 237; on public speaking by justices, 253–54; seniority of, on supreme court, 230; on SMS's supreme court appointment, 258; at swearing-in ceremonies, 236–37, 244

Devin, William A., 170, 216

Dilday v. Beaufort County Board of Education, 279–81

District court judges: appointment and removal of, by SMS, 372, 373, 416–17, 419; creation of, 269; first black woman as, 348, 349; Judge-Be-Lawyer bill and, 381; in judicial salary package, 414–15; as members of Judicial Standards Commission, 373–74, 509 (n. 26); as members of merit selection nominating committee, 383, 511 (n. 66); nonlawyers as, 361, 373, 381–82; salary increases for, 417

Divorce: in Sharp family tragedies, 432–34; SMS's legal opinion on, 289–91, 492 (n. 79); stigma of, 68

Dixie Classic, 211

Dole, Elizabeth, 449 (n. 13)

Dotzenrod, Ralph, 399, 400

Douglas, William O., 313, 317, 318

Drum, Nancy, 399

Duke University, 363, 433, 434; hospital/Medical Center, 65, 76, 78, 88, 291; nursing school, 72, 94, 96. *See also* Trinity College

Durham Herald, 344

Earnhardt, Caroline, 341–42

Eason, Joe, 417

Edenton, 410–11

Edmisten, Rufus, 365, 367

Education: in Blackwell family, 11; in 1960 gubernatorial election, 221, 227; law school requirements for, 36–37; segregation in, 196, 222, 276–81; sexism in, 395; in Sharp family, 27. *See also* Legal education

Efird, Oscar O., 81, 173, 174

Eisenhower, Dwight D., 175, 182, 217, 314

Elections: campaign work by SMS in, 100, 103–4, 109–15, 134–36, 138; gerrymandering in, 10; get-out-the-vote efforts in, 189–90; voting irregularities in, 112–15; women's votes in, 23, 103–4, 134, 190, 227. *See also specific types of elections (gubernatorial, presidential, etc.)*

Elliott, Bette, 342

Elliott, Harriet Wiseman, 27, 447 (nn. 41, 42, 44)

Elliott, Lucille, 44–45, 79

Equal Rights Amendment (ERA), 389–405; Congress on, 389, 390; effects on statutory protections, 107, 390, 392, 394–95; failure of, 389, 390, 396, 404–5; General Assembly on, 391, 396–98, 401–5; media coverage of, 400, 401, 403–4, 514 (n. 43); provisions of, 389, 390; SMS's opposition to, 389, 393–405, 426; in supreme court elections, 363, 398; in U.S. Supreme Court appointments, 313

Equitable Distribution Act of 1981, 290–91

ERA. *See* Equal Rights Amendment

Erlichman, John D., 310

Ervin, Paul, 220

Ervin, Samuel J., Jr.: career of, 393; on desegregation, 196; on ERA, 390, 393–94, 396–99, 401, 402, 405; on 1960 presidential election, 224; Senate appointment of, 216; on SMS in federal courts, 303, 306, 311; on *stare decisis*, 286; superior court appointment of, 100; in Watergate investigation, 362, 393

Ervin, Samuel J., III, 503 (n. 50)

Ethics. *See* Judicial conduct

Evans, May Thompson, 101

Everett, Mrs. B. B., 108

Everett, Kathrine Robinson, 30, 39, 55, 448 (n. 57)

Everett, Reuben Oscar, 448 (n. 57)

Exum, James G., Jr., 245; on death penalty, 386; on judicial merit selection system, 384; as supreme court candidate, 365, 502 (n. 30); on 1974 supreme court election, 349, 360–61, 503 (n. 50)

Ezrol, Stanley, 356–57

Faggart, L. F. "Mule," 381

Fagge, Harry, 83

Fahs, Dorothy. *See* Beck, Dorothy Fahs

Farming: by Blackwell family, 9–10; in 1948 gubernatorial campaign, 131–33, 135; by Sharp family, 7, 12, 17, 180, 213

Federal Bureau of Investigation (FBI), SMS on search committee to find new head of, 368, 412–14, 516 (n. 31)

Federal courts: partisanship in appointments to, 314, 315; SMS as candidate for, 298–318

Feminism, SMS's views on, 194, 369. *See also* Equal Rigths Amendment; Women's rights

Ferrell, W. L., 463 (n. 60)

Fillman, Margaret. *See* Chaney, Margaret Fillman

Fleishman, Joel, 232

Flogging, 151, 469 (n. 23)

Fogleman, Clay, 85

Folger, A. D., 100

Folger, John H., 109–15, 463 (n. 60)

Folger, W. A. "Lon," 109

Ford, Betty, 313, 366

Ford, Gerald, 313, 317, 318, 362

Fordham, Jefferson B., 56, 57, 276, 285, 452 (n. 13)

Fortas, Abe, 305, 309, 315, 317, 318

Fountain, George M., 208

Fourteenth Amendment (U.S. Constitution): and ERA, 363, 394, 395; provisions of, 513 (n. 11); and segregation, 197, 278–79; and women jurors, 106, 109

Frankfurter, Felix, 41, 298–99

Freeman, Franklin, 346, 371–74, 376, 437, 512 (n. 73)

Free speech. *See* Speaker Ban Law

Freund, Paul A., 394

Friday, Herschel H., 316–17

Friday, William, 312

Friedan, Betty: *The Feminine Mystique*, 274

Fry, Lilian Rowe, 449 (n. 12)

Fultz quadruplets, 89, 212–13, 231, 459 (n. 48)

Furman v. Georgia, 358–59, 506 (n. 128)

Galifinakis, Nick, 352

Gardner, Dillard: death of, 485 (n. 52); in high school, 21, 25, 446 (n. 29); at law school, 39, 43; as marshal-librarian, 236–37, 253, 485 (n. 52)

Gardner, O. Max, 23, 104, 130, 131

Garment, Leonard, 316

Garrett, A. Earle, Jr.: on destruction of journals, xv; in law school, 71; on SMS's superior court appointment, 142; at swearing-in ceremonies, 236

Garrett, A. Earle, Sr.: marriage of, 12; Sharps living with, 12, 14, 407; tragedies in family of, 432

Garrett, Eliza Merritt. *See* Sharp, Eliza Merritt Garrett

Garrett, Susie Blackwell, 12, 14, 30, 407, 432

Gender: in language, 143, 484 (n. 38); in 1974 supreme court election, 343, 349, 354–55, 362

General Assembly, N.C.: on death penalty, 387; on ERA, 391, 396–98, 401–5; judicial input in, 385–86, 404;

77, 84–85; on U.S. Supreme Court vacancies, 305, 306; and work-release program, 158–59
—SMS's affair with, xv, 157–61, 163; end of, 166, 176–77, 212
Gwyn, Allen H., Jr.: on 1948 gubernatorial election, 133–34; on support for SMS's nomination to U.S. Supreme Court, 306; in supreme court appointment of SMS, 220–21, 229, 232, 237; and 1974 supreme court election, 341, 354; at swearing-in ceremonies, 236
Gwyn, Janie Johnston: marriage of, 159; SMS's relationship with, 501 (n. 12); in 1952 supreme court election, 173, 175–76; at swearing-in ceremonies, 236, 367

Hall, Clarence, 219
Halstead, William, 468 (n. 87)
Hanes, Robert M., 463 (n. 60)
Hanft, Frank W., 121, 234
Happer, Gladys Morgan, 163, 456 (n. 124)
Harlan, John M., 310, 316
Harris, Lou, 223
Harris, Shearon, 410
Harvard Law School, 36, 39, 449 (n. 13)
Hatch, William T., 468 (n. 87)
Hayden, Carl, 390
Hayden Rider, 390, 512 (n. 1)
Haynsworth, Clement, 309, 315
Helms, Fred, 412
Helms, Jesse, 179, 313, 339, 355
Helms, Parks, 382
Hester, William S., 64–65
Higgins, Carlisle W.: age of, 218, 336, 501 (n. 10); career of, 259; chambers of, 256; on charitable immunity, 284; in conferences, 265; on custody case injustice, 84–85; on death penalty, 359; and geographic composition of court, 233, 478 (n. 55); on implied warranty of fitness, 287–88; and

judicial reform, 207, 270; in local elections, 64, 100; in luncheon procession, 327–28; on mirror for court, 257; personality of, 259; on privity of contract, 288–89; retirement of, 336–38, 339, 400, 412; and safety of SMS, 267–68; seniority of, on supreme court, 336, 337; Sharp & Sharp working with, 85; on succession in supreme court, 420; supreme court appointment of, 217, 478 (n. 45); on supreme court appointment of SMS, 259; on 1974 supreme court election, 340, 341, 344; at swearing-in ceremonies, 367
Highway and Public Works Commission, 150–51, 231, 256
Hills, Carla, 366
Hiss, Alger, 139
Hobgood, Frank P., 143, 145
Hobgood, Hamilton H., 361, 363, 376, 385, 416
Hobson's choice, 265, 295, 486 (n. 93)
Hodges, Luther H.: Branch working for, 419; as commerce secretary, 298; and constitutional amendments, 218; court reform under, 268; in 1956 gubernatorial election, 217; judicial appointments by, 207–8, 217–19, 478 (n. 50), 479 (n. 65); Judicial Council under, 497 (n. 1); segregation under, 196
Hoey, Clyde R., 100, 216, 461 (n. 6)
Holshouser, James E., Jr.: on ERA, 391; as governor-elect, 337, 338; in 1972 gubernatorial election, 333, 336, 339; judicial appointments by, 339, 341; on 1974 supreme court election, 355; and swearing-in ceremonies, 367
Holt, Bertha, 387
Holton, Tabitha Anne, 39
Hood, Grady M., 453 (n. 45)
Hooks, Jack, 243
Hoover, Herbert, 51, 52, 224, 227
Hoover, J. Edgar, 412

Horton, Hamilton C., Jr., 398
Hotel Sir Walter: alcohol at, 295; Kesler and SMS at, 162, 211; political activities at, 258; residents of, 257–58; SMS living in, 235, 252, 257–58, 319, 332, 406; in 1974 supreme court election, 363
House of Representatives, N.C. *See* General Assembly, N.C.
House of Representatives, U.S.: 1946 elections for, 109–15; 1974 elections for, 365; ERA in, 390
Hruska, Roman, 309
Huffman, Robert L., 484 (n. 36)
Hughes, Sarah T., 274, 488 (n. 2)
Humphrey, Hubert, 223
Humphreys, Ira, 14, 62, 444 (n. 44)
Hunt, George, *241*, 462 (n. 20)
Hunt, James B.: career of, 419; on death penalty, 388; on ERA, 391, 397, 403; in 1976 gubernatorial election, 402, 419, 420; gubernatorial terms of, 419, 502 (n. 30); judicial appointments by, 419–21, 422; on judicial merit selection system, 383, 384, 385; on judicial salaries, 416; at swearing-in ceremonies, 367
Hunt, Patricia, 404, 405
Huskins, J. Frank, 245; on divorce law, 290; retirement of, 492 (n. 90); seniority of, on supreme court, 337; and stress in SMS, 408; as supreme court candidate, 219, 482 (n. 147), 490 (n. 50); on workers' compensation, 492 (n. 90)
Hutchins, Robert, 74
Hyde, Herbert L., 391

Income, judicial, 252, 338, 368, 371, 414–18, 483 (n. 26)
Income taxes, 180, 212, 231
Institute of Government (UNC), 108–9, 463 (n. 54)
Integration. *See* Segregation
Intelligence (town), 8, 11

International Labor Defense, 87
Iredell, James, 410–11

Jackson, Walter Clinton, 27–28, 31, 53, 447 (nn. 44, 45)
James, Murray G., 168–69
J. E .B. v. Alabama ex rel. T.B., 462 (n. 39)
Johnson, Charles M., 115, 130–35
Johnson, Frank M., Jr., 414
Johnson, Guion, 221, 228, 233, 234; *Ante-Bellum North Carolina*, 221
Johnson, Jefferson D., Jr., 168, 169, 218, 478 (n. 55)
Johnson, Lyndon B.: and Civil Rights Act, 276; Great Society of, 274, 389; in 1960 presidential election, 222–25; SMS's opinion of, 275; Supreme Court appointments by, 302, 304–8, 309, 315, 317–18; swearing-in of, 274
Jones, E. Richard "Dick," 261–62, 263–65
Jordan, B. Everett, 303, 306, 311
Jordan, Barbara, 354, 366
Jordan, Henry, 152
Josey, Claude Kitchin, 397
Joyner, William T., 112, 113–14
Judge-Be-Lawyer bill, 381–82, 385
Judges: assignments of, 338, 373, 382; first black woman as, in district court, 347–48, 504 (n. 71); lawyers' friendships with, 83; merit selection system for, 379–85; political activities of, 253–54, 275, 360; political nature of, 99, 140; removal from office, 372–74; Republican appointment of, 336, 339, 502 (n. 30); salaries of, 338, 368, 371, 414–18; verdicts by, vs. juries, 190–91. *See also* Lay judges; Women—as judges and justices
Judicial activism: in charitable immunity case, 285; in divorce case, 289; in judicial standards cases, 376; in privity of contract case, 287–89; in workers' compensation cases, 291–93

Index

Judicial conduct: Code of, 345, 360, 368, 374, 385–86, 396, 398, 400; in custody case, 84–85; grounds for evaluating, 374, 509 (n. 27); under SMS as chief justice, 371–79, 425–26; supreme court opinions on, 374–79

Judicial Council, 205, 206, 331, 385, 480 (n. 108), 497 (n. 1)

Judicial Department Act of 1965, 488 (n. 121)

Judicial elections: in merit selection system, 379–81; partisanship in, 343, 379–81, 503 (n. 37). *See also* North Carolina Supreme Court—elections for

Judicial philosophy: of Lake, 331, 500 (n. 73); of R. Hunt Parker, 259, 375; of SMS, 281, 284, 286–87, 375–76, 425; strict constructionism, 285, 393

Judicial Redistricting Act of 1955, 205–6

Judicial Standards Commission, 368, 373–79, 509 (nn. 3, 26)

Judicial system, N.C.: budget of, 414–18; chief justice as head of, 357–58, 368; civil procedure rules in, 293; constitutional amendments and, 218; inefficiency in, 204–5; intermediate appellate court in, 296–97; organization of courts in, 268–69; pace of justice in, 145; 1950s reform of, 204–8, 480 (n. 108); 1960s reform of, 268–72, 296, 368, 488 (n. 121); in 1974 supreme court election, 345

Junior Order of United American Mechanics, 15–16, 25

Juries: eavesdropping on, 60–61, 453 (nn. 38, 42); nullification by, 191, 474 (n. 36); selection of, 83; in small-town environment, 83; SMS's approach to, as judge, 191–92; SMS's defense of system of, 190–92; SMS's first experience with, 60; women as members of, 60, 99, 104–9, 144–45, 192, 462 (n. 39)

Justices of the peace, 268, 269, 271

Katzenbach, Nicholas, 305

Kelley, Clarence M., 412, 414

Kennedy, Ethel, 227

Kennedy, Jackie, 260, 274, 275

Kennedy, John F.: assassination of, 274–75, 302, 318, 488 (n. 1); Fultz quadruplets and, 89; personal life of, 428; in 1960 presidential election, 222–27; Supreme Court appointments by, 298–99, 302, 313–15, 317–18

Kennedy, Robert, 223–24, 227, 275, 315

Kesler, Frances Sue, 162, 235, 333, 367, 409, 432

Kesler, John Columbus, 122; career of, 163; on career of SMS, 177, 409; death of, 438; on 1960 gubernatorial election, 222; in Judicial Council, 331, 497 (n. 1); and judicial reform, 270; in law school, 44, 46–48; marriage of, 93, 162, 209; nature of relationship with SMS, xiv–xvi, 44, 177; on 1960 presidential election, 225, 226–27; on supreme court appointment of SMS, 170, 215, 235; on 1952 supreme court election, 172, 174; on 1974 supreme court election, 344; at swearing-in ceremonies, 236, 367

—SMS's affair with, 162–66; and Bobbitt, 325–26, 328, 329, 331, 333, 335; decline of, 301–2, 307–8, 319–20, 325, 409; end of, 432; expectations for future of, 209–10, 302, 334–35; heartbreak over, 48, 50, 163; hesitancy in, 163, 301, 302, 333; hiatus in, 47–48, 177, 212; jealousy in, 174, 209; love in, 48, 50, 93, 163, 166, 209–10, 212, 428, 432; marriage prospect in, 47, 50, 93, 212, 428; physical aspect of, 162; records of, xv–xvi, 162, 470 (n. 50); after retirement, 431–32; revival of, after death of wife, 332–35; start of, 44, 46–48, 162; during superior court judgeship, 163–66, 209–12; during supreme court justiceship, 301–2, 319–20, 409; travels in, 164–

66, 296; and U.S. Supreme Court candidacy, 302

—SMS's correspondence with, xiv–xv; on Bobbitt, 325; breach in security of, 301–2; copies of, 439, 477 (n. 14); on death penalty, 203; on Democratic Party, 189; details of life in, 210; difficulty of, 164; on family, 180, 181, 214; on governorship, 272; handling of, xiv–xv, 164, 210; on home county superior court term, 185; on Kennedy assassination, 275; on law clerks, 264–65; on public speaking, 254–55; race in, 198, 199, 277; on religion, 228; on supreme court appointments, 218, 220, 221, 228, 236, 252; on supreme court life, 260, 261, 267–68, 319–20, 485 (n. 71); on telephone calls, 258; on U.S. Supreme Court, 301; on women's roles, 250

Kesler, Sudie Grace West: death of, 332–33; health problems of, 307; marriage of, 93, 162; relationship with SMS, 209, 235, 301

Key, V. O., Jr., 104, 130

Kierkegaard, Søren, 424

King, Billie Jean, 366

King, Martin Luther, Jr. 223, 295

Kitchin, W. W., 8

Klenner, Annie Hill Sharp (sister of SMS), 118; birth of, 13; children of, 95, 323, 433–35; education of, 72; marriage of, 89, 94–95; on SMS's care of siblings, 24, 72; SMS's support of, 72; in 1974 supreme court election, 364; tragedies in family of, 432–34

Klenner, Frederick Robert: children of, 95, 323; death of, 434; and Fultz quadruplets, 89, 459 (n. 48); marriage of, 89, 94–95; medical practice of, 95, 179, 180, 433; tragedies in family of, 433–34

Klenner, Fritz, 95, 323, 433–36

Klenner, Gertrude, 95, 436

Klenner, Mary Anne, 95

Kreps, Juanita, 391

Ku Klux Klan, 159, 199, 219

Kurfees, Marshall, 111, 112

Kurland, Philip, 394

Labor Party, 356–57

Labor unions, 87, 103, 130

Ladies' Home Journal, 172

Lake, I. Beverly, 245; associate justice appointment of, 280; on charitable immunity, 285; as chief justice candidate, 337, 338, 340, 341; in 1960 gubernatorial election, 221–22, 224, 225, 350, 427; judicial philosophy of, 331, 500 (n. 73); Morgan (Robert) and, 337, 500 (n. 3); on segregation, 196, 280; seniority of, on supreme court, 337; on succession in supreme court, 419, 420; in 1974 supreme court election, 340, 341

Lambeth, Tom, 232

Lane, J. Foust, 466 (n. 32)

Langdell, Christopher C., 36

Langston, Allen: on death penalty, 85; on eavesdropping on juries, 61; SMS dating, 71, 77, 79; on superior court appointment of SMS, 141; on trial experience, 82

Language, gender in, 143, 484 (n. 38)

Law clerks of SMS: in charitable immunity case, 282–83; on decisionmaking process, 417; first woman, 368–69; role in opinions, 263–65, 282, 486 (n. 84); on stand-up desk, 273; and U.S. Supreme Court candidacy of SMS, 306–7

Law school. *See* Legal education; University of North Carolina School of Law

Lawyers: judges' friendships with, 83; wives of, 156. *See also* Women—as lawyers

Lay judges (nonlawyers): assignments of, 373, 382; elimination of, 385; limits on skills of, 381–82; merit selection system and, 379–82; in 1974 supreme court election, 350, 351, 356, 361–62, 380

Leaksville News, 137

Leatherman v. Leatherman, 289–91

Lee, Robert E., 396

Legal education: casebook system in, 36; Jim Sharp on, 42–43; modernization of, 35–37, 42–43; for women, 39, 347–48, 421, 429. *See also* University of North Carolina School of Law

Legislature. *See* General Assembly, N.C.

Lewis, Rhoda V., 253

Liberalism, judicial, 286–87, 425

Life imprisonment, vs. death penalty, 358–59

Lillie, Mildred L., 312, 314, 316–17

Lindh, Pat, 313

Link, Arthur A., 399

Llewellyn, Karl: *Jurisprudence,* 287

Lobdell, Hugh L. "Cicero": SMS dating, 71, 74, 77; SMS's introduction to, 70–71; on supreme court appointment of SMS, 234, 251; and 1952 supreme court election, 174; at swearing-in ceremonies, 367

Local courts, organization of, 268–69

Local elections: of 1928, 53; of 1930, 64; of 1946, 107–8

Lockwood, Lorna E., 253

London, Henry M., 90, 91

Los Angeles Times, 414

Lynch, Delores, 433, 434, 435

Lynch, Janie, 434, 435

Lynch, Jim, 433–35

Lynch, John, 433–35

Lynch, Susie Newsom: birth of, 97; family tragedy involving, 408, 432–36; marriage of, 323, 408; SMS as guardian of, 480 (n. 104)

Lynch, Tom, 323, 408, 432–35

Lyon, Virginia: on ERA, 401; hiring of, 261; after retirement of SMS, 431; SMS's relationship with, 261–62; SMS's romances and, 308, 328, 437; and 1974 supreme court election, 340; on women law clerks, 368–69

Maddrey, Mabel Claire, 257–58

Madison (town), 12–13

Magistrates, 269, 345

Manning, Henry, 282–83, 307, 308, 490 (n. 50), 495 (n. 62)

Manor, Blanche, 258

Markham, Donald W., *121*

Marshall, Thurgood, 308, 315

Martin, James G., 502 (n. 30)

Matthews, Burnita Shelton, 488 (n. 2)

McAnally, Charlie, 449 (n. 28)

McCall, Frederick B., 51, *121*

McCormick, Charles T., 45, 56, 65–69

McDonald, Ralph, 130

McGehee, Lucius Polk, 35–36

McIntosh, A. C., 41, *121*

McIver, Charles Duncan, 27

McKay, Martha: on ERA, 397, 398; in 1960 gubernatorial election, 221, 227; in supreme court appointment of SMS, 232, 481 (n. 139); in Women's Political Caucus, 390; on women's roles, 250

McKee, Gertrude Dills, 102, 462 (n. 17)

McLean, Carrie L., 102

McMichael, P. D., 465 (n. 26)

McMullan, Harry, 107

McRae, John A., 324

Mebane, Jessie, 277, 278

Mebane, Lillie M., 102

Mecca (restaurant), 437

Media coverage: courtroom cameras in, 418; of death penalty cases, 201, 202; of ERA debate, 400, 401, 403–4, 514 (n. 43); of FBI search committee, 413, 414; of Jim Sharp's death, 181; of judicial misconduct case,

378–79; of judicial reform, 270–71; photographs in, 55–56, 343, 365, 452 (n. 5), 503 (n. 40); of prison reform speech, 371; of Sharp family tragedies, 435; of Sharp & Sharp, establishment of, 55–56; of SMS's trial practice, 59, 62, 81, 84; of superior court appointment of SMS, 129–30, 136–37, 139, 141, 142–44; of superior court judgeship of SMS, 146–49, 155, 185–86, 201, 202; of supreme court appointments, 217–19, 235, 249–51, 421; of supreme court elections, 171, 173, 341–44, 346, 353–54, 364, 365; of U.S. Supreme Court appointments, 316; of women jurors, 105, 107

Merit selection system, judicial, 379–85, 511 (n. 71)

Methodist Church, 18–19, 228, 237

Meyer, Louis B., 422

Mitchell, John, 310, 311, 312, 315–16

Mitchell, Martha, 310

Mondale, Walter F., 412, 413

Montague, Bert M., 372, 381, 493 (n. 112)

Moore, Clifton L., 219–20, 259, 270, 284

Moore, Dan K., 245; as chief justice candidate, 337; judicial appointments by, 71, 280, 344, 354, 419, 422, 490 (n. 50); seniority of, on supreme court, 337; on Speaker Ban Law, 275–76; on supreme court appointments, 338, 420; on 1974 supreme court election, 341; on U.S. Supreme Court and SMS, 306

Moore, Jeannelle, 329

Morgan, Gladys. *See* Happer, Gladys Morgan

Morgan, James F., 404

Morgan, Robert, 257, 337, 338, 352, 365, 500 (n. 3)

Morris, Naomi Elizabeth: as appellate court judge, 354, 421–24, 429; on judicial merit selection system, 385; law clerks of, 369

Morrison, Cameron, 23, 37

Mountain Farm, 13, 14–15, 407

Mulder, John E., 121

National Association for the Advancement of Colored People (NAACP), 197, 198, 223

National League of Women Voters, 107

National Organization for Women (NOW), 389, 390

National Women's Political Caucus, 311

National Women's Political Council, 316

NCCW. *See* North Carolina College for Women

Neaves, W. A., 464 (n. 60)

Nelson, W. H., 137

New Bethel Township, 7, 8

Newcomb, Betty, 350

Newcomb, James M., in 1974 supreme court election, 349–56, 362, 365–66, 380

Newnam, Margaret Reid, 20, 90, 145, 236, 302

News and Observer: on Bobbitt, 323; on death penalty, 360; on ERA, 401; on FBI search committee, 413; on gubernatorial elections, 134, 135, 272, 465 (n. 26); on judicial misconduct, 378; on judicial reform, 270; on superior court appointment of SMS, 139, 142, 143; on supreme court appointments, 218, 229–30; on supreme court elections, 171, 173, 303, 344, 346, 353–54, 355; on supreme court opinions, 286, 360; on trial practice of SMS, 59; on women jurors, 105, 107; on women's equality, 391; on women's roles, 249–51

Newsom, Florence Abigail Sharp (sister of SMS): Annie Sharp living with, 321–23; birth of, 18; children of, 97, 272, 432–35, 480 (n. 104); financial troubles of, 407–8; on Hotel Sir Walter, 332; marriage of, 97; murder of, 435–36; on religion, 227; on 1974 supreme court election, 364; tragedies in family of, 432–36; visits home by, 230; youth of, 24, 96–97

Newsom, Robert W., Jr.: career of, 323, 407, 408; children of, 97, 432–35, 480 (n. 104); marriage of, 97; murder of, 435–36; tragedies in family of, 432–36

Newsom, Robert W., III, 97, 407, 408, 434

Newsom, Susie. *See* Lynch, Susie Newsom

Newsweek, 365

New York: SMS's travels to, 90, 139, 164–66, 296

New York Times, 70, 191, 249, 316, 438

Nineteenth Amendment (U.S. Constitution), 23, 102, 105, 391

Nixon, Julie, 310

Nixon, Pat, 310

Nixon, Richard M.: in 1956 presidential election, 217; in 1960 presidential election, 223, 225, 226; in 1972 presidential election, 333–34, 339; resignation of, 362; SMS's views on, 217, 226; Supreme Court appointments by, 308–13, 315–17; and 1974 supreme court election, 362–63; tapes of, 310; Watergate and, 362, 393, 412

Nixon, Tricia, 310

North Carolina Association of Black Lawyers, 383

North Carolina Association of Women Attorneys, 423

North Carolina Bar Association: on court reform, 268–69; SMS's speeches before, 369–71; on U.S. Supreme Court candidates, 306; and women judges, 423

North Carolina Business and Professional Women's Clubs, 390

North Carolina College for Women (NCCW; later Woman's College of the University of North Carolina [1932] and University of North Carolina at Greensboro [1963]):

accreditation of, 28, 447 (n. 48); faculty of, 27–28; honorary degrees given by, 169–70; Louise Sharp at, 96; name changes of, 27; Sallie Sharp at, 64, 72, 78, 94; SMS attending, 26–31; SMS's involvement in, 218; SMS's speeches at, 61; teachers educated at, 20, 28

North Carolina Courts Commission, 377–78, 380

North Carolina Federation of Women's Clubs, 106–7, 144, 299

North Carolina Law Review, 44, 45, 46, 70, 71, 422

North Carolina Museum of Art, 255

North Carolina State Bar: SMS's speeches before, 171, 205; swearing in of SMS to, 50–51, 237, 366

North Carolina Supreme Court: appeal to, right of, 296; camaraderie on, 267–68; caseload of, 296; chambers of, 255–57, 431; conferences of, 265; court reform affecting, 268–72; geographic composition of, 219, 233, 478 (n. 55); luncheon procession by, 260, 267, 327–28, 368; media coverage of, 59; oral arguments in, 508 (n. 1); retirement age for justices on, 312, 334, 336, 339, 367; routines of, 262–67; seniority on, 259, 262–63, 482 (n. 164); SMS's first cases argued before, 58–59, 62, 77; social and political issues facing, 274, 276; succession in, 416–21; terms of, 262

— chief justice of: duties of, 343, 357–58, 368; election vs. appointment of, 336; judicial reform and, 270; length of service as, 345–46, 504 (n. 54); non-lawyers as, 350, 351, 356, 361–62, 380; power of, 270, 338–39; retirement age and, 334; seniority in selection of, 337, 342, 344–45, 419–21

— elections for: of 1952, 171–76; of 1954, 216; of 1962, 268, 272–73; of 1966, 280–81, 302–3; of 1974, 339–66

—opinions: announcement of, 266–
67; on antitrespass laws, 278–79;
assignment of, 265–66; on baseball,
295–96; on brown-bagging, 294–95;
on charitable immunity, 281–87, 490
(nn. 44, 51); circulation of drafts of,
266; on civil procedure rules, 293;
color-coded jackets for, 267; copying
of, 257; on death penalty, 201, 202,
203, 358–60, 386, 512 (n. 74); dissenting, 260, 266; on divorce law, 289–91,
492 (n. 79); on judicial conduct,
374–79; law clerks' role in, 263–65;
per curiam, 282; on prison discipline,
152; on privity of contract, 287, 288,
289; on school integration, 279–80;
volume of, 296–97; on women in
political office, 102, 461 (n. 15); on
women jurors, 104–6; on workers'
compensation, 291–93
See also Sharp, Susie Marshall—
supreme court–related subentries
NOW. *See* National Organization for
Women
Nowell, W. Milton, 375, 509 (n. 23)
Nutbush District, 9

Oakes, Roy, 202–3
Occupational diseases, 291–93
O'Connor, Sandra Day, 298, 318, 421
Odum, Howard, 70
O'Herron, Ed, 420
Olive, Hubert E., 175
Order of the Coif, 56, 57, 70, 71
Osborne, Floyd, 178

Parker, Frank, 338
Parker, John J., 175, 203, 317, 324, 472
(n. 32)
Parker, R. Hunt: age of, 218, 259; and
camaraderie of justices, 267; career
of, 259; on charitable immunity,
284–85; chief justice appointment
of, 490 (n. 50); conservatism of,
258–59; on court facilities, 256; death

of, 331, 337; and geographic composition of court, 478 (n. 55); health
problems of, 218; at Hotel Sir Walter,
257; judicial philosophy of, 259, 375;
on judicial reform, 270; personality
of, 259; reaction to SMS's appointment, 258–59, 260; in supreme court
elections, 172–73, 175; at swearing-in
ceremonies, 236
Parker, Roy, Jr., 249, 251
Partisanship: in ABA, 314; in federal
court appointments, 314, 315; in
judicial elections, 343, 379–81, 503
(n. 37); in supreme court, 254;
SMS's views on, 189–90, 343
Patronage, 99, 136, 193, 206
Patton, Frank C., 104
Patton, George B., 468 (n. 87)
Pearsall Plan, 196, 475 (n. 62)
Pearson, Drew, 112, 224, 226
Penn, Charles A., 15
Peoples, Linwood T., 376–79, 510
(n. 49)
Per curiam (PC) opinion, 282
Pet Milk Company, 89, 459 (n. 48)
Petty, Mary Macy, 448 (n. 54)
Phillips, Dickson, 368
Phillips, F. Donald, 152, 172–73, 482
(n. 147)
Photographs: in courtrooms, 418, 420;
in media coverage, 55–56, 343, 365,
452 (n. 5), 503 (n. 40); SMS's efforts
to purge, 436–37
Pipkin, W. Benton, 113
Pittard, Sallie Royster. *See* Blackwell,
Sallie Royster Pittard
Pless, J. William, Jr.: associate justice
appointment of, 285, 490 (n. 50); as
associate justice candidate, 219, 233,
234, 251; on charitable immunity,
285; on judicial reform, 269, 270–71,
488 (n. 114); on judicial robes, 188;
on succession in supreme court, 420;
on 1974 supreme court election, 347
Plessy v. Ferguson, 285

Scott, William Kerr, *241*; death of, 221; in death penalty cases, 201; in 1948 gubernatorial election, 115, 130–36, 160, 465 (n. 26), 466 (n. 40); judicial appointments by, 137, 167–71, 284, 337–38, 429, 466 (n. 54), 468 (n. 87); prison system under, 152–53; roads program of, 139–40, 151; SMS's campaign work for, 134–36; SMS's superior court appointment by, 129, 135–37, 139–40, 145, 215; SMS's support for, 115, 133, 135; on supreme court, SMS in, 216, 218, 231; on 1952 supreme court election, 171–72; on women in government, 137, 466 (n. 54)

Seawell, A. A. F., 152, 168, 284

Segal, Bernard G., 314, 315

Segregation: Annie Sharp on, 19; in 1946 congressional elections, 110–11; end of, 196–99, 276–80; and ERA, 392; in 1960 gubernatorial election, 221–22, 224; and racial intermarriage, 195; SMS's superior court rulings on, 196–98, 234, 427; SMS's supreme court opinions on, 278–81, 508 (n. 168); SMS's views on, 88, 195–99, 277, 427

Senate, N.C. *See* General Assembly, N.C.

Senate, U.S.: 1974 elections for, 365; ERA in, 390, 394; and U.S. Supreme Court appointments, 315, 317

Seniority: order of, on supreme court, 259, 262–63, 482 (n. 164); in selection of chief justice, 337, 342, 344–45, 419–21

"Separate but equal" doctrine, 195, 222, 285

Separation of powers doctrine, 278, 281, 360, 385–86

Shackleford, Claude E., 200–202

Shapiro, Irving S., 413, 516 (n. 31)

Sharp, Annie Britt Blackwell (mother of SMS), *116*; aristocratic origins of,

8, 10–11, 14, 407; birth of children of, 12, 13, 16, 17, 18, 24, 26; career of, 8, 11, 26; on careers for daughters, 26, 72; death of, 332; death of children of, 16–17, 24, 182–83; as Democrat, 189; depression of, 24–25, 446 (n. 26); education of, 11; family of, 8–11; during financial troubles, 12–15, 407; grandchildren of, 213–14; on hard work, 10–11; health problems of, 78, 307, 310, 321–23; marriage of, 11, 180; on marriage of daughters, 94–95; and prospect of SMS on U.S. Court of Appeals, 303, 304; religious views of, 18; on segregation, 19; SMS caring for, 212–13, 300–301, 320–23; on SMS's secretarial job, 71–72; and supreme court appointment of SMS, 235, 300–301; and swearing-in ceremonies, 367; visit to supreme court by, 321; visits to UNC by, 70

Sharp, Annie Hill (sister of SMS). *See* Klenner, Annie Hill Sharp

Sharp, Bob (uncle of SMS), 13

Sharp, Bobbie (sister-in-law of SMS), 227–28, 313, 321, 323

Sharp, Eliza Merritt Garrett (grandmother of SMS), 18–19, 97, 441 (n. 1)

Sharp, Florence Abigail (sister of SMS). *See* Newsom, Florence Abigail Sharp

Sharp, Frances (cousin of SMS), 46–47, 50

Sharp, Gwen (sister-in-law of SMS), 321

Sharp, James Blackwell (brother of SMS), 24, 446 (n. 23)

Sharp, James Marshall (grandfather of SMS), 12, 441 (n. 1)

Sharp, James Merritt (father of SMS), *116*, *124*; anti-Catholicism of, 16; birth of children of, 12, 13, 16, 17, 18, 24, 26; on careers for daughters, 26; in civic groups, 15–16; death of, 177–81, 184; death of children of, 16–17, 24; early legal career of, 12–15, 23–24; education of, 7, 12,

(n. 14) (*see also specific correspondents*); scrapbooks, 91, 439

—physical appearance and clothing of, 2; complexion, 2, 323; hair, 21, 46, 88, 231, 234; hats, 143, 267–68; judicial robes, 187–88; and media coverage, 155, 186; regal bearing, 2, 372; in retirement, 436–37; in school, 21, 31, 46; as superior court judge, 143, 148, 155, 186, 187–88; as supreme court associate justice, 236, 260; as supreme court chief justice, 372, 424; in 1974 supreme court election, 342; at swearing-in ceremonies, 143, 236; as trial lawyer, 88

—political activism by, as judge: in death penalty legislation, 386–88; in ERA debate, 275, 394, 396–401, 403–5; generally, 385–86; in Judge-Be-Lawyer legislation, 381–82, 385; in merit selection controversy, 379–85; in prison reform, 370–71; in Speaker Ban Law controversy, 275–76

—public speaking by: anecdotes in, 186–87; at Bar Association, 369–71; in early career, 61–62; in 1948 gubernatorial election, 134, 138; on jury duty, 108–9, 144; memory problems in, 408–9; political role of, 203; popularity of, 61–62, 188–89; on race, 195, 198–99; at State Bar, 171, 205; as superior court judge, 154, 188–89; as supreme court associate justice, 253–55; as supreme court chief justice, 369–71; during 1974 supreme court election, 363–64; on women's roles, 190–94; writing for, 231

—romantic relationships of: friendships after end of, xvi; during law school, 44, 46–48, 53–54; during law school secretarial job, 71, 77; loyalty vs. exclusivity in, 92–93; records of, xiv–xvi, 54, 157–58, 160, 162; after retirement, 431–32, 437–38; significance

of, xvi, 427–28; during superior court tenure, 156–66; during supreme court tenure, 323–35, 409–12; during trial practice, 63–64, 91–93. *See also* Bobbitt, William Haywood—SMS's affair with; Breckenridge, Millard Sheridan—SMS's affair with; Gwyn, Allen H.—SMS's affair with; Kesler, John Columbus—SMS's affair with

—superior court appointment of (1949), 2, 135–45; announcement of, 141; circumstances leading to, 129, 215, 429; expectations regarding, 140; Gwyn's role in, 129, 136, 138, 140, 160; hesitation in acceptance of, 98, 99, 139–40, 145, 167; Jim Sharp's health and, 98, 99, 140; media coverage of, 129–30, 136–37, 139, 141, 142–44; opponents of, 137; reactions to, 141–45; supporters of, 136–38, 144; swearing-in ceremony for, 143, 145

—as superior court judge (1949–62), 146–237; advice given to, 146; duties of, vs. supreme court justice, 252–53; first term of, 146–53, 169–70; in home county, 184–85; judicial reform affecting, 204–8; media coverage of, 146–49, 155, 185–86, 201, 202; order in court of, 155; personal life during, 156–66, 176–83, 209–15; political aspect of, 203–4; public attention to, 146–47, 154–55, 185–86, 203–4; reappointment of, 170, 176, 177, 181, 203–8; reasons for success of, 155–56; reputation of, 2, 155–56, 171, 185, 208, 215; travels of, 153–54

—supreme court appointment of (1962), 2, 228–37; announcement of, 235; circumstances leading to, 228–35, 251–52, 429; governors considering, 169–71, 217–19; Gwyn's role in, 215, 220–21, 228, 232, 237; hopes for, 167, 215, 217, 237; media coverage of, 235, 249–51; predictions of, 167, 216;

reactions to, 235–37, 251–53, 258–59; supporters of, 232, 234; swearing-in ceremony for, 236–37

—as supreme court associate justice (1962–74), 249–335; Bobbitt's collaboration with, 330–31; chambers of, 255–57, 484 (n. 39); duties of, 252–53, 254, 263; in election of 1962, 268, 272–73; in election of 1966, 280–81, 302–3; in election of 1974, 339; enjoyment of job, 303–4, 305; vs. federal job offers, 303–4, 305; judicial philosophy of, 281, 284, 286–87; loneliness of, 319–20; other justices' acceptance of, 258–60; personal life of, 319–35; political activities of, 253–54, 275; public speaking by, 253–55; reputation of, 314; retirement considered by, 334, 339; salary of, 252, 304, 483 (n. 26); secretary of, 261; as secretary to court, 254; vs. superior court judge, 252–53; women justices preceding, 253; workload of, 253, 254, 260, 287, 296–97

—supreme court chief justice, election of (1974), 2, 336–66; announcement of candidacy, 341–43; death penalty in, 358–61; decision to run, 339–41; Democratic opponent, 344–47; ERA in, 363, 398; fundraising for, 346; justices' support for, 340–43; Labor opponent, 356–57; media coverage of, 341–44, 346, 353–54, 364, 365; organization of campaign, 353, 363–64, 507 (n. 153); reasons for running, 342, 363; Republican opponents, 347–56; Republican rise and, 334, 336–38; results of, 364–66; stamina in, 351–52; voter apathy in, 361; voter ignorance in, 352, 357–62

—as supreme court chief justice (1974–79), 367–430; on cameras in courtrooms, 418, 420; on death penalty statutes, 386–88; duties of, 368; ERA and, 399–405; on FBI search committee, 368, 412–14; influence and legacy of, 424–30; issues facing, scope of, 368; on judicial conduct, 371–79, 425–26; and judicial input into legislation, 385–86, 404; judicial philosophy of, 375–76, 425; on judicial salaries, 414–18; on merit selection system, 379–85, 511 (n. 71); personal life of, 406–12; political activities of, 386–88, 396–97; public speaking by, 369–71; stress of, 408–9; successor to, 416–21; swearing-in ceremony for, 367–68, 399–400

—supreme court opinions by, 274–97; activism of, 285; on antitrespass law, 278–79; on baseball, 295–96; on brown-bagging, 294–95; on charitable immunity, 281–87, 490 (nn. 44, 51); as chief justice, 368; on civil procedure rules, 293; color-coded jackets for, 267; on death penalty, 358–60, 386, 512 (n. 74); "dissenting concurrence," 288–89; dissenting opinions, 289–91, 358–60; on divorce law, 289–91, 492 (n. 79); evidence in, 490 (n. 34); first, 264; influence of, 425; on judicial conduct, 374–79; law clerks' role in, 264–65, 282, 486 (n. 84); vs. personal views, 276; on privity of contract, 287–89; on school integration, 279–80, 508 (n. 168); and 1974 supreme court election, 363, 364; on workers' compensation, 291–93

—travels of: after retirement, 431; in Sharp & Sharp era, 90–91; as superior court judge, 153–54, 164–66; as supreme court justice, 319–20 *See also* Sharp & Sharp; United States Supreme Court—possible appointment of SMS to

Sharp, Thomas Adolphus (brother of SMS): on bartering, 86; birth of, 16; in chemistry, 96, 448 (n. 54); daughter of, 96, 227–28, 323; education of, 96, 460 (n. 74); marriage of, 96; SMS's correspondence with, 317; and SMS's declining health, 438; and swearing-in ceremonies, 236

Sharp, Tyrrell (niece of SMS), 96, 227–28, 323

Sharp & Sharp (law firm), 80–98; cola contamination cases of, 491 (n. 70); difficulty of starting career at, for SMS, 57–60; equality of partners in, 55; establishment of, 55; expanding role of SMS in, 80, 82, 98; fees charged by, 86–88; Jim Sharp's plans for, 47, 53, 55; media coverage of, 55–56, 62, 81, 84; offices of, 55, 452 (n. 1); Robinson working for, 177–79, 181; SMS's clients and superior court appointment, 140; SMS's 1930 departure from, 65, 69, 77; SMS's first cases, 58–60, 62–63; SMS's 1932 return to, 80; travels during, 90–91; trial practice of, 81–89

Sharp family, 7–19, 117–19; aristocratic origins of, 10; Breckenridges' friendship with, 67; children leaving home, 94–97; Civil War legacy in, 1, 7; in Democratic Party, 189; financial support by SMS, 72, 78, 408; financial troubles of, 12–15, 64, 65, 72, 407–8; illnesses and deaths in, 16–17, 24, 177–83, 446 (n. 23); after Jim Sharp's death, 181, 212–15; moves of, 12–13, 14; SMS caring for siblings in, 18, 24–25, 94, 97; SMS living with, as adult, 63, 93–94; during SMS's superior court tenure, 181, 212–15; during SMS's supreme court tenure, 300–301, 320–23, 406–8; in 1974 supreme court election, 364; tragedies in, 432–36

Sharp Institute, 8, 11

Shaw, George, 48–49

Shelby Dynasty, 104

Sheridan, Belle, 68–69

Sheridan, Millard, 68

Simmons, Furnifold, 51

Sink, H. Hoyle, 141–42

Sit-ins, 221, 274, 278–79

Slade, Dorothy M., 397

Smith, Al, 51, 52, 100, 224, 227

Smith, Dollie, 400, 514 (n. 43)

Smith, Donald L., 503 (n. 38)

Smith, Estelle T., 134

Smith, Janie Sands: in high school, 20, 21; and judicial misconduct, 379; on Kesler, 44, 46; on law school, 39; marriage of, 64; at swearing-in ceremonies, 145, 236, 367

Smith, Wade, 295

Smith, Willis, 109, 171, 179

Snider, William, 251, 303–4, 305, 341

Somers, Robert V., 346–47

South: Civil War legacy in, 1; legal education in, 35–36; paradoxes of, 1, 3, 441 (n. 2)

Speaker Ban Law, 159, 275–76, 489 (n. 9)

Special superior court judges: assignments of, 204–5; history of, 147–48; judicial system reform and, 204–8; political nature of, 99, 140, 203, 206; public standing of, 148; role of, 99, 147–48, 204, 206; term length of, 140, 206, 208, 216; travel by, 99, 153–54, 204; vacations for, 153

Stacey, Janie, 25, 26

Stacy, Walter P., 49, 145, 146, 169, 504 (n. 54)

State v. Carpenter, 149–53, 469 (n. 20)

State v. Cobb, 278–79

State v. Emery, 104–6

State v. Jarrette, 359–60

State v. Waddell, 358–59

State v. Woodson, 386

Stevens, John Paul, 313, 318

Stevenson, Adlai, 304; in presidential elections, 175, 182, 217, 222–23, 224

Stewart, Carl, 416

Stewart, D. K., 243

Stewart, Dan E., 507 (n. 153)

critique of, 278, 285, 307, 308; and volume of cases in North Carolina, 296; on women jurors, 106, 109, 462 (n. 39); on women lawyers, 39
— appointments to: ABA role in, 312, 314–17; of first woman, 298, 318; by Ford, 313, 317, 318; by Johnson, 302, 304–8, 309, 315, 317–18; by Kennedy, 298–99, 302, 313–15, 317–18; by Nixon, 308–13, 315–17
— possible appointment of SMS to: chances of, 313–18; under Ford, 313; under Johnson, 302, 304–8; under Kennedy, 298–302, 313–15; under Nixon, 308–13; SMS's reaction to, 299–302, 305–9, 312, 313; supporters of, 298–99, 305, 306, 310, 313
University of North Carolina (UNC; Chapel Hill): campus of, 37, 449 (n. 7); and ERA, 392; establishment of, 37; flu outbreak at, 53; network of state leaders from, 37–38; and State Triangular Debate, 22; women's admission to, 20, 38–39; women's dormitory at, 38–39, 40; women's experiences at, 40–41. *See also* University of North Carolina School of Law
University of North Carolina at Greensboro. *See* North Carolina College for Women
University of North Carolina School of Law: admission requirements for, 36–37, 449 (n. 6); casebook system at, 36; commencement at, 56, 57; faculty of, 41, 43, 44, 51, 121, 449 (n. 14), 450 (n. 50); growth of, 44; history of, 35–39; law review at, 45; library of, 45; moot court at, 36, 41, 43, 46, 49, 52; modernization of, 35–37; and SMS's supreme court appointment, 234; women at, 30, 39, 421–22, 449 (n. 12)
— SMS at: admission, 31; arrival, 38–41; bar exam taken, 49–50; departure

of, 53–54; family obligations after, 47, 53; first year, 41–44; friendships, 40, 43–44, 70–71; grades, 42, 49, 56; graduation, 56, 57; interactions with classmates, 48–49; and law review, 45, 46, 48, 53; and moot court, 43, 46, 48, 49, 52; return visits after leaving, 56–57; romances, 44, 46–48, 53–54; second year, 45–49; as secretary for dean, 65–79; summer session, 43–44, 49; third year, 51–54
UPI, 270, 400, 401, 403
U.S. News and World Report, 429

Valentine, Itimous T., 168, 170–75
Valley Home, 9, 11
Van Alstyne, William, 401
Vance, Zebulon B., 10
Vance County, 10
Van Hecke, Maurice T., 51, 69, 121, 236
Vanore, Andrew A., Jr., 453 (n. 38)
Vietnam War, 274, 304, 362, 389
Viguerie, Richard, 402
Voters: apathy of, 361; ignorance of, 352, 357–62; straight-ticket, 355–57, 362, 365–66; turnout of, 189–90; women as, 23, 103–4, 134, 190, 227 (*see also* Women's suffrage)

Wall Street Journal, 294, 344
Walters, Barbara, 389
Ware v. Knight, 62
Warren, Earl, 276, 285, 300, 309, 315, 377
Washington, Booker T., 195
Washington, D.C.: Breck in, 79, 92, 459 (n. 57); FBI search committee in, 413–14, 516 (n. 35)
Washington Post, 316, 393
Watergate, 362, 393, 412–13
Webster, James A., Jr., 306
Webster, Wesley D., 387, 398, 403, 515 (nn. 56, 58)
Webster, William H., 414
Wells, Samuel F., Jr., 470 (n. 37)

West, Sudie Grace. *See* Kesler, Sudie Grace West

Wettach, Robert H., 45, *121*

Whichard, Willis P. "Bill," 324–25, 391, 396, 502 (n. 24)

White, Byron R., 298, 315

White, William S., 189

Whitley, Pauline, 25, 26

Whitsett Institute, 7

Whittaker, Charles E., 298

Willebrandt, Mabel Walker, 30

Willis, Emmitt C., 459 (n. 57)

Wilmington 10 case, 427

Wilson, Duncan C., 243

Wilson, Henry Hall, Jr., 493 (n. 2)

Winborne, John Wallace: age of, 218; chief justice appointment of, 217; and geographic composition of court, 478 (n. 55); at Hotel Sir Walter, 258; law clerks of, 263–64; retirement of, 229–34

Windsor, Duke and Duchess of, 91

Winston, Ellen, 391

Winston-Salem Journal, 139, 217–18, 425, 436

Winston-Salem Sentinel, 378–79

Wiseman, Myrtle E., 387, 388, 512 (n. 84)

Woman's College of the University of North Carolina. *See* North Carolina College for Women

Women: colleges for, 20, 27; domestic responsibilities of, 193, 249–50; on juries, 60, 99, 104–9, 144–45, 192, 462 (n. 39); in law school, 39, 347–48; male network's exclusion of, 38; public affairs role of, 23, 103, 190, 192–93; SMS's influence on, 1; SMS's views on, 19, 190–94, 249–50, 426; in supreme court appointment of SMS, 230, 231, 234; at UNC, 20, 38–39, 40–41; voting power of, 23, 103–4, 134, 190, 227; during World War II, 103
— careers of: equality in, 55, 391; in FBI, 413; male network and, 38; marriage combined with, 28, 29, 193, 249–50, 428; in North Carolina, 391; SMS's views on, 193–94, 249–50
— as judges and justices: in appellate courts, 253, 421–24, 429; first, 253, 298, 318; first black, 347–48; Ford's consideration of, 313; Nixon's consideration of, 310–13, 316; rarity in 1920s, 30; rarity in 1940s, 99; rarity in 1970s, 422–23, 429–30; SMS on need for, 422–23
— as lawyers: ERA and, 405; first in North Carolina, 39; in judicial merit selection system, 383–84; as law clerks, 368–69; loyalty among, 90; number of, in 1920s, 30; number of, in 1930s, 55; number of, in 1970s, 429; in office vs. trial practice, 81; opportunities for, 421, 423; referrals among, 90; rhetorical style of, 81–82; separate classification for, SMS on, 194, 384, 423; state laws allowing, 39
— in politics: and ERA, 390–91; in 1960 gubernatorial campaign, 221, 227; Sanford's appointment of, 231–32; scarcity of, 99, 101–3, 192; Scott's appointment of, 137, 466 (n. 54); SMS on need for, 190, 192–93, 249; in 1974 state and national elections, 354–55, 365

Women's clubs, 106–7, 144, 299, 390

Women's rights/equality: 1920s backsliding in, 28–29; expansion of, 1; and jury duty, 107; at NCCW, 27, 28–29; resistance to, 391; SMS's views on, 395–96, 426; in workplace, 55, 391. *See also* Equal Rights Amendment; Women's suffrage

Women's suffrage, 23, 102, 105, 106, 391

Wood v. J. P. Stevens & Co., 293

Woodward, C. Vann, 87

Woolen, Charles T., 65

Workers' Compensation Act of 1929, 291–92

Work-release program, 158–59

World War I, 15–18
World War II, 103
Worsham, Leon, 61
Wortham, Sallie Green. *See* Blackwell, Sallie Green Wortham
Wright, Richard, 387
Wyrick, Louise Tesh, 91

Yale Law School, 74
Yarborough, Ed, 487 (n. 105)
Young, Bernard, 184, 252
Young, Ina, 54
Young Democrats Club, 101, 102–3, 189